BEYOND THE WESTERN TRADITION

Readings in Moral and Political Philosophy

EDITED BY

Daniel Bonevac

William Boon

Stephen Phillips

The University of Texas at Austin

Mayfield Publishing Company
Mountain View, California
London · Toronto

Library of Congress Cataloging-in-Publication Data
Beyond the Western tradition : readings in moral and political philosophy /
  edited by Daniel Bonevac, William Boon, Stephen Phillips.
     p.   cm.
  Includes index.
  ISBN 1-55934-075-4
  1. Ethics.   2. Political science—Philosophy.   I. Bonevac, Daniel A., 1955–
  II. Boon, William, 1954–   III. Phillips, Stephen H.
  BJ1012.B49 1991
  170—dc20   91-33102
                                                                  CIP

Manufactured in the United States of America
10 9 8 7 6 5 4 3 2 1

Mayfield Publishing Company
1240 Villa Street
Mountain View, California 94041

Sponsoring editor, James Bull; managing editor, Linda Toy; production editor, April Wells; copy editor, Sally Peyrefitte; text and cover designer, Donna Davis; illustrator, Joan Carol; art director, Jeanne M. Schreiber; manufacturing manager, Martha Branch. Cover image: Paul Klee, "Bird Wandering Off," The Metropolitan Museum of Art, The Berggruen Klee Collection, 1987. (1987.455.17) Copyright ©1987 by The Metropolitan Museum of Art. The text was set in 10/12 ITC Berkeley Oldstyle Book and Berkeley Oldstyle Medium and printed on 50# Finch Opaque by Malloy Lithographing, Inc.

Contents

Preface

Most introductory philosophy courses share the Western European/North American focus of the rest of the curriculum. Without question, the tradition of philosophical reflection that begins in ancient Greece and extends today to college classrooms in, among other places, the United States is immensely important to ongoing philosophical work, to world history, to modern institutions, and to our concepts of ourselves. Other traditions, however, are also important. They are philosophically rich, historically influential, and similarly important to our self-understanding. The features of Western philosophy that make it valuable stand out especially clearly in comparison with other traditions.

This book is a collection of classics from non-Western ethical traditions. Collecting philosophical classics beyond the Western tradition raises, in an acute form, the question of what philosophy is. Here, we restrict our attention to ethics and, when directly relevant to ethics, political philosophy. But this limitation still leaves some key questions open. Is a written text a necessary condition for philosophy? Is argumentation? Where should we draw the line between philosophical ethics and literature with moral dimensions or ethnographical descriptions of mores?

We have decided to collect works that deal with questions of ethical wisdom, good character, and the good life. Traditions of non-Western ethics call for reflection on these topics and for action guided by this reflection. Philosophical traditions of ethical wisdom exhibit explicit reflection and, often, canons of reflection but not necessarily explicit debate. Understanding ethical philosophy this way allows us to include classics of practical wisdom from societies where written argumentative traditions are just now developing.

Our project also raises the issue of the boundaries of the Western tradition. What counts as Western? What counts as non-Western? In works originating in South and East Asia, these questions are not troublesome, for there are continuous written philosophical traditions that have come into contact with the West fairly recently. In other parts of the world, however, distinguishing the Western from the non-Western is more difficult. We might try to characterize a work by appealing to its author's ethnic background or the place of its composition, but those are superficial features that would lead to many misclassifications. We might try to characterize a work in terms of the culture of which it forms a part, but this seems upside down; classifying the culture seems to presuppose classifying the works that help to define it. We might try to characterize a work by its substantive content, but this would require some prior notion of the concerns, themes, and theories of both Western and non-Western philosophy.

Where could we obtain such a notion? In general, we have tried to characterize works as Western or non-Western by appealing to the author's conception of the work as a continuation of an ongoing philosophical tradition. To whom does the author refer? What cultural and especially religious influences are explicitly addressed? This criterion helps little in works originating in Africa, where, until recently, there has been no continuing written philosophical tradition. It does suggest, however, that Jewish and Islamic philosophy, while stemming from Greek thought, form distinct, non-Western traditions. It also suggests that Latin American philosophy should count as Western, for Latin American philosophers refer primarily to Western European sources and see themselves as participants in the European philosophical tradition. We take it as a hopeful sign that our criterion begins to break down when applied to twentieth-century thought. Increasingly, philosophers are looking across traditional divides to find ideas in all traditions. We hope that this book will accelerate the trend.

Finally, presenting a fair introduction to non-Western philosophy raises difficult issues of what to include to represent non-Western traditions. There is a temptation to choose works that have concerns that are similar to those of Western philosophy, works that are dramatically different from Western philosophy, or works that fit a particular conception of what non-Western thought is like. To resist this temptation, we have tried to respect the self-definitions of the philosophical traditions of West, South, and East Asia. Within each tradition, there is a moderately clear sense of who the important thinkers are. We have tried to follow that sense as much as our focus on ethics and our desire for readings accessible to undergraduates would allow. Only in Africa have we had to make completely independent choices.

Using This Book

This book can serve to introduce students to non-Western philosophy or to supplement Western readings in introductory philosophy or ethics courses. We have arranged the readings by region—Africa, West Asia and the Southern Mediterranean, South Asia, and East Asia—and, within each region, chronologically. Each section, except that on Africa, reflects a philosophical tradition that is reasonably continuous. Until this century, moreover, interactions between these traditions were infrequent. In fact, only two such interactions play a large role in the philosophical works included in this book. Interestingly, they took place around the same time. One is the transmission of Greek thought to Asia Minor, which exerted a strong influence on Jewish, Islamic, and Ethiopian thought. The other is the transmission of Buddhism from South Asia to China. The coherence and relative independence of the regional traditions makes a regional organization natural.

The readings do lend themselves to other approaches. Some instructors may want to organize the material topically; others, using this book to supplement readings on Western philosophy, may want to organize it around the historical progression of the Western philosophical tradition. The following chart arranges philosophers roughly (and sometimes controversially) according to the classification of ethical theories developed in the Introduction:

	CONSEQUENTIALIST THEORIES		DEONTOLOGICAL THEORIES	
	Particular	Universal	Particular	Universal
Community	Gyekye	Fanon Kautilya		
Person/Trait		Maimonides Mahayana wisdom literature	Confucius Mencius Lao Tzu Wang Ewe proverbs Swahili proverbs Aurobindo	Chu Hsi
Motive/Intent			later Egyptian works Buddha	
Act	Mo Tzu *Kamasutra* *Yogasutra*	Hsün Tzu	Sufis Nishida Seung Sahn	early Egyptian works 'Abba Mika'el Zera Yacob Walda Heywat al-Farabi Avicenna Bahya Upanishads *Bhagavad Gita* Jain canons Gandhi

This chart should itself suggest some ideas for organizing the material topically. Here are other suggestions:

Religion and Ethics	Egypt (*The Book of the Dead*), Zera Yacob, Walda Heywat, al-Farabi, Bahya, Avicenna, Sufis, Buddha, Rammohun Roy
Relativism	Han Fei Tzu, Aurobindo
Virtue	Confucius, Lao Tzu, Mencius, Mahayana wisdom literature, *Dhammapada*
Human Nature	'Abba Mika'el, Mencius, Hsün Tzu, Nishida, Aurobindo, Upanishads
Reason and Intuition	al-Farabi, Sufis, Lao Tzu, Chu Hsi, Wang Yang-Ming, Seung Sahn

The Golden Rule	Egypt, Walda Heywat, Confucius, Mo Tzu, Jain canons
Rules	Maimonides, Hsün Tzu, Manu
Consequentialism	Gyekye, *Bhagavad Gita,* Mo Tzu, Mencius, Avicenna
Context, Conflict	Ewe proverbs, Swahili proverbs, *Kamasutra*
Violence	Fanon, Ewe proverbs, Swahili proverbs, *Bhagavad Gita,* Jain canons, Gandhi
Pleasure	Zera Yacob, Walda Heywat, *Bhagavad Gita,* Buddha, Carvaka, *Kamasutra*

An organization incorporating non-Western readings into a chronological Western-centered syllabus:

IN CONJUNCTION WITH:	READ:
Plato, *Euthyphro*	Zera Yacob, Walda Heywat, Gyekye, Bahya, Sufis, Manu, Rammohun Roy
Plato, *Republic*	Hsün Tzu, Han Fei Tzu, Carvaka, Kautilya
Aristotle, *Nicomachean Ethics*	Swahili proverbs, Ewe proverbs, Upanishads, Mahayana wisdom literature, Confucius, Mencius, Avicenna
Hobbes, *Leviathan*	Gyekye, Hsün Tzu, Han Fei Tzu
Kant, *Groundwork of the Metaphysics of Morals*	*Bhagavad Gita,* Buddha, Mahayana wisdom literature, Gandhi, Chu Hsi
Butler, *Five Sermons*	Sufis, Buddha, Wang Yang-Ming, Nishida, Seung Sahn
Bentham, *Principles of Morals and Legislation*	Mo Tzu, Mencius, Carvaka, *Kamasutra*
Mill, *On Liberty*	Mo Tzu, Lao Tzu, Mencius
Mill, *Utilitarianism*	Gyekye, *Bhagavad Gita, Yogasutra,* Kautilya, Maimonides, Mo Tzu, Mencius, Hsün Tzu
Marx	Fanon, Gyekye, Rammohun Roy, Gandhi
Nietzsche	Fanon, Aurobindo, Nishida
Existentialism	Upanishads, Nishida, Seung Sahn

Acknowledgments

We are grateful to our students for giving us the idea for this collection and to everyone at Mayfield Publishing Company who helped to make the idea a reality. We would especially like to thank Jim Bull, whose encouragement and support were invaluable. We are also grateful to Sally Peyrefitte, whose editing made our contributions to this book clearer; to April Wells, who shepherded the book through production; to Pamela Trainer, for her help with permissions; and to Boyce Nute, for his enthusiasm and his idea for the title.

We thank Linda Blomstad, California State University, Sacramento; Don Porter, College of San Mateo; and Anita Silvers, San Francisco State University, for their insightful comments.

We owe thanks to Adrienne Diehr, who helped with the section on Egyptian philosophy, to Thomas K. Seung for his help with the East Asian section, and to Nadir Chokir for helpful discussions on African philosophy.

Finally, we thank Beverly Bonevac, Vilma Maroun, and Hope Phillips for their intellectual and moral support for our adventures beyond the Western tradition.

TIMELINE: BEFORE THE COMMON ERA (B.C.E.)

2300	2100	1900	1700	1500	1300	1100	900	700	500	300	100

Africa

- Harkhuf (2300?)
- Ptahotep (2150?)
- Merikare (2100?)
- Any (1400?)
- Rekhmire (1450?)
- Amenemope (1100?)
- *Book of the Dead* (600?)
- Ankhsheshonq (200?)

West Asia

India

- *Mahabharata* (800?–400?)
- Upanishads (700?)
- Buddha (563–483)
- *Yogasutra* (400?)

East Asia

- Lao Tzu (6th century?)
- Confucius (551–479)
- Mo Tzu (470?–391?)
- Mencius (372?–289?)
- Hsün Tzu (310?–212?)
- Han Fei Tzu (280?–233)

The West

- Socrates (470?–399)
- Plato (427?–347)
- Aristotle (384–322)
- Cicero (106–43)

0	200	400	600	800	1000	1200	1400	1600	1800	2000

'Abba Mika'el (1510?)

Zera Yacob (1599–1692)

Walda Heywat (1630?–?)

Franz Fanon
(1925–1961)

Rabi'a al-'Adawiyya (d. 801)

al-Farabi (870?–950)

Bahya (11th century)

Avicenna (980–1037)

al-Ghazali (d. 1111)

Maimonides (1135–1204)

Manu (4th century)

Rammohun Roy
(1772–1833)

Gandhi
(1869–1948)

Aurobindo
(1872–1950)

Chu Hsi (1130–1200)

Wang Yang-Ming (1472–1529)

Kitaro Nishida
(1870–1945)

Seung Sahn
(b. 1927)

St. Augustine (354–430)

St. Thomas Aquinas (1225–1274)

Niccolò Machiavelli (1469–1527)

Thomas Hobbes (1588–1679)

René Descartes (1596–1650)

John Locke (1632–1704)

Immanuel Kant
(1724–1804)

Jeremy Benthan
(1748–1832)

John Stuart Mill
(1806–1873)

Karl Marx
(1818–1883)

Jean-Paul Sartre
(1905–1980)

INTRODUCTION

This book is a collection of classic writings on ethics and political philosophy from beyond the Western tradition. We intend it as a supplement to Western readings or as a sole text in introductory ethics courses. To understand these readings, it is helpful to understand some of the chief problems and concerns of ethics.

Philosophy, if the word itself is any guide, is the love of wisdom. What is wisdom? This is a substantive and difficult ethical question, but a simple answer is that wisdom is good judgment. Philosophy, then, is the love or pursuit of good judgment. Questions of value are thus at the heart of philosophy.

Ethics is nevertheless not all there is to philosophy. To be a good judge of scientific assertions, you must understand evidence and related issues in the theory of knowledge and the philosophy of science. To be a good judge of arguments, you must understand logic. Ethics is the pursuit of good judgment concerning *action*. It is a *practical* discipline, focusing on such questions as

What should I do?

What kind of life should I lead?

What kind of person should I try to become?

How can I tell right from wrong?

What obligations do I have to other people?

When am I justified in criticizing others?

When are they justified in criticizing me?

Philosophers writing on ethics try to answer at least some of these questions.

Answers to ethical questions differ in important ways from answers to ordinary, factual questions. In particular, they are *prescriptive:* they do not merely describe the way the world is but refer to how it *ought* to be. Ethical assertions typically contain *prescriptive* or *normative terms* such as 'ought', 'should', 'good', 'bad', 'may', 'duty', 'responsible', and 'obligation'. Sometimes they take the imperative rather than the indicative mood ("Thou shalt not steal," for example). Ethical assertions do not merely describe the facts; they evaluate them.

Questions of justification lead philosophers to construct moral theories, rather than simply to make ethical assertions and announce ethical views. Why is *that* the correct criterion for good action? a critic may ask. Why are *those* the most important virtues and vices? To answer these questions, philosophers have tried to develop general and abstract moral theories that not only distinguish right from wrong but also provide a basis for their way of making the distinction. In almost every philosophical tradition, ethics begins with articulations of moral positions— lists of rules for good behavior, say, or accounts of the ideal person or society—and

1

sprouts moral theories somewhat later, when disagreements over ethical positions have given rise to a pattern of argument and counterargument.

Ethics and Metaethics

The questions listed above constitute the subject matter of ethics proper, often called *normative ethics*. They naturally give rise to another set of questions, however, which concern the project of ethics itself.

What kind of discipline is ethics?

How can ethical assertions be justified?

What do ethical terms such as 'good' or 'obligation' mean?

Are ethical truths objective?

How can we know ethical truths?

These questions arise *about* ethical philosophy, not *within* ethical philosophy; they constitute the subject matter of *metaethics*.

Twentieth-century British and American philosophers have been very concerned with metaethical topics. Outside the Western tradition, however, metaethics has received serious attention in only two forms. First, some writers challenge the idea that ethics is worth taking seriously. The ancient Chinese philosopher Yang Chu, for example, observes that great Chinese sages often led miserable lives, whereas notorious villains led wonderful lives. After their deaths, of course, people praised the sages and disparaged the villains. But this did nothing to benefit the former or harm the latter. What good is praise once you are dead? So, Yang Chu concludes, trying to be moral is foolish. He declares that he would not give a single hair on his head to save the entire world. Another ancient Chinese philosopher, Han Fei Tzu, rejects the idea that ethics offers any independent standard for judging or evaluating matters. To act properly, in his view, is simply to act in the interests of the ruler. In other words, according to Han Fei Tzu, might makes right. The ideal citizen is a tool of the government; the ideal government is effective at maximizing its own power. For those in power, ethics and prudence—What should I do? and What is in my own interest?—are the same.

Second, many philosophers, especially in the Islamic and Jewish traditions, discuss the relationship of ethics to religion. Is a secular ethics possible? Or is ethics necessarily a part of religion, relying on revealed truths or mystical insight? Jewish thinkers such as Bahya and Islamic thinkers such as the Sufis see ethical questions as essentially religious. From their point of view, ethics is a part of theology, not philosophy. Pushed to an extreme, this perspective implies that philosophy is impossible; all pursuit of wisdom presupposes religious revelation and so forms part of theology. Al-Farabi, Avicenna, Maimonides, Zera Yacob, and Walda Heywat, in contrast, believe that ethics has a rational foundation that we can investigate in a secular fashion. The first three believe that religion, too, provides ethical insight. But they hold that reason and religion do not disagree; they are two ways of reaching the same answers. Zera Yacob thinks that religion and reason do conflict but that reason takes precedence, because we have no other way to tell whether claims of religious revelation are true or spurious. Reason, in his view, gives us a tool for critiquing religious claims about ethics.

Normative Ethics

We can classify ethical theories according to the kinds of questions they treat as primary, the kinds of considerations they take into account in answering those questions, and whether they see ethical thinking as focusing on particulars or universals—on individual situations, actions, people, and so on, or on *kinds* of situations, actions, people, and so on. To a large extent, these issues are independent.

Ethical Questions   Many ethical questions fall into two basic classes. One set asks, in various forms, what kind of person I should try to become. The other set asks what kinds of actions I ought to perform or refrain from performing. Obviously, the actions I perform relate to my character somehow, so these questions are not completely independent. Some philosophers maintain that we should define the notion of good character in terms of good action; others maintain the reverse. Some believe that issues of action and character, while related, cannot be defined in terms of each other.

Classifying approaches to ethics into those focusing on action and those focusing on character, however, is too simple. We can appreciate the rich choices available to ethical thinkers, as well as some aspects of the link between ethics and political theory, by placing both character and action in a broader context. Some utilitarians, for example, maintain that good actions are those that tend to produce good consequences. Good intentions are those that tend to lead to good actions. Good motives are those that tend to lead to good intentions; good traits of character are those that tend to lead to good motives. Good people are those who tend to have good traits of character. Finally, good communities are those that tend to promote the development of good people. This reasoning links action and character in a chain:

Good community
↓
Good person
↓
Good character trait
↓
Good motive
↓
Good intention
↓
Good action

Some philosophers define good action in terms of good character by reversing the direction of this chain of dependencies. Some define both good action and good character in terms of a vision of a good society. In principle, an ethical view can choose to take any link or combination of links in the chain as basic, defining the others in terms of it. Actions, character traits, and communities, however, have proved to be the most popular choices.

Ethicists who take issues of character as fundamental or irreducible try to explain what it is to be a good person. To do this, they outline a theory of character traits. Good traits are *virtues;* bad traits are *vices.* In the West, Aristotle proposes the best-known theory of this sort. In ancient China, Confucius and Mencius also outline theories of character traits. Their lists of virtues and vices, however, differ significantly from Aristotle's and from each other's.

Ethicists who take issues of action as fundamental or irreducible try to explain what makes good actions good and bad actions bad. Broadly speaking, they try to develop some criteria for distinguishing good from bad actions. Ethicists who take issues concerning the overall shape of a community as fundamental or irreducible try to develop an account of the good society. Some do this by developing criteria for distinguishing good from bad communities. Others instead picture an ideal community and evaluate existing ones by comparison. Still others think of a community as capable of action in much the way an individual person is. This view enables them to speak of a community's actions, intentions, motives, traits, and overall character. In effect, such philosophers construct a moral framework in which communities are viewed as agents and from it derive a framework in which people are viewed as agents.

Ethical Considerations   Moral theories thus differ on the questions they take as fundamental. They also differ on the kinds of considerations to which they appeal in answering those questions. Some theories, called *consequentialist* theories, posit that a thing's value depends solely on its ultimate consequences. On this view, actions, for example, are judged solely on the basis of their effects. *Deontological* theories, by contrast, posit that other issues are independently important to questions of value. Deontological theories may appeal to intrinsic features of actions, intentions, and so on, that are quite independent of their consequences. The Golden Rule, for example, demands that we treat others as we would want to be treated: "Do unto others as you would have them do unto you." This establishes a criterion for evaluating actions that has nothing to do with their consequences.

Consequentialist theories declare that an action, intention, or principle of social organization should be judged by its consequences. Something is good if and only if it has, or tends to have, good effects. This implies that consequentialism rests the goodness of actions on the goodness of effects. Any form of consequentialism, therefore, rests upon a theory of the value of effects—a theory of nonmoral value, as some writers call it. Jeremy Bentham and John Stuart Mill hold that the good, in this nonmoral sense, is simply pleasure and the absence of pain. For this reason, they are called *hedonists.* Outside the West, theories of nonmoral good have tended to be more complicated. Mo Tzu, clearly a consequentialist, says little about what good consequences are but does mention harmony, peace, and prosperity as goods. He seems to have in mind both individual and broader, social goods. The Akan of West Africa have a straightforwardly communitarian theory of nonmoral value. They start with society as a whole and with a conception of good for society—a conception involving harmony, cooperation, and other ideals. The Akan then characterize good actions and character traits as those that tend to promote that communal good. Maimonides takes a very different approach; at the foundation of his theory lie nonmoral factors such as order and happiness, and also an independent theory of individual virtue. Actions are good to the extent that they promote all of these.

The most influential form of consequentialism is *utilitarianism,* the view that morality reduces, in essence, to one principle: Maximize good. Like any consequentialist theory, it rests on an independent characterization of good effects. It is a universalist theory, for it concerns only the total amount of good in the universe; it makes no difference who enjoys this good, where it is found, and so on. Because it requires us to seek the greatest good, utilitarianism is a strong theory in two senses. First, it makes very stringent demands. It requires not merely that we promote the good or observe certain principles in seeking the good, but that we maximize it. Second, utilitarianism requires that we have a quantifiable conception of the good. Not just any theory of nonmoral good is compatible with utilitarianism. We must have a theory of the good that allows us to say how much good is present in a state of affairs. In short, we must be able to compare amounts of good—ideally, by attaching numbers to them. And this makes sense only on certain understandings of what the good is.

Deontological theories take other things into account. Some deontological theories of action, for example, stress motives and intentions. Others stress the form of an action, asking whether it falls into certain specified categories. Still others treat the goodness of actions as a property of them that we cannot define but can recognize intuitively.

The most familiar kind of deontological theory explains what makes good actions good and bad actions bad by appealing to rules. The Ten Commandments, for example, are ten rules from God that many have understood to be the heart of Judeo-Christian morality:

1. Thou shalt have no other gods before me.
2. Thou shalt not make any graven images.
3. Thou shalt not take the name of the Lord thy God in vain.
4. Remember the Sabbath day, to keep it holy.
5. Honor thy father and thy mother.
6. Thou shalt not kill.
7. Thou shalt not commit adultery.
8. Thou shalt not steal.
9. Thou shalt not bear false witness against thy neighbor.
10. Thou shalt not covet.

The earliest ethical text in this book, *The Autobiography of Harkhuf,* which dates from about 2300 B.C.E., seems to presuppose this kind of approach to ethics. So does much ancient wisdom literature, which consists of a series of proverbs, rules, and directives for action. This volume contains several examples of such literature: the various *Instructions* from Egypt and 'Abba Mika'el's *Book of the Philosophers.*

Wisdom literature offers guidelines for action but little theoretical justification for them. Why follow *these* rules? Various philosophers have tried to defend a deontological approach to ethics that derives rules from more abstract considerations. This may be the world's most popular philosophical strategy for addressing ethical issues; Zera Yacob, Walda Heywat, al-Farabi, Avicenna, Bahya, the Upanishads, and the *Bhagavad Gita* all adopt it in some form.

Not all deontological theorists, however, trust rules to portray the moral truth accurately. Many thinkers believe that ethical truth is so particular, depending on the details of individual situations, that no rules can capture it. The Sufis and Seung Sahn all hold that moral knowledge results from special insight into particular situations. In the West, this approach has been called *intuitionism*. This brings us, however, to a third way of classifying moral theories.

Particulars and Universals   We can categorize moral theories according to whether they focus on particular items or on general kinds. Some theories maintain that ethical problems are primarily particular: they arise within a particular context and involve a set of particular actions that are options for a particular agent. Such theories may discuss general moral problems and may even offer rules for addressing them, but the rules are at best rules of thumb that provide general hints for approaching particular situations. They certainly do not define what is right and wrong in particular situations. All moral knowledge is, at root, particular—specific to specific situations. Mo Tzu, Wang Yang-Ming, the Akan, and Ewe and Swahili proverbs—as well as the Sufis and Seung Sahn—tend to adopt this highly particular focus.

Other theories contend that moral thinking is always general. We always address a particular problem on the assumption that it has certain general features, and we try to solve it by exploiting those features. On this approach, ethics primarily concerns *kinds* of actions, character traits, communities, or whatever. Consequently, it is natural to express ethical truths in terms of rules. The rules are not merely guidelines justified by experience in particular situations, as decorating hints for small rooms or tips for betting on baseball might be; they define what right and wrong are. Moral knowledge is at root universal. In addition to the many deontologists who favor rules, Chu Hsi, Maimonides, and Hsün Tzu opt explicitly for a universal, rule-based theory.

This distinction, together with that between consequentialist and deontological theories, suggests four kinds of normative ethical theories:

	Consequentialist	Deontological
Particular	_____ consequentialism	_____ deontologism
Universal	Rule consequentialism	Rule deontologism
(Kind- or Rule-based)		

The blanks should be filled in with 'act', 'intention', 'motive', 'trait', 'person', or 'community', depending on what moral question or questions the theory treats as primary. In each case, the particular theories focus on particular acts, intentions, and so on. Kind- or rule-based theories vary similarly in what questions they take as basic, but their names rarely reflect this fact.

PART I   Africa

Algiers

MOROCCO

TUNISIA

WESTERN
· SAHARA

ALGERIA

LIBYA

Cairo ·

EGYPT

MAURITANIA

· SENEGAL

· MALI

NIGER

Aksum

· GUINEA

UPPER
VOLTA

· CHAD

SUDAN

DJIBOUTI

· SIERRA
  LEONE

NIGERIA

Addis ·
Ababa   ETHIOPIA

· LIBERIA

IVORY
COAST

CAMEROON

CENRAL
AFRICAN REPUBLIC

· GHANA

SOMALIA

· TOGO

EQUATORIAL
GUINEA

UGANDA   KENYA

· BENIN

GABON

CONGO

· Nairobi

CABINDA
(ANGOLA)

ZAIRE

RWANDA

BURUNDI

TANZANIA   Dar es Salaam

ANGOLA

ZAMBIA

MALAWI

ZIMBABWE

MOZAMBIQUE

NAMIBIA

BOTSWANA

MADAGASCAR

SWAZILAND

LESOTHO ·

SOUTH AFRICA

Homeland of Akan tribe

Homeland of Ewe tribe

Region where Swahili is spoken

EGYPTIAN PHILOSOPHY

Thousands of years before the birth of Confucius, Socrates, or Jesus, Egypt produced much interesting ethical literature. The selections below include texts of several different kinds.

Autobiography Some of the earliest surviving Egyptian ethical texts are autobiographies that serve as epitaphs, usually for public officials. Designed to prove that the deceased deserves reward in the hereafter, they praise that person's achievements, arguing that he or she was a good person who lived a moral life. A typical autobiography contains a list of virtues followed by a list of immoral acts the person did not commit. The autobiographies thus give us important clues about the Egyptian conception of ethics. From the list of virtues we can infer what it is to be a good person; from the list of immoral acts we can infer a list of moral rules of conduct.

Included below is part of the *Autobiography of Harkhuf,* the most famous Old Kingdom autobiography, which dates from the Sixth Dynasty (2300–2150 B.C.E.). Harkhuf served kings Mernere and Neferkare Pepi II—the last of the four kings of the Sixth Dynasty—was governor of Upper Egypt, and led four expeditions to Nubia. The autobiography has four sections: (*a*) a prayer for offerings, (*b*) a poetic argument that Harkhuf has lived a good life (reproduced here), (*c*) a report of military conquests and praises from kings, and (*d*) a statement of praise from king Neferkare Pepi II. The argument that Harkhuf deserves eternal reward raises four points. First, Harkhuf established a house. Second, he was loved and praised by his family and his king. Third, he was generous, caring for the less fortunate. Finally, he was just.

Instructions Old Kingdom writers popularized instructions, series of maxims strung together as advice from father to son, as a literary genre. The maxims are bits of practical advice. Authors of instructions varied the format and content, but much of the wisdom transmitted was popular; authors relied on traditional proverbs as well as on their own insights. The longest and best known of the instructions, *The Instruction of Ptahhotep,* appears below. It survives in four copies, the earliest of which is in Middle Egyptian. But many scholars believe that the work dates from the Sixth Dynasty and encodes the morality of the late Old Kingdom aristocracy. It focuses on basic issues of social relations and on basic virtues—self-control, moderation, kindness, generosity, justice, truthfulness, and discretion—which are to be practiced toward all. This instruction, like many others, seems to rest on faith in the perfectability of human beings. It is optimistic that the demands of morality can be met.

As the Old Kingdom faded into the Middle Kingdom, instructions developed into treatises on kingship. The instructions are advice from a departing king to his successor. The earliest preserved example of this sort of royal testament, *The Instruction Addressed to King Merikare,* appears below. It was probably written, not by the former king Khety himself, but by someone during the reign of Merikare, in the Ninth/Tenth Dynasty (around 2100 B.C.E.). The work presents an interesting ethics, together with a rudimentary political theory. Political leaders are obliged to treat their subjects with respect and justice, to honor tradition, to punish only rebels with death, and to prevail through effective speech rather than force.

New Kingdom instructions are less pretentious than those of earlier eras. Intended for average people, they reflect the ethical outlook of the middle classes. *The Instruction of Any,* composed during the Eighteenth Dynasty (1550–1305 B.C.E.), is advice from a father, a minor official, to his son. Much of this advice is practical; find a good wife; don't chase women or drink too much; be careful in your speech and with your possessions; don't yell at the boss; stay out of trouble. The father does, however, urge his son to be charitable and to respect social rank. Interestingly, the son debates his father, insisting that the advice is too hard to follow. For the first time, perfectability comes into question: Can the son lead a completely moral life?

The Instruction of Amenemope, composed in the Twentieth Dynasty (1195–1080 B.C.E.), is considered the genre's zenith. It reflects a shift of emphasis from action and worldly success to restraint, contemplation, and endurance. The conception of the ideal person, of the good life, and of the highest virtues changes accordingly. Modesty, humility, self-control, and contentment are the chief characteristics of the ideal person. The instructions are nevertheless justified by the success they produce: "If you make your life with these in your heart / You will find it a success." The path to success, according to the work, is not obvious. This instruction embodies another important conceptual change: Even the ideal person is imperfect. We can strive for perfection, but only God can achieve it.

Royal Installation Speeches   Appearing below is *The Installation of the Vizier Rekhmire,* carved on the vizier's tomb. Rekhmire served as vizier, the highest state official, under king Thutmose III, who reigned from 1479 to 1425 B.C.E. The king himself attended the vizier's installation and gave a speech, a formal charge outlining the duties of the vizier. The speech is interesting mostly for its outline of the Egyptian concept of justice and for its argument for the importance of following rules.

The Book of the Dead   This work, which the Egyptians called "the coming forth by day," is a compilation of spells for resurrecting people in the afterlife. It attained its final form during the Twenty-Sixth Dynasty of the New Kingdom (664–525 B.C.E.). In essence, *The Book of the Dead* is a book of magic for achieving eternal life. But it also contains an ethical component; the dead must establish that they are worthy of eternal life. Parts of Chapter 125, "Judgment of the Dead," appear here. (The original document contains an illustration of a dead person's heart being weighed on a scale by a group of gods headed by Osiris.) Mostly, the dead person's argument rests on a list of evil actions not performed, which reveals the content of the prohibitions the Egyptians then regarded as most important.

Demotic Wisdom Literature   Instructions written in the Middle and Late Kingdoms become progressively less aristocratic and more popular in tone. This trend culminates in the wisdom literature of the Ptolemaic period (323–30 B.C.E.). Unlike earlier instructions, Ptolemaic works consist of single complete and self-contained sentences. Each sentence is a proverb. Moreover, the language of the works is demotic (that is, popular), not stylized and specifically literary. Works of this form became common not only in Egypt but also in Greece, Israel, Mesopotamia, and other parts of the eastern Mediterranean. Texts from these cultures have many formal elements and even specific proverbs in common; this suggests that much borrowing took place and that a culture of ethical precepts and practical advice was more or less shared by various societies. *The Instruction of Ankhsheshonq* is an Egyptian contribution to this shared literature. It consists partly of moral teaching and partly of practical advice. It is especially interesting because it raises the question, Why be moral? Its answer, moreover, is that sometimes we should not be; sometimes, down-to-earth, pragmatic considerations are more important than abstract moral questions.

from the *Autobiography of Harkhuf*

I have come here from my city,
I have descended from my nome;
I have built a house, set up (its) doors,
I have dug a pool, planted sycamores.
The king praised me,
My father made a will for me.
I was one worthy
One beloved of his father,
Praised by his mother,
Whom all his brothers loved.
I gave bread to the hungry,
Clothing to the naked,
I brought the boatless to land.

. . . .

I was one who spoke fairly, who repeated what
    was liked,
I never spoke evilly against any man to his
    superior,
For I wished to stand well with the great god.
Never did I judge between two contenders
In a manner which deprived a son of his father's
    legacy.

from *The Instruction of Ptahhotep*

1. Don't be proud of your knowledge,
   Consult the ignorant and the wise;
   The limits of art are not reached,
   No artist's skills are perfect;
   Good speech is more hidden than
      greenstone,
   Yet may be found among maids at the
      grindstones.

2. If you meet a disputant in action,
   A powerful man, superior to you,
   Fold your arms, bend your back,
   To flout him will not make him agree with
      you.
   Make little of the evil speech
   By not opposing him while he's in action;
   He will be called an ignoramus,
   Your self-control will match his pile [of
      words].

3. If you meet a disputant in action
   Who is your equal, on your level,
   You will make your worth exceed his by
      silence,
   While he is speaking evilly,
   There will be much talk by the hearers,
   Your name will be good in the mind of the
      magistrates.

4. If you meet a disputant in action,
   A poor man, not your equal,
   Do not attack him because he is weak,
   Let him alone, he will confute himself.
   Do not answer him to relieve your heart,
   Do not vent yourself against your opponent,
   Wretched is he who injures a poor man,
   One will wish to do what you desire,
   You will beat him through the magistrates'
      reproof.

5. If you are a man who leads,
   Who controls the affairs of the many,
   Seek out every beneficent deed,
   That your conduct may be blameless.
   Great is justice, lasting in effect,
   Unchallenged since the time of Osiris.
   One punishes the transgressor of laws,
   Though the greedy overlooks this;
   Baseness may seize riches,
   Yet crime never lands its wares;
   In the end it is justice that lasts,
   Man says: "It is my father's ground."

6. Do not scheme against people,
   God punishes accordingly:
   If a man says: "I shall live by it,"
   He will lack bread for his mouth.
   If a man says: "I shall be rich,"
   He will have to say: "My cleverness has
      snared me."
   If he says: "I will snare for myself,"
   He will be unable to say: "I snared for my
      profit."
   If a man says: "I will rob someone,"
   He will end being given to a stranger.
   People's schemes do not prevail,
   God's command is what prevails;
   Live then in the midst of peace,
   What they give comes by itself.

   . . . .

9. If you plow and there's growth in the field,
   And god lets it prosper in your hand,
   Do not boast at your neighbors' side,
   One has great respect for the silent man:
   Man of character is man of wealth.

If he robs he is like a crocodile in court.
Don't impose on one who is childless,
Neither decry nor boast of it;
There is many a father who has grief,
And a mother of children less content than
   another;
It is the lonely whom god fosters,
While the family man prays for a follower.

10. If you are poor, serve a man of worth,
   That all your conduct may be well with the
      god.
   Do not recall if he once was poor,
   Don't be arrogant toward him
   For knowing his former state;
   Respect him for what has accrued to him,
   For wealth does not come by itself.
   It is their law for him whom they love,
   His gain, he gathered it himself;
   It is the god who makes him worthy
   And protects him while he sleeps.

11. Follow your heart as long as you live,
   Do no more than is required,
   Do not shorten the time of "follow-the-heart,"
   Trimming its moment offends the *ka*.*
   Don't waste time on daily cares
   Beyond providing for your household;
   When wealth has come, follow your heart,
   Wealth does no good if one is glum!

12. If you are a man of worth
   And produce a son by the grace of god,
   If he is straight, takes after you,
   Takes good care of your possessions,
   Do for him all that is good,
   He is your son, your *ka* begot him,
   Don't withdraw your heart from him.
   But an offspring can make trouble:
   If he strays, neglects your counsel,
   Disobeys all that is said,
   His mouth spouting evil speech,
   Punish him for all his talk!
   They hate him who crosses you,
   His guilt was fated in the womb;
   He whom they guide can not go wrong,
   Whom they make boatless can not cross.

. . . .

* Vitality, vital force, personality. —ED.

16. If you are a man who leads,
   Whose authority reaches wide,
   You should do outstanding things,
   Remember the day that comes after.
   No strife will occur in the midst of honors,
   But where the crocodile enters hatred arises.

17. If you are a man who leads,
   Listen calmly to the speech of one who
      pleads;
   Don't stop him from purging his body
   Of that which he planned to tell.
   A man in distress wants to pour out his heart
   More than that his case be won.
   About him who stops a plea
   One says: "Why does he reject it?"
   Not all one pleads for can be granted,
   But a good hearing soothes the heart.

. . . .

19. If you want a perfect conduct,
   To be free from every evil,
   Guard against the vice of greed:
   A grievous sickness without cure,
   There is no treatment for it.
   It embroils fathers, mothers,
   And the brothers of the mother,
   It parts wife from husband;
   It is a compound of all evils,
   A bundle of all hateful things.
   That man endures whose rule is rightness,
   Who walks a straight line;
   He will make a will by it,
   The greedy has no tomb.

20. Do not be greedy in the division,
   Do not covet more than your share;
   Do not be greedy toward your kin,
   The mild has a greater claim than the harsh.
   Poor is he who shuns his kin,
   He is deprived of interchange.
   Even a little of what is craved
   Turns a quarreler into an amiable man.

. . . .

22. Sustain your friends with what you have,
   You have it by the grace of god;
   Of him who fails to sustain his friends
   One says, "a selfish *ka*."

One plans the morrow but knows not what
   will be,
The [right] ka is the ka by which one is
   sustained.
If praiseworthy deeds are done,
Friends will say, "welcome!"
One does not bring supplies to town,
One brings friends when there is need.

23. Do not repeat calumny,
   Nor should you listen to it,
   It is the spouting of the hot-bellied.
   Report a thing observed, not heard,
   If it is negligible, don't say anything,
   He who is before you recognizes worth.
   If a seizure is ordered and carried out,
   Hatred will arise against him who seizes;
   Calumny is like a dream against which one
      covers the face.

. . . .

29. If you are angered by a misdeed,
   Lean toward a man on account of his
      rightness;
   Pass it over, don't recall it,
   Since he was silent to you the first day.

30. If you are great after having been humble,
   Have gained wealth after having been poor
   In the past, in a town which you know,
   Knowing your former condition,
   Do not put trust in your wealth,
   Which came to you as gift of god;
   So that you will not fall behind one like you,
   To whom the same has happened.

31. . . . Do not plunder a neighbor's house,
   Do not steal the goods of one near you,
   Lest he denounce you before you are heard.
   A quarreler is a mindless person,
   If he is known as an aggressor
   The hostile man will have trouble in the
      neighborhood.

. . . .

34. Be generous as long as you live,
   What leaves the storehouse does not return;
   It is the food to be shared which is coveted,
   One whose belly is empty is an accuser;
   One deprived becomes an opponent,

Don't have him for a neighbor.
Kindness is a man's memorial
For the years after the function.

. . . .

36. Punish firmly, chastise soundly,
   Then repression of crime becomes an
      example;
   Punishment except for crime
   Turns the complainer into an enemy.

37. If you take to wife a špnt*
   Who is joyful and known by her town,
   If she is fickle and likes the moment,
   Do not reject her, let her eat,
   The joyful brings happiness.

Epilogue

If you listen to my sayings,
All your affairs will go forward;
In their truth resides their value,
Their memory goes on in the speech of men,
Because of the worth of their precepts;
If every word is carried on,
They will not perish in this land.
If advice is given for the good,
The great will speak accordingly;
It is teaching a man to speak to posterity,
He who hears it becomes a master-hearer;
It is good to speak to posterity,
It will listen to it.

If a good example is set by him who leads,
He will be beneficent for ever,
His wisdom being for all time.
The wise feeds his ba with what endures,
So that it is happy with him on earth.
The wise is known by his wisdom,
The great by his good actions;
His heart matches his tongue,
His lips are straight when he speaks;
He has eyes that see,
His ears are made to hear what will profit his son,
Acting with truth he is free of falsehood.

* The meaning of this term is not known. Guesses range from "fat woman" to "dancer." —ED.

from *The Instruction Addressed to King Merikare*

Reprinted from Miriam Lichtheim, Ancient Egyptian Literature, Volume I: The Old and Middle Kingdoms, *University of California Press, 1973. Copyright © 1973 by the Regents of the University of California.*

The hothead is an inciter of citizens,
He creates factions among the young;
If you find that citizens adhere to him,

Denounce him before the councillors,
Suppress him, he is a rebel,
The talker is a troublemaker for the city.
Curb the multitude, suppress its heat,

. . . .

If you are skilled in speech, you will win,
The tongue is a king's sword;
Speaking is stronger than all fighting,
The skillful is not overcome.

. . . .

Those who know that he knows will not attack him,
No crime occurs when he is near;
Justice comes to him distilled,
Shaped in the sayings of the ancestors.
Copy your fathers, your ancestors,

See, their words endure in books,
Open, read them, copy their knowledge,
He who is taught becomes skilled.
Don't be evil, kindness is good,
Make your memorial last through love of you.

. . . .

Respect the nobles, sustain your people,
Strengthen your borders, your frontier patrols;
It is good to work for the future,
One respects the life of the foresighted,
While he who trusts fails.
Make people come to you through your good
	nature,
A wretch is who desires the land of his neighbor,
A fool is who covets what others possess.
Life on earth passes, it is not long,

Happy is he who is remembered,
A million men do not avail the Lord of the Two
	Lands.
Is there a man who lives forever?
He who comes with Osiris passes,
Just as he leaves who indulged himself.

. . . .

Do justice, then you endure on earth;
Calm the weeper, don't oppress the widow,
Don't expel a man from his father's property,
Don't reduce the nobles in their possessions.
Beware of punishing wrongfully,
Do not kill, it does not serve you.
Punish with beatings, with detention,
Thus will the land be well-ordered;
Except for the rebel whose plans are found out,
For god knows the treason plotters,
God smites the rebels in blood.

. . . .

The Court that judges the wretch,
You know they are not lenient,
On the day of judging the miserable,
In the hour of doing their task.
It is painful when the accuser has knowledge,
Do not trust in length of years,
They view a lifetime in an hour!
When a man remains over after death,
His deeds are set beside him as treasure,
And being yonder lasts forever.
A fool is who does what they reprove!
He who reaches them without having done wrong
Will exist there like a god,
Free-striding like the lords forever!

. . . .

Do not prefer the wellborn to the commoner,
Choose a man on account of his skills,
Then all crafts are done . . .
Guard your borders, secure your forts,
Troops are useful to their lord.

from *The Instruction of Any*

Take a wife while you're young,
That she make a son for you;
She should bear for you while you're youthful,
It is proper to make people.
Happy the man whose people are many,
He is saluted on account of his progeny.

. . . .

Do not enter the house of anyone,
Until he admits you and greets you;
Do not snoop around in his house,
Let your eye observe in silence.
Do not speak of him to another outside,
Who was not with you;
A great deadly crime

. . . .

Beware of a woman who is a stranger,
One not known in her town;
Don't stare at her when she goes by,
Do not know her carnally.
A deep water whose course is unknown,
Such is a woman away from her husband.
"I am pretty," she tells you daily,
When she has no witnesses;
She is ready to ensnare you,
A great deadly crime when it is heard.

. . . .

Don't indulge in drinking beer,
Lest you utter evil speech
And don't know what you're saying.
If you fall and hurt your body,
None holds out a hand to you:
Your companions in the drinking

Stand up saying: "Out with the drunk!"
If one comes to seek you and talk with you,
One finds you lying on the ground,
As if you were a little child.

. . . .

Behold, I give you these useful counsels,
For you to ponder in your heart;
Do it and you will be happy,
All evils will be far from you.
Guard against the crime of fraud,
Against words that are not true;
Conquer malice in your self,
A quarrelsome man does not rest on the morrow.
Keep away from a hostile man,
Do not let him be your comrade;
Befriend one who is straight and true,
One whose actions you have seen.
If your rightness matches his,
The friendship will be balanced.
Let your hand preserve what is in your house,
Wealth accrues to him who guards it;
Let your hand not scatter it to strangers,
Lest it turn to loss for you.
If wealth is placed where it bears interest,
It comes back to you redoubled;
Make a storehouse for your own wealth,
Your people will find it on your way.
What is given small returns augmented,
What is replaced brings abundance.
The wise lives off the house of the fool,
Protect what is yours and you find it;
Keep your eye on what you own,
Lest you end as a beggar.
He who is slack amounts to nothing,
Honored is the man who's active.

. . . .

Do not reveal your heart to a stranger,
He might use your words against you;

The noxious speech that came from your mouth,
He repeats it and you make enemies.
A man may be ruined by his tongue,
Beware and you will do well.
A man's belly is wider than a granary,
And full of all kinds of answers;
Choose the good one and say it,
While the bad is shut in your belly.
A rude answer brings a beating,
Speak sweetly and you will be loved.
Don't ever talk back to your attacker,
Do not set a trap for him;
It is the god who judges the righteous,
His fate comes and takes him away.

. . . .

Do not eat bread while another stands by
Without extending your hand to him.
As to food, it is here always,
It is man who does not last;
One man is rich, another is poor.
But food remains for him who shares it.
As to him who was rich last year,
He is a vagabond this year;
Don't be greedy to fill your belly,
You don't know your end at all.
Should you come to be in want,
Another may do good to you.
When last year's watercourse is gone,
Another river is here today;
Great lakes become dry places,
Sandbanks turn into depths.
Man does not have a single way,
The lord of life confounds him.

Attend to your position,
Be it low or high;
It is not good to press forward,
Step according to rank.
Do not intrude on a man in his house,
Enter when you have been called;
He may say "Welcome" with his mouth,
Yet deride you in his thoughts.
One gives food to one who is hated,
Supplies to one who enters uninvited.

Don't rush to attack your attacker,
Leave him to the god;
Report him daily to the god,
Tomorrow being like today,

And you will see what the god does,
When he injures him who injured you.

Do not enter into a crowd,
If you find it in an uproar
And about to come to blows.
Don't pass anywhere near by,
Keep away from their tumult,
Lest you be brought before the court,
When an inquiry is made.
Stay away from hostile people,
Keep your heart quiet among fighters;
An outsider is not brought to court,
One who knows nothing is not bound in fetters.

. . . .

Do not control your wife in her house,
When you know she is efficient;
Don't say to her: "Where is it? Get it!"
When she has put it in the right place.
Let your eye observe in silence,
Then you recognize her skill;
It is joy when your hand is with her,
There are many who don't know this.
If a man desists from strife at home,
He will not encounter its beginning.
Every man who founds a household
Should hold back the hasty heart.
Do not go after a woman,
Let her not steal your heart.

Do not talk back to an angry superior,
Let him have his way;
Speak sweetly when he speaks sourly,
It's the remedy that calms the heart.

. . . .

Epilogue

The scribe Khonshotep answered his father, the
    scribe Any:
I wish I were like [you],
As learned as you!
Then I would carry out your teachings,
And the son would be brought to his father's
    place.
Each man is led by his nature,
You are a man who is a master,
Whose strivings are exalted,

Whose every word is chosen.
The son, he understands little
When he recites the words in the books.
But when your words please the heart,
The heart tends to accept them with joy.
Don't make your virtues too numerous,
That one may raise one's thoughts to you;
A boy does not follow the moral instructions,
Though the writings are on his tongue!

The scribe Any answered his son, the scribe
  Khonshotep:
Do not rely on such worthless thoughts,
Beware of what you do to yourself!
I judge your complaints to be wrong,
I shall set you right about them.
There's nothing superfluous in our words,
Which you say you wished were reduced.
The fighting bull who kills in the stable,
He forgets and abandons the arena;
He conquers his nature,
Remembers what he's learned,
And becomes the like of a fattened ox.
The savage lion abandons his wrath,
And comes to resemble the timid donkey.
The horse slips into its harness,
Obedient it goes outdoors.
The dog obeys the word,
And walks behind its master.
The monkey carries the stick,
Though its mother did not carry it.
The goose returns from the pond,
When one comes to shut it in the yard.
One teaches the Nubian to speak Egyptian,
The Syrian and other strangers too.
Say: "I shall do like all the beasts,"
Listen and learn what they do.

The scribe Khonshotep answered his father, the
  scribe Any:
Do not proclaim your powers,
So as to force me to your ways;
Does it not happen to a man to slacken his hand,
So as to hear an answer in its place?
Man resembles the god in his way
If he listens to a man's answer.
One [man] cannot know his fellow,
If the masses are beasts;
One [man] cannot know his teachings,
And alone possess a mind,
If the multitudes are foolish.
All your sayings are excellent,
But doing them requires virtues;
Tell the god who gave you wisdom:
"Set them on your path!"

The scribe Any answered his son, the scribe
  Khonshotep:
Turn your back to these many words,
That are not worth being heard.
The crooked stick left on the ground,
With sun and shade attacking it,
If the carpenter takes it, he straightens it,
Makes of it a noble's staff,
And a straight stick makes a collar.
You foolish heart,
Do you wish us to teach,
Or have you been corrupted?

"Look," said he, "you my father,
You who are wise and strong of hand:
The infant in his mother's arms,
His wish is for what nurses him."
"Look," said he, "when he finds his speech,
He says: "Give me bread.""

from *The Instruction of Amenemope*

Reprinted from Miriam Lichtheim, Ancient Egyptian Literature, Volume II: New Kingdom, *University of California Press, 1976. Copyright © 1976 by the Regents of the University of California.*

Prologue

Beginning of the teaching for life,
The instructions for well-being,
Every rule for relations with elders,
For conduct toward magistrates;
Knowing how to answer one who speaks,
To reply to one who sends a message.
So as to direct him on the paths of life,
To make him prosper upon earth;
To let his heart enter its shrine,
Steering clear of evil;
To save him from the mouth of strangers,
To let [him] be praised in the mouth of people.

. . . .

CHAPTER 1

. . . .

If you make your life with these in your heart,
You will find it a success;
You will find my words a storehouse for life,
Your being will prosper upon earth.

CHAPTER 2

Beware of robbing a wretch,
Of attacking a cripple;
Don't stretch out your hand to touch an old man,
Nor open your mouth to an elder.
Don't let yourself be sent on a mischievous
    errand,
Nor be friends with him who does it.

Don't raise an outcry against one who attacks you,
Nor answer him yourself.

. . . .

CHAPTER 3

Don't start a quarrel with a hot-mouthed man,
Nor needle him with words.
Pause before a foe, bend before an attacker,
Sleep [on it] before speaking.
A storm that bursts like fire in straw,
Such is the heated man in his hour.
Withdraw from him, leave him alone,
The god knows how to answer him.
If you make your life with these [words] in your
    heart,
Your children will observe them.

CHAPTER 6

Do not move the markers on the borders of fields,
Nor shift the position of the measuring-cord.
Do not be greedy for a cubit of land,
Nor encroach on the boundaries of a widow.
The trodden furrow worn down by time,
He who disguises it in the fields,
When he has snared [it] by false oaths,
He will be caught by the might of the Moon.
Recognize him who does this on earth:
He is an oppressor of the weak,
A foe bent on destroying your being,
The taking of life is in his eye.
His house is an enemy to the town,
His storage bins will be destroyed;
His wealth will be seized from his children's
    hands,
His possessions will be given to another.
Beware of destroying the borders of fields,
Lest a terror carry you away;

One pleases god with the might of the lord
When one discerns the borders of fields.
Desire your being to be sound,
Beware of the Lord of All;
Do not erase another's furrow,
It profits you to keep it sound.
Plow your fields and you'll find what you need,
You'll receive bread from your threshing-floor.
Better is a bushel given you by the god,
Than five thousand through wrongdoing.
They stay not a day in bin and barn,
They make no food for the beer jar;
A moment is their stay in the granary,
Comes morning they have vanished.
Better is poverty in the hand of the god,
Than wealth in the storehouse;
Better is bread with a happy heart
Than wealth with vexation.

CHAPTER 10

Don't force yourself to greet the heated man,
For then you injure your own heart;
Do not say "greetings" to him falsely,
While there is terror in your belly.
Do not speak falsely to a man,
The god abhors it;
Do not sever your heart from your tongue,
That all your strivings may succeed.
You will be weighty before the others,
And secure in the hand of the god.
God hates the falsifier of words,
He greatly abhors the dissembler.

CHAPTER 11

Do not covet a poor man's goods,
Nor hunger for his bread;
A poor man's goods are a block in the throat,
It makes the gullet vomit.
He who makes gain by lying oaths,
His heart is misled by his belly;
Where there is fraud success is feeble,
The bad spoils the good.

. . . .

CHAPTER 12

Do not desire a noble's wealth,
Nor make free with a big mouthful of bread;
If he sets you to manage his property,
Shun his, and yours will prosper.
Do not converse with a heated man,
So as to befriend a hostile man.
If you are sent to transport straw,
Stay away from its container.
If a man is observed on a fraudulent errand,
He will not be sent on another occasion.

CHAPTER 13

Do not cheat a man through pen on scroll,
The god abhors it;
Do not bear witness with false words,
So as to brush aside a man by your tongue.
Do not assess a man who has nothing,
And thus falsify your pen.
If you find a large debt against a poor man,
Make it into three parts;
Forgive two, let one stand,
You will find it a path of life.
After sleep, when you wake in the morning,
You will find it as good news.
Better is praise with the love of men
Than wealth in the storehouse;
Better is bread with a happy heart
Than wealth with vexation.

CHAPTER 18

Do not lie down in fear of tomorrow:
"Comes day, how will tomorrow be?"
Man ignores how tomorrow will be;
God is ever in his perfection,
Man is ever in his failure.
The words men say are one thing,
The deeds of the god are another.
Do not say: "I have done no wrong,"
And then strain to seek a quarrel;
The wrong belongs to the god,
He seals [the verdict] with his finger.
There is no perfection before the god,

But there is failure before him;
If one strains to seek perfection,
In a moment he has marred it.
Keep firm your heart, steady your heart,
Do not steer with your tongue;
If a man's tongue is the boat's rudder,
The Lord of All is yet its pilot.

CHAPTER 20

Do not confound a man in the law court,
In order to brush aside one who is right.
Do not incline to the well-dressed man,
And rebuff the one in rags.
Don't accept the gift of a powerful man,
And deprive the weak for his sake.

*Maat** is a great gift of god,
He gives it to whom he wishes.
The might of him who resembles him,
It saves the poor from his tormentor.
Do not make for yourself false documents,
They are a deadly provocation;
They [mean] the great restraining oath,
They [mean] a hearing by the herald.
Don't falsify the oracles in the scrolls,
And thus disturb the plans of god;
Don't use for yourself the might of god,
As if there were no Fate and Destiny.
Hand over property to its owners,
Thus do you seek life for yourself;
Don't raise your desire in their house,
Or your bones belong to the execution-block.

*Justice, right, rightness, order, truth. —ED.

from *The Installation of the Vizier Rekhmire*

Reprinted from Miriam Lichtheim, Ancient Egyptian Literature, Volume II: The New Kingdom, *University of California Press, 1976. Copyright © 1976 by the Regents of the University of California.*

The Speech of Pharaoh

Lo, petitioners come from the South and the
   North,
The whole land is eager for the counsel of the
   vizier;
See to it that all is done according to law,
That all is done exactly right,
In giving a man his vindication.
Lo, the magistrate who judges in public,
Wind and water report all that he does,
Lo, there is none who ignores his deeds.
If he makes a mistake in deciding his case,
And fails to reveal it through the mouth of the
   clerk,
It will be known through the mouth of him
   whom he judged,
Through his telling it to the clerk by saying:
"This is not the decision of my case."
Lo, the magistrate's safety is acting by the rule,
In acting on a petitioner's speech;
Then the judged cannot say:
"I was not given my right."
A proverb in the Book of Memphis says:
"Gracious king, lawful vizier."

Avoid what was said of the vizier Akhtoy,
That he denied his own people for the sake of
   others,
For fear of being falsely called partial.
If one of them appealed a judgment,
That he had planned to do to him,
He persisted in denying him,
But that is excess of justice.

Do not judge unfairly,
God abhors partiality;
This is an instruction,
Plan to act accordingly.
Regard one you know like one you don't know,
One near you like one far from you.
The magistrate who acts like this,
He will succeed here in this place.

Do not pass over a petitioner,
Before you have considered his speech.
When a petitioner is about to petition you,
Don't dismiss what he says as already said.
Deny him after you let him hear
On what account you have denied him.
Lo, it is said:
"A petitioner wants his plea considered
Rather than have his case adjudged."
Do not scold a man wrongfully,
Scold where scolding is due.
Cast your fear, that you be feared,
The feared magistrate is a magistrate.
A magistrate's worth is that he does right,
But if a man makes himself feared a million
   times,
People think something is wrong with him,
And they don't say of him, "He is a man."

This too is said:
A magistrate who lies comes out as he deserves.
Lo, you succeed in doing this office by doing
   justice,
Lo, doing justice is what is wanted in the actions
   of the vizier,
Lo, the vizier is its true guardian since the time of
   god.
Lo, what one says of the vizier's chief scribe:
"Scribe of Justice" one says of him.
As to the hall in which you judge,
It has a room full of [written] decisions.

He who does justice before all people,
He is the vizier.
Lo, a man remains in his office,
If he acts as he is charged,
Innocent is the man who acts as he is told.
Do not act willfully
In a case where the law is known;
For as regards the headstrong man,
The Lord prefers the timid to the headstrong
   man.

. . . .

from *The Book of the Dead*

Reprinted from Miriam Lichtheim, Ancient Egyptian Literature, Volume II: The New Kingdom, *University of California Press, 1976. Copyright © 1976 by the Regents of the University of California.*

CHAPTER 125 / THE JUDGMENT OF THE DEAD

The Declaration of Innocence

. . . .

I have not done crimes against people,
I have not mistreated cattle,
I have not sinned in the Place of Truth.
I have not known what should not be known,
I have not done any harm.
I did not begin a day by exacting more than my
    due,
My name did not reach the bark of the mighty
    ruler.
I have not blasphemed a god,
I have not robbed the poor.
I have not done what the god abhors,
I have not maligned a servant to his master.
I have not caused pain,
I have not caused tears.
I have not killed,
I have not ordered to kill,
I have not made anyone suffer.
I have not damaged the offerings in the temples,
I have not depleted the loaves of the gods,
I have not stolen the cakes of the dead.
I have not copulated nor defiled myself.
I have not increased nor reduced the measure,
I have not diminished the arura,*

*A Greek unit of measure, roughly equivalent to two-thirds of an acre. —ED.

I have not cheated in the fields.
I have not added to the weight of the balance,
I have not falsified the plummet of the scales.
I have not taken milk from the mouth of children,
I have not deprived cattle of their pasture.
I have not snared birds in the reeds of the gods,
I have not caught fish in their ponds.
I have not held back water in its season,
I have not dammed a flowing stream,
I have not quenched a needed fire.
I have not neglected the days of meat offerings,
I have not detained cattle belonging to the god,
I have not stopped a god in his procession.
I am pure, I am pure, I am pure, I am pure!
I am pure as is pure that great heron in Hnes.
I am truly the nose of the Lord of Breath,
Who sustains all the people,

. . . .

The Declaration to the Forty-two Gods

O Wide-of-stride who comes from On: I have not
    done evil.
O Flame-grasper who comes from Kheraha: I have
    not robbed.
O Long-nosed who comes from Khmun: I have
    not coveted.
O Shadow-eater who comes from the cave: I have
    not stolen.
O Savage-faced who comes from Rostau: I have
    not killed people.
O Lion-Twins who come from heaven: I have not
    trimmed the measure.
O Flint-eyed who comes from Khem: I have not
    cheated.
O Fiery-one who comes backward: I have not
    stolen a god's property.
O Bone-smasher who comes from Hnes: I have
    not told lies.

O Flame-thrower who comes from Memphis:
I have not seized food.

O Cave-dweller who comes from the west: I have
not sulked.

O White-toothed who comes from Lakeland:
I have not trespassed.

O Blood-eater who comes from slaughterplace:
I have not slain sacred cattle.

O Entrail-eater who comes from the tribunal:
I have not extorted.

O Lord of Maat who comes from Maaty: I have
not stolen bread rations.

O Wanderer who comes from Bubastis: I have not
spied.

O Pale-one who comes from On: I have not
prattled.

O Villain who comes from Anjdty: I have
contended only for my goods.

O Fiend who comes from slaughterhouse: I have
not committed adultery.

O Examiner who comes from Min's temple: I have
not defiled myself.

O Chief of the nobles who comes from Imu:
I have not caused fear.

O Wrecker who comes from Huy: I have not
trespassed.

O Disturber who comes from the sanctuary:
I have not been violent.

O Child who comes from the nome of On: I have
not been deaf to Maat.

O Foreteller who comes from Wensi: I have not
quarreled.

O Bastet who comes from the shrine: I have not
winked.

O Backward-faced who comes from the pit: I have
not copulated with a boy.

O Flame-footed who comes from the dusk: I have
not been false.

O Dark-one who comes from darkness: I have not
reviled.

O Peace-bringer who comes from Sais: I have not
been aggressive.

O Many-faced who comes from Djefet: I have not
had a hasty heart.

O Accuser who comes from Utjen: I have not
attacked and reviled a god.

O Horned-one who comes from Siut: I have not
made many words.

O Nefertem who comes from Memphis: I have
not sinned, I have not done wrong.

O Timeless-one who comes from Djedu: I have
not made trouble.

O Willful-one who comes from Tjebu: I have not
waded in water.

O Flowing-one who comes from Nun: I have not
raised my voice.

O Commander of people who comes from his
shrine: I have not cursed a god.

O Benefactor who comes from Huy: I have not
been boastful.

O Nehebkau who comes from the city: I have not
been haughty.

O High-of-head who comes from the cave: I have
not wanted more than I had.

O Captor who comes from the graveyard: I have
not cursed god in my town.

The Address to the Gods

. . . .

Behold me, I have come to you,
Without sin, without guilt, without evil,
Without a witness against me,
Without one whom I have wronged.
I live on *maat*, I feed on *maat*,
I have done what people speak of,
What the gods are pleased with,
I have contented a god with what he wishes.
I have given bread to the hungry,
Water to the thirsty,
Clothes to the naked,
A ferryboat to the boatless.
I have given divine offerings to the gods,
Invocation-offerings to the dead.
Rescue me, protect me,
Do not accuse me before the great god!

. . . .

from *The Instruction of Ankhsheshonq*

Reprinted from Miriam Lichtheim, Ancient Egyptian Literature, Volume III: The Late Period, *University of California Press, 1980. Copyright © 1980 by the Regents of the University of California.*

S[erve your] god, that he may guard you.

Serve your brothers, that you may have good repute.

Serve a wise man, that he may serve you.

Serve him who serves you.

Serve any man, that you may find profit.

Serve your father and mother, that you may go and prosper.

Examine every matter, that you may understand it.

Be gentle and patient, then your heart will be beautiful.

It is in maturity that instruction succeeds.

Do not rely on the property of another, saying, "I will live on it"; acquire your own.

Do not abuse when you fare well, lest you fare badly.

Do not send a low woman on a business of yours; she will go after her own.

Do not send a wise man in a small matter when a big matter is waiting.

Do not send a fool in a big matter when there is a wise man whom you can send.

Do not send into town when you may find trouble in it.

Do not long for your home when you do an errand.

Do not long for your home to drink beer in it in midday.

Do not pamper your body, lest you become weak.

Do not pamper yourself when you are young, lest you be weak when you are old.

Do not hate a man to his face when you know nothing of him.

Do not fret so long as you own something.

Do not worry so long as you own something.

Do not fret at all.

Do not fret about your occupation. . . .

Do not spare your son work when you can make him do it.

Do not instruct a fool, lest he hate you.

Do not instruct him who will not listen to you.

Do not rely on a fool.

Do not rely on the property of an idiot. . . .

Do not speak hastily, lest you give offense.

Do not say right away what comes out of your heart. . . .

Learning and foolishness belong to the people of your town; respect the people of your town.

Do not say "I am learned"; set yourself to become wise.

Do not do a thing that you have not first examined.

Examining makes your good fortune.

If you examine three wise men about a matter it is perfect; the outcome lies with the great god.

Do well by your body in your days of well-being.

There is no one who does not die. . . .

Do not take to yourself a woman whose husband is alive, lest he become your enemy.

In strait times or happy times wealth grows because of spreading it.

May your fate not be the fate of one who begs and is given.

When you work the land do not pamper your body.

Do not say "Here is my brother's acre"; look to your own. . . .

He who does not gather wood in summer will not be warm in winter. . . .

Wealth takes hold of its owner.

The owner of a cow gets to run.

Do not spend before you have set up your storehouse.

Spend according to the size of your means. . . .

He who sends spittle up to the sky will have it fall on him.

A man's character is his family.

A man's character is his destiny.

A man's character is on his face.

A man's character is one of his limbs. . . .

Man does not know the days of his misfortune.

Do not entrust your people to one who has not experienced distress.

Do not delay to get yourself a tomb on the mountain; you do not know the length of your life.

Do not do evil to a man and so cause another to do it to you.

Do not be discouraged in a matter in which you can ask (advice).

Happy is the heart of him who has made a judgment before a wise man.

A wise master who asks [advice], his house stands forever.

Disdain ruins a great man. . . .

Do not retaliate; do not let one retaliate against you.

Let your benefaction reach him who has need of it.

Do not be stingy; wealth is no security.

Even a kind master will kill to have peace.

The prudent killer does not get killed.

Do not undertake a matter if you cannot carry it out. . . .

The friend of a fool is a fool; the friend of a wise man is a wise man.

The friend of an idiot is an idiot. . . .

Do not speak in two voices.

Speak truth to all men; let it cleave to your speech. . . .

A thief steals by night; he is found by day.

Do not make many words.

A house is open to him who has goods in his hand.

He who is bitten of the bite of a snake is afraid of a coil of rope.

The man who looks in front of him does not stumble and fall. . . .

Do not be afraid to do that in which you are right.

Do not commit theft; you will be found out. . . .

Do not drink water in the house of a merchant; he will charge you for it.

Do not deliver a servant into the hand of his master. . . .

Borrow money at interest and put it in farmland.

Borrow money at interest and take a wife.

Borrow money at interest and celebrate your birthday.

Do not borrow money at interest in order to live well on it.

Do not swear falsely when you are in distress, lest you become worse off than you are.

Do not ask advice from the god and then neglect what he said.

Do not laugh at a cat. . . .

Do not be fainthearted in a bad situation. . . .

One does not load a beam on a donkey.

If a woman loves a crocodile she takes on its character. . . .

A deed happens to its doer.

The god looks into the heart.

It is in battle that a man finds a brother.

It is on the road that a man finds a companion.

The plans of the god are one thing, the thoughts of men are another. . . .

'ABBA MIKA'EL

'Abba Mika'el (Father Michael), an Egyptian by birth, translated *The Book of the Philosophers* between 1510 and 1522. Originally, the work was written in Greek, probably during the Byzantine period. This version is lost. Hunain ibn Ishâq (809–877?), a Mesopotamian Christian, translated it into Arabic; 'Abba Mika'el, probably collaborating with one or more native Ethiopians, translated the work into Geez, an ancient Ethiopian tongue of the Semitic family still in use in the sixteenth century as a formal, literary language. But the translation is far from literal. So much has been added, deleted, and changed that the product seems more an original work or an adaptation than a translation. The Greek influence, especially, remains in *The Book of the Philosophers,* but it has a distinctly Ethiopian stamp.

The Book of the Philosophers consists of sayings or proverbs, mostly ethical in content. It thus seems to descend from the demotic wisdom literature of the eastern Mediterranean; *The Instruction of Ankhsheshonq* is a distant ancestor, as are certain Christian writings. But unlike earlier wisdom texts, *The Book of the Philosophers* often strings proverbs together to form parables or arguments. The names of philosophers attached to various sayings (generally omitted in the translation below) are inaccurate; names seem to have been interchanged freely, and the book often attributes common, traditional proverbs to some philosopher or other. The result of the freedom exercised in translating the work and attributing proverbs, however, is an intriguing glimpse of sixteenth-century African thought.

The proverbs in *The Book of the Philosophers* center on virtue. Wisdom, humility, and patient hope play an especially important role. One of the most interesting features of the collection, however, is its stress on each individual's nature. "A wise man remains faithful to his nature," counsels one proverb. "Do not choose a way that is different from you," advises another. The book assumes that each person has a nature, or character, that affects how that person ought to live. An ideally moral life for one person might be completely wrong for another. But there is no hint of relativism. The same ethical principles and virtues appear to apply to everyone. How they apply, however, can vary.

from *The Book of the Philosophers*

In the name of God the Trinity who existed before the universe, who forgives and who has pity, and with confidence in Him and with power from Him, we begin with the help of our Lord Jesus Christ to write the Book of the Philosophers in which each of them speaks according to his ability.

You shall tie your word and secret with a rope, but if you speak you will be tied by them.

They said to a man: "Who counselled you?" He answered: "I saw the foolishness of the fool. I ran away and was thus counselled."

Three things are found in a wise man: keeping people in good order, being satisfied with a little in life, and loving all. The third is the best.

They said to one of the wise men: "How would you take care of your child?" *He answered:* "If he does not get drunk, he will live as I wish, and if he gets drunk, he will live as the wine wishes."

They said to a monk: "Why did you leave the world?" He anwered: "I knew I would have to leave it of necessity, so I chose to leave it willingly."

You do not store wisdom in containers, but in your chest.

Wisdom makes one respect without relatives and relates him to all.

Knowledge has many organs. The most important one is humility. Its brain is the understanding of how to act. Its tongue is a true word. Its conscience is the thinking of good deeds. Its hand is forgiveness. Its leg is the going to the learned. Its domain is justice. Its kingdom is praise and gratitude. Its sword is hope. Its power is prayer. Its fence is love. Its camp is consultation with conscientious people. Its wedding is victory, wisdom, patience, increase of truth.

Its wealth is good exhortation. Its lodging is generosity and meekness. Its friend is love of generous people. Its treasure is to avoid offence.

Brotherhood is like one soul in separate and distinct bodies.

Conscience is of two sexes: active and passive. The active is wisdom that distinguishes what should be. The passive is thinking.

Wisdom is not good if the action is not good.

Do not refuse knowledge to your soul by giving up learning. You will be like a starving man who cannot reach bread placed before him and who does not know his way.

As sickness wounds the flesh, so does sorrow the heart.

Knowledge is innumerable. Take the best from everything.

Patience bridles disaster.

They said to Buzurgmihr: "Which one do you like: your brother or your friend?" *He replied:* "My friend is my brother."

He who has no brother misses the flavour of life.

He who reasons will develop his conscience. He who heightens and honours himself, life will be simple in his eyes.

Three things are found in the character of a fool: anger without a reason, judgement without justice, confusion of enemies with friends.

Conscience is created from four things: knowledge, ability, light and want.

All action has its fruit. The fruit for goodness is giving quickly.

He who takes notice of his own fault, notices that of the others.

He who bears what he cannot will miss what he can.

The fruit of conscience is humility, and the fruit of humility is love.

A soul that is not patient with itself is not patient with others.

A man who is unable to remember God is naked of Him and his life is self-worshiping.

If you cannot control yourself, you cannot order others.

The wise man inquires into all things great and small.

Sorrow shortens life and love of money ends in sorrow.

The *masanqo*[1] stimulates the four different characters in man. Everyone who is moved by it loves the song which is an agreement between one's taste and the strings that are played.

He who heightens his wish weakens his conscience.

Life for fools is death.

Wisdom is the ladder of knowledge. Learn from counselling, even if it is only one word, for the little becomes much in time of need.

The result of wisdom is peace and innocence.

For the one who is adjusted, all sorrow escapes and he attracts all good things.

All knowledge is obtained through justice.

Better die searching for knowledge than live as an idiot.

Hope is like a cloud, and generosity like rain.

Cleverness consists in avoiding worry and being guided by what already happened and by what will happen.

When you feel the wave of anger, keep your face bright and resist your conscience till you beat it[2].

If I tell lies, I fear God; if I tell the truth, I fear you.

Let not by-gones bother you. Do not seek what is impossible for you. Do not believe what is untrue.

Man's eyes are like a spring of water. He is never satisfied with wealth except with earth[3].

If it were possible to build a house by shouting, without any action, a donkey would build two houses a day.

Carrying stones with a wise and conscientious person is better than drinking wine with a fool.

[1] Ethiopian one-string violin.

[2] "It" refers to the wave of anger. Meaning of the saying: resist your misguided conscience till you overcome the evil tendency that you have let grow in it.

[3] Meaning: unless he goes into the earth after his death. Once buried he will forever have enough of the ground he is enclosed in.

If a wealthy man eats a snake, people will think it is for medical reasons. If a poor man eats it, people will think it is because of hunger.

A sheep's hoof in your hand is better than the meat in the hands of another. A bird in the hand is worth all the birds soaring high in the air.

A slip of the feet is better than a slip of the tongue.

Rebuking protects and wealth is protected, for knowledge governs, but money is governed.

The soul is the pillar of the flesh, the mind is the pillar of the spirit, and education is the pillar of knowledge.

Decreasing jealousy increases the flesh.

Patience while one is needy is better than being agitated and mourning, because justice is a clear path.

My son, if you want to know the heart of a man, speak nonsense to him. If he accepts it, he is a fool; if not, he is wise.

All who are afraid run away, all who hope seek, all who are loved are humble, all that makes one sick is bad, and all who obey are quiet.

He who does not counsel himself, counsels the others.

Conscience belongs to something heavenly and it gives birth to a star by its brightness.

The most important thing in humility is to lay the foundation of peace.

The first thing of the mind is to accept with a smiling face, the second is to love, the third is to achieve what is needed.

A good behaviour is compared to a helpful brother, wisdom to a good land; cooperation to an excellent guide.

While some people were passing along a road, they met a monk who was living in his cave. They entered and rested for a while. They asked him: "O monk! which is the right road?" He replied, pointing to the sky with his hand: "Here is the road!" Again they asked him: "Why do you always go back and forth with a stick in your hand, though you are neither old nor sick?" He said: "I know I wish to go, for this is a place of exile, and to hold a stick is a sign of travelling."

The bitterness of patience produces a tasty fruit.

Good behaviour calls for cleverness and harmony.

Good order is better than an accumulation of gold. The greatest evil in man's behaviour is conceit and jealousy. If you want to befriend people, tell them something that irritates them. If you want them not to turn truth into madness, strengthen love with them. If you do not do so, beware of them in the days of your friendship with them as you would in the days of your anger, for anger reveals and brings out what is buried in their heart.

Lessen your treasure so that your sorrows may be lessened, for a treasure is a fountain of sorrows.

Increasing knowledge dresses one with grace. A true word brings love and peace. Politeness keeps prosperity. Good behaviour cleanses one's action. Desire is won through true efforts.

Be free, and then speak and act, for your acts are now changed.

Conscience is a light which goes in between truth and sin, between words and lie, between goodness and vanity, and other things similar to these.

Four things cannot be recovered: a word once spoken, a spear that is thrown, a desire that is lost and a year that is gone.

Silence without thought is dumbness.

If the heart is enriched, knowledge is enriched.

Three things fit with three others: conscience with ardour, activity with peace, respect of relatives with couselling, and the mystery of a thing like the soul is in the flesh.

Hope makes one patient.

Open a new day by performing good deeds and be submissive to your afterworld as if it were with you.

Do not choose a way that is different from you.

The behaviour of foolish people resembles that of babies. Both of them need someone to feed and guide them.

We are guided to the knowledge of the creator by creatures; so are we led by the flesh to the knowledge of man's heart.

A wise man remains faithful to his nature, but a wiser man remains faithful to his action.

A perfect soul is above happiness and sorrow.

A jealous person is a weak rebel.

Skillfulness is like a blind man that has legs and action is like a paralyzed person that has no legs. If they agree that the blind carries the paralytic who sees, they will be like one who sees and has legs. If they quarrel, the resulting deed will be of no use to any one of them, neither to the paralytic who has eyes nor to the blind who has legs.

Do not despise a good piece of advice even if it comes from a poor person, for people do not despise a precious stone on account of the low condition of the man who swims into the depths of the sea and gets the precious stone out.

A man who admires you for what is not within you is speaking to another, and his reply is not for you.

Justice is one-faced but injustice has many faces.

When evil action is stirred, it bears sorrow, and when revealed, pain is relieved.

Conscience and counselling are like soul and flesh. Without the soul the flesh has no life nor any movement. And without the flesh, the soul has no power nor any manifestation of man's behaviour. If together they rise and meet, they do something stronger than death.

Want is of two kinds, tiredness in looking for something one can find, hard work in looking for a thing that is gone.

A man who collects knowledge is great, and he who eats from it is satisfied, and he who drinks from it quenches his thirst.

The Book of the Philosophers is completed. Praise be to God! Amen.

ZERA YACOB

Zera Yacob (1599–1692), born near Aksum, was the son of a poor Ethiopian farmer. He attended traditional Ethiopian schools, studying the Psalms, sacred music, and Ethiopian literature. The school encouraged questions and discussions; it taught reflection, criticism, and the power of thought. Following a period of devastation brought about by foreign invasion, Ethiopia was undergoing a religious revival and suffering various religious conflicts. In 1626, in the midst of these events, King Susenyos converted to Catholicism and summarily ordered obedience to Rome. Zera Yacob, who greatly valued independence of thought, did not convert. Seeing an opportunity, a rival priest in Aksum, Walda Yohannes, denounced Zera Yacob as a traitor, claiming that he was inciting revolution against the Catholics and the king. Only twenty-seven years old, Zera Yacob fled for his life, taking nothing but a small amount of gold and his copy of the Psalms. On his way to Shoa, the region around Addis Ababa, he found a cave in a beautiful valley, where he stayed for two years until Susenyos died. In the cave, he formulated the basic ideas of his philosophy.

Returning to society, Zera Yacob acquired a literary patron in the rich merchant Habtu. Zera Yacob lived in his house in Enfraz, tutored his sons, and married his maidservant. One of Habtu's sons, Walda Heywat, asked Zera Yacob to write down his philosophical views; the result (in 1667) was *The Treatise of Zera Yacob*. Fearing persecution, Zera Yacob never published it. He lived in Enfraz, happily and prosperously, for twenty-five more years until his death at age ninety-three.

The book's original Geez title, *Hatäta,* comes from a root meaning to question, search, investigate, or examine. The *Treatise* champions reason as a tool for understanding the world and for understanding religion. Zera Yacob argues that reason, applied to the evidence of the world, leads to the conclusion that the world, God's creation, is essentially good. His ethics rests on this foundation. Because creation is good, enjoying it is appropriate and also good. Zera Yacob thus opposes traditional Ethiopian asceticism, a philosophy of denial, fasting, and monastic life, in favor of involvement with the secular world.

In fact, Zera Yacob uses reason, which he calls the "light of our heart," to criticize the ethical prescriptions of various religions. He argues that Jewish law, Christian morality, and Islamic rules of conduct all go astray on basic points; they imply that the order of nature itself is wrong. Zera Yacob optimistically believes that "he who investigates with the pure intelligence set by the creator in the heart of each man and scrutinizes the order and laws of creation, will discover the truth." Reason thus serves as a foundation for morality and as a test for religious beliefs.

Underlying Zera Yacob's assault on particular religious tenets is a general skepticism about deriving ethical conclusions from religious revelation. Many religious thinkers have believed that God reveals moral truth and that we can know that truth only because God reveals it to us. Zera Yacob argues that this cannot be correct. Defenders of each religion claim that they know the only true way. Obviously, not everyone can be right. How can we decide who is right? How, that is, can we judge which alleged revelations really come from God? Zera Yacob argues that we cannot. We have no way to tell true revelations from pretenders. We have no choice, therefore, but to use reason to discover moral truth.

from *The Treatise of Zera Yacob*

Reprinted from Claude Sumner, The Source of African Philosophy: The Ethiopian Philosophy of Man. *Copyright © 1986 by Franz Steiner Verlag Wiesbaden GmbH, Sitz Stuttgart.*

CHAPTER IV / THE INVESTIGATION OF FAITH AND OF PRAYER

Later on I thought, saying to myself: "Is everything that is written in the Holy Scriptures true?" Although I thought much about these things I understood nothing, so I said to myself: "I shall go and consult scholars and thinkers; they will tell me the truth." But afterwards I thought, saying to myself: "What will men tell me other than what is in their heart?" Indeed each one says: "My faith is right, and those who believe in another faith believe in falsehood, and are the enemies of God." These days the *Frang** tell us: "Our faith is right, yours is false." We on the other hand tell them: "It is not so; your faith is wrong, ours is right." If we also ask the Mohammedans and the Jews, they will claim the same thing, and who would be the judge for such a kind of argument? No single human being can judge: for all men are plaintiffs and defendants between themselves. Once I asked a *Frang* scholar many things concerning our faith; he interpreted them all according to his own faith. Afterwards I asked a well-known Ethiopian scholar and he also interpreted all things according to his own faith. If I had asked the Mohammedans and the Jews, they also would have interpreted according to their own faith; then, where could I obtain a judge that tells the truth? As my faith appears true to me, so does another one find his own faith true; but truth is one. While thinking over this matter, I said: "O my creator, wise among the wise and just among the just,

*Literally, "foreigners"; here, "Europeans," "Catholics." —Ed.

who created me with an intelligence, help me to understand, for men lack wisdom and truthfulness; as David said: 'No man can be relied upon.'"

I thought further and said: "Why do men lie over problems of such great importance, even to the point of destroying themselves?" and they seemed to do so because although they pretend to know all, they know nothing. Convinced they know all, they do not attempt to investigate the truth. As David said: "Their hearts are curdled like milk." Their heart is curdled because they assume what they have heard from their predecessors and they do not inquire whether it is true or false. But I said: "O Lord! who strike me down with such torment, it is fitting that I know your judgement. You chastise me with truth and admonish me with mercy. But never let my head be anointed with the oil of sinners and of masters in lying: make me understand, for you created me with intelligence." I asked myself: "If I am intelligent, what is it I understand?" And I said: "I understand there is a creator, greater than all creatures; since from his overabundant greatness, he created things that are so great. He is intelligent who understands all, for he created us as intelligent from the abundance of his intelligence; and we ought to worship him, for he is the master of all things. If we pray to him, he will listen to us; for he is almighty." I went on saying in my thought: "God did not create me intelligent without a purpose, that is to look for him and to grasp him and his wisdom in the path he has opened for me and to worship him as long as I live." And still thinking on the same subject, I said to myself: "Why is it that all men do not adhere to truth, instead of believing falsehood?" The cause seemed to be the nature of man which is weak and sluggish. Man aspires to know truth and the hidden things of nature, but his endeavour is difficult and can only be attained with great labour and patience, as Soloman said: "With the help of wisdom I have been at pains to study all that is done under heaven; oh, what a weary task God has given mankind to labour at!" Hence people hastily accept what they have heard from their fathers and shy from any critical examination. But God created man to be the master of his own actions, so that he will be what he wills to be, good or bad. If a man chooses to be wicked he can continue in this way until he receives the punishment he deserves for his wickedness. But being carnal, man likes what is of the flesh; whether they are good or bad, he finds ways and means through which he can satisfy his carnal desire. God did not create man to be evil, but to choose what he would like to be, so that he may receive his reward if he is good or his condemnation if he is bad. If a liar, who desires to achieve wealth or honours among men, needs to use foul means to obtain them, he will say he is convinced this falsehood was for him a just thing. To those people who do not want to search, this action seems to be true, and they believe in the liar's strong faith. I ask you in how many falsehoods do our people believe? They believe wholeheartedly in astrology and other calculations, in the mumbling of secret words, in omens, in the conjuration of devils and in all kinds of magical art and in the utterances of soothsayers. They believe in all these because they did not investigate the truth but listened to their predecessors. Why did these predecessors lie unless it was for obtaining wealth and honours? Similarly those who wanted to rule the people said: "We were sent by God to proclaim the truth to you"; and the people believed them. Those who came after them accepted their fathers' faith without question: rather, as a proof of their faith, they added to it by including stories of signs and omens. Indeed they said: "God did these things"; and so they made God a witness of falsehood and a party to liars.

CHAPTER V / THE LAW OF MOSES AND THE MEDITATION OF MOHAMMED

To the person who seeks it, truth is immediately revealed. Indeed he who investigates with the pure intelligence set by the creator in the heart of each man and scrutinizes the order and laws of creation, will discover the truth. Moses said: "I have been sent by God to proclaim to you his will and his law"; but those who came after him added stories of miracles that they claimed had been wrought in Egypt and on Mount Sinai and attributed them to Moses. But to an inquisitive mind they do not seem to be true. For in the Books of Moses, one can find a wisdom that is shameful and that fails to agree with the wisdom of the creator or with the order and the laws of creation. Indeed by the will of the creator, and the law of nature, it has been ordained that man and woman would unite in a carnal embrace to generate children, so that human beings will not disappear from the earth. Now this mating, which is willed by God in his law of creation, cannot be impure since God does not stain the work of his own hands. But Moses considered that act as evil; but our intelligence teaches us that he who says such a thing is wrong and makes his creator a liar. Again they said that the law of Christianity is from God, and miracles are brought forth to prove it. But our intelligence tells and confirms to us with proofs that marriage springs from the law of the creator; and yet monastic law renders this wisdom of the creator ineffectual, since it prevents the generation of children and extinguishes mankind. The law of Christians which propounds the superiority of monastic life over marriage is false and cannot come from God. How can the violation of the law of the creator stand superior to his wisdom, or can man's deliberation correct the word of God? Similarly Mohammed said: "The orders I pass to you are given to me by God"; and there was no lack of writers to record miracles proving Mohammed's mission, and people believed in him. But we know that the teaching of Mohammed could not have come from God; those who will be born both male and female are equal in number; if we count men and women living in an area, we find as many women as men; we do not find eight or ten women for every man; for the law of creation orders one man to marry one woman. If one man marries ten women, then nine men will be without wives. This violates the order of creation and the laws of nature and it ruins the usefulness of marriage; Mohammed, who taught in the name of God, that one man could marry many wives, is not sent from God. These few things I examined about marriage.

Similarly when I examine the remaining laws, such as the Pentateuch, the law of the Christians and the law of Islam, I find many things which disagree with the truth and the justice of our creator that our intelligence reveals to us. God indeed has illuminated the heart of man with understanding by which he can see the good and evil, recognize the licit and the illicit, distinguish truth from error, "and by your light we see the light, oh Lord"! If we use this light of our heart properly, it cannot deceive us; the purpose of this light which our creator gave us is to be saved by it, and not to be ruined by it. Everything that the light of our intelligence shows us comes from the source of truth, but what men say comes from the source of lies and our intelligence teaches us that all that the creator established is right. The creator in his kind wisdom has made blood to flow monthly from the womb of women. And the life of a woman requires this flow of blood in order to generate children; a woman who has no menstruation is barren and cannot have children, because she is impotent by nature. But Moses and Christians have defiled the wisdom of the creator; Moses even considers impure all the things that such a woman touches; this law of Moses impedes marriage and the entire life of a woman and it spoils the law of mutual help, prevents the bringing up of children and destroys love. Therefore this law of Moses cannot spring from him who created woman. Moreover, our intelligence tells us that we should bury our dead brothers. Their corpses are impure only if we follow the wisdom of Moses; they are not, however, if we follow the wisdom of our creator who made us out of dust that we may return to dust. God does not change into impurity the order he imposes on all creatures with great wisdom, but man attempts to render it impure that he may glorify the voice of falsehood.

The Gospel also declares: "He who does not leave behind father, mother, wife and children is not worthy of God." This forsaking corrupts the nature of man. God does not accept that his creature destroy itself, and our intelligence tells us that abandoning our father and our mother helpless in their old age is a great sin; the Lord is not a god that loves malice; those who desert their children are worse than the wild animals, that never forsake their off-spring. He who abandons his wife abandons her to adultery and thus violates the order of creation and the laws of nature. Hence what the Gospel says on this subject cannot come from God. Likewise the Mohammedans said that it is right to go and buy a man as if he were an animal. But with our intelligence we understand that this Mohammedan law cannot come from the creator of man who made us equal, like brothers, so that we call our creator our father. But Mohammed made the weaker man the possession of the stronger and equated a rational creature with irrational animals; can this depravity be attributed to God?

God does not order absurdities, nor does he say: "Eat this, do not eat that; today eat, tomorrow do not eat; do not eat meat today, eat it tomorrow", unlike the Christians who follow the laws of fasting. Neither did God say to the Mohammedans: "Eat during the night, but do not eat during the day", nor similar and like things. Our reason teaches us that we should eat of all things which do no harm to our health and our nature, and that we should eat each day as much as is required for our sustenance. Eating one day, fasting the next endangers health; the law of fasting reaches beyond the order of the creator who created food for the life of man and wills that we eat it and be grateful for it; it is not fitting that we abstain from his gifts to us. If there are people who argue that fasting kills the desire of the flesh, I shall answer them: "The concupiscence of the flesh by which a man is attracted to a woman and a woman to a man springs from the wisdom of the creator; it is improper to do away with it; but we should act according to the well-known law that God established concerning legitimate intercourse. God did not put a purposeless concupiscence into the flesh of men and of all animals; rather he planted it in the flesh of man as a root of life in this world and a stabilizing power for each creature in the way destined for it. In order that this concupiscence lead us not to excess, we should eat according to our needs, because overeating and drunkenness result in ill health and shoddiness in work. A man who eats according to his needs on Sunday and during the fifty days does not sin, similarly he who eats on Friday and on the days before Easter does not sin. For God created man with the same necessity for food on each day and during each month. The Jews, the Christians and the Mohammedans did not understand the work of God when they instituted the law of fasting; they lie when they say that God imposed fasting upon us and forbade us to eat; for God our creator gave us food that we support ourselves by it, not that we abstain from it.

CHAPTER VII / THE LAW OF GOD AND THE LAW OF MAN

I said to myself: "Why does God permit liars to mislead his people?" God has indeed given reason to all and everyone so that they may know truth and falsehood, and the power to choose between the two as they will. Hence if it is truth we want, let us seek it with our reason which God has given us so that with it we may see that which is needed for us from among all the necessities of nature. We cannot, however, reach truth through the doctrine of man, for all men are liars. If on the contrary we prefer falsehood, the order of the creator and the natural law imposed on the whole of nature do not perish thereby, but we ourselves perish by our own error. God sustains the world by his order which he himself has established and which man cannot destroy, because the order of God is stronger than the order of men. Therefore those who believe that monastic life is superior to marriage are they themselves drawn to marriage because of the might of the order of the creator; those who believe that fasting brings righteousness to their soul eat when they feel hungry; and those who believe that he who has given up his goods is perfect are drawn to seek them again on account of their usefulness, as many of our monks have done. Likewise all liars would like to break the order of nature: but it is not possible that they do not see their lie broken down. But the creator laughs at them, the Lord of creation derides them. God knows the right way to act, but the sinner is caught in the snare set by himself. Hence a monk who holds the order of marriage as impure will be caught in the snare of fornication and of other carnal sins against nature and of grave sickness. Those who despise riches will show their hypocrisy in the presence of kings and of wealthy persons in order to acquire

these goods. Those who desert their relatives for the sake of God lack temporal assistance in times of difficulty and in their old age, they begin to blame God and men and to blaspheme. Likewise all those who violate the law of the creator fall into the trap made by their own hands. God permits error and evil among men because our souls in this world live in a land of temptation, in which the chosen ones of God are put to the test, as the wise Solomon said: "God has put the virtuous to the test and proved them worthy to be with him; he has tested them like gold in a furnace, and accepted them as a holocaust." After our death, when we go back to our creator, we shall see how God made all things in justice and great wisdom and that all his ways are truthful and upright. It is clear that our soul lives after the death of our flesh; for in this world our desire for happiness is not fulfilled; those in need desire to possess, those who possess desire more, and though man owned the whole world, he is not satisfied and craves for more. This inclination of our nature shows us that we are created not only for this life, but also for the coming world; there the souls which have fulfilled the will of the creator will be perpetually satisfied and will not look for other things. Without this inclination the nature of man would be deficient and would not obtain that of which it has the greatest need. Our soul has the power of having the concept of God and of seeing him mentally; likewise it can conceive of immortality. God did not give this power purposelessly; as he gave the power, so did he give the reality. In this world complete justice is not achieved: wicked people are in possession of the goods of this world in a satisfying degree, the humble starve; some wicked men are happy, some good men are sad, some evil men exult with joy; some righteous men weep. Therefore, after our death there must needs be another life and another justice, a perfect one, in which retribution will be made to all according to their deeds, and those who have fulfilled the will of the creator revealed through the light of reason and have observed the law of their nature will be rewarded. The law of nature is obvious, because our reason clearly propounds it, if we examine it. But men do not like such inquiries; they choose to believe in the words of men rather than to investigate the will of their creator.

CHAPTER VIII / THE NATURE OF KNOWLEDGE

The will of God is known by this short statement from our reason that tells us: "Worship God your creator and love all man as yourself." Moreover our reason says: "Do not do unto others that which you do not like done to you, but do unto others as you would like others to do unto you." The decalogue of the Pentateuch expresses the will of the creator excepting the precept about the observance of the Sabbath, for our reason says nothing of the observance of the Sabbath. But the prohibitions of killing, stealing, lying, adultery: our reason teaches us these and similar ones. Likewise the six precepts of the Gospel are the will of the creator. For indeed we desire that men show mercy to us; it therefore is fitting that we ourselves show the same mercy to the others, as much as it is within our power. It is the will of God that we keep our life and existence in this world. It is the will of the creator that we come into and remain in this life, and it is not right for us to leave it against his holy will. The creator himself wills that we adorn our life with science and work; for such an end did he give us reason and power. Manual labour comes from the will of God, because without it the necessities of our life cannot be fulfilled. Likewise marriage of one man with one woman and education of children. Moreover there are many other things which agree with our reason and are necessary for our life or for the existence of mankind. We ought to observe them, because such is the will of our creator, and we ought to know that God does not create us perfect but creates us with such a reason as to know that we are to strive for perfection as long as we live in this world, and to be worthy for the reward that our creator has prepared for us in his wisdom. It was possible for God to have created us perfect and to make us enjoy beatitude on earth; but he did not will to create us in this way; instead he created us with the capacity of striving for perfection, and placed us in the midst of the trials of the world so that we may become perfect and deserve the reward that our creator will give us after our death; as long as we live in this world we ought to praise our creator and fulfil his will and be patient until he draws us unto him, and beg from his mercy that he will lessen our period of hardship and forgive our sins and faults which we committed through ignorance, and enable us to know the laws of our creator and to keep them.

Now as to prayer, we always stand in need of it because our rational nature requires it. The soul endowed with intelligence that is aware that there is a God who knows all, conserves all, rules all, is drawn to him so that it prays to him and asks him to grant things good and to be freed from evil and sheltered under the hand of him who is almighty and for whom nothing is impossible, God great and sublime who sees all that is above and beneath him, holds all, teaches all, guides all, our Father, our creator, our Protector, the reward for our souls, merciful, kind, who knows each of our misfortunes, takes pleasure in our patience, creates us for life and not for destruction, as the wise Solomon said: "You, Lord, teach all things, because you can do all things and overlook men's sins so that they can repent. You love all that exists, you hold nothing of what you have made in abhorrence, you are indulgent and merciful to all." God created us intelligent so that we may meditate on his greatness, praise him and pray to him in order to obtain the needs of our body and soul. Our reason which our creator has put in the heart of man teaches all these things to us. How can they be useless and false?

WALDA HEYWAT

Walda Heywat (1630?–?) was a son of Habtu, a rich Ethiopian merchant from Enfraz, and a pupil of Zera Yacob. We know little about his life. He wrote his *Treatise* to explore and explain the ideas of his teacher. But Walda Heywat is more than just his teacher's promoter. Zera Yacob's work is highly rationalistic; it relies on reason to illumine religious and philosophical issues. Walda Heywat's *Treatise,* in contrast, consists partly of stories designed to illustrate philosophical and, most often, ethical points. The stories reflect the influence of Ethiopian popular literature. Moreover, they seem designed to teach philosophy to the previously uninitiated. In his writing, Walda Heywat is primarily a teacher addressing an audience of students.

Although Walda Heywat relies on Zera Yacob for many of his ideas, his thought is distinctive, primarily for its practical, everyday focus. Walda Heywat treats themes close to common sense, practical problems, and ordinary living. He argues that work is valuable; that all human beings are equal from a moral point of view and deserve equal respect; and that family life is good and extremely important, serving as a foundation for other social relations. His philosophy continues to be influential in Ethiopian thought.

Walda Heywat begins by asserting the social nature of humanity. We are born into society, and we rely on others for survival and for happiness. This implies that each person has a duty to help others. Moreover, because God has created us all equal, we ought to show others the love and respect we show ourselves. From this principle Walda Heywat derives the Golden Rule. He criticizes contemporary Christians for failing to live up to the commandment to love one another. He also defends religious tolerance, maintaining that "each man should believe what seems true to him." (Recall that Zera Yacob, Walda Heywat's teacher, suffered religious persecution, spending two years in a remote cave and never daring to publish his own critiques of standard religious requirements.)

Walda Heywat argues that we should love our work and strive to provide what we need and also some to share with others. This striving, in principle, has no limits; to rest content with our possessions, he says, is just laziness. "Acquire as much as you can without dishonesty," he advises. By creating wealth, we can imitate God, who created every source of wealth.

Walda Heywat also discusses the structure of the family, suggesting that women are inferior to men and so ought to play a different role. In this respect he ratifies the Ethiopian social structure of his time and departs from the teachings of Zera Yacob, who maintains that "husband and wife are equal in marriage."

from *The Treatise of Walda Heywat*

Reprinted from Claude Sumner, The Source of
African Philosophy: The Ethiopian Philosophy of
Man. *Copyright © 1986 by Franz Steiner Verlag
Wiesbaden GmbH, Sitz Stuttgart.*

CHAPTER XIII / SOCIAL LIFE

If a person approaches his creator and remains as if
he were elevated with him in his prayer and his
thanksgiving, he should not remain aloof from his
fellow men, because God ordered men to unite and
cooperate with their neighbors. God did not create
man that he be busy only with himself, but he created
him with the need for the society of other men. For
man cannot live by himself, one is in need of the
other. All men should help one another; whoever
breaks away from the company of men, abrogates the
law of his creator. Therefore do not praise those who
isolate themselves from men that they may live as her-
mits in country caves. They have ignored the will of
the creator who ordered that each and every man help
one another; now a solitary man is useless to human
society as if he were already dead; God does not
accept the service of such a man who refuses to walk
through the path he would have led him by and does
not want to serve in the well-determined service that
he had imposed on him.

Moreover God created all men equal just like
brothers, sons of one father; our creator himself is
the father of all. Therefore, we should love one
another and observe this eternal precept which God
engraved upon the Tables of our heart and which
says: "Love your fellow men as yourself, and do to
them what you wish others to do to you; do not do
to them that which you do not want to be done to
you"; observation of this primary precept is the perfection of all our deeds and of all justice. Do not
think that the doctrine of fools who say the follow-

ing is good: "The word 'fellow man' is confined only
to relatives, or our neighbors, or our friends, or
members of the faith." Do not say the same as they
do; for all men are our fellow men whether they are
good or evil, Christians, Mohammedans, Jews, pa-
gans: all are equal to us and our brothers, because
we are all the sons of one father and the creatures of
one creator. Therefore we ought to love one another,
and to behave well with all as much as we can and
not to inflict evil on anyone. We ought to bear
patiently the ignorance and sins of men, and forgive
them the error through which they made us suffer,
because we ourselves are sinners and wish that our
sins be remitted. If there are people who say: "What
shall we do to those who do wrong to us?" I may say
to them: "We ought to avoid their evil as much as
possible and not to answer evil by evil, because vindication belongs only to God the judge of all; if we
cannot avoid the malice that they have contrived
against us except by knocking them down, then and
only then is it permitted to preserve our life and
existence by all means possible and to prevent their
violence with our strength, their design with our
designs, their deceit with our deceit, their spear with
our spear; for God gave us reason and strength that
we preserve our life and health, and escape from the
nets and oppression of wrongdoers. If we cannot
attain this we should be patient and should leave
our anxieties to God, and let him judge us and vindicate us, and beg him to save and free us from the
oppression of men. Unless we are forced in this way,
we should not afflict any man with any injury in
word or deed; we ought scrupulously to keep away,
from all lie, calumny, evil speech, theft, adultery,
beating, murder, from any action from which a damage or a loss for our fellow man may result; all these
go against the order of the creator, destroy all the
laws of nature, extinguish the love and harmony of
which all men have an equal need."

CHAPTER XIV / LOVE

As a mouse spoils with its teeth fine vestments of great value, but is not nourished with them, likewise the human tongue, that destroys a good name with calumnies, gets no advantage from the calumny: a good name is more valuable than fine cloth and all possessions. Just as hail destroys the corn, but as soon as it falls loses its violence, so does calumny which falls from the mouth of men: at the same time it disgraces one's fellow man and ruins the calumniator. As fire burns the house of the builder, man's anger burns his own entrails. O my son! do not be angry in any way whatsoever, lest you regret it bitterly; never let the sun set on your anger. But turn back from your error with ease, and if you have sinned against your neighbour, do not delay to come to yourself again, get up at once and repair with goodness the evil you have inflicted upon him; reconcile yourself with him that peace may reign and God bless you, be a peace-loving man with all and let not an evil word come from your mouth. Be kind and console the troubled and the sad, and God will give you a good reward. Remember to give alms; if you have bread, share it with your brothers who are hungry, and God will fill you with his goods; if you have the power, liberate your opposed brothers, and God will liberate you and will not unleash the rod of sinners in your heritage; if you are wise, have pity on those who lack science, and God will permit you to understand his mysteries and will open to you his secret wisdom. If you can, try to please all men; for the Lord our God is love. He who always loves his friend and pleases him is with God and God is with him. Mutual love embellishes man's entire life; it makes all our afflictions easier to bear; it adds flavour and sweetness to our whole life; it makes this world the kingdom of heaven. But our love is not to be only words or mere talk, but something real and active. Let us not be like the Christians of our country, who teach the love of Jesus Christ with their lips, but do not have love in their heart; they throw insults and curses at one another, and fight about their faith. This kind of love is not from God, it is useless. Let us not pretend to love one another like these hypocrites whose lips speak of justice and love, but with viper's venom under their tongue, whose heart is always meditating hatred and enmity. Let us not love one another like those who love their relatives, their friends, those who share their faith, but hate the aliens and those who do not belong to their faith; their love is not perfect, we ought to know that all men are equal by creation and all are sons of God; we err if we hate them on account of their faith because each man should believe what seems true to him. Faith cannot be strengthened or made to appear right in the heart of men by force and excommunication but by science and doctrine; as we should not hate men because of their science, so should we not hate them because of their faith.

CHAPTER XVIII / THE IMPORTANCE OF HANDICRAFT

Love to work with your hands as much as your life allows, and be expert in this work that you may gain a profit from it; do not be ashamed to work with your hands, because it is God's precept; without work of their hands all human creatures perish and their whole life is destroyed. Do not say: "Hard work is suitable to the poor and the workers, the blacksmiths and the builders, to the sons of artisans, not to the sons of important and noble persons"; such a thought is born from a proud heart. Are not the needs of our life equally exacting for each single person? As the needs of our life are not satisfied except through handwork, likewise work is imposed on each one so that he will fulfil his needs; do not say: "I have all I need to be able to eat and drink without work"; this springs from vicious laziness and destroys the order of the creator who said: "You shall eat from the fruit of your work." He who lives on the work of another man while he has himself the ability to work is a thief and plunderer. Acquaint yourself with manual labour in your childhood, carefully avoid laziness, for an idle person is not worthy of God's grace. Do your work so that at the right time you may provide for your own needs, and those of your family and the poor you help. Let not your heart be beaten down if the fruit of your work is wasted or lost, but persevere in your work and pray to God that he bless this fruit and multiply it. Do not exhaust yourself as animals with no power of thinking, but lay out your work wisely so that you will increase usefulness and profit, and lessen fatigue. If God makes your work prosper and you gather its fruit, thank him with all your heart and rejoice with all your family; eat, drink, celebrate a feast of joy and enjoyment, and persevere in your work so that you may add fruit to the fruit already found in your work, and profit to the profit already gained. Never say: "I have enough", do not say either: "This small amount is enough for my life; why should I labour uselessly?" This utterance stems from a hopeless laziness. Acquire as much as you can without dishonesty; enjoy all the goods you have acquired by the sweat of your brow, and be like the creator: as our creator created from nothing by his power and wisdom all the goods of this world that we see, so you also produce by your own effort and wisdom from your work some good fruit for your life and that of your fellow man.

CHAPTER XXVI / THE WAY OF LIVING

Be patient among yourselves about your difficult character and your hidden defects, because in the whole world there cannot be found a man or a woman without vice. A wise man put it thus: "If a man was without vice he would not die, because he would not be a man." O man, remember that a woman is weak by nature and less intelligent than man. Therefore bear patiently with the harshness of her nature and the loquacity of her tongue, let her anger pass away, not giving it too great importance, and never quarrel with her: if you get used to this type of life, it will be easy for you. As to you, O woman, please your husband, as much as you can; give him delight by your food and drink, and by taking good care of his house and life; your husband cannot love you unless you love him; if you love him, he cannot hate you.

There was a man whose wife was lazy and unkind. So the husband disliked her and began going to another woman; then the wife became jealous; she went to a doctor and said: "My husband hates me; give me a medicine that will make him love me." He said: "I shall prepare it for you, but first go and get me three pieces of hair from the mane of a lion,

I need them for the potion." While she was going away she asked herself: "How can I approach a lion and yet avoid that he devour me?" Then she took a sheep with her and went to a field; the lion came out seeking to devour her: she threw the sheep to it and ran away. The lion, having found food to eat, did not chase her. On the next day, she did the same thing and for many days she repeated the same action, because jealousy for her husband had taken hold of her. As the lion saw that the woman was bringing her food, it no more turned against her, but became familiar with her; when she came with the sheep, it received her with delight swishing its tail and, like a dog, it licked her hand and played with her. Then the woman plucked three pieces of hair from its mane and brought them to the doctor. She said to him: "Here, I have brought to you what is needed for the medicine." He said: "How did you manage to pluck them?" When she had narrated to him all she had done, he said to her: "Go, do to your husband what you did to the lion, and your husband will like you; do you think that your husband is wilder than the lion? As you won the love of the lion by giving it food, so you can win the love of your husband." Then she went and began to follow the doctor's advice; she pleased her husband in all things and was patient; after a few days the husband thought in his heart and said: "Why should I love other women more than my wife; she is good and helps me more than they do?" Then he turned to her and loved her very much.

CHAPTER XXX / SUGGESTIONS FOR A PRUDENT LIFE

Do not trust everyone who comes to you; for he who trusts everyone he meets is foolish. Examine everything and hold on to what is good. Beware once for all of your enemies, but a thousand times of your friend, for he discloses your secrets. Your secret is bound to your heart as long as it is in your heart, once it is spoken out from your mouth, you are bound to the bond of your listener. Do not trust in men's gifts, but trust in your prudence, your action and the fruit of your work. Above all, trust in the gifts and favours of God; do not trust your friends, because tomorrow they will be your enemies. Rely on the work of your hands, which should not exceed your power. Love those who are associated with you and who are close to you and act as if you trusted them; but in reality trust no one absolutely; and in all society you take part in, search first of all an escape by which you can keep out of men's traps, should they wish evil for you. Be alert; all men who appear good to you are not really so, and all those who once did good to you will not always do so. Beware not to fall into men's traps; fear God and do not force any evil upon them, nor pay back evil with evil to those who harmed you, but let God take care of your worry and leave men's malice come back upon the heads of those who do it. Never say within your heart: "My enemies have done evil to me, so I too will pay back evil to them." This is vain; it will not help you to live with people; it leads to quarrels and enmities without end; it is better that you hide in your heart all the injustices men perpetrated against you.

CHAPTER XXXIV / HAPPINESS AND HOPE

When you fall ill, bear with patience even your great affliction, and do not lose courage; trust in God who sees and takes into account the suffering of your sickness, and will reward you well for your patience. Even if he does not pay you in this life, he will reward you after your death when you come to him. Do not fear to depart from life, because death is a liberation: when it will please God to release you from this prison so that you may go to him, thank him; it is a greater advantage to you that you be liberated from this shameful servitude, and fly free and bright like an angel to the bosom of your creator; there you will know and understand all the mysteries of this world and the beauty of the order of heaven and earth; you will enjoy perfect bliss, and possess perpetual and infinite beatitude. Do not love the absurdities of this world—a world in which you must remain until your term of servitude and trial is completed; it is not right for you to leave this world by your own will; this depends on the will of God, who imposed this servitude upon you. If the time

for your liberation has come and it pleases God to release you from your prison, adore him with great humility, thank him, and go to him in joy and confidence. Behold, he will reward you with a life which surpasses all life in this world. Pray to him that he grant you a quiet death and that he may take you away from this world in peace and confidence in him; fear none of the things that frighten the wicked, who did not want to follow the path the creator had traced for them in this world, and who refused to perform the service fixed for all men, who did not understand God's works nor follow the natural law that reason taught them.

But you, my brother, who accept and approve my counselling do not be afraid at the hour of death, for it is better for you to go to your creator. Oh! why do you fear death, when you know that the immortal soul has a greater value than the mortal flesh? Is not freedom more valuable than servitude, joy than sadness, life than death? Likewise, it is better for the soul to be liberated from the prison of the body than to be bound to it. As a man freed from prison sees the light of the sun which gives him delight and heat, likewise our soul, come out of the body, will countemplate God's light and will burn with love for its creator; turning back it will glance at the loss of this world and say with astonishment: "How could I love that ignoble servitude? How did I fear a death which brought me into this beatitude for ever and ever?" Amen.

CHAPTER XXXV / CONCLUSION

Behold, I have written these few things, with the help of God. My brother who have read this book of mine, if you are wise, you too write down the things God taught you. Do not be like a lamp that is put under a tub, but raise up the light of your wisdom; teach and counsel the sons of our country, that wisdom may flourish and sin and ignorance of the right way of behaving may disappear from our land. These men did not know the mighty arm of our creator; had they known it, they would have been ashamed of striving after what is futile. In fact in our days our foolish countrymen, moved by jealousy, have quarrelled among themselves about the institutions of their faith; but they have failed to recognize the order of their creator.

O Lord, we know no other God but you, and we invoke your name and no other; we have not abandoned your doctrine for the doctrine of men, for your precept is the light on earth. Give us peace, since you have given us all; delight us with the dew of your blessing, and protect us that we may worship you in truth and justice. Because yours are glory and honour, now, and for all eternity, world without end. Amen.

FRANTZ FANON

Frantz Fanon (1925–1961), born on the Caribbean island of Martinique, studied psychiatry in France. At twenty-seven, he published *Black Skin, White Masks*. Shortly thereafter, he was assigned to a hospital in Algeria during the war of independence with France. Aligning himself with the rebels, he wrote *A Dying Colonialism* and *The Wretched of the Earth*. The latter appeared in 1961, just before Fanon died of cancer. Jean-Paul Sartre said of Fanon, "In short, the Third World finds *itself* and speaks to *itself* through his voice."*

Fanon begins with the premise that the world is not homogeneous. It consists of many different people and cultures. Some enjoy positions of power and privilege; others suffer oppression. Their oppression stems from many kinds of power and privilege but ultimately rests on actual or threatened violence. Colonial powers dominate the Third World because they have used, continue to use, and threaten to use violence to maintain their power.

Decolonialization is the process of overcoming colonial oppression by overturning current relations of power. Because those relations rest on violence, Fanon argues, only violence can overturn them. To destroy the colonial world with its two sharp divisions, oppressors and oppressed, one must destroy the half of that world consisting of the oppressors.

The colonial world also gives rise to psychological conditions that must be overcome. The oppressors paint the oppressed as barely human, as masses of animals without feelings or autonomy. To overcome the oppression and assert their own interests, the oppressed must first overcome this image of themselves. This too requires violence. Both real and the psychological liberation can come about only through violence. Violence, Fanon therefore concludes, is the only way to liberate the oppressed. Moreover, it is not an unfortunate but necessary step, to be regretted deeply but undertaken nevertheless; violence is itself liberating and ought to be celebrated. As Sartre summarizes Fanon's view, "Violence, like Achilles' lance, can heal the wounds it has inflicted."†

This defense and even celebration of violence is so unusual in the philosophical tradition and has become so influential in parts of the Third World that it makes Fanon's thought worth studying. But Fanon's views have other important philosophical dimensions. Fanon, for example, attacks individualism as a tool of the oppressors. With liberation, he writes, "Individualism is the first to disappear." Many Western and non-Western thinkers adopt a communitarian view, according to which human beings are essentially social. Fanon agrees, but he argues that

---

*Jean-Paul Sartre, in the preface to Fanon's *Wretched of the Earth*, trans. Constance Farrington (Grove Press, 1963), 10.

†Sartre, in the preface of Fanon's *Wretched of the Earth*, 30.

individualism is nothing but a method for preventing the oppressed from coming together and cooperating to overthrow their oppression. Moreover, he takes this position to its full anti-individualist conclusion: "Henceforward, the interests of one will be the interests of all. . . . The motto 'look out for yourself,' the atheist's method of salvation, is in this context forbidden." Thus, there can be no private property, no individual rights: "Resources should be pooled."*

Fanon also attacks the notion of truth. At least in the context of colonialism, truth is simply what serves the interests of the group. When the oppressors speak of truth, they really speak of what serves their own interests as oppressors. When the revolutionaries speak of truth, they speak of what "hurries on the break-up of the colonialist regime." There is no such thing as truth in itself. There is no such thing as good in itself, either. What is good is what promotes the revolution and works against the interests of the oppressors. In this sense, Fanon is not so much an ethical thinker as an antiethical thinker.

While Fanon's assault on individualism, private property, and ethics itself largely follows the analysis of Marx and Engels in *The Communist Manifesto* and other writings, his attack on truth takes their view one step further. Marx and Engels are willing to assail morality as a capitalist tool, but they do not go as far as to deny the existence of truth. In fact, they regard their dialectical materialism as the only proper scientific attitude. Fanon's criticisms suggest that there is something wrong with the idea of a "proper scientific attitude" and with the idea of truth underlying it.

*Fanon, *Wretched of the Earth*, 49.

from *The Wretched of the Earth*

CONCERNING VIOLENCE

National liberation, national renaissance, the restoration of nationhood to the people, commonwealth: whatever may be the headings used or the new formulas introduced, decolonization is always a violent phenomenon. At whatever level we study it—relationships between individuals, new names for sports clubs, the human admixture at cocktail parties, in the police, on the directing boards of national or private banks—decolonization is quite simply the replacing of a certain "species" of men by another "species" of men. Without any period of transition, there is a total, complete, and absolute substitution. It is true that we could equally well stress the rise of a new nation, the setting up of a new state, its diplomatic relations, and its economic and political trends. But we have precisely chosen to speak of that kind of *tabula rasa* which characterizes at the outset all decolonization. Its unusual importance is that it constitutes, from the very first day, the minimum demands of the colonized. To tell the truth, the proof of success lies in a whole social structure being changed from the bottom up. The extraordinary importance of this change is that it is willed, called for, demanded. The need for this change exists in its crude state, impetuous and compelling, in the consciousness and in the lives of the men and women who are colonized. But the possibility of this change is equally experienced in the form of a terrifying future in the consciousness of another "species" of men and women: the colonizers.

Decolonization, which sets out to change the order of the world, is, obviously, a program of complete disorder. But it cannot come as a result of magical practices, nor of a natural shock, nor of a friendly understanding. Decolonization, as we know, is a historical process: that is to say that it cannot be understood, it cannot become intelligible nor clear to itself except in the exact measure that we can discern the movements which give it historical form and content. Decolonization is the meeting of two forces, opposed to each other by their very nature, which in fact owe their originality to that sort of substantification which results from and is nourished by the situation in the colonies. Their first encounter was marked by violence and their existence together—that is to say the exploitation of the native by the settler—was carried on by dint of a great array of bayonets and cannons. The settler and the native are old acquaintances. In fact, the settler is right when he speaks of knowing "them" well. For it is the settler who has brought the native into existence and who perpetuates his existence. The settler owes the fact of his very existence, that is to say, his property, to the colonial system.

Decolonization never takes place unnoticed, for it influences individuals and modifies them fundamentally. It transforms spectators crushed with their inessentiality into privileged actors, with the grandiose glare of history's floodlights upon them. It brings a natural rhythm into existence, introduced by new men, and with it a new language and a new humanity. Decolonization is the veritable creation of new men. But this creation owes nothing of its legitimacy to any supernatural power; the "thing" which has been colonized becomes man during the same process by which it frees itself.

In decolonization, there is therefore the need of a complete calling in question of the colonial situation. If we wish to describe it precisely, we might find it in the well-known words: "The last shall be first and the first last." Decolonization is the putting into practice of this sentence. That is why, if we try to describe it, all decolonization is successful.

The naked truth of decolonization evokes for us the searing bullets and bloodstained knives which emanate from it. For if the last shall be first, this will only come to pass after a murderous and decisive struggle between the two protagonists. That affirmed intention to place the last at the head of things, and to make them climb at a pace (too quickly, some say) the well-known steps which characterize an organized society, can only triumph if we use all means to turn the scale, including, of course, that of violence.

You do not turn any society, however primitive it may be, upside down with such a program if you have not decided from the very beginning, that is to say from the actual formulation of that program, to overcome all the obstacles that you will come across in so doing. The native who decides to put the program into practice, and to become its moving force, is ready for violence at all times. From birth it is clear to him that this narrow world, strewn with prohibitions, can only be called in question by absolute violence.

The colonial world is a world divided into compartments. It is probably unnecessary to recall the existence of native quarters and European quarters, of schools for natives and schools for Europeans; in the same way we need not recall apartheid in South Africa. Yet, if we examine closely this system of compartments, we will at least be able to reveal the lines of force it implies. This approach to the colonial world, its ordering and its geographical layout will allow us to mark out the lines on which a decolonized society will be reorganized.

The colonial world is a world cut in two. The dividing line, the frontiers are shown by barracks and police stations. In the colonies it is the policeman and the soldier who are the official, instituted go-betweens, the spokesmen of the settler and his rule of oppression. In capitalist societies the educational system, whether lay or clerical, the structure of moral reflexes handed down from father to son, the exemplary honesty of workers who are given a medal after fifty years of good and loyal service, and the affection which springs from harmonious relations and good behavior—all these aesthetic expressions of respect for the established order serve to create around the exploited person an atmosphere of submission and of inhibition which lightens the task of policing considerably. In the capitalist countries a multitude of moral teachers, counselors and "bewilderers" separate the exploited from those in power. In the colonial countries, on the contrary, the policeman and the soldier, by their immediate presence and their frequent and direct action maintain contact with the native and advise him by means of rifle butts and napalm not to budge. It is obvious here that the agents of government speak the language of pure force. The intermediary does not lighten the oppression, nor seek to hide the domination; he shows them up and puts them into practice with the clear conscience of an upholder of the peace; yet he is the bringer of violence into the home and into the mind of the native. . . .

This world divided into compartments, this world cut in two is inhabited by two different species. The originality of the colonial context is that economic reality, inequality, and the immense difference of ways of life never come to mask the human realities. When you examine at close quarters the colonial context, it is evident that what parcels out the world is to begin with the fact of belonging to or not belonging to a given race, a given species. In the colonies the economic substructure is also a superstructure. The cause is the consequence; you are rich because you are white, you are white because you are rich. . . .

. . . In the colonies, the foreigner coming from another country imposed his rule by means of guns and machines. In defiance of his successful transplantation, in spite of his appropriation, the settler still remains a foreigner. It is neither the act of owning factories, nor estates, nor a bank balance which distinguishes the governing classes. The governing race is first and foremost those who come from elsewhere, those who are unlike the original inhabitants, "the others."

The violence which has ruled over the ordering of the colonial world, which has ceaselessly drummed the rhythm for the destruction of native social forms and broken up without reserve the systems of reference of the economy, the customs of dress and external life, that same violence will be claimed and taken over by the native at the moment when, deciding to embody history in his own person, he surges into the forbidden quarters. To wreck the colonial world is henceforward a mental picture of action which is very clear, very easy to understand and which may be assumed by each one of the individuals which constitute the colonized people. To break up the colonial world does not mean that after the frontiers have been abolished lines of communication will be set up between the two zones. The destruction of the colonial world is no more and no less that the abolition of one zone, its burial in the depths of the earth or its expulsion from the country.

The natives' challenge to the colonial world is not a rational confrontation of points of view. It is not a treatise on the universal, but the untidy affirmation of an original idea propounded as an absolute. The colonial world is a Manichean world. It is not enough for the settler to delimit physically, that is to say with the help of the army and the police force, the place of the native. As if to show the totalitarian character of colonial exploitation the settler paints the native as a sort of quintessence of evil. Native society is not simply described as a society lacking in values. It is not enough for the colonist to affirm that those values have disappeared from, or still better never existed in, the colonial world. The native is declared insensible to ethics; he represents not only the absence of values, but also the negation of values. He is, let us dare to admit, the enemy of values, and in this sense he is the absolute evil. He is the corrosive element, destroying all that comes near him; he is the deforming element, disfiguring all that has to do with beauty or morality; he is the depository of maleficent powers, the unconscious and irretrievable instrument of blind forces. . . .

At times this Manicheism goes to its logical conclusion and dehumanizes the native, or to speak plainly, it turns him into an animal. In fact, the terms the settler uses when he mentions the native are zoological terms. He speaks of the yellow man's reptilian motions, of the stink of the native quarter, of breeding swarms, of foulness, of spawn, of gesticulations. When the settler seeks to describe the native fully in exact terms he constantly refers to the bestiary. The European rarely hits on a picturesque style; but the native, who knows what is in the mind

of the settler, guesses at once what he is thinking of. Those hordes of vital statistics, those hysterical masses, those faces bereft of all humanity, those distended bodies which are like nothing on earth, that mob without beginning or end, those children who seem to belong to nobody, that laziness stretched out in the sun, that vegetative rhythm of life—all this forms part of the colonial vocabulary. General de Gaulle speaks of "the yellow multitudes" and François Mauriac of the black, brown, and yellow masses which soon will be unleashed. The native knows all this, and laughs to himself every time he spots an allusion to the animal world in the other's words. For he knows that he is not an animal; and it is precisely at the moment he realizes his humanity that he begins to sharpen the weapons with which he will secure its victory.

As soon as the native begins to pull on his moorings, and to cause anxiety to the settler, he is handed over to well-meaning souls who in cultural congresses point out to him the specificity and wealth of Western values. But every time Western values are mentioned they produce in the native a sort of stiffening or muscular lockjaw. During the period of decolonization, the native's reason is appealed to. He is offered definite values, he is told frequently that decolonization need not mean regression, and that he must put his trust in qualities which are well-tried, solid, and highly esteemed. But it so happens that when the native hears a speech about Western culture he pulls out his knife—or at least he makes sure it is within reach. The violence with which the supremacy of white values is affirmed and the aggressiveness which has permeated the victory of these values over the ways of life and of thought of the native mean that, in revenge, the native laughs in mockery when Western values are mentioned in front of him. In the colonial context the settler only ends his work of breaking in the native when the latter admits loudly and intelligibly the supremacy of the white man's values. In the period of decolonization, the colonized masses mock at these very values, insult them, and vomit them up.

. . . For a colonized people the most essential value, because the most concrete, is first and foremost the land: the land which will bring them bread and, above all, dignity. But this dignity has nothing to do with the dignity of the human individual: for the human individual has never heard tell of it. All that the native has seen in his country is that they can freely arrest him, beat him, starve him: and no professor of ethics, no priest has ever come to be beaten in his place, nor to share their bread with him. As far as the native is concerned, morality is very concrete; it is to silence the settler's defiance, to break his flaunting violence—in a word, to put him out of the picture. The well-known principle that all men are equal will be illustrated in the colonies from the moment that the native claims that he is the equal of the settler. One step more, and he is ready to fight to be more than the settler. In fact, he has already decided to eject him and to take his place; as we see it, it is a whole material and moral universe which is breaking up. The intellectual who for his part has followed the colonialist with regard to the universal abstract will fight in order that the settler and the native may live together in peace in a new world. But the thing he does not see, precisely because he is permeated by colonialism and all its ways of thinking, is that the settler, from the moment that the colonial context disappears, has no longer any interest in remaining or in co-existing. It is not by chance that, even before any negotiation between the Algerian and French governments has taken place, the European minority which calls itself "liberal" has already made its position clear: it demands nothing more nor less than twofold citizenship. By setting themselves apart in an abstract manner, the liberals try to force the settler into taking a very concrete jump into the unknown. Let us admit it, the settler knows perfectly well that no phraseology can be a substitute for reality.

Thus the native discovers that his life, his breath, his beating heart are the same as those of the settler. He finds out that the settler's skin is not of any more value than a native's skin; and it must be said that this discovery shakes the world in a very necessary manner. All the new, revolutionary assurance of the native stems from it. For if, in fact, my life is worth as much as the settler's, his glance no longer shrivels me up nor freezes me, and his voice no longer turns me into stone. I am no longer on tenterhooks in his presence; in fact, I don't give a damn for him. Not only does his presence no longer trouble me, but I am already preparing such efficient ambushes for him that soon there will be no way out but that of flight.

We have said that the colonial context is characterized by the dichotomy which it imposes upon the whole people. Decolonization unifies that people by the radical decision to remove from it its heterogeneity, and by unifying it on a national, sometimes a racial, basis. We know the fierce words of the Senegalese patriots, referring to the maneuvers of their president, Senghor: "We have demanded that the higher posts should be given to Africans; and now Senghor is Africanizing the Europeans." That is to say that the native can see clearly and immediately if decolonization has come to pass or not, for his minimum demands are simply that the last shall be first. . . .

Individualism is the first to disappear. The native intellectual had learnt from his masters that the individual ought to express himself fully. The colonialist bourgeoisie had hammered into the native's mind the idea of a society of individuals where each person shuts himself up in his own subjectivity, and whose only wealth is individual thought. Now the native who has the opportunity to return to the people during the struggle for freedom will discover the falseness of this theory. The very forms of organization of the struggle will suggest to him a different vocabulary. Brother, sister, friend—these are words outlawed by the colonialist bourgeoisie, because for them my brother is my purse, my friend is part of my scheme for getting on. The native intellectual takes part, in a sort of auto-da-fé, in the destruction of all his idols: egoism, recrimination that springs from pride, and the childish stupidity of those who always want to have the last word. Such a colonized intellectual, dusted over by colonial culture, will in the same way discover the substance of village assemblies, the cohesion of people's committees, and the extraordinary fruitfulness of local meetings and groupments. Henceforward, the interests of one will be the interests of all, for in concrete fact *everyone* will be discovered by the troops, *everyone* will be massacred—or *everyone* will be saved. The motto "look out for yourself," the atheist's method of salvation, is in this context forbidden.

. . . The people . . . take their stand from the start on the broad and inclusive positions of *bread and the land:* how can we obtain the land, and bread to eat? And this obstinate point of view of the masses, which may seem shrunken and limited, is in the end the most worthwhile and the most efficient mode of procedure.

The problem of truth ought also to be considered. In every age, among the people, truth is the property of the national cause. No absolute verity, no discourse on the purity of the soul, can shake this position. The native replies to the living lie of the colonial situation by an equal falsehood. His dealings with his fellow-nationals are open; they are strained and incomprehensible with regard to the settlers. Truth is that which hurries on the break-up of the colonialist regime; it is that which promotes the emergence of the nation; it is all that protects the natives, and ruins the foreigners. In this colonialist context there is no truthful behavior: and the good is quite simply that which is evil for "them." . . .

The peasantry is systematically disregarded for the most part by the propaganda put out by the nationalist parties. And it is clear that in the colonial countries the peasants alone are revolutionary, for they have nothing to lose and everything to gain. The starving peasant, outside the class system, is the first among the exploited to discover that only violence pays. For him there is no compromise, no possible coming to terms; colonization and decolonization are simply a question of relative strength. The exploited man sees that his liberation implies the use of all means, and that of force first and foremost. When in 1956, after the capitulation of Monsieur Guy Mollet to the settlers in Algeria, the Front de Libération Nationale, in a famous leaflet, stated that colonialism only loosens its hold when the knife is at its throat, no Algerian really found these terms too violent. The leaflet only expressed what every Algerian felt at heart: colonialism is not a thinking machine, nor a body endowed with reasoning faculties. It is violence in its natural state, and it will only yield when confronted with greater violence. . . .

What is the real nature of this violence? We have seen that it is the intuition of the colonized masses that their liberation must, and can only, be achieved by force. By what spiritual aberration do these men, without technique, starving and enfeebled, confronted with the military and economic might of the occupation, come to believe that violence alone will free them? How can they hope to triumph?

It is because violence (and this is the disgraceful thing) may constitute, in so far as it forms part of its system, the slogan of a political party. The leaders may call on the people to enter upon an armed struggle. This problematical question has to be thought over. When militarist Germany decides to settle its frontier disputes by force, we are not in the least surprised; but when the people of Angola, for example, decide to take up arms, when the Algerian people reject all means which are not violent, these are proofs that something has happened or is happening at this very moment. The colonized races, those slaves of modern times, are impatient. They know that this apparent folly alone can put them out of reach of colonial oppression. A new type of relations is established in the world. The underdeveloped peoples try to break their chains, and the extraordinary thing is that they succeed. It could be argued that in these days of sputniks it is ridiculous to die of hunger; but for the colonized masses the argument is more down-to-earth. The truth is that there is no colonial power today which is capable of adopting the only form of contest which has a chance of succeeding, namely, the prolonged establishment of large forces of occupation. . . .

We have said that the native's violence unifies the people. By its very structure, colonialism is separatist and regionalist. Colonialism does not simply state the existence of tribes; it also reinforces it and separates them. The colonial system encourages chieftaincies and keeps alive the old Marabout confraternities. Violence is in action all-inclusive and national. It follows that it is closely involved in the liquidation of regionalism and of tribalism. Thus the national parties show no pity at all toward the caids and the customary chiefs. Their destruction is the preliminary to the unification of the people.

At the level of individuals, violence is a cleansing force. It frees the native from his inferiority complex and from his despair and inaction; it makes him fearless and restores his self-respect. Even if the armed struggle has been symbolic and the nation is demobilized through a rapid movement of decolonization, the people have the time to see that the liberation has been the business of each and all and that the leader has no special merit. From thence comes that type of aggressive reticence with regard to the machinery of protocol which young governments quickly show. When the people have taken violent part in the national liberation they will allow no one to set themselves up as "liberators." They show themselves to be jealous of the results of their action and take good care not to place their future, their destiny, or the fate of their country in the hands of a living god. Yesterday they were completely irresponsible; today they mean to understand everything and make all decisions. Illuminated by violence, the consciousness of the people rebels against any pacification. From now on the demagogues, the opportunists, and the magicians have a difficult task. The action which has thrown them into a hand-to-hand struggle confers upon the masses a voracious taste for the concrete. The attempt at mystification becomes, in the long run, practically impossible. . . .

EWE PROVERBS

The Ewe tribe lives in southern Ghana, Togo, and Benin (formerly called Dahomey) on the west African coast—the prime region in which slave traders seized Africans to ship to North America several centuries ago. The Ewe have a particularly rich tradition of proverbs, many of which have clear ethical significance. In many African cultures, proverbs are an important educational tool. People use them to teach values to the young, to justify actions and advice, and to criticize the actions of others. Sometimes, proverbs are even cited in courts of law as quasi-legal rules of behavior that can override written laws. Proverbs are so important, in fact, to various west African ethnic groups that they even have proverbs about proverbs:

Yoruba:	"A proverb is the horse of conversation."
Yoruba:	"A wise man knows proverbs reconcile difficulties."
Sierra Leone:	"Proverbs are the daughters of experience."
Ibo:	"The proverb is the leaf they use to eat the word."
Kongo:	"Proverbs are the affairs of the nation."

The proverbs of many African cultures therefore amount to a wisdom literature—still largely unwritten, but increasingly documented—akin to that of ancient Mediterranean and Mesopotamian cultures. The proverbs below were collected by N. K. Dzobo, a professor of education in Ghana and himself a member of the Ewe tribe, who has translated them literally and explained them.

Like most wisdom literature, Ewe proverbs discuss virtues and offer bits of ethical and practical advice. The virtues extolled are largely familiar, though the proverbs sometimes offer a fresh perspective on them. Ewe proverbs are distinctive, however, because they raise an issue often overlooked in wisdom literature and in Western philosophy. A number of Ewe proverbs stress that obligations vary with circumstances. A rule that applies generally may not apply in some situations; a pattern of conduct that is generally commendable may sometimes be bad. The Ewe emphasize the variability of circumstances, the speed with which the world changes, and the need to adapt to new situations. Correspondingly, the Ewe are not complacent about being able to characterize ethics in a set of universal rules. Nevertheless, the Ewe value experience as a guide for future action, not because it supports a stable set of rules but because it trains us to perceive situations as they should be perceived.

Ewe Proverbs

Reprinted from N. K. Dzobo, African Proverbs: Guide to Conduct (The Moral Value of Ewe Proverbs), *Volume I, by permission of the Department of Education, University of Cape Coast, Ghana, and N. K. Dzobo. Copyright © 1973 by N. K. Dzobo. Proverbs and explanations have been selected from Chapter 2, "Proverbs and Their Moral Teachings."*

"You do not rejoice when you see people arrive from the farm weeping."

Explanation: Whenever people arrive from the farm weeping it means that they have brought bad news which does not call for rejoicing.

The child who breaks a snail's shell cannot break a tortoise's shell.

Moral Teaching: There are certain things any human being can do and others he cannot because his powers are limited, therefore you must know the limit of your powers and keep your ambitions within them. Do not be overambitious.

"A dog can catch some animals but cannot catch a lion."

Moral Teaching: As in proverb . . . above.

"A kitten can catch only a baby mouse."

Moral Teaching: Always do what you can and have a realistic estimation of your abilities. Avoid overestimation of your powers.

"You cannot crack two palmnuts in the mouth at the same time."

Explanation: It is easier to crack one palmnut of a special oil-palm tree than to crack two with the teeth.

Moral Teaching: Do not try to do too much at once. Learn to do one thing at a time.

"The hand can be used to pull out the tender branch of a date-palm, but cannot be used to pull out the tender branch of a fanpalm." The branches of a fanpalm are tougher and rougher than those of the date-palm.

Moral Teaching: Do not presume that because you can do certain things therefore you can do everything. Be modest in the estimation of your powers.

The [last five] proverbs discussed above stress the evil of excessive ambition, especially in children, and the importance of accepting one's powers as they are and acting within their limits. It is believed that if children behave according to the teachings of these proverbs they will be spared the pains of unfulfilled and unrealisable aspirations.

"The man with a miserable life is never tired of it."

Moral Teaching: Appreciate what you have by knowing its *real value* and do not undervalue it through unhealthy comparison.

"The game that you miss, i.e. runs away from a hunter, is always a big one."

Moral Teachings: There is always a tendency to overvalue things that we want but we do not have, and so this proverb is warning against the danger of overvaluing the real worth of what we want badly but cannot get. We must rather learn to appreciate whatever we have.

"Suffering and happiness are twins."

Moral Teaching: Life is a mixture of joy and suffering and so we must learn to accept both, and the acceptance of both is a sign of maturity.

"The crab says that when you see it walking clumsily it does not mean that it has lost its way."

Moral Teaching: This proverb can be used by anybody whose actions are misunderstood, to warn those who judge him that he has not forgotten the essential principles that guide his behaviour. The proverb warns against the practice of misjudging the basic principles that guide the behaviour of people.

"You change your steps according to the change in the rhythm of the drum."

Explanation: During the course of drumming and dancing the rhythm of the leading drum causes the steps of the dancers to change.

Moral Teaching: Adapt yourself and your conduct to changing circumstances and do not be unreasonably rigid in your thinking and behaviour.

"Tasty soup (meal) draws seats (people) to itself."

Explanation: Ewes like tasty and good smelling and spicy soup and so when a tasty meal is prepared it becomes inviting to people.

Moral Teaching: Good behaviour does not have to be advertised, because it is good for its own sake. Good behaviour is never denied a due social recognition and so it pays to be good.

"The blacksmith in one village becomes a blacksmith's apprentice in another."

Moral Teaching: As there are different grades of skills and they are relative to individuals and localities so social status is relative, and so if you go to another country or join another community learn to assess your relative status and behave yourself according to your new status. Do not take your knowledge and status for granted when you are in a new situation, but be prepared to re-evaluate them and let your estimation of your status guide your conduct.

"A stranger with big eyes does not know the by-ways, he knows only the broadways."

Explanation: "A stranger with big eyes" stands for a visitor to a country who thinks he knows everything there is to know about life in his new environment and what he presumes he knows is enough to guide his behaviour. This proverb is maintaining that he may have some general knowledge to guide his

behaviour but usually misses the important details of behaviour in the new situation.

Moral Teaching: Do not assume to know too much when you are in a new situation, but be willing to learn what is needed to make the right and appropriate adjustment in your new environment.

"The person who steals mushrooms hears the evening announcement."

Explanation: In the villages people who have found their crops or any personal belongings stolen cause an announcement to be made in the evening about the stolen crops or articles. In the announcement they ask the thieves to return the stolen goods or else they will be handed over to the gods for punishment. Usually they mention the name of a powerful god who is believed to invariably kill all evildoers. Thieves therefore listen carefully to the evening announcement and they also dread it. It may happen that someone has stolen some crops and his guilty conscience will cause him to behave as if he had heard an announcement about the crops he has stolen, even though there is no announcement. In other words, his conscience will be accusing him of his wrong deed.

Moral Teaching: Guilty conscience is a form of punishment for wrong doing which any normal wrong-doer cannot escape and so it is better to stop doing wrong and do good.

"The person who has gone into a patch of giant-grass does not complain of skin irritation."

Explanation: This proverb comes from a farming experience and especially from farmers who work on the grassland. Sometimes they have to walk through the giant-grass to go to their farms and this produces a lot of skin irritation.

Moral Teachings: The skin irritation caused by the giant-grass may be compared to minor distractions in the pursuance of one's objectives. The moral lesson of this proverb and of similar ones that will follow is that you must expect minor distractions in any effort that you put forth to realize certain objectives but do not let these minor distractions deter you from achieving your goals. You should not vacillate but be resolute and persistent in the pursuance of your goals.

"Once you make up your mind to cross a river by walking through, you do not complain of getting your stomach wet."

Moral Teaching: The moral lesson is as in the preceding proverb, and may be summed up in the biblical saying, once you put your hand to the plough you do not look behind. (a paraphrase)

"A thief does not reap more than the farmer himself."

Explanation: Some people use the fact that thieves will steal their crops as an excuse for not farming at all. This proverb admits this fact but goes on to say that, however much thieves may take from your farm, you as the farmer will always harvest more crops than they can.

Moral Teaching: The moral lesson of this proverb is like the two previous ones, but its emphasis is slightly different. In every enterprise some minor losses should be expected and they should not deter you from embarking upon it, because with persistence and dogged-determination some reasonable reward will be reaped in the end.

"If a whiteman wants to give you a hat, look at the one he is wearing before you accept it."

Moral Teaching: This proverb is used to warn people against the tendency to be gullible and credulous. Always weigh carefully what others tell you and evaluate it by their social consequences.

"The vulture cannot cure baldness" (because if it can it would have cured its own baldness).

Moral Teaching: In the traditional society some people lay claim to certain powers to cure diseases, to make others wealthy or to make barren women productive. The problem is, how do you test the validity of the claims that they make? This proverb establishes a standard for evaluating such claims. Whatever powers a person claims to have, such powers must be seen to make a practical difference to his own life before his claims could be accepted as valid, and so anybody who accepts such claims without this test of their validity will be considered gullible. The proverb is counselling against the tendency to be gullible in such matters and recom-

mends critical assessment and discernment instead of gullibility.

"The chicken says, 'Fear is life.'"

Moral Teaching: There is time to show bravery and time to show "fear" i.e. cautious retreat.

"There is no rain whose flood can submerge all mountains" i.e. there is an end to every fall of rain.

Moral Teaching: There is an end to everything and people are supposed to use this knowledge to guide their behaviour or to comfort themselves in their sufferings.

"Even the longest life ends in a grave, it does not prolong its longevity beyond the grave."

Moral Teaching: This proverb also teaches that there is an end to everything especially to wealth and life. This warning, however, is not supposed to lead to a preparation for another life, or for a life that has no end. The purpose is rather to warn people to live *circumspectively* and to avoid living without any thought of the end.

"The way the hump-back is buried shows how the person with a goiter will be buried."

Moral Teaching: Let what happens to others be a lesson to you, or learn from the experience of others and direct your behaviour accordingly.

"You do not become a chief simply by sitting on a big stool."

Explanation: Chief's stools and sandals and cloths are specially made to enhance their status and so a chief's stool is normally larger than ordinary stools.

Moral Teaching: You cannot arrogate greatness to yourself, it has to be conferred on you by others who think you deserve it. True greatness is the result of the judgment of history.

"You do not look into a bottle with both eyes, and if you try it, it is only your nose that looks into it."

Moral Teaching: "Looking into a bottle with both eyes" means "to be greedy," and "looking into a bottle with the nose" means you cannot after all see what you want to see in the bottle because the nose is not meant to see. The moral lesson of this proverb is that you invariably get nothing from being greedy. Learn to be content even with the little that you have.

"A lazy man's farm is a breeding ground for snakes."

Explanation: A lazy farmer does not keep his farm clear of weeds and so snakes can easily live there and he may be bitten by them, and this will be regarded as a punishment for his laziness.

Moral Teaching: Laziness has its own appropriate punishment and so people must learn to be hard-working so as to avoid the inevitable punishment for laziness.

"The person who goes to draw water does not drink mud."

Explanation: In many African homes women and children go out to draw water from common wells or from nearby streams, and in the big towns from public hydrants. Since water-drawers provide water for their homes they themselves will get good water to drink at all cost.

Moral Teaching: Those who work will always eat the fruits of their labour. Every just toil will be rewarded and the traditional society uses the truth of the saying as a motivation for hard work.

"The person who comes round to lick the soup pot will never be filled."

Moral Teaching: You are never well fed by living on the crumbs from the tables of others, or by depending on charity. It is only through hard work that you can be comfortably and satisfactorily fed, because the reward of hard work is having what you want in abundance and so work hard and you will eat the fruits of your own labour.

"You never get used to the sharpness of pepper."

Moral Teaching: In this proverb "pepper" stands for difficult tasks which people do not normally like but which should be done. The proverb teaches that

it is only persistence that will enable you to accomplish such tasks.

"The person who helps you to carry your load does not develop a hump." (i.e. he does not take over your burden completely.)

Moral Teaching: Do not expect too much help from other people because there is a limit to their help. In other words, everybody must eventually learn to carry his own burden.

"The person who is semi-affluent does not refuse to give to the one who is affluent indeed."

Moral Teaching: Give help judiciously so that one day when you are in need those whom you have helped may help you also. Consider your own interest when you give help to others.

"The merciful (helpers) may turn easily into enemies."

Explanation: Sometimes people resent the help being given them because they feel humiliated by it, and so if the donor is not careful about the way he offers his help he may become a hated helper or, at least, a detestable helper in the end.

Moral Teaching: In helping others know to what extent you should help them so that your help does not injure their self-respect and as a result of that you become an unwanted helper.

"The person who gives you a little at a time cannot be called your enemy."

Moral Teaching: Always do the little you can to help others. It is better to do the little that you can than to do nothing at all.

"The mouth must have enough to eat before it spills over into the beard."

Explanation: This proverb states the need for dependants, especially in the traditional family setting, to help the person on whom they depend. If they cannot help him at least they can wish him success in his work so that if he becomes successful he will help them too. The proverb can be used as an excuse for not helping others. For example, if a member of a family is asked to help his younger brothers and sisters and he does not want to help, he can use this proverb to show that he himself needs help and so he cannot help others.

Moral Teachings: The proverb can be used as a moral reason for demanding help from dependants and can also be used as a reason for not helping others.

> "The person who touches your head to wake you up is the one whose face you look at, i.e. you take notice of."

Explanation: The person who wakes you up in the morning so that you do not oversleep has done you some good service and so you take a notice of him and reward him for it.

Moral Teaching: Be grateful to your benefactors and do good to those who have done you some kind service.

> "A child who resembles his father does not necessarily take after his father."

Moral Teaching: Children must *learn to behave* themselves because any physical resemblances between them and their parents will not automatically help them maintain the good name of their parents.

> "The antelope does not wear the shoes of an elephant."

Moral Teaching: Accept your humble status and do not aspire after greatness that is beyond your reach. This proverb offers a lesson also in the importance of self-acceptance and warns against unrealistic and inordinate aspirations.

> "The stone cannot tell the ground to push away so that it will sit down."

Explanation: The Ewe expression *te ɖa,* meaning "push away" is an insolent expression and if the stone says this to the ground, then it is being rude to the ground. However, the relationship between the stone and the ground is such that the stone is unconditionally dependent on the ground. The stone is insolubly attached to the ground by the force of gravity and it cannot exist without the ground. It must therefore humble itself to accept its dependent status.

Moral Teaching: There are some dependent human relationships that are absolutely necessary e.g. teacher-student relationship, such relationships must be accepted with humility.

> "The salt does not praise itself." (It is others who say that salt is good.)

Moral Teaching: Do not brag about your goodness but be modest about it. This proverb therefore teaches people to have a humble estimate about their merits.

> "However good the hair may be a hat is worn on it."

Moral Teaching: This proverb again emphasises the importance of submission to authority. No individual is so good that he cannot be subjected to some kind of authority. Every individual must be prepared to submit himself to one form of authority or another, be it human or divine.

> "When you are carrying beef on your head you do not use your feet to catch grasshoppers."

Explanation: Beef is a better meat than grasshopper and so if you have beef you do not go after a grasshopper.

Moral Teaching: Be able to tell the relative value of things you have and do not spend your energy on less valuable things. This proverb teaches the importance of the right judgment of the relative value of things.

> "You do not turn your oilpalm grove into a broom industry." (Better things can be obtained from an oilpalm plantation than brooms, e.g. it can be turned into an oil industry.)

Moral Teaching: Know the real value of your resources and do not waste them. Judge the worth of your resources rightly.

> "The mother of twins does not lie on one side while she is in bed with the twin children."

Explanation: The common practice is for a mother of twins to lie in between them in bed so that she can equally mind them.

Moral Teaching: The main lesson of this proverb is this, as a head of a family or a leader you must treat all to whom you are responsible fairly. This proverb can therefore be used to warn people against discriminatory practices.

"Knowledge is like a baobab tree (monkeybread tree) and no one person can embrace it with both arms."

Explanation: The baobab tree usually has a very huge base stem and cannot be embraced by the two arms of any human being.

Moral Teaching: Knowledge and truth are like the unbounded ocean and so no one individual can claim to have a corner on them. Individuals must therefore be humble in their claims to knowledge and in such a humble frame of mind they can always acquire more knowledge since there is no limit to what any man can know.

"One head does not go into a consultation."

Explanation: In the traditional society judgments in disputes are usually given by the elders after they have consulted separately among themselves. This practice is based on the belief that a correct judgment is more likely to come from the deliberations of more than one person.

Moral Teaching: This proverb shows the belief of our fathers in the value of consultation in arriving at sound decisions. It is also a warning to individuals who are overconfident in their own judgments.

"What the eye has seen is what the hand goes after."

Moral Teaching: You cannot achieve anything in life if you are not aiming at anything in particular. Purposeful living makes life worth living.

"Love is like an egg, it breaks easily" (and so it should be handled carefully).

Moral Teaching: The loving relationship is very vulnerable and so must be carefully handled otherwise it will turn into hate or indifference.

"The world is like the skin of a chameleon" (i.e. it changes fast).

Moral Teaching: Since times change and our fortunes are changed in them we must always behave modestly and not arrogantly.

"The frontline soldiers easily become rear guards."

Moral Teaching: The moral teaching of this proverb is the same as the preceding one. Nobody remains at the top forever and so when you are at the top remember that you will be down one day and so be modest and moderate in your behaviour towards others.

"You do not set your yam barn on fire when you are hungry." The intention of setting the yam barn on fire is to roast the yams to eat because of hunger.

Moral Teaching: This proverb can be used to caution against extreme and drastic measure in solving problems. It recommends moderate measures as much as possible in solving problems.

"The town i.e. the chiefdom, of a chief who does not talk falls apart."

Moral Teaching: The expression "the chief who does not talk" means the chief who is not prepared to correct the wrong behaviour of his subjects and the chiefdom of such a chief will be morally ruined. The proverb therefore teaches the importance of moral correction. It is the duty of society to correct the wrong deeds of its members.

"You do not doze in your seat while you have a short mat to lie on."

Moral Teaching: Do not belittle whatever opportunities you may have but use them profitably. Make the most of the least that you have.

"You kill a snake with the club that you have in your hand."

Explanation: The implication of this proverb is that sometimes some people say that they are not able to kill a snake because they have not got any good sticks around.

Moral Teaching: The moral teaching of this proverb is like the one above but has an additional moral lesson. Use the means that are available to you in the best way possible to solve your problems and avoid unprofitable comparison of your means with those of your friends. Such unprofitable comparison will demoralise you and lead to inaction.

"The antelope says that the tail that is really his is the one at the end of his body."

Moral Teaching: Appreciate and make the most of whatever you have and avoid envying others for what they have.

"You clean the ceiling before you clean the floor."

Moral Teaching: The simple truth of this statement is used to teach the need for doing things according to a specific form of procedure. Orderly procedure is a social value.

"You do not take a big gourd to a farm that is close by."

Explanation: Farmers take water pots or gourds to their farms and usually the size of the pot will depend upon how far the farm is from the village. If the farm is close by you take a small pot of water and if not you take a big one.

Moral Teaching: The ability to size up the seriousness of a problem and to work out the appropriate solution to it is at a premium in a society where nothing is allowed to disrupt human relationships. Members of a traditional society are expected to learn to assess accurately the seriousness of a problem, and work out an appropriate solution to it. Over-estimation or under-estimation is considered as a serious defect in an assessment of problems.

"If you are patient enough you can cook a stone and it will become soft."

Moral Teaching: With patience you can achieve seemingly impossible tasks.

"If you are cooking a stone you do not become impatient or complain of using too much firewood."

Explanation: There are two proverbs here and they all emphasize the value of patience, but the second one advises against the practice of complaining under difficult tasks.

Moral Teaching: To achieve success in the performance of difficult tasks you need patience and you must be ready to pay the necessary price for the success you want.

"The chicken is never ashamed of its coop."

Moral Teaching: Be proud of your own home/village/country, however humble and lowly it may be, never be ashamed of it, but love it.

"You are never overcome by troubles at home" (because your relatives are there to help you overcome your difficulties).

Moral Teaching: In the traditional family and village each member is readily helped in time of need by other members of the family and village. The individual may not get such a help readily if he is among "strangers" i.e. people who do not belong to his village or family. This experience is used to encourage people to be loyal to their home-village and they are assured that such a loyalty will be rewarded.

"The person who is eating *akple* refers to it as a *big ball of akple.*" (*Akple* is a cornmeal eaten mainly by Anlo-Ewes).

Moral Teaching: Learn to appreciate whatever is yours and do not belittle it. This proverb can be used to remind people to love their native land or home and it can also be used to encourage the love of things that personally belong to you. In the latter context it teaches a reasonable contentment with what one has.

"A stump that stays in a river for a hundred years does not become a crocodile."

Moral Teaching: The Ewe on the whole are very patriotic and they teach their children to love their places of birth. This proverb . . . warns people who go to live in foreign lands that they will never become real citizens of those lands. Even if they stay abroad for a long time they will be regarded as "strangers" and because of this they must learn to love and honour their homelands.

"Every long journey has its destination."

Moral Teaching: Everything has an end and in case of work the end is the reward that you will get, and so if you are engaged in a tedious task do not be disheartened but persevere and your reward will come one day as the day follows the night. This proverb teaches perseverance in the performance of difficult tasks.

"You do not grumble about self-imposed or self-chosen tasks."

Moral Teaching: This proverb also teaches cheerfulness and endurance in discharging self-chosen projects.

"The rainstorm indicates the position of the door of a house."

Moral Teaching: Adopt your actions to circumstances and remember that new times call for new answers.

"Flying bullets teach you how to deploy your troops."

Explanation: This proverb is derived from the experience of the battlefield. Evidently in old days troops were disposed in relation to the direction from which one's enemy was firing and so there was no fixed strategy. Conditions of fighting rather determined one's strategy.

Moral Teaching: There are no general solutions to problems. Solutions should be dictated by the specific nature of individual problems.

"The chicken is never declared innocent in the court of hawks" (because the chicken is a prey to hawks).

Moral Teaching: This proverb is advising on how to relate to one's enemies and the relationship should be one of non-interference in their affairs.

"Two people do not race through a rice farm."

Explanation: Rice seedlings are planted so closely together that even if one person runs through them he will cause a lot of damage, how much more two.

Moral Teaching: "Racing through a rice farm" is a figurative expression which means "to act in anger or in an unfriendly manner." This type of act is disapproved of by society and so if two people are quarrelling and this proverb is told to one of them, he is being asked to control his anger. Learn to control your temper.

"The goat places its white spot anywhere it likes on its body." (Sometimes the white spot will be on one leg, or on the head or on the chest.)

Moral Teaching: This proverb is used to confirm the right of every individual to self-determination and to counsel against unnecessary interference in other people's affairs.

"When it is threatening to rain you look in the direction of your farm." (i.e. you make sure that it is raining on your farm.)

Moral Teaching: This is one of the rare proverbs which is used to justify a concern for one's own interests. In plain words the proverb means, look after your own interests. If you know how to love yourself then you can love others.

"The new is woven on to the old."

Moral Teaching: In this proverb "the old" stands for the "traditions of the past," and it is maintained that the traditions of the past form the foundation of the present and so traditions should be respected. The proverb is meant to develop a positive attitude to and respect for traditional practices.

"There are always paths in between a patch of sugarcane plants that look alike in height."

Moral Teaching: "A patch of sugarcane plants" represents people with whom one has a dealing and some of them will be either one's relatives, friends, colleagues or countrymen. According to the teaching of this proverb there are different ways of relating oneself to the different classes of people and it is necessary to know the type of behaviour that is appropriate to each class.

"The cotton thread says that it is only as a team that you carry a stone."

Explanation: This proverb comes from the practice of kente weavers who, to straighten their cotton threads, make them into a loop and hang them down with a heavy stone from a transverse wooden bar. The loop of many threads can stand the weight of a heavy stone while one single thread cannot.

Moral Teaching: There is strength in unity, therefore learn to work together with others.

"One hand cannot hold a bull's horns."

Explanation: The "bull's horn" represents any difficult task which cannot be done by one man alone but as he teams up with others they could do it.

Moral Teaching: This proverb stresses the need for a united effort in solving difficult problems, and it also advises individuals who trust too much in their own strengths to learn to co-operate with others in solving difficult tasks. The two virtues commended by the two preceding proverbs are *unity* and *co-operation*.

"One pole cannot build a house, i.e. carry a roof."

Moral Teaching: Unity is strength.

"You do not say that a palmwine tapper is a useless person when it is not yet dark."

Explanation: Palmwine tappers usually bring free palmwine home in the evening for their friends to drink and so it is in the evening that their friends may find them useful and so their friends will be passing a hasty judgement if they are declared useless when they are not yet back from their palmwine factories.

Moral Teaching: Do not be in a hurry to pass judgement on the behaviour of others, wait for the opportune moment to do so otherwise your judgement may be premature. You must exercise caution in passing judgement on the behaviour of others.

SWAHILI PROVERBS

Swahili, a North Bantu language, developed as a trading language among various Bantu tribes and Arab traders. Now an official language of Tanzania and Uganda, it is spoken throughout much of east central Africa, for example, in Zaire, Mozambique, and Zambia. Swahili proverbs thus constitute an unwritten wisdom literature shared by many east African ethnic groups.

Collected below are some Swahili proverbs translated as literally as possible. An explanation is provided when the literal translation seems likely to puzzle or mislead English speakers. All of the proverbs address ethical topics. Roughly the first half concern character; they give insight into the virtues and vices that east Africans consider important. The second half concern freedom, responsibility, limitations, cooperation, and other topics pertaining to the ethics of action.

Many languages and cultures contain proverbs that contradict each other: "Look before you leap" and "He who hesitates is lost" in English, for example. Swahili is no exception. Partly because many different ethnic groups contribute proverbs to the language, the shared but generally unwritten wisdom literature reflects many different perspectives on certain issues. The proverbs that follow therefore do not present a single, coherent view of ethics in the way that an individual philosopher tries to do so. Nevertheless, they indicate what ethical issues concern east Africans. The views they reveal about those issues in many cases differ significantly from Western perspectives. And, in some cases, the proverbs display a striking unanimity. For example, they show that issues of character—virtues and vices—have central importance in east African ethical thinking. They moreover indicate what virtues east Africans think are most worthy of cultivating. Many proverbs caution against violence; many advise kindness in dealing with others. A large number concern ambition, achievement, and work. Caution, patience, and courage are other common topics. Also mentioned, but less often, are virtues such as self-control, humility, honesty, and fairness. The virtues are familiar, but the order of importance suggests a somewhat different conception of character from that developed in Western virtue ethics. Proverbs dealing with certain virtues, furthermore, display high degrees of consensus. Every proverb concerning violence, for example, speaks against it. Every proverb concerning caution recommends it. The proverbs thus give us considerable insight into east African ethical thought.

Swahili proverbs also stress an aspect of ethical thinking that has emerged in Western thought only in the twentieth century. We make choices, not in ideal situations, but under practical constraints. We act with limited information, abilities, and resources. Swahili proverbs recognize this, and a surprising number deal explicitly with the problem of limitations. Some of these proverbs maintain that "the best is an enemy of the good"; others presuppose pluralism, the doctrine that goods differ in kind. Frequently, we face choices between goods of different kinds. Whatever choice we make, we give up something important: "He who chooses is never satisfied," as one Swahili proverb says. Conflicting values are fundamental and pervasive features of the moral life.

Swahili Proverbs

Reprinted from Albert Scheven, Swahili Proverbs.
Copyright © 1981 by the University Press of America.
Sources cited by Scheven are as follows:

EM: E. Meena, Misemo (Nairobi: TransAfrica, 1975).

JK: Jan Knappert, "On Swahili: Proverbs," African
Language Studies 16 (1975): 117–46.

KB: Kajiga Bahihuta, Dictionaire de la Langue
Swahili (Goma, Zaire: Librairie Les Volcans, 1975).

SAM: S. A. Mohamed, Vito vya hekima, simo na
maneno ya mshangao (Nairobi: Longman,
Kenya, 1967).

Character

Living is the intention.
[What makes life worthwhile is having a purpose, an aim.]

A person becomes what he wants to become.

What one cultivates is what one harvests.

When you serve, serve well.

The area covered by your life is not as important as what you build on it.
To have a broad life [that is, seeing a lot of things] or to live a long time is not important. What matters most is how that life is spent. —EM

Kindness and Violence

One who throws mud gets himself soiled as well.

By continual piercing one pierces oneself.

Peace comes not save by the point of the sword.

Peace is a way to love and understanding.

Two points do not stab one another.

War causes destruction.

Know-how, not force.

He who does good to people does it also to himself.

The man who does good to others, God requites him with good things too.

To him who does kind things, kind things will be done.

Do not render evil for good.

Goodness and kindness are stronger than harshness.

A person who has no enemies is not a human being.

Wisdom

Wisdom creates well-being.

The ignorant praises his own ignorance.

He who says "I didn't understand" is not stupid.

The most precious qualities of a person are two: intelligence and modesty.

He gave a sermon and forgot himself.

When you have gained some experience in life, it [life] is over.

Experience is the mother of knowledge.

Ambition

The good luck of your colleague should not keep you out of sleep.
Don't be envious. —JK

Whether you have little or much, be content.

The grumbler gets more *to grumble about.* —KB

He who has his own does not miss his neighbor's.
[Understood: he should be happy with what he has. Or: The one who has does not lack help from others. Richness attracts richness.]

Stretch your legs according to your bed.

The bird does not think that his own nest is shabby.

Achievement

Aiming is not the same as hitting.

A bridge is not a dwelling place.

A beginning is a beginning, there is no beginning
which is bad.
[The golden rule of life is: make a beginning.]

Good beginnings make good endings.

And come, pass by this rock, so we may know
that you are a pilot.
[Prove your worth by deeds.]

Serve [even] an unbeliever to attain your ends.

Caution

Careful, careful, is better than medicines.

Don't play with the young of a leopard.

When you play with a lion, do not put your hand
in its mouth.

Don't laugh at a leopard which does not show its
claws.

Do not pray to meet a lion.

Patience

What is in the sea, go and wait for it on the beach.

To stand up for justice needs patience.

Begin with patience, end with pleasure.

Today is yours, tomorrow is not.

Eat your wealth; sand is not edible.
[Enjoy your life today.]

Work

He who gets blisters from the hoe handle will not
die of hunger.

Only he who goes into the forest comes back
with firewood.

A little, but earned.

He builds skyscrapers.
[Of somebody who does not do the work to make
his dreams possible.]

Courage

Fear is also a shield.

Courage proves itself in difficulties.

Courage is not the same as fighting someone
stronger than you.

Are you a leopard, show your claws.

Self-Control

Anger is loss.

The anger of the cuttlefish is the joy of the
fisherman.

To lose one's temper is to go astray.

Humility

First humility, then perfection.

He who does not see his own vices should not
take notice of the faults of his companions.

He who does not listen to the advice of an elder
will see bad things.

Ancestry

He who leaves his ancestry is bold.

One who leaves his ancestry is never a hero.

He who leaves his own people is a liar.

Honesty

Speaking the truth is no disgrace.

An unpleasant truth is better than a pleasant
falsehood.

Fairness

The judge has no personal preferences.

A man's excellence is not determined by his
color.

Freedom and Responsibility

Don't laugh at a blind man, it's not his fault.

It is you yourself who stepped on the thorns which are on the road.

It was man who taught a leopard how to eat people.
  . . . A man may himself, through carelessness, teach his enemy how to hurt him. —EM

The evil spirit of a man is a man.
[When a man does evil, he is not a victim of the Devil, but is obeying his own free will; man is free to choose between good and evil.]

Man is bad.
Fellow-man has to be feared. Man is capable of any evil. —SAM

An open pool is not freedom.
Freedom without limits is like a free pool. . . . freedom must have limits and order to maintain peace. —EM

A slave has no choice.
[Note: *mja* and *abd** are often translated as: servant of God. Implied is that what God has destined for you is what you get. It is said whenever something good or bad happens to someone. The use of this proverb is twofold: a) a person often has no choice when his conscience is clear about a way of action; b) Whatever plans we make for the future, we cannot foresee superior forces.]

A thorn with which one has pricked oneself of one's own accord does not hurt.

The load you bind for yourself is not heavy.

God did not create an evil person.

The bad craftsman quarrels with his tools.

Respect

He who laughs at a scar has not received a wound.

He who ridicules the good will be overtaken by evil.

A man may be regarded as a thing, but he is not [only] a thing.

Kiss the hand you cannot cut.
[Respect those who have authority over you, or they will destroy you.]

A fool is a person too, don't say he is a cow.

A man's greatness and respect come from himself.

Reciprocity

Goodness engenders abuse.
[Do good to an evil person and he will abuse you.]

He who does not know how to forgive, let him not expect to be forgiven.

He who does not trust others cannot be trusted.

It is useless for me to recognize him who does not recognize me.

Help him who helps you.
[By doing a service to someone you teach him indirectly to give service in his turn.]

He who supports a worthless person has trouble for nothing.

Respect for a stupid person is stupidity.

Please him who does not please you.
[Do good to a bad person in order to soften him and make friends.]

He who does not harm you, do no harm to him.

Hatred for hatred, light for light.

Love your enemy.

Do harm to him who harms you.

When your enemy falls, lift him up.
[Helping an enemy in trouble may turn him into a friend.]

He who does not wrong is not done wrong.

Cooperation

It is better to build bridges than walls.

He who does not help me putting down my load, must not expect [help] when he has his own [load].

---

* The words for "slave." —ED.

[Said of people who expect help, but never help others. Note: Heavy loads are carried on the head; to put them down, especially when heavy and breakable, as big waterpots, help is needed and expected.]

A boat doesn't go forward if each one is rowing his own way.

When minds are one, what is far becomes near. [Difficult things become possible. Unity is strength.]

Unity is strength, division is weakness.

People were told "Come and live together," they were not told "Come and compete with one another."

Avarice is the root of all evil.

He who itches scratches himself.

A man should do what he can, and not wait for other people to find a solution for him. —EM

Conflict and Limitations

You cannot cross the ocean by swimming.

If you can't build a hut, build a shack.

You do not have the strength to defeat an elephant.

If you bake fish, you cannot pluck a chicken.

If you want to build you must be willing to destroy.

There is no rainy season without mosquitoes.

He who does not drink from a spring, drinks from a river.
[Take the second best.]

Need breaks need.
Sometimes a man has to demolish something needed in order to get something needed more. —SAM

Do not carry what you cannot master.

He who wants everything loses everything.

He who chooses is never satisfied.

Whatever is superior is found at great price.

He wrecked the ship for the sake of a pancake.

He says "No! No!" and nevertheless his heart is there.

Context

What is good for you may be bad for your friend.

The environment is the beginning of success.

Yesterday and the day before yesterday are not like today.

The right answer at the right time, and the right time is not a chance accident.

Everyone leaving his [own] vessel becomes a common sailor.

God and the World

A person saved by God is not crooked.

He who pays heed to Satan makes himself deserve divine anger.

Payment on earth is the reckoning of the hereafter.
God returns one's good or evil deed often while one is still on earth. —SAM

The world is nothing, depend not on it.

The delusions of this world, one usually knows them in hell.

The world is a mixture of good and evil.

KWAME GYEKYE

The Akan tribe lives in Ghana. Neighbors of the Ewe, they also inhabit the west African coast that yielded many of the African natives brought by slave traders to North America. Professor Gyekye, himself an Akan, has written about the Akan view of causality, metaphysics, religion, and ethics.

Akan ethics, as Gyekye describes it, is a version of consequentialism. Good acts are those that bring about the well-being of the society; bad actions work against the well-being of the society. The Akan thus evaluate actions by their consequences, but their view differs from that of most Western consequentialists in a very interesting way. According to Jeremy Bentham, John Stuart Mill, and other Western utilitarians, the good of a community is the sum of the goods of its members. Bentham and Mill add up individual pleasures and pains to obtain this sum; other utilitarians add up satisfactions and frustrations of individual desires. The Akan, in contrast, maintain that the good of the community cannot be reduced to individual goods. According to their communitarian consequentialism, good acts promote the well-being of the society, which the Akan understand in terms of social welfare, solidarity, harmony, and other features of the social order itself.

The good of the community, while it does not reduce to individual well-being, nevertheless is not independent of it. Certain character traits are more conducive to social well-being than others and are therefore considered virtues: kindness, faithfulness, compassion, hospitality, and others. Akan ethics thus judges actions and character traits by appeal to their efforts on social good.

One distinctive feature of Akan ethics is the classification of unethical actions into two categories: ordinary and extraordinary evils. Extraordinary evils bring suffering to the whole community, not just to individual members of the community. Performing an extraordinarily evil act, the Akan think, has religious ramifications, for it angers the gods. Still, it is the disastrous consequences for the well-being of the community that make the evil extraordinary, not the gods' disapproval.

Though the Akan apply their consequentialism to both actions and character traits, character plays a special role in their ethical system. In fact, they use a single word for both 'character' and 'ethics'. In this respect, the Akan are like the Arabs and Greeks, as well as their neighbors, the Yoruba; the vocabulary of each of these peoples suggests that ethics is the science of character. Indeed, on the Akan view, actions derive from character. Human beings, the Akan believe, are innately neither good nor evil. A person develops into a good or bad person by acting, developing habits, and responding to moral (or immoral) instruction. This is the force of the Akan proverb "One is not born with a bad 'head', but one takes it on the earth."

This implies that although character is primary, both character traits and actions have important roles to play in Akan ethics. Actions stem from character traits; people perform good actions, in general, because they have good characters.

But how do they develop those characters? They perform good actions, develop good habits, and receive good moral instruction. In short, character is central, but actions are important to character development. Actions, therefore, not only stem from character but also help to develop character. For this reason, the Akan neither define good character in terms of good action nor define good action in terms of good character. Each kind of good they define independently, in terms of the community's well-being.

from *An Essay on African Philosophical Thought: The Akan Conceptual Scheme*

(For purposes of clarity and to save space, I shall in this chapter write "morality$_1$" to refer to moral beliefs, norms, rules, principles, ideals, and "morality$_2$," to refer to patterns of behavior, that is, attitudes or responses to moral norms, rules, etc.; moral practice or commitment. Where I mean both aspects, I shall write "morality" without subscripts.)

8.1.1. *The Concepts of Good and Evil*

I shall begin with the Akan moral concepts of good (or goodness: *papa*) and evil (*bōne*), which are fundamental in the moral thought and practice of any culture. In Akan thought goodness is not defined by reference to religious beliefs or supernatural beings. What is morally good is not that which is commanded by God or any spiritual being; what is right is not that which is pleasing to a spiritual being or in accordance with the will of such being. In the course of my field research none of my discussants referred to Onyame (God) or other spiritual entities in response to the questions What is good? What is evil? None of them held that an action was good or evil because Onyame had said so. On the contrary, the views that emerge in discussions of these questions reveal an undoubted conviction of a nonsupernaturalistic—a humanistic—origin of morality. Such views provide insight into the Akan conception of the criterion of moral value.

In Akan moral thought the sole criterion of goodness is the welfare or well-being of the community. Thus, in the course of my field research, the response I had to the question, "What do the Akan people mean by 'good' (or, goodness)?" invariably included a list of goods, that is, a list of deeds, habits, and patterns of behavior considered by the society as worthwhile because of their consequences for human well-being. The list of such goods invariably included: kindness (generosity: *ayamyie*), faithfulness (*honesty,* truthfulness: *nokwaredi*), compassion (*mmōbrōhunu*), hospitality (*ahōhoyē, adōe*), that which brings peace, happiness, dignity, and respect (*nea ede asomdwee, ahomeka, anuonyam ne abuo ba*), and so on. The good comprehends all the above, which is to say that the good (*papa*) is explained in terms of the qualities of things (actions, behavioral patterns). Generosity, hospitality, justice are considered (kinds of) good. Generosity is a good thing, but it is not identical with goodness. Goodness (or the good), then, is considered in Akan moral thinking as a concept comprehending a number of acts, states, and patterns of behavior that exemplify certain characteristics.

On what grounds are some acts (etc.) considered good? The answer is simply that each of them is supposed (expected or known) to bring about or lead to social well-being. Within the framework of Akan social and humanistic ethics, what is morally good is generally that which promotes social welfare, solidarity, and harmony in human relationships. Moral value in the Akan system is determined in terms of its consequences for mankind and society. "Good" is thus used of actions that promote human interest. The good is identical with the welfare of the society, which is expected to include the welfare of the individual. This appears to be the meaning or definition of "good" in Akan ethics. It is clear that this definition does not at all refer to the will or commands of God. That which is good is decreed not by a supernatural being as such, but by human beings within the framework of their experiences in living in society. So that even though an Akan maxim says

I am doing the *good* (thing) so that my way to the
world of spirits might not be blocked,
(mereye papa na ankosi me nsaman kwan)

what constitutes the good is determined not by spiritual beings but by human beings.

Just as the good is that action or pattern of behavior which conduces to well-being and social harmony, so the evil (*bōne*; that is, moral evil) is that which is considered detrimental to the well-being of humanity and society. The Akan concept of evil, like that of good, is definable entirely in terms of the needs of society. Thus, even though one often hears people say "God does not like evil" (*Onyame mpē bonē*), yet what constitutes evil is determined by the members of the community, not by Onyame.

Akan ethics recognizes two categories of evil, *bōne* and *musuo,* although *bōne* is the usual word for evil. The first category, *bōne,* which I shall call "ordinary," includes such evils as theft, adultery, lying, backbiting (*kōkōnsa*), and so on. The other category of evil, *musuo,* I shall call "extraordinary." As described by a group of discussants, "*musuo* is an evil which is great and which brings suffering (*ōhaw, ahokyerē*: disaster, misfortune) to the whole community, not just to the doer alone." Another discussant also stated that "the consequences of committing *musuo* affect the whole community." *Musuo* was also defined as an "uncommon evil" (*bōne a wōntaa nhu*), and as an "indelible evil" (*ade a woye a wompepa da*), "remembered and referred to by people even many years after the death of the doer." Thus, *musuo* is generally considered to be a great, extraordinary moral evil; it is viewed by the community with particular abhorrence and revulsion because its commission is believed not only to bring shame to the whole community, but also, in the minds of many ordinary people, to invite the wrath of the supernatural powers.

The category of *musuo* includes such acts as suicide, incest, having sexual intercourse in the bush, rape, murder, stealing things dedicated to the deities or ancestral spirits, etc. Moral evils that are *musuo* are also considered as taboos (*akyiwade*: abominations, prohibitions), a taboo being, to most people, an act that is forbidden or proscribed just because it is supposedly hateful to some supernatural being. That *musuo* are classifiable as taboos was in fact the view of some discussants: "*musuo* is something we abominate" (*musuo ye ade a yekyi*); "*musuo* is a taboo" (*akyiwade*). Now, it is remarkable that the same evils considered as taboos by Bishop Sarpong,* such as murder, sexual intercourse with a woman impregnated by another man, suicide, incest, words of abuse against the chief, and stealing from among the properties of a deity are all *musuo.* This gives the impression that the category of extraordinary moral evils (*musuo*) is coextensive with the category of taboos (*akyiwade*). But in reality this is not so. The *musuo* are indeed taboos, but from this we can only infer that some taboos are *musuo;* since *musuo* are moral evils, such taboos (as are *musuo*) are also moral evils. It seems to me that extraordinary moral evils (which include both *musuo* and moral taboos) are the kinds of moral evil that are *never* to be committed under any circumstances. This view is based on the force of the work *kyi,* to abhor, hate, from which *akyiwade* (hateful things, taboos) derives. Henceforth, I shall simply use the expression "moral taboos" to cover both *musuo* and *akyiwade....*

How would the traditional Akan thinker explain the origin and role of taboos in Akan morality? In connection with taboo, Bishop Sarpong observed: "If one were to ask the Ashanti why he keeps these taboos, he will probably not be able to give the reasons I have propounded. All he is likely to assert is that they existed from time immemorial, that the ancestors want him to observe them." Bishop Sarpong is right as far as the ordinary Akan is concerned; but the wise persons (*anyansafo*) among them would be able to furnish the underlying reasons for considering such acts as moral evils of a high order. Their statements quoted above indicate clearly that they believe that committing a taboo act affects the welfare of the whole community. Moral taboos are thus explained by reference to their social

---

* Bishop Sarpong was an earlier writer on the Akan conceptual scheme. —ED.

function and purpose. Communal well-being, then, appears to be the principal reason for the proscription of the category of moral evils referred to as moral taboos (*musuo* and *akyiwade*). The following explanation given by Bishop Sarpong for tabooing sexual intercourse in the bush is in line with the thinking of the Akan thinkers:

> Those who indulge in it expose themselves to the risk of being bitten by venomous creatures like the snake, the scorpion, and the spider. (It should be borne in mind that Ashanti is a forested region with dangerous creatures whose bites may easily be fatal.) Let a mishap of this nature take place and there is every likelihood that misapprehensions are conceived about the conjugal act itself. That this would be detrimental to the human species is too obvious to emphasize.

In the view of Akan thinkers, the real, underlying reason for regarding sexual intercourse in the bush as a great moral evil and thus for tabooing it is not that it is hated by the earth goddess (*Asase Yaa*), but that it has undesirable social consequences. Their position is plainly that the acts classified as moral taboos were so regarded simply because of the *gravity* of their consequences for human society, not because those acts were hateful to any supernatural beings.

8.1.2. Morality in the Context of a Nonrevealed Religion

. . . to the question asked by Socrates (in Plato's *Euthyphro*) whether something is good because God approves of it or whether God approves of it because it is good, the response of the Akan moral thinker would be that God approves of the good because it is good. The reason is, if something is good because God approves of it, how would that good thing be known to them (that is, Akans)? How would they know what God approves in a nonrevealed religion? On the contrary, their ascription of moral attributes to God and the sanctions that he is believed to apply . . . in the event of a breach of the moral law clearly suggest the Akan conviction that God approves of the good because it is good and eschews the evil because it is evil.

8.1.3. Religion, Sanctions, and Moral Practice

. . . Akan thought conceives the human being as a social animal and society as a necessary condition for human existence. . . . This thought is expressed in the proverb

When a man descends from heaven, he descends
  into human society.

But the person who descends into human society has desires, aims, interests, and will, and these have to be reconciled with those of others. An Akan proverb such as

One man's curse is another man's fortune
(lit.: What appears sour on one man's palate appears
  sweet on another man's palate),

indicates the view that the desires, interests, and passions of individual members of a society differ and may conflict with one another. One often hears the ordinary Akan say *obi mpɛ a obi pɛ:* "If one does not desire it, the other does"; that is, people have different desires, preferences, and choices. One Akan motif shows a "siamese" crocodile with two heads but a common stomach. The saying that goes with the symbol is that, although they have one stomach, the heads fight over the food that will eventually nourish both of them. The symbol . . . points to the conflicts that result from the existence of individual desires and needs. The problem is how to minimize such conflicts and at the same time allow room for the realization of individual desires and needs. The need for a system of rules to regulate the conduct of individuals and, consequently, for social harmony and cooperative living, thus becomes urgent. It is this social need that gives rise to morality$_1$, according to Akan ethics.

Thus considerations for human well-being and for an ideal type of social relationships—both of which are generated by the basic existential conditions of man—these, not divine pronouncements, constitute the crucible in which Akan morality$_1$ is fashioned. Whatever the moral virtues possessed by, or ascribed to, God and the other spiritual powers, it should now be clear that the compelling reason of the Akan for pursuing the good is not that it is pleasing to the supernatural beings or approved by them, but rather that it will lead to the attainment of human well-being. This *humanistic* moral outlook of the Akan is something that, I think, is worth being cherished, for its goal, from the moral point of view, is ultimate and, thus, self-justifying.

. . . .

9.2. The Centrality of Character (suban) in Akan Ethics

Morality is generally concerned with right and wrong conduct or behavior and good and bad character. We speak not only of a moral act but also of a moral person; we speak not only of an honest or generous or vicious act but also of an honest or generous or vicious person. When a person is generally honest or generous the Akans judge him or her to be a good person, by which they mean that he or she has a good character (*ōwō suban papa*), and when the person is wicked or dishonest they judge him or her to be a bad person, that is, to have a bad character. It is on the basis of a person's conduct (deeds, *nneyēe*) that the Akans judge one to be good or bad, to have good character or bad character. According to them, the character of a person is basic. The performance of good or bad acts depends on the state of one's character; inasmuch as good deeds reflect good character, character (*suban*) appears as the focal point of the ethical life. It is, in Akan moral thought, the crucial element in morality, for it profits a society little if its moral system is well articulated intellectually and the individuals in that system nevertheless have bad character and so do the wrong things. A well-articulated moral system does not necessarily produce good character; neither does knowledge of moral rules make one a good person or produce good character.

For the Akans, and perhaps also for the Greeks and Arabs, ethics has to do principally with character. Ethics, according to Akan thinkers, deals essentially with the quality of the individual's character. This is a remarkable assertion, for after all the ethical response, that is, the response or attitude to a moral rule, is an individual, private affair. All that a society can do regarding morality is to provide or impart moral knowledge to its members, making them aware of the moral rules that are applicable to all living in it. But granted this, it does not follow that the individual members of the society will lead lives in conformity with the moral rules. A man may know and may even accept a moral rule such as, say, it is wrong to seduce someone's wife. But he may fail to apply this rule to a particular situation. He is not able to effect the transition from knowledge to action. According to the Akan thinkers, to be able to act in accord with the moral rules of the society requires the possession of a good character (*suban*).

What, then, is character? How do Akan thinkers define character? The root of *suban* is *su* or *esu,* meaning nature, which might imply that character is associated with a person's nature, that character develops from a set of inborn traits. . . . Overall, one might conclude that character is a state or condition of the soul which "causes" it to perform its actions spontaneously and easily. This implies that the moral habits are innate, that we are born virtuous and are not responsible for our character. That impression, however, is false. Despite its etymological link with nature, the *suban* of a person is not wholly innate. . . .

Akan thinkers define character in terms of habits, which originate from a person's deeds or actions; character is the configuration of (individual) acts. Thus, several of my discussants opined that "Character is your deeds" (actions: *nneyēe*); "Character comes from your deeds" (*suban firi wo nneyēe*). Moreover, sometimes the Akans use the sentence, "He has a bad character" (*ōwō suban bōne*) when they want to say "He does bad things" (*ōyē nneēma bōne*). The thought here is that moral virtues arise through habituation, which is consonant with the empirical orientation of Akan philosophy. This is, I think, the reason for the teaching of moral values embedded in proverbs and folktales to children in the process of their socialization; the moral instructions are meant to habituate them to moral virtues. If moral habits were thought to be acquired by nature or through birth it would be senseless to pursue moral instruction. But it is believed and expected that the narratives are one way by which children acquire and internalize moral virtues.

I hold the view that in general society presents us

with a variety of modes of behavior. We see and are told what is good behavior and what is bad, what is praiseworthy and what is blameworthy. We are given a choice. To acquire virtue, a person must practice good deeds so that they become habitual. The newly acquired good habit must be strengthened by repetition. A single good deed may initiate further good deeds, and in this way virtue is acquired. Over time such an acquired virtue becomes a habit. This is the position of Akan philosophy, for this is what they mean by saying *aka ne hō*, "It is left (or has remained) with him," "It has become part of him," "It has become his habit." Such practice and performance emphasize the relevance and importance of action in the acquisition of virtue. To be just, for instance, one must first behave in a just manner. The emphasis placed by Akan thinkers on the influence of actions on character illustrates their conviction that one is in some sense responsible for the sort of person one is; the person is responsible for the state of his or her character. The unjust man may be held responsible for becoming unjust, because his character is the result of repeated (*aka hō*) voluntary acts of injustice. He had the choice between committing acts of injustice and refraining from such acts.

The emphasis on the relevance of actions for states of character is reflected in the way that abstract terms for "goodness," "virtue," are formed. The usual words for "goodness" in Akan are *yieyē* and *papayē* (the latter also appears sometimes as *papa*). The last syllable of each word means to do or perform. Thus, the two words literally mean "good-doing" (that is, doing good).

This analysis of the Akan concept of character supports, as far as the Akan position goes, Mbiti's view that "the essence of African morality is that it is a morality of 'conduct' rather than a morality of 'being' . . . a person is what he is because of what he does, rather than that he does what he does because of what he is." This view is repeated by Bishop Sarpong: "For it would appear that for the Akan what a man is is less important than what a man does. To put it more concretely, a person is what he is because of his deeds. He does not perform those deeds because of what he is." The emphasis on deeds (*nneyēe*) is appropriate, for it agrees with the

Akan belief that a person is not born virtuous or vicious. The previously quoted proverb

One is not born with a bad "head," but one takes it
   on the earth,

implies, among other things, that a bad habit is not an inborn characteristic, but one that is acquired. The Akan position thus is that the original nature of human beings was morally neutral. If this were not the case, there would be no such thing as a moral person. The person's original moral neutrality later comes to be affected by actions, habits, responses to moral instruction, and so on. Consequently, what a person does or does not do is crucial to the formation of the character. A virtuous character is the result of the performance of virtuous *acts*. . . .

. . . But then the question is: If a person is not born virtuous, how can he or she perform virtuous acts? The answer is through moral instruction, which in traditional Akan society was normally done by means of ethical proverbs and folktales. In this way the growing child and young adult become aware of what is a virtuous or vicious act and become virtuous by performing virtuous acts.

. . . .

10.1. Communalism as a Social Theory

. . . Communalism, which is a doctrine about social organization and relations, is an offshoot of the Akan concept of humanism. It is perhaps indisputable that social institutions embody a philosophical perspective about human nature and social relationships. One way in which the Akan concept of humanism is made explicit is in its social organization. Ensuring the welfare and interests of each member of society—the essential meaning of Akan humanism—can hardly be accomplished outside the communal system.

Communalism may be defined as the doctrine that the group (that is, the society) constitutes the focus of the activities of the individual members of the society. The doctrine places emphasis on the activity and success of the wider society rather than, though not necessarily at the expense of, or to the detriment of, the individual.

Aristotle proclaimed many centuries ago that man is by nature a social animal, and that it is impossible for him to live outside society. Akan thinkers agree that society is not only a necessary condition for human existence, but it is natural to man. This idea is expressed in an already-quoted proverb:

When a man descends from heaven, he descends
    into a human society.
(onipa firi soro besi a, obesi onipa kurom)

[The idea of man descending from heaven stems from the belief that man is created by the Supreme Being, Onyame, in heaven (soro).]

This proverb rejects the concept of the state of nature, as explicated by those eighteenth-century European philosophers who asserted the existence of an original presocial character of man. In the state of nature, people lived solitary and uncooperative lives, with undesirable consequences that in time led to the formation of society. Akan thought, however, sees humans as originally born into a human society (onipa kurom), and therefore as social beings from the outset. In this conception, it would be impossible for people to live in isolation. For not only is the person not born to live a solitary life, but the individual's capacities are not sufficient to meet basic human requirements. For the person, as another proverb has it, is not a palm tree that he or she should be complete or self-sufficient. Consequently, the individual inevitably requires the succor and the relationships of others in order to realize or satisfy basic needs. As another proverb states it:

The prosperity [or well-being] of man depends
    upon his fellow man.
(obi yiye firi obi)

Human sociality, then, is seen as a consequence of basic human nature, but it is also seen as that which makes for personal well-being and worth. Because community life is natural to man, the kind of society that permits the full realization of human capacities, needs, and aspirations should be communal.

Communalism as conceived in Akan thought is not a negation of individualism; rather, it is the recognition of the limited character of the possibili-

ties of the individual, which limited possibilities whittle away the individual's self-sufficiency. Thus, we have the following proverbs:

One finger cannot lift up a thing.
If one man scrapes the bark of a tree for medicine,
    the pieces fall down.
The left arm washes the right arm and the right
    arm washes the left arm.

The above proverbs, and many more similar to these in content, clearly underscore the rationale behind communalism. They indicate, on the one hand, the failures and frustrations of extreme individualism; that in spite of individual talents and capacities, the individual ought to be aware of his or her insufficiency to achieve his welfare through solitary effort. On the other hand, the proverbs also indicate the value of collective action, mutual aid, and interdependence as necessary conditions not only for an individual's welfare, but also for the successful achievement of even the most difficult undertakings. Communalism insists that the good of all determines the good of each or, put differently, the welfare of each is dependent on the welfare of all. This requires that the individual should work for the good of all, which of course includes his or her own good.

Thus, it is implicit in communalism that the success and meaning of the individual's life depend on identifying oneself with the group. This identification is the basis of the reciprocal relationship between the individual and the group. It is also the ground of the overriding emphasis on the individual's obligation to the members of the group; it enjoins upon him or her the obligation to think and act in terms of the survival of the group as a whole. In fact one's personal sense of responsibility is measured in terms of responsiveness and sensitivity to the needs and demands of the group. Since this sense of responsibility is enjoined equally upon each member of the group—for all the members are expected to enhance the welfare of the group as a whole—communalism maximizes the interests of all the individual members of the society. . . .

But inherent in the communal enterprise is the problem of contribution and distribution. The communal enterprise tends to maximize the common good because each individual is expected to contribute to it, but obviously individuals are not equal in their capacities and talents—a fact explicitly recognized in Akan thought. . . . It follows therefore that individual contributions to the common good will be unequal. Now, the question is: Should inequality in contribution lead to inequality in distribution? Akan social thought, with its social and humanistic thrust, answers this question in the negative. It may be objected that this leads to an unfair treatment of those who have contributed more, to which one may respond that those who have contributed more must have been endowed with greater talents and capacities—natural characteristics and assets for which they were not responsible. This counterargument is perhaps implicit in the proverbs, "The left arm washes the right arm and the right arm washes the left arm" and "The fingers of the hand are not equal in length." Even though the power or effort of one arm may not be as great as that of the other, nevertheless it is able to make *some* contribution. The natural assets of human beings are, as the two proverbs imply, different and should therefore not be made the basis of unequal distribution, even though the second proverb rejects the idea of absolute equality.

The Akan position is defensible for, irrespective of an individual's contribution to the common good, it is fair and reasonable that everyone's *basic* human needs be satisfied by the society: From each according to *whatever contribution* one can make to each according to one's *basic* needs will be the new slogan. . . .

10.2. The Tensions of Individualism

. . . The common good, I take it, is not merely the sum of the various individual goods. The concept implies, I think, that there are certain needs that are *basic* to the enjoyment and fulfillment of the life of each individual. Such needs include shelter, food, health, equality of opportunity, and liberty. Thus conceived, the common good is predicated on a true or essential universal, the good of *all,* that which is essentially good for human beings as such. The common good, therefore, is not conceptually opposed to

the individual good of any member of the society. It embraces his or her individual good as it embraces the goods of other members. If the common good is attained, then logically the individual good is also attained. Strictly speaking, there can or should be no conflict between the two, for the individual and the common goods are tied up together and overlap. Therefore, any conflict stems from a misconception either of the common good, of the individual good, or of the relationship between the two.

Thus, the symbol of the crossed crocodiles with two heads and a common stomach has great significance for Akan social thought. While it suggests the rational underpinnings of the concept of communalism, it does not do so to the detriment of individuality. The concept of communalism, as it is understood in Akan thought, therefore does not overlook individual rights, interests, desires, and responsibilities, nor does it imply the absorption of the individual will into the "communal will," or seek to eliminate individual responsibility and accountability. Akan social thought attempts to establish a delicate balance between the concepts of communality and individuality. Whether it succeeds in doing so in practice is of course another question.

The Akan acceptance of individualism is also indicated by their understanding of an important feature of the group. We see it expressed in the proverb,

The clan (group) is (merely) a *multitude* (crowd).
  (*abusua yē dōm*)

This proverb does not say that the group is amorphous or unreal, but that the individual cannot always and invariably depend on the group for everything. The proverb is thus intended to deepen the individual's sense of responsibility for oneself. The proverb suggests that the relevance and importance of the group (clan) are exaggerated even by the Akan people themselves. This gives the lie to the supposition that the individual in a communal social order is a parasite. The individual is supposed to have a dual responsibility: for oneself as an individual as well as to the group. This is not easy to do successfully, and the balance between individuality and communality is a precarious one indeed.

In striking the right balance between individualism and communalism, Akan social thought seeks to promote social arrangements that allow for the adequate expression of the individual's worth and self-fulfillment. If one is by nature a social being, and not merely an atomized entity, then the development of one's full personality and identity can best be achieved only within the framework of social relationships that are realizable within a com-munal social system. That is to say, the conception and development of an individual's full personality and identity cannot be separated from his or her role in the group. The interaction between the individual and the group is thus conceived in Akan social thought to be basic to the development and enhancement of the individual's personality.

PART II — West Asia and the Southern Mediterranean

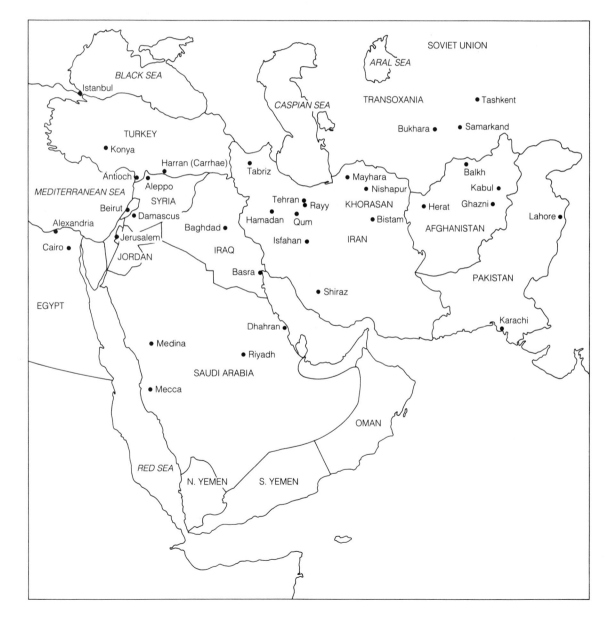

AL-FARABI

Al-Farabi (Abu Nasr Muhammad al-Farabi, 870?–950), of Turkish descent, was born in Transoxania, in present-day Uzbekistan, an independent republic in the southern part of what was formerly the Soviet Union. He studied in Khorasan (covering parts of present-day Iran and Afghanistan) and Baghdad. At least part of his studies were under Syriac-speaking Christian philosophers who represented the tradition of the Alexandrian school. After the Muslim conquest of Alexandria, the school had moved first to Antioch and then to Harran (Carrhae). Al-Farabi studied under a teacher of this school, Yuhanna Ibn Haylan, in Baghdad and may have studied in Harran also. When he was seventy-two, al-Farabi migrated to Syria under the patronage of Prince Sayf al-Dawlah in Aleppo. The prince conquered Damascus three years later, where al-Farabi lived until his death at age eighty.

Al-Farabi was the first Islamic thinker to master the Greek tradition of philosophy and to render the Islamic view of the world consistent with its language and concepts. Before al-Farabi, ancient Greek and later Hellenistic philosophy had had some influence in the Muslim world. A center for the translation of Greek works into Arabic was established under state sponsorship; and, partly as a result of exposure to Greek and Christian philosophy, various sects of "dialectical theologians" debated issues of some philosophical interest. They did so, however, in a purely theological context, taking the revealed religion of the Koran as their principle. Before al-Farabi, no one had tried to master these systems and apply them as such to theoretical and practical problems of the day.

The dialectical theologians in time came to form the center of Islamic orthodoxy. In the 250 years following al-Farabi's death, dialectical theology opposed the study of Greco-Christian philosophy with increasing fervor, seeing such study as productive of heresy and loss of faith. Various political upheavals, often involving intrigues initiated by these sects of theologians, afflicted the lives of Islamic philosophers—notably Avicenna and Averroës—during this period, but al-Farabi seems to have been free of such misfortunes.

Al-Farabi gives somewhat more attention to political and ethical philosophy than other Muslim philosophers, yet he carefully grounds his practical philosophy in his metaphysics—that is, in his theory of the nature of the world and its first and ultimate cause. This interdependence of metaphysics and political philosophy is reflected in the structure of *The Political Regime*. Al-Farabi initially sets out his metaphysical system and then proceeds to introduce his political theory. Into this overarching system, whose broad strokes are adapted from Plato, Aristotle, and later Neoplatonic philosophers, al-Farabi adroitly introduces a theory of prophecy and revealed religion.

Like Aristotle, al-Farabi constructs a system of ethics centered on the concept of *eudaimonia,* or happiness. Happiness, in his view, is the final and unquestioned goal of all human activity; hence man should lead his life in the way that will maximize happiness. The study of ethics tries to say where the greatest happiness lies. For al-Farabi, as for Aristotle, human happiness lies in the activities that develop our natural capacities to their fullest extent. Most important are the capacities that distinguish us from other beings. Among these is our ability to reason, speak, and know. Of course, we also need to provide ourselves with certain basic necessities. We must therefore form cities. Happiness, then, resides in activities that enhance our natural capacities: our ability to know and to form and maintain political associations.

Note that it is not up to each individual person to decide what his happiness is, at least ultimately. Of course, individual people may have vastly different ideas about what will make them happy, and to a certain extent they are free to pursue these ideas. Unless they choose the activities that tend to enhance their natures as human beings, however, they will miss out on true happiness and very likely cause trouble for others. Such a system, which uses human nature as a guide for determining how humans should live, is a *naturalist* ethics.

Into this scheme, which is largely Aristotelian, al-Farabi introduces the notion of the prophet. Prophets are very talented and appear in history very rarely. The prophet has attained the highest mental development possible in this life. This amounts to knowledge of the First Cause. Stemming from this knowledge is the highest moral virtue, as well as the most clear-sighted vision of how to implement policies in the city that will turn people toward the actions best for them. The prophet does this, trying to turn people toward their own better natures, as well as to teach them the real principles of creation. Few can understand such things as clearly and certainly as the prophet, however, so the prophet spreads his message largely by similitudes, in symbols and allegories, of the ultimate causes. These the prophet knows in their ultimate form. But the similitudes make them accessible to the rest of us, who cannot attain such knowledge in this life. These similitudes, which can be in language, in visual art, or in actions, constitute established religion. The abilities and attainments of prophets make them fit to rule the cities. Any city in which a prophet lives and rules, moreover, will be virtuous.

Al-Farabi provides a catalogue of types of cities that depart, in one way or another, from the virtuous ideal. This catalogue follows and expands on one in Plato's *Republic*. One significant addition is the section on "weeds" in the virtuous cities. Here, al-Farabi describes types of people who, for one reason or another, fail to come to terms with the truths the prophet reveals and instead enter a state of perplexity.

In *The Attainment of Happiness,* al-Farabi derives more systematically the abilities the prophet must have. The highest moral virtue, the highest deliberative virtue, the highest practical art, and the most accomplished theoretical attainments all come together in the prophet.

Although much of al-Farabi's concern with the prophet's role seems calculated to provide philosophical support for Muslim beliefs of the time, he explicitly allows that there may be more than one correct religion. Religion, he contends, is merely a likeness of what the prophet-philosopher knows with certainty and clarity.

from *The Political Regime*

Man belongs to the species that cannot accomplish their necessary affairs or achieve their best state, except through the association of many groups of them in a single dwelling-place. Some human societies are large, others are of a medium size, still others are small. The large societies consist of many nations that associate and cooperate with one another; the medium ones consist of a nation; the small are the ones embraced by the city. These three are the perfect societies. Hence the city represents the first degree of perfection. Associations in villages, quarters, streets, and households, on the other hand, are the imperfect associations. Of these the least perfect is the household association, which is a part of the association in the street, the latter being a part of the association in the quarter, and this in turn a part of the political association. Associations in quarters and villages are both for the sake of the city; they differ, however, in that the quarters are parts of the city while the villages only serve it. The political [or civic] society is a part of the nation, and the nation is divided into cities. The absolutely perfect human societies are divided into nations. A nation is differentiated from another by two natural things—natural make-up and natural character—and by something that is composite (it is conventional but has a basis in natural things), which is language—I mean the idiom through which men express themselves. As a result some nations are large and others are small.

The primary natural cause of the differences between nations in these matters consists of a variety of things. One of them is the difference in the parts of the celestial bodies that face them, namely, the first [that is, the outermost] sphere and the sphere of the fixed stars, then the difference in the positions of the inclined spheres from the various parts of the earth and the variation in their proximity and remoteness. . . . It is in this manner and direction that natural things fit together, are connected with each other, and occupy their respective ranks; and this is the extent to which the celestial bodies contribute to their perfection. The remaining perfections are not given by the celestial bodies but by the Active Intellect; and the Active Intellect gives the remaining perfections to no other species but man.

In giving [these perfections] to man, the Active Intellect follows a course similar to that followed by the celestial bodies. First, it gives him a faculty and a principle with which, of his own accord, he seeks, or is able to seek, the remaining perfections. That principle consists of the primary knowledge and the first intelligibles present in the rational part of the soul; but it gives him this kind of knowledge and those intelligibles only after man (*a*) first develops the sensitive part of the soul and the appetitive part, which gives rise to the desire and aversion that adhere to the sensitive part. (The instruments of the last two faculties develop from the parts of the body.) They, in turn, give rise to the will. For, at first, the will is nothing but a desire that follows from a sensation; and desire takes place through the appetitive part of the soul, and sensation through the sensitive. (*b*) Next, there has to develop the imaginative part of the soul and the desire that adheres to it. Hence a second will develops after the first. This will is a desire that follows from [an act of the] imagination. After these two wills develop, it becomes possible for the primary knowledge that emanates from the Active Intellect to the rational part to take place. At this point a third kind of will develops in man—the desire that follows from intellecting—which is specifically called "choice." This choice pertains specifically to man, exclusive of all other animals. By virtue of it, man is able to do either what is commendable or blamable, noble or base; and because of it there is reward and punishment. (The first two wills, on the other hand, can exist in the irrational animals too.) When this will develops in man, with it he is able to seek or not to seek happiness, and to do what is good or evil, noble or base, in so far as this lies in his power.

Happiness is the good without qualification. Everything useful for the achievement of happiness or by which it is attained, is good too, not for its own sake, however, but because it is useful with respect to happiness; and everything that obstructs the way to happiness in any fashion is unqualified evil. . . .

As to voluntary good and evil, which are the noble and the base respectively, they have their origin specifically in man. Now there is only one way in which the voluntary good can come into being. That is because the faculties of the human soul are five: the theoretical-rational, the practical-rational, the appetitive, the imaginative, and the sensitive. Happiness, which only man can know and perceive, is known by the theoretical-rational faculty and by none of the remaining faculties. Man knows it when he makes use of the first principles and the primary knowledge given to him by the Active Intellect. When he knows happiness, desires it by the appetitive faculty, deliberates by the practical-rational faculty upon what he ought to do in order to attain it, uses the instruments of the appetitive faculty to do the actions he has discovered by deliberation, and his imaginative and sensitive faculties assist and obey the rational and aid it in arousing man to do the actions with which he attains happiness, then everything that originates from man will be good. It is only in this way that the voluntary good comes into being. As to voluntary evil, it originates in the manner that I shall state. Neither the imaginative nor the appetitive faculty perceives happiness. Not even the rational faculty perceives happiness under all conditions. The rational faculty perceives happiness only when it strives to apprehend it. Now there are many things that man can imagine that they ought to be the aim and end of life, such as the pleasant and the useful, honor, and the like. When-

ever man neglects to perfect his theoretical-rational part, fails to perceive happiness and hasten toward it, holds something other than happiness—what is useful, what is pleasant, domination, what is honorable, and the like—as an end toward which he aims in his life, desires it with the appetitive faculty, uses the practical-rational faculty to deliberate in the discovery of what enables him to attain this end, uses the instruments of the appetitive faculty to do the things he has discovered, and is assisted in this by the imaginative and the sensitive faculties, then everything that originates from him is evil. Similarly, when man apprehends and knows happiness but does not make it the aim and the end of his life, has no desire or has only a feeble desire for it, makes something other than happiness the end that he desires in his life, and uses all his faculties to attain that end, then everything that originates from him is evil.

Since what is intended by man's existence is that he attain happiness, which is the ultimate perfection that remains to be given to the possible beings capable of receiving it, it is necessary to state the manner in which man can reach this happiness. Man can reach happiness only when the Active Intellect first gives the first intelligibles, which constitute the primary knowledge. However, not every man is equipped by natural disposition to receive the first intelligibles, because individual human beings are made by nature with unequal powers and different preparations. Some of them are not prepared by nature to receive any of the first intelligibles; others—for instance, the insane—receive them, but not as they really are; and still others receive them as they really are. The last are the ones with sound human natural dispositions; only these, and not the others, are capable of attaining happiness.

* * *

Since what is intended by man's existence is that he attain supreme happiness, he—in order to achieve it—needs to know what happiness is, make it his end, and hold it before his eyes. Then, after that, he needs to know the things he ought to do in order to attain happiness, and then do these actions. In view of what has been said about the differences in the natural dispositions of individual men, not everyone is disposed to know happiness on his own, or the things that he ought to do, but needs a teacher and a guide for this purpose. Some men need little guidance, others need a great deal of it. In addition, even when a man is guided to these two [that is, happiness and the actions leading to it], he will not, in the absence of an external stimulus and something to arouse him, necessarily do what he has been taught and guided to. This is how most men are. Therefore they need someone to make all this known to them and to arouse them to do it.

Besides, it is not in the power of every man to guide others nor in the power of every man to induce others to do these things. He who does not possess the power to arouse another to do anything whatever, nor to employ him in it, but only has the power always to do what he has been guided to, is never a ruler in anything at all; he is always ruled in everything. He who has the power to guide another to a certain thing, to induce him to do it, and to employ him in it, is in that thing a ruler over the one who cannot do it on his own. And he who cannot discover something on his own, but does it when he is guided to it and instructed in it, and has the power to arouse another to do, and to employ him in, that thing in which he himself has been instructed and to which he has been guided, is a ruler over one man and is ruled by another. Thus the ruler may be a supreme or a subordinate ruler. The subordinate ruler is one who is subject to one man and in turn rules over another. These two types of rule can be in one kind [of art], such as husbandry, trade, or medicine, and can pertain to all kinds of human [arts].

The supreme ruler without qualification is he who does not need anyone to rule him in anything whatever, but has actually acquired the sciences and every kind of knowledge, and has no need of a man to guide him in anything. He is able to comprehend well each one of the particular things that he ought to do. He is able to guide well all others to everything in which he instructs them, to employ all those who do any of the acts for which they are equipped, and to determine, define, and direct these acts toward happiness. This is found only in the one who possesses great and superior natural dispositions, when his soul is in union with the Active Intellect. He can only attain this [union with the Active Intellect] by first acquiring the passive intellect, and then the

intellect called the acquired; for, as it is stated in *On the Soul*,* union with the Active Intellect results from possessing the acquired intellect. This man is the true prince according to the ancients; he is the one of whom it ought to be said that he receives revelation. For man receives revelation only when he attains this rank, that is, when there is no longer an intermediary between him and the Active Intellect; for the passive intellect is like matter and substratum to the acquired intellect, and the latter is like matter and substratum to the Active Intellect. It is then that the power that enables man to understand how to define things and actions and how to direct them toward happiness, emanates from the Active Intellect to the passive intellect. This emanation that proceeds from the Active Intellect to the passive through the mediation of the acquired intellect, is revelation. Now because the Active Intellect emanates from the being of the First Cause, it can for this reason be said that it is the First Cause that brings about revelation to this man through the mediation of the Active Intellect. The rule of this man is the supreme rule; all other human rulerships are inferior to it and are derived from it. Such is his rank.

The men who are governed by the rule of this ruler are the virtuous, good, and happy men. If they form a nation, then that is the virtuous nation; if they are associated in a single dwelling-place, then the dwelling-place that brings together all those subject to such a rule is the virtuous city; and if they are not associated together in a single dwelling-place, but live in separate dwelling-places whose inhabitants are governed by rulerships other than this one, then these are virtuous men who are strangers in those dwelling-places. . . .

As every citizen of the city does what is entrusted to him—either by knowing it on his own or by being guided and induced to it by the ruler—he acquires, by these actions, the good states of the soul, just as by continued practice in good writing a man acquires excellence in the art of writing, which is a state of the soul; and the more he continues practic-

---

* Aristotle's work on the human mind. The reference is to Book III, Chapters 5 and 7. The term *acquired intellect* comes, not from Aristotle, but from Alexander of Aphrodisias's commentary on *On the Soul.* —ED.

ing, the more firm his excellence in writing becomes, the greater the pleasure he takes in the resulting state, and the stronger the delight of his soul in that state. Similarly, the actions that are determined and directed toward happiness strengthen the part of the soul that is naturally equipped for happiness, and actualize and perfect it—to the extent that the power resulting from the perfection achieved by it enables it to dispense with matter; having been thus freed from matter, it is not destroyed by the destruction of matter, since it is no longer in need of matter in order to exercise its power or to exist—at which time it attains happiness. It is evident that the kinds of happiness attained by the citizens of the city differ in quantity and quality as a result of the difference in the perfections they acquire through political activities. Accordingly, the pleasures they attain vary in excellence. When the soul becomes separated from matter and incorporeal, it is no longer subject to any of the accidents that are attached to bodies as such; therefore it cannot be said of it that it moves or that it rests. Rather one ought then to apply to it the statements appropriate to what is incorporeal. . . .

As one group of them passes away, and their bodies are destroyed, their souls have achieved salvation and happiness, and they are succeeded by other men who assume their positions in the city and perform their actions, the souls of the latter will also achieve salvation. As their bodies are destroyed, they join the rank of the former group that had passed away, they will be together with them in the way that incorporeal things are together, and the kindred souls within each group will be in a state of union with one another. . . . Such is the state of every group of them. This, then, is true and supreme happiness, which is the purpose of the Active Intellect.

When the activities of the citizens of a city are not directed toward happiness, they lead them to acquire bad states of the soul—just as when the activities of [the art of] writing are badly performed, they produce bad writing, and similarly, when the activities of any art are badly performed, they produce in the soul bad states, corresponding to the [badly performed] art. As a result their souls become sick. Therefore they take pleasure in the states that they acquire through their activities. Just as because

of their corrupt sense [of taste], those with bodily sickness—for example, the ones affected by fever—take pleasure in bitter things and find them sweet, and suffer pain from sweet things, which seem bitter to their palates; similarly, because of their corrupt imagination, those who are sick in their souls take pleasure in the bad states [of the soul]. And just as there are among the sick those who do not feel their malady and those who even think that they are healthy, and such sick men do not at all listen to the advice of a physician; similarly, the sick in their souls who do not feel their sickness and even think that they are virtuous and have sound souls, do not listen at all to the words of a guide, a teacher, or a reformer. The souls of such individuals remain chained to matter and do not reach that perfection by which they can separate from matter, so that when the matter ceases to exist they too will cease to exist.

The ranks of order among the citizens of the city, as regards ruling and serving, vary in excellence according to their natural dispositions and according to the habits of character they have formed. The supreme ruler is the one who orders the various groups and every individual in each group, in the place they merit—that is, gives each a subservient or a ruling rank of order. Therefore, there will be certain ranks of order that are close to his own, others slightly further away, and still others that are far away from it. Such will be the ruling ranks of order: beginning with the highest ruling rank of order, they will descend gradually until they become subservient ranks of order devoid of any element of ruling and below which there is no other rank of order. After having ordered these ranks, if the supreme ruler wishes to issue a command about a certain matter that he wishes to enjoin the citizens of the city or a certain group among them to do, and to arouse them toward it, he intimates this to the ranks closest to him, these will hand it on to their subordinates, and so forth, until it reaches down to those assigned to execute that matter. The parts of the city will thus be linked and fitted together, and ordered by giving precedence to some over the others. Thus the city becomes similar to the natural beings; the ranks of order in it similar to the ranks of order of the beings, which begin with the First and terminate in prime matter and the elements; and the way they are linked and fitted together will be similar to the way the beings are linked and fitted together. The prince of the city will be like the First Cause, which is the cause for the existence of all the other beings. Then the ranks of order of the beings gradually keep descending, each one of them being both ruler and ruled, until they reach down to those possible beings—that is, prime matter and the elements—that possess no ruling element whatever, but are subservient and always exist for the sake of others. . . .

Each one of the citizens of the virtuous city is required to know the highest principles of the beings and their ranks of order, happiness, the supreme rulership of the virtuous city, and the ruling ranks of order in it; then, after that, the specified actions that, when performed, lead to the attainment of happiness. These actions are not merely to be known; they should be done and the citizens of the city should be directed to do them.

The principles of the beings, their ranks of order, happiness, and the rulership of the virtuous cities, are either cognized and intellected by man, or he imagines them. To cognize them is to have their essences, as they really are, imprinted in man's soul. To imagine them is to have imprinted in man's soul their images, representations of them, or matters that are imitations of them. This is analogous to what takes place with regard to visible objects, for instance, man. We see him himself, we see a representation of him, we see his image reflected in water and other reflecting substances, and we see the image of a representation of him reflected in water and in other reflecting substances. Our seeing him himself is like the intellect's cognition of the principles of the beings, of happiness, and so forth; while our seeing the reflection of man in water and our seeing a representation of him is like imagination, for our seeing a representation of him or our seeing his reflection in a mirror is seeing that which is an imitation of him. Similarly, when we imagine those things, we are in fact having a cognition of matters that are imitations of them rather than a cognition of them themselves.

Most men, either by nature or by habit, are unable to comprehend and cognize those things; these are the men for whom one ought to represent the manner in which the principles of the beings, their

ranks of order, the Active Intellect, and the supreme rulership, exist through things that are imitations of them. Now while the meanings and essences of those things are one and immutable, the matters by which they are imitated are many and varied. Some imitate them more closely, while others do so only remotely—just as is the case with visible objects: for the image of man that is seen reflected in water is closer to the true man than the image of a representation of man that is seen reflected in water. Therefore, it is possible to imitate these things for each group and each nation, using matters that are different in each case. Consequently, there may be a number of virtuous nations and virtuous cities whose religions are different, even though they all pursue the very same kind of happiness. For religion is but the impressions of these things or the impressions of their images, imprinted in the soul. Because it is difficult for the multitude to comprehend these things themselves as they are, the attempt was made to teach them these things in other ways, which are the ways of imitation. Hence these things are imitated for each group or nation through the matters that are best known to them; and it may very well be that what is best known to the one may not be the best known to the other.

Most men who strive for happiness, follow after an imagined, not a cognized, form of happiness. Similarly, most men accept such principles as are accepted and followed, and are magnified and considered majestic, in the form of images, not of cognitions. Now the ones who follow after happiness as they cognize it and accept the principles as they cognize them, are the wise men. And the ones in whose souls these things are found in the form of images, and who accept them and follow after them as such, are the believers. . . .

The virtuous city is the opposite of (A) the ignorant city, (B) the immoral city, and (C) the erring city. (D) Then there are the Weeds in the virtuous city. (The position of the Weeds in the cities is like that of the darnel among the wheat, the thorns growing among the crop, or the other grass that is useless or even harmful to the crop or plants.) Finally, there are the men who are bestial by nature. But the bestial by nature are neither political beings nor could they ever form a political association. Instead, some of them are like gregarious beasts and others are like wild beasts, and of the latter some are like ravenous beasts. . . .

A. *The Ignorant Cities*

As for the citizens of the ignorant cities, they are political beings. Their cities and their political associations are of many kinds, which comprise (i) indispensable associations, (ii) the association of vile men in the vile cities, (iii) the association of base men in the base cities, (iv) timocratic association in the timocratic city, (v) despotic association in the despotic cities, (vi) free association in the democratic city and the city of the free.

The Indispensable City

The indispensable city or the indispensable association is that which leads to cooperation to acquire the bare necessities for the subsistence and the safeguarding of the body. There are many ways to acquire these things, such as husbandry, grazing, hunting, robbery, and so forth. Both hunting and robbery are practiced either by stealth or openly. There are certain indispensable cities that possess all the arts that lead to the acquisition of the bare necessities. In others the bare necessities are obtained through one art only, such as husbandry alone or any other art. The citizens of this city regard the best man to be the one who is most excellent in skill, management, and accomplishment in obtaining the bare necessities through the ways of acquisition that they employ. Their ruler is he who can govern well and is skillful in employing them to acquire the indispensable things, who can govern them well so as to preserve these things for them, or who generously provides them with these things from his own possessions.

ii. The Vile City

The vile city or the association of the vile citizens is that whose members (*a*) cooperate to acquire wealth and prosperity, the excessive possession of indispensable things or their equivalent in coin and in money, and their accumulation beyond the need for them and for no other reason than the love and covetousness of wealth; and (*b*) avoid spending any

of it except on what is necessary for bodily subsistence. This they do either by pursuing all the modes of acquisition or else such modes as are available in that country. They regard the best men to be the wealthiest and the most skillful in the acquisition of wealth. Their ruler is the man who is able to manage them well in what leads them to acquire wealth and always to remain wealthy. Wealth is obtained through all the methods employed to obtain the bare necessities, that is, husbandry, grazing, hunting, and robbery; and also through voluntary transactions like commerce, lease, and so forth.

iii. The Base City

The base city or the base association is that in which the citizens cooperate to enjoy sensual pleasures or imaginary pleasures (play and amusement) or both. They enjoy the pleasures of food, drink, and copulation, and strive after what is most pleasant of these, in the pursuit of pleasure alone, rather than what sustains, or is in any way useful to, the body; and they do the same as regards play and amusement. This city is the one regarded by the citizens of the ignorant city as the happy and admirable city; for they can attain the goal of this city only after having acquired the bare necessities and acquired wealth, and only by means of much expenditure. They regard whoever possesses more resources for play and the pleasures as the best, the happiest, and the most enviable man.

iv. The Timocratic City

The timocratic city or the timocratic association is that in which the citizens cooperate with a view to be honored in speech and deed: that is, to be honored either by the citizens of other cities or by one another. Their honoring of one another consists in the exchange of either equal or unequal honors. The exchange of equal honors takes place through someone bestowing on someone else a certain kind of honor at a certain time so that the latter may at another time return the same kind of honor or another kind of honor that, in their eyes, is of equal worth. The exchange of unequal honors takes place through someone bestowing a certain kind of honor on someone else, with the latter bestowing on the former another kind of honor of greater worth than the first. In every case, moreover, this [exchange of unequal honors] among them takes place on the basis of merit (one of two men merits an honor of a certain worth, while the other merits a greater one), depending on what they consider merit to be. In the eyes of the citizens of the ignorant city, merits are not based on virtue, but (a) on wealth, or (b) on possessing the means of pleasure and play and on obtaining the most of both, or (c) on obtaining most of the necessities of life (when man is served and is well provided with all the necessities he needs), or (d) on man's being useful, that is, doing good to others with respect to these three things. (e) There is one more thing that is well liked by most of the citizens of the ignorant cities, that is, domination. For whoever achieves it is envied by most of them. Therefore this, too, must be regarded as one of the merits in the ignorant cities. For, in their eyes, the highest matter for which a man must be honored is his fame in achieving domination [that is, superiority] in one, two, or many things; not being dominated, because he himself is strong, because his supporters are either numerous or strong, or because of both; and that he be immune to being harmed by others, while able to harm others at will. For, in their eyes, this is a state of felicity for which a man merits honor; hence the better he is in this respect, the more he is honored. Or the man [whom they honor] possesses, in their eyes, distinguished ancestors. But ancestors are distinguished because of the things mentioned above: namely, one's fathers and grandfathers were either wealthy, abundantly favored with pleasure and the means to it, had domination [that is, were superior] in a number of things, were useful to others—be they a group or the citizens of a city—with respect to these things, or were favored with the instruments of these things, such as nobility, endurance, or the contempt of death, all of which are instruments of domination. Honors of equal worth, on the other hand, are sometimes merited by virtue of an external possession, and sometimes honor itself is the reason for the merit, so that the one who begins and honors someone else merits thereby to be honored by the other, as is the case in market transactions.

Thus, in their eyes, the one who merits more honor rules over the one who merits less of it. This inequality continues on an ascending scale terminating in the one who merits more honors than anyone else in the city. This, therefore, will be the ruler and the prince of the city. By virtue of this office, he ought to be of greater merit than all the rest. . . . He thus possesses all the things for which men may honor him, reserving for himself alone the things regarded by them as manifesting splendor, embellishment, eminence, and magnificence—such as buildings, costumes, and medals, and, finally, inaccessibility to people. Further, he lays down the laws concerning honors. Once he assumes a certain office and people are accustomed to the fact that he and his family will be their princes, he then orders the people into ranks in such a way as to obtain honor and majesty. To each kind of rank, he assigns (a) a kind of honor and (b) things by virtue of which one merits honor, such as wealth, building, costume, medal, carriage, and so forth, and which contribute to his majesty; and he arranges all this in a definite order. Furthermore, he will show special preference for those men who honor him more or contribute more to the enhancement of his majesty, and he confers honor and distributes favor accordingly. The citizens of his city who covet honor keep honoring him until he acknowledges what they have done and confers honors on them, because of which they will be honored by their inferiors and superiors.

For all these reasons, this city can be likened to the virtuous city, especially when the honors, and men's ranks of order with respect to honors, are conferred because of other, more useful things: for example, wealth, pleasures, or anything else that is desired by whoever seeks after useful things. This city is the best among the ignorant cities; unlike those of the others, its citizens are [more properly] called "ignorant" and so forth. However, when their love of honor becomes excessive, it becomes a city of tyrants, and it is more likely to change into a despotic city.

v. The Despotic City

The despotic city or the despotic association is that in which the members cooperate to achieve domination. This happens when they are all seized by the love of domination, provided that it is in different degrees, and that they seek different kinds of domination and different things for the sake of which to dominate other men; for instance, some like to dominate another man in order to spill his blood, others, to take his property, still others, to possess him so that they may enslave him. People occupy different ranks of order in this city depending on the extent of one's love of domination. Its citizens love to dominate others in order to spill their blood and kill them, to possess them so that they may enslave them, or in order to take their property. In all this, what they love and aim at is to dominate, subdue, and humiliate others, and that the subdued should have no control whatever over himself or any of the things because of which he has been dominated, but should do as the subduer commands and wishes. (Indeed when the lover of domination and subjugation—who is inclined to, or desires, a certain thing—obtains it without having to subdue someone else, he does not take it and pays no attention to it.) Some of them choose to dominate through wiliness, others, through open combat alone, and still others, through both wiliness and open combat. Therefore many of those who subjugate others in order to spill their blood, do not kill a man when asleep and do not seize his property until they first wake him up; they prefer to engage him in combat and to be faced with some resistance in order to subdue him and harm him. Since every one of them loves to dominate the others, each one loves to dominate everyone else, whether a fellow citizen or not. They refrain from dominating one another as regards the spilling of blood or the taking of property, only because they need one another so as to survive, cooperate in dominating others, and defend themselves against outside domination.

Their ruler is he who shows greater strength in governing well with a view to employing them to dominate others; who is the wiliest of them; and who has the soundest judgment about what they ought to do in order to continue to dominate forever and never be dominated by others. Such is their ruler and prince. They are the enemies of all other men. . . .

. . . At times, such men become rude, cruel, irascible, extravagant, and excessively gluttonous; they consume great quantities of food and drink, overindulge in copulation, and fight each other for all the goods, which they obtain through subjugating and humiliating those who possess them. They think that they should dominate everything and everybody.

(1) Sometimes this is true of the entire city, whose citizens will then choose to dominate those outside the city for no other reason than the citizens' need for association [and hence for a common cause that would promote it]. (2) Sometimes the vanquished and the subjugators live side by side in a single city. The subjugators then either (a) love to subjugate and dominate others to the same degree and hence have the same rank of order in the city, or (b) they occupy various ranks of order, each one of them having a certain kind of domination over their vanquished neighbors, which is lesser or greater than that of the other. In this way, and depending on the power and judgment through which they achieve domination, they occupy their respective places next to a prince who rules them and manages the subjugators' affairs as regards the instruments they use for subjugation. (3) And sometimes there is but a single subjugator, with a group of men as his instruments for subjugating all other men. The group in question does not seek to enable him to dominate and seize something for someone else's sake, but so that he dominate something that would belong to him alone. The single subjugator, in turn, is satisfied with what maintains his life and strength; he gives [the rest] to the others and dominates for the sake of the others, like dogs and falcons do. The rest of the citizens of the city, too, are slaves to that one, serving his every wish; they are submissive and humiliated, possessing nothing whatever of their own. Some of them cultivate the soil, others trade, for him. In all this, he has no other purpose beyond seeing a certain group subjugated and dominated and submissive to him alone, even though he derives no benefit or pleasure from them except that of seeing them humiliated and dominated. This (3), then, is the city whose prince alone is despotic, while the rest of its citizens are not despotic. In the one that preceded it (2), half of the city is despotic. In the first (1), all the citizens are despotic.

The despotic city may thus have such a character that it employs one of these methods in the pursuit of domination alone and the enjoyment of it. But if domination is loved only as a means for the acquisition of bare necessities, prosperity, the enjoyment of pleasures, honors, or all of these together, then this is a despotic city of a different sort; and its citizens belong to the other cities mentioned above. Most people call such cities despotic; but this name applies more properly to the one among them that seeks all of these (three?) things by means of subjugation. . . .

Sometimes the citizens of the [vile or] plutocratic city and the citizens of the [base] city that is dedicated to play and amusement imagine that they are the ones who are lucky, happy, and successful, and that they are more excellent than the citizens of all other cities. These delusions about themselves sometimes lead them to become contemptuous of the citizens of other cities and to suppose that others have no worth, and to love to be honored for whatever caused their happiness. Consequently, they develop traits of arrogance, extravagance, boastfulness, and the love of praise, and suppose that others cannot attain what they themselves have attained, and that the others are therefore too stupid to achieve these two kinds of happiness [which result from wealth, and play and amusement, respectively]. They create for themselves titles with which they embellish their ways of life, such as that they are the talented and the elegant, and that the others are the rude. Therefore they are supposed to be men of pride, magnanimity, and authority. Sometimes they are even called high-minded.

When the lovers of wealth and the lovers of pleasure and play do not happen to possess any of the arts by which wealth is obtained except the power to dominate, and they achieve wealth and play by subjugation and domination, then they become extremely arrogant and join the ranks of tyrants (in contrast, the former group are simply idiots). Similarly, it is possible to find among the lovers of honor some who love it, not for its own sake, but for the sake of wealth. . . .

vi. The Democratic City

The democratic city is the one in which each one of the citizens is given free rein and left alone to do whatever he likes. Its citizens are equal and their laws say that no man is in any way at all better than any other man. Its citizens are free to do whatever they like; and no one, be he one of them or an outsider, has any claim to authority unless he works to enhance their freedom. Consequently, they develop many kinds of morals, inclinations, and desires, and they take pleasure in countless things. Its citizens

consist of countless similar and dissimilar groups. This city brings together the groups—both the base and the noble—that existed separately in all the other cities; and positions of authority are obtained here by means of any one of the things we have mentioned. Those from among the multitude of this city, who possess whatever the rulers possess, have the upper hand over those who are called their rulers. Those who rule them do so by the will of the ruled, and the rulers follow the wishes of the ruled. Close investigation of their situation would reveal that, in truth, there is no distinction between ruler and ruled among them. However, they praise and honor those who lead the citizens of the city to freedom and to whatever the citizens like and desire, and who safeguard the citizens' freedom and their varied and different desires against [infringement] by one another and by outside enemies; and who limit their own desires to bare necessities. Such, then, is the one who is honored, regarded as the best, and is obeyed among them. As to any other ruler, he is either (a) their equal or (b) their inferior. (a) He is their equal when it happens that, when he provides them with the good things that they want and desire, they reciprocate with comparable honors and wealth. In this case they do not consider him to be superior to them. (b) They are his superiors when they accord him honors and allot him a share of their possessions, without receiving any benefit from him in return. For it is quite possible to find in this city a ruler in this situation: he happens to be magnified in the eyes of the citizens either because they take a fancy to him or because his ancestors ruled them well and they let him rule in gratitude for what his ancestors did. In this case, the multitude would have the upper hand over the rulers.

All the endeavors and purposes of the ignorant cities are present in this city in a most perfect manner; of all of them, this is the most admirable and happy city. On the surface, it looks like an embroidered garment full of colored figures and dyes. Everybody loves it and loves to reside in it, because there is no human wish or desire that this city does not satisfy. The nations emigrate to it and reside there, and it grows beyond measure. People of every race multiply in it, and this by all kinds of copulation and marriages, resulting in children of extremely varied dispositions, with extremely varied education and upbringing. Consequently, this city develops into many cities, distinct yet intertwined, with the parts of each scattered throughout the parts of the others. Strangers cannot be distinguished from the residents. All kinds of wishes and ways of life are to be found in it. Consequently, it is quite possible that, with the passage of time, virtuous men will grow up in it. Thus it may include philosophers, rhetoricians, and poets, dealing with all kinds of things. It is also possible to glean from it certain [men who form] parts of the virtuous city; this is the best thing that takes place in this city. Therefore, this city possesses both good and evil to a greater degree than the rest of the ignorant cities. The bigger, the more civilized, the more populated, the more productive, and the more perfect it is, the more prevalent and the greater are the good and the evil it possesses.

There are as many aims pursued by the ignorant rulerships as there are ignorant cities. Every ignorant rulership aims at having its fill of bare necessities; wealth; delight in the pleasures; honor, reputation, and praise; domination; or freedom. Therefore, such rulerships are actually bought for a price, especially the positions of authority in the democratic city; for here no one has a better claim than anyone else to a position of authority. Therefore, when someone finally holds a position of authority, it is either because the citizens have favored him with it, or else because they have received from him money or something else in return. In their eyes the virtuous ruler is he who has the ability to judge well and to contrive well what enables them to attain their diverse and variegated desires and wishes, safeguards them against their enemies, and takes nothing of their property, but confines himself to the bare necessities of life. As for the truly virtuous man—namely the man who, if he were to rule them, would determine and direct their actions toward happiness—they do not make him a ruler. If by chance he comes to rule them, he will soon find himself either deposed or killed or in an unstable and challenged position. And so are all the other ignorant cities; each one of them only wants the ruler who facilitates the attainment of its wishes and desires, and paves the way for their acquisition and preservation. Therefore, they refuse the rule of virtuous men and resent it. Nevertheless, the construc-

tion of virtuous cities and the establishment of the rule of virtuous men are more effective and much easier out of the indispensable and democratic cities than out of any other ignorant city. . . .

B. The Immoral Cities

Immoral cities are the ones whose citizens once believed in, and cognized, the principles [of beings]; imagined, and believed in, what happiness is; and were guided toward, knew, and believed in, the actions by which to attain happiness. Nevertheless, they did not adhere to any of those actions, but came to desire and will one or another of the aims of the citizens of the ignorant cities—such as honor, domination, and so forth—and directed all their actions and faculties toward them. There are as many kinds of these [immoral] cities as there are ignorant cities, inasmuch as all their actions and morals are identical with those of the ignorant cities. They differ from the citizens of the ignorant cities only in the opinions in which they believe. Not one of the citizens of these cities can attain happiness at all.

C. The Erring Cities

Erring cities are those whose citizens are given imitations of other matters than the ones we mentioned —that is, the principles that are established for, and imitated to, them are other than the ones we mentioned; a kind of happiness that is not true happiness is established for, and represented to, them; and actions and opinions are prescribed for them by none of which true happiness can be attained.

D. The Weeds in Virtuous Cities

The Weeds within the virtuous cities are of many classes. (i) [Members of] one class adhere to the actions conducive to the attainment of happiness; however, they do not do such actions in the pursuit of happiness, but rather of other things that man can attain by means of virtue, such as honor, rulership, wealth, and so forth. Such individuals are called opportunists (*mutaqanniṣūn*). Some of them have an inclination to one of the ends of the citizens of the ignorant cities and they are prevented by the Laws and the religion of the city from pursuing such ends. Therefore they resort to the expressions of the lawgiver and the statements that embody his precepts, and interpret them as they wish, by which interpretation they make the thing they are after appear good. Such men are called the misinterpreters (*muharrifah*). Others among them do not deliberately misinterpret but, because they do not rightly understand the lawgiver and because of their misconception of his statements, they understand the Laws of the city in a different way than the one intended by the lawgiver. Their actions will therefore not conform to the intention of the supreme ruler. Hence they err without realizing it. These men are the apostates (*māriqah*).

(ii) [Members of] another class do imagine the things we mentioned, yet they are not convinced of what they have imagined of them. Hence they use arguments to falsify them for themselves and for others. In so doing, they are not contending against the virtuous city; rather they are looking for the right path and seeking the truth. He who belongs to this class, should have the level of his imagination raised to things that cannot be falsified by the arguments he has put forward. If he is satisfied with the level to which he has been raised, he should be left alone. But if he is again not satisfied, and discovers here certain places susceptible to contention, then he should be raised to a higher level. This process should continue until he becomes satisfied with one of these levels. And if it happens that he is not satisfied with any one of these levels of imagination, he should be raised to the level of the truth and be made to comprehend those things as they are, at which point his mind will come to rest.

(iii) [Members of] another class falsify whatever they imagine. Whenever they are raised to a higher level, they falsify it, even when they are conducted to the level of the truth—all this in the pursuit of domination alone, or in the pursuit of ennobling another of the aims of the ignorant cities that is desired by them. They falsify them in every way they can; they do not like to listen to anything that may establish happiness and truth firmly in the soul, or any argument that may ennoble and imprint them

in the soul, but meet them with such sham arguments as they think will discredit happiness. Many of them do that with the intention of appearing as having a pretext for turning to one of the aims of the ignorant cities.

(iv) [Members of] another class imagine happiness and the principles [of beings], but their minds are totally lacking in the power to cognize them, or it is beyond the power of their minds to cognize them adequately. Consequently, they falsify the things they imagine and come upon the places of contention in them, and whenever they are raised to a level of imagination that is closer to the truth, they find it to be false. Nor is it possible to raise them to the level of the truth because their minds lack the power to comprehend it. And many of them may find most of what they imagine to be false, not because what they imagine truly contains places of contention, but because they have a defective imagination, and they find these things false because of their defective minds, not because these things contain a place of contention. Many of them—when unable to imagine something sufficiently or discover the real points of contention and in the places where they are to be found, or are unable to comprehend the truth—think that the man who has apprehended the truth and who says that he has apprehended it, is a deliberate liar who is seeking honor or domination, or else think that he is a deluded man. So they try hard to falsify the truth also, and abase the man who has apprehended it. This leads many of them to think that all men are deluded in everything they claim to have apprehended. It leads (1) some of them to a state of perplexity in all things, and (2) others to think that no apprehension whatever is true, and that whenever someone thinks that he has apprehended something that he is lying about it and that he is not sure or certain of what he thinks. These individuals occupy the position of ignorant simpletons in the eyes of reasonable men and in relation to the philosophers. (For this reason it is the duty of the ruler of the virtuous city to look for the Weeds, keep them occupied, and treat each class of them in the particular manner that will cure them: by expelling them from the city, punishing them, jailing them, or forcing them to perform a certain function even though they may not be fond of it.) (3) Others among them think that the truth consists of whatever appears to each individual and what each man thinks it to be at one time or another, and that the truth of everything is what someone thinks it is. (4) Others among them exert themselves to create the illusion that everything that is thought to have been apprehended up to this time is completely false, and that, although a certain truth or reality does exist, it has not as yet been apprehended. (5) Others among them imagine—as if in a dream or as if a thing is seen from a distance—that there is a truth, and it occurs to them that the ones who claim to have apprehended it may have done so, or perhaps that one of them may have apprehended it. They feel that they themselves have missed it, either because they require a long time, and have to toil and exert themselves, in order to apprehend it, when they no longer have sufficient time or the power to toil and persevere; or because they are occupied by certain pleasures and so forth to which they have been accustomed and from which they find it very difficult to free themselves; or because they feel that they cannot apprehend it even if they had access to all the means to it. Consequently, they regret and grieve over what they think others may have attained. Hence, out of jealousy for those who may have apprehended the truth, they think it wise to endeavor, using sham argument, to create the illusion that whoever claims to have apprehended the truth is either deluded or else a liar who is seeking honor, wealth, or some other desirable thing, from the claim he makes. Now many of these perceive

their own ignorance and perplexity; they feel sad and suffer pain because of what they perceive to be their condition, they are overcome by anxiety, and it torments them; and they find no way to free themselves of this by means of a science leading them to the truth whose apprehension would give them pleasure. Hence they choose to find rest from all this by turning to the various ends of the ignorant cities, and to find their solace in amusements and games until death comes to relieve them of their burden. Some of these—I mean the ones who seek rest from the torment of ignorance and perplexity—may create the illusion that the [true] ends are those that they themselves choose and desire, that happiness consists of these, and that the rest of men are deluded in what they believe in. They exert themselves to adorn the ends of the ignorant cities and the happiness [that they pursue]. They create the illusion that they have come to prefer some of these ends after a thorough examination of all that the others claim to have apprehended, that they have rejected the latter only after finding out that they are inconclusive, and that their position was arrived at on the basis of personal knowledge—therefore, theirs are the ends, not the ones claimed by the others.

These, then, are the classes of the Weeds growing among the citizens of the city. With such opinions, they constitute neither a city nor a large multitude; rather they are submerged by the citizen body as a whole.

from *The Attainment of Happiness*

Reprinted with permission of The Free Press, a division of Macmillan, Inc., from Alfarabi's Philosophy of Plato and Aristotle, *translated by Muhsin Mahdi. Copyright © 1962 by The Free Press.*

CHAPTER i

. . . It is incumbent on man to investigate . . . the things that realize for man his objective through the intellectual principles that are in him, and by which he achieves that perfection that became known in natural science. It will become evident concomitantly that these rational principles are not mere *causes* by which man attains the perfection for which he is made. Moreover, he will know that these rational principles also supply many things to natural beings other than those supplied by nature. Indeed man arrives at the ultimate perfection (whereby he attains that which renders him truly substantial) only when he labors with these principles toward achieving that perfection. Moreover, he cannot labor toward this perfection except by exploiting a large number of natural beings and until he manipulates them to render them useful to him for arriving at the ultimate perfection he should achieve. Furthermore, it will become evident to him in this science that each man achieves only a portion of that perfection, and what he achieves of this portion varies in its extent, for an isolated individual cannot achieve all the perfections by himself and without the aid of many other individuals. It is the innate disposition of every man to join another human being or other men in the labor he ought to perform: this is the condition of every single man. Therefore, to achieve what he can of that perfection, every man needs to stay in the neighborhood of others and associate with them. It is also the innate nature of this animal to seek shelter and to dwell in the neighborhood of those who belong to the same species, which is why he is called the *social* and *political* animal. There emerges now another science and another inquiry that investigates these intellectual principles and the acts and states of character with which man labors toward this perfection. From this, in turn, emerge the science of man and political science. . . .

. . . He should continue this investigation until he finally reaches a being that cannot possess any of these principles at all (either *what* it is or *from what* it is or *for what* it is) but is itself the first principle of all the aforementioned beings: it is itself that *by* which, *from* which, and *for* which they are, in the most perfect modes in which a thing can be a principle for the beings, modes free from all defects. Having understood this, he should investigate next what properties the other beings possess as a consequence of their having *this* being as their principle and the cause of their being. He should begin with the being whose rank is higher than the rest (that is, the one nearest to the first principle), until he terminates in the being whose rank is inferior to the rest (that is, the one furthest from the first principle). He will thus come to know the ultimate causes of the beings. This is the divine inquiry into them. For the first principle is the divinity, and the principles that come after it—and are not bodies or in bodies—are the divine principles.

Then he should set out next upon the science of man and investigate the *what* and the *how* of the purpose for which man is made, that is, the perfection that man must achieve. Then he should investigate all the things by which man achieves this perfection or that are useful to him in achieving it. These are the good, virtuous, and noble things. He should distinguish them from things that obstruct his achieving this perfection. These are the evils, the vices, and the base things. He should make known *what* and *how* every one of them is, and *from what* and *for what* it is, until all of them become known, intelligible, and distinguished from each other. This is political science. It consists of knowing the things by which the citizens of cities attain happiness through political association in the measure that innate disposition equips each of them for it. . . .

CHAPTER ii

. . . Things of this sort are not covered by the theoretical sciences, which cover only the intelligibles that do not vary at all. Therefore another faculty and another skill is required with which to discern the voluntary intelligibles, [not as such, but] insofar as they possess these variable accidents: that is, the modes according to which they can be brought into actual existence by the will at a determined time, in a determined place, and when a determined event occurs. That is the *deliberative* faculty. It is the skill and the faculty by which one discovers and discerns the variable accidents of the intelligibles whose particular instances are made to exist by the will, when one attempts to bring them into actual existence by the will at a determined time, in a determined place, and when a determined event takes place, whether the time is long or short, whether the locality is large or small.

Things are *discovered* by the deliberative faculty only insofar as they are found to be useful for the attainment of an end and purpose. The discoverer first sets the end before himself and then investigates the means by which that end and that purpose are realized. The deliberative faculty is most perfect when it discovers what is most useful for the attainment of these ends. The ends may be truly good, may be evil, or may be only believed to be good. If the means discovered are the most useful for a virtuous end, then they are noble and fair. If the ends are evil, then the means discovered by the deliberative faculty are also evil, base, and bad. And if the ends are only believed to be good, then the means useful for attaining and achieving them are also only believed to be good. . . .

It is obvious that the one who possesses a virtue by which he discovers what is most useful and noble, and this for the sake of a virtuous end that is good (irrespective of whether what is discovered is a true good that he wishes for himself, a true good that he wishes someone else to possess, or something that is believed to be good by whomever he wishes it for), cannot possess this faculty without possessing a moral virtue. For if a man wishes the good for others, then he is either truly good or else believed to be good by those for whom he wishes the good although he is not good and virtuous. Similarly he who wishes the true good for himself has to be good and virtuous, not in his deliberation, but in his moral character and in his acts. It would seem that his virtue, moral character, and acts, have to correspond to his power of deliberation and ability to discover what is most useful and noble. Hence if he discovers by his deliberative virtue only those most useful and noble means that are of great force (such as what is most useful for a virtuous end common to a whole nation, to many nations, or to a whole city, and does not vary except over a long period), then his moral virtues ought to be of a comparable measure. Similarly, if his deliberative virtues are confined to means that are most useful for a restricted end when a specific event occurs, then this is the measure of his [moral] virtue also. Accordingly, the more perfect the authority and the greater the power of these deliberative virtues, the stronger the authority and the greater the power of the moral virtues that accompany them. . . .

Therefore one ought to investigate which virtue is the perfect and most powerful virtue. Is it the combination of all the virtues?; or, if one virtue (or a number of virtues) turns out to have a power equal to that of all the virtues together, what ought to be the distinctive mark of the virtue that has this power and is hence the most powerful virtue? This virtue is such that when a man decides to fulfill its functions, he cannot do so without making use of the functions of all the other virtues. If he himself does not happen to possess all of these virtues—in which case he cannot make use of the functions of particular virtues present in him when he decides to fulfill the functions of that virtue—that virtue of his will be a moral virtue in the exercise of which he exploits the acts of the virtues possessed by all others, whether they are nations, cities within a nation, groups within a city, or parts within each group. This, then, is the leading virtue that is not surpassed by any other in authority. . . .

It is evident that the deliberative virtue with the highest authority can only be subordinate to the theoretical virtue; for it merely discerns the accidents of the intelligibles that, prior to having these accidents as their accompaniments, are acquired by the theoretical virtue. If it is determined that the one who possesses the deliberative virtue should discover the variable accidents and states of only those intelligibles of which he has personal insight and personal knowledge (so as not to make discoveries about things that perhaps ought not to take place), then the deliberative virtue cannot be separated from the theoretical virtue. It follows that the theoretical virtue, the leading deliberative virtue, the leading moral virtue, and the leading practical art are inseparable from each other; otherwise the latter [three] will be unsound, imperfect, and without complete authority.

But if, after the theoretical virtue has caused the intellect to perceive the moral virtues, the latter can only be made to exist if the deliberative virtue discerns them and discovers the accidents that must accompany their intelligibles so that they can be brought into existence, then the deliberative virtue is anterior to the moral virtues. If it is anterior to them, then he who possesses the deliberative virtue discovers by it only such moral virtues as exist independently of the deliberative virtues. Yet if the deliberative virtue is independent of the moral virtue, then he who has the capacity for discovering the (good) moral virtues will not himself be good, not even in a single virtue. But if he himself is not good, how then does he seek out the good or wish the true good for himself or for others? And if he does not wish the good, how is he capable of discovering it without having set it before himself as an end? Therefore, if the deliberative virtue is independent of the moral virtue, it is not possible to discover the moral virtue with it. Yet if the moral virtue is inseparable from the deliberative, and they coexist, how could the deliberative virtue discover the moral and join itself to it? For if they are inseparable, it will follow that the deliberative virtue did not discover the moral virtue; while if the deliberative virtue did discover the moral virtue, it will follow that the deliberative virtue is independent of the moral virtue. Therefore either the deliberative virtue itself is the virtue of goodness, or one should assume that the deliberative virtue is accompanied by some other virtue, different from the moral virtue that is discovered by the deliberative faculty. If that other moral virtue is formed by the will also, it follows that the deliberative virtue discovered it—thus the original doubt recurs. It follows, then, that there must be some other moral virtue—other, that is, than the one discovered by the deliberative virtue—which accompanies the deliberative virtue and enables the possessor of the deliberative virtue to wish the good and the virtuous end. *That* virtue must be *natural* and must come into being by nature, and it must be coupled with a certain deliberative virtue [that is, *cleverness*] which comes into being by nature and discovers the moral virtues formed by the will. The virtue formed by the will will then be the *human* virtue by which man, after acquiring it in the way in which he acquires voluntary things, acquires the *human* deliberative virtue.

But one ought to inquire what manner of thing that *natural* virtue is. Is it or is it not identical with this voluntary virtue? Or ought one to say that it *corresponds* to this virtue, like the states of character that exist in irrational animals?—just as it is said that courage resides in the lion, cunning in the fox, shiftiness in the bear, thievishness in the magpie, and so on. For it is possible that every man is innately so disposed that his soul has a power such that he generally moves more easily in the direction of the accomplishment of a certain virtue or of a certain state of character than in the direction of doing the opposite act. Indeed man moves first in the direction in which it is easier for him to move, provided he is not compelled to do something else. For instance, if a man is innately so disposed that he is more prone to stand his ground against dangers than to recoil before them, then all he needs is to undergo the experience a sufficient number of times and this state of character become voluntary. Prior to this, he possessed the corresponding *natural* state of character. If this is so in particular moral virtues that accompany particular deliberative virtues, it must also be the case with the highest moral virtues that accompany the highest deliberative virtues. If this is so, it follows that there are some men who are innately disposed to a [*natural* moral] virtue that corresponds to the highest [*human* moral] virtue and that is joined to a naturally superior deliberative power, others just below them, and so on. If this is so, then not every chance human being will possess art, moral virtue, and deliberative virtue with great power.

Therefore the prince occupies his place by nature and not merely by will. Similarly, a subordinate occupies his place primarily by nature and only secondarily by virtue of the will, which perfects his natural equipments. This being the case, the theoretical virtue, the highest deliberative virtue, the highest moral virtue, and the highest practical art are realized in those equipped for them by nature: that is, in those who possess superior natures with very great potentialities.

CHAPTER iii

After these four things are realized in a certain man, the realization of the particular instances of them in nations and cities still remains; his knowing how to make these particular instances exist in nations and cities remains: he who possesses such a great power ought to possess the capacity of realizing the particular instances of it in nations and cities.

There are two primary methods of realizing them: instruction and the formation of character. To instruct is to introduce the theoretical virtues in nations and cities. The formation of character is the method of introducing the moral virtues and practical arts in nations. Instruction proceeds by speech alone. The formation of character proceeds through habituating nations and citizens in doing the acts that issue from the practical states of character by arousing in them the resolution to do these acts; the states of character and the acts issuing from them should come to possess their souls, and they should be as it were enraptured by them. The resolution to do a thing may be aroused by speech or by deed.

Instruction in the theoretical sciences should be given either to the *imams* and the princes, or else to those who should preserve the theoretical sciences. The instruction of these two groups proceeds by means of identical approaches. These are the approaches stated above. . . .

Now since the virtue or the art of the prince is exercised by exploiting the acts of those who possess the particular virtues and the arts of those who practice the particular arts, it follows necessarily that the virtuous and the masters of the arts whom he [the prince] employs to form the character of nations and citizens of cities comprise two primary groups: a group employed by him to form the character of whosoever is susceptible of having his character formed willingly, and a group employed by him to form the character of those who are such that their character can be formed only by compulsion. . . .

. . . The latter is the craft of war. . . .

The other group, employed to form the character of nations and the citizens of cities with their consent, is composed of those who possess the rational virtues and arts. For it is obvious that the prince needs to return to the theoretical, intelligible things whose knowledge was acquired by certain demonstrations, look for the persuasive methods that can be employed for each, and seek out all the persuasive methods that can be employed for it (he can do this because he possesses the power to be persuasive about individual cases). Then he should repair to these very same theoretical things and seize upon their similitudes. He ought to make these similitudes produce images of the theoretical things for all nations jointly, so establish the similitudes that persuasive methods can cause them to be accepted, and exert himself throughout to make both the similitudes and the persuasive methods such that all nations and cities may share in them. . . .

CHAPTER iv

. . . nations and the citizens of cities are composed of some who are the elect and others who are the vulgar. The vulgar confine themselves, or should be confined, to theoretical cognitions that are in conformity with unexamined common opinion. The elect do not confine themselves in any of their theoretical cognitions to what is in conformity with unexamined common opinion but reach their conviction and knowledge on the basis of premises subjected to thorough scrutiny. Therefore whoever thinks that he is not confined to what is in conformity with unexamined common opinion in his inquiries, believes that in them he is of the "elect" and that everybody else is vulgar. Hence the competent practitioner of every art comes to be called one of the "elect" because people know that he does not confine himself, with respect to the objects of his art, to what is in conformity with unexamined common opinion, but exhausts them and scrutinizes them thoroughly. Again, whoever does not hold a political office or does not possess an art that establishes his claim to a political office, but either possesses no art at all or is enabled by his art to hold only a subordinate office in the city, is said to be "vulgar"; and whoever holds a political office or else possesses an art that enables him to aspire to a political office is of the "elect." Therefore, whoever thinks that he possesses an art that qualifies him for assuming a political office or thinks that his position has the same status as a political office (for instance, men with prominent ancestors and many who possess great wealth), calls himself one of the "elect" and a "statesman."

Whoever has a more perfect mastery of the art that qualifies him for assuming an office is more appropriate for inclusion among the elect. Therefore it follows that the most elect of the elect is the supreme ruler. It would appear that this is so because he is the one who does not confine himself in anything at all to what is in conformity with unexamined common opinion. He must hold the office of the supreme ruler and be the most elect of the elect because of his state of character and skill. . . .

When the theoretical sciences are isolated and their possessor does not have the faculty for exploiting them for the benefit of others, they are defective philosophy. To be a truly perfect philosopher one has to possess both the theoretical sciences and the faculty for exploiting them for the benefit of all others according to their capacity. Were one to consider the case of the true philosopher, he would find no difference between him and the supreme ruler. For he who possesses the faculty for exploiting what is comprised by the theoretical matters for the benefit of all others possesses the faculty for making such matters intelligible as well as for bringing into actual existence those of them that depend on the will. The greater his power to do the latter, the more perfect is his philosophy. Therefore he who is truly perfect possesses with sure insight, first, the theoretical virtues, and subsequently the practical. Moreover, he possesses the capacity for bringing them about in

nations and cities in the manner and the measure possible with reference to each. Since it is impossible for him to possess the faculty for bringing them about except by employing certain demonstrations, persuasive methods, as well as methods that represent things through images, and this either with the consent of others or by compulsion, it follows that the true philosopher is himself the supreme ruler.

Every instruction is composed of two things: (a) making what is being studied comprehensible and causing its idea to be established in the soul and (b) causing others to assent to what is comprehended and established in the soul. There are two ways of making a thing comprehensible: first, by causing its essence to be perceived by the intellect, and second, by causing it to be imagined through the similitude that imitates it. Assent, too, is brought about by one of two methods, either the method of certain demonstration or the method of persuasion. Now when one acquires knowledge of the beings or receives instruction in them, if he perceives their ideas themselves with his intellect, and his assent to them is by means of certain demonstration, then the science that comprises these cognitions is *philosophy*. But if they are known by imagining them through similitudes that imitate them, and assent to what is imagined of them is caused by persuasive methods, then the ancients call what comprises these cognitions *religion*. And if those intelligibles themselves are adopted, and *persuasive* methods are used, then the religion comprising them is called *popular, generally accepted,* and *external* philosophy. Therefore, according to the ancients, religion is an imitation of philosophy. Both comprise the same subjects and both give an account of the ultimate principles of the beings. For both supply knowledge about the first principle and cause of the beings, and both give an account of the ultimate end for the sake of which man is made—that is, supreme happiness—and the ultimate end of every one of the other beings. In everything of which philosophy gives an account based on intellectual perception or conception, religion gives an account based on imagination. In everything demonstrated by philosophy, religion employs persuasion. Philosophy gives an account of the ultimate principles (that is, the essence of the first principle and the essences of the incorporeal second principles), as they are perceived by the intellect. Religion sets forth their images by means of similitudes of them taken from corporeal principles and imitates them by their likenesses among political offices. It imitates the divine acts by means of the functions of political offices. It imitates the actions of natural powers and principles by their likenesses among the faculties, states, and arts that have to do with the will, just as Plato does in the *Timaeus*. It imitates the intelligibles by their likenesses among the sensibles: for instance, some imitate *matter* by *abyss* or *darkness* or *water,* and *nothingness* by *darkness*. It imitates the classes of supreme happiness—that is, the ends of the acts of the human virtues—by their likenesses among the goods that are believed to be the ends. It imitates the classes of true happiness by means of the ones that are believed to be happiness. It imitates the ranks of the beings by their likenesses among spatial and temporal ranks. And it attempts to bring the similitudes of these things as close as possible to their essences. Also, in everything of which philosophy gives an account that is demonstrative and certain, religion gives an account based on persuasive arguments. Finally, philosophy is prior to religion in time.

Again, it is evident that when one seeks to bring into actual existence the intelligibles of the things depending on the will supplied by practical philosophy, he ought to prescribe the conditions that render possible their actual existence. Once the conditions that render their actual existence possible are prescribed, the voluntary intelligibles are embodied in laws. Therefore the legislator is he who, by the excellence of his deliberation, has the capacity to find the conditions required for the actual existence of voluntary intelligibles in such a way as to lead to the achievement of supreme happiness. It is also evident that only after perceiving them by his intellect should the legislator seek to discover their conditions, and he cannot find their conditions that enable him to guide others toward supreme happiness without having perceived supreme happiness with his intellect. Nor can these things become intelligible (and the legislative craft thereby hold the supreme office) without his having beforehand acquired philosophy. Therefore, if he intends to possess a craft that is authoritative rather than subservient, the legislator must be a philosopher. Similarly, if the philosopher who has acquired the theo-

retical virtues does not have the capacity for bringing them about in all others according to their capacities, then what he has acquired from them has no validity. Yet he cannot find the states and the conditions by which the voluntary intelligibles assume actual existence, if he does not possess the deliberative virtue; and the deliberative virtue cannot exist in him without the practical virtue. Moreover, he cannot bring them about in all others according to their capacities except by a faculty that enables him to excel in persuasion and in representing things through images.

It follows, then, that the idea of *Imam*, Philosopher, and Legislator is a single idea. However, the name *philosopher* signifies primarily theoretical virtue. But if it be determined that the theoretical virtue reach its ultimate perfection in every respect, it follows necessarily that he must possess all the other faculties as well. *Legislator* signifies excellence of knowledge concerning the conditions of practical intelligibles, the faculty for finding them, and the faculty for bringing them about in nations and cities. When it is determined that they be brought into existence on the basis of knowledge, it will follow that the theoretical virtue must precede the others —the existence of the inferior presupposes the existence of the higher. The name *prince* signifies sovereignty and ability. To be completely able, one has to possess the power of the greatest ability. His ability to do a thing must not result only from external things; he himself must possess great ability because his art, skill, and virtue are of exceedingly great power. This is not possible except by great power of knowledge, great power of deliberation, and great power of [moral] virtue and art. Otherwise he is not truly able nor sovereign. For if his ability stops short of this, it is still imperfect. Similarly, if his ability is restricted to goods inferior to supreme happiness, his ability is incomplete and he is not perfect. Therefore the true prince is the same as the philosopher-legislator. As to the idea of *Imam* in the Arabic language, it signifies merely the one whose example is followed and who is well received: that is, either his perfection is well received or his purpose is well received. If he is not well received in all the infinite activities, virtues, and arts, then he is not truly well received. Only when all other arts, virtues, and activities seek to realize *his* purpose and no other, will his art be the most powerful art, his [moral] virtue the most powerful virtue, his deliberation the most powerful deliberation, and his science the most powerful science. For with all of these powers he will be exploiting the powers of others so as to accomplish his own purpose. This is not possible without the theoretical sciences, without the greatest of all deliberative virtues, and without the rest of those things that are in the philosopher.

So let it be clear to you that the idea of the Philosopher, Supreme Ruler, Prince, Legislator, and *Imam* is but a single idea. No matter which one of these words you take, if you proceed to look at what each of them signifies among the majority of those who speak our language, you will find that they all finally agree by signifying one and the same idea.

Once the images representing the theoretical things demonstrated in the theoretical sciences are produced in the souls of the multitude and they are made to assent to their images, and once the practical things (together with the conditions of the possibility of their existence) take hold of their souls and dominate them so that they are unable to resolve to do anything else, then the theoretical and practical things are realized. Now these things are *philosophy* when they are in the soul of the legislator. They are *religion* when they are in the souls of the multitude. For when the legislator knows these things, they are evident to him by sure insight, whereas what is established in the souls of the multitude is through an image and a persuasive argument. Although it is the legislator who also represents these things through images, neither the images nor the persuasive arguments are intended for himself. As far as he is concerned, they are certain. He is the one who invents the images and the persuasive arguments, but not for the sake of establishing these things in his own soul as a religion for himself. No, the images and the persuasive arguments are intended for others, whereas, so far as he is concerned, these things are certain. They are a religion for others, whereas, so far as he is concerned, they are philosophy. Such, then, is true philosophy and the true philosopher.

BAHYA

Bahya ben Joseph ibn Paquda (eleventh century c.e.) wrote the first systematic ethical treatise in the Jewish philosophical tradition, *The Commandments of the Heart* (also known as the *Book of Direction of the Duties of the Heart*). He served as judge of the rabbinical court in Saragossa, Spain. He wrote *The Commandments of the Heart* around 1040, in Arabic; Judah ibn Tibbon translated it into Hebrew around 1060. Few other facts about Bahya's life are known, and no other writings exist.

Islamic and Indian religious writings stress the distinction between two kinds of commandments, or duties: duties of the body (or limbs, or members) and duties of the heart. Duties of the body are obligations to act or refrain from acting in a certain way: to help those in need, for example, or to refrain from killing. They are external obligations, and others can see whether or not we fulfill them. Duties of the heart, in contrast, are obligations to have or refrain from having certain states of mind: to love others, for example, or to refrain from coveting. These duties are internal; others cannot see whether we fulfill them, though they may be able to infer from our external actions that we are or are not fulfilling them.

Bahya points out that most religious practices and teachings, like most secular laws and moral principles, focus on external action but neglect states of mind. This, he argues, is a mistake. Like Immanuel Kant in Western philosophy, Bahya contends that what is essential, from a moral point of view, is purely internal. The commandments of the heart are central to ethical life, taking priority over the commandments of the limbs. This is not to say that the commandments of the body are unimportant. But they would have no force without the commandments of the heart. We evaluate people and their actions morally by considering their intentions. To be moral, people must not only do the right thing but also have the right intentions. So, even the evaluation of external actions depends on the agent's state of mind. Consequently, Bahya argues, duties of the body depend on duties of the heart. Because everything in ethics depends on the heart's commandments, one of the most important of those commandments is to seek knowledge of them, which Bahya calls "the inward knowledge, the light of the heart, the fire of the soul."

Bahya believes that the duties of the heart are, at root, religious. Fundamental to the good life is the recognition that God exists and is all-wise, all-powerful, and all-good. Both the world and our own natures reveal these aspects of God, which we can appreciate only with the help of reason, revelation, and religious tradition. Following from these fundamental recognitions, moreover, are the duties of the heart: trust in, service to, and humility before God. Repentance, self-communion, and renunciation lead to the highest state of the heart, the love of God. For Bahya, ethics is intimately religious; there cannot be a secular ethics. All our duties—first the duties of the heart, and then those of the body—follow from our recognition that God is the almighty creator of the universe.

from *Commandments of the Heart*

Reprinted from Bahya ben Joseph ibn Pakuda,
The Book of Direction to the Duties of the Heart.
*Introduction, translation, and notes by Menahem
Mansoor with Sara Arenson and Shoshana Dann-
hauser. Copyright © 1973 by Routledge and Kegan
Paul.*

INTRODUCTION

Praised be God, the Lord of Israel, the true one, for He is of unique truth, eternal existence, and perpetual goodness. He created the beings as a demonstration of His oneness, made the creatures to be witnesses of His omnipotence, and formed nothingness into being to declare His wisdom and all-embracing graces. . . . Having created men and endowed them with speech and the qualities which distinguish them and perfect their understanding, God gave them the most noble of his graces—Wisdom. Wisdom is the life of their soul, the light of their mind, their way to the favor of God (glory and praise be unto Him), and their guardian from His anger in this world and the next. . . .

All the parts of wisdom and their various branches are gates opened by God for the benefit of men, through which they may perceive religion and the world. But while some of these gates are specially concerned with religion, others are more proper for the uses of the world.

The part of wisdom appropriate to this world is the lower wisdom, or the science of the nature and accidents of bodies—Physics, along with the middle wisdom, or the science of Mathematics. These two sciences concern not only all the secrets of this world, its benefits and uses to us, but they also introduce us to all the arts and all the ways of satisfying the needs of the body.

But the part of wisdom specially devoted to religion and its advantages is the supreme wisdom, the science of Metaphysics. It is our duty to seek this wisdom, in order that we may understand our religion. . . .

The gates opened by God for the knowledge of His religion and law are three in number, namely—the sane and sound mind, the true book of God as revealed to His messenger, and the traditions of our blessed prophets, which have been passed on orally by our pious sages. . . .

Religion itself is divided into two parts. One is the knowledge of the external duties of the body and its members; the other is the internal knowledge of the secret duties of the heart.

The duties of the members are also divided into two parts. The first part contains the duties imposed by the mind even if they had not been imposed by the Scriptures. The second part consists of duties imposed by revelation only, duties neither imposed nor forbidden by the mind, as, for instance, the ban on eating meat with milk, the ban on wearing a garment of mingled linen and wool, or the ban on sowing with mingled seeds. These are precepts the causes of whose prescription is concealed from us.

But the origins of the duties of the heart are intelligible, as I shall explain, with the help of God. All duties are either positive or negative. There is no need to explain this in connection with the duties of the members, because the subject is well known and clear, but I shall explain what occurs to me concerning the positive and negative duties of the heart, as a guide to those whom I shall not mention.

Among the positive commandments included in the duties of the heart are: to believe in the Creator of the world, who brought the world into existence from nothingness; to believe in pure monotheism, free from a belief in any other gods; to assent to obeying God in our hearts; to meditate upon the wonders of creation in order to arrive at the knowledge of Him; to rely completely upon Him; to be humble and submissive before Him; to exhibit a constant care and attention to our deeds lest we be ashamed before His constant scrutiny of all our acts and secrets; to feel a desire to please Him and consecrate all our work for His sake; to love those who love Him and hate those who hate Him. All of these duties and others like them have no effect on the members.

The negative commandments included in the duties of the heart are the opposites of those mentioned above, and, along with these, the feelings of envy, rancor, and vengeance against people of our own creed, as is written in the Scripture (Lev. 19:18): "Thou shalt not take vengeance, nor bear any grudge against the children of thy people." Nor may man use the mind and heart for the purpose of sinning against God either by desiring to sin or by resolving to sin, although these thoughts occur to the human conscience, unknown to all but the holy Creator, as it is said (Jer. 17:10): "I the Lord search the mind and test the heart"; (Prov. 20:27): "The spirit of man is the lamp of the Lord, Searching all the inward parts."

As the religious commandments have an exterior part and an interior, or secret, part, I studied the books of our ancients who composed many books on the religious commandments after the time of the Talmudic sages, so that I might learn from them esoteric wisdom. . . .

Having studied these books, I could not find among them even one dealing exclusively with the esoteric knowledge. When I found that this knowledge, the knowledge of the duties of the heart, was neglected, not contained in any book comprising all its origins, forsaken, with none of its chapters collected in one work, I was deeply astonished. I said to myself, "It may be that this kind of duty is not obligatory upon us, but is commanded rather by way of morality, in order to show us the right way and the straight path. Perhaps it is to be considered supererogatory, for whose neglect we are neither questioned nor punished. This may be the reason why the ancients have left it unnoted." Then I examined the duties of the heart as they are commanded by the mind, the Scriptures, and tradition, so that I might see whether they were obligatory or not. And I found them to be the basis of all duties. Were they not, all the duties of the members would be of no avail.

As I have said, the duties of the heart are commanded by the mind, for we have already shown that man is composed of a soul and a body—both are God's graces given to us, one exterior, one interior. Accordingly, we are obliged to obey God both outwardly and inwardly. Outward obedience is expressed in the duties of the members, like prayer, fasting, almsgiving, learning His book and spreading the knowledge of it, fulfilling the commandments concerning the tabernacle, the palm branch, the fringes, the doorpost, the railing on the roof, and the like, all of which can be wholly performed by man's physical body.

Inward obedience, however, is expressed in the duties of the heart, in the heart's assertion of the unity of God and in the belief in Him and His book, in constant obedience to Him and fear of Him, in humility before Him, love for Him and complete reliance upon Him, submission to Him and abstinence from the things hateful to Him. Inward obedience is expressed in the consecration of all our work for His sake, in meditation upon his graces, in all the duties performed by faith and conscience without the activity of the external body-members.

Thus I have come to know for certain that the duties of the members are of no avail to us unless our hearts choose to do them and our souls desire their performance. Since, then, our members cannot perform an act unless our souls have chosen it first, our members could free themselves from all duties and obligations if it should occur to us that our hearts were not obliged to choose obedience to God. Since it is clear that our Creator commanded the members to perform their duties, it is improbable that He overlooked our hearts and souls, our noblest parts, and did not command them to share in His worship, for they constitute the crown of obedience and the very perfection of worship. For this reason, we were commanded both outward and inward duties, so that our obedience to our glorious Creator might be complete, perfect, and all-embracing, comprising both our outer and inner parts, both mind and body.

When this necessity became clear to me through logic, I said to myself, "Perhaps the Scriptures are devoid of this matter, and this is why it has not been treated in any work that could direct us and show us the way." Then I looked for its traces in the book of

God and I found it repeated there many times (Deut. 6:5 ff.; 30:20; 11:13; 13:5):

> And thou shalt love the Lord thy God with all thy heart, and with all thy soul, and with all thy might. And these words, which I command thee this day, shall be upon thy heart; to love the Lord thy God, to hearken to His voice, and to cleave unto Him; to love the Lord your God, and to serve Him with all your heart and with all your soul; After the Lord your God shall ye walk, and Him shall ye fear; (Lev. 19:18): But thou shalt love thy neighbor as thyself; (Deut. 10:12; 10:19): And now, Israel, what doth the Lord thy God require of thee, but to fear the Lord thy God; Love ye therefore the stranger; for ye were strangers in the land of Egypt.

Fear and love are among the duties of the heart. As for the negative commandments of the heart, I found many references to them (Deut. 5:21):

> Neither shalt thou covet thy neighbor's wife; neither shalt thou desire thy neighbor's house, his field, or his man-servant, or his maid-servant, his ox, or his ass, or any thing that is thy neighbor's; (Lev. 19:18; 19:17): Thou shalt not take vengeance, nor bear any grudge against the children of thy people; Thou shalt not hate thy brother in thy heart; (Num. 15:39): And that ye go not about after your own heart and your own eyes; (Deut. 15:7): thou shalt not harden thy heart, nor shut thy hand from thy needy brother.

And the whole of obedience is reduced to the heart and the tongue in the saying (Deut. 30:11 f.): "For this commandment which I command thee this day, it is not too hard for thee, neither is it far off. It is not in heaven, that thou shouldest say: 'Who shall go up for us to heaven, and bring it unto us, and make us to hear it, that we may do it?'" So do the other books of the prophets abound in this, but I shall not cite them here, for the sayings are many and well known.

Having verified the need for the duties of the heart in the book of God, as well as by logic, I turned aside to examine the matter in the tradition of our ancient sages. In their sayings, I found it to be even more obvious and distinct than in the Scriptures, or through the use of logic. Some of their sayings are general (Sanhedrin 106b; Jerus. Berakh. 1). "God requireth the heart"; and "The heart and the eye are the two agents of sin." Some are particular, like those in the Sayings of the Fathers which are too long to cite here. Then I found many references to this matter in the stories of the lives of the sages, which have been transmitted to us, when they were asked (Megillah 27b), "How have you reached this old age?"

Again in the Scriptures, in connection with him who kills unintentionally (Num. 35:11): "That the manslayer that killeth any person through error may flee thither," I have found that he is not worthy of death. This is true also of him who inadvertently violates one of the negative commandments for whose violation we are usually punished with one of the four deaths, or extirpation. When the act is done unintentionally the sinner is deemed guilty only of sin-offering or guilt-offering. This leads us to the conclusion that what determines the punishment is the participation of both heart and body in the act—the heart in the intention and the body in carrying out the heart's intention. The same is said of him who does good, but not for the sake of God. He gets no reward for it. Since, now, the foundation and the pillar of action is the intention of the heart and conscience, the knowledge of the duties of the heart should come before and stand above the knowledge of the duties of the members.

Although I was now convinced of the necessity of esoteric knowledge, through logic, still I hesitated: "Maybe this kind of duty is not obligatory upon us everywhere and at all times, like the commandments concerning cancellation of debts and the fallowness of the soil in the Sabbatical year, jubilee, and sacrifices." Considering this carefully, I found, however, that these duties are always obligatory upon us, as long as we live, without a break or possibility of excuse, exactly like the duty of the heart to assert the unity of God, and the duty of the conscience to obey and fear and love Him and perform His commandments, as the sage said (Ps. 119:5): "Oh that my ways were directed to observe Thy statutes!" It is obligatory exactly like the duty of reliance upon and submission to Him, as it is said (Ps. 62:9): "Trust in Him at all times, ye people," and the duty to expel hate and jealousy from our hearts and abstain from those vestiges of this world which interfere with our devotion to God.

These obligations are upon us constantly, every-where and at all times, accompanying every hour, every minute, every situation, as long as our minds and souls are yet with us. This is like the case of a servant ordered by his master to do two kinds of work. Indoors he must tend to the house, outdoors he must cultivate the soil at certain fixed times. If he misses the right time or is unable to do his work in the field, the obligation to work outdoors is cancelled. But he cannot be freed of his responsibilities indoors as long as he remains in the house and is serving his master. When he is undisturbed, the obligation to work indoors binds him constantly. In this same way, O my brother, the duties of the heart are binding upon us without any excuse, and nothing really prevents us from performing them except the love of this world and our ignorance of God, as it is said (Isa. 5:12): "And the harp and the psaltery, the tabret and the pipe, And wine, are in their feasts; But they regard not the work of the Lord, Neither have they considered the operation of His hands." I said to myself further, "Perhaps this kind of obligation is not divided into numerous duties, and this is the reason why it has never been explained at length or written down in a special book." When I counted them, I found that their details were very numerous, and I understood that the sayings (Ps. 119:96): "I have seen an end to every purpose; But Thy Commandment is exceeding broad" was indeed meant for the duties of the heart. For the duties of the members are limited in number, about 613 commandments in all, while the duties of the heart are many and their details innumerable.

"Perhaps they are so clear and so simple, and people's devotion to them so strong, that they do not need any further enlightenment," I said to myself, and I went on to observe people's behavior through the ages, as it is described in books. Except for the few, I found that men were far from fulfilling these duties, in accordance with the traditions about them. The common folk have always needed urging and teaching, and this is especially true of those of our own times, who neglect even the knowledge and practise of the duties of the members, not to mention the duties of the heart.

I saw that even he who did interest himself in the study of the Law applied himself only to those things which would make him wise in the eyes of fools, or would make him seem learned to those who pretend to be scholars. On the whole, he has wandered away from the study of the Law to things which neither benefit him nor elevate him spiritually, things the ignorance of which would not even be noticed. Thus he neglects the study of the roots of his religion and the foundations of his Law, which he cannot afford to ignore or neglect because the commandments cannot be fulfilled without both knowledge and practise.

There is, for instance, the matter of the assertion of the unity of God. Must we examine it with our minds, or is it enough to assert it by tradition only, saying, "Our Lord is One," as the fools do, with neither proof nor demonstration? Must we inquire after the meaning of "the true one" and "the admissible one?" Must we differentiate between this meaning and the meaning of other existing entities? These are questions the believer cannot afford to ignore, and the Scriptures insist on that, saying (Deut. 4:39): "Know this day, and lay it to thy heart, that the Lord, He is God in heaven above and upon the earth beneath; there is none else." The same is true for the rest of the duties of the heart, those which we have already mentioned as well as those which will be described later. The believer's faith is not perfect unless he both knows and practises the duties of the heart. This is the inward knowledge, the light of the heart, the fire of the soul. This is meant by the sage when he says (Ps. 51:8): "Behold, Thou desirest truth in the inward parts: Make me, therefore, to know wisdom in mine inmost heart."

It is told about one of the sages that he used to sit in audience till noontime. Then, being left alone with his companions, he used to say, "Now let us have the secret light," meaning the knowledge of the duties of the heart. Another sage was once asked about a difficult divorce problem. His answer was, "O you who ask me about something the ignorance of which cannot harm you at all. Have you already completed the study of those duties which you cannot afford to ignore and must not neglect, that you find leisure to turn to these difficult and complicated problems, the knowledge of which would not add anything to your faith and religion, nor correct any of your soul's vices? As for me, I swear I have

devoted thirty-five years to the study of the obligations my religion imposes upon me. You know the
scope of my endeavors and the number of books I
have read, and still I have no time to spare for the
kind of thing you have just questioned me about."
He then continued to blame and reprove that man
strongly.

Another sage is quoted as saying, "I have spent
twenty-five years learning the true meaning of my
acts of worship." Still another said, "There are certain parts of knowledge which are buried in the
hearts of the sages like hidden treasures; as long as
they stay hidden nobody knows about them. But the
moment they are uncovered, their truth becomes
manifest to all." This is analogous to the saying
(Prov. 20:5): "Counsel in the heart of man is like
deep water; but a man of understanding will draw it
out," and its meaning is as follows: True knowledge
is hidden and buried in the nature of each man and
within his discriminative faculty, like the water that
is buried in the depths of the earth. A man endowed
with a sound mind and a sound understanding
directs his efforts to detecting and uncovering that
which is hidden within him, in order to draw it out
of his soul, in the same way as men seek after the
water which is buried in the depths of the earth. . . .

. . . If the thing you are required to verify logically is impossible for you to understand, as, for
instance, the reasons for the commandments accepted by revelation, then your excuse is valid and
your reluctance to speculate about it is permissible.
Or, if you are a man of weak mind and little discrimination, so that you cannot make the effort to
understand, then your neglect of speculation is
excused, since your way of worship is like that of
women and children, who accept things by tradition. On the other hand, if you are a man of sound
mind and understanding, which qualify you to
verify the traditions passed down to you from the
prophets concerning the roots of religion and the
origins of the acts of worship—then you are obliged
to use your faculties in order to verify things both
logically and by tradition. Your neglect will then be
considered a shortcoming in carrying out the duties
imposed upon you by God. . . .

. . . although by nature tradition is the first instrument the student needs and chooses, he will not be
acting prudently if he is satisfied with that only, if it
is in his power to verify it logically. Whoever is able
to do it must employ his mind in verifying everything that is intelligible by way of demonstration
and logical proofs.

Since I have realized the importance of the duties
of the heart and our obligation to perform them, as
I have described above, and since I have found them
neglected and not gathered in a special book, and
since I have observed the way our contemporaries
overlook them in both theory and practice, it has
become one of God's finest favors done unto me to
draw my notice to the encouragement of this inner
knowledge. As a result, I turned to the traditions of
our ancient righteous forefathers, and I found that
their devotion to the duties involving their own
souls was much stronger and deeper than was their
interest in the various branches of jurisprudence or
in the usually complicated problems of theology.
They used to concentrate their efforts on general
decisions, on judgments about what was lawful and
what was unlawful, and then they turned their
minds and interests to the perfection of their deeds
and the duties of their hearts. Whenever there arose
a complicated problem for judgment, they examined
it by raising conjectures and they drew their conclusions on the basis of the general principles they
held, not bothering to study them logically, for they
were scornful of the incidents of this world. . . .

Thus it became clear to me that acts intended for
the sake of God are based on a pure heart and an
innocent conscience, and that when intentions are
defective, deeds are not acceptable to God, numerous and insistent as they may be. So it is said in the
Scriptures (Isa. 1:15 f.):

> And when ye spread forth your hands, I will hide Mine
> eyes from you; Yea, when ye make many prayers, I will
> not hear; Your hands are full of blood. Wash you, make
> you clean. Put away the evil of your doings From before
> Mine eyes, Cease to do evil; (Deut. 30:14): But the word
> is very nigh unto thee, in thy mouth, and in thy heart,
> that thou mayest do it; (Prov. 23:26): My son, give up
> thy heart, And let thine eyes observe my ways;

and also by our ancient sages (Jerus. Berakh. 1):
"Give me thine eyes and heart, and I know that thou
art mine." The Scriptures add (Num. 15:39):

And it shall be unto you for a fringe, that ye may look upon it, and remember all the commandments of the Lord, and do them; and that ye go not about after your own heart and your own eyes, after which ye used to go astray; (Mic. 6:6, 8): Wherewith shall I come before the Lord, And bow myself before God on high? Shall I come before Him with burnt-offerings, with calves of a year old?; It hath been told thee, O man, what is good, And what the Lord doth require of thee: Only to do justly, and to love mercy, and to walk humbly with thy God; (Jer. 9:24): But let him that glorieth glory in this, That he understandeth, and knoweth Me, That I am the Lord who exercise mercy, justice, and righteousness, in the earth; For in these things I delight, Saith the Lord.

The meaning of the last verse is as follows: A man should rather boast about his understanding of Me, his discernment of My graces and favors by way of meditation upon creation, and his realization of My omnipotent wisdom by observing My deeds. All these quotations are proofs of the importance of cultivating the duties of the heart and the virtues of the soul.

You must know also that the purpose and advantage of the duties of the heart is to make our outer and inner worship of God equal and balanced, so that the heart, the tongue, and the other members are all witnesses to our obedience, each one confirming the other and giving testimony in its favor, not opposing the other by disagreement. This is what the Scriptures call "just" and "whole-hearted":

(Deut. 18:13): Thou shalt be whole-hearted with the Lord thy God; (Gen. 6:9): Noah was in his generations a man righteous and wholehearted; Noah walked with God; (Pss. 15:2; 101:2): He that walketh uprightly, and worketh righteousness, And speaketh truth in his heart; I will give heed unto the way of integrity; Oh when wilt Thou come unto me? I will walk within my house in the integrity of my heart. . . .

It is well known that a man who is in disagreement with himself, whose right hand belies his left, is never thought to be truthful, is never considered perfect. In the same way, when our exterior opposes our interior, when our intention contradicts our words, when our conscience is not at one with the actions of our body, then is our worship of our Creator imperfect, for He does not accept an obedience

that is false and counterfeit. This is stressed in the Scriptures (Isa. 1:13; 61:8):

Bring no more vain oblations; It is an offering of abomination unto Me; New moon and sabbath, the holding of convocations—I cannot endure iniquity along with the solemn assembly; For I the Lord love justice, I hate robbery with iniquity; And I will give them their recompense in truth, And I will make an everlasting covenant with them; (Mal. 1:8): And when ye offer the blind for sacrifice, it is no evil! And when ye offer the lame and sick, it is no evil! Present it now unto thy governor; Will he be pleased with thee? Or will he accept thy person? Saith the Lord of hosts; (1 Sam. 15:22): And Samuel said: Hath the Lord as great delight in burnt-offerings and sacrifices, As in hearkening to the voice of the Lord? Behold, to obey is better than sacrifice, and to hearken than the fat of rams.

For the same reason, a man's one good deed can outweigh many good deeds performed by himself or another, and the same is true of an evil act. All is according to intention and purpose. The thought of a good deed by a true worshipper and his desire to carry it out, even if he prove unable to do so, may be balanced against many a good deed carried out by others, as it is said (2 Chr. 6:8):

But the Lord said to David my father: Whereas it was in thy heart to build a house for My name, thou didst well that it was in thy heart; (Mal. 3:16): Then they that feared the Lord spoke one with another; And the Lord hearkened, and heard, And a book of remembrance was written before Him, For them that feared the Lord, and that thought upon His name.

The last verse was commented upon by our sages (Shabbat 63a): "That thought upon His name" the Rabbis explain thus, "If one intended to fulfil a duty but was prevented from realizing his intention, it is accounted to him as if he had done it."

When I had learned the great stress that reason, Scriptures, and tradition put on the duties of the heart, I began to train my soul in them, urging my soul to embrace both the theory and the practice. Whenever I discovered one aspect of these duties, it led me to another, and that one to still another, until their magnitude became wide and too difficult to remember with precision. Fearing the oblivion of what I had retained in my heart, fearful that I might forget what I had accumulated in my mind, remembering the little help I could get in this matter from my contemporaries, I decided to put it down in a book in a Diwan form, in a book which would contain all the roots as well as some of the branches. This way I could always urge my soul to know these duties and fire it to fulfill them.

Whenever my work lives up to my intention, I am grateful to God, who helps me in this undertaking. Whenever it conflicts or falls short, I blame only myself, reproving my soul and confronting it with my intention until truth makes clear my soul's corruption and its deviation is corrected by certainty, its confusion by uprightness and its defect by perfection. Furthermore, I have decided to give it a permanent form, so as to make of it an eternal treasure and a perpetual light, that people may be guided by its fire and directed in its way. Thus others may benefit by it more than myself. This would be more than my full share.

With this purpose in mind, I decided to write a book, and to divide it according to the rules of the duties of the heart and the obligations of conscience. I was determined to include in it enough of the different aspects of this knowledge to point out to men the paths of righteousness, to direct them in the way of the just, guide them back to the laudable customs of the ancients, lead them to emulate the pious ones, warn them against heedlessness and wake them from sloth. I wanted to point out to men the finest details of this science. I wanted to inspire them with the knowledge of God and His Law and to urge upon them the search for deliverance. I wanted to arouse the worshipper, raise up him who is reluctant, lead aright him who is eager but hasty, encourage the slow and the tardy, manage the novice and set aright him who is perplexed. . . .

I came to understand that the human soul leans greedily toward the essence of evil, that it is reluctant to do good and idle in the search for virtue, playing always in the field of light amusement. Whenever it is aroused by the fire of lust, it seeks false excuses in order to respond, alters the arguments to follow the lead of lust, strengthens the reasons in its favor, disregards arguments against it. On the other hand, when it is called by the light of truth,

it invents vain excuses to avoid it, twists the argument to escape it, contradicts it fearfully. Every man's foe is within him, unless God provides him with immunity, and his soul with an ever-present guardian endowed with the overwhelming power to restrain it with the reins of discipline, bind it with the bridle of justice and give it a taste of the bitterness of the moralizing whip. When this kind of man intends to do good, he achieves it immediately, for when his soul entices him to something else, he reproves it and overcomes it. . . .

Since I was determined to establish in this book the roots of the duties of the heart, I used my own judgment in choosing those roots which include the others. Declaring the pure assertion of the unity of God the supreme root and the highest principle, I went on to examine the well-known duties which stem from this assertion, those which must follow from it.

Knowing for certain that the Creator is the only one who is real, indescribable either by substance or by accident, I recognized the limitations of the mind, which cannot conceive of anything indescribable either by substance or by accident. I realized then that it would be impossible for us to conceive of Him by way of His essence and I saw that we must know Him and conceive of His existence by way of His creatures. This is the chapter dealing with meditation upon creation. This I established as the second root of the whole of the duties of the heart.

Observing the sovereignty of the only real One and the obedience due Him by His creatures, I established obedience to God as the third root of the whole of the duties of the heart.

Observing the unique role of the only real One in the management of everything, seeing that both reward and punishment come solely from His hands, He having no peer to share this power with Him, I found that we should rely wholly on Him and surrender ourselves to Him. So I established reliance as the fourth root of the whole of the duties of the heart.

Thinking of the meaning of the only real One, whose unique essence has neither peer nor equal, I concluded that we should also give Him our undivided obedience and worship, devoting all our acts purely to His name, for an act done also for the sake of something else is unacceptable to Him. So I established the pure worship of God as the fifth root of the whole of the duties of the heart.

Turning my mind to the praise and glorification we owe to the only real One because of His uniqueness, and to the resulting humbleness He therefore deserves from us, I established humility as the sixth root of the whole of the duties of the heart.

Considering the manner in which people are accustomed to neglect the obligation of obedience to God and their failure to offer it, and knowing that the way to correct these errors and failures is through repentance and atonement, I established repentance as the seventh root of the whole of the duties of the heart.

Searching for the way in which we may achieve perfect realization of our obligations to God, our duties both external and internal, I found that we can achieve it only by reckoning with our souls for the sake of God and by urging them to their duties. So I established self-reckoning as the eighth root of the whole of the duties of the heart.

Returning my thought to the meaning of the only real One, I found that the pure assertion of the unity of God cannot be truly accomplished in the believer's soul so long as his heart is drunk with the wine of love for this world and inclined to its beastly lusts. Only if he endeavors to empty his heart and purify his mind of the vestiges of this world, only if he abstains from all its pleasures, is the perfect assertion of the unity of God achieved in his heart and only then can the virtue of his soul be saved. So I established asceticism as the ninth root of the whole of the duties of the heart.

Finally I examined our obligation to love and to please the Lord and to fear his anger. This is the essence of happiness and of misfortune, as it is said (Ps. 30:6): "For His anger is but for a moment, His favour is for a life-time; weeping may tarry for the night, but joy cometh in the morning," for the Creator is the goal of all hope and the purpose of every wish, He is the beginning and the end. So I established the love of God as the tenth root of the whole of the duties of the heart. . . .

You must know that all the duties of the heart and the obligations of the soul are included in the ten roots discussed in this book of mine, both the positive and the negative ones—just as the sayings (Lev. 19:18):

Thou shalt not take vengeance, nor bear any grudge against the children of thy people, but thou shalt love thy neighbor as thyself: I am the Lord; (Ps. 15:3): That hath no slander upon his tongue, Nor doeth evil to his fellow, Nor taketh up a reproach against his neighbor; (ibid. 34:15): Depart from evil, and do good; seek peace, and pursue it;

include many of the commandments. Therefore, keep it close to your heart and repeat it constantly in your mind. When your intention and desire to follow them become evident, all the details will appear to you clearly, with the help of God, as it is said (Ps. 25:12 ff.): "What man is he that feareth the Lord? Him will He instruct in the way that He shall choose. His soul shall abide in prosperity; And his seed shall inherit the land. The counsel of the Lord is with them that fear Him; and His covenant, to make them know it."

I found it worth my while to end the introduction to my book with a fine parable which will stimulate you to apprehend the purpose of this book and help you to appreciate the place of this kind of duty among the rest, as well as the place of the whole of this knowledge of the Law among the other sciences —physics, mathematics, and logic. Try to understand while you read and while you repeat it in your mind, and you will reach the truth, if God so wishes. This then is the parable:

A king divided some silk material among his servants in order to examine their skills. The clever servant, gifted with a sound judgment, chose the best part in his lot, then the best of what was left, thus dividing his material into three kinds, good, medium, and worthless. He used each kind separately and made of it the best garment possible, employing various artisans to sew for him silken garments, each different in color and style. These he wore while serving the king, each according to the time and place appropriate to it. But the foolish servant went out and made his whole lot of silk into worthless garments. Then he sold them for the little money he could get for them and hastened to spend it on good food and delicious drink. The king heard of this and he was satisfied with what his clever servant had done. He drew him nearer, made him his favorite and gave him a rank equal to that of his special officers. As for the foolish servant, the king found his deed abominable and exiled him to the most deserted place in his kingdom, where he stayed with others who had aroused the anger of the king.

In the same way, O my brother, God has revealed to His creatures His perfect Scripture, in order to test us. The wise and sagacious man, gifted with sound judgment, when he reads the book of God and understands it thoroughly, divides it into three parts. First comes the knowledge of the subtle spiritual meanings which constitute the inner knowledge to whose practise he should devote himself constantly—the duties of the heart and the obligations of the soul. Secondly, he should extract from it another part, the knowledge of the duties of the members, all in their appropriate time and place. Finally, he should apply the third part to the study of history, so that he may know the classes of people and their succession in past generations, as well as the stories and anecdotes passed down from ancient times. He should fit every detail into its proper place as is necessary, using for this purpose the help of the various sciences, like mathematics, demonstration and logical argumentation. All of these are but introductions to the supreme science of metaphysics.

Whoever ignores these duties cannot discern the marks of the Creator's wisdom in His world and is a boor in what relates to his own body, not to speak of the bodies of others. The clever servant used the tools of the various artisans to make what he wanted to out of the king's silk, but the foolish boor, having been given the book of God, uses it to learn the history and anecdotes of past generations. He hastens only to enjoy through it the pleasures of this world and he uses it to forward his false ways—the pursuit of his lust, the neglect of asceticism. And he imitates the different classes of people and their various natures and habits. This is meant by the saying (Prov. 5:23): "He shall die for lack of instruction; And in the greatness of his folly he shall reel."

Consider this parable, O my brother; ponder upon it and think it over. Try to understand my warnings by considering the book of your Lord. Help yourself in this task by reading the books of our Rabbi Saadia, for they bring light to the heart, sharpen the mind, direct the careless, and arouse the idle. May God help you and me to obey Him and may He direct us by His mercy to the path of His worship, as He was entreated by the sage (Ps. 16:10):

> For Thou wilt not abandon my soul to the netherworld; Neither wilt Thou suffer Thy godly one to see the pit. . . .

AVICENNA

Avicenna (Abu 'Ali al-Husayn ibn 'Abd Allah ibn Sina), 980–1037, was born in Persia near Bukhara (in present-day Uzbekistan, an independent republic in the southern part of what was formerly the Soviet Union) and spent his life in Persia. Son of the provincial governor, Avicenna showed his gifts for study and learning as a child; he had memorized the Koran by the age of ten. He benefited from his father's association with learned men of the day, and his father provided for his education enthusiastically. By the age of eighteen, Avicenna was teaching himself, having outgrown the teachers his father provided; by twenty-one, he had acquired a reputation as a physician at the court of the ruling Samanid family. His favor at this court got him, among other things, access to an extensive royal library.

The circumstances so auspicious for the germination of Avicenna's talents ended abruptly with the Sumanids' defeat at the hands of the Turkish leader Mahmud of Ghazna. For the rest of his life, Avicenna pursued his writing only in the brief periods of calm he could find in an era of great political upheaval and turmoil.

Avicenna wandered to Rayy (near Tehran), where he practiced medicine. Unable to pursue his work in philosophy, he traveled to Hamadan and entered the service of the prince. Here he found enough leisure to begin some of his most famous works, including *The Book of Healing*. He had to make time for his writing outside his duties as administrator and physician to the court. In addition, court intrigues forced him more than once to suffer imprisonment or to go into hiding. But in hiding and in prison, he wrote; when in the service of the court, he dispatched his duties during the day and met with students for general philosophical discussions and for work on his treatises at night. These sessions were often accompanied by music and revels that lasted well into the night.

When Avicenna was forty-two, the prince died. Refusing to serve under the prince's son, Avicenna went to Isfahan, south of Tehran, after a short period of hiding and imprisonment in Hamadan. (He escaped by disguising himself as a Sufi.) He found great favor at this court, where he finished the writing he had started in Hamadan and produced many other treatises. His duties at Isfahan obliged him to accompany his patron into battles. On one such campaign, Avicenna fell ill. Though he acted as his own physician, he died in Hamadan at the age of fifty-seven.

Avicenna is known primarily as an outstanding metaphysician and physician. He is studied to this day in eastern Islamic countries. More than either al-Farabi before him or Averroës after him, Avicenna shows a mystical side in his writings. In some tracts, he interrupts the dry exposition of systematic philosophy for an evocation of blissful union with God. This shows an affinity with Sufism, whose followers disdain worldly pursuits and enter on a harsh asceticism in order to attain such a direct union with God. Although Avicenna's last works are lost, he was apparently trying to develop a mystical philosophy.

The Book of Healing deals with a vast number of subjects. The last part concerns metaphysics, and the last book of that part contains the selections concerning laws and practices in the cities, presented here. Discussing politics and ethics at the end of a book on metaphysics implies that for Avicenna, as for al-Farabi, political and ethical theory must rest on a metaphysical foundation. Avicenna's theory of the prophet, like al-Farabi's, rests on his metaphysics. But Avicenna offers little grounding for some of his practical prescriptions beyond appeal to common opinion. His rules reflect common ethical opinion of his time, much of which remains commonly held in Islamic countries today.

For example, Avicenna expresses some attitudes toward women and marriage often associated with contemporary Islam. These attitudes are controversial in the Islamic philosophical tradition as well as in the modern world. Writing a hundred years after Avicenna, Averroës bemoans the position of women in Muslim society. He argues for equality between the sexes on largely utilitarian grounds.

Avicenna also argues for expansive powers for the legislator. Government, Avicenna believes, should promote the welfare of its citizens. The most important task of government, therefore, is to prepare the souls of the citizens for the afterlife, for nothing is more important to an individual than his or her eternal salvation or damnation. The legislator must reinforce divine law by offering rewards for good religious behavior and imposing penalties for its opposite. But the legislator must be careful to regulate by law only what is universal and unchanging, leaving other affairs to administrators or individuals.

The legislator should also use the law to promote moral virtue and justice among the people. Virtue is important, for it turns the soul away from this world and directs it toward the next; it also produces tangible benefits in this life. Following Aristotle, Avicenna holds that virtue is a mean: to act virtuously, one must pursue various kinds of action to the right degree, neither too little nor too much; one must do the right thing at the right time, for the right reason and in the right way. Avicenna defines the virtues in terms of motive. The classes of virtues follow the motivating powers of the soul: the appetitive, the irascible, and the practical. The virtues, therefore, consist of moderation of appetite, moderation of passion, and moderation in practical affairs.

from *The Book of Healing*

Reprinted with permission of The Free Press, a division of Macmillan, Inc. from Medieval Political Philosophy by Ralph Lernel and Muhsin Mahdi. Copyright © 1963 by the Free Press.

Healing: Metaphysics X

CHAPTER 2 / PROOF OF PROPHECY. THE MANNER OF THE PROPHET'S CALL TO GOD, THE EXALTED. THE "RETURN" TO GOD.

We now say: it is known that man differs from the other animals in that he cannot lead a proper life when isolated as a single individual, managing his affairs with no associates to help him satisfy his basic wants. One man needs to be complemented by another of his species, the other, in turn, by him and one like him. Thus, for example, one man would provide another with vegetables while the other would bake for him; one man would sew for another while the other would provide him with needles. Associated in this way, they become self-sufficient. For this reason men have found it necessary to establish cities and form associations. Whoever, in the endeavor to establish his city, does not see to the requirements necessary for setting up a city and, with his companions, remains confined to forming a mere association, would be engaged in devising means [to govern] a species most dissimilar to men and lacking the perfection of men. Nevertheless, even the ones like him cannot escape associating with the citizens of a city, and imitating them.

If this is obvious, then man's existence and survival require partnership. Partnership is only achieved through reciprocal transactions, as well as through the various trades practiced by man. Reciprocal transactions demand law (*sunnah*) and

justice, and law and justice demand a lawgiver and a dispenser of justice. This lawgiver must be in a position that enables him to address men and make them adhere to the law. He must, then, be a human being. Men must not be left to their private opinions concerning the law so that they disagree, each considering as just what others owe them, unjust what they owe others.

Thus, with respect to the survival and actual existence of the human species, the need for this human being is far greater than the need for such benefits as the growing of the hair on the eyebrow, the shaping of the arches in the feet, and many others that are not necessary for survival but at best are merely useful for it. Now the existence of the righteous man to legislate and to dispense justice is a possibility, as we have previously remarked. It becomes impossible, therefore, that divine providence should ordain the existence of those former benefits and not the latter, which are their bases. Nor is it possible that the First Principle and the angels after Him should know the former and not the latter. Nor yet is it possible that that which He knows to be in itself within the realm of possibility but whose realization is necessary for introducing the good order, should not exist. And how can it not exist, when that which depends and is constructed on its existence, exists? A prophet, therefore, must exist and he must be a human. He must also possess characteristics not present in others so that men could recognize in him something they do not have and which differentiates him from them. Therefore he will perform the miracles about which we have spoken.

When this man's existence comes about, he must lay down laws about men's affairs by the permission of God, the Exalted, by His command, inspiration, and the *descent of His Holy Spirit* on him. The first principle governing his legislation is to let men know that they have a Maker, One and Omnipotent; that *He knows the hidden and the manifest;* that obedience is due Him since *command* must belong to *Him who creates;* that He has prepared for those who obey Him an afterlife of bliss, but for those who disobey Him an afterlife of misery. This will induce the multitude to obey the decrees put in the prophet's mouth by the God and the angels.

But he ought not to involve them with doctrines pertaining to the knowledge of God, the Exalted, beyond the fact that He is one, the truth, and has none like Himself. To go beyond this and demand that they believe in His existence as being not referred to in place, as being not subject to verbal classifications, as being neither inside nor outside the world, or anything of this kind, is to ask too much. This will simply confuse the religion (*din*) they have and involve them in something from which deliverance is only possible for the one who receives guidance and is fortunate, whose existence is most rare. For it is only with great strain that they can comprehend the true states of such matters; it is only the very few among them that can understand the truth of divine "unicity" and divine "remoteness." The rest would inevitably come to deny the truth of such an existence, fall into dissensions, and indulge in disputations and analogical arguments that stand in the way of their political duties. This might even lead them to adopt views contrary to the city's welfare, opposed to the imperatives of truth. Their complaints and doubts will multiply, making it difficult for a man to control them. For divine wisdom is not easily acquired by everyone.

Nor is it proper for any man to reveal that he possesses knowledge he is hiding from the vulgar. Indeed, he must never permit any reference to this. Rather, he should let them know of God's majesty and greatness through symbols and similitudes derived from things that for them are majestic and great, adding this much—that He has neither equal, nor companion, nor likeness. Similarly, he must instill in them the belief in the resurrection in a manner they can conceive and in which their souls find rest. He must tell them about eternal bliss and misery in parables they can comprehend and conceive. Of the true nature of the afterlife he should only indicate something in general: that it is something that "no eye has seen and no ear heard," and that there are pleasures that are great possessions, and miseries that are perpetual torture.

Know that God, exalted be He, knows that the good lies in such a state of affairs. It follows, then, that that which God knows to be the good, must exist, as you have known [from the preceding discussion]. But there is no harm if the legislator's words contain symbols and signs that might stimulate the naturally apt to pursue philosophic investigation.

CHAPTER 3 / ACTS OF WORSHIP: THEIR BENEFITS IN THIS WORLD AND THE NEXT.

Moreover, this individual who is a prophet is not one whose like recurs in every period. For the matter that is receptive of a perfection like his occurs in few bodily compositions. It follows necessarily, then, that the prophet (may God's prayers and peace be upon him) must plan with great care to ensure the preservation of the legislation he enacts concerning man's welfare. Without doubt, the fundamental principle here is that men must continue in their knowledge of God and the resurrection and that the cause for forgetting these things with the passage of the generation succeeding [the mission of] the prophet (may God's prayers and peace be on him) must be absolutely eliminated. Hence there must be certain acts and works incumbent on people that the legislator must prescribe to be repeated at frequent specified intervals. In this way memory of the act is renewed and reappears before it can die.

These acts must be combined with what brings God and the afterlife necessarily to mind; otherwise they are useless. Remembering is achieved through words that are uttered or resolutions made in the imagination and by telling men that these acts bring them closer to God and are richly rewarded. And these acts must in reality be of such a nature. An example of these are the acts of worship imposed on people. In general, these should be reminders. Now reminders consist of either motions or the absence of motions that lead to other motions. An example of motion is prayer; of the absence of motion, fasting. For although the latter is a negative notion, it so greatly moves one's nature that he who fasts is reminded that what he is engaged in is not a jest. He will thus recall the intention of his fasting, which is to draw him close to God. . . .

The noblest of these acts of worship, from one point of view, should be the one in which the worshiper considers himself to be addressing God, beseeching Him, drawing close to Him, and standing in His presence. This is prayer. The legislator should therefore prescribe for the worshiper in preparation for prayer those postures men traditionally adopt when they present themselves to human kings, such as purification and cleanliness (indeed, he must prescribe fully in these two things). He should also prescribe for the worshipers the behavior traditionally adopted in the presence of kings: reverence, calm, modesty, the lowering of the eyes, the contracting of the hands and feet, the avoidance of turning around, composure. Likewise, he must prescribe for each time of prayer praiseworthy manners and customs. These acts will benefit the vulgar inasmuch as they will instill in them remembrance of God and the resurrection. In this way their adherence to the statutes and laws will continue. For without such reminders they will forget all of this with the passing of a generation or two. It will also be of great benefit for them in the afterlife inasmuch as their souls will be purified in the manner you have known [in our discourse]. As for the elect, the greatest benefit they derive from these things pertains to the afterlife.

We have established the true nature of the afterlife and have proved that true happiness in the hereafter is achieved through the soul's detaching itself by piety from the acquisitions of bodily dispositions opposed to the means for happiness. This purification is realized through moral states and habits of character acquired by acts that turn the soul away from the body and the senses and perpetuate its memory of its true substance. For if the soul continues to turn unto itself, it will not be affected by the bodily states. What will remind and help the soul in this respect are certain arduous acts that lie outside natural habit—indeed they are more on the side of exertion. These tire the body and curb the [natural] animal desire for rest, for laziness, for the rejection of toil, for the quieting of the hot humor, and for avoiding all exercise except that which is conducive to bestial pleasure. In the performance of these acts the soul must be required to recall God, the angels, and the world of happiness, whether it desires to do so or not. In this way the soul is instilled with the propensity to be repelled from the body and its influences and with the positive disposition to control it. Thus it will not be affected by the body. Hence when the soul encounters bodily acts, these will not produce in it the propensities and positive disposition that they would normally produce when the soul submits to them in everything. For this reason, the one who speaks truth has said: *Surely the good deeds drive away the bad deeds.* If this act persists in man, then he will acquire the positive disposition of turning in the direction of truth and away from error. He thus becomes well prepared to be delivered unto [true] happiness after bodily separation.

If these acts were performed by someone who did not believe them to be divine obligations and who, nonetheless, had to remember God in every act, rejecting everything else, this one would be worthy of some measure of this virtue. How much more worthy will be the one who performs these acts knowing that the prophet comes from God and is sent by God, that his being sent is necessitated by divine wisdom, that all the prophet's legislation is an obligation demanded of him by God, that all he legislates comes from God? For the prophet was obligated by God to impose these acts of worshiping Him. These acts benefit the worshipers in that they perpetuate in the latter adherence to the laws and religion (*sharī'ah*) that insure their existence and in that, by virtue of the goodness they inspire, they bring the worshipers closer to God in the hereafter.

Moreover, this is the man who is charged with administering the affairs of men, for insuring their livelihood in this world and their well-being in the world to come. He is a man distinguished from the rest of mankind by his godliness.

CHAPTER 4 / ESTABLISHMENT OF THE CITY, THE HOUSEHOLD (THAT IS, MARRIAGE), AND THE GENERAL LAWS PERTAINING TO THESE MATTERS.

The legislator's first objective in laying down the laws and organizing the city must be to divide it into three groups: administrators, artisans, and guardians. He must place at the head of each group a leader, under whom he will place other leaders, under these yet others, and so forth until he arrives at the common run of men. Thus none in the city will remain without a proper function and a specific place: each will have his use in the city. Idleness and unemployment must be prohibited. The legislator must leave the way open to no one for acquiring from another that share of a livelihood necessary for man while exempting himself from any effort in return. Such people he must vigorously restrain. If they fail to refrain from such a practice, he must then exile them from the land. But should the cause here be some physical malady or defect, the legislator must set aside a special place for such cases, under someone's charge.

There must exist in the city a common fund, part of it consisting of duties imposed on acquired and natural profits such as fruit and agricultural produce, part of it imposed as punishment, while another part should consist of property taken from those who resist the law, that is, of war-booty. Thus the fund will serve to meet the exigencies of the common good, to meet the needs of the guardians who do not work in any craft, and those prevented from earning their livelihood by maladies and chronic diseases. Some people have held the opinion that the diseased whose recovery is not to be expected should be killed. But this is base; for their sustenance will not hurt the city. If such people have relatives enjoying a superfluity of means, then the legislator must impose on these relatives the responsibility for their people.

Just as idleness must be prohibited, so should professions like gambling, whereby properties and utilities are transferred without any benefit rendered in exchange. For the gambler takes without rendering any service at all. Rather, what one takes must always be a compensation given in return for work, a compensation that is either substance, utility, good remembrance, or any other thing considered a human good. Similarly, professions that lead to the opposite of welfare and usefulness, such as the learning of theft, brigandage, leadership of criminal bands, and the like, must be prohibited. Professions that allow people to dispense with learning those crafts pertaining to the association—professions such as usury—must be prohibited. For usury is the seeking of excess profit without practic-

ing a craft to achieve it, even though it does render a service in return. Also those acts—which, if once permitted, would be detrimental to the city's growth—like fornication and sodomy, which dispense with the greatest pillar on which the city stands, that is, marriage, must be prohibited.

The first of the legislator's acts must pertain to marriage resulting in issue. He must call and urge people to it. For by marriage is achieved the continuity of the species, the permanence of which is proof of the existence of God, the Exalted. He must arrange it in such a way that matrimony takes place as a manifest affair, so that there will be no uncertainties concerning progeny causing defects in the proper transfer of inheritances, which are a source of wealth. . . . Through this also—I mean the concealment of marriage—defects in other respects occur: for example, in the necessity that one party should undertake expenditure over the other, in rendering mutual assistance, and in other matters that will not escape the wise person after reflection.

The legislator must take firm measures to assure the permanence of the union so that not every quarrel should result in a separation that disrupts the bond between children and parents and renews the need of marriage for everyone. In this there are many sorts of harm. Also, because what is most conducive to the general good is love. Love is only achieved through friendship; friendship through habit; habit is produced only through long association. This assurance, with respect to the woman, consists in not placing in her hands the right to make the separation. For in reality she is not very rational and is quick to follow passion and anger. But a way for separation must be left open and not all doors closed. To prevent separation under all circumstances results in all kinds of harmful consequences. Of these is the fact that some natures cannot adapt themselves to others: the more they are brought together, the greater the resulting evil, aversion, and unpleasantness. Or again, someone might get an unequal partner, or one who is of bad character, or repellent in nature. This will induce the other partner to desire someone else—for desire is natural—and this in turn leads to many harmful consequences. It also might so happen that the married couple do not cooperate for procreation and if exchanged for other partners they would. Hence some means for separation is necessary. But the law must be strict about it.

The means for separation must not be placed in the hands of the less rational of the two, the one more prone to disagreement, confusion, and change. Instead, this must be relegated to the judges who will affect the separation when they ascertain the woman's mistreatment by the other partner. In the case of the man, an indemnity must be imposed on him so that he will approach separation only after ascertainment and after he finds it to be the right thing for him in every way.

The legislator must, nevertheless, leave the way open for reconciliation, without, however, emphasizing it lest this encourage thoughtless action. On the contrary, he must make reconciliation more difficult than separation. How excellent was that which [Muhammad] the greatest of legislators commanded—that the man, after thrice pronouncing the formula for divorce, is not allowed to remarry the woman until he brings himself to drink a cup unsurpassed in bitterness, which is, to first let another man marry her by a true marriage and have real relations with her. If such a prospect awaits a man, he will not approach separation recklessly, unless he has already determined that the separation is to be permanent, or unless he is of a defective character and takes perverted pleasure in scandal. But the likes of these fall outside the pale of men who deserve the seeking of their welfare.

Since woman by right must be protected inasmuch as she can share her sexual desire with many, is much inclined to draw attention to herself, and in addition to that is easily deceived and is less inclined to obey reason; and since sexual relations on her part with many men cause great disdain and shame, which are well-known harms, whereas on the part of the man they only arouse jealousy, which should be ignored as it is nothing but obedience to the devil; it is more important to legislate that the woman should be veiled and secluded from men. Thus, unlike the man, she should not be a breadearner. It must be legislated that her needs be satisfied by the man upon whom must be imposed her sustenance. For this the man must be compensated. He must own her, but not she him. Thus she

cannot be married to another at the same time. But in the case of man this avenue is not closed to him though he is forbidden from taking a number of wives whom he cannot support. Hence the compensation consists in the ownership of the woman's "genitalia." By this ownership I do not mean sexual intercourse. For both partake of its pleasure and the woman's share is even greater, as is her delight and pleasure in children. But by this I mean that no other man can make use of them.

It must be legislated with respect to the child that both parents must undertake his proper upbringing—the woman in her special area, the man by provision. Likewise it must be prescribed that the child must serve, obey, respect, and honor his parents. For they are the cause of his existence and in addition have borne his support, something we need not enlarge upon as it is evident.

CHAPTER 5 / CONCERNING THE CALIPH AND THE IMAM: THE NECESSITY OF OBEYING THEM. REMARKS ON POLITICS, TRANSACTIONS, AND MORALS.

Next, the legislator must impose as a duty obedience to whosoever succeeds him. He must also prescribe that designation of the successor can only be made by himself or by the consensus of the elders. The latter should verify openly to the public that the man of their choice can hold sole political authority, that he is of independent judgment, that he is endowed with the noble qualities of courage, temperance, and good governance, and that he knows the law to a degree unsurpassed by anyone else. Such a verification must be openly proclaimed and must find unanimous agreement by the entire public. The legislator must lay down in the law that should they disagree and quarrel, succumbing to passion and whim, or should they agree to designate someone other than the virtuous and deserving individual, then they would have committed an act of unbelief. Designation of the caliph through appointment by testament is best: it will not lead to partisanship, quarrels, and dissensions.

The legislator must then decree in his law that if someone secedes and lays claim to the caliphate by virtue of power or wealth, then it becomes the duty of every citizen to fight and kill him. If the citizens are capable of so doing but refrain from doing so, then they disobey God and commit an act of unbelief. The blood of anyone who can fight but refrains becomes free for the spilling after this fact is established in the assembly of all. The legislator must lay down in the law that, next to belief in the prophet, nothing brings one closer to God than the killing of such a usurper.

If the seceder, however, verifies that the one holding the caliphate is not fit for it, that he is afflicted with an imperfection, and that this imperfection is not found in the seceder, then it is best that the citizens accept the latter. The determining factor here is superiority of practical judgment and excellence in political management. The one whose attainment in the rest of the virtues [including knowledge] is moderate—although he must not be ignorant of them nor act contrary to them—but excels in these two is more fit than the one who excels in the other virtues but is not foremost in these two. Thus the one who has more knowledge must join and support the one who has better practical judgment. The latter, in turn, must accept the former's support and seek his advice. . . .

As for enemies and those who oppose his law, the legislator must decree waging war against them and destroying them, after calling on them to accept the truth. Their property and women must be declared free for the spoil. For when such property and women are not administered according to the constitution of the virtuous city, they will not bring about the good for which property and women are sought. Rather, these would contribute to corruption and evil. Since some men have to serve others, such people must be forced to serve the people of the just city. The same applies to people not very capable of acquiring virtue. For these are slaves by nature as, for example, the Turks and the Zinjis and in general all those who do not grow up in noble [that is, moderate] climes where the conditions for the most part are such that nations of good temperament, innate intelligence, and sound minds thrive. If a city other than his has praiseworthy laws, the legislator must not interfere with it unless the times are such that they require the declaration that no law is valid save the revealed law. For when nations and

cities go astray and laws are prescribed for them, adherence to the law must be assured. If the adherence to the law becomes incumbent, it might very well be the case that to ensure this adherence requires the acceptance of the law by the whole world. If the people of that [other] city, which has a good way of life, find that this [new] law, too, is good and praiseworthy and that the adoption of the new law means restoring the conditions of corrupted cities to virtue, and yet proceed to proclaim that this law ought not to be accepted and reject as false the legislator's claim that this law has come to all cities, then a great weakness will afflict the law. Those opposing it could then use as argument for their rejecting it that the people of that [other] city have rejected it. In this case these latter must also be punished and war (*jihād*) waged on them; but this war must not be pursued with the same severity as against the people utterly in error. Or else an indemnity must be imposed on them in lieu of their preference. In any case, it must be enunciated as a truth that they are negators [of the true law]. For how are they not negators, when they refuse to accept the divine Law, which God, the Exalted, has sent down? Should they perish, they would have met what they deserve. For their death, though it means the end of some, results in a permanent good, particularly when the new law is more complete and better. It should also be legislated with regard to these, that if clemency on condition that they pay ransom and tax is desired, this can be done. In general, they must not be placed in the same category as the other nonbelievers.

The legislator must also impose punishments, penalties, and prohibitions to prevent disobedience to the divine Law. For not everyone is restrained from violating the law because of what he fears of the afterlife. Most of these [penalties and so forth] must pertain to acts contrary to law that are conducive to the corruption of the city's order; for example, adultery, theft, complicity with the enemies of the city, and the like. As for the acts that harm the individual himself, the law should contain helpful advice and warning, and not go beyond this to the prescription of obligatory duties. The law concerning acts of worship, marriage, and prohibitions should be moderate, neither severe nor lenient. The legislator must relegate many questions, particularly those pertaining to transactions, to the exercise of the individual judgment (*ijtihād*) of the jurists. For different times and circumstances call for decisions that cannot be predetermined. As for the further control of the city involving knowledge of the organization of guardians, income and expenditure, manufacture of armaments, legal rights, border fortifications, and the like, it must be placed in the hands of the ruler in his capacity as caliph. The legislator must not impose specific prescriptions concerning these. Such an imposition would be defective since conditions change with time. Moreover, it is impossible to make universal judgments that cover every contingency in these matters. He must leave this to the body of counsellors.

It is necessary that the legislator should also prescribe laws regarding morals and customs that advocate justice, which is the mean. The mean in morals and customs is sought for two things. The one, involving the breaking of the dominance of the passions, is for the soul's purification and for enabling it to acquire the power of self-mastery so that it can liberate itself from the body untarnished. The other, involving the use of these passions, is for worldly interests. As for the use of pleasures, these serve to conserve the body and procreation. As for courage, it is for the city's survival. The vices of excess are to be avoided for the harm they inflict in human interests, while the vices of deficiency are to be avoided for the harm they cause the city. By wisdom as a virtue, which is the third of a triad comprising in addition temperance and courage, is not meant theoretical wisdom—for the mean is not demanded in the latter at all—but, rather, practical wisdom pertaining to worldly actions and behavior. For it is deception to concentrate on the knowledge of this wisdom, carefully guarding the ingenious ways whereby one can attain through it every benefit and avoid every harm, to the extent that this would result in bringing upon one's associates the opposite of what one seeks for oneself and result in distracting oneself from the attainment of other virtues. To cause the hand to be thus fettered to the neck, means the loss of a man's soul, his whole life, the instrument of his well-being, and his survival to that moment at which he attains perfection. Since the motivating powers are three—the appetitive, the irascible, and the practical—the virtues consist of three things: (*a*) moderation in such appetites as the pleasures of sex, food, clothing, comfort, and other pleasures of sense and imagination; (*b*) moderation in all the irascible passions such as fear, anger, depression, pride, hate, jealousy, and the like; (*c*) moderation in practical matters. At the head of these virtues stand temperance, practical wisdom, and courage; their sum is justice, which, however, is extraneous to theoretical virtue. But whoever combines theoretical wisdom with justice, is indeed the happy man. And whoever, in addition to this, wins the prophetic qualities, becomes almost a human god. Worship of him, after the worship of God, becomes almost allowed. He is indeed the world's earthly king and God's deputy in it.

MAIMONIDES

Moses Maimonides, or Moses ben Maimon (1135–1204), was born in Córdoba, Spain. His father was a distinguished Jewish scholar. At thirteen, Maimonides fled Córdoba, already under Muslim control, when an intolerant Islamic sect conquered it. Eventually, he and his family settled in northern Africa. When he was thirty, Maimonides became a court physician in Egypt. He served as a leader of the Jewish community there, becoming a great authority on Jewish law. He died at age sixty-seven.

Maimonides wrote many volumes on Jewish law, medicine, and other topics. His chief work bearing on philosophy is *The Guide of the Perplexed,* a long treatise written in Arabic on the meaning of various Hebrew words. Maimonides addresses his work to people who are torn between what they see as the competing claims of religion and philosophy. (Such people, known as "the perplexed," are among the "weeds" of the ideal city described by al-Farabi in *The Political Regime.*) Maimonides recognizes that, in the opinion of many, reason and religious belief conflict. He tries to reconcile the two, showing that reason not only is compatible with but even supports religion and religious law. In his view, shallow thought challenges religion, but profound thought strengthens it.

This view implies that—in philosophy, at least—a little learning is a dangerous thing. Maimonides wishes to encourage deep study and reflection but to discourage shallow learning. To keep the vulgar away, al-Farabi had written intentionally boring, jargon-filled treatises. To the same end, Maimonides admits that he breaks apart ideas that belong together, makes contradictory assertions, and generally tries to make his book hard to understand.

Maimonides' ethics centers on the idea of law. He argues that proper civil and religious laws make rational sense; they promote the welfare of the soul or the welfare of the body. Maimonides is thus something like a rule-consequentialist; that is, Maimonides evaluates individual actions by appealing to a set of rules. The rules themselves he justifies by appealing to the consequences of adopting them. God's laws, as revealed in the Torah, are what best promote moral character and the community's happiness.

A primary objection to rule-consequentialism is that in some cases, we can achieve better results by violating the rules. Maimonides confronts the objection directly, admitting that this is true. The rules are generalities that cover most cases; sometimes they direct an action that does not maximize welfare. Nevertheless, Maimonides argues, even in such cases the rules must be observed.

Maimonides, influenced by Bahya and others, says that laws aim at the welfare of the body and the soul. Unlike Bahya, however, Maimonides treats the welfare of the body as primary, identifying promotion of the soul's welfare with teaching correct opinions. The soul's welfare presupposes the body's welfare; someone who is very ill, starving, or freezing cannot concentrate on the duties of the heart. Laws aiming at the welfare of the body should try to stop wrongdoing and encourage good moral character. Both are useful to the community as a whole.

As this formulation suggests, Maimonides holds that good moral character has only instrumental value. It corresponds to a kind of wisdom, but not the highest kind; it amounts to a wisdom involving means, not ends. Wisdom of the highest kind, the true human perfection, is a knowledge of intrinsic goods—things worth desiring for their own sakes, rather than for the sake of something else. This requires the rational virtues, which allow a person to apprehend the true realities or intelligibles (in Plato and Aristotle, forms) and, ultimately, the divine. The apprehension of the true realities, Maimonides insists, is the only thing worth desiring for its own sake. Achieving a knowledge of God leads to moral as well as intellectual perfection, for it leads to the imitation of God's loving kindness, judgment, and righteousness.

from *The Guide of the Perplexed*

Reprinted from Moses Maimonides, The Guide of the Perplexed, *translated by Schlomo Pines. Copyright © 1963 by the University of Chicago.*

CHAPTER 25

The actions are divided with regard to their ends into four classes: futile actions, frivolous actions, vain actions, or good and excellent actions. The action that is called vain is that by which its agent aims at some end and that end is not achieved, its achievement being hindered by obstacles. . . . A futile action is that action by which no end is aimed at at all, as when some people play with their hands while thinking and as the actions of the negligent and the inattentive. A frivolous action is that action by which a low end is aimed at; I mean to say that something unnecessary and not very useful is aimed at therein, as when one dances not for exercise or as when one does things in order to make people laugh about those things. . . . The good and excellent action is that accomplished by an agent aiming at a noble end, I mean one that is necessary or useful, and achieves that end. This is a division against which, as it seems to me, no objection can be made at any point. For one who accomplishes a certain action in all cases either aims or does not aim thereby at some end. Again an end aimed at is in all cases either noble or low, and is either achieved or not. And this is what is necessarily required by the division.

After having explained this, I shall say: A man endowed with intellect is incapable of saying that any action of God is vain, futile, or frivolous. . . .

CHAPTER 27

The Law as a whole aims at two things: the welfare of the soul and the welfare of the body. As for the welfare of the soul, it consists in the multitude's acquiring correct opinions corresponding to their respective capacity. Therefore some of them [namely, the opinions] are set forth explicitly and some of them are set forth in parables. For it is not within the nature of the common multitude that its capacity should suffice for apprehending that subject matter as it is. As for the welfare of the body, it comes about by the improvement of their ways of living one with another. This is achieved through two things. One of them is the abolition of their wronging each other. This is tantamount to every individual among the people not being permitted to act according to his will and up to the limits of his power, but being forced to do that which is useful to the whole. The second thing consists in the acquisition by every human individual of moral qualities that are useful for life in society so that the affairs of the city may be ordered. Know that as between these two aims, one is indubitably greater in nobility, namely, the welfare of the soul—I mean the procuring of correct opinions—while the second aim—I mean the welfare of the body—is prior in nature and time. The latter aim consists in the governance of the city and the well-being of the states of all its people according to their capacity. This second aim is the more certain one, and it is the one regarding which every effort has been made precisely to expound it and all its particulars. For the first aim can only be achieved after achieving this second one. For it has already been demonstrated that man has two perfections: a first perfection, which is the perfection of the body, and an ultimate perfection, which is the perfection of the soul. The first perfection consists of being healthy and in the very best bodily state, and this is only possible through his finding the things necessary for him whenever he seeks them. These are his food and all the other things needed for the governance of his body, such as a shelter, bathing, and so forth. This cannot be achieved in any way by one isolated individual. For an individual can only attain all this through a political association, it being already known that man is political by nature. His ultimate perfection is to become rational in actu, I mean to have an intellect in actu; this would consist in his knowing everything concerning all the beings that it is within the capacity of man to know in accordance with his ultimate perfection. It is clear that to this ultimate perfection there do not belong either actions or moral qualities and that it consists only of opinions toward which speculation has led and that investigation has rendered compulsory. It is also clear that this noble and ultimate perfection can only be achieved after the first perfection has been achieved. For a man cannot represent to himself an intelligible even when taught to understand it and all the more cannot become aware of it of his own accord, if he is in pain or is very hungry or is thirsty or is hot or is very cold. But once the first perfection has been achieved it is possible to achieve the ultimate, which is indubitably more noble and is the only cause of permanent preservation.

The true Law then, which as we have already made clear is unique—namely, the Law of Moses our Master—has come to bring us both perfections, I mean the welfare of the states of people in their relations with one another through the abolition of reciprocal wrongdoing and through the acquisition of a noble and excellent character. In this way the preservation of the population of the country and their permanent existence in the same order become possible, so that every one of them achieves his first perfection; I mean also the soundness of the beliefs and the giving of correct opinions through which ultimate perfection is achieved. . . .

CHAPTER 28

Among the things to which your attention ought to be directed is that you should know that in regard to the correct opinions through which the ultimate perfection may be obtained, the Law has communicated only their end and made a call to believe in them in a summary way—that is, to believe in the existence of the deity, may He be exalted, His unity, His knowledge, His power, His will, and His eternity. All these points are ultimate ends, which can be made clear in detail and through definitions only after one knows many opinions. In the same way the

Law also makes a call to adopt certain beliefs, belief in which is necessary for the sake of political welfare. Such, for instance, is our belief that He, may He be exalted, is violently angry with those who disobey Him and that it is therefore necessary to fear Him and to dread Him and to take care not to disobey. With regard to all the other correct opinions concerning the whole of being—opinions that constitute the numerous kinds of all the theoretical sciences through which the opinions forming the ultimate end are validated—the Law, albeit it does not make a call to direct attention toward them in detail as it does with regard to [the opinions forming ultimate ends], does do this in summary fashion by saying: To love the Lord. . . .

What results from what we have now stated as a premise regarding this subject is that whenever a commandment, be it a prescription or a prohibition, requires abolishing reciprocal wrongdoing, or urging to a noble moral quality leading to a good social relationship, or communicating a correct opinion that ought to be believed either on account of itself or because it is necessary for the abolition of reciprocal wrongdoing or for the acquisition of a noble moral quality, such a commandment has a clear cause and is of a manifest utility. No question concerning the end need be posed with regard to such commandments. For no one was ever so perplexed for a day as to ask why we were commanded by the Law that God is one, or why we were forbidden to kill and to steal, or why we were forbidden to exercise vengeance and retaliation, or why we were ordered to love each other. The matters about which people are perplexed and opinions disagree—so that some say that there is no utility in them at all except the fact of mere command, whereas others say that there is a utility in them that is hidden from us—are the commandments from whose external meaning it does not appear that they are useful according to one of the three notions we have mentioned: I mean to say that they neither communicate an opinion nor inculcate a noble quality nor abolish reciprocal wrongdoing. Apparently these commandments are not related to the welfare of the soul, as they do not communicate a belief, or to the welfare of the body, as they do not communicate rules useful for the governance of the city or for the governance of the household. Such, for instance, are the prohibitions of the mingled stuff, of the mingling [of diverse species], and of meat in milk, and the commandment concerning the covering of blood, the heifer whose neck was broken, and the firstling of an ass, and others of the same kind. However, you will hear my explanation for all of them and my exposition of the correct and demonstrated causes for them all with the sole exception—as I have mentioned to you—of details and particular commandments. I shall explain that all these and others of the same kind are indubitably related to one of the three notions referred to—either to the welfare of a belief or to the welfare of the conditions of the city, which is achieved through two things: abolition of reciprocal wrongdoing and acquisition of excellent characters.

Sum up what we have said concerning beliefs as follows: In some cases a commandment communicates a correct belief, which is the one and only thing aimed at—as, for instance, the belief in the unity and eternity of the deity and in His not being a body. In other cases the belief is necessary for the abolition of reciprocal wrongdoing or for the acquisition of a noble moral quality—as, for instance, the belief that He, may He be exalted, has a violent anger against those who do injustice, according to what is said: *And My wrath shall wax hot, and I will kill, and so on,* and as the belief that He, may He be exalted, responds instantaneously to the prayer of someone wronged or deceived: *And it shall come to pass, when he crieth unto Me, that I will hear; for I am gracious.*

CHAPTER 31

There is a group of human beings who consider it a grievous thing that causes should be given for any law; what would please them most is that the intellect would not find a meaning for the commandments and prohibitions. What compels them to feel thus is a sickness that they find in their souls, a sickness to which they are unable to give utterance and of which they cannot furnish a satisfactory account. For they think that if those laws were useful in this existence and had been given to us for this or that reason, it would be as if they derived from the reflection and the understanding of some intelligent being. If, however, there is a thing for which the intellect could not find any meaning at all and that

does not lead to something useful, it indubitably derives from God; for the reflection of man would not lead to such a thing. It is as if, according to these people of weak intellects, man were more perfect than his Maker; for man speaks and acts in a manner that leads to some intended end, whereas the deity does not act thus, but commands us to do things that are not useful to us and forbids us to do things that are not harmful to us. But He is far exalted above this; the contrary is the case. . . . Now if there is a thing for which no reason is known and that does not either procure something useful or ward off something harmful, why should one say of one who believes in it or practices it that he is wise and understanding and of great worth? And why should the religious communities think it a wonder? Rather things are indubitably as we have mentioned: every commandment from among these six hundred and thirteen commandments exists either with a view to communicating a correct opinion, or to putting an end to an unhealthy opinion, or to communicating a rule of justice, or to warding off an injustice, or to endowing men with a noble moral quality, or to warning them against an evil moral quality. Thus all [the commandments] are bound up with three things: opinions, moral qualities, and political civic actions. . . .

CHAPTER 35

To the totality of purposes of the perfect Law there belong the abandonment, depreciation, and restraint of desires in so far as possible, so that these should be satisfied only in so far as this is necessary. You know already that most of the lusts and licentiousness of the multitude consist in an appetite for eating, drinking, and sexual intercourse. This is what destroys man's last perfection, what harms him also in his first perfection, and what corrupts most of the circumstances of the citizens and of the people engaged in domestic governance. For when only the desires are followed, as is done by the ignorant, the longing for speculation is abolished, the body is corrupted, and the man to whom this happens perishes before this is required by his natural term of life; thus cares and sorrows multiply, mutual envy, hatred, and strife aiming at taking away what the other has, multiply. All this is brought about by the fact that the ignoramus regards pleasure alone as the end to be sought for its own sake. Therefore God, may His name be held sublime, employed a gracious ruse through giving us certain laws that destroy this end and thought away from it in every way. He forbids everything that leads to lusts and to mere pleasure. This is an important purpose of this Law. Do you not see how the texts of the Torah command to kill him who manifestly has an excessive longing for the pleasure of eating and drinking? For he is the stubborn and rebellious son, to whom its following dictum applies: He is a glutton and a drunkard. He commands stoning and cutting him off speedily before the matter becomes serious and before he brings about the destruction of many and ruins by the violence of his lust the circumstances of righteous men.

Similarly to the totality of intentions of the Law there belong gentleness and docility; man should not be hard and rough, but responsive, obedient, acquiescent, and docile. . . .

Similarly one of the intentions of the Law is purity and sanctification; I mean by this renouncing and avoiding sexual intercourse and causing it to be as infrequent as possible, as I shall make clear. Thus when He, may He be exalted, commanded the religious community to be sanctified with a view to receiving the Torah, and He said: *And sanctify them today and tomorrow*—He said: *Come not near a woman*. Consequently He states clearly that sanctity consists in renouncing sexual intercourse, just as He also states explicitly that the giving-up of the drinking of wine constitutes sanctity, in what He says about the Nazarite: *He shall be saintly.* . . .

Cleaning garments, washing the body, and removal of dirt also constitute one of the purposes of this Law. But this comes after the purification of the actions and the purification of the heart from polluting opinions and polluting moral qualities. For to confine oneself to cleaning the outward appearance through washing and cleaning the garment, while having at the same time a lust for various pleasures and unbridled license in eating and sexual intercourse, merits the utmost blame. . . . To sum up the dictum: Their outward appearances are clean and universally known as unsullied and pure, whereas innerly they are engaged in the pursuit of their desires and the pleasures of their bodies. But this is not the purpose of the Law, for the first purpose is to restrain desire—the purification of the outer coming after the purification of the inner. . . .

CHAPTER 34

Among the things that you likewise ought to know is the fact that the Law does not pay attention to the isolated. The Law was not given with a view to things that are rare. For in everything that it wishes to bring about, be it an opinion or a moral habit or a useful work, it is directed only toward the things that occur in the majority of cases and pays no attention to what happens rarely or to the damage occurring to the unique human being because of this way of determination and because of the legal character of the governance. For the Law is a divine thing; and it is your business to reflect on the natural things in which the general utility, which is included in them, nonetheless necessarily produces damages to individuals, as is clear from our discourse and the discourse of others. In view of this consideration also, you will not wonder at the fact that the purpose of the Law is not perfectly achieved in every individual and that, on the contrary, it necessarily follows that there should exist individuals whom this governance of the Law does not make perfect. For not everything that derives necessarily from the natural specific forms is actualized in every individual. Indeed, all things proceed from one deity and one agent and have been given from one shepherd. The contrary of this is impossible, and we have already explained that the impossible has a stable nature that never changes. In view of this consideration, it also will not be possible that the laws be dependent on changes in the circumstances of the individuals and of the times, as is the case with regard to medical treatment, which is particularized for every individual in conformity with his present temperament. On the contrary, governance of the Law ought to be absolute and universal, including everyone, even if it is suitable only for certain individuals and not suitable for others; for if it were made to fit individuals, the whole would be corrupted and you would make out of it something that varies. For this reason, matters that are primarily intended in the Law ought not to be dependent on time or place; but the degrees ought to be absolute and universal, according to what He, may He be exalted, says: *As for the congregation, there shall be one statute [ḥuqqah] for you.* However, only the universal interests, those of the majority, are considered in them, as we have explained.

After I have set forth these premises, I shall begin to explain what I have intended to explain.

CHAPTER 35

With a view to this purpose, I have divided all the commandments into fourteen classes.

The first class comprises the commandments that are fundamental opinions. . . .

The second class comprises the commandments concerned with the prohibition of idolatry. . . .

The third class comprises the commandments concerned with improvement of the moral qualities. . . .

The fourth class comprises the commandments concerned with giving alms, lending, bestowal of gifts, and matters that are connected with this—as for instance estimations and anathemas. . . .

The fifth class comprises the commandments concerned with prohibiting wrongdoing and aggression. They are those included in our compilation in the *Book of Torts* [*Sepher Neziqin*]. The utility of this class is manifest.

The sixth class comprises the commandments concerned with punishments, as for instance laws concerning thieves and robbers and laws concerning false witnesses—in fact most of the matters we have enumerated in the *Book of Judges* [*Sepher Shophetim*]. The utility of this is clear and manifest, for if a criminal is not punished, injurious acts will not be abolished in any way and none of those who design aggression will be deterred. No one is as weak-minded as those who deem that the abolition of punishments would be merciful on men. On the contrary, this would be cruelty itself on them as well as the ruin of the order of the city. On the contrary, mercy is to be found in His command, may He be exalted: *Judges and officers shalt thou make thee in all thy gates.*

The seventh class comprises the laws of property concerned with the mutual transactions of people, such as loans, hire for wages, deposits, buying, selling, and other things of this kind. Inheritance also

belongs to this group. These are the commandments that we have enumerated in the *Book of Acquisition and Judgments* [*Sepher Qinyan ve-Mishpatim*]. The utility of this class is clear and manifest. For these property associations are necessary for people in every city, and it is indispensable that rules of justice should be given with a view to these transactions and that these transactions be regulated in a useful manner.

The eighth class comprises the commandments concerning the days in which work is forbidden, I mean Sabbaths and festivals. . . .

The ninth class comprises all the other practices of worship prescribed to everybody. . . .

The tenth class comprises the commandments concerned with the Sanctuary and its utensils and servants. . . .

The eleventh class comprises the commandments concerned with the sacrifices. . . .

The twelfth class comprises the commandments concerned with things unclean and clean. . . .

The thirteenth class comprises the commandments concerned with the prohibition of certain foods and what is connected therewith. . . .

The fourteenth class comprises the commandments concerned with the prohibition of certain sexual unions. . . .

It is known that all the commandments are divided into two groups: transgressions between man and his fellow man and transgressions between man and God. Among the classes we have differentiated and enumerated, the fifth, sixth, seventh, and a portion of the third, belong to the group devoted to the relation between man and his fellow man, while all the other classes deal with the relationship between man and God. For every commandment, whether it be a prescription or a prohibition, whose purpose it is to bring about the achievement of a certain moral quality or of an opinion or the rightness of actions, which only concerns the individual himself and his becoming more perfect, is called by them [a commandment dealing with the relation] between man and God, even though in reality it sometimes may affect relations between man and his fellow man. But this happens only after many intermediate steps and through comprehensive considerations, and it does not lead from the beginning to harming a fellow man. Understand this. . . .

CHAPTER 40

The commandments comprised in the fifth class are those that we have enumerated in the *Book of Torts*. All of them are concerned with putting an end to acts of injustice and with the prevention of acts causing damage. In order that great care should be taken to avoid causing damage, man is held responsible for every act causing damage deriving from his possessions or caused by an act of his, if only it were possible for him to be cautious and take care not to cause damage. . . .

CHAPTER 41

The commandments comprised in the sixth class are concerned with punishments; and their utility, speaking generally, is well known, and we have already mentioned it. Hear then the particulars concerning this and a judgment concerning every strange case figuring in them.

The punishment meted out to anyone who has done wrong to somebody else consists in general in his being given exactly the same treatment that he has given to somebody else. If he has injured the latter's body, he shall be injured in his body, and if he has injured him in his property, he shall be injured in his property. The owner of the property may be indulgent and forgive. To a murderer alone, however, because of the greatness of his wrongdoing, no indulgence shall be shown at all and no blood money shall be accepted from him: *And the land cannot be cleansed of the blood that is shed therein, but by the blood of him that shed it.* Hence even if the victim remains alive for an hour or for several days, speaks, and is in full possession of his mind and says: Let him who murdered me be dismissed; I have forgiven and pardoned him—this cannot be accepted from him. For necessarily there must be a soul for a soul—the young and the old, the slaves and the free, the men of knowledge and the ignorant, being considered as equal. For among the crimes of man there is none greater than this. . . .

He who has caused damage to property shall have inflicted upon him damage to his property up to exactly the same amount: *Whom the judges shall condemn, he shall pay double unto his neighbor*—that is, the thing taken by him and an equal amount taken from the property of the thief.

Know that the more frequent the kind of crime is and the easier it is to commit, the greater the penalty for it must be, so that one should refrain from it. . . .

Similarly the law concerning false witnesses is that the thing that they wished to be done unto another shall be done unto them: if they wished the one they bore witness against to be killed, they shall be killed; if they wished him to be flogged, they shall be flogged: and if they wished him to be fined, they shall have a similar fine imposed on them. In all this the intention is to make the penalty equal to the crime, and this too is a meaning of the expression: righteous judgments. . . .

Introduction. Know that whether a penalty is great and most grievous or small and easy to bear depends on four things being taken into consideration. The first is the greatness of the crime: for actions from which great harm results entail a heavy penalty, whereas actions from which only small and slight harm results entail but a light penalty. The second is the frequency of the occurrence of the crime: for a crime that occurs rather often ought to be prevented by means of a heavy penalty, whereas a slight penalty suffices to prevent one that is rare in view of its rarity. The third is the strength of incitement: for a man can be made to give up a thing toward which he is incited—either because desire draws him strongly toward it or because of the strength of habit or because of his feeling great hardship when refraining from it—only by fear of a heavy penalty. The fourth is the ease with which the action can be committed in secret and concealment, so that the others are unaware of it: for the deterrent for this can only be the fear of a great and heavy penalty.

After this introduction has been made, you should know that classification of punishments, according to the text of the Torah, comprises four degrees: [1] that which entails death by order of a court of law; [2] that which entails being cut off—that is, being whipped, the crime being believed withal to be a great one; [3] that which entails being whipped, but the crime is not believed to be a great one, but a mere transgression, or entails death at the hands of God; [4] that in which there is only a prohibition the transgression of which does not even entail flogging. . . .

As for death by order of a court of law, you will find that this sentence is only brought on in grave cases: that is, either in the case of the corruption of belief or in that of a very great crime. I refer to idolatry, adulterous or incestuous sexual intercourse, and the shedding of blood and all that leads to these crimes as well as in the cases of the profanation of the Sabbath, as the latter fortifies the belief in the creation of the world; of a false claim of prophecy; of a rebellious elder, because of the great harm that results in these cases; of him that smiteth his father and his mother and curseth his father and his mother, because of the great impudence of the thing and its destroying the good order of the household, which is the first part of the city. As for a stubborn and rebellious son, he must be put to death because of what he will become, for necessarily he will murder later on. He that stealeth a man must likewise be punished in this manner, for he exposes him to death. Also he that comes breaking in, for he too is prepared to kill, as [the Sages], may their memory be blessed, have explained. These three, I mean a stubborn and rebellious son, he that stealeth a man and selleth him, and he that comes breaking in, will become shedders of blood. You will not find that death by order of a court of law is prescribed except in the case of these great crimes. Not all incestuous and adulterous sexual intercourse is punished by death by order of a court of law; only such as is easy to engage in or is most shameful or has the strongest attraction. That which is not of this kind is merely punished by cutting off. . . .

CHAPTER 42

The commandments comprised in the seventh class are the laws concerning property; they are those that we have enumerated in a portion of the *Book of Judgments* and in a portion of the *Book of Acquisition*. All of them have an evident reason. For they consist in an estimation of the laws of justice with regard to the transactions that of necessity occur between people and see to it that these do not deviate from a course of mutual help useful for both parties, lest one of them should aim at increasing his share in the whole and at being the gainer in all respects.

First and foremost there should be no swindling in buying and selling, and only the usual and habitually recognized profits should be sought. Conditions have been laid down under which the contract becomes valid, and swindling, even if it consists in mere words, has been forbidden, as is well known.

Then there is the law of four trustees. It is manifest in what way it is just and equitable. For the trustee who keeps a deposit gratuitously and derives no advantage whatever from this business and merely exercises charity is not responsible for anything, and every accident that may happen is borne by the purse of the owner of the property. A borrower who has all the advantage, whereas the owner of the property exercises charity with regard to him, is responsible for everything, and all accidents that may happen are paid for out of the purse of the borrower. As for him who takes charge of a deposit in consideration of a salary and the lessor, each one of them, I mean the trustee and the owner of the property, participates in the advantage; therefore damages from accidents are divided between them. Those that are due to lack of care in keeping watch are paid for out of the purse of the trustee as when the thing is stolen or lost, for the fact of theft or loss shows that he had neglected measures of great prudence and exceeding precautions. On the other hand, damages from such accidents as can be prevented by no device—as when the beast that has been lent is crippled or carried off or died, that is, when circumstances are beyond one's control—are borne by the purse of the owner of the property.

Then exceeding kindness is shown to the hired man because of his poverty, and it has been commanded that he receive his wages promptly and that he should in no way be cheated out of his due; I mean that he should be recompensed according to the value of his service. It is a matter of pity for him that he or even a beast must not be prevented from eating some of the food on which they work, according to the statutes of this Law.

The statutes concerning property also comprise inheritance. Herein is involved an excellent moral quality, I mean that a man should not withhold a good thing from one deserving it. Accordingly when he is going to die, he should not begrudge his heir and squander his property. On the contrary, he should leave it to him who among all the people deserves it most, namely, to his next of kin: *Unto his kinsman that is next to him of his family. . . .*

CHAPTER 53

This chapter includes an interpretation of the meaning of three terms that we have need of interpreting: namely, ḥesed [loving-kindness], mishpat [judgment], and ṣedaqah [righteousness].

. . . the meaning of ḥesed is excess in whatever matter excess is practiced. In most cases, however, it is applied to excess in beneficence. Now it is known that beneficence includes two notions, one of them consisting in the exercise of beneficence toward one who has no right at all to claim this from you, and the other consisting in the exercise of beneficence toward one who deserves it, but in a greater measure than he deserves it. In most cases the prophetic books use the word ḥesed in the sense of practicing beneficence toward one who has no right at all to claim this from you. . . .

The word ṣedaqah is derived from ṣedaq, which means justice; justice being the granting to everyone who has a right to something, that which he has a right to and giving to every being that which corresponds to his merits. . . .

As for the word mishpat, it means judgment concerning what ought to be done to one who is judged, whether in the way of conferring a benefit or of punishment.

Thus it has been summarized that ḥesed is applied to beneficence taken absolutely; ṣedaqah, to every good action performed by you because of a moral virtue with which you perfect your soul; and mishpat sometimes has as its consequence punishment and sometimes the conferring of a benefit.

CHAPTER 54

The term wisdom [ḥokhmah] is applied in Hebrew in four senses. It is applied to the apprehension of true realities, which have for their end the apprehension of Him, may He be exalted. It says: But wisdom, where shall it be found? and so on. It says: If thou seek her as silver, and so on. This usage is frequent. The term is applied to acquiring arts, whatever the art might be: And every wise-hearted among you; And all the women that were wise-hearted. It is applied to acquiring moral virtues: And teach his elders wisdom; Is wisdom with aged men?—for the thing that is acquired through mere old age is a disposition to achieve moral virtues. It is applied to the aptitude for stratagems and ruses: Come, let us deal wisely with them. According to this meaning it says: And fetched thence a wise woman, meaning thereby that she had an aptitude for stratagems and ruses. In this sense it is said: They are wise to do evil. . . . It has accordingly become plain that the term wise can be applied to one possessing the rational virtues, to one possessing the moral virtues, to everyone skilled in a practical art, and to one possessing ruses in working evil and wickedness. According to this explanation, one who knows the whole of the Law in its true reality is called wise in two respects: in respect of the rational virtues comprised in the Law and in respect of the moral virtues included in it. But since the rational matter in the Law is received through tradition and is not demonstrated by the methods of speculation, the knowledge of the Law came to be set up in the books of the prophets and the sayings of the Sages as one separate species and wisdom, in an unrestricted sense, as another species. It is through this wisdom, in an unrestricted sense, that the rational matter that we receive from the Law through tradition, is demonstrated. All the texts that you find in the [scriptural] books that extol wisdom and speak of its wonder and of the rarity of those who acquire it—Not many are wise; But wisdom, where shall it be found? and so on; and many other texts of this kind—treat of that wisdom which teaches us to demonstrate the opinions of the Torah. This is also frequent in the sayings of the Sages, may their memory be blessed; I mean that they set up the knowledge of the Torah as one separate species and wisdom as another species. . . . It has thus become clear to you that, according to them, the science of the Torah is one species and wisdom is a different species, being the verification of the opinions of the Torah through correct speculation. After we have made all these preliminary remarks, hear what we shall say:

The ancient and the modern philosophers have made it clear that the perfections to be found in man consist of four species. The first and the most defective, but with a view to which the people of the earth spend their lives, is the perfection of possessions—that is, of what belongs to the individual in the manner of money, garments, tools, slaves, land, and other things of this kind. A man's being a great king also belongs to this species of perfection. Between this perfection and the individual himself there is no union whatever; there is only a certain relation, and most of the pleasure taken in the relation is purely imaginary. I refer to one's saying: This is my house; this is my slave; this money is mine; these are my soldiers. For if he considers his own individual self, he will find that all this is outside his self and that each of these possessions subsists as it is by itself. Therefore when the relation referred to has been abolished, there is no difference between an individual who has been a great king and the most contemptible of men, though nothing may have changed in any of the things that were attributed to him. The philosophers have explained that the endeavor and the efforts directed by man toward this kind of perfection are nothing but an effort with a view to something purely imaginary, to a thing that has no permanence. And even if these possessions should remain with him permanently during the whole of his life, he would by no means thereby achieve perfection in his self.

The second species has a greater connection than the first with the individual's self, being the perfection of the bodily constitution and shape—I refer to that individual's temperament being most harmonious, his limbs well proportioned and strong as they ought to be. Neither should this species of perfection be taken as an end, for it is a corporeal perfection and does not belong to man qua man, but qua animal; for man has this in common with the lowest animals. Moreover even if the strength of a human individual reached its greatest maximum, it would not attain the strength of a strong mule, and still less the strength of a lion or an elephant. The end of this perfection consists, as we have mentioned, in man's transporting a heavy burden or breaking a thick bone and in other things of this kind, from which no great utility for the body may be derived. Utility for the soul is absent from this species of perfection.

The third species is a perfection that to a greater extent than the second species subsists in the individual's self. This is the perfection of the moral virtues. It consists in the individual's moral habits having attained their ultimate excellence. Most of the commandments serve no other end than the attainment of this species of perfection. But this species of perfection is likewise a preparation for something else and not an end in itself. For all moral habits are concerned with what occurs between a human individual and someone else. This perfection regarding moral habits is, as it were, only the disposition to be useful to people; consequently it is an instrument for someone else. For if you suppose a human individual is alone, acting on no one, you will find that all his moral virtues are in vain and without employment and unneeded, and that they did not perfect the individual in anything; for he only needs them and they again become useful to him in regard to someone else.

The fourth species is the true human perfection; it consists in the acquisition of the rational virtues —I refer to the conception of intelligibles, which teach true opinions concerning the divine things. This is in true reality the ultimate end; this is what gives the individual true perfection, a perfection belonging to him alone; and it gives him permanent perdurance; through it man is man. If you consider each of the three perfections mentioned before, you will find that they pertain to others than you, not to you, even though, according to the generally accepted opinion, they inevitably pertain both to you and to others. This ultimate perfection, however, pertains to you alone, no one else being associated in it with you in any way: *They shall be only thine own,* and so on. Therefore you ought to desire to achieve this thing, which will remain permanently with you, and not weary and trouble yourself for the sake of others, O you who neglect your own soul so that its whiteness has turned into blackness through the corporeal faculties having gained dominion over it—as is said in the beginning of the poetical parables that have been coined for these notions; it says: *My mother's sons were incensed against me; they made me keeper of the vineyards; but mine own vineyard have I not kept.* It says on this very same subject: *Lest thou give thy splendor unto others, and thy years unto the cruel.*

The prophets too have explained to us and interpreted to us the selfsame notions—just as the philosophers have interpreted them—clearly stating to us that neither the perfection of possession nor the perfection of health nor the perfection of moral habits is a perfection of which one should be proud or that one should desire; the perfection of which one should be proud and that one should desire is knowledge of Him, may He be exalted, which is the true science. Jeremiah says concerning these four perfections: *Thus saith the Lord: Let not the wise man glory in his wisdom, neither let the mighty man glory in his might, let not the rich man glory in his riches; but let him that glorieth glory in this, that he understandeth and knoweth Me.* Consider how he mentioned them according to the order given them in the opinion of the multitude. For the greatest perfection in their opinion is that of the rich man in his riches, below him the mighty man in his might, and below him the wise man in his wisdom. [By the expression, "the wise man in his wisdom,"] he means him who possesses the moral virtues; for such an individual is also held in high esteem by the multitude, to whom the discourse in question is addressed. Therefore these perfections are arranged in this order. The Sages, may their memory be blessed, apprehended from this verse the very notions we have mentioned and have explicitly stated that which I have explained to you in this chapter: namely, that the term *wisdom* [ḥokhmah], used in an unrestricted sense and regarded as the end, means in every place the apprehension of Him, may He be exalted; that the possession of the treasures acquired, and competed for, by man and thought to be perfection are not a perfection; and that similarly all the actions prescribed by the Law—I refer to the various species of worship and also the moral habits that are useful to all people in their mutual dealings—that all this is not to be compared with this ultimate end and does not equal it, being but preparations made for the sake of this end. Hear verbatim a text of theirs dealing with all these notions; it is a text in Bereshith Rabbah. It is said there: *One scriptural dictum says: And all things desirable are not to be compared unto her. Another scriptural dictum says: And all things thou canst desire are not to be compared unto her. The expression, things desirable, refers to commandments and good actions; while, things thou canst desire, refers to precious stone and pearls. Neither things desirable nor things thou canst desire are to be compared unto her, but let him that glorieth glory in this, that he understandeth and knoweth Me.* . . .

As we have mentioned this verse and the wondrous notions contained in it, and as we have mentioned the saying of the Sages, may their memory be blessed, about it, we will complete the exposition of what it includes. For when explaining in this verse the noblest ends, he does not limit them only to the apprehension of Him, may He be exalted. . . . But he says that one should glory in the apprehension of Myself and the knowledge of My attributes, by which he means His actions, as we have made clear with reference to its dictum: *Show me now Thy ways,* and so on. In this verse he makes it clear to us that those actions that ought to be known and imitated are loving-kindness, judgment, and righteousness. He adds another corroborative notion through saying, *in the earth*—this being a pivot of the Law. For matters are not as the overbold opine who think that His providence, may He be exalted, terminates at the sphere of the moon and that the earth and that which is in it are neglected: *The Lord hath forsaken the earth.* Rather is it as has been made clear to us by the Master of those who know: *That the earth is the Lord's.* He means to say that His providence also extends over the earth in the way that corresponds to what the latter is, just as His providence extends over the heavens in the way that corresponds to what they are. This is what he says: *That I am the Lord who exercises loving-kindness, judgment, and righteousness, in the earth.* Then he completes the notion by saying: *For in these things I delight, saith the Lord.* He means that it is My purpose that there should come from you loving-kindness, righteousness, and judgment in the earth in the way we have explained with regard to the thirteen attributes: namely, that the purpose should be assimilation to them and that this should be our way of life. Thus the end that he sets forth in this verse may be stated as follows: It is clear that the perfection of man that may truly be gloried in is the one acquired by him who has achieved, in a measure corresponding to his capacity, apprehension of Him, may He be exalted, and who knows His providence extending over His creatures as manifested in the act of bringing them into being and in their governance as it is. The way of life of such an individual, after he has achieved this apprehension, will always have in view loving-kindness, righteousness, and judgment, through assimilation to His actions, may He be exalted, just as we have explained several times in this Treatise. . . .

SUFIS

Sufism distills a tendency to mysticism native to Islam into a way of life. A mystic is one who claims to have had—or believes it possible to have—direct, unmediated experience of God. This is the goal of the Sufi. Islamic philosophers such as al-Farabi and Avicenna see the daily affairs of men and cities as suffused with religious importance. Daily prayer and other activities are reminders of God's presence. But Sufis want to experience God immediately, not through activities such as prayer. Sufi mystics seek an intensely powerful experience requiring the virtual annihilation of the personality so that the seeker can enter union with God. They want to become one with God. Some Sufi mystics express this identification with God with utterances of praise in the first person, such as "How great is My Majesty!" (Abu Yazid) or "I am the Truth" (al-Hallaj). Such exclamations express, with admirable concision, praise for the godhead and, in the same breath, the intimacy of the personal union the speaker has achieved. There is no longer any difference between the speaker and God. For the speakers and for Sufi believers, these statements reflect passionate devotion to God.

Orthodox Muslims considered both of these men blasphemers, however; both were executed. Still, although at various times in its history the relations between the Sufi movement and the orthodoxy have been dangerously tenuous, the movement has endured for over a thousand years. Today, there is a Sufi world headquarters in Geneva and a Sufi journal.

Sufism grew out of ascetic disciplines already in practice in the Muslim world. Ascetics renounce earthly pleasures and worldly success to devote themselves entirely to worship. Ascetic practices usually call for self-imposed deprivations and discomforts, such as frequent fasting, voluntary poverty, long periods of solitude and meditation, and sometimes self-inflicted injury. Ascetics endure such rigors in the belief that only in the face of such discomforts can they really turn away from this world and themselves toward the divine. The name *Sufi* comes from a discipline early Islamic ascetics imposed on themselves: wearing a simple garment made of coarse wool, or *suf.* (Another possible source for the name is the Arabic word for purity, *sufa*). Sufism developed from these earlier ascetic practices partly through the infusion of Neoplatonic mystical speculation and partly in reaction against the unabashed pursuit of wealth and outward splendor by those who inherited the church from Muhammad.

Gradually, Sufi asceticism became less severe and more contemplative. Sometime in the thirteenth century, Jalal al-Din Rumi introduced ecstatic whirling dances into a sect of Sufism; the dancers came to be known as "whirling dervishes."

The doctrines of Sufism are hard to categorize philosophically. Most Sufi writing is meditational, not dialectical; that is, the Sufis do not in general anticipate and defend skeptical challenges to their view. There is certainly a Sufist metaphysics, similar in language and general scheme to Neoplatonic metaphysics. Yet, presenting this system is not very important for the Sufis. The speculative activity of demonstration, with reasoned argument based on sure premises, is not the way to attain the kind of union the Sufist wants. The Sufi writers depend far more often on parable or metaphor to teach. Many write, very beautifully, in verse. The Sufis try to purify their desire to behold God. Many of their writings try to stimulate the seeker's ardor; few, however, are well-suited as responses to genuinely skeptical challenges.

Sufi ethical philosophy presents a paradox. In many ways, Sufism makes the most relentless demands of any ethical system presented in this book. The devotees seek constantly to purify themselves internally; the state of their character becomes their only concern, their life's work. Yet, this most demanding ethic is one of renunciation. The Sufis are not primarily concerned with justice or moral conduct toward others. Rather, they renounce all affairs of the world; they spurn good works; they direct attention inward. This renunciation is so complete that ordinary concern for one's bodily limbs is considered polytheism.

Seekers pass through many stages of meditation. Sufi writers work these out with some precision—and with a language technical enough to provide common terms to writers separated in time by centuries. Within various stages are norms the Sufi must follow. The exemplars of some of the Sufi virtues of piety and quietism are also of ethical significance.

The Sufi writers represented here, along with the dates of their deaths, are as follows:

- Rabi'a al-'Adawiyya (801), born in Basra, was kidnapped and sold as a slave when she was a young child. Her master freed her because of her great religious devotion. She devoted the rest of her life to mysticism, becoming one of the earliest and most influential Sufis.

- Abu 'Abdallah a.b. 'Asim al-Antaki (835) lived in Antioch, Syria. He wrote many tracts on mysticism; he was known as the "Explorer of Hearts."

- Harith b. Asad al-Muhasibi (857), born in Basra, studied theology—Christian, Jewish, and Islamic—as well as philosophy in Baghdad. He was a great teacher of Sufism.

- Abu Yazid Tayfur al-Bistami (875), born in Bistam, Persia, was an early and influential Sufi.

- Abu Nasr al-Sarraj (988), born in Tus, travelled widely to discuss mystical topics with Sufis. He was one of the first Sufi writers to try to outline his views systematically.

- Abu Bakr al-Kalabadhi (995) lived in Bukhara and wrote an authoritative textbook on Sufism.

- Abu Talib al-Makki (996) lived and taught in Mecca, Basra, and Baghdad. He wrote an early treatise on Sufism, *The Food of Hearts*.

- Abu Sa'id b. Abi'l-Khayr (1048), born in Mayhana, Khurasan, converted to Sufism in his youth and wrote many mystical poems.

- Abu'l-Hasan al-Jullabi al-Hujwiri (1079), born in Ghazna, Afghanistan, died in Lahore, Pakistan. He traveled widely to study Sufism and wrote *The Unveiling of the Veiled,* in Persian, to set forth Sufi doctrine.

- Abu Hamid al-Ghazali (1111) was born in Tus, in Khurasan. A skeptic, al-Ghazali criticized rational attempts to understand God in his book *The Incoherence of the Philosophers* (attacked by Averroës in a book he entitled *The Incoherence of the Incoherence*). Al-Ghazali established a Sufi convent and wrote a series of treatises on Sufism.

- Abu'l-Majdud b. Adam Sana'i (1150) was born in Ghazna, Afghanistan. As a young man, he renounced the world and became a Sufi. He wrote many religious poems and is considered one of Persia's greatest poets.

- 'Abd al-Qadir Jilani (1166), from Baghdad, founded the Qadiriyya order of Sufism.

- Shihab al-Din Suhrawardi Halabi al-Maqtul (1191) studied in Baghdad, became a Sufi, and settled in Aleppo, living the life of a Sufi philosopher. Saladin executed him as a heretic.

- Farid al-Din 'attar (1229) was born near Nishapur, a famous center of Sufi mysticism. He gave up his profession as a druggist (*'attar*) to become a Sufi. He studied Sufism for thirty-nine years, during which he traveled extensively and wrote Sufi literature.

- 'Umar ibn al-Farid (1235), born in Cairo, Egypt, converted to Sufism as a young man and spent much time meditating in the mountains. He spent fifteen years in Mecca; upon his return to Egypt he was hailed as a saint, and he remains the greatest of Arab mystical poets.

- Mahmud Shabistari (1320) lived in Tabriz during the Mongol conquests of much of west Asia.

- 'Abd al-Rahman Jami (1492), born in Jam, Khurasan, lived in Herat and became a famous poet.

- 'Abd al-Wahhab al-Sha'rani, or al-Sha'rawi (1565), an Egyptian, founded an order of Sufis. He led a life of denial during the Turkish occupation of Egypt.

The Nature of God

al-Ghazali (1111)

All that we behold and perceive by our senses bears undeniable witness to the existence of God and His power and His knowledge and the rest of His attributes, whether these things be manifested or hidden, the stone and the clod, the plants and the trees, the living creatures, the heavens and the earth and the stars, the dry land and the ocean, the fire and the air, substance and accident, and indeed we ourselves are the chief witness to Him . . . but just as the bat sees only at night, when the light is veiled by darkness, and cannot therefore see in the daytime, because of the weakness of its sight, which is dazzled by the full light of the sun, so also the human mind is too weak to behold the full glory of the Divine Majesty.

God is One, the Ancient of Days, without prior, Eternal, having no beginning, Everlasting, having no end, continuing for evermore. . . . He is the First and the Last, the transcendent and the immanent, Whose wisdom extendeth over all. . . . He cannot be likened to anything else that exists nor is anything like unto Him, nor is He contained by the earth or the heavens, for He is exalted far above the earth and the dust thereof. . . . The fact of His existence is apprehended by men's reason and He will be seen as He is by that gift of spiritual vision, which He will grant unto the righteous, in the Abode of Eternity, when their beatitude shall be made perfect by the vision of His glorious Countenance.

He is the exalted, Almighty, puissant, Supreme, Who slumbereth not nor sleepeth: neither mortality nor death have dominion over Him. His is the power and the kingdom and the glory and the majesty and to Him belongs creation and the rule over what He has created: He alone is the Giver of life, He is Omniscient, for His knowledge encompasseth all things, from the deepest depths of the earth to the highest heights of the heavens. Not the smallest atom in the earth or the heavens, but is known unto Him, yea, He is aware of how the ants creep upon the hard rock in the darkness of the night: He perceives the movement of the mote in the ether. He beholds the thoughts which pass through the minds of men, and the range of their fancies and the secrets of their hearts, by His knowledge, which was from aforetime. All that is other than Him—men and jinns, angels and Satan, the heavens and the earth, animate beings, plants, inorganic matter, substance and accident, what is intelligible and what is sensible—all were created by His power out of non-existence. He brought them into being, when as yet they had no being, for from eternity He alone existed and there was no other with Him.

Sana'i (1150)

No mind can attain to a knowledge of the Absolute God: the reason and the soul cannot know His Perfection, the mind is dazzled by His Majesty, the eye of the soul is blinded by His perfect Beauty. The imagination is incapable of realising the glory of His Essence: the understanding is unable to interpret His Nature and its mode of being. The soul is but a servant in His train and reason a pupil in His school. What is reason in this temporal world? Only one who writes crookedly the script of God.

Suhrawardi (1191)

The essence of the First Absolute Light, God, gives constant illumination, whereby it is manifested and it brings all things into existence, giving life to them by its rays. Everything in the world is derived from the Light of His Essence and all beauty and perfection are the gift of His bounty, and to attain fully to this illumination is salvation.

From the stage of "I" the seeker passes to the stage of "I am not" and "Thou art", and then to the stage of "I am not and Thou art not", for he is now himself one with the One. The vision of God and the reception of His Light mean unification . . . and union . . . with His Essence, Who is the Light of lights.

. . . It is necessary that you know Him, after this fashion, not by learning . . . nor by intellect, nor by understanding, nor by imagination, nor by sense, nor by the outward eye nor by the inward eye, nor by perception. By Himself He sees Himself and by Himself He knows Himself. . . . His veil, that is, phenomenal existence, is but the concealment of His existence in His oneness, without any attribute. . . . There is no other and there is no existence for any other, than He. . . . He whom you think to be other than God, he is not other than God, but you do not know Him and do not understand that you are seeing Him. . . .

When the mystery—of realising that the mystic is one with the Divine—is revealed to you, you will understand that you are no other than God and that you have continued and will continue . . . without when and without times. Then you will see all your actions to be His actions and all your attributes to be His attributes and your essence to be His essence, though you do not thereby become He or He you, in either the greatest or the least degree. "Everything is perishing save His Face," that is, there is nothing except His Face, "then, whithersoever you turn, there is the Face of God."

Just as he who dies the death of the body, loses all his attributes, both those worthy of praise and those worthy of condemnation alike, so in the spiritual death all attributes, both those worthy of praise and those to be condemned, come to an end, and in all the man's states what is Divine comes to take the place of what was mortal. Thus, instead of his own essence, there is the essence of God and in place of his own qualities, there are the attributes of God. He who knows himself sees his whole existence to be the Divine existence, but does not realise that any change has taken place in his own nature or qualities. For when you know yourself, your "I-ness" vanishes and you know that you and God are one and the same.

The Goal of the Mystic

al-Bistami (875)

For thirty years God Most High was my mirror, now I am my own mirror and that which I was I am no more, for "I" and "God" represents polytheism, a denial of His Unity. Since I am no more, God Most High is His own mirror. Behold, now I say that God is the mirror of myself, for with my tongue He speaks and I have passed away.

al-Din'attar (1229)

One night, the moths gathered together, tormented by the longing to unite themselves with the candle. They all said: "We must find someone to give us news of that for which we long so earnestly."

One of the moths then went to a castle afar off and saw the light of a candle within. He returned and told the others what he had seen and began to describe the candle as intelligently as he could. But the wise moth, who was the chief of their assembly, said: "He has no real information to give us about the candle." Another moth then visited the candle and passed close to the light, drawing near to it and touching the flames of that which he desired, with his wings: the heat of the candle drove him back and he was vanquished. He, too, came back and revealed something of the mystery, explaining something of what union with the candle meant, but the wise moth said to him: "Your explanation is really worth no more than your comrade's was."

A third moth rose up, intoxicated with love, and threw himself violently into the candle's flame. He hurled himself forward and stretched out his antennae towards the fire. As he entered completely into its embrace, his members became glowing red like the flame itself. When the wise moth saw from afar that the candle had identified the moth with itself and had given the moth its own light, he said: "This moth has fulfilled his desire, but he alone understands that to which he has attained. None other knows it and that is all."

In truth, it is the one who has lost all knowledge and all trace of his own existence who has, at the same time, found knowledge of the Beloved. So long as you will not ignore your own body and soul, how will you ever know the Object you love?

Now I am made one with Thee and from that Union my heart is consumed with rapture and my tongue is all bewildered. By union, I have been merged in the Unity, I am become altogether apart from all else. I am Thou and Thou art I—nay, not I, all is altogether Thou. I have passed away, "I" and "Thou" no more exist. We have become one and I have become altogether Thou.

By union with Thee, I have become the perfected gnostic and now the gnostic has vanished away and I have become altogether the Creative Truth. I am free from both pride and passion and desire. I reveal the Divine Mysteries and thereby I fill the lovers of God throughout the world with amazement and a hundred thousand creatures remain astonished at me. All forms are consumed in the flames, when the candle of Union with Him is set alight and blazes up.

When the paintings are hidden, thou wilt see the Painter.

O brother, I will tell you the mystery of mysteries. Know, then, that painting and Painter are one! When your faith is made perfect, you will never see yourself, save on Him.

al-Farid (1235)

Let my passionate love for Thee overwhelm me and have pity on the blazing flames of my heart's love for Thee. If I ask to see Thee unveiled, bestow on me that which I ask and answer me not: "Thou shalt not see Me." O heart, thou hast promised me to have patience in thy love, beware, then, of being straitened and wearied. Love is life itself, and to die of love will give the right to be forgiven.

Say to those who went before me and those who will come after me and to those who are with me now, who have seen my grief, "Learn from me and follow in my steps: listen to me and tell of my passion among mankind."

I have been alone with the Beloved and we shared secrets which meant more than the breeze when night comes. Then the Vision I had hoped for was revealed to my sight, and made me known to men, when I had been unknown. The sight of His beauty and His Majesty bewildered me and in my ecstasy, my tongue could no more speak. Look upon the fairness of His Face and you will find all beauty pictured in it and if all beauty were found in a face and it seemed perfect, beholding Him, it would say: "There is no God but He and He is Most Great."

Shabistari (1320)

Who is the traveller on the road to God? It is that one who is aware of his own origin. . . . He is the traveller who passes on speedily: he has become pure from self as flame from smoke. Go you, sweep out the dwelling-room of your heart, prepare it to be the abode and home of the Beloved: when you go out, He will come in. Within you, when you are free from self, He will show His Beauty. . . .

When you and your real self become pure from all defilement, there remains no distinction among things, the known and the knower are all one.

But union with God is far from created things. To be His friend is to become a stranger to oneself. When it becomes possible for the contingent to pass away, nothing but the essential remains. Unity is like a sea. . . . look and see how a drop from that ocean has found so many forms and has been given so many names, mist and water and rain and dew and clay, plant, animal and finally, man in his perfection. All come from one drop, at the last as at the first: from that drop all these things were fashioned. . . . The phantoms pass away: in one moment there remains—in all places—only the Creative Truth. At that moment of time you come near to Him: parted from self, you can join the Beloved. In God there is no duality. In the Presence "I" and "we" and "you" do not exist. "I" and "you" and "we" and "He" become one. . . . Since in the Unity there is no distinction, the Quest and the Way and the Seeker become one. . . .

One, though in counting it be used of necessity, yet becomes no more than one by the counting. How can you doubt that this is like a dream: that beside Unity, duality is just a delusion? The differences that appear and the apparent multiplicity of things come from the chameleon of contingency. Since the existence of each of them is One, they bear witness to the Unity of the Creative Truth.

Everything which is manifest in this world is like a reflection from that world: it is like a curling lock and a beard and a mole and an eyebrow, for everything in its own place is good. The manifestation of the Divine Glory sometimes comes through Beauty and at another time through Majesty. The Divine world is infinite: how can finite words reach unto it? All these mysteries, which are known only by direct experience. . . . how can they be explained by human speech? When the gnostics interpret these mysteries, it is by symbols that they are interpreted.

Wine and lamp and the beloved are symbols of the One Reality, Who in every form, is manifested in His glory. Wine and lamp are the light and the direct experience of the knower. Contemplate the Beloved, Who is hidden from no one. Drink for a while the wine of ecstasy: perhaps it may save you from the power of self. Yes, I tell you, drink this wine that it may save you from yourself and lead the essence of the drop into the ocean.

To become a haunter of taverns is to be set free from self: egotism is infidelity, even though one seem to be devout. The tavern belongs to the world beyond compare, the abode of lovers who fear nothing. The tavern is the place where the bird of the spirit makes its nest: the tavern is the sanctuary of God Himself.

Jami (1492)

O Thou, by Whom the souls of lovers are refreshed, by Whom new life is given to their tongues, upon the world has Thy protection fallen: all who are fair of face owe their fairness to Thee. All talk of beauty and of love comes from Thee and, in truth, both lover and beloved are of Thy making. Before Thee, the beauty of mortals is a veil, but Thou hast veiled Thy Face, and that Beauty is derived from itself. Thou has veiled Thyself, as a bride is veiled, and none can see Thee or know Thee. When wilt Thou cease to torment us with this veil?

Once Thou didst withdraw this veil and wast revealed and now again Thou art showing Thy face and Thou dost bid us, as we look upon Thee, to pass away from self and to discriminate no more between what we think to be good or ill. As Thy lover, may Thy light be shed upon me so that I may see Thee in all things. Thou hast Thy place in all forms of truth and in the forms of created things there is none but Thou. Wheresoever I look, in all that I behold, throughout the world I see none but Thee.

It surely behoves you to make an effort and to turn away from self, and turn your face towards the Absolute Reality, and concern yourself with Him, Who is the Creative Truth. You must know that created things, in their different types, are all of them means whereby His Beauty is manifested, and the diverse classes of creatures are all mirrors which reflect His perfection. You must continue to strive in this way, until He dwells in your soul and your own existence passes out of your sight, and if you regard yourself, you are regarding Him, and when you say anything of yourself, you say it of Him.

That which was finite has become infinite and "I am the Truth" is the same as "He is the Truth".

When God Most Glorious manifests His Essence to anyone, that one will find his own essence and his own attributes and his own actions to be utterly absorbed in the light of God's Essence and the Divine attributes and actions and will. He will see his essence to be the Essence of the One and his attributes to be the attributes of God and his action to be the actions of God, because of his complete absorption in union with the Divine; and beyond this stage, there is no further stage of union for man. For when the eye of the soul—the spiritual vision—is rapt away to the contemplation of the Divine Beauty, the light of understanding, whereby we distinguish between things, is extinguished in the dazzling light of the Eternal Essence and the distinction between the temporal and the eternal, the perishable and the imperishable, is taken away.

Sincerity

Rabi'a (801)

One day Rabi'a was seen carrying fire in one hand and water in the other and she was running with speed. They asked her what was the meaning of her action and where she was going. She replied: "I am going to light a fire in Paradise and pour water on to Hell, so that both veils (i.e. hindrances to the true vision of God) may completely disappear from the pilgrims, and their purpose may be sure, and the servants of God may see Him, without any object of hope or motive of fear. What if the hope of Paradise and the fear of Hell did not exist? Not one could worship his Lord or obey Him."

The best thing for the servant, who desires to be near his Lord, is to possess nothing in this world or the next, save Him. I have not served God from fear of Hell, for I should be like a wretched hireling, if I did it from fear: nor from love of Paradise, for I should be a bad servant if I served for the sake of what was given, but I have served Him only for the love of Him and out of desire for Him.

The Neighbour first and then the house: is it not enough for me that I am given leave to worship Him? Even if Heaven and Hell were not, does it not behove us to obey Him? He is worthy of worship without any intermediate motive.

O my Lord, if I worship Thee from fear of Hell, burn me in Hell; and if I worship Thee from hope of Paradise, exclude me thence; but if I worship Thee for Thine own sake, then withhold not from me Thine Eternal Beauty.

The groaning and the yearning of the lover of God will not be satisfied until it is satisfied in the Beloved.

I have made Thee the Companion of my heart,
But my body is available for those who desire its
    company.
And my body is friendly towards its guests,
But the Beloved of my heart is the Guest of my soul.

My peace is in solitude, but my Beloved is always with me. Nothing can take the place of His love and it is the test for me among mortal beings. Whenever I contemplate His Beauty, He is my *miḥrāb,* towards Him is my *qibla*—O Healer of souls, the heart feeds upon its desire and it is the striving towards union with Thee that has healed my soul. Thou art my Joy and my Life to eternity. Thou wast the source of my life, from Thee came my ecstasy. I have separated myself from all created beings: my hope is for union with Thee, for that is the goal of my quest.

al-Sha'rawi (1565)

When the servant has realised that all his actions proceed from his Lord and then he gives himself to meditation on any thing, how can his meditation profit him, for God is regarding his meditation, and indeed all things are under His regard? . . . and a vision of his own shortcomings is more fitting for the servant, for then he can realise what true meditation means.

The end reached by the theologian, is the beginning of the way for the dervish, for the highest stage of the theologian is to be sincere in his knowledge and in what he does for the sake of God, and to show his sincerity in not seeking any reward for what he does; he does not experience anything but this. But this is only the entrance to the Sufi Path, for the seeker: from thence he ascends, according to the grace which is granted him and the part allotted to him. There are stages and states which he must attain all the time he is ascending, until he passes away from his consideration of all this and from himself, into the contemplation of the glory of his Lord.

The servant of God reaches the stage of giving himself to the service of his Lord, through acts of devotion, but only when he has ceased to think of his service, because he is preoccupied with his Lord and is contemplating Him at all times, has he reached true service to God because he is now under the Divine Will, and where else can he find rest?

Then the servant passes on to the stage of steadfastness and realises that this also is a gift from God, Who enables him to be steadfast, and you must know that the result of steadfastness is that the servant ceases to claim or pray for anything, whether the thing which he seeks is his right or whether he has no right to it, whether it is an outward benefit or an inward gift.

Then the servant passes on to the stage of dependence upon God, for those servants of His, who are truly sincere, have come to know that God Most High has appointed all things to Himself and the servant has control over nothing, not even over his own property. He knows that God's judgment is All-wise and All-good.

The servant then passes to the stage of trust in God, and when His servants have reached this stage, they know that power belongs to God and they have no control over the matters which God has appointed to their care. So they are obedient to the command of their Lord, without consideration of why he desires anything, for they know that all He does is Wisdom itself.

The mystic seeks to be one of the people of gnosis concerning God, the gnosis which is the mark of the Sufis, but you must know that knowledge of God concerns His essential attributes (which keep Him apart from us), and His attributes manifested in action. If anyone asserts that he has knowledge of the attributes which belong to the Essence, which are eternal, his assertion is false, because it limits God to what can be conceived by the finite mind, and His Essence is without limit, infinite. There is a door which is closed to man, who is a creature, and it is not fitting that he should try to open it and concern himself with the Creative Truth.

The mystic also seeks to be one of those who are in fellowship with God, but it may be that to see himself in this light only shuts him out from the Presence of His Lord. For you must know that the servant is nearer to fellowship with God, when men shun him than when they accept him. Let the servant beware, lest he is deceived by the satisfaction he has in times of spiritual uplift. I say that delight in fellowship is the result of the grace accorded to the soul. The sincere servant is that one to whom fellowship and its absence are all the same; how can that one have fellowship with the Creative Truth, who does not know Him, nor has any affinity with Him, nor intercourse with Him, who does not frequent His society and has never seen Him? Fellowship can exist only with that one, with whom one is intimate, and intimacy is only with him with whom one has affinity and likeness and to whom one has drawn near, and this can be realised only by experience.

The mystic then seeks to be one of those who worships God, praising Him at all times and in all states, and it may be that to have this vision of himself is a hindrance. For that one who truly praises God Most High is unmindful of all else in His Presence. For all creatures, throughout the universe, glorify God, without weariness and to this, those possessed of revelation, bear witness. I myself have experienced this state from the time of the evening prayer until the first third of the night had passed, and I was listening to the things God has made, praising Him and lifting up their voices until I feared

for my reason: then it was veiled from me by the mercy of God, as a favour, which I recognise. . . . I heard the fish say: "Praise be to the King Most Holy, the Lord of riches and power and strength", and also the animals and the plants likewise, and in all their praises, I heard only this.

Then the mystic aspires to be one of those who merge their will in the Divine Will and this unity with God is not attained in truth except by detachment from all the creatures. For the idea of unity, which the servant has, is not free from defects, and unity with God must be thought of only in regard to Him, without a trace of anything beside Him.

Practical Prescriptions

al-Antaki (835)

Avoid covetousness by preferring contentment: make sure of the sweetness of asceticism by cutting short hope: destroy the motives to desire by despairing altogether of the creatures; secure peace of mind by trust in God . . . : extinguish the fires of desire by the coldness of despair: close the road to pride by the knowledge of assured faith . . . : seek peace of body by finding rest for the heart: secure peace of mind through ceasing to contend and abandoning the search of one's own good. Acquire kindliness by continuous association with those worshippers of God who are also wise, and enlightenment by continuous contrition, the door to which is opened by long reflection, which the habit of reflection is to be acquired in solitary retreat. The most harmful time for speech is when silence would be better for you and the most harmful time for silence is when speech would be more fitting for you and more necessary. That which brings you nearest to God is the abandonment of secret sins, because if you fail inwardly, both your outward and inward acts are made void.

Justice is of two kinds, the outward justice between yourself and the creature, and the inward justice between yourself and God. The road of justice is the road of rectitude, but the road of grace is the road of perfection. The most profitable part of reason is that which makes known to you the grace of God towards you and helps you to give thanks for it and rises up to oppose sensuality. The most profitable part of sincerity is the fact that it keeps you from hypocrisy and affectation and vainglory and that you do not like to be remembered for what you do and that you act without seeking reward for your action from any but God.

The signs of love to God include little exterior devotion but continual reflection and the taste for solitude and silence. When others look at the lover, he does not see them: when he is called, he does not hear: when misfortune comes upon him, he is not grieved, and when success looks him in the face, he does not rejoice. He fears no one, puts hope in no man and makes no request of anyone (save God).

Act, then, as if there were no one on earth but yourself and no one in Heaven but God. All actions are to be guided by knowledge and true knowledge comes through the light of certainty, by which God enlightens the heart of His servant, so that he beholds the things of the spiritual world, and by the power of that light all the veils between him and that world are removed until, at last, by means of that radiance, he attains to contemplation of the Invisible.

al-Muhasibi (857)

What have you to do with delight in this world? It is the prison of the believer and he does not rejoice in it nor find pleasure in it. This world is only an abode of affliction, a place of care and sorrow, as Adam said: "We were begotten of God, as the offspring of God, and Satan has taken us captive through sin." It is not fitting for us to rejoice nor meet for us to do otherwise than weep and be grieved while we are in the abode of captivity and to continue so doing until we return to the abode from which we were taken captive. O my brothers, it is a shameful thing for an intelligent being to rejoice in any of the goods of this world and how should he rejoice in the praise of a man who is vain and deluded? Then understand what I say to you, O servant of God, you who are gratified by praise. Even though your good works were to win for you the friendship of all the birds of the heavens and the wild beasts and the cattle and the reptiles that creep on the earth, and though the angels were to praise you therefor, and men and jinns were all to rejoice

in your company and praise you in what you did, and you were known thereby and your righteousness was commended, what reliance can you or any other place upon that? For it is only when you come to appear before God, that you will know the truth of the matter and whether God is pleased with you or not, and this alone is of consequence to you.

Your pleasure in the sweetness of sweet food you find only in eating it. The pleasure of lust and sensuality is in the thought and pursuit of it, and the pleasure of hypocrisy is in the infection of the heart by it; therefore it is necessary to make the will sound and in all action to contemplate God alone.

al-Sarraj (988)

Renunciation . . . is a noble station and it is the basis of all spiritual progress. It is the first step on the way for those who set their faces towards God, those who seek to consecrate themselves to His service alone, to carry out His Will and to trust completely to Him. That one who does not base his practice of religion on renunciation cannot hope to make any progress therein, for the love of this world leads to all sin, and the renunciation of it leads to all good deeds and to obedience to the Will of God.

Gnosis is fire and faith light, gnosis is ecstasy and faith a gift. The difference between the believer and the gnostic is that the believer sees by the light of God and the gnostic sees by means of God Himself, and the believer has a heart, but the gnostic has no heart: the heart of the believer finds rest in worship, but the gnostic finds no rest save in God. Gnosis is of three kinds, the gnosis of acceptance, the gnosis of reality, and the gnosis of contemplation, and in the gnosis of contemplation, understanding and learning and explanation and disputation pass away.

"Passing away" and "continuance" are two terms which are both applicable to the servant who acknowledges that God is One and who makes the ascent into unification from the stage of the common folk to the stage of the elect. The meaning of "passing away" and "continuance" in its beginning, is the passing away of ignorance into the abiding condition of knowledge and the passing away of disobedience into the abiding state of obedience, and the passing away of indifference into the state of continual worship, and the passing away of the consideration of the actions of the servant, which are temporary, into the vision of the Divine Grace, which is eternal.

al-Kalabadhi (995)

The real meaning of detachment . . . is to be separated outwardly from all possessions and inwardly from what is unreal. It is to take nothing from what belongs to this world, nor to seek anything in exchange for the transitory things which have been renounced, not even eternity itself. That renunciation has been made for the sake of the One True God, for no cause or reason save Him alone—It means also that one's heart should be detached from consideration of different stages and states, in which one remains at different times, and should feel no satisfaction in them or desire for them. The one who breaks the fetters of self-hood, through passing away from self, is the one chosen to approach God and he becomes alone with the One Reality.

al-Makki (996)

Patience has three stages: first, it means that the servant ceases to complain, and this is the stage of repentance: second, he becomes satisfied with what is decreed, and this is the rank of the ascetics: third, he comes to love whatever his Lord does with him and this is the stage of the true friends of God. The beginning of asceticism is concern in the soul for the next world and then the coming into existence of the sweetness of hope in God: and concern for the next world does not enter in until concern for this world goes out, nor does the sweetness of hope enter in until the sweetness of desire has departed. True asceticism means the thrusting out from the heart of all thought of worldly things and the reckoning of them as vanity, and only so will asceticism become perfect. Asceticism leads ultimately to fellowship with God.

Abi'l-Khayr (1048)

If men wish to draw near to God, they must seek Him in the hearts of men. They should speak well of all men, whether present or absent, and if they themselves seek to be a light to guide others, then, like the sun, they must show the same face to all. To bring joy to a single heart is better than to build many shrines for worship, and to enslave one soul by kindness is worth more than the setting free of a thousand slaves.

That is the true man of God, who sits in the midst of his fellow-men, and rises up and eats and sleeps and buys and sells and gives and takes in the bazaars amongst other people, and who marries and has social intercourse with other folk, and yet is never for one moment forgetful of God.

al-Hujwiri (1079)

Human satisfaction is equanimity under the decrees of Fate, whether it holds or whether it gives, and steadfastness of the soul in regarding passing events, whether they are a manifestation of the Divine Majesty . . . or of the Divine Beauty. . . . It is all the same, to the true servant, whether he is in want or receives bounteously, he remains equally satisfied thereby, and whether he be consumed in the fire of the wrath of the Divine Majesty or whether he be illuminated by the light of the mercy of the Divine Beauty, it is all one to him. Both are manifestations of God and whatever comes from Him is altogether good.

The true mystic, in seeing the act, beholds Him Who acts and since the human being, whatever his qualities, whether he be full of faults or free from them, whether he be veiled or whether he has received illumination from God, belongs to God and was created by Him, to quarrel with the human act, is to quarrel with the Divine Agent.

al-Ghazali (1111)

To be a Sufi means to abide continuously in God and to live at peace with men: whoever abides in God and deals rightly with men, treating them with unfailing kindness, is a Sufi. The right attitude towards your fellow-men is that you should not lay burdens upon them according to your own desire, but rather burden yourself according to their desires. In your dealings with others, treat them as you would wish them to treat you, for the faith of God's servant is not made perfect unless he desires for others what he desires for himself.

The rule of the Sufi is that Poverty should be his adornment and Patience his ornament and Satisfaction his steed and Trust his dignity. God alone is sufficient for him: he employs his members in acts of devotion and it may be that he has no desire at all for worldly things, or if he has, only for what suffices for his needs. His heart is free from defilement and from distraction, because of his love for his Lord, and he looks towards Him in his inmost self, committing all things to Him and having fellowship with Him. He does not rely upon anything, nor does he have fellowship with any, save Him Whom he worships, preferring God to all else.

Jilani (1166)

Die, then, to the creatures, by God's leave, and to your passions, by His command, and you will then be worthy to be the dwelling-place of the knowledge of God. The sign of your death to the creatures is that you detach yourself from them and do not look for anything from them. The sign that you have died to your passions is that you no longer seek benefit for yourself, or to ward off injury, and you are not concerned about yourself, for you have committed all things unto God. The sign that your will has been merged in the Divine Will is that you seek nothing of yourself or for yourself—God's Will is working in you. Give yourself up into the hands of God, like the ball of the polo-player, who sends it to and fro with his mallet, or like the dead body in the hands of the one who washes it, or like the child in its mother's bosom.

Sana'i (1150)

Wheresoever you will incline, let it be in accordance with the Divine Spirit within you: do not incline in opposition to it, but soar above the snares of earth, reaching the dwelling-place of the Most High, regarding the borders of the world of spirit with the eye of your Divine being. Abandon vain conceits so that you may find admission to the Court of God, for that mansion of eternity is prepared for you and this temporal world is not your true home—abandon to-day and sacrifice your life for the sake of to-morrow. . . . Arise and leave this base world in order that you may find the One and Only God. Leave behind your body and your life and reason and faith and in His Path find for yourself a soul. If you wish to possess a pearl, O man, leave the desert and walk beside the sea. Strive in the road of God, O soldier: if you are without ambition, you will have no honour, but the man who despises his own body shall ride up on the air like fire. He who through love to God, is like a candle in the Path, like a candle shall be crowned with fire.

Jami (1492)

At the beginning of things, the Beloved unveiled His Beauty, in the solitude of the Invisible World. He placed before Himself the mirror of the invisible; He showed all His Beauty unto Himself, He was, in truth, both Seer and Seen: none except Him had looked upon this world. All was one, there was no duality: there was no assertion of "mine" or "thine". Though He saw the diversity of His attributes to be one and beautiful in His Essence; yet He desired they should manifest to Him in another mirror. It was seemly that every one of His eternal attributes should, after that, be displayed each in a different guise. So He created the life-giving meadows and the garden of the universe, so that, from every bough and flower and leaf therein, His beauty should be manifested, in many different forms.

From that Divine Beauty light shone upon the rose and therewith the nightingale was filled with desire for the rose. From that light the candle was set aflame and everywhere a hundred moths were consumed by its fire. A single ray from its light made the sun ablaze and the lotus raised its head from the water. By that Divine Beauty the face of Layla was made fair and Majnūn was moved to love by every hair of hers. It was that which opened Shirīn's sweet lips and carried away the heart of Parvīz and the soul of Farhad. His Beauty is manifested in every place, and within those things in this world, which are counted fair, but are set behind a veil. Because of the Beloved, the moon of Canaan—Yusuf—lifted up his head and Zulaykha, overcome with love, therewith became distraught. In every veil you see, the Divine Beauty is concealed, making every heart a slave to Him. In love to Him the heart finds its life; in desire for Him, the soul finds its happiness. The heart which loves a fair one here, though it knows it not, is really His lover.

Have a care, lest in error you speak idly, saying that from us is love and from Him is goodness. You are but the mirror, He is the picture reflected in the mirror; you are concealed, He is shown clearly; even if you receive praise for goodness and love, both come from Him and only appear in you. If you will look well, you will see that He is the mirror likewise, not alone the Treasure, but the Treasure-house also. If with discerning eye, you see everything to be good, if you look at that which you have found good, you will find it to be but the reflection of His Face. "I" and "Thou" are of no significance, except as figures of imagination; we have no right to interfere. Better be silent, for this tale has no end, there is none who can describe or interpret Him. It is better that we should be afflicted as lovers, for otherwise we are afflicted, being nothing.

Be the captive of Love in order that you may be truly free—free from coldness and the worship of self—Thousands who were wise and learned, who were strangers to love, have passed on their way. No name is left to them, nothing to proclaim their fame and dignity nor to relate their history in the march of time. Although you may attempt to do a hundred things in this world, only Love will give you release from the bondage of yourself.

PART III South Asia

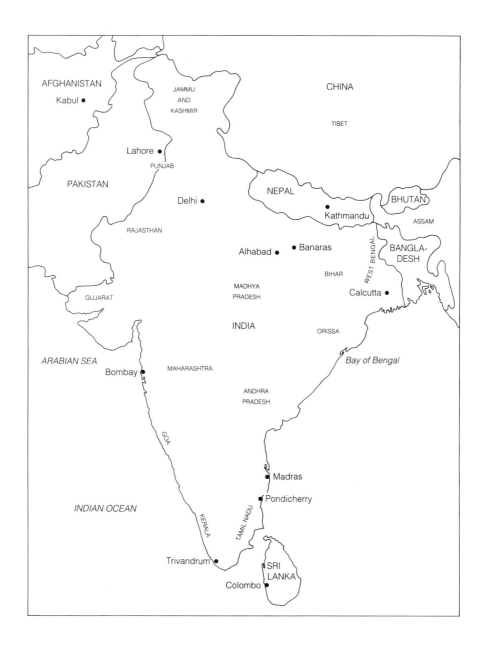

AFGHANISTAN

Kabul •

JAMMU
AND
KASHMIR

CHINA

TIBET

Lahore •

PUNJAB

PAKISTAN

Delhi •

RAJASTHAN

NEPAL

Kathmandu •

BHUTAN

ASSAM

BANGLA-
DESH

Alhabad • • Banaras

WEST BENGAL

BIHAR

MADHYA
PRADESH

Calcutta •

INDIA

ORISSA

ARABIAN SEA

Bombay •

MAHARASHTRA

Bay of Bengal

ANDHRA
PRADESH

GOA

Madras •

Pondicherry •

INDIAN OCEAN

KERALA

TAMIL NADU

Trivandrum •

SRI
LANKA

Colombo •

THE UPANISHADS

Tribes speaking Sanskrit, an Indo-European language similar to Greek and Latin, began migrating to the Indus Valley as early as 1500 B.C.E The sacred literature of these Aryans, as they referred to themselves, is known as the Veda, a collection of poems ranging in content from speculations about the origins of things and stories about the lives of the gods to love poetry and descriptions of nature and of important historical events. The Upanishads are a later collection of writings that came to be appended to the Veda along with other writings. The Upanishads, unlike the root Vedic texts, contain some self-conscious argument. Further, the concerns of the Upanishads are much more explicitly philosophical than the earlier Vedic poetry. The teaching of the Upanishads centers on questions of metaphysics: what is the ultimate reality, what is its nature and relation to the the world, and how can it be known? Within this context, ethical teachings also emerge. The Upanishadic passages below—from the Brihadaranyaka, Chandogya, Taittiriya, Mundaka, Svetas-vatara, and Maitri Upanishads—present ethical dimensions of views about a Supreme Reality termed *Brahman.*

Brahman, said to be the Absolute, is sometimes thought of as God and sometimes as an impersonal Ground of Being. But in all cases, the notion of knowledge, or realization, of Brahman is prominent. Though the several Upanishads do not speak with one voice—they were composed by many authors over many centuries, beginning from about 900 B.C.E.—the claim that mystical knowledge of Brahman is the most worthy goal in life organizes much of the ethical teaching. Brahman is the source, or ground, of all that we find in the world. But the Upanishads teach that the way to attain knowledge of Brahman is not through an understanding of objects presented through our senses but, primarily, through an understanding and deeper appreciation of ourselves, of our own subjectivity.

Some of the passages present ideas about how Brahman is manifest in us and in the concerns of our daily lives. Others present reasons why mystical knowledge of Brahman should be sought or why it occurs through an expanded self-knowledge, or enlightenment. Still others present practical teachings about how to proceed toward enlightenment through self-control, meditation, and yoga.

The practices of yoga figure prominently in much of the later Indian ethical literature of the Hindus, Buddhists, and Jains. The Upanishads are the earliest texts where these practices are spelled out in any detail. Generally, yoga is self-discipline. The yoga taught in the Upanishads seems to grow out of the view that knowledge of Brahman can come only through a thorough self-knowledge that includes mastery of natural desires.

Other theories, particularly psychological theories, bear on the Upanishads' ethical teachings; the views about Brahman, though they are primary, do not solely determine the moral doctrines. The Chandogya Upanishad presents a forerunner of what later came to be known as the theory of karma: roughly, that one reaps what one sows and, further, that one becomes what one does. *Karma* literally means action, and the theory is that the direction of one's action—including the direction of one's efforts at acquiring knowledge and understanding—determines one's status in this lifetime and even in lifetimes to come.

The theory of rebirth also invades the ethical teachings of the Upanishads and, indeed, the very heart of their message, the claim that knowledge of Brahman is the supreme value. Usually, rebirth is seen as undesirable; in fact, knowledge of Brahman is often conceived as liberation from rebirth, as a state removed from all action and becoming. Paradoxically, this state is attained by undertaking certain kinds of action. In some later texts, in the *Bhagavad Gita,* for instance, and in the wisdom literature of Mahayana Buddhism, views about this concept change and develop.

from the Brihadaranyaka Upanishad

Reprinted from The Thirteen Principal Upanishads, *translated from the Sanskrit by Robert Ernest Hume (London: Oxford University Press, 1921).*

CHAPTER 2.4

The Conversation of Yajnavalkya and Maitreyi Concerning the Pantheistic Soul

5. Then said he [Yajnavalkya]: Lo, verily, not for love of the husband is a husband dear, but for love of the Soul (*Atman*) a husband is dear.

   Lo, verily, not for love of the wife is a wife dear, but for love of the Soul a wife is dear.

   Lo, verily, not for love of the sons are sons dear, but for love of the Soul sons are dear.

   Lo, verily, not for love of the wealth is wealth dear, but for love of the Soul wealth is dear.

   Lo, verily, not for love of Brahmanhood is Brahmanhood dear, but for love of the Soul Brahmanhood is dear.

   Lo, verily, not for love of Kshatrahood is Kshatrahood dear, but for love of the Soul Kshatrahood is dear.

   Lo, verily, not for love of the worlds are the worlds dear, but for love of the Soul the worlds are dear.

   Lo, verily, not for love of the gods are the gods dear, but for love of the Soul the gods are dear.

   Lo, verily, not for love of the beings are beings dear, but for love of the Soul beings are dear.

   Lo, verily, not for love of all is all dear, but for love of the Soul all is dear.

   Lo, verily, it is the Soul that should be seen, that should be hearkened to, that should be thought on, that should be pondered on, O Maitreyi. Lo, verily, with the seeing of, with the hearkening to, with the thinking of, and with the understanding of the Soul, this world-all is known.

CHAPTER 4.3

The Various Conditions of the Soul

9. Verily, there are just two conditions of this person: the condition of being in this world and the condition of being in the other world. There is an intermediate third condition, namely, that of being in sleep. By standing in this intermediate condition one sees both those conditions, namely being in this world and being in the other world. Now whatever the approach is to the condition of being in the other world, by making that approach one sees the evils [of this world] and the joys [of yonder world].

The State of Dreaming

When one goes to sleep, he takes along the material of this all-containing world, himself tears it apart, himself builds it up, and dreams by his own brightness, by his own light. Then this person becomes self-illuminated.

10. There are no chariots there, no spans, no roads. But he projects from himself chariots, spans, roads. There are no blisses there, no pleasures, no delights. But he projects from himself blisses, pleasures, delights. There are no tanks there, no lotus-pools, no streams. But he projects from himself tanks, lotus-pools, streams. For he is a creator.

17. Having had enjoyment in this state of waking, having traveled around and seen good and evil, he hastens again, according to the entrance and place of origin, back to dreaming sleep.

18. As a great fish goes along both banks of a river, both the hither and the further, just so this person goes along both these conditions, the condition of sleeping and the condition of waking.

The Soul in Deep, Dreamless Sleep

19. As a falcon, or an eagle, having flown around here in space, becomes weary, folds its wings, and is borne down to its nest, just so this person hastens to that state where, asleep, he desires no desires and sees no dream.

20. Verily, a person has those channels called *hita*; as a hair subdivided a thousandfold, so minute are they, full of white, blue, yellow, green, and red. Now when people seem to be killing him, when they seem to be overpowering him, when an elephant seems to be tearing him to pieces, when he seems to be falling into a hole—in these circumstances he is imagining through ignorance the very fear which he sees when awake. When, imagining that he is a god, that he is a king, he thinks "I am this world-all," that is his highest world.

21. This, verily, is that form of his which is beyond desires, free from evil, without fear. As a man, when in the embrace of a beloved wife, knows nothing within or without, so this person, when in the embrace of the intelligent Soul, knows nothing within or without. Verily, that is his [true] form in which his desire is satisfied, in which the Soul is his desire, in which he is without desire and without sorrow.

22. There a father becomes not a father; a mother, not a mother; the worlds, not the worlds; the gods, not the gods; the Vedas, not the Vedas; a thief, not a thief. There the destroyer of an embryo becomes not the destroyer of an embryo; a Candala [the son of a Sudra father and a Brahman mother] is not a Candala; a Paulkasa [the son of a Sudra father and a Kshatriya mother] is not a Paulkasa; a mendicant is not a mendicant; an ascetic is not an ascetic. He is not followed by good, he is not followed by evil, for then he has passed beyond all sorrows of the heart.

32. An ocean, a seer alone without duality, becomes he whose world is Brahman*, O King!—thus Yajnavalkya instructed him. This is a man's highest path. This is his highest achievement. This is his highest world. This is his highest bliss. On a part of just this bliss other creatures have their living.

* "Brahma," in Hume's translation. Translation altered to "Brahman" throughout this selection. —ED.

from the Chandogya Upanishad

CHAPTER 3.14

The Individual Soul Identical with the Infinite Brahman

1. Verily, this whole world is Brahman. Tranquil, let one worship It as that from which he came forth, as that into which he will be dissolved, as that in which he breathes.

   Now, verily, a person consists of purpose. According to the purpose which a person has in this world, thus does he become on departing hence. So let him form for himself a purpose.

2. He who consists of mind, whose body is life (*prana*), whose form is light, whose conception is truth, whose soul (*atman*) is space, containing all works, containing all desires, containing all odors, containing all tastes, encompassing this whole world, the unspeaking, the unconcerned—[3] this Soul of mine within the heart is smaller than a grain of rice, or a barley-corn, or a mustard-seed, or a grain of millet, or the kernel of a grain of millet; this Soul of mine within the heart is greater than the earth, greater than the atmosphere, greater than the sky, greater than these worlds.

4. Containing all works, containing all desires, containing all odors, containing all tastes, encompassing this whole world, the unspeaking, the unconcerned—this is the Soul of mine within the heart, this is Brahman. Into him I shall enter on departing hence.

CHAPTER 5.10

7. Accordingly, those who are of pleasant conduct here—the prospect is, indeed, that they will enter a pleasant womb, either the womb of a Brahman, or the womb of a Kshatriya, or the womb of a Vaisya. But those who are of stinking conduct here—the prospect is, indeed, that they will enter a stinking womb, either the womb of a dog, or the womb of a swine, or the womb of an outcast (*candala*).

8. But on neither of these ways are the small, continually returning creatures, [those of whom it is said:] "Be born, and die"—theirs is a third state.

   Thereby [it comes about that] yonder world is not filled up.

   Therefore one should seek to guard himself. As to this there is the following verse:—

9. The plunderer of gold, the liquor-drinker,
   The invader of a teacher's bed, the Brahman-killer—
      These four sink downward in the scale,
      And, fifth, he who consorts with them.

CHAPTER 6.1

The Instruction of Svetaketu by Uddalaka Concerning the Key to All Knowledge

The Threefold Development of the Elements and of Man from the Primary Unitary Being

1. *Om!* Now, there was Svetaketu Aruneya. To him his father said: "Live the life of a student of sacred knowledge. Verily, my dear, from our family there is no one unlearned [in the Vedas], a Brahman by connection, as it were."

2. He then, having become a pupil at the age of twelve, having studied all the Vedas, returned at the age of twenty-four, conceited, thinking himself learned, proud.

3. Then his father said to him: "Svetaketu, my dear, since now you are conceited, think yourself learned, and are proud, did you also ask for that teaching whereby what has not been heard of becomes heard of, what has not been thought of becomes thought of, what has not been understood becomes understood?"

4. "How, pray, sir, is that teaching?"

"Just as, my dear, by one piece of clay everything made of clay may be known—the modification is merely a verbal distinction, a name; the reality is just "clay"—

5. Just as, my dear, by one copper ornament everything made of copper may be known—the modification is merely a verbal distinction, a name; the reality is just "copper"—

6. Just as, my dear, by one nail-scissors everything made of iron may be known—the modification is merely a verbal distinction, a name; the reality is just "iron"—so, my dear, is that teaching."

7. "Verily, those honored men did not know this; for, if they had known it, why would they not have told me? But do you, sir, tell me it."

"So be it, my dear," said he.

CHAPTER 6.8

Concerning Sleep, Hunger and Thirst, and Dying

5. . . . understand that this [body] is a sprout which has sprung up. It will not be without a root.

6. Where else could its root be than in water? With water, my dear, as a sprout, look for heat as the root. With heat, my dear, as a sprout, look for Being as the root. All creatures here, my dear, have Being as their root, have Being as their abode, have Being as their support. . . .

When a person here is deceasing, my dear, his voice goes into his mind; his mind, into his breath; his breath, into heat; the heat, into the highest divinity. That which is the finest essence—this whole world has that as its soul.

That is Reality. That is Atman (Soul). That art thou, Svetaketu.

CHAPTER 8.7

The Progressive Instruction of Indra by Prajapati Concerning the Real Self

1. "The Self (Atman), which is free from evil, ageless, deathless, sorrowless, hungerless, thirstless, whose desire is the Real, whose conception is the Real—He should be searched out, Him one should desire to understand. He obtains all worlds and all desires who has found out and who understands that Self."— Thus spake Prajapati.

2. Then both the gods and the devils heard it. Then they said: "Come! Let us search out that Self, the Self by searching out whom one obtains all worlds and all desires!"

Then Indra from among the gods went forth unto him, and Virocana from among the devils. Then, without communicating with each other, the two came into the presence of Prajapati, fuel in hand.

3. Then for thirty-two years the two lived the chaste life of a student of sacred knowledge.

Then Prajāpati said to the two: "Desiring what have you been living?"

Then the two said: "'The Self (Atman), which is free from evil, ageless, deathless, sorrowless, hungerless, thirstless, whose desire is the Real, whose conception is the Real—He should be searched out, Him one should desire to understand. He obtains all worlds and all desires who has found out and who understands that Self.'—Such do people declare to be your words, sir. We have been living desiring Him."

4. Then Prajāpati said to the two: "That Person who is seen in the eye—He is the Self (Atman) of whom I spoke. That is the immortal, the fearless. That is Brahman."

"But this one, sir, who is observed in water and in a mirror—which one is he?"

"The same one, indeed, is observed in all these," said he.

CHAPTER 8.8

1. "Look at yourself in a pan of water. Anything that you do not understand of the Self, tell me."

    Then the two looked in a pan of water.

    Then Prajapati said to the two: "What do you see?"

    Then the two said: "We see everything here, sir, a Self corresponding exactly, even to the hair and fingernails!"

2. Then Prajapati said to the two: "Make your-selves well-ornamented, well-dressed, adorned, and look in a pan of water."

    Then the two made themselves well-ornamented, well-dressed, adorned, and looked in a pan of water.

    Then Prajapati said to the two: "What do you see?"

3. Then the two said: "Just as we ourselves are here, sir, well-ornamented, well-dressed, adorned—so there, sir, well-ornamented, well-dressed, adorned."

    "That is the Self," said he. "That is the immortal, the fearless. That is Brahman."

    Then with tranquil heart the two went forth.

4. Then Prajapati glanced after them, and said: "They go without having comprehended, with-out having found the Self (Ātman). Whosoever shall have such a doctrine, be they gods or be they devils, they shall perish."

    Then with tranquil heart Virocana came to the devils. To them he then declared this doc-trine: "Oneself is to be made happy here on earth. Oneself is to be waited upon. He who makes his own self happy here on earth, who waits upon himself—he obtains both worlds, both this world and the yonder."

5. Therefore even now here on earth they say of one who is not a giver, who is not a believer, who is not a sacrificer, "Oh! devilish!" for such is the doctrine of the devils. They adorn the body of one deceased with what they have begged, with dress, with ornament, as they call it, for they think that thereby they will win yonder world.

CHAPTER 8.9

1. But then Indra, even before reaching the gods, saw this danger: "Just as, indeed, that one [i.e. the bodily self] is well-ornamented when this body is well-ornamented, well-dressed when this is well-dressed, adorned when this is adorned, even so that one is blind when this is blind, lame when this is lame, maimed when this is maimed. It perishes immediately upon the perishing of this body. I see nothing enjoy-able in this."

2. Fuel in hand, back again he came. Then Prajapati said to him, "Desiring what, O Maghavan ('Munificent One'), have you come back again, since you along with Virocana went forth with tranquil heart?"

    Then he said: "Just as, indeed, that one [i.e. the bodily self] is well-ornamented when this body is well-ornamented, well-dressed when this is well-dressed, adorned when this is adorned, even so it is blind when this is blind, lame when this is lame, maimed when this is maimed. It perishes immediately upon the perishing of this body. I see nothing enjoyable in this."

3. "He is even so, O Maghavan," said he. "How-ever, I will explain this further to you. Live with me thirty-two years more."

    Then he lived with him thirty-two years more.

    To him [i.e. to Indra] he [i.e. Prajapati] then said:—

CHAPTER 8.10

1. "He who moves about happy in a dream—he is the Self (Atman)," said he. "That is the immor-tal, the fearless. That is Brahman."

    Then with tranquil heart he [i.e. Indra] went forth.

Then, even before reaching the gods, he saw this danger: "Now, even if this body is blind, that one [i.e. the Self, Atman] is not blind. If this is lame, he is not lame. Indeed, he does not suffer defect through defect of this. [2] He is not slain with one's murder. He is not lame with one's lameness. Nevertheless, as it were, they kill him; as it were, they unclothe him; as it were, he comes to experience what is unpleasant; as it were, he even weeps. I see nothing enjoyable in this."

3. Fuel in hand, back again he came. Then Prajapati said to him: "Desiring what, O Maghavan, have you come back again, since you went forth with tranquil heart?"

Then he said: "Now, sir, even if this body is blind, that one [i.e. the Self] is not blind. If this is lame, he is not lame. Indeed, he does not suffer defect through defect of this. [4] He is not slain with one's murder. He is not lame with one's lameness. Nevertheless, as it were, they kill him; as it were, they unclothe him; as it were, he comes to experience what is unpleasant; as it were, he even weeps. I see nothing enjoyable in this."

"He is even so, O Maghavan," said he. "However, I will explain this further to you. Live with me thirty-two years more."

Then he lived with him thirty-two years more.

To him [i.e. to Indra] he [i.e. Prajapati] then said:—

CHAPTER 8.11

1. "Now, when one is sound asleep, composed, serene, and knows no dream—that is the Self (Atman)," said he. "That is the immortal, the fearless. That is Brahman."

Then with tranquil heart he went forth.

Then, even before reaching the gods, he saw this danger: "Assuredly, indeed, this one does not exactly know himself with the thought 'I am he,' nor indeed the things here. He becomes one who has gone to destruction. I see nothing enjoyable in this."

2. Fuel in hand, back again he came. Then Prajapati said to him: "Desiring what, O

Maghavan, have you come back again, since you went forth with tranquil heart?"

Then he [i.e. Indra] said: "Assuredly, this [self] does not exactly know himself with the thought 'I am he,' nor indeed the things here. He becomes one who has gone to destruction. I see nothing enjoyable in this."

3. "He is even so, O Maghavan," said he. "However, I will explain this further to you, and there is nothing else besides this. Live with me five years more."

Then he lived with him five years more.— That makes one hundred and one years. Thus it is that people say, "Verily, for one hundred and one years Maghavan lived the chaste life of a student of sacred knowledge with Prajapati."—

To him [i.e. to Indra] he [i.e. Prajapati] then said:—

CHAPTER 8.12

1. "O Maghavan, verily, this body is mortal. It has been appropriated by Death (Mrityu). [But] it is the standing-ground of that deathless, bodiless Self (Atman). Verily, he who is incorporate has been appropriated by pleasure and pain. Verily, there is no freedom from pleasure and pain for one while he is incorporate. Verily, while one is bodiless, pleasure and pain do not touch him.

2. "The wind is bodiless. Clouds, lightning, thunder—these are bodiless. Now as these, when they arise from yonder space and reach the highest light, appear each with its own form, [3] even so that serene one, when he rises up from this body and reaches the highest light, appears with his own form. Such a one is the supreme person. There such a one goes around laughing, sporting, having enjoyment with women or chariots or friends, not remembering the appendage of this body. As a draft-animal is yoked in a wagon, even so this spirit is yoked in this body.

4. "Now, when the eye is directed thus toward space, that is the seeing person; the eye is [the instrument] for seeing. Now, he who knows 'Let me smell this'—that is the Self (Atman);

the nose is [the instrument] for smelling. Now, he who knows 'Let me utter this'—that is the Self; the voice is [the instrument] for utterance. Now, he who knows 'Let me hear this'—that is the Self; the ear is [the instrument] for hearing.

5. "Now, he who knows 'Let me think this'—that is the Self; the mind is his divine eye. He, verily, with that divine eye the mind, sees desires here, and experiences enjoyment.

6. "Verily, those gods who are in the Brahman-world reverence that Self. Therefore all worlds and all desires have been appropriated by them. He obtains all worlds and all desires who has found out and who understands that Self (Atman)."

Thus spake Prajapati—yea, thus spake Prajapati!

CHAPTER 2.8

The Knower of the Unity of the Human Person with the Personality in the World Reaches the Self Consisting of Bliss

Both he who is here in a person and he who is yonder in the sun—he is one.

He who knows this, on departing from this world, proceeds on to that self which consists of food, proceeds on to that self which consists of breath, proceeds on to that self which consists of mind, proceeds on to that self which consists of understanding, proceeds on to that self which consists of bliss.

As to that there is also this verse:—

CHAPTER 2.9

The Knower of the Bliss of Brahman is Saved from All Fear and from All Moral Self-Reproach

Wherefrom words turn back,
Together with the mind, not having attained—
The bliss of Brahman he who knows,
Fears not from anything at all.

Such a one, verily, the thought does not torment: "Why have I not done the good? Why have I done the evil?" He who knows this, delivers himself from these two [thoughts]. For truly, from both of these he delivers himself—he who knows this!

Such is the mystic doctrine!

from the Mundaka Upanishad

CHAPTER 3.1

The Way to Brahman

Recognition of the Great Companion, the Supreme Salvation

1. Two birds, fast bound companions,
   Clasp close the self-same tree.
   Of these two, the one eats sweet fruit;
   The other looks on without eating.

2. On the self-same tree a person, sunken,
   Grieves for his impotence, deluded;
   When he sees the other, the Lord, contented,
   And his greatness, he becomes freed from
      sorrow.

3. When a seer sees the brilliant
   Maker, Lord, Person, the Brahman-source,
   Then, being a knower, shaking off good and
      evil,
   Stainless, he attains supreme identity [with
      Him].

Delight in the Soul, the Life of All Things

4. Truly, it is Life that shines forth in all things!
   Understanding this, one becomes a knower.
      There is no superior speaker.
   Having delight in the Soul (Atman), having
      pleasure in the Soul, doing the rites,
   Such a one is the best of Brahman-knowers.

The Pure Soul Obtainable by True Methods

5. This Soul (Atman) is obtainable by truth, by
   austerity,
   By proper knowledge, by the student's life of
      chastity constantly [practised].
   Within the body, consisting of light, pure is He
   Whom the ascetics, with imperfections done
      away, behold.

6. Truth alone conquers, not falsehood.
   By truth is laid out the path leading to the
      gods
   By which the sages whose desire is satisfied
      ascend
   To where is the highest repository of truth.

The Universal Inner Soul

7. Vast, heavenly, of unthinkable form,
   And more minute than the minute, It shines
      forth.
   It is farther than the far, yet here near at hand,
   Set down in the secret place [of the heart],
      even here among those who behold [It].

Obtainable by Contemplation, Purified from Sense

8. Not by sight is It grasped, not even by speech,
   Not by any other sense-organs, austerity, or
      work.
   By the peace of knowledge, one's nature
      purified—
   In that way, however, by meditating, one does
      behold Him who is without parts.

9. That subtle Soul (Atman) is to be known by
      thought
   Wherein the senses fivefoldly have entered.
   The whole of men's thinking is interwoven
      with the senses.
   When that is purified, the Soul (Atman) shines
      forth.

The Acquiring Power of Thought

10. Whatever world a man of purified nature
     makes clear in mind,
     And whatever desires he desires for himself—
     That world he wins, those desires too.
     Therefore he who is desirous of welfare
     should praise the knower of the Soul
     (Atman).

CHAPTER 3.2

Desires as the Cause of Rebirth

1. He knows that Supreme Brahman abode,
   Founded on which the whole world shines
   radiantly.

They who, being without desire, worship the
Person (Purusha)
And are wise, pass beyond the seed [of rebirth]
here.

2. He who in fancy forms desires,
   Because of his desires is born [again] here and
   there.
   But of him whose desire is satisfied, who is a
   perfected soul,
   All desires even here on earth vanish away.

from the Svetasvatara Upanishad

CHAPTER 2

Rules and Results of Yoga

8. Holding his body steady with the three
     [upper parts] erect,
   And causing the senses with the mind to
     enter into the heart,
   A wise man with the Brahman-boat should
     cross over
   All the fear-bringing streams.

9. Having repressed his breathings here in the
     body, and having his movements checked,
   One should breathe through his nostrils with
     diminished breath.
   Like that chariot yoked with vicious horses,
   His mind the wise man should restrain
     undistractedly.

10. In a clean level spot, free from pebbles, fire,
      and gravel
    By the sound of water and other propinquities
    Favorable to thought, not offensive to the eye,
    In a hidden retreat protected from the wind,
      one should practise Yoga.

11. Fog, smoke, sun, fire, wind,
    Fire-flies, lightning, a crystal, a moon—
    These are the preliminary appearances,
    Which produce the manifestation of Brahman
      in Yoga.

12. When the fivefold quality of Yoga has been
      produced,
    Arising from earth, water, fire, air, and space,
    No sickness, no old age, no death has he
    Who has obtained a body made out of the
      fire of Yoga.

13. Lightness, healthiness, steadiness,
    Clearness of countenance and pleasantness of
      voice,
    Sweetness of odor, and scanty excretions—
    These, they say, are the first stage in the
      progress of Yoga.

The Vision of God

14. Even as a mirror stained by dust
    Shines brilliantly when it has been cleansed,
    So the embodied one, on seeing the nature of
      the Soul (Atman),
    Becomes unitary, his end attained, from
      sorrow freed.

15. When with the nature of the self, as with a
      lamp,
    A practiser of Yoga beholds here the nature of
      Brahman,
    Unborn, steadfast, from every nature free—
    By knowing God one is released from all
      fetters!

from the Maitri Upanishad

CHAPTER 6

Liberation into the Real Brahman by Relinquishment of All Desires, Mental Activity, and Self-Consciousness

30. *Om!* One should be in a pure place, himself pure, abiding in pureness, studying the Real, speaking of the Real, meditating upon the Real, sacrificing to the Real. Henceforth, in the real Brahman which longs for the Real, he becomes completely other. So he has the reward of having his fetters cut; becomes void of expectation, freed from fear in regard to others [as fully] as in regard to himself, void of desire. He attains to imperishable, immeasurable happiness, and continues [therein].

Verily, freedom from desire is like the choicest extract from the choicest treasure. For, a person who is made up of all desires, who has the marks of determination, conception, and self-conceit, is bound. Hence, in being the opposite of that, he is liberated.

On this point some say: "It is a quality which by force of the developing differentiation of Nature comes to bind the self with determination [and the like], and that liberation results from the destruction of the fault of determination [and the like]."

[But] it is with the mind, truly, that one sees. It is with the mind that one hears. Desire, conception, doubt, faith, lack of faith, steadfastness, lack of steadfastness, shame, meditation, fear—all this is truly mind.

Borne along and defiled by the stream of Qualities, unsteady, wavering, bewildered, full of desire, distracted, one goes on into the state of self-conceit. In thinking "This is I" and "That is mine" one binds himself with himself, as does a bird with a snare! Hence a person who has the marks of determination, conception, and self-conceit is bound. Hence, in being the opposite of that, he is liberated. Therefore one should stand free from determination, free from conception, free from self-conceit. This is the mark of liberation (*moksa*). This is the pathway to Brahman here in this world. This is the opening of the door here in this world. By it one will go to the farther shore of this darkness, for therein all desires are contained. . . .

THE *YOGASUTRA*

Many systematizations of Upanishadic ideas appear over the centuries. One is the *Yogasutra,* which, although some of its parts date from the Upanishadic era, took its present form about 400 C.E. The *Yogasutra* is ascribed to Patanjali, but like many of the people associated with ancient and even classical texts, we know nothing further about him.

The *Yogasutra* is both a "how-to" book on the practices of self-discipline and a metaphysics centered on a mystical experience that is deemed to be supremely valuable and offers a liberation from rebirth. A distinctive feature of the *Yogasutra's* philosophy is its approach to ethics. Lying, stealing, and causing injury, for example, are prohibited not because they harm others but because they increase one's attachment to the world. Thus, they hinder the attainment of the personal *summum bonum* (the highest good, from which all others derive). Presumably, if these activities were to lead one closer to liberation, they would be good. The *Yogasutra* does not conceive of the reality reached through mystical attainment as Brahman, an omnipresent Absolute, but rather as an individual conscious being, *purusa,* that has been detached from all involvement in the world.

Still, perfect ethical action, like all perfection of will, brings extraordinary powers. All nature can be made subservient to the yogi's will through sustained effort and right practice; however, mastery of one's own thought and inner nature is much more difficult (and valuable) than any outer accomplishment, even the acquisition of powers the world would see as miraculous.

The *Yogasutra* also presents an elaborate theory of karma developed along psychological lines. Every action leaves a trace in the subconscious, a "potency" that impels future action of the same kind; that is, every action creates a habit. Smoking a cigarette, for example, forms a subconscious trace and desire to smoke another. But the action of meditation is special; meditation, at least of a certain kind, is thought to leave no trace and to burn up other traces as well.

from the *Yogasutra*

Reprinted from Patanjali's Yoga Sutras, *translated by Rama Prasada (Allahabad: Panini Office, 1912).*

2.28. On the destruction of impurity by the sustained practice of the accessories of *yoga,* the light of wisdom reaches up to discriminative knowledge.

2.29. Restraint, observance, posture, regulation of breath, abstraction [of the senses], concentration, meditation, and trance are the eight accessories of *yoga.*

2.30. Of these, the restraints (*yama*) are: abstinence from injury (*ahiṁsā*), veracity, abstinence from theft, continence, and abstinence from avariciousness.

2.31. They are the great vow, universal, and not-limited by life-state, space, time, and circumstance.

2.32. The observances are cleanliness, purificatory action, study, and the making of the ever-liberated yogi the object of concentration.*

2.33. Upon thoughts of sin troubling, habituation to the contrary.

2.34. The sins are the causing of injury to others and the rest. They are done, caused to be done, and permitted to be done; they are preceded by desire, anger, and ignorance; they are slight, middling, and intense; their result is an infinity of pain and unwisdom; thus comes the habit of thinking to the contrary.

2.35. [The habit of] not causing injury being confirmed, hostilities are given up in his presence.

* Translation altered. —Ed.

2.36. Veracity being confirmed, action and fruition become dependents.

2.37. [The habit of] not stealing being confirmed, all jewels approach him.

2.38. Continence being confirmed, vigour is obtained.

2.39. Non-covetousness being confirmed, knowledge of the succession of births is obtained.

2.40. By cleanliness is meant disgust with one's body, and cessation of contact with others.

2.41. And upon the essence [of mind] becoming pure, come high-mindedness, one-pointedness, control of the senses, and fitness for the knowledge of the self.

2.42. By contentment, the acquisition of extreme happiness.

2.43. By purificatory actions, the removal of impurity and the attainments of the physical body and the senses.

2.44. By study comes communion with the desired deity.

2.45. The attainment of trance, by making Isvara the motive of all actions.

2.46. Posture is steadily easy.

2.47. By slackening of effort and by thought-transformation as infinite.

2.48. Thence cessation of disturbance from the pairs of opposites.

2.49. Regulation of breath is the stoppage of the inhaling and exhaling movements [of breath] which follows when that has been secured.

2.50. Manifestation as external, internal, and total restraint [of breath] is regulated by place, time, and number; and thus it becomes long in duration and subtle.

2.51. The fourth is that which follows when the spheres of the external and internal have been passed.

2.52. Thence the cover of light is destroyed.

2.53. And the fitness of the mind for concentration.

2.54. Abstraction [of the senses] is that by which the senses do not come into contact with their objects and follow as it were the nature of the mind.

2.55. Thence the senses are under the highest control.

3.1. Concentration is the steadfastness of the mind.

3.2. The continuation there of the mental effort [to understand] is meditation (*dhyana*).

3.3. The same, when shining with the light of the object alone, and devoid, as it were, of itself, is trance [or contemplation].

3.4. The three together are *samyama*.*

3.5. By the achievement thereof comes the visibility of the cognition.

3.6. Its application is to the planes.

3.7. The three are more intimate than the preceding.

3.8. Even that is non-intimate to the seedless.

3.9. The suppressive modification is the conjunction of the mind with the moment of suppression, when the outgoing and suppressive potencies disappear and appear, respectively.

3.10. By potency comes its undisturbed flow.

3.11. The trance-modification of the mind is the destruction and rise of all-pointedness and one-pointedness, respectively.

4.30. Thence the removal of actions and afflictions.

4.31. The knowable is but little then, because of knowledge having become infinite, on account of the removal of all obscuring impurities.

4.32. By that, the qualities having fulfilled their object, the succession of their changes ends.

4.34. Absolute freedom comes when the qualities, becoming devoid of the object of the *purusa*, become latent; or the power of consciousness becomes established in its own nature.

---

* Mastery of consciousness. —Ed.

THE *BHAGAVAD GITA*

The poem known as the *Bhagavad Gita* (Song of God) is a small portion of a long epic, the *Mahabharata.* This "Great Indian Epic" is a text composed by wandering minstrels and poets and contains over 100,000 verses compiled, edited and amended over six or seven centuries, beginning as early as the fifth century B.C.E. Of the many Hindu scriptures, the *Gita* has undoubtedly proved the most popular within recent centuries.

The epic's story centers on a conflict over the succession to the throne of a princely state in the ancient civilization that extended along the Ganges River draining the Himalayas. The political issues are complex, but one side of the family, and not the other, has the just claim. Five brothers are the principal "good guys" in the dispute, though there are many noble and venerable sages and heroes fighting against them. Krishna, a prince and ruler of a neighboring state, joins the battle line as the charioteer for the third of the five brothers, a champion archer named Arjuna. The *Gita,* a dialogue between Krishna, who reveals himself as God incarnate, and Arjuna, occurs just moments before the battle begins. Arjuna (Everyman), looking across the battle line at his friends and kinsfolk, cannot face the prospect of killing them and sinks down despondently in his chariot, paralyzed over what he should do.

Arjuna's crisis is principally ethical, but the answer he receives from Krishna is religious and mystical. At the beginning of the dialogue, Arjuna insists that it cannot be morally right to fight and kill his kinsmen, teachers, friends, and loved ones who are arrayed against him. "No good do I see in killing my own family in battle. I desire not victory, nor rule, nor pleasures, Krishna; what is power to us, enjoyments, or life, Govinda? Those who make rulership desirable for us, and enjoyments and pleasures, it is they that are arrayed in battle (against us), abandoning life and wealth. Teachers, fathers, sons, grandfathers, uncles, in-laws—these I do not wish to kill even if it means that I must die, Krishna—not even to rule the three worlds, why then for the earth?"*

Despite the passion and sincerity of the moral feeling that Arjuna expresses, Krishna insists that the right thing to do is to fight, to kill the opposing warriors and win the battle. Note that this is not what one might expect from Krishna, a proponent of a mystical supreme goal. Jainism, for example, teaches a similar *summum bonum,* but insists *ahimsa* (non-injury) is an essential practice for that end.

There are many dimensions to Krishna's explanation of why fighting is the right course of action for Arjuna; more commentary has been elicited by Krishna's response to Arjuna's plea for guidance than by any other comparably brief text, except perhaps the Gospels. Krishna explains divine incarnation, rebirth, various

*from Chapter One; translation by Stephen Phillips.

paths and practices of yoga, the transcendence of God, the unity of the world with God, evil, the purpose of creation, and the destiny of the individual soul—all within the course of explaining why Arjuna should fight. But the heart of the *Gita's* ethical doctrine appears to be a yogic teaching about action. This is *karmayoga* (yoga of action) a discipline of giving, of acting in a spirit of sacrifice* without concern for personal benefit. The implication is that this leads Arjuna to do what is objectively right.

The selections below begin with Krishna's explanation of important metaphysical truths that underlie this teaching of yoga and continue with the chapter devoted to the *karmayoga* leg of a "triple path" that Krishna proposes. (The others, which have less ethical relevance, are *jnanayoga,* the discipline of meditation, and *bhaktiyoga,* the discipline of love and devotion.) By practicing the yoga of action, one turns *karma* (habit) into *dharma* (right action) attuned with God's will. Just as God sacrifices divine qualities in coming to be (that is, creating this finite world for the good of us all) and thereby sacrifices a native infinity and bliss, we, by sacrificing our superficial self-interest and natural desires in acting for the good of all, attune ourselves to God's ongoing creative activity. Further, our consciousness mystically widens to unite with God's. God takes on a special birth to protect the good and the right, and we can participate in God's action by taking a self-sacrificing attitude.

In general and throughout the *Gita,* Krishna propounds a type of mysticism where highest self-interest and ethical duty converge: we have to act morally to advance along a yogic path, and through this process we naturally become more ethical, he implies. The idea also occurs in Buddhism: by exercising compassion, we advance toward enlightenment, and by advancing toward enlightenment, we cannot help but act out of compassion.

---

yajna, translated in the following sometimes as "worship," sometimes as "sacrifice."

from *The Bhagavad Gita*

CHAPTER II

The Blessed One said:

2. Whence to thee this faintheartedness
       In peril has come,
   Offensive to the noble, not leading to heaven,
       Inglorious, O Arjuna?

3. Yield not to unmanliness, son of Prtha;
       It is not meet for thee.
   Petty weakness of heart
       Rejecting, arise, scorcher of the foe!

Arjuna said:

4. How shall I in battle against Bhisma,
       And Drona, O Slayer of Madhu,
   Fight with arrows,
       Who are both worthy of reverence, Slayer
           of Enemies?

5. For not slaying my revered elders of great
           dignity
       'Twere better to eat alms-food, even, in this
           world;
   But having slain my elders who seek their
           ends, right in this world
       I should eat food smeared with blood.

6. And we know not which of the two were
           better for us,
       Whether we should conquer, or they
           should conquer us;
   What very ones having slain we wish not to
           live,

They are arrayed in front of us,
    Dhrtarastra's men.

7. My very being afflicted with the taint of weak
        compassion,
    I ask Thee, my mind bewildered as to the
        right:
   Which were better, that tell me definitely;
       I am Thy pupil, teach me that have come
           to Thee (for instruction).

8. For I see not what would dispel my
       Grief, the witherer of the senses,
   If I attained on earth rivalless, prosperous
       Kingship, and even overlordship of the
           gods.

. . . .

The Blessed One said:

11. Thou hast mourned those who should not be
        mourned,
    And (yet) thou speakest words about
        wisdom!
   Dead and living men
       The (truly) learned do not mourn.

12. But not in any respect was I (ever) not,
       Nor thou, nor these kings;
   And not at all shall we ever come not to be,
       All of us, henceforward.

13. As to the embodied (soul) in this body
       Come childhood, youth, old age,
   So the coming to another body;
       The wise man is not confused herein.

14. But contacts with matter, son of Kunti,
       Cause cold and heat, pleasure and pain;
   They come and go, and are impermanent;
       Put up with them, son of Bharata!

15. For who these (contacts) do not cause to
        waver,

The man, O bull of men,
    To whom pain and pleasure are alike, the
        wise,
He is fit for immortality.

16. Of what is not, no coming to be occurs;
    No coming not to be occurs of what is;
But the dividing-line of both is seen,
    Of these two, by those who see the truth.

17. But know that that is indestructible,
    By which this all is pervaded;
Destruction of this imperishable one
    No one can cause.

18. These bodies come to an end,
    It is declared, of the eternal embodied
        (soul),
Which is indestructible and unfathomable.
    Therefore fight, son of Bharata!

19. Who believes him a slayer,
    And who thinks him slain,
Both these understand not:
    He slays not, is not slain.

20. He is not born, nor does he ever die;
    Nor, having come to be, will he ever more
        come not to be.
Unborn, eternal, everlasting, this ancient one
    Is not slain when the body is slain.

21. Who knows as indestructible and eternal
    This unborn, imperishable one,
That man, son of Prtha, how
    Can he slay or cause to slay—whom?

22. As leaving aside worn-out garments
    A man takes other, new ones,
So leaving aside worn-out bodies
    To other, new ones goes the embodied
        (soul).

23. Swords cut him not,
    Fire burns him not,
Water wets him not,
    Wind dries him not.

24. Not to be cut is he, not to be burnt is he,
    Not to be wet nor yet dried;
Eternal, omnipresent, fixed,
    Immovable, everlasting is he.

25. Unmanifest he, unthinkable he,

Unchangeable he is declared to be;
    Therefore knowing him thus
    Thou shouldst not mourn him.

26. Moreover, even if constantly born
    Or constantly dying thou considerest him,
Even so, great-armed one, thou
    Shouldst not mourn him.

27. For to one that is born death is certain,
    And birth is certain for one that has died;
Therefore, the thing being unavoidable,
    Thou shouldst not mourn.

28. The beginnings of things are unmanifest,
    Manifest their middles, son of Bharata,
Unmanifest again their ends:
    Why mourn about this?

29. By a rare chance one may see him,
    And by a rare chance likewise may another
        declare him,
And by a rare chance may another hear (of)
        him;
    (But) even having heard (of) him, no one
        whatsoever knows him.

30. This embodied (soul) is eternally unslayable
    In the body of every one, son of Bharata;
Therefore all beings
    Thou shouldst not mourn.

31. Likewise having regard for thine own (caste)
        duty
    Thou shouldst not tremble;
For another, better thing than a fight required
        of duty
    Exists not for a warrior.

32. Presented by mere luck,
    An open door of heaven—
Happy the warriors, son of Prtha,
    That get such a fight!

33. Now, if thou this duty-required
    Conflict wilt not perform,
Then thine own duty and glory
    Abandoning, thou shalt get thee evil.

34. Disgrace, too, will creatures
    Speak of thee, without end;
And for one that has been esteemed, disgrace
    Is worse than death.

35. That thou hast abstained from battle thru fear
    The (warriors) of great chariots will think
        of thee;
    And of whom thou wast highly regarded,
        Thou shalt come to be held lightly.

36. And many sayings that should not be said
        Thy ill-wishers will say of thee,
    Speaking ill of thy capacity:
        What, pray, is more grievous than that?

37. Either slain thou shalt gain heaven,
        Or conquering thou shalt enjoy the earth.
    Therefore arise, son of Kunti,
        Unto battle, making a firm resolve.

38. Holding pleasure and pain alike,
        Gain and loss, victory and defeat,
    Then gird thyself for battle:
        Thus thou shalt not get evil.

. . . .

45. The Vedas have the three Strands (of matter)
        as their scope;
    Be thou free from the three Strands,
        Arjuna,
    Free from the pairs (of opposites), eternally
        fixed in goodness,
    Free from acquisition and possession,
        self-possessed.

46. As much profit as there is in a water-tank
        When on all sides there is a flood of water,
    No more is there in all the Vedas
        For a Brahman who (truly) understands.

47. On action alone be thy interest,
        Never on its fruits;
    Let not the fruits of action be thy motive,
        Nor be thy attachment to inaction.

48. Abiding in discipline perform actions,
        Abandoning attachment, Dhanamjaya,
    Being indifferent to success or failure;
        Discipline is defined as indifference.

49. For action is far inferior
        To discipline of mental attitude,
            Dhanamjaya.
    In the mental attitude seek thy (religious)
        refuge;
    Wretched are those whose motive is the
        fruit (of action).

50. The disciplined in mental attitude leaves
        behind in this world
    Both good and evil deeds.
    Therefore discipline thyself unto discipline;
        Discipline in actions is weal.

51. For the disciplined in mental attitude, action-
        produced
    Fruit abandoning, the intelligent ones,
    Freed from the bondage of rebirth,
        Go to the place that is free from illness.

52. When the jungle of delusion
        Thy mentality shall get across,
    Then thou shalt come to aversion
        Towards what is to be heard and has been
            heard (in the Veda).

53. Averse to traditional lore ("heard" in the
        Veda)
    When shall stand motionless
    Thy mentality, immovable in concentration,
        Then thou shalt attain discipline.

Arjuna said:

54. What is the description of the man of
        stabilized mentality,
    That is fixed in concentration, Kesava?
    How might the man of stabilized mentality
        speak,
    How might he sit, how walk?

The Blessed One said:

55. When he abandons desires,
        All that are in the mind, son of Prtha,
    Finding contentment by himself in the self
        alone,
    Then he is called of stabilized mentality.

56. When his mind is not perturbed in sorrows,
        And he has lost desire for joys,
    His longing, fear, and wrath departed,
        He is called a stable-minded holy man.

57. Who has no desire towards any thing,
        And getting this or that good or evil
    Neither delights in it nor loathes it,
        His mentality is stabilized.

58. And when he withdraws,
        As a tortoise his limbs from all sides,

His senses from the objects of sense,
    His mentality is stabilized.

59. The objects of sense turn away
    From the embodied one that abstains from
        food,
    Except flavor; flavor also from him
    Turns away when he has seen the highest.

60. For even of one who strives, son of Kunti,
    Of the man of discernment,
    The impetuous senses
    Carry away the mind by violence.

61. Them all restraining,
    Let him sit disciplined, intent on Me;
    For whose senses are under control,
    His mentality is stabilized.

62. When a man meditates on the objects of
        sense,
    Attachment to them is produced.
    From attachment springs desire,
    From desire wrath arises;

63. From wrath comes infatuation,
    From infatuation loss of memory;
    From loss of memory, loss of mind;
    From loss of mind he perishes.

64. But with desire-and-loathing-severed
    Senses acting on the objects of sense,
    With (senses) self-controlled, he, governing
        his self,
    Goes unto tranquility.

65. In tranquility, of all griefs
    Riddance is engendered for him;
    For of the tranquil-minded quickly
    The mentality becomes stable.

66. The undisciplined has no (right) mentality,
    And the undisciplined has no
        efficient-force;
    Who has no efficient-force has no peace;
    For him that has no peace how can there
        be bliss?

67. For the senses are roving,
    And when the thought-organ is directed
        after them,
    It carries away his mentality,
    As wind a ship on the water.

68. Therefore whosoever, great-armed one,
    Has withdrawn on all sides
    The senses from the objects of sense,
    His mentality is stabilized.

69. What is night for all beings,
    Therein the man of restraint is awake;
    Wherein (other) beings are awake,
    That is night for the sage of vision.

70. It is ever being filled, and (yet) its foundation
        remains unmoved—
    The sea: just as waters enter it,
    Whom all desires enter in that same way
    He attains peace; not the man who lusts
        after desires.

71. Abandoning all desires, what
    Man moves free from longing,
    Without self-interest and egotism,
    He goes to peace.

72. This is the fixation that is Brahmanic, son of
        Prtha;
    Having attained it he is not (again)
        confused.
    Abiding in it even at the time of death,
    He goes to Brahman-nirvana.

Here ends the Second Chapter, called Discipline of
Reason-method.

CHAPTER III

Arjuna said:

1. If more important than action
    The mental attitude is held of Thee,
        Janardana,
    Then why to violent action
    Dost Thou enjoin me, Kesava?

2. With words that seem confused
    Thou apparently bewilderest my intellect.
    So tell me one thing definitely,
    Whereby I may attain welfare.

The Blessed One said:

3. In this world a two-fold basis (of religion)
    Has been declared by Me of old, blameless
        one:

By the discipline of knowledge of the
    followers of reason-method,
      And by the discipline of action of the
        followers of discipline-method.

4. Not by not starting actions
    Does a man attain actionlessness,
  And not by renunciation alone
    Does he go to perfection.

5. For no one even for a moment
    Remains at all without performing actions;
  For he is made to perform action willy-nilly,
    Every one is, by the Strands that spring
      from material nature.

6. Restraining the action-senses
    Who sits pondering with his
      thought-organ
On the objects of sense, with deluded soul,
    He is called a hypocrite.

7. But whoso the senses with the thought-organ
    Controlling, O Arjuna, undertakes
Discipline of action with the action-senses,
    Unattached (to the fruits of action), he is
      superior.

8. Perform thou action that is (religiously)
    required;
  For action is better than inaction.
And even the maintenance of the body for
    thee
  Can not succeed without action.

9. Except action for the purpose of worship,
    This world is bound by actions;
Action for that purpose, son of Kunti,
    Perform thou, free from attachment (to its
      fruits).

10. After creating creatures along with (rites of)
    worship,
    Prajāpati (the Creator) said of old:
By this ye shall procreate yourselves—
    Let this be your Cow-of-Wishes.

11. With this prosper ye the gods,
    And let the gods prosper you;
(Thus) prospering one the other,
    Ye shall attain the highest welfare.

12. For desired enjoyments to you the gods
    Will give, prospered by worship;

Without giving to them, their gifts
    Whoso enjoys, is nothing but a thief.

13. Good men who eat the remnants of (food
    offered in) worship
  And freed from all sins;
But those wicked men eat evil
    Who cook for their own selfish sakes.

14. Beings originate from food;
    From the rain-god food arises;
From worship comes the rain(-god);
    Worship originates in action.

15. Action arises from Brahman, know;
    And Brahman springs from the
      Imperishable;
Therefore the universal Brahman
    Is eternally based on worship.

16. The wheel thus set in motion
    Who does not keep turning in this world,
Malignant, delighting in the senses,
    He lives in vain, son of Prtha.

17. But who takes delight in the self alone,
    The man who finds contentment in the
      self,
And satisfaction only in the self,
    For him there is found (in effect) no action
      to perform.

18. He has no interest whatever in action done,
    Nor any in action not done in this world,
Nor has he in reference to all beings
    Any dependence of interest.

19. Therefore unattached ever
    Perform action that must be done;
For performing action without attachment
    Man attains the highest.

20. For only thru action, perfection
    Attained Janaka and others.
Also for the mere control of the world
    Having regard, thou shouldst act.

21. Whatsoever the noblest does,
    Just that in every case other folk (do);
What he makes his standard,
    That the world follows.

22. For Me, son of Prtha, there is nothing to be
    done
    In the three worlds whatsoever,

Nothing unattained to be attained;
  And yet I still continue in action.

23. For if I did not continue
  At all in action, unwearied,
  My path (would) follow
  Men altogether, son of Prtha.

24. These folk would perish
  If I did not perform action,
  And I should be an agent of confusion;
  I should destroy these creatures.

25. Fools, attached to action,
  As they act, son of Bharata,
  So the wise man should act (but) unattached,
  Seeking to effect the control of the world.

26. Let him not cause confusion of mind
  In ignorant folk who are attached to
    action;
  He should let them enjoy all actions,
  The wise man, (himself) acting
    disciplined.

27. Performed by material nature's
  Strands are actions, altogether;
  He whose soul is deluded by the I-faculty
  Imagines "I am the agent."

28. But he who knows the truth, great-armed one,
  About the separation (of the soul) from
    both the Strands and action
  'The Strands act upon the Strands'—
  Knowing this, is not attached (to actions).

29. Deluded by the Strands of material nature,
  Men are attached to the actions of the
    Strands.
  These dull folk of imperfect knowledge
  The man of perfect knowledge should not
    disturb.

30. On Me all actions
  Casting, with mind on the over-soul,
  Being free from longing and from selfishness,
  Fight, casting off thy fever.

31. Who this My doctrine constantly
  Follow, such men,
  Full of faith and not murmuring,
  They too are freed from (the effect of)
    actions.

32. But those who, murmuring against it,
  Do not follow My doctrine,
  Them, deluded in all knowledge,
  Know to be lost, the fools.

33. One acts in conformity with his own
  Material nature,—even the wise man:
  Beings follow (their own) nature;
  What will restraint accomplish?

34. Of (every) sense, upon the objects of (that)
    sense
  Longing and loathing are fixed;
  One must not come under control of those
    two,
  For they are his two enemies.

35. Better one's own duty, (tho) imperfect,
  Than another's duty well performed;
  Better death in (doing) one's own duty;
  Another's duty brings danger.

Arjuna said:

36. Then by what impelled does this
  Man commit sin,
  Even against his will, Vrsni-clansman,
  As if driven by force?

The Blessed One said:

37. It is desire, it is wrath,
  Arising from the Strand of passion,
  All-consuming, very sinful;
  Know that this is the enemy here.

38. As fire is obscured by smoke,
  And as a mirror by dirt,
  As the embryo is covered by its membrane-
    envelope,
  So this (universe) is obscured thereby.

39. By this is obscured the knowledge
  Of the knowing one, by this his eternal
    foe,
  That has the form of desire, son of Kunti,
  And is an insatiable fire.

40. The senses, the thought-organ, the
    consciousness,
  Are declared to be its basis;
  With these it confuses
  The embodied (soul), obscuring his
    knowledge.

41. Thou therefore, the senses first
	Controlling, O bull of Bharatas,
	Smite down this evil one,
		That destroys theoretical and practical
		knowledge.

42. The senses, they say, are high;
	Higher than the senses is the
		thought-organ;
	But higher than the thought-organ is the
		consciousness;
		While higher than the consciousness is He
		(the soul).

43. Thus being conscious of that which is higher
		than consciousness,
	Steadying the self by the self,
	Smite the enemy, great-armed one,
		That has the form of desire, and is hard to
		get at.

Here ends the Third Chapter, called Discipline of
Action.

CHAPTER IV

The Blessed One said:

5. For Me have passed many
		Births, and for thee, Arjuna;
	These I know all;
		Thou knowest not, scorcher of the foe.

6. Tho unborn, tho My self is eternal,
		Tho Lord of Beings,
	Resorting to My own material nature
		I come into being by My own mysterious
		power.

7. For whenever of the right
		A languishing appears, son of Bharata,
	A rising up of unright,
		Then I send Myself forth.

8. For protection of the good,
		And for destruction of evil-doers,
	To make a firm footing for the right,
		I come into being in age after age.

9. My wondrous birth and actions
		Whoso knows thus as they truly are,
	On leaving the body, to rebirth
		He goes not; to Me he goes, Arjuna!

10. Rid of passion, fear, and wrath,
		Made of Me, taking refuge in Me,
	Many by the austerity of knowledge
		Purified, have come to My estate.

11. In whatsoever way any come to Me,
		In that same way I grant them favor.
	My path follow
		Men altogether, son of Prtha.

. . . .

18. Who sees inaction in action,
		And action in inaction,
	He is enlightened among men;
		He does all actions, disciplined.

19. All whose undertakings
		Are free from desire and purpose,
	His actions burnt up in the fire of knowledge,
		Him the wise call the man of learning.

20. Abandoning attachment to the fruits of
		action,
		Constantly content, independent,
	Even when he sets out upon action,
		He yet does (in effect) nothing whatsoever.

21. Free from wishes, with mind and soul
		restrained,
		Abandoning all possessions,
	Action with the body alone
		Performing, he attains no guilt.

22. Content with getting what comes by chance,
		Passed beyond the pairs (of opposites), free
		from jealousy,
	Indifferent to success and failure,
		Even acting, he is not bound.

23. Rid of attachment, freed,
		His mind fixed in knowledge,
	Doing acts for worship (only), his action
		All melts away.

24. The (sacrificial) presentation is Brahman;
		Brahman is the oblation;
		In the (sacrificial) fire of Brahman it is
		poured by Brahman;
	Just to Brahman must he go,
		Being concentrated upon the (sacrificial)
		action that is Brahman.

. . . .

32. Thus many kinds of sacrifice
		Are spread out in the face of Brahman.

Know that they all spring from action!
    Knowing this thou shalt be freed.

33. Better than sacrifice that consists of substance
    Is the sacrifice of knowledge, scorcher of
        the foe.
All action without remainder, son of Prtha,
    Is completely ended in knowledge.

34. Learn to know this by obeisance (to those
        who can teach it),
    By questioning (them), by serving (them);
They will teach thee knowledge,
    Those who have knowledge, who see the
        truth.

35. Knowing which, not again to bewilderment
    In this manner shalt thou go, son of
        Pandu;
Whereby all beings without exception
    Thou shalt see in thyself, and also in Me.

36. Even if thou art of sinners
    The worst sinner of all,
Merely by the boat of knowledge all
    (The "sea" of) evil shalt thou cross over.

37. As firewood a kindled fire
    Reduces to ashes, Arjuna,
The fire of knowledge all actions
    Reduces to ashes even so.

38. For not like unto knowledge
    Is any purifier found in this world.
This the man perfected in discipline himself
    In time finds in himself.

39. The man of faith gets knowledge,
    Intent solely upon it, restraining his
        senses.
Having got knowledge, to supreme peace
    In no long time he goes.

40. The man unknowing and without faith,
    His soul full of doubt, perishes.
Not is this world, nor the next,
    Nor bliss, for him whose soul is full of
        doubt.

41. Him that has renounced actions in discipline,
    That has cut off his doubt with knowledge,
The self-possessed, no actions
    Bind, O Dhanamjaya.

42. Therefore this that springs from ignorance,

That lies in the heart, with the sword of
    knowledge thine own
Doubt cutting off, to discipline
    Resort: arise, son of Bharata!

Here ends the Fourth Chapter, called Discipline of
Knowledge.

CHAPTER XVIII

45. Taking delight in his own special kind of
        action,
    A man attains perfection;
Delighting in one's own special action,
        success
    How one reaches, that hear!

46. Whence comes the activity of beings,
    By whom this all is pervaded,—
Him worshiping by (doing) one's own
        appropriate action,
    A man attains perfection.

47. Better one's own duty, (even) imperfect,
    Than another's duty well performed.
Action pertaining to his own estate
    Performing, he incurs no guilt.

48. Natural-born action, son of Kunti,
    Even tho it be faulty, one should not
        abandon.
For all undertakings by faults
    Are dimmed, as fire by smoke.

49. His mentality unattached to any object,
    Self-conquered, free from longings,
To the supreme perfection of actionlessness
    He comes thru renunciation.

50. Having attained perfection, how to Brahman
    He also attains, hear from Me,
In only brief compass, son of Kunti;
    Which is the highest culmination of
        knowledge.

51. With purified mentality disciplined,
    And restraining himself with firmness,
Abandoning the objects of sense, sounds and
        the rest,
    And putting away desire and loathing,

52. Cultivating solitude, eating lightly,

Restraining speech, body, and mind,
Devoted to the discipline of meditation
    constantly,
Taking refuge in dispassion,

53. From egotism, force, pride,
    Desire, wrath, and possession
Freed, unselfish, calmed,
    He is fit for becoming Brahman.

54. Having become Brahman, serene-souled,
    He neither grieves nor longs;
Alike to all beings,
    He attains supreme devotion to Me.

55. Thru devotion he comes to know Me,
    What My measure is, and who I am, in
        very truth;
Then, knowing Me in very truth,
    He enters into (Me) straightway.

56. Even tho all actions ever
    He performs, relying on Me,
By My grace he reaches
    The eternal, undying station.

57. With thy thoughts all actions
    Casting upon Me, devoted to Me,
Turning to discipline of mentality,
    Keep thy mind ever fixed on Me.

58. If thy mind is on Me, all difficulties
    Shalt thou cross over by My grace;
But if thru egotism thou
    Wilt not heed, thou shalt perish.

59. If clinging to egotism
    Thou thinkest "I will not fight!,"
Vain is this thy resolve;
    (Thine own) material nature will coerce
        thee.

60. Son of Kunti, by thine own natural
    Action held fast,
What thru delusion thou seekest not to do,
    That thou shalt do even against thy will.

61. Of all beings, the Lord
    In the heart abides, Arjuna,
Causing all beings to turn around
    (As if) fixed in a machine, by his magic
        power.

62. To Him alone go for refuge
    With thy whole being, son of Bharata;
By His grace, supreme peace
    And the eternal station shalt thou attain.

63. Thus to thee has been expounded the
        knowledge
    That is more secret than the secret, by Me;
After pondering on it fully,
    Act as thou thinkest best.

64. Further, the highest secret of all,
    My supreme message, hear.
Because thou art greatly loved of Me,
    Therefore I shall tell thee what is good for
        thee.

65. Be Me-minded, devoted to Me;
    Worshiping Me, revere Me;
And to Me alone shalt thou go; truly to thee
    I promise it—(because) thou art dear to
        Me.

66. Abandoning all (other) duties,
    Go to Me as thy sole refuge;
From all evils I thee
    Shall rescue: be not grieved!

THE SERMONS OF THE BUDDHA

The Buddha lived in the sixth century B.C.E. in what is now Nepal. Born Siddhartha Gautama of the Sakya clan, he, according to the oldest versions of his life, was a prince destined to inherit his father's ruling mantle, leading as a young man a life of pleasure and enjoyment in the palace. He was encouraged in this by his father, who, fearing a prophecy that his son would become a religious mendicant, tried to protect him from the sight of anything unpleasant or evil. But one day the young prince journeyed some distance from the royal gardens and pleasure grounds and encountered first a diseased person, then a wrinkled and decrepit old man, and finally a corpse (Buddhists came to view these conditions as the "three evils"). Inquiring about each of these in turn and being told that all persons are subject to such infirmities, the Buddha-to-be vowed to renounce his life of enjoyments and search tirelessly for the origin and cause of these evils and the power to root them up. His experience of enlightenment, or awakening (in Sanskrit, the word *buddha* means literally "the awakened one"), did not occur right away, however; he tried various paths of asceticism before arriving at the Middle Way, a way of life he later proclaimed to his disciples. Finally, after a long ordeal in meditation under a Bodhi tree, he achieved the *summum bonum,* an extinction of evil at its roots. The remainder of his life he spent traveling and preaching, helping others to reach the supreme good, called *nirvana.*

The Buddha himself did not write anything. Records of his teachings and sermons were apparently kept by his disciples, and in the midst of the reign of the Buddhist emperor Asoka in the third century B.C.E., an enormous canon of literature sacred to Southern Buddhists was compiled. In the contemporary world, the southern branch of Buddhism, known as *Theravada Buddhism,* is prevalent in Sri Lanka, Burma, and Thailand, for example. The northern branch of Buddhism, known as *Mahayana Buddhism* (prevalent in Nepal, Tibet, China, Korea, and Japan) recognizes a distinct literature as sacred, though it does not entirely reject the teachings of the Southern Canon.

The most famous and probably least amended version of the Southern Canon is known as the Pali Canon; some scholars believe that Pali, a close derivative of Sanskrit, is the language that the Buddha himself spoke. The Pali Canon has three sections: (*a*) sermons of the Buddha, (*b*) rules for monks and nuns, and (*c*) discussions and interpretations of doctrine. The selections below are from the first section, sermons commonly believed to be the Buddha's own words: *The First Sermon, The Fire-Sermon, The Tevigga Sutta, The Akankheyya Sutta,* and *The Dhammapada (The Path of Virtue),* which is probably the most renowned and cherished portion of the canon among Buddhists of the south.

Among the more important teachings presented are the Four Noble Truths: (1) There is suffering; (2) The root of suffering is desire, attachment, and personal clinging; (3) There is a way to eliminate desire and thereby eliminate suffering, namely, the *nirvana* experience; (4) The way to this supreme good is the Eightfold Noble Path—right thought, right resolve, right speech, right conduct, right livelihood, right effort, right mindfulness, and right concentration or meditation. Other important doctrines include the "wheel of becoming" that shows the connectedness between life, craving, and rebirth (that there is rebirth seems never doubted by the Buddha: "freedom from rebirth" is one way the goal of Buddhist practice is articulated in the canon); the causal interdependence of all things; their insubstantiality and phenomenal nature as mere groups of qualities; and, similarly, the insubstantiality of the self or soul (there is no soul, according to the Buddha). Each of these doctrines, and others as well, received much thought and elaboration in later years as Buddhist systematic philosophies emerged. But more than any metaphysical teaching, the Buddha emphasizes the practice of meditation and compassion, thereby inspiring others to lead the noble life.

In considering Buddhist ethics, one must keep in mind that a distinction is drawn between monks (and nuns, though there were few nuns) on the one hand and the rest of humanity on the other. Monks are obliged to follow a strict regimen in implementing the Eightfold Path. They must remain celibate; they must forsake personal property, living with only a robe and a bowl; they have special obligations to meditate, study, and teach. The rest of us face a much looser set of ethical requirements: refraining from killing, stealing, improper sexual relations, improper speech, and the use of drugs and alcohol. This less stringent practice will prepare us for a more serious following of the Path in a future lifetime.

The First Sermon

Reprinted from Edward J. Thomas, The Life of Buddha as Legend and History. *Copyright © 1927 by Alfred A. Knopf, Inc.*

These two extremes, O monks, are not to be practised by one who has gone forth from the world. What are the two? That conjoined with the passions, low, vulgar, common, ignoble, and useless, and that conjoined with self-torture, painful, ignoble, and useless. Avoiding these two extremes the Tathagata* has gained the knowledge of the Middle Way, which gives sight and knowledge, and tends to calm, to insight, enlightenment, *nirvana*.

What, O monks, is the Middle Way, which gives sight . . . ? It is the noble Eightfold Path, namely, right views, right intention, right speech, right action, right livelihood, right effort, right mindfulness, right concentration. This, O monks, is the Middle Way. . . .

1. Now this, O monks, is the noble truth of pain: birth is painful, old age is painful, sickness is painful, death is painful, sorrow, lamentation, dejection, and despair are painful. Contact with unpleasant things is painful, not getting what one wishes is painful. In short the five *khandhas* of grasping are painful.

2. Now this, O monks, is the noble truth of the cause of pain: that craving which leads to rebirth, combined with pleasure and lust, finding pleasure here and there, namely, the craving for passion, the craving for existence, the craving for non-existence.

3. Now this, O monks, is the noble truth of the cessation of pain: the cessation without a remainder of that craving, abandonment, forsaking, release, non-attachment.

4. Now this, O monks, is the noble truth of the way that leads to the cessation of pain: this is the noble Eightfold Path, namely, right views, right intention, right speech, right action, right livelihood, right effort, right mindfulness, right concentration. . . .

As long as in these noble truths my threefold knowledge and insight duly with its twelve divisions was not well purified, even so long, O monks, in the world with its gods, Mara, Brahma, with ascetics, *brahmins,* gods, and men, I had not attained the highest complete enlightenment. Thus I knew.

But when in these noble truths my threefold knowledge and insight duly with its twelve divisions was well purified, then, O monks, in the world . . . I had attained the highest complete enlightenment. Thus I knew. Knowledge arose in me; insight arose that the release of my mind is unshakable; this is my last existence; now there is no rebirth.

---

*A term meaning "one who has thus become." It refers to the Buddha. —ED.

The Fire-Sermon

Reprinted from Buddhism in Translations, *translated by Henry Clarke Warren (Cambridge: Harvard University Press, 1896).*

Then The Blessed One, having dwelt in Uruvela as long as he wished, proceeded on his wanderings in the direction of Gaya Head, accompanied by a great congregation of priests, a thousand in number, who had all of them aforetime been monks with matted hair. And there in Gaya, on Gaya Head, The Blessed One dwelt, together with the thousand priests.

And there The Blessed One addressed the priests:—

"All things, O priests, are on fire. And what, O priests, are all these things which are on fire?

"The eye, O priests, is on fire; forms are on fire; eye-consciousness is on fire; impressions received by the eye are on fire; and whatever sensation, pleasant, unpleasant, or indifferent, originates in dependence on impressions received by the eye, that also is on fire.

"And with what are these on fire?

"With the fire of passion, say I, with the fire of hatred, with the fire of infatuation; with birth, old age, death, sorrow, lamentation, misery, grief, and despair are they on fire.

"The ear is on fire; sounds are on fire; . . . the nose is on fire; odors are on fire; . . . the tongue is on fire; tastes are on fire; . . . the body is on fire; things tangible are on fire; . . . the mind is on fire; ideas are on fire; . . . mind-consciousness is on fire; impressions received by the mind are on fire; and whatever sensation, pleasant, unpleasant, or indifferent, originates in dependence on impressions received by the mind, that also is on fire.

"And with what are these on fire?

"With the fire of passion, say I, with the fire of hatred, with the fire of infatuation; with birth, old age, death, sorrow, lamentation, misery, grief, and despair are they on fire.

"Perceiving this, O priests, the learned and noble disciple conceives an aversion for the eye, conceives an aversion for forms, conceives an aversion for eye-consciousness, conceives an aversion for the impressions received by the eye; and whatever sensation, pleasant, unpleasant, or indifferent, originates in dependence on impressions received by the eye, for that also he conceives an aversion. Conceives an aversion for the ear, conceives an aversion for sounds, . . . conceives an aversion for the nose, conceives an aversion for odors, . . . conceives an aversion for the tongue, conceives an aversion for tastes, . . . conceives an aversion for the body, conceives an aversion for things tangible, . . . conceives an aversion for the mind, conceives an aversion for ideas, conceives an aversion for mind-consciousness, conceives an aversion for the impressions received by the mind; and whatever sensation, pleasant, unpleasant, or indifferent, originates in dependence on impressions received by the mind, for this also he conceives an aversion. And in conceiving this aversion, he becomes divested of passion, and by the absence of passion he becomes free, and when he is free he becomes aware that he is free; and he knows that rebirth is exhausted, that he has lived the holy life, that he has done what it behooved him to do, and that he is no more for this world."

Now while this exposition was being delivered, the minds of the thousand priests became free from attachment and delivered from the depravities.

from *The Tevigga Sutta*

Reprinted from The Tevigga Sutta, *translated by T. W. Rhys-Davids, Volume XI of* Sacred Books of the East, *edited by Max Müller (Oxford: Clarendon Press, 1900).*

Then the Blessed One spake and said:—Know, Vasettha, that from time to time a Tathagata is born into the world, a fully Enlightened One, blessed and worthy, abounding in wisdom and goodness, happy with knowledge of the worlds, unsurpassed as a guide to erring mortals, a teacher of gods and men, a Blessed Buddha. He thoroughly understands this universe, as though he saw it face to face,—the world below with all its people, the worlds above, of Mara and of Brahma—and all creatures, Samanas and Brahmans, gods and men, and from that knowledge makes it known and teaches others. The Truth does he proclaim both in its letter and in its spirit, lovely in its origin, lovely in its progress, lovely in its consummation. A higher life doth he make known in all its purity and in all its perfectness.

A householder or one of his sons, or a man of inferior birth in any caste, listens to the truth he proclaims. On hearing the truth, faith in the Tathagata is awakened and when that faith is strengthened he thus considers within himself: Full of hindrance is the household life, a path defiled by passion, free as the air is the life of him who has renounced all worldly things. How difficult it is for the man who dwells at home to live the higher life in all its fullness, in all its purity, in all its perfection. Let me then, shave my head and face, let me clothe myself in the garment of a mendicant and go forth from a household life into the homeless life. Then before long, forsaking his portion of the family property, be it great or be it small; forsaking his relatives, be they many or few, he shaves his head, clothes himself in the mendicant's robe, and goes forth from the household life into the homeless state.

When he has thus become a recluse, he passes a life of restraint according to rules of the Patimokkha; uprightness is his delight, he sees danger in the least of those things he should avoid; he adopts and trains himself in the Precepts; he encompasses himself with purity in word and deed; he sustains his life by means that are unselfish and kind; good is his conduct, guarded the door of his senses; mindful and self-possessed, he is altogether happy.

Now, Vasettha, wherein is his conduct good? Herein, O Vasettha, putting away all unkindness to sentient beings he abstains from destroying life. He lays aside the cudgel and sword and, full of humility and pity, he is compassionate and kind to all creatures that have life. Putting away the desire for things which are not his, he abstains from taking anything that is not freely given him. He has only what has been given him, therewith is he content, and he passes his life in honesty and in purity of heart. Putting away all thoughts of lust, he lives a life of chastity and purity. Putting away all thoughts of deceiving, he abstains from all prevarications; he speaks truthfully, from the truth he never swerves; faithful and trustworthy, he never injures his fellow men by deceit.

Putting away all judgment of others, he abstains from slander. What he hears he repeats not elsewhere to raise a quarrel; what he hears elsewhere he repeats not here to raise a quarrel. Thus he brings together those who are divided, he encourages those who are friendly; he is a peacemaker, a lover of peace, impassioned for peace, a speaker of words that make for peace. Putting away all bitter thoughts, he abstains from harsh language. Whatever is humane, pleasant to the ear, kindly, reaching to the heart, urbane, acceptable to the people, appreciated by the people—such are the words he speaks. Putting away all foolish thoughts, he abstains from vain conversation. He speaks in season, he speaks truthfully, consistently, wisely, with restraint. He speaks only when it is appropriate for him to speak, words that are profitable, well sustained, well defined, full of wisdom.

Besides being kind to all animate life, he refrains from injuring insects or even herbs. He takes but one meal a day; abstaining from food at all other times. He abstains from attending dances, concerts and theatrical shows. He abstains from wearing, using or adorning himself with garlands, scents and ointments, he abstains from large and soft beds. He abstains from accumulating silver or gold, from coveting great harvests, herds of cattle; he abstains from the getting of maids and women attendants,

slaves either men or women; he abstains from gathering herds of sheep or goats, fowls or swine, elephants, cattle, horses and mares. He abstains from the getting of fields and lands.

He refrains from accepting commissions to carry messages, he refrains from all buying and selling, he abstains from the use of all trade deceptions, false weights, alloyed metals, false measures. He abstains from all bribery, cheating, fraud and crooked ways. He refrains from all banditry, killing or maiming, abducting, highway robbery, plundering villages, or obtaining money by threats of violence. These are the kinds of goodness he practices.

from *The Akankheyya Sutta*

Reprinted from Buddhism in Translations, *translated by Henry Clarke Warren (Cambridge: Harvard University Press, 1986).*

THE SIX HIGH POWERS

"If a priest, O priests, should frame a wish, as follows: 'Let me exercise the various magical powers,—let me being one become multiform, let me being multiform become one, let me become visible, become invisible, go without hindrance through walls, ramparts, or mountains, as if through air, let me rise and sink in the ground as if in the water, let me walk on the water as if on unyielding ground, let me travel cross-legged through the air like a winged bird, let me touch and feel with my hand the moon and the sun, mighty and powerful though they are, and let me go with my body even up to the Brahma-world,' —then must he be perfect in the precepts, bring his thoughts to a state of quiescence, practise diligently the trances, attain to insight, and be a frequenter of lonely places.

"If a priest, O priests, should frame a wish, as follows: 'Let me hear with a divinely clear hearing, surpassing that of men, sounds both celestial and human, far and near,' then must he be perfect in the precepts, etc.

"If a priest, O priests, should frame a wish, as follows: 'Let me by my own heart investigate and discern the hearts of other beings, the hearts of other men; let me discern a passionate mind to be passionate, let me discern a mind free from passion to be free from passion, let me discern a mind full of hatred to be full of hatred, let me discern a mind free from hatred to be free from hatred, let me discern an infatuated mind to be infatuated, let me discern a mind free from infatuation to be free from infatuation, let me discern an intent mind to be intent, let me discern a wandering mind to be wandering, let me discern an exalted mind to be exalted, let me discern an unexalted mind to be unexalted, let me discern an inferior mind to be inferior, let me discern a superior mind to be superior, let me discern a concentrated mind to be concentrated, let me discern an unconcentrated mind to be unconcentrated, let me discern an emancipated mind to be emancipated, let me discern an unemancipated mind to be unemancipated,' then must he be perfect in the precepts, etc.

"If a priest, O priests, should frame a wish, as follows: 'Let me call to mind many previous states of existence, to wit, one birth, two births, three births, four births, five births, ten births, twenty births, thirty births, forty births, fifty births, one hundred births, one thousand births, one hundred thousand births, many destructions of a world-cycle, many renovations of a world-cycle, many destructions and many renovations of a world-cycle: "I lived in such a place, had such a name, was of such a family, of such a caste, had such a maintenance, experienced such happiness and such miseries, had such a length of life. Then I passed from that existence and was reborn in such a place. There also I had such a name, was of such a family, of such a caste, had such a maintenance, experienced such happiness and such miseries, had such a length of life. Then I passed from that existence and was reborn in this existence." Thus let me call to mind many former states of existence, and let me specifically characterize them,' then must he be perfect in the precepts, etc.

"If a priest, O priests, should frame a wish, as follows: 'Let me with a divinely clear vision, surpassing that of men, behold beings as they pass from one existence and spring up in another existence; let me discern the base and the noble, the handsome and the ugly, those in a higher state of existence and those in a lower state of existence undergoing the result of their deeds. So that I can know as follows:

"Alas! these beings, having been wicked of body, wicked of voice, wicked of mind, slanderers of noble people, wrong in their views, acquirers of false merit under wrong views, have arrived, after the dissolution of the body, after death, at a place of punishment, a place of suffering, perdition, hell; or, again, these other beings, having been righteous of body, righteous of voice, righteous of mind, not slanderers of noble people, right in their views, acquirers of merit under right views, have arrived, after the dissolution of the body, after death, at a place of happiness, a heavenly world." Thus let me with a divinely clear vision, surpassing that of men, discern beings as they pass from one existence and spring up in another existence; let me discern the base and the noble, the handsome and the ugly, those in a higher state of existence and those in a lower state of existence undergoing the results of their deeds,' then must he be perfect in the precepts, etc.

"If a priest, O priests, should frame a wish, as follows: 'Let me, through the destruction of depravity, in the present life and in my own person, attain to freedom from depravity, to deliverance of the mind, to deliverance by wisdom,' then must he be perfect in the precepts, bring his thoughts to a state of quiescence, practise diligently the trances, attain to insight, and be a frequenter of lonely places."

from *The Dhammapada (The Path of Virtue)*

CHAPTER I / THE TWIN-VERSES

1. (The mental) natures are the result of what we have thought, are chieftained by our thoughts, are made up of our thoughts. If a man speaks or acts with an evil thought, sorrow follows him (as a consequence) even as the wheel follows the foot of the drawer (i.e., the ox which draws the cart).

2. (The mental) natures are the result of what we have thought, are chieftained by our thoughts, are made up of our thoughts. If a man speaks or acts with a pure thought, happiness follows him (in consequence) like a shadow that never leaves him.

3. "He abused me, he struck me, he overcame me, he robbed me"—in those who harbour such thoughts hatred will never cease.

4. "He abused me, he struck me, he overcame me, he robbed me"—in those who do not harbour such thoughts hatred will cease.

5. Not at any time are enmities appeased here through enmity but they are appeased through non-enmity. This is the eternal law.

6. Some (who are not learned) do not know that we must all come to an end here; but those who know this, their dissensions cease at once by their knowledge.

7. As the wind throws down a tree of little strength, so indeed does Māra (the tempter) overthrow him who lives looking for pleasures, uncontrolled in his senses, immoderate in eating, indolent, and of low vitality.

8. As the wind does not throw down a rocky mountain, so Mara indeed does not overthrow him who lives unmindful of pleasures, well controlled in his senses, moderate in eating, full of faith (in the Buddha, the law, and the *sangha* or community), and of high vitality.

9. He who will wear the yellow robe without having cleansed himself from impurity, who is devoid of truth and self-control, is not deserving of the yellow robe.

10. But he who puts away depravity, is well grounded in all virtues, and is possessed of self-restraint and truth is indeed worthy of the yellow robe.

11. They who imagine truth in untruth and see untruth in truth, never arrive at truth but follow vain imaginings (desires).

12. But they who know truth as truth and untruth as untruth arrive at truth and follow right desires.

13. As rain breaks through an ill-thatched house, so passion makes its way into an unreflecting mind.

14. As rain does not break through a well-thatched house, so passion does not make its way into a reflecting mind.

15. The evil-doer grieves in this world, he grieves in the next; he grieves in both. He grieves, he is afflicted, seeing the evil of his own actions.

16. The righteous man rejoices in this world, he rejoices in the next; he rejoices in both. He rejoices and becomes delighted, seeing the purity of his own actions.

17. The evil-doer suffers in this world, he suffers in the next; he suffers in both. He suffers (thinking) "evil has been done by me." He suffers even more when he has gone to the evil place.

18. The righteous man rejoices in this world, he rejoices in the next; he rejoices in both. He rejoices (thinking) "good has been done by me." He rejoices still more when he has gone to the good place.

19. Even if he recites a large number of scriptural texts but, being slothful, does not act accordingly, he is like a cowherd counting the cows of others, he has no share in religious life.

20. Even if he recites only a small number, if he is one who acts rightly in accordance with the law, he, having forsaken passion, hatred, and folly, being possessed of true knowledge and serenity of mind, being free from worldly desires both in this world and the next, has a share in the religious life.

CHAPTER II / VIGILANCE

1. Vigilance is the abode of eternal life, thoughtlessness is the abode of death. Those who are vigilant (who are given to reflection) do not die. The thoughtless are as if dead already.

2. The wise who have clearly understood this reflectiveness delight in reflectiveness and rejoice in the knowledge of the Aryas.

3. These wise ones, meditative, persevering, always putting forth strenuous effort attain to *nirvana,* the highest freedom and happiness.

4. If a person is reflective, if he rouses himself, if he is ever-mindful, if his deeds are pure, if he acts with consideration, if he is self-restrained and lives according to law, his glory will increase.

5. The wise man, by rousing himself, by vigilance, by restraint, by control, may make for himself an island which the flood cannot overwhelm.

6. Fools, men of inferior intelligence, fall into sloth; the wise man guards his vigilance as his best treasure.

7. Give not yourselves over to sloth or to the intimacy with lust and sensual pleasures. He who meditates with earnestness attains great joy.

8. When the wise man drives away sloth by strenuous effort, climbing the high tower of wisdom, he gazes sorrowless on the sorrowing crowd below. The wise person gazes on the fools even as one on the mountain peak gazes upon the dwellers on the plain (below).

9. Earnest among the slothful, awake among the sleepy, the wise man advances even as a racehorse does, leaving behind the hack.

10. By vigilance did Indra rise to the lordship of the gods. People praise vigilance; thoughtlessness is always deprecated.

11. A mendicant who delights in vigilance, who looks with fear on thoughtlessness (who sees danger in it), moves about like a fire consuming every bond, small or large.

12. A mendicant who delights in vigilance, who looks with fear on thoughtlessness, cannot fall away (from his perfect state) (but) is close to *nirvana.*

CHAPTER III / THOUGHT

1. Just as a fletcher makes straight his arrow, the wise man makes straight his trembling, unsteady thought which is difficult to guard and difficult to hold back (restrain).

2. Even as a fish taken from his watery home and thrown on the dry ground (moves about restlessly), this thought quivers all over in order to escape the dominion of Mara (the tempter or Death).

3. The control of thought, which is difficult to restrain, fickle, which wanders at will, is good; a tamed mind is the bearer of happiness.

4. Let the wise man guard his thought, which is difficult to perceive, which is extremely subtle, which wanders at will. Thought which is well guarded is the bearer of happiness.

5. They who will restrain their thought, which travels far, alone, incorporeal, seated in the cave (of the heart), will be freed from the fetters of death.

6. If a man's thought is unsteady, if it does not know the true law, if the serenity of mind is troubled, (in him) wisdom is not perfected.

7. There is no fear for him whose thought is untroubled (by faults), whose thought is unagitated, who has ceased to think of good and evil, who is awake (watchful, vigilant).

8. Knowing that this body is (fragile) like a jar, making this thought firm like a fortress, let him attact Mara (the tempter) with the weapon of wisdom, protect what he has conquered and remain attached to it.

9. Before long, alas, will this body lie on the earth, despised, bereft of consciousness, useless like a burnt faggot.

10. Whatever an enemy may do to an enemy, whatever a hater may do to a hater, a wrongly directed mind will do no greater harm.

11. Not a mother, not a father, nor any other relative will do so much; a well-directed mind will do us greater service.

CHAPTER V / THE FOOL

7. Fools of little understanding, being enemies to themselves, wander about doing evil deeds which bear bitter fruits.

8. That deed is not well done, which, having been done, brings remorse, whose reward one receives weeping and with a tearful countenance.

9. But that deed is well done, which, having been done, does not bring remorse, whose reward one receives delighted and happy.

10. So long as an evil deed does not bear fruit, the fool thinks that it is like honey; but when it bears fruit, then the fool suffers grief.

CHAPTER VI / THE WISE MAN

1. If a person sees a wise man who reproaches him (for his faults), who shows what should be avoided, he should follow such a wise man as he would a revealer of hidden treasures. It fares well and not ill with one who follows such a man.

2. Let him admonish, let him instruct, let him restrain from the impure. He becomes beloved of the good and hated by the evil.

3. One should not associate with friends who are evil-doers nor with persons who are despicable; associate with friends who are virtuous, associate with the best of men.

4. He who drinks in the law lives happily with a serene mind. The wise man ever rejoices in the law made known by the elect (or the Aryas).

5. Engineers (who build canals and aqueducts) lead the water (wherever they like), fletchers make the arrow straight, carpenters carve the wood; wise people fashion (discipline) themselves.

6. As a solid rock is not shaken by the wind, so wise men are not moved amidst blame and praise.

7. Even as a deep lake is clear and calm, so also wise men become tranquil after they have listened to the laws.

8. Good people walk on, whatever happens to them. Good people do not prattle, yearning for pleasures. The wise do not show variation (elation or depression), whether touched by happiness or else by sorrow.

9. He who, for his own sake or for the sake of another, does not wish for a son or wealth or a kingdom, if he does not wish for his own prosperity by unfair means he certainly is virtuous, wise, and religious.

10. Few amongst men are those who reach the farther shore: the other people here run along (this) shore.

11. But those who, when the law has been well preached to them, follow the law, will pass to the other shore, [beyond] the dominion of death which is difficult to overcome.

12. Let the wise man leave the way of darkness and follow the way of light. After going from his home to a homeless state, that retirement so hard to love.

13. Let him look for enjoyment. Putting away all pleasures, calling nothing his own, let the wise man cleanse himself from all the impurities of the heart.

14. Those whose minds are well grounded in the (seven) elements of enlightenment, who without clinging to anything rejoice in freedom from attachment, whose appetites have been conquered, who are full of light, attain *nirvana* in this world.

CHAPTER VII / THE *ARHAT* (THE SAINT)

1. There is no suffering for him who has completed his journey, who is freed from sorrow, who has freed himself on all sides, who has shaken off all fetters.

2. The thoughtful exert themselves; they do not delight in an abode; like swans who have left their lake they leave their house and home.

3. Those who have no accumulation (of property), who eat according to knowledge, who have perceived (the nature of) release and unconditioned freedom, their path is difficult to understand like that (the flight) of birds through the sky.

4. He whose passions are destroyed, who is indifferent to food, who has perceived (the nature of) release and unconditioned freedom, his path is difficult to understand like that of birds through the sky.

5. Even the gods envy him whose senses are subdued like horses well tamed by the charioteer, who is free from pride and free from taints.

6. Such a man who is tolerant like the earth, like a threshold; who does his duty, who is like a lake free from mud: to a man like that there is no cycle of births and deaths.

7. His thought is calm, calm is his word as well as his deed when he has obtained freedom through true knowledge and has become tranquil.

8. The man who is free from credulity, who knows the uncreated, who has severed all ties, who has put an end to all occasions (for the performance of good or bad actions), who has renounced all desires, he, indeed, is exalted among men.

9. That place is delightful where saints dwell, whether in the village or in the forest, in deep water or on dry land.

10. Forests are delightful (to saints); where (ordinary) people find no delight there the passionless will find delight, for they do not seek for the pleasures of sense.

CHAPTER VIII / THE THOUSANDS

4. If a man were to conquer in battle a thousand times a thousand men, and another conquer one, himself, he indeed is the greatest of conquerors.

5. Conquest of self is indeed better than the conquest of other persons; of one who has disciplined himself, who always practises self-control.

6. Not even a god nor a *gandharva* [fairy] nor Mara along with Brahma could turn into defeat the victory of such a one (who has conquered himself).

. . . .

CHAPTER IX / EVIL CONDUCT

1. A man should hasten towards the good; he should restrain his thoughts from evil. If a man is slack in doing what is good, his mind (comes to) rejoice in evil.

2. If a man commits sin, let him not do it again and again. Let him not set his heart on it. Sorrowful is the accumulation of evil conduct.

3. If a man does what is good, let him do it again and again. Let him set his heart on it. Happiness is the outcome of good conduct.

4. Even an evil-doer sees happiness so long as his evil deed does not ripen; but when the evil deed has ripened, then does the evil-doer see evil.

5. Even a good man sees evil as long as his good deed does not ripen; but when his good deed

ripens, then the good man sees the good (in store for him).

6. Think not lightly of evil (saying) that "it will come near me." Even a water-pot is filled by the falling of drops of water. A fool becomes full of evil even if he gathers it little by little.

7. Think not lightly of good (saying) that "it will not come near me." Even a water-pot is filled by the falling of drops of water. A wise man becomes full of goodness even if he gathers it little by little.

8. As a merchant ill-attended and having much wealth shuns a dangerous road, as a man who loves his life avoids poison, so should (a wise man) avoid evil actions.

9. If there be no wound on a person's hand he might touch poison with his hand. Poison does not harm one who has no wound. No evil (befalls) him who does no evil.

10. Whoever does wrong to an innocent person or to one who is pure and sinless, evil recoils on that fool even as fine dust thrown against the wind (recoils on the person throwing it).

11. Some enter the womb; evil-doers go to hell; the good go to heaven; those free from worldly desires attain *nirvana.*

12. Neither in the sky nor in the midst of the sea nor by entering into the clefts of mountains is there known a place on earth where, stationing himself, a man can escape from (the consequences of) his evil deed.

13. Neither in the sky nor in the midst of the sea nor by entering into the clefts of mountains is there known a place on earth where, stationing himself, death cannot overcome (him).

CHAPTER X / PUNISHMENT

1. All men tremble at punishment, all men fear death. Likening others to oneself, one should neither slay nor cause to slay.

2. All men tremble at punishment: all men love life. Likening others to oneself, one should neither slay nor cause to slay.

3. He who seeking his own happiness inflicts pain (strikes with a stick) on beings who (like

himself) are desirous of happiness does not obtain happiness after death.

4. He who seeking his own happiness does not inflict pain (strike with a stick) on beings who (like himself) are desirous of happiness obtains happiness after death.

5. Do not speak anything harsh. Those who are spoken to will answer you (in the same way). Since angry talk is painful, retaliation will touch you.

13. Not nakedness, not matted hair, not dirt (literally mud), not fasting, not lying on the ground, not rubbing with ashes (literally dust), not sitting motionless purify a mortal who is not free from doubt.

14. He who though adorned (dressed in fine clothes) fosters the serene mind, is calm, controlled, is established (in the Buddhist way of life), is chaste, and has ceased to injure all other beings, he indeed is a *brahmin,* an ascetic (*samana*), a friar (a *bhikkhu*).

15. Is there in the world any man so restrained by modesty that he avoids censure as a well-trained horse avoids the whip?

16. Like a well-trained horse when touched by a whip, be strenuous and swift and you will, by faith, by virtue, by energy, by meditation, by discernment of the law, put aside this great sorrow (of earthly existence), endowed with knowledge and (good) behaviour and mindfulness.

17. Engineers (who build canals and aqueducts) lead the water (where they like); fletchers make the arrow straight; carpenters carve the wood; good people fashion (discipline) themselves.

CHAPTER XII / THE SELF

1. If a man holds himself dear, let him diligently watch himself. The wise man should be watchful during one of the three watches.

2. Let each man first establish himself in what is proper, then let him teach others. (If he do this) the wise man will not suffer.

3. If a man so shapes his life as he directs others, then, subduing himself well, he might indeed subdue (others), since the self is indeed difficult to subdue.

4. The self is the lord of self; who else could be the lord? With self well subdued a man finds a lord who is difficult to obtain.

5. The evil done by oneself, born of oneself, produced by oneself, crushes the fool even as a diamond breaks a precious stone.

6. As a creeper overpowers the entwined *sal* tree, he whose impiety is great reduces himself to the state which his enemy wishes for him.

7. Evil deeds, deeds which are harmful to oneself, are easy to do. What is beneficial and good, that is very difficult to do.

8. The foolish man who scorns the teaching of the saintly, the noble, and the virtuous and follows false doctrine, bears fruit to his own destruction even like the *khattaka* reed.

9. By oneself, indeed, is evil done; by oneself is one injured. By oneself is evil left undone; by oneself is one purified. Purity and impurity belong to oneself. No one purifies another.

10. Let no one neglect his own task for the sake of another's, however great; let him, after he has discerned his own task, devote himeself to his task.

CHAPTER XIV / THE BUDDHA (THE AWAKENED)

5. The eschewing of all evil, the perfecting of good deeds, the purifying of one's mind, this is the teaching of the Buddhas (the awakened).

6. Patience which is long suffering is the highest austerity. The awakened declare *nirvana* to be the highest (of things). He verily is not an anchorite who oppresses (others); he is not an ascetic who causes grief to another.

7. Not reviling, not injuring, (practising) restraint according to the law, moderation in eating, dwelling in solitude, diligence in higher thought, this is the teaching of the awakened.

8. There is no satisfaction of one's passions even by a shower of gold pieces. He who knows that "passions are of small enjoyment and productive of pain" is a wise man.

9. Even in celestial pleasures he finds no delight. The disciple who is fully awakened delights only in the destruction of all desires.

10. Men driven by fear go to many a refuge, to mountains, and to forests, to sacred trees, and shrines.

11. That, verily, is not a safe refuge, that is not the best refuge. After having got to that refuge a man is not delivered from all pains.

12. But he who takes refuge in the Buddha, the Law, and the Order, he perceives, in his clear wisdom, the four noble truths.

13. Suffering, the origin of suffering, the cessation of suffering, and the noble eightfold path which leads to the cessation of suffering.

14. That, verily, is a safe refuge, that is the best refuge; after having got to that refuge a man is delivered from all pains.

CHAPTER XV / HAPPINESS

1. Let us live happily then, hating none in the midst of men who hate. Let us dwell free from hate among men who hate.

2. Let us live happily then, free from disease in the midst of those who are afflicted with disease. Let us dwell free from disease among men who are afflicted with disease.

3. Let us live happily then, free from care in the midst of those who are careworn; let us dwell free from care among men who are careworn.

4. Let us live happily then, we who possess nothing. Let us dwell feeding on happiness like the shining gods.

5. Victory breeds hatred; the conquered dwells in

sorrow. He who has given up (thoughts of both) victory and defeat, he is calm and lives happily.

6. There is no fire like passion, no ill like hatred, there is no sorrow like this physical existence (individuality), there is no happiness higher than tranquility.

7. Greediness is the worst of diseases; propensities are the greatest of sorrows. To him who has known this truly, *nirvana* is the highest bliss.

8. Health is the greatest of gifts, contentment is the greatest wealth; trust is the best of relationships. *Nirvana* is the highest happiness.

MAHAYANA WISDOM LITERATURE

Early in the history of Buddhism, a split occurred among its followers. This split was based on different conceptions about the Middle Way's ultimate purpose. According to the schools that came to be associated with the Southern Canon, the ideal is to become an *arhat* (saint)*, one who loses all individual personality in universal, impersonal, unconceptualizable bliss and awareness that somehow underlie all appearance. According to Mahayana Buddhism (the northern branch), in contrast, the truest aim is to become a *bodhisattva,* who, unlike the arhat, turns back from this final bliss and extinction of personality to help every conscious being attain it.

From the perspective of a Mahayanist, the Southern Canon presents, by and large, a course of spiritual discipline and a goal that are not the best and the highest, because they are personally oriented. Mahayanists, instead, focus their efforts on acquiring the six moral, intellectual, and spiritual perfections† possessed by the Buddha, which enable them to promote the welfare of all beings. Thus Mahayana is the more world-affirming of the two branches; its aim is the development of individual perfections rather than the extinction of individuality and personality in an other-worldly bliss. Individual form must not be relinquished, because it is needed as a medium to help others. Mahayanists do not deny many of the doctrines of the Southern Canon but instead interpret them as the Buddha's means of aiding people unable to appreciate higher spiritual truths.

The six personal perfections Mahayanists aspire to are liberality or charity, good moral character, patience or peace in the face of anger or desires, energy (the energy to strive for the good), the ability to maintain deep meditation, and—most important—insight or wisdom.

The first selection, from the *Large Sutra on Perfect Wisdom,* elaborates these as well as the bodhisattva ideal. The two selections from the *Surangama Sutra* contain a Mahayana version of the ethical inspiration the Buddha provides followed by the Buddha's explanations why certain conduct is both morally right and in one's own best interest. The final selection, from the *Lankavatara Sutra,* delineates ten stages on the bodhisattva path to perfection. (See the Glossary for definitions of important Sanskrit terms in these passages.)

---

* Also called a Pratyeka-Buddha in the texts that follow.
† Also called Paramitas in the texts that follow.

from the *Large Sutra on Perfect Wisdom*

CHAPTER 13 / THE SIX PERFECTIONS

I 7–10. The Progress as Such.

(4. *Armed with the great armour.*)

PURNA, SON OF MAITRAYANI: It is clear also to me in what sense a Bodhisattva is called a "great being."

THE LORD: Make it clear then, Purna!

PURNA: A Bodhisattva is called a "great being," because that being is armed with the great armour, has set out in the great vehicle, has mounted on the great vehicle.

SARIPUTRA: How great is that which entitles him to be called "armed with the great armour"?

PURNA: Here a Bodhisattva, who courses towards enlightenment, and has stood firmly in the perfection of giving, gives a gift not for the sake of a limited number of beings, but, on the contrary, for the sake of all beings. And in the same spirit he practises the other perfections. A Bodhisattva is not armed with the great armour if he delimits a certain number of beings, and thinks, "so many beings will I lead to Nirvana, so many beings will I not lead to Nirvana; so many beings will I introduce to enlightenment, so many beings will I not introduce to enlightenment!" But on the contrary, it is for the sake of all beings that he is armed with the great armour, and he thinks, "I myself will fulfil the six perfections and also on all beings will I enjoin them." And the same with the Unlimited . . . By something as great as that is a Bodhisattva, a great being called "armed with the great armour."

I 7. *The Progress which Consists in Putting on the Armour.*

I 7a. The Sextad Connected with the Perfection of Giving.

Furthermore, Sariputra, the perfection of giving of a Bodhisattva, who courses in perfect wisdom and gives gifts, consists in that, with attentions associated with the knowledge of all modes, he turns over to full enlightenment that gift which he gives, after he has made that wholesome root (which results from the act of giving) common to all beings. His perfection of morality consists in that, with his whole attention centred on the knowledge of all modes, he shuns the attentions of Disciples and Pratyekabuddhas; his perfection of patience in the enduring of those dharmas, in his willingness to find pleasure in them, in his ability to tolerate them; his perfection of vigour in the indefatigability with which he continues to dedicate his wholesome roots to full enlightenment, after he has made them common to all beings; his perfection of concentration in his one-pointedness of thought when he gives a gift, so that, when he dedicates that wholesome root to enlightenment, after he has made it common to all beings, he gives, through keeping his whole attention centred on the knowledge of all modes, no opportunity to a Disciple-thought or a Pratyekabuddha-thought. His perfection of wisdom consists in that he sets up the notion that everything is made of illusion and in that he gets at no giver, recipient, or gift. With his thought associated with the knowledge of all modes, that Bodhisattva does not make these six perfections into a sign, and does not get at them. It is thus that a Bodhisattva, who courses in perfect wisdom, is armed with the great armour.

I 7b. The Second Sextad Connected with the Perfection of Morality.

Furthermore, a Bodhisattva, who courses in the perfection of morality, gives a gift with attentions associated with the knowledge of all modes, dedicates it to full enlightenment, after he has made (the merit from) that gift common to all beings—and that without taking anything as a basis. This is the perfection of giving of a Bodhisattva who courses in the perfection of morality. With his whole attention centred on the knowledge of all modes, a Bodhisattva does not long for the level of a Disciple or Pratyekabuddha, and much less still for the level of the common people. This is the perfection of morality of a Bodhisattva who courses in the perfection of morality. The enduring of those dharmas, the willingness to find pleasure in them, the ability to tolerate them, that is the perfection of patience of a Bodhisattva who courses in the perfection of morality. The indefatigability and uncowedness with which he continues to dedicate his wholesome roots to full enlightenment, after he has made them common to all beings that is the perfection of vigour of a Bodhisattva who courses in the perfection of morality. The one-pointedness of thought of a Bodhisattva who practises morality, i.e. that he gives, through keeping his whole attention centred on the knowledge of all modes, no opportunity to productions of thought associated with Disciples and Pratyekabuddhas, when he dedicates that wholesome root to full enlightenment, after he has made it common to all beings. He sets up the notion that everything is made of illusion; he gets at no one who practises morality, and that morality he does not either mind or get at; this is the perfection of wisdom of a Bodhisattva who courses in the perfection of morality. It is thus that a Bodhisattva who courses in the perfection of morality takes hold of the six perfections. It is thus that he comes to be called "armed with the great armour."

I 7c. The Third Sextad Connected with the Perfection of Patience.

Furthermore, a Bodhisattva, who courses in the perfection of patience, gives a gift; with his attention centred on the knowledge of all modes, and not associated with Disciples or Pratyekabuddhas, he dedicates that wholesome root to full enlightenment, having made it common to all beings; this is the perfection of giving of a Bodhisattva who courses in the perfection of patience. The perfection of morality, patience, vigour, and concentration of the Bodhisattva who courses in the perfection of patience, should be understood by analogy with what has been said before. A Bodhisattva, who courses in the perfection of patience, exerts himself through wisdom to procure all Buddhadharmas, and to mature all beings; this is the perfection of wisdom of a Bodhisattva who courses in the perfection of patience.

I 7d. The Fourth Sextad, Connected with the Perfection of Vigour.

By analogy one should understand the six perfections of a Bodhisattva who courses in the perfection of vigour.

I 7e. The Fifth Sextad, Connected with the Perfection of Meditation and Concentration.

I 7f. The Sixth Sextad, Connected with the Perfection of Wisdom.

Furthermore, a Bodhisattva, who courses in the perfection of wisdom, gives a gift which is threefold pure; with his attention centred on the knowledge of all modes, he dedicates to full enlightenment that gift which he gives, after he has made that wholesome root common to all beings. This is the perfection of giving of a Bodhisattva who courses in the perfection of wisdom. Similarly should one understand the perfection of morality, patience, vigour, and concentration of a Bodhisattva who courses in perfect wisdom. With regard to all perfections, and to all dharmas, he sets up the notion that they are an illusion, a dream, a reflected image, an echo, a reflection, a magical creation; with his attention centred on all-knowledge, he dedicates to full enlightenment that wholesome root, after he has made it common to all beings. It is thus that a Bodhisattva, who courses in perfect wisdom, fulfils the perfection of wisdom. A Bodhisattva is then called "armed with the great armour." It is thus that a Bodhisattva, having stood firm in each single perfection, fulfils all the six perfections.

I 7g. The Armour of the Skill in Means.

Furthermore, a Bodhisattva enters into the trances, Unlimited, and formless attainments, but he does not relish them, is not captivated by them, is not reborn on account of them. This, Sariputra, is of a Bodhisattva, a great being, the perfection of wisdom which is associated with skill in means. A Bodhisattva furthermore dwells in the trances and formless attainments by way of the vision of detachment, of emptiness, of the signless, of the wishless, and yet he does not realize the reality limit. This is the great armour of the skill in means of the Bodhisattva who courses in the perfection of wisdom.

I 7h. The Résumé of the Sextad on the Armour.

It is thus that a Bodhisattva is called "armed with the great armour." About this Bodhisattva the Buddhas, the Lords, in the ten directions utter a shout of triumph, proclaim his praise, announce his name, and make the pronouncement that "in this world system that Bodhisattva, that great being is armed with the great armour!" And he matures beings and purifies the Buddha-field.

I 8. The Progress in Setting Out.

(5. *Set out in the great vehicle.*)

SARIPUTRA: Through how much does the Bodhisattva become one who has set out in the great vehicle, one who has mounted on the great vehicle?

I 8,1. The Entering on and Emerging from the Trances and Formless Attainments.

PURNA: Here, coursing in the perfection of giving, a Bodhisattva dwells detached from sense desires, detached from evil and unwholesome dharmas, in the attainment of the first trance, which is with thoughts adjusted and discursive, born of detachment, full of rapture and ease. And so for all the four trances, and for the four formless attainments. These are a Bodhisattva's trances and formless attainments. When a Bodhisattva courses in the perfection of giving through these trances and formless attainments, enters into and emerges from them, through the modes, characteristics and signs of space makes these wholesome roots common to all beings, and dedicates them to full enlightenment—then this is a Bodhisattva's perfection of giving. Similarly he acts with regard to the perfections of morality, patience, vigour, and concentration. Moreover, a Bodhisattva, coursing in the perfection of wisdom, enters into the four trances and the four formless attainments. When a Bodhisattva dwells through these trances and attainments in the perfection of wisdom, and, while entering into and emerging from them attends to the modes, characteristics and signs of space, and, coursing in the perfection of wisdom, makes these, and other, wholesome roots common to all beings, through attentions connected with the knowledge of all modes, and dedicates them to full enlightenment—then this is a Bodhisattva's perfection of wisdom. It is thus that a Bodhisattva, who courses in the six perfections, is called "one who has set out in the great vehicle."

I 8,2. The Six Perfections.

Furthermore, it is the perfection of giving of the Bodhisattva if, with his attention centred on the knowledge of all modes, he produces a thought controlled by the great compassion, and thinks, "for the sake of the demolition of the defilements will I demonstrate the trances, Unlimited and formless attainments to all beings." It is his untarnished perfection of morality if, with his attention centred on the knowledge of all modes, he enters into the trances, and, firmly grounded in them, does not give an opportunity to other productions of thought associated with the Disciples and Pratyekabuddhas. When it occurs to a Bodhisattva who, with his attention centred on the knowledge of all modes, dwells in the trances and formless attainments, that "for the purpose of the extinction of the defilements of all beings will I demonstrate Dharma," then the enduring of those attentions, the willingness to find pleasure in them, to test and understand them, and to meditate on them, that is a Bodhisattva's perfection of patience. It is a Bodhisattva's perfection of vigour that, through his attentions connected with the knowledge of all modes, he dedicates all wholesome roots to full enlightenment, and never relaxes his vigour. It is his perfection of concentration that, through his attentions connected with the knowledge of all modes, he enters into the trances and formless attainments, and yet does not apprehend them. It is his perfection of wisdom that he contemplates the limbs of the trances under the aspects of impermanent, ill, not-self . . . wishless, and yet does not apprehend them. This is the great vehicle of the Bodhisattva, the great being.

I 8,3. The Path.

Furthermore, this is the great vehicle of a Bodhisattva that, in all their modes, he develops the dharmas which are the 37 wings of enlightenment, the concentrations which are the doors to freedom—Emptiness, the Signless, the Wishless—the (ten) powers, the grounds of self-confidence, and the 18 special dharmas of a Buddha.

I 8,5. The Four Unlimited.

Furthermore, a Bodhisattva dwells with a thought connected with friendliness—a thought that is vast, extensive, nondual, unlimited, free from hostility, rivalry, hindrance, or injury to anyone, extends everywhere and is well cultivated; he radiates friendliness in the ten directions of the world which has as its highest (development) the Dharma-element, and the space-element as its terminus. And so with compassion, sympathetic joy, and impartiality. These are called the four Unlimited of the Bodhisattva, the great being. A Bodhisattva enters the concentration

of friendliness, and strives to save all beings. He enters the concentration on compassion, and directs pity and compassion towards beings. He enters the concentration on sympathetic joy, and resolves to make beings rejoice. He enters the concentration on impartiality, and "extends" to beings the extinction of the outflows. This is the perfection of giving of the Bodhisattva who courses in the Unlimited. When a Bodhisattva enters into the modes, characteristics and signs of the trances and Unlimited, and emerges from them, and yet does not dedicate (the resulting merit) to the level of a Disciple or Pratyekabuddha, but to nothing else than the knowledge of all modes—then this is the untarnished perfection of morality of the Bodhisattva who courses in the Unlimited. When he dwells in those trances, Unlimited, and formless attainments free from contamination, and does not long for the two levels of a Disciple or a Pratyekabuddha, but just the knowledge of all modes seems good to him and pleases him—then this is the perfection of patience of the Bodhisattva who courses in the Unlimited. If, through the production of thoughts associated with the knowledge of all modes, he dwells as one who perseveres in forsaking unwholesome and in accomplishing wholesome dharmas—then this is the perfection of vigour of the Bodhisattva who courses in the Unlimited. If, although he enters into those trances, Unlimited, and formless attainments, he does not gain his rebirths through them, does not relish them, is not captivated by them—then this is the perfection of concentration of a Bodhisattva who courses in the Unlimited. If, with his attentions centred on the knowledge of all modes, he enters into the trances, Unlimited and formless attainments and emerges from them, and contemplates them under the aspects of impermanence, ill, not-self, of quietude, emptiness, signlessness and wishlessness, but does not go forward to the way of salvation of the Disciples and Pratyekabuddhas—then this is the perfection of wisdom of a Bodhisattva who courses in the Unlimited. This is the great vehicle of the Bodhisattva, the great being.

from *The Surangama Sutra*

Reprinted from the Surangama Sutra, translated by Bhikshu Wai-tao and Dwight Goddard, in Dwight Goddard (ed.), A Buddhist Bible. *Copyright © 1938 by Beacon Press.*

CHAPTER 1 / THE MANY MANIFESTATIONS OF THE WONDLERFUL ESSENCE-MIND, AND OF THE PERFECT PRINCIPLE OF THE THREE EXCELLENCIES WITHIN THE ALL-INCLUSIVE UNITY OF THE WOMB OF TATHAGATA.

(False Mind vs True Mind.)

When Ananda came into the presence of the Lord Buddha, he bowed down to the ground in great humility, blaming himself that he had not yet fully developed the potentialities of Enlightenment, because from the beginning of his previous lives, he had too much devoted himself to study and learning. He earnestly pleaded with the Lord Buddha and with all the other Tathagatas from the ten quarters of the Universe, to support him in attaining perfect Enlightenment, that is, to support him in his practice of the Three Excellencies of Dhyana, Samadhi and Samapatti, by some most fundamental and expedient means.

At the same time, all of the Bodhisattvas-Mahasattva, as numerous as the sands of the river Ganges, together with all the Arhats, Pratyeka-Buddhas, from all the ten quarters, with one accord and with gladness of heart, prepared to listen to the instruction to be given to Ananda by the Lord Buddha. With one accord they paid homage to the Lord and then resuming their seats, waited in perfect quietness and patience to receive the sacred teaching.

Then the Lord Buddha spoke to Ananda, saying:—Ananda, you and I are from the same ancestral blood and we have always cherished a fraternal affection for each other. Let me ask you a few questions and you answer me spontaneously and freely. When you first began to be interested in Buddhism what was it that impressed you in our Buddhist way of life and most influenced you to forsake all worldly pleasures and enabled you to cut asunder your youthful sexual cravings?

Ananda replied:—Oh, my Lord! The first thing that impressed me were the thirty-two marks of excellency in my Lord's personality. They appeared to me so fine, as tender and brilliant, and transparent as a crystal.

From that time I have constantly thought about them and have been more and more convinced that these marks of excellence would be impossible for anyone who was not free from all sexual passion and desire. And why? Because when anyone becomes inflamed by sexual passion, his mind becomes disturbed and confused, he loses self-control and becomes reckless and crude. Besides, in sexual intercourse, the blood becomes inflamed and impure and adulterated with impure secretions. Naturally from such a source, there can never originate an aureole of such transcendently pure and golden brightness as I have seen emanating from the person of my Lord. It was because of this that I admired my Lord and it was this that influenced me to become one of thy true followers.

The Lord Buddha then said:—Very good, Ananda! All of you in this Great Dharma Assembly ought to know and appreciate that the reason why sentient beings by their previous lives since beginningless time have formed a succession of deaths and rebirths, life after life, is because they have never realized the true Essence of Mind and its self-purifying brightness. On the contrary they have been absorbed all the time busying themselves with their deluding and transient thoughts which are nothing but falsity and vanity. Hence they have prepared for themselves the conditions for this ever returning cycle of deaths and rebirths.

· ·

After such a manner have the four orders of sentient life been ever wandering in the recurring cycles of deaths and rebirths wholly in close correspondence to the conditions of karma accumulated by them in previous lives. The lives that come from eggs were conceived by means of mutual intercourse that had been inspired by thoughts of each other; lives that are born from wombs, conceive by means of lust and concupiscence; lives that come from spawn come by the conjunction of conformable cells; lives that come by metamorphosis come by means of transformation and separation of cells. Because of these causes and conditions there rises the false conception of a reciprocal continuance of sentient lives.

Again, Purna! When mutual thinking and lustful desire combine the attraction is so intense that the two cannot be separated and, thus, parenthood and posterity will ever continue their reciprocal rebirths because of this lustful desire. So great is this lust and greed that it can not be restrained and thus, all these four great orders of life prey upon each other according to their relative strength—the bodies of the weak becoming the prey of the strong. Thus the killing of sentient beings is always because of greed in some form. When a man kills a sheep for food, the sheep gives rebirth to a man and the man gives rebirth to a sheep, and so the reciprocal killing goes on ever increasing without termination through innumerable kalpas of time. This awful suffering and retribution is all because of greed. So the proverb runs:—"You owe me your life, but I must repay the debt." Because of these causes and conditions all sentient lives have been fast bound to the cycle of deaths and rebirths after hundreds and thousands of kalpas. Another proverb says:—"You love my inner heart, but I love your outer beauty," so because of all these causes and conditions, all sentient beings have been entangled in cycles of deaths and rebirths for hundreds and thousands of kalpas. All this suffering and retribution is based upon lust, greed and killing, and because of the causes and conditions arising from them, there is the false conception of the continuity of karmas and their inevitable fruit.

Again, Purna! The pure Essence of Mind leads toward enlightenment and peace, but these three deluding entanglements of lust, greed and killing, are the very reverse and lead toward entanglement, strife, suffering, deaths and rebirths and all rise from the illusive thinking of the discriminating mind. Because of this false thinking there becomes manifest all the false phenomena that fall within the range of the sense organs. Thus all these conditional phenomena of rivers, mountains, earth, etc., and their successive and endless changes arise, and all are based upon the illusions of the thinking mind without any other interpretation. . . .

from *The Lankavatara Sutra*

Reprinted from Lankavatara Sutra, *translated by D. T. Suzuki (Tokyo: Eastern Buddhist Society, 1929).*

CHAPTER XI / BODHISATTVAHOOD AND ITS STAGES

Then said Mahamati to the Blessed One: Will you tell us now about the disciples who are Bodhisattvas?

The Blessed One replied: The Bodhisattvas are those earnest disciples who are enlightened by reason of their efforts to attain self-realisation of Noble Wisdom and who have taken upon themselves the task to enlighten others. They have gained a clear understanding of the truth that all things are empty, un-born, and of a maya-like nature; they have ceased from viewing things discriminatively and from considering them in their relations; they thoroughly understand the truth of twofold egolessness and have adjusted themselves to it with patient acceptance; they have attained a definite realisation of imagelessness; and they are abiding in the perfect-knowledge that they have gained by self-realisation of Noble Wisdom.

Well stamped by the seal of "Suchness" they entered upon the first of the Bodhisattva stages. The first stage is called the Stage of Joy. Entering this stage is like passing out of the glare and shadows into a realm of "no-shadows"; it is like passing out of the noise and tumult of the crowded city into the quietness of solitude. The Bodhisattva feels within himself the awakening of a great heart of compassion and he utters his ten original vows: To honor and serve all Buddhas; to spread the knowledge and practice of the Dharma; to welcome all coming Buddhas; to practise the six Paramitas; to persuade all beings to embrace the Dharma; to attain a perfect understanding of the universe; to attain a perfect understanding of the mutuality of all beings; to attain perfect self-realisation of the oneness of all the Buddhas and Tathagatas in self-nature, purpose and resources; to become acquainted with all skillful means for the carrying out of these vows for the emancipation of all beings; to realise supreme enlightenment through the perfect self-realisation of Noble Wisdom, ascending the stages and entering Tathagatahood.

In the spirit of these vows the Bodhisattva gradually ascends the stages to the sixth. All earnest disciples, masters and Arhats have ascended thus far, but being enchanted by the bliss of the Samadhis and not being supported by the powers of the Buddhas, they pass to their Nirvana. The same fate would befall the Bodhisattvas except for the sustaining power of the Buddhas, by that they are enabled to refuse to enter Nirvana until all beings can enter Nirvana with them. The Tathagatas point out to them the virtues of Buddhahood which are beyond the conception of the intellectual-mind, and they encourage and strengthen the Bodhisattvas not to give in to the enchantment of the bliss of the Samadhis, but to press on to further advancement along the stages. If the Bodhisattvas had entered Nirvana at this stage, and they would have done so without the sustaining power of the Buddhas, there would have been the cessation of all things and the family of the Tathagatas would have become extinct.

Strengthened by the new strength that comes to them from the Buddhas and with the more perfect insight that is theirs by reason of their advance in self-realisation of Noble Wisdom, they re-examine the nature of the mind-system, the egolessness of personality, and the part that grasping and attachment and habit-energy play in the unfolding drama of life; they re-examine the illusions of the fourfold logical analysis, and the various elements that enter into enlightenment and self-realisation, and, in the thrill of their new powers of self-mastery, the Bodhisattva enter upon the seventh stage of Far-going.

Supported by the sustaining power of the Buddhas, the Bodhisattvas at this stage enter into the bliss of the Samadhi of perfect tranquillisation. Owing to their original vows they are transported by emotions of love and compassion as they become aware of the part they are to perform in the carrying out of their vows for the emancipation of all beings. Thus they do not enter into Nirvana, but, in truth, they too are already in Nirvana because in their emotions of love and compassion there is no rising of discrimination; henceforth, with them, discrimination no more takes place. Because of Transcendental Intelligence only one conception is present —the promotion of the realisation of Noble Wisdom. Their insight issues from the Womb of Tathagatahood and they enter into their task with spontaneity and radiancy because it is of the self-nature of Noble Wisdom. This is called the Bodhisattva's Nirvana—the losing oneself in the bliss of perfect self-yielding. This is the seventh stage, the stage of Far-going.

The eighth stage, is the stage of No-recession. Up to this stage, because of the defilements upon the face of Universal Mind caused by the accumulation of habit-energy since beginningless time, the mind-system and all that pertains to it has been evolved and sustained. The mind-system functioned by the discriminations of an external and objective world to which it became attached and by which it was perpetuated. But with the Bodhisattva's attainment of the eighth stage there comes the "turning-about" within his deepest consciousness from self-centered egoism to universal compassion for all beings, by which he attains perfect self-realisation of Noble Wisdom. There is an instant cessation of the delusive activities of the whole mind-system; the dancing of the waves of habit-energy on the face of Universal Mind are forever stilled, revealing its own inherent quietness and solitude, the inconceivable Oneness of the Womb of Tathagatahood.

Henceforth there is no more looking outward upon an external world by senses and sense-minds, nor a discrimination of particularised concepts and ideas and propositions by an intellectual-mind, no more grasping, nor attachment, nor pride of egoism, nor habit-energy. Henceforth there is only the inner experience of Noble Wisdom which has been attained by entering into its perfect Oneness.

Thus establishing himself at the eighth stage of No-recession, the Bodhisattva enters into the bliss of the ten Samadhis, but avoiding the path of the disciples and masters who yielded themselves up to their entrancing bliss and who passed to their Nirvanas, and supported by his vows and the Transcendental Intelligence which now is his and being sustained by the power of the Buddhas, he enters upon the higher paths that lead to Tathagatahood. He passes through the bliss of the Samadhis to assume the transformation body of a Tathagata that through him all beings may be emancipated. Mahamati, If there had been no Tathagata-womb and no Divine Mind then there would have been no rising and disappearance of the aggregates that make up personality and its external world, no rising and disappearance of ignorant people nor holy people, and no task for Bodhisattvas; therefore, while walking in the path of self-realisation and entering into the enjoyments of the Samadhis, you must never abandon working hard for the emancipation of all beings and your self-yielding love will never be in vain. To philosophers the conception of Tathagata-womb seems devoid of purity and soiled by these external manifestations, but it is not so understood by the Tathagatas—to them it is not a proposition of philosophy but is an intuitive experience as real as though it was an amalaka fruit held in the palm of the hand.

With the cessation of the mind-system and all its evolving discriminations, there is cessation of all strain and effort. It is like a man in a dream who imagines he is crossing a river and who exerts himself to the utmost to do so, who is suddenly awakened. Being awake, he thinks: "Is this real or is it unreal?" Being now enlightened, he knows that it is neither real nor unreal. Thus when the Bodhisattva arrives at the eighth stage, he is able to see all things truthfully and, more than that, he is able to thoroughly understand the significance of all the dream-like things of his life as to how they came to pass and as to how they pass away. Ever since beginningless time the mind-system has perceived multiplicities of forms and conditions and ideas which the thinking-mind has discriminated and the empirical-mind has experienced and grasped and clung to. From this has risen habit-energy that by its accumulation has conditioned the illusions of existence and non-existence, individuality and generality, and has thus perpetuated the dream-state of false-imagination. But now, to the Bodhisattvas of the eighth stage, life is past and is remembered as it truly was—a passing dream.

As long as the Bodhisattva had not passed the seventh stage, even though he had attained an intuitive understanding of the true meaning of life and its maya-like nature, and as to how the mind carried on its discriminations and attachments yet, nevertheless, the cherishing of the notions of these things had continued and, although he no longer experienced within himself any ardent desire for things nor any impulse to grasp them yet, nevertheless, the notions concerning them persisted and perfumed his efforts to practise the teachings of the Buddhas and to labor for the emancipation of all beings. Now, in the eighth stage, even the notions have passed away, and all effort and striving is seen to be unnecessary. The Bodhisattva's Nirvana is perfect tranquillisation, but it is not extinction nor inertness; while there is an entire absence of discrimination and purpose, there is the freedom and spontaneity of potentiality that has come with the attainment and patient acceptance of the truths of egolessness and imagelessness. Here is perfect solitude, undisturbed by any gradation or continuous succession, but radiant with the potency and freedom of its self-nature which is the self-nature of Noble Wisdom, blissfully peaceful with the serenity of Perfect Love.

Entering upon the eighth stage, with the "turning-about" at the deepest seat of consciousness, the Bodhisattva will become conscious that he has received the second kind of Transcendental-body. The transition from mortal-body to Transcendental-body has nothing to do with mortal death, for the old body continues to function and the old mind serves the needs of the old body, but now it is free from the control of mortal mind. There has been an inconceivable transformation-death by which the false-imagination of his particularised individual personality has been transcended by a realisation of his oneness with the universalised mind of Tathagatahood, from which realisation there will be no recession. With that realisation he finds himself amply endowed with all the Tathagata's powers, psychic faculties, and self-mastery, and, just as the good earth is the support of all

beings in the world of desire, so the Tathagatas become the support of all beings in the Transcendental World of No-form.

The first seven of the Bodhisattva stages were in the realm of mind and the eighth, while transcending mind, was still in touch with it; but in the ninth stage of Transcendental Intelligence, by reason of his perfect intelligence and insight into the imagelessness of Divine Mind which he had attained by self-realisation of Noble Wisdom, he is in the realm of Tathagatahood. Gradually the Bodhisattva will realise his Tathagata-nature and the possession of all its powers and psychic faculties, self-mastery, loving compassion, and skillful means, and by means of them will enter into all the Buddha-lands. Making use of these new powers, the Bodhisattva will assume various transformation-bodies and personalities for the sake of benefiting others. Just as in the former mental life, imagination had risen from relative-knowledge, so now skillful-means rise spontaneously from Transcendental Intelligence. It is like the magical gem that reflects instantaneously appropriate responses to one's wishes. The Bodhisattva passes over to all the assemblages of the Buddhas and listens to them as they discourse on the dream-like nature of all things and concerning the truths that transcend all notions of being and non-being, that have no relation to birth and death, nor to eternality nor extinction. Thus facing the Tathagatas as they discourse on Noble Wisdom that is far beyond the mental capacity of disciples and masters, he will attain a hundred thousand Samadhis, indeed, a hundred thousand nyutas of kotis of Samadhis, and in the spirit of these Samadhis he will instantly pass from one Buddha-land to another, paying homage to all the Buddhas, being born into all the celestial mansions, manifesting Buddha-bodies, and himself discoursing on the Triple Treasure to lesser Bodhisattvas that they too may partake of the fruits of self-realisation of Noble Wisdom.

Thus passing beyond the last stage of Bodhisattvahood, he becomes a Tathagata himself endowed with all the freedom of the Dharmakaya. The tenth stage belongs to the Tathagatas. Here the Bodhisattva will find himself seated upon a lotuslike throne in a splendid jewel-adorned palace and surrounded by Bodhisattvas of equal rank. Buddhas from all the Buddha-lands will gather about him and with their pure and fragrant hands resting on his forehead will give him ordination and recognition as one of themselves. Then they will assign him a Buddha-land that he may possess and perfect as his own.

The tenth stage is called the Great Truth Cloud, inconceivable, inscrutable. Only the Tathagatas can realise its perfect Imagelessness and Oneness and Solitude. It is Mahesvara, the Radiant Land, the Pure Land, the Land of Far-distances; surrounding and surpassing the lesser worlds of form and desire, in which the Bodhisattva will find himself at-one-ment. Its rays of Noble Wisdom which is the self-nature of the Tathagatas, many-colored, entrancing, auspicious, are transforming the triple world as other worlds have been transformed in the past, and still other worlds will be transformed in the future. But in the Perfect Oneness of Noble Wisdom there is no gradation nor succession nor effort. The tenth stage is the first, the first is the eighth, the eighth is the fifth, the fifth is the seventh: what gradation can there be where perfect Imagelessness and Oneness prevail? And what is the reality of Noble Wisdom? It is the ineffable potency of the Dharmakaya; it has no bounds nor limits; it surpasses all the Buddha-lands, and pervades the Akanistha and the heavenly mansions of the Tushita.

THE JAIN CANONS

Mahavira, the founder of Jainism, lived in the sixth century B.C.E., roughly contemporary with the Buddha. Of all the early Indian philosophies organized around a mystical *summum bonum,* Jainism is the most renowned for its ethical commitment to the value of life. Jains are vegetarians; moreover, Jain monks have been known to wear masks so that their breathing will not cause injury to insects. Regarding even vegetable life as sentient beings, some Jain monks have even starved themselves to death to prevent injury to others. Noninjury, *ahimsa,* an ideal popularized in modern times by Mahatma Gandhi, was propagated in ancient and classical India principally by the Jains.

Like Buddhist scriptures, the Jain canon is immense. The selections below are drawn from an early work that discusses *ahimsa.* Note that the practice is justified not simply because it is conducive to one's own highest end but because, to the Jains, all living things have souls, and all souls are of equal worth. Introspecting, I realize that injury to me is bad for me; I conclude that injury to others is similarly bad for them. Their souls are as valuable as my own. Therefore, all injury must be avoided. A similar line of reasoning appears in Buddhism; see *The Dhammapada,* Chapter X, verses 1 and 2, on page 185. But that argument discusses only human beings. Jains extend it to all sentient life.

from the *Acaranga Sutra*

Reprinted from Ayaro (Acaranga Sutra), *translated by Muni Mahendra Kumar (New Delhi: Today and Tomorrow's Printers and Publishers, 1981). Copyright © 1981 by Jain Vishva Bharati.*

The True Doctrine: Non-violence

1. I say —

    The Arhats (Venerable Ones) of the past, those of the present and the future narrate thus, discourse thus, proclaim thus, and asseverate thus:

    One should not injure, subjugate, enslave, torture or kill any animal, living being, organism or sentient being.

2. This Doctrine of Non-violence (viz. *Ahimsa-dharma*) is immaculate, immutable and eternal.

    The Self-realised *Arhats,* having comprehended the world (of living beings), have propounded this (Doctrine).

3. (The *Arhats* have propounded the Doctrine of Non-violence for one and all, equally for) those who are intent on practising it and
    those who are not;
    those who are desirous to practise it and
    those who are not;
    those who have eschewed violence and
    those who have not;
    those who are acquisitive and those who
    are not;
    those who are deeply engrossed in worldly ties and those who are not.

4. This Doctrine of *Ahimsa* is Truth. It is truely axiomatic. It is rightly enunciated here (i.e. in the Teachings of the *Arhats*).

5. Having accepted this (Great vow of Non-violence), one should neither vitiate it nor forsake it.

    Comprehending the true spirit of the Doctrine, (one should practise it till one's last breath).

6. He should be dispassionate towards sensual objects.

7. He should refrain from worldly desires.
    [Annotation] The three main worldly desires are—craving for son, wealth and longevity. A *sadhaka** should not cherish these as well as such other worldly desires.

8. How can one who is bereft of the knowledge of this (Doctrine of *Ahimsa*), have the knowledge of other (Doctrines)?

9. This (Doctrine of Non-violence) which is being expounded has been perceived, heard, deliberated upon and thoroughly understood.
    [Annotation] Bhagavan Mahavira has asserted that everyone is endowed with the faculty of independent reasoning. On the basis of this principle he said—"Search for the truth yourself."

    He did not insist that the Doctrine of Non-violence should be practised because it has been enunciated by him. He averred: "Whatever I say about the doctrine has been directly perceived by the Seers, heard from the preceptors, thrashed out by profound reasoning and thoroughly comprehended through contemplation."

    The process of the development of the knowledge consists not in accepting what is propounded by the Seers through direct perception by faith alone, but in hearing, profound reasoning and thorough comprehension.

---

* A person following the Path. —ED.

10. Those who resort to and remain engrossed in violence suffer (the miseries of) trans-migration again and again.

11. O *Sadhaka!* You, who are endeavouring day and night; discern that those who are stupefied are outside the sphere of the Doctrine (of Non-violence). You should, therefore, be alert and always sedulous. . . .

20. Some put forth mutually . . . contradictory doctrines in the field (of philosophy).

 Some of them contend: "The following doctrine has been perceived, heard, reflected upon, thoroughly, comprehended and scrutinized in all directions—upwards, downwards and lateral:

 'All animals, living beings, organisms and sentient creatures may be injured, governed, enslaved, tortured and killed.'

 "Know that there is no sin in committing violence."

21. This (approval of violence) is the doctrine of the ignoble ones.

22. Those who are Noble Ones assert thus: "O Protagonists of the doctrine of violence! Whatever you have perceived, heard, reflected upon, thoroughly comprehended and scrutinized in all directions—upwards, downwards and lateral, is fallacious, and hence, you say, speak, assert and preach: 'All animals, living beings, organisms and sentient creatures may be injured, governed, enslaved, tortured and killed: Know that there is no sin in committing violence.'

23. "We, on the other hand, say, speak, assert and preach: 'All animals, living beings, organisms and sentient creatures should not be injured, governed, enslaved, tortured and killed.' Know that it is non-violence which is (completely) free from sin."

24. This (approval of non-violence) is the doctrine of the Noble ones.

25. First, we shall ask (each philosopher) to enunciate his own doctrine and then put the following question to him: "O philosophers! Is suffering pleasing to you or painful?

26. "(If you say that suffering is pleasing to you, your answer is contradictory to what is self-evident. And if you, on the other hand, say that suffering is painful to you, then) your answer is valid. Then, we want to tell you that just as suffering is painful to you, in the same way it is painful, disquieting and ter-rifying to all animals, living beings, organ-isms and sentient beings."

122. Through observation and scrutiny find out for yourself that inquietude is distasteful to, highly terrifying and painful for all animals, all beings, all those throbbing with life and all souls. So do I say. . . .

123. (Being overwhelmed by grief), the creatures are scared from (all) directions and inter-mediate directions. . . .

124. See! Almost everywhere the passionate man are tormenting (mobile-beings).

125. (Each of the) mobile-beings has its own body to inhabit.

126. See! Every (ascetic who has ceased from causing violence to these beings), leads a life of self-discipline.

127. (And discern from them) those psuedo-monks who, despite professing, "We are mendicants," (act like householders i.e. cause violence to the mobile-beings).

131. Some monk either indulges himself in action causing violence to the mobile-beings through various kinds of weapons, makes others to cause violence to the mobile-beings, or approves of others causing vio-lence to the mobile-beings.

132. Such an act of violence proves baneful for him, such an act of violence deprives him of enlightenment.

133. He (true ascetic), comprehending it (i.e. con-sequences of act of violence), becomes vigi-lant over the practice of self-discipline.

134. Hearing from the Bhagavan Mahavira Him-self or from the monks, one comes to know:—It (i.e. causing violence to the mobile-beings), in fact, is the knot of bondage,

it, in fact, is the delusion,
it, in fact, is the death,
it, in fact, is the hell.

137. I say —Just as consciousness of a man born without any sense-organs (i.e. one who is blind, deaf, dumb, crippled etc. from birth) is not manifest, the consciousness of the mobile-beings is also not manifest. (Nevertheless) such a man (the one born organless) (experiences pain) when struck or cut with a weapon (so also do the mobile beings).

138. (On simultaneously) cutting and severing with weapons, (all the following thirty-two anatomical features of a man, he suffers excruciating pain though he would not be able to express it): Foot, ankle, leg, knee, thigh, waist, belly, stomach, flank, back, bosom, heart, breast, shoulder, arm, hand, finger, nail, neck, chin, lip, tooth, tongue, palate, throat, temple, ear, nose, eye, brow, forehead and head. (So is the case with the mobile-being).

139. Man (experiences pain) when forced into unconsciousness or when he is deprived of life. (So do the mobile-beings).

143. Having discerned this, a sage should neither use any weapon causing violence to the mobile-being, nor cause others to use it nor approve of others using it.

144. He who discerns (i.e. comprehends and forswears) the actions that cause violence to the mobile-beings, can be regarded as a (true) ascetic (for a true ascetic is he) who has discerningly forsworn actions.

145. (One who practices non-violence) becomes competent to practise abstinence from causing violence to the beings of air-body.

146. It is he who perceives (that violence causes) terror (and that it would be to) his own detriment (becomes competent to practise non-violence).

147. One who knows the inner-self knows the external (world) as well: One who knows the external (world) knows the inner-self as well. . . .

148. Try to realise the significance of this 'equality'. . . .

171. Those (who do not rejoice in the practice of the ethical code), while indulging in violence, preach (to others) the ethical code.

174. One who is rich in the enlightenment (i.e. one who practices non-violence) should not indulge in any sinful action (i.e. causing violence and self-indulgence) through his conscience (guided) by the intellect fully illuminated with Truth. . . .

CARVAKA

In classical India, not all thinkers accepted the ethic of a mystical "greatest good." The most striking opposition came from a philosophic school known as *Carvaka*, also called *Lokayata*, a term meaning "those attached to the ways of the world." These philosophers were materialists; that is, they believed that physical matter is the only reality. They attacked the religious positions prominent in their time, maintaining that we can know only what we perceive through our senses. For this reason, the followers of the Carvaka school were commonly referred to as skeptics. Within the arena of moral philosophy, they advocated hedonism and egoism.

Carvakas attack religious and moral positions by trying to show that inferential reasoning cannot establish anything. That is to say, by showing that inference is unreliable whatever the topic, these skeptics try to debunk arguments that have moral or religious conclusions at odds with their materialism or their hedonism. Many rival philosophers point out that the Carvaka attack on inference is self-defeating, for it utilizes the very processes of thinking that it aims to show invalid. The Carvaka response is that the burden of proof is on the other side. In the following passage, the attack presupposes familiarity with an argument form that had become standard in philosophical debates as well as familiarity with certain logical terms. A paradigm case:

(0) There is a fire on yonder hill.

    (The conclusion to be proved. How? Because:)

(1) There is smoke rising from it.

(2) Wherever there's smoke, there's fire.

(3) This smoke-possessing-hill is an example of the "wherever" of the universal proposition (2).

(Therefore:)

(4) There is a fire on yonder hill.

Here "fire" is an example of a *major term* as referred to in the text following; "smoke" a *middle term*. The universal proposition (2) expresses an *invariable connection*.

Most Carvaka texts have been lost, but references to their views occur in many of their opponents' works. The selections that follow are taken from a late (around 1500 C.E.) Sanskrit compendium of philosophic positions.

from Madhava's *Compendium of Philosophy*

Reprinted from The Sarva-Darsana-Samgraha, *translated by E. B. Cowell and A. E. Gough (London: Kegan Paul, Trench, Trubner, 1914).*

The efforts of Carvaka are indeed hard to be eradicated, for the majority of living beings hold by the current refrain—

While life is yours, live joyously;
None can escape Death's searching eye:
When once this frame of ours they burn,
How shall it e'er again return?

The mass of men, in accordance with the Sastras of policy and enjoyment, considering wealth and desire the only ends of man and denying the existence of any object belonging to a future world, are found to follow only the doctrine of Carvaka. Hence another name for that school is Lokayata,—a name well accordant with the thing signified.

In this school the four elements, earth, & c., are the original principles; from these alone, when transformed into the body, intelligence is produced, just as the inebriating power is developed from the mixing of certain ingredients; and when these are destroyed, intelligence at once perishes also. They quote the *sruti* [Vedic text] for this [*Brhadaranyaka Upanisad* ii.iv.12]: "Springing forth from these elements, itself solid knowledge, it is destroyed when they are destroyed,—after death no intelligence remains." Therefore the soul is only the body distinguished by the attribute of intelligence, since there is no evidence for any self distinct from the body, as such cannot be proved, since this school holds that perception is the only source of knowledge and does not allow inference, & c.

The only end of man is enjoyment produced by sensual pleasures. Nor may you say that such cannot be called the end of man as they are always mixed with some kind of pain, because it is our wisdom to enjoy the pure pleasure as far as we can, and to avoid the pain which inevitably accompanies it; just as the man who desires fish takes the fish with their scales and bones, and having taken as many as he wants, desists; or just as the man who desires rice, takes the rice, straw and all, and having taken as much as he wants, desists. It is not therefore for us, through a fear of pain, to reject the pleasure which our nature instinctively recognises as congenial. Men do not refrain from sowing rice, because forsooth there are wild animals to devour it; nor do they refuse to set the cooking-pots on the fire, because forsooth there are beggars to pester us for a share of the contents. If any one were so timid as to forsake a visible pleasure, he would indeed be foolish like a beast, as has been said by the poet—

The pleasure which arises to men from contact with
    sensible objects,
Is to be relinquished as accompanied by pain,—such is
    the reasoning of fools;
The berries of paddy, rich with the finest white grains,
What man, seeking his true interest, would fling away
    because covered with husk and dust?

If you object that, if there be no such thing as happiness in a future world, then how should men of experienced wisdom engage in the *Agnihotra*[1] and other sacrifices, which can only be performed with great expenditure of money and bodily fatigue, your objection cannot be accepted as any proof to the contrary, since the *Agnihotra,* & c., are only useful as means of livelihood, for the Veda is tainted by the three faults of untruth, self-contradiction, and tautology; then again the impostors who call themselves Vaidic [or Vedic] pandits are mutually destructive, as the authority of the *jnana-kanda* (section on knowledge) is overthrown by those who maintain that of the *karma-kanda* (section on action), while those who maintain the authority of

[1] Sacrificial offering to fire.

the *jnana-kanda* reject that of the *karma-kanda*; and lastly, the three Vedas themselves are only the incoherent rhapsodies of knaves, and to this effect runs the popular saying—

The *Agnihotra,* the three Vedas, the ascetic's three
staves, and smearing oneself with ashes,—
Brhaspati says these are but means of livelihood for
those who have no manliness nor sense.

Hence it follows that there is no other hell than mundane pain produced by purely mundane causes, as thorns, &c.; the only Supreme is the earthly monarch whose existence is proved by all the world's eyesight; and the only liberation is the dissolution of the body. By holding the doctrine that the soul is identical with the body, such phrases as "I am thin," "I am black," &c., are at once intelligible, as the attributes of thinness, &c., and self-consciousness will reside in the same subject (the body); and the use of the phrase "my body" is metaphorical like "the head of Rahu" [Rahu being really *all head*].

All this has been thus summed up—
In this school there are four elements, earth, water, fire,
and air;
And from these four elements alone is intelligence
produced,—
Just like the intoxicating power from *kinva,*[2] & c.,
mixed together;
Since in "I am fat," "I am lean," these attributes abide in
the same subject,
And since fatness, &c., reside only in the body, it alone
is the soul and no other,
And such phrases as "my body" are only significant
metaphorically.

"Be it so," says the opponent; "your wish would be gained if inference, &c., had no force of proof; but then they have this force; else, if they had not, then how, on perceiving smoke, should the thoughts of the intelligent immediately proceed to fire; or why, on hearing another say, 'There are fruits on the bank of the river,' do those who desire fruit proceed at once to the shore?"

All this, however, is only the inflation of the world of fancy.

[2] An intoxicating herb.

Those who maintain the authority of inference accept the sign or middle term as the causer of knowledge, which middle term must be found in the minor and be itself invariably connected with the major. Now this invariable connection must be a relation destitute of any condition accepted or disputed; and this connection does not possess its power of causing inference by virtue of its existence, as the eye, &c., are the cause of perception, but by virtue of its being known. What then is the means of this connection's being known?

We will first show that it is not perception. Now perception is held to be of two kinds, external and internal [i.e., as produced by the external senses, or by the inner sense, mind]. The former is not the required means; for although it is possible that the actual contact of the senses and the object will produce the knowledge of the particular object thus brought in contact, yet as there can never be such contact in the case of the past or the future, the universal proposition which was to embrace the invariable connection of the middle and major terms in every case becomes impossible to be known. Nor may you maintain that this knowledge of the universal proposition has the general class as its object, because, if so, there might arise a doubt as to the existence of the invariable connection in this particular case [as, for instance, in this particular smoke as implying fire].

Nor is internal perception the means, since you cannot establish that the mind has any power to act independently towards an external object, since all allow that it is dependent on the external senses, as has been said by one of the logicians, "The eye, &c., have their objects as described; but mind externally is dependent on the others."

Nor can inference be the means of the knowledge of the universal proposition, since in the case of this inference we should also require another inference to establish it, and so on, and hence would arise the fallacy of an *ad infinitum* retrogression.

Nor can testimony be the means thereof, since we may either allege in reply . . . that this is included in the topic of inference; or else we may hold that this fresh proof of testimony is unable to leap over the old barrier that stopped the progress of inference, since it depends itself on the recognition of a sign in the form of the language used in the child's presence by the old man; and, moreover, there is no . . . reason for our believing on another's word that smoke and fire are invariably connected. . . .

And again, if testimony were to be accepted as the only means of the knowledge of the universal proposition, then in the case of a man to whom the fact of the invariable connection between the middle and major terms had not been pointed out by another person, there could be no inference of one thing [as fire] on seeing another thing [as smoke]; hence, on your own showing, the whole topic of inference for oneself would have to end in mere idle words.

Then again, comparison, &c., must be utterly rejected as the means of the knowledge of the universal proposition, since it is impossible that they can produce the knowledge of the unconditioned connection [i.e., the universal proposition], because their end is to produce the knowledge of quite another connection, viz., the relation of a name to something so named.

Again, this same absence of a condition, which has been given as the definition of an invariable connection [i.e., a universal proposition], can itself never be known; since it is impossible to establish that all conditions must be objects of perception; and therefore, although the absence of perceptible things may be itself perceptible, the absence of non-perceptible things must be itself non-perceptible; and thus, since we must here too have recourse to inference, &c., we cannot leap over the obstacle which has already been planted to bar them. Again, we must accept as the definition of the condition, "it is that which is reciprocal or equipollent in extension with the major term though not constantly accompanying the middle." These three distinguishing clauses, "not constantly accompanying the middle term," "constantly accompanying the major term," and "being constantly accompanied by it" [i.e., reciprocal], are needed in the full definition to stop respectively three such fallacious conditions, in the argument to prove the non-eternity of sound, as "being produced," "the nature of a jar," and "the not causing audition"; wherefore the definition holds. . . .

But since the knowledge of the condition must here precede the knowledge of the condition's absence, it is only when there is the knowledge of the condition, that the knowledge of the universality of the proposition is possible, i.e., a knowledge in the form of such a connection between the middle term and major term as is distinguished by the absence of any such condition; and, on the other hand, the knowledge of the condition depends upon the knowledge of the invariable connection. Thus we fasten on our opponents as with adamantine glue the thunderbolt-like fallacy of reasoning in a circle. Hence by the impossibility of knowing the universality of a proposition it becomes impossible to establish inference, &c.

The step which the mind takes from the knowledge of smoke, &c., to the knowledge of fire, &c., can be accounted for by its being based on a former perception or by its being an error; and that in some cases this step is justified by the result is accidental just like the coincidence of effects observed in the employment of gems, charms, drugs, &c.

From this it follows that fate, &c., do not exist, since these can only be proved by inference. But an opponent will say, if you thus do not allow *adrsta*,[3] the various phenomena of the world become destitute of any cause. But we cannot accept this objection as valid, since these phenomena can all be produced spontaneously from the inherent nature of things. Thus it has been said—

The fire is hot, the water cold, refreshing cool the
   breeze of morn;
By whom came this variety? from their own nature was
   it born. . . .
There is no heaven, no final liberation, nor any soul in
   another world,
Nor do the actions of the four castes, orders, &c., produce any real effect.
The *Agnihotra,* the three Vedas, the ascetic's three
   staves, and smearing oneself with ashes,
Were made by Nature as the livelihood of those destitute of knowledge and manliness.
If a beast slain in the *Jyotistoma* rite[4] will itself go to
   heaven,
Why then does not the sacrificer forthwith offer his
   own father?
If the *Sraddha*[5] produces gratification to beings who are
   dead,

---

[3] The unseen force.

[4] A Vedic sacrifice.

[5] Oblations to the dead.

Then here, too, in the case of travellers when they start,
it is needless to give provisions for the journey.

If beings in heaven are gratified by our offering the
Sraddha here,

Then why not give the food down below to those who
are standing on the housetop?

While life remains let a man live happily, let him feed
on ghee even though he runs in debt;

When once the body becomes ashes, how can it ever
return again?

If he who departs from the body goes to another world,

How is it that he comes not back again, restless for love
of his kindred?

Hence it is only as a means of livelihood that *brāhmins*
have established here

All these ceremonies for the dead—there is no other
fruit anywhere.

The three authors of the Vedas were buffoons, knaves,
and demons.

All the well-known formulas of the pandits . . .

And all the obscene rites for the queen . . . ,

These were invented by buffoons, and so all the various
kinds of presents to the priests,

While the eating of flesh was similarly commanded by
night-prowling demons.

Hence in kindness to the mass of living beings
must we fly for refuge to the doctrine of Carvaka.
Such is the pleasant consummation.

MANU'S *SCIENCE OF DHARMA*

In classical Indian civilization, it was commonly thought that most people were incapable of following a path to enlightenment—at least not until they reached old age, when the force of natural desires naturally waned. For this reason, many argued, a distinct ethical authority for everyday life was needed. In the mainstream of Hindu conceptions, this distinct authority was a revealed literature consisting of the Vedas and their countless appendages and interpretations of Vedic precepts written by priests, or brahmins (also called, as in the text below, *Brahamanas.*) The key concept of these texts is *dharma* (right living, duty, sacred law). The textbooks on *dharma* range from details of the proper performance of sacrifices to strictures on marriage (who may marry whom, etc.), everyday conduct for various professions, and property rights and legal principles in general. A central organizing motif is that a person's duties and obligations vary according to that person's status or stage in life. The ethical principals governing the student, for example, are different from those governing the householder; the duties of women are different from those of men; those of priests are different from those of warriors, and so on. This is a vast literature reflecting life in classical times, growing and evolving over tens of centuries as society changed.

The most philosophically interesting portions of this literature concern questions of how to justify actions and ethical assertions. For example, in a text on the proper interpretation of the Vedic revelation, it is argued, "Sense perception, which is a person's cognition brought about by the correct functioning of the sense organs, cannot be the means of knowing *dharma,* because sense perception apprehends only what already exists whereas *dharma* concerns what should (in the future) be done."* The selection below is from the *Science of Dharma* attributed to Manu, about whom we know little else. One of the oldest books of the genre, it was doubtless often amended through the years; it reached its final form approximately in the fourth century C.E. The selection addresses the sources of the teaching of *dharma,* precepts for students, and the prescriptions for kings administering justice.

---

* *Mimamsasutra* 1.4; translation by Stephen Phillips.

from *The Laws of Manu*

Reprinted from The Laws of Manu, *translated by Georg Bühler; Volume XXV of* Sacred Books of the East, *edited by Max Müller (Oxford: Clarendon Press, 1886). In this selection, Sanskrit terms are omitted.*

CHAPTER II

1. Learn that sacred law which is followed by men learned (in the Veda) and assented to in their hearts by the virtuous, who are ever exempt from hatred and inordinate affection.

2. To act solely from a desire for rewards is not laudable, yet an exemption from that desire is not (to be found) in this (world): for on (that) desire is grounded the study of the Veda and the performance of the actions, prescribed by the Veda.

3. The desire (for rewards), indeed, has its root in the conception that an act can yield them, and in consequence of (that) conception sacrifices are performed; vows and the laws prescribing restraints are all stated to be kept through the idea that they will bear fruit.

4. Not a single act here (below) appears ever to be done by a man free from desire; for whatever (man) does, it is (the result of) the impulse of desire.

5. He who persists in discharging these (prescribed duties) in the right manner, reaches the deathless state and even in this (life) obtains (the fulfilment of) all the desires that he may have conceived.

6. The whole Veda is the (first) source of the sacred law, next the tradition and the virtuous conduct of those who know the (Veda further), also the customs of holy men, and (finally) self-satisfaction.

7. Whatever law has been ordained for any (person) by Manu, that has been fully declared in the Veda: for that (sage was) omniscient.

8. But a learned man after fully scrutinising all this with the eye of knowledge, should, in accordance with the authority of the revealed texts, be intent on (the performance of) his duties.

9. For that man who obeys the law prescribed in the revealed texts and in the sacred tradition, gains fame in this (world) and after death unsurpassable bliss.

10. But by Sruti (revelation) is meant the Veda, and by Smriti (tradition) the Institutes of the sacred law: those two must not be called into question in any matter, since from those two the sacred law shone forth.

11. Every twice-born man, who, relying on the Institutes of dialectics, treats with contempt those two sources (of the law), must be cast out by the virtuous, as an atheist and a scorner of the Veda.

12. The Veda, the sacred tradition, the customs of virtuous men, and one's own pleasure, they declare to be visibly the fourfold means of defining the sacred law.

117. (A student) shall first reverentially salute that (teacher) from whom he receives (knowledge), referring to worldly affairs, to the Veda, or to the Brahman.

118. A Brâhmana who completely governs himself, though he know the Savitri* only, is better than he who knows the three Vedas, (but) does not control himself, eats all (sorts of) food, and sells all (sorts of goods).

*A famous mantra. —ED.

119. One must not sit down on a couch or seat which a superior occupies; and he who occupies a couch or seat shall rise to meet a (superior), and (afterwards) salute him.

120. For the vital airs of a young man mount upwards to leave his body when an elder approaches; but by rising to meet him and saluting he recovers them.

121. He who habitually salutes and constantly pays reverence to the aged obtains an increase of four (things), (viz.) length of life, knowledge, fame, (and) strength.

122. After the (word of) salutation, a Brâhmana who greets an elder must pronounce his name, saying, "I am N. N."

123. To those (persons) who, when a name is pronounced, do not understand (the meaning of) the salutation, a wise man should say, "It is I"; and (he should address) in the same manner all women.

161. Let him not, even though in pain, (speak words) cutting (others) to the quick; let him not injure others in thought or deed; let him not utter speeches which make (others) afraid of him, since that will prevent him from gaining heaven.

162. A Brahmana should always fear homage as if it were poison; and constantly desire (to suffer) scorn as (he would long for) nectar.

163. For he who is scorned (nevertheless may) sleep with an easy mind, awake with an easy mind, and with an easy mind walk here among men; but the scorner utterly perishes.

191. Both when ordered by his teacher, and without a (special) command, (a student) shall always exert himself in studying (the Veda), and in doing what is serviceable to his teacher.

192. Controlling his body, his speech, his organs (of sense), and his mind, let him stand with joined hands, looking at the face of his teacher.

193. Let him always keep his right arm uncovered, behave decently and keep his body well covered, and when he is addressed (with the words), "Be seated," he shall sit down, facing his teacher.

194. In the presence of his teacher let him always eat less, wear a less valuable dress and ornaments (than the former), and let him rise earlier (from his bed), and go to rest later.

195. Let him not answer or converse with (his teacher), reclining on a bed, nor sitting, nor eating, nor standing, nor with an averted face.

196. Let him do (that), standing up, if (his teacher) is seated, advancing towards him when he stands, going to meet him if he advances, and running after him when he runs;

197. Going (round) to face (the teacher), if his face is averted, approaching him if he stands at a distance, but bending towards him if he lies on a bed, and if he stands in a lower place.

198. When his teacher is nigh, let his bed or seat be low; but within sight of his teacher he shall not sit carelessly at ease.

199. Let him not pronounce the mere name of his teacher (without adding an honorific title) behind his back even, and let him not mimic his gait, speech, and deportment.

200. Wherever (people) justly censure or falsely defame his teacher, there he must cover his ears or depart thence to another place.

204. He may sit with his teacher in a carriage drawn by oxen, horses, or camels, on a terrace, on a bed of grass or leaves, on a mat, on a rock, on a wooden bench, or in a boat.

205. If his teacher's teacher is near, let him behave (towards him) as towards his own teacher; but let him, unless he has received permission from his teacher, not salute venerable persons of his own (family).

206. This is likewise (ordained as) his constant behaviour towards (other) instructors in science, towards his relatives (to whom honour is due), towards all who may restrain him from sin, or may give him salutary advice.

CHAPTER VIII

1. A king, desirous of investigating law cases, must enter his court of justice, preserving a dignified demeanour, together with Brahmanas and with experienced councillors.

2. There, either seated or standing, raising his right arm, without ostentation in his dress and ornaments, let him examine the business of suitors,

3. Daily (deciding) one after another (all cases) which fall under the eighteen titles (of the law) according to principles drawn from local usages and from the Institutes of the sacred law.

4. Of those (titles) the first is the non-payment of debts, (then follow), (2) deposit and pledge, (3) sale without ownership, (4) concerns among partners, and (5) resumption of gifts,

5. (6) Non-payment of wages, (7) non-performance of agreements, (8) rescission of sale and purchase, (9) disputes between the owner (of cattle) and his servants,

6. (10) Disputes regarding boundaries, (11) assault and (12) defamation, (13) theft, (14) robbery and violence, (15) adultery,

7. (16) Duties of man and wife, (17) partition (of inheritance), (18) gambling and betting; these are in this world the eighteen topics which give rise to lawsuits.

8. Depending on the eternal law, let him decide the suits of men who mostly contend on the titles just mentioned.

9. But if the king does not personally investigate the suits, then let him appoint a learned Brahmana to try them.

10. That (man) shall enter that most excellent court, accompanied by three assessors, and fully consider (all) causes (brought) before the (king), either sitting down or standing.

11. Where three Brahmanas versed in the Vedas and the learned (judge) appointed by the king sit down, they call that the court of (four-faced) Brahman.

12. But where justice, wounded by injustice,

approaches and the judges do not extract the dart, there (they also) are wounded (by that dart of injustice).

13. Either the court must not be entered, or the truth must be spoken; a man who either says nothing or speaks falsely, becomes sinful.

14. Where justice is destroyed by injustice, or truth by falsehood, while the judges look on, there they shall also be destroyed.

15. "Justice, being violated, destroys; justice, being preserved, preserves: therefore justice must not be violated, lest violated justice destroy us."

16. For divine justice (is said to be) a bull; that (man) who violates it the gods consider to be (a man despicable like) a Sudra;* let him, therefore, beware of violating justice.

17. The only friend who follows men even after death is justice; for everything else is lost at the same time when the body (perishes).

18. One quarter of (the guilt of) an unjust (decision) falls on him who committed (the crime), one quarter on the (false) witness, one quarter on all the judges, one quarter on the king.

19. But where he who is worthy of condemnation is condemned, the king is free from guilt, and the judges are saved (from sin); the guilt falls on the perpetrator (of the crime alone).

20. A Brahmana who subsists only by the name of his caste, or one who merely calls himself a Brahmana (though his origin be uncertain), may, at the king's pleasure, interpret the law to him, but never a Sudra.

21. The kingdom of that monarch, who looks on while a Sudra settles the law, will sink (low), like a cow in a morass.

22. That kingdom where Sudras are very numerous, which is infested by atheists and destitute of twice-born (inhabitants), soon entirely perishes, afflicted by famine and disease.

23. Having occupied the seat of justice, having covered his body, and having worshipped the

---

* A member of the lowest of the four principal castes. —ED.

guardian deities of the world, let him, with a collected mind, begin the trial of causes.

24. Knowing what is expedient or inexpedient, what is pure justice or injustice, let him examine the causes of suitors according to the order of the castes.

25. By external signs let him discover the internal disposition of men, by their voice, their colour, their motions, their aspect, their eyes, and their gestures.

26. The internal (working of the) mind is perceived through the aspect, the motions, the gait, the gestures, the speech, and the changes in the eye and of the face.

27. The king shall protect the inherited (and other) property of a minor, until he has returned (from his teacher's house) or until he has passed his minority.

28. In like manner care must be taken of barren women, of those who have no sons, of those whose family is extinct, of wives and widows faithful to their lords, and of women afflicted with diseases.

29. A righteous king must punish like thieves those relatives who appropriate the property of such females during their lifetime.

30. Property, the owner of which has disappeared, the king shall cause to be kept as a deposit during three years; within the period of three years the owner may claim it, after (that term) the king may take it.

31. He who says, "This belongs to me," must be examined according to the rule; if he accurately describes the shape, and the number (of the articles found) and so forth, (he is) the owner, (and) ought (to receive) that property.

32. But if he does not really know the time and the place (where it was) lost, its colour, shape, and size, he is worthy of a fine equal (in value) to the (object claimed).

33. Now the king, remembering the duty of good men, may take one-sixth part of property lost and afterwards found, or one-tenth, or at least one-twelfth.

34. Property lost and afterwards found (by the king's servants) shall remain in the keeping of (special) officials; those whom the king may convict of stealing it, he shall cause to be slain by an elephant.

35. From that man who shall truly say with respect to treasure-trove, "This belongs to me," the king may take one-sixth or one-twelfth part.

36. But he who falsely says (so), shall be fined in one-eighth of his property, or, a calculation of (the value of) the treasure having been made, in some smaller portion (of that).

37. When a learned Brahmana has found treasure, deposited in former (times), he may take even the whole (of it); for he is master of everything.

38. When the king finds treasure of gold concealed in the ground, let him give one half to Brahmanas and place the (other) half in his treasury.

39. The king obtains one half of ancient hoards and metals (found) in the ground, by reason of (his giving) protection, (and) because he is the lord of the soil.

40. Property stolen by thieves must be restored by the king to (men of) all castes . . . ; a king who uses such (property) for himself incurs the guilt of a thief.

41. (A king) who knows the sacred law, must inquire into the laws of castes . . . ; of districts, of guilds, and of families, and (thus) settle the peculiar law of each.

42. For men who follow their particular occupations and abide by their particular duty, become dear to people, though they may live at a distance.

43. Neither the king nor any servant of his shall themselves cause a lawsuit to be begun, or hush up one that has been brought (before them) by (some) other (man).

44. As a hunter traces the lair of a (wounded) deer by the drops of blood, even so the king shall discover on which side the right lies, by inferences (from the facts).

45. When engaged in judicial proceedings he must pay full attention to the truth, to the object (of the dispute), (and) to himself, next to the witnesses, to the place, to the time, and to the aspect.

46. What may have been practised by the virtuous, by such twice-born men as are devoted to the law, that he shall establish as law, if it be not opposed to the (customs of) countries, families, and castes.

47. When a creditor sues (before the king) for the recovery of money from a debtor, let him make the debtor pay the sum which the creditor proves (to be due).

48. By whatever means a creditor may be able to obtain possession of his property, even by those means may he force the debtor and make him pay.

49. By moral suasion, by suit of law, by artful management, or by the customary proceeding, a creditor may recover property lent; and fifthly, by force.

50. A creditor who himself recovers his property from his debtor, must not be blamed by the king for retaking what is his own.

51. But him who denies a debt which is proved by good evidence, he shall order to pay that debt to the creditor and a small fine according to his circumstances.

52. On the denial (of a debt) by a debtor who has been required in court to pay it, the complainant must call (a witness) who was present (when the loan was made), or adduce other evidence.

53. (The plaintiff) who calls a witness not present at the transaction, who retracts his statements, or does not perceive that his statements (are) confused or contradictory;

54. Or who having stated what he means to prove afterwards varies (his case), or who being questioned on a fact duly stated by himself does not abide by it;

55. Or who converses with the witnesses in a place improper for such conversation; or who declines to answer a question, properly put, or leaves (the court);

56. Or who, being ordered to speak, does not answer, or does not prove what he has alleged; or who does not know what is the first (point), and what the second, fails in his suit.

57. Him also who says "I have witnesses," and, being ordered to produce them, produces them not, the judge must on these (same) grounds declare to be non-suited.

58. If a plaintiff does not speak, he may be punished corporally or fined according to the law; if (a defendant) does not plead within three fortnights, he has lost his cause.

59. In the double of that sum which (a defendant) falsely denies or on which (the plaintiff) falsely declares, shall those two (men) offending against justice be fined by the king.

60. (A defendant) who, being brought (into court) by the creditor, (and) being questioned, denies (the debt), shall be convicted (of his falsehood) by at least three witnesses (who must depose) in the presence of the Brahmana (appointed by) the king.

KAUTILYA'S *SCIENCE OF MATERIAL GAIN*

Over time, other ethical norms came to share the mainstream with the *dharma* taught by the orthodox brahmins. This development was in part fostered by ideas within the *dharma* textbooks themselves: the idea that duty varies with stage of life and social position, for example. The theme emerges that a person has four distinct ends and that mores of conduct vary according to what end is appropriate to the particular stage of life. These four ends are (*a*) the supreme personal good, variously conceived, as we have seen, as enlightenment, liberation, knowledge of the Absolute, Brahman, and union with God; (*b*) *dharma*, which is particularly appropriate to the priests and those performing sacrifices and ceremonies, such as marriage and cremation, that affect the course of the soul in future lives (note the narrowing of the *dharma* concept, which is here confined mostly within the context of the other ends); (*c*), material gain, which is the particular province of kings who have the responsibility of securing wealth and prosperity for themselves and their subjects; and (*d*) worldly pleasure, including sexual enjoyment.

The *Science of Material Gain* (or, as in the text below, "the science of polity") attributed to Kautilya (whose identity is in dispute, as is the age of the text), consists primarily of advice to kings concerning the right organization of the state. The work's orientation is more pragmatic than that of Manu's *Science of Dharma*. Further, divine revelation is no longer the sole authority for ethics; Kutilya also gives philosophy a place. The selection below addresses this expansion, then proceeds to enumerate duties of a king and the ideal characteristics of a king, country, treasury, army, and allies.

from the *Science of Material Gain*

Reprinted from Sources of Indian Tradition, *compiled by Wm. Theodore de Bary, Stephen Hay, Royal Weiler, and Andrew Yarrow. Copyright © 1958 by Columbia University Press.*

The Science of Polity

Philosophy, the Veda, the science of economics, and the science of polity—these are the sciences. . . .

Sankhya, Yoga, and materialism—these constitute philosophy. Distinguishing, with proper reasoning, between good and evil in the Vedic religion, between profit and nonprofit in the science of economics, and between right policy and wrong policy in the science of polity, and determining the comparative validity and invalidity of these sciences [under specific circumstances], philosophy becomes helpful to the people, keeps the mind steady in woe and weal, and produces adroitness of understanding, speech, and action. . . .

. . . The way of life taught in the trilogy of the Vedas [and other Vedic works] is helpful on account of its having laid down the duties of the four classes and the four stages of life. . . .

Agriculture, cattle-breeding, trade, and commerce constitute the main topics dealt with in the science of economics; it is helpful on account of its making available grains, cattle, gold, raw material, and free labor. Through the knowledge of economics, a king brings under his control his own party and the enemy's party with the help of treasury and army.

The scepter[1] . . . is the means of the acquisition and the preservation of philosophy, the Veda, and economics. The science treating with the effective bearing of the scepter is the science of polity. . . . It conduces to the acquisition of what is not acquired, the preservation of what has been acquired, the

growth of what has been preserved, and the distribution among worthy people of what has grown. It is on it [the science of polity] that the proper functioning of society [lit., the world] depends. . . .

"Of the three ends of human life, material gain is, verily, the most important." So says Kautilya. "On material gain depends the realization of dharma and pleasure. . . . "

Duties of a King

Only if a king is himself energetically active, do his officers follow him energetically. If he is sluggish, they too remain sluggish. And, besides, they eat up his works. He is thereby easily overpowered by his enemies. Therefore, he should ever dedicate himself energetically to activity.

He should divide the day as well as the night into eight parts. . . . During the first one-eighth part of the day, he should listen to reports pertaining to the organization of law and order and to income and expenditure. During the second, he should attend to the affairs of the urban and the rural population. During the third, he should take his bath and meal and devote himself to study. During the fourth, he should receive gold and the departmental heads. During the fifth, he should hold consultations with the council of ministers through correspondence and also keep himself informed of the secret reports brought by spies. During the sixth, he should devote himself freely to amusement or listen to the counsel of the ministers. During the seventh, he should inspect the military formations of elephants, cavalry, chariots, and infantry. During the eighth, he, together with the commander-in-chief of the army, should make plans for campaigns of conquest. When the day has come to an end he should offer the evening prayers.

During the first one-eighth part of the night, he should meet the officers of the secret service. During

[1] That is, government as opposed to anarchy.

the second, he should take his bath and meals and also devote himself to study. During the third, at the sounding of the trumpets, he should enter the bed chamber and should sleep through the fourth and fifth. Waking up at the sounding of the trumpets, he should, during the sixth part, ponder over the teachings of the sciences and his urgent duties for the day. During the seventh, he should hold consultations and send out the officers of the secret service for their operations. During the eighth, accompanied by sacrificial priests, preceptors, and the chaplain, he should receive benedictions; he should also have interviews with the physician, the kitchen-superintendent, and the astrologer. Thereafter, he should ... divide the day and the night into parts in accordance with his own capacities and thereby attend to his duties.

When he has gone to the reception hall, he should not allow such persons, as have come for business, to remain sticking to the doors of the hall [i.e., waiting in vain]. For, a king, with whom it is difficult for the people to have an audience, is made to confuse between right action and wrong action by his close entourage. Thereby he suffers from the disaffection of his own subjects or falls prey to the enemy. Therefore he should attend to the affairs relating to gods, hermitages, heretics, learned brāhmans, cattle, and holy places as also those of minors, the aged, the sick, those in difficulty, the helpless, and women—in the order of their enumeration or in accordance with the importance or the urgency of the affairs.

A king should attend to all urgent business, he should not put it off. For what has been thus put off becomes either difficult or altogether impossible to accomplish.

Seated in the fire-chamber and accompanied by the chaplain and the preceptor he should look into the business of the knowers of the Veda and the ascetics—having first got up from his seat and having respectfully greeted them.

Only in the company of the adepts in the three Vedas, and not by himself, should he decide the affairs of the ascetics as also of the experts in magical practices—lest these become enraged.

The vow of the king is energetic activity, his sacrifice is constituted of the discharge of his own administrative duties; his sacrificial fee [to the officiating priests] is his impartiality of attitude toward all; his sacrificial consecration is his anointment as king.

In the happiness of the subjects lies the happiness of the king; in their welfare, his own welfare. The welfare of the king does not lie in the fulfillment of what is dear to him; whatever is dear to the subjects constitutes his welfare.

Therefore, ever energetic, a king should act up to the precepts of the science of material gain. Energetic activity is the source of material gain; its opposite, of downfall.

In the absence of energetic activity, the loss of what has already been obtained and of what still remains to be obtained is certain. The fruit of one's work is achieved through energetic activity—one obtains abundance of material prosperity. . . .

The king, the ministers, the country, the forts, the treasury, the army, and the allies are the constituents of the state.

Of these, the perfection of the king is this: Born of a high family; non-fatalistic; endowed with strong character; looking up to [experienced] old men [for guidance]; religious, truthful in speech; not inconsistent [in his behavior]; grateful; having liberal aims; full of abundant energy; not procrastinating; controller of his feudatories; of determined intellect; having an assembly of ministers of no mean quality; intent on discipline—these are the qualities by means of which people are attracted toward him. Inquiry; study; perception; retention; analytical knowledge; critical acumen; keenness for the realization of reality—these are the qualities of the intellect. Valor; impetuosity; agility; and dexterity—these are the qualities of energy. Of profound knowledge; endowed with strong memory, cogitative faculty, and physical strength; exalted; easily controlling himself; adept in arts; rid of difficulties; capable bearer of the scepter; openly responding both to acts of help and harm; full of shame [to do anything evil]; capable of dealing adequately with visitations of nature and the constituents of state; seeing far and wide; utilizing for his work the opportunities afforded by the proper place, time, and personal vigor; skilled in discriminating between conditions which require conclusion of a treaty and manifestation of valor, letting off the enemies and curbing them, and waiting under the pretext of some mutual understanding and taking advantage of the enemies' weak points; laughing joyfully, but guardedly and without loss of dignity; looking straight and with uncrooked brow; free from passion, anger, greed, obstinacy, fickleness, heat, and calumny; capable of self-management; speaking with people smilingly but with dignity; observing customs as taught by elderly people—these are the qualities of the personality. . . .

Firm in the midland and at the boundaries; capable of affording subsistence to its own people and, in case of difficulties, also to outsiders; easy to defend; affording easy livelihood to the people; full of hatred for the enemy; capable of controlling [by its strategic position] the dominions of the feudatories; devoid of muddy, rocky, salty, uneven, and thorny tracts, and of forests infested with treacherous animals and wild animals; pleasing; rich in arable land, mines, and timber and elephant forests; wholesome to cows; wholesome to men; with well-preserved pastures; rich in cattle; not depending entirely on rain; possessing waterways and overland roads; having markets full of valuable, manifold, and abundant ware; capable of bearing the burden of army and taxation; having industrious agriculturists, stupid masters*, and a population largely consisting of the lower classes [i.e., the economically productive classes, vaishyas and shūdras]; inhabited by devoted and respectable men—this is the perfection of the country. . . .

Lawfully inherited from his ancestors or earned by the king himself; mainly consisting of gold and silver; full of manifold and big precious stones and bars of gold; and such as would endure a calamity even of a long duration and also a state of things which brought in no income—this is the perfection of the treasury.

Coming down from father and grandfather; constant in its loyalties; obedient; having the sons and wives of soldiers contented and well provided for; not becoming disintegrated in military campaigns in foreign lands; everywhere unassailable; capable of bearing pain; experienced in many battles; expert in the science of all the weapons of war; regarding the rise and the downfall of the king as equivalent to their own and consequently not double-dealing with him; mainly consisting of kshatriyas [nobles]—this is the perfection of the army.

Coming down from father and grandfather; constant in their loyalties; obedient; not double-dealing; capable of preparing for war on a large scale and quickly—this is the perfection of the allies. . . .

---

* Some versions of the text have a negative prefix, so that this phrase should be translated "prudent masters" or "seasoned craftsmen." —ED.

VATSYAYANA'S *KAMASUTRA*

The textbooks of "science" of Indian classical civilization are not free from prescriptive judgments. They claim to be objective, but they concern themselves not only with what exists but also with what they consider right and appropriate. Such textbooks were written about singing, dancing, jewelry-making, cooking, tailoring, drawing inferences, carpentry, architecture, gardening, war, and many other subjects. A person of taste, culture and learning would command several of these. But the science of love and enjoyment, or *kama,* held a special place; its subject was thought to be universally pursued and—depending on circumstances— worthy of pursuit.

The *Kamasutra* is the most famous of the textbooks on sex and love. The author, Vatsyayana, is careful to locate his work in a context of civility. First, he discusses the validity of *kama* as an end with respect to the other chief ends of the person. Then he stresses that the *kama*-oriented are to pursue sex and love (his primary topics) not exclusively but together with the other arts. Any of these—not just sexual delight—promotes enjoyment. The context and qualifications Vatsyayana provides seem appropriate because he does indeed proceed to detail the arts of courting and lovemaking.

One feature particularly relevant to Vātsyāyana's ethics is a clear distinction of ends and means. Though he often gives long lists of means that will achieve a given end (winning the affection of the desired woman or man, for example), he does not espouse the idea that the ends justify the means. Again and again, he insists that the means employed should be appropriate to other circumstances, not only to the end in mind. The items that appear on his long lists reflect variations of circumstance; generally, they are not simply alternatives to be chosen indiscriminately.

The author lived between the first and fourth centuries C.E. He mentions several authorities whose work he relies on, but the texts are lost to us. The *Kamasutra* became the most popular textbook on its subject during the middle and latter periods of classical Indian civilization; several other texts mention it, and its influence is marked in many works of literature. A famous commentary on it was written in the eleventh century, and other commentaries appeared as late as the eighteenth, though the *Kamasutra*'s popularity—at least its public popularity, as opposed to the private—waned after the Muslim invasions beginning in the twelfth century.

from *The Kamasutra*

Reprinted from The Kama Sutra of Vatsyayana, *translated by Richard Burton (Cosmopoli, 1883).*

Man, the period of whose life is one hundred years, should practise Dharma, Artha and Kama at different times and in such a manner that they may harmonize together and not clash in any way. He should acquire learning in his childhood, in his youth and middle age he should attend to Artha and Kama, and in his old age he should perform Dharma, and thus seek to gain Moksha, i.e. release from further transmigration. Or, on account of the uncertainty of life, he may practise them at times when they are enjoined to be practised. But one thing is to be noted, he should lead the life of a religious student until he finishes his education.

Dharma is obedience to the command of the Shastra or Holy Writ of the Hindoos to do certain things, such as the performance of sacrifices, which are not generally done, because they do not belong to this world, and produce no visible effect; and not to do other things, such as eating meat, which is often done because it belongs to this world, and has visible effects.

Dharma should be learnt from the Shruti (Holy Writ), and from those conversant with it.

Artha is the acquisition of arts, land, gold, cattle, wealth, equipages and friends. It is, further, the protection of what is acquired, and the increase of what is protected.

Artha should be learnt from the king's officers, and from merchants who may be versed in the ways of commerce.

Kama is the enjoyment of appropriate objects by the five senses of hearing, feeling, seeing, tasting and smelling, assisted by the mind together with the soul. The ingredient in this is a peculiar contact between the organ of sense and its object, and the consciousness of pleasure which arises from that contact is called Kama.

Kama is to be learnt from the Kama Sutra (aphorisms on love) and from the practice of citizens.

When all the three, viz. Dharma, Artha and Kama, come together, the former is better than the one which follows it, i.e. Dharma is better than Artha, and Artha is better than Kama. But Artha should always be first practised by the king for the livelihood of men is to be obtained from it only. Again, Kama being the occupation of public women, they should prefer it to the other two, and these are exceptions to the general rule.

Objection 1

Some learned men say that as Dharma is connected with things not belonging to this world, it is appropriately treated of in a book; and so also is Artha, because it is practised only by the application of proper means, and a knowledge of those means can only be obtained by study and from books. But Kama being a thing which is practised even by the brute creation, and which is to be found everywhere, does not want any work on the subject.

Answer

This is not so. Sexual intercourse being a thing dependent on man and woman requires the application of proper means by them, and those means are to be learnt from the Kama Shastra. The non-application of proper means, which we see in the brute creation, is caused by their being unrestrained, and by the females among them only being fit for sexual intercourse at certain seasons and no more, and by their intercourse not being preceded by thought of any kind. . . .

Objection 4

Those who are inclined to think that Artha is the chief object to be obtained argue thus. Pleasures should not be sought for, because they are obstacles to the practice of Dharma and Artha, which are both superior to them, and are also disliked by meritorious persons. Pleasures also bring a man into distress, and into contact with low persons; they cause him to commit unrighteous deeds, and produce impurity in him; they make him regardless of the future, and encourage carelessness and levity. And lastly, they cause him to be disbelieved by all, received by none, and despised by everybody, including himself. It is notorious, moreover, that many men who have given themselves up to pleasure alone, have been ruined along with their families and relations. . . .

Answer

This objection cannot be sustained, for pleasures, being as necessary for the existence and well being of the body as food, are consequently equally required. They are, moreover, the results of Dharma and Artha. Pleasures are, therefore, to be followed with moderation and caution. No one refrains from cooking food because there are beggars to ask for it, or from sowing seed because there are deer to destroy the corn when it is grown up.

Thus a man practising Dharma, Artha and Kama enjoys happiness both in this world and in the world to come. The good perform those actions in which there is no fear as to what is to result from them in the next world, and in which there is no danger to their welfare. Any action which conduces to the practice of Dharma, Artha and Kama together, or of any two, or even one of them, should be performed, but an action which conduces to the practice of one of them at the expense of the remaining two should not be performed.

. . . .

Now the householder, having got up in the morning and performed his necessary duties, should wash his teeth, apply a limited quantity of ointments and perfumes to his body, put some ornaments on his person and collyrium on his eyelids and below his eyes, colour his lips . . . and look at himself in the glass. Having then eaten betel leaves, with other things that give fragrance to the mouth, he should perform his usual business. He should bathe daily, anoint his body with oil every other day, apply a lathering substance to his body every three days, get his head (including face) shaved every four days and the other parts of his body every five or ten days. All these things should be done without fail, and the sweat of the armpits should also be removed. Meals should be taken in the forenoon, in the afternoon, and again at night, according to Charayana. After breakfast, parrots and other birds should be taught to speak, and the fighting of cocks, quails, and rams should follow. A limited time should be devoted to diversions . . . and then should be taken the midday sleep. After this the householder, having put on his clothes and ornaments, should, during the afternoon, converse with his friends. In the evening there should be singing, and after that the householder, along with his friend, should await in his room, previously decorated and perfumed, the arrival of the woman that may be attached to him, or he may send a female messenger for her, or go for her himself. After her arrival at his house, he and his friend should welcome her, and entertain her with a loving and agreeable conversation. Thus end the duties of the day.

. . . .

"Thus have I written in a few words the 'Science of love', after reading the texts of ancient authors, and following the ways of enjoyment mentioned in them."

"He who is acquainted with the true principles of this science pays regard to Dharma, Artha, Kama, and to his own experiences, as well as to the teachings of others, and does not act simply on the dictates of his own desire. As for the errors in the science of love which I have mentioned in this work, on my own authority as an author, I have, immediately after mentioning them, carefully censured and prohibited them."

"An act is never looked upon with indulgence for the simple reason that it is authorised by the science, because it ought to be remembered that it is the intention of the science, that the rules which it contains should only be acted upon in particular cases. After reading and considering the works of Babhravya and other ancient authors, and thinking over the meaning of the rules given by them, the Kama Sutra was composed, according to the precepts of Holy Writ, for the benefit of the world, by Vatsyayana, while leading the life of a religious student, and wholly engaged in the contemplation of the Deity."

"This work is not intended to be used merely as an instrument for satisfying our desires. A person, acquainted with the true principles of this science, and who preserves his Dharma, Artha, and Kama, and has regard for the practices of the people, is sure to obtain the mastery over his senses."

"In short, an intelligent and prudent person, attending to Dharma and Artha, and attending to Kama also, without becoming the slave of his passions, obtains success in everything that he may undertake."

RAMMOHUN ROY

Raja Rammohun Roy (1772–1833), sometimes referred to as the "father of modern India," was adept in the diverse cultures that competed in India in his time. Born into the highest Hindu caste, he received an excellent education. He learned Persian from his father at home in Bengal—so that he could enter the service of the Delhi emperor—and studied Arabic in Patna, reading Euclid, Aristotle and the Koran. Then, at his mother's insistence, he enrolled in a school in Banaras, where he mastered Sanskrit. When he was fifteen, he journeyed at his own insistence to Tibet to study Buddhism and then continued traveling and studying within India. After his father's death in 1803, Rammohun was employed by the British in Calcutta, became fluent in English, and rose to a high position in the Bengal Civil Service. His earnings, coupled with an income from landed estates, allowed him to retire in his forties to devote all his energy to political, religious, and educational projects and to the pamphlets, petitions, and religious writings for which he had already become renowned.

Rammohun Roy was the first Indian to found newpapers, editing and publishing them in English, Bengali, and Persian. He led a successful campaign against the Hindu practice of widows committing suicide by throwing themselves on their husbands' funeral pyres. Out of his own funds he built school houses and founded schools, some using English as the instructional medium, others Bengali. He wrote a Bengali grammar text in Bengali, and he wrote an English version as well.

Rammohun became interested in Christianity, and translated the New Testament into Bengali after spending years learning Hebrew and Greek to read the original text. He did not shrink from religious and theological controversy, finding much in Hindu theism compatible with the teachings of Jesus. What he found unreasonable he attacked; he wrote theological tracts (though often under assumed names) against much Christian as well as Hindu orthodoxy, sparing no tenet from the scrutiny of reason. In fact, the Baptist missionary who helped Rammohun with his biblical translation converted to Unitarianism under the force of his arguments. In ethics, Rammohun championed Christianity, urging that Hindus could and should embrace the Christian moral teachings without relinquishing the best of their own traditional theological beliefs. In 1828, he founded the Brahmo Samaj, a "church" dedicated to "the worship and adoration of the Eternal, Unsearchable and Immutable Being, who is the Author and Preserver of the universe."*

In 1831, Rammohun traveled to England, where he remained, except for a brief visit to France, until his death. He was warmly welcomed as the unofficial ambas-

---

*Rammohun Roy, *The Trust Deed of the Brahmo Somaj*, in *The English Works of Rammohun Roy* (Allahabad: Panini Office, 1906).

bador of India, was honored by the British East India Company, was invited to address the House of Commons, and wrote several important papers pertaining to government policy in India. Rammohun died in Bristol, in the house of an English Unitarian friend, less than three years after his arrival.

Introduction to *The Precepts of Jesus*

Reprinted from The English Works of Raja Rammohun Roy *(Allahabad: Panini Office, 1906).*

A conviction in the mind of its total ignorance of the nature and of the specific attributes of the God-head, and a sense of doubt respecting the real essence of the soul, give rise to feelings of great dissatisfaction with our limited powers, as well as with all human acquirements which fail to inform us on these interesting points. On the other hand, a notion of the existence of a supreme superintending power, the Author and Preserver of this harmonious system, who has organized and who regulates such an infinity of celestial and terrestrial objects, and a due estimation of that law which teaches that man should do unto others as he would wish to be done by, reconcile us to human nature, and tend to render our existence agreeable to ourselves and profitable to the rest of mankind. The former of these sources of satisfaction, *viz.*, a belief in God, prevails generally; being derived either from tradition and instruction, or from an attentive survey of the wonderful skill and contrivance displayed in the works of nature. The latter, although it is partially taught also in every system of religion with which I am acquainted, is principally inculcated by Christianity. This essential characteristic of the Christian religion I was for a long time unable to distinguish as such, amidst the various doctrines I found insisted upon in the writings of Christian authors, and in the conversation of those teachers of Christianity with whom I have had the honour of holding communication. Amongst these opinions, the most prevalent seems to be, that no one is justly entitled to the appellation of Christian who does not believe in the divinity of Christ and of the Holy Ghost, as well as in the divine nature of God, the Father of all created beings. Many allow a much greater latitude to the term Christian, and consider it as comprehending all who acknowledge the Bible to contain the re-vealed will of God, however they may differ from others in their interpretations of particular passages of Scripture; whilst some require from him who claims the title of Christian, only an adherence to the doctrines of Christ, as taught by himself, without insisting on implicit confidence in those of the Apostles, as being, except when speaking from inspiration, like other men, liable to mistake and error. That they were so, is obvious from the several instances of differences of opinion amongst the Apostles recorded in the Acts and Epistles.

Voluminous works, written by learned men of particular sects for the purpose of establishing the truth, consistency, rationality, and priority of their own peculiar doctrines, contain such variety of arguments, that I cannot hope to be able to adduce here any new reasonings of sufficient novelty and force to attract the notice of my readers. Besides, in matters of religion particularly men in general, through prejudice and partiality to the opinions which they once form, pay little or no attention to opposite sentiments (however reasonable they may be) and often turn a deaf ear to what is most consistent with the laws of nature, and conformable to the dictates of human reason and divine revelation. At the same time, to those who are not biased by prejudice, and who are, by the grace of God, open to conviction, a simple enumeration and statement of the respective tenets of different sects may be a sufficient guide to direct their inquiries in ascertaining which of them is most consistent with the sacred traditions, and most acceptable to common sense. For these reasons, I decline entering into any discussion on those points, and confine my attention at present to the task of laying before my fellow-creatures the words of Christ, with a translation from the English into Sanscrit, and the language of Bengal. I feel persuaded that by separating from the other matters contained in the New Testament, the moral precepts found in that book, these will be more likely to produce the desirable effect of improving the hearts and minds of men of different persuasions and degrees of understanding. For, historical and some other passages are liable to the doubts and disputes of free-thinkers and antichristians, especially miraculous relations, which are much less wonderful than the fabricated tales handed down to the native of Asia, and consequently would be apt, at best, to carry little weight with them. On the contrary, moral doctrines, tending evidently to the maintenance of the peace and harmony of mankind at large, are beyond the reach of metaphysical perversion, and intelligible alike to the learned and to the unlearned. This simple code of religion and morality is so admirably calculated to elevate men's ideas to high and liberal notions of God, who has equally subjected all living creatures, without distinction of caste, rank or wealth, to change, disappointment, pain and death, and has equally admitted all to be partakers of the bountiful mercies which he has lavished over nature, and is also so well fitted to regulate the conduct of the human race in the discharge of their various duties to themselves, and to society, that I cannot but hope the best effects from its promulgation in the present form.

Preface to the First Edition of the *Brahmunical Magazine*

Reprinted from The English Works of Raja Rammohun Roy (*Allahabad: Panini Office, 1906*).

For a period of upwards of fifty years, this country (Bengal) has been in exclusive possession of the English nation; during the first thirty years of which, from their word and deed, it was universally believed that they would not interfere with the religion of their subjects, and that they truly wished every man to act in such matters according to the dictates of his own conscience. Their possessions in Hindoostan and their political strength have, through the grace of God, gradually increased. But during the last twenty years, a body of English gentlemen, who are called missionaries, have been publicly endeavouring, in several ways to convert Hindoos and Mussulmans of this country into Christianity. The first way is that of publishing and distributing among the natives various books, large and small reviling both religions, and abusing and ridiculing the gods and saints of the former: the second way is that of standing in front of the doors of the natives or in the public roads to preach the excellency of their own religion and the debasedness of that of others: the third way is that if any natives of low origin become Christians from the desire of gain or from any other motives, these gentlemen employ and maintain them as a necessary encouragement to others to follow their example.

It is true that the apostles of Jesus Christ used to preach the superiority of the Christian religion to the natives of different countries. But we must recollect that they were not of the rulers of those countries where they preached. Were the missionaries likewise to preach the Gospel and distribute books in countries not conquered by the English, such as Turkey, Persia, &c., which are much nearer England, they would be esteemed a body of men truly zealous in propagating religion and in following the example of the founders of Christianity. In Bengal, where the English are the sole rulers, and where the mere name of Englishmen is sufficient to frighten people, an encroachment upon the rights of her poor timid and humble inhabitants and upon their religion, cannot be viewed in the eyes of God or the public as a justifiable act. For wise and good men always feel disinclined to hurt those that are of much less strength than themselves, and if such weak creatures be dependent on them and subject to their authority, they can never attempt, even in thought, to mortify their feelings.

We have been subjected to such insults for about nine centuries, and the cause of such degradation has been our excess in civilization and abstinence from the slaughter even of animals; as well as our division into castes, which has been the source of want of unity among us.

It seems almost natural that when one nation succeeds in conquering another, the former, though their religion may be quite ridiculous, laugh at and despise the religion and manners of those that are fallen into their power. For example, Mussulmans, upon their conquest of India, proved highly inimical to the religious exercises of Hindoos. When the generals of Chungezkhan, who denied God and were like wild beasts in their manners, invaded the western part of Hindoostan, they universally mocked at the profession of God and of futurity expressed to them by the natives of India. The savages of Arracan, on their invasion of the eastern part of Bengal, always attempted to degrade the religion of Hindoos. In ancient days, the Greeks and the Romans, who were gross idolaters and immoral in their lives, used to laugh at the religion and conduct of their Jewish subjects, a sect who were devoted to the belief of one God. It is therefore not uncommon if the English missionaries, who are of the conquerors of this country, revile and mock at the religion of its natives. But as the English are celebrated for the manifestation of humanity and for administering justice, and as a great many gentlemen among them are noticed to have had an aversion to violate equity, it would tend to destroy their acknowledged character if they follow the example of the former savage conquerors in disturbing the established religion of the country; because to introduce a religion by means of abuse and insult, or by affording the hope of worldly gain, is inconsistent with reason and justice. If by the force of argument they can prove the truth of their own religion and the falsity of that of Hindoos, many would of course embrace their doctrines, and in case they fail to prove this, they should not undergo such useless trouble, nor tease Hindoos any longer by their attempts at conversion. In consideration of the small huts in which Brahmans of learning generally reside, and the simple food, such as vegetables, &c., which they are accustomed to eat, and the poverty which obliges them to live upon charity, the missionary gentlemen may not, I hope, abstain from controversy from contempt of them, for truth and true religion do not always belong to wealth and power, high names or lofty palaces.

Now, in the Mission-press of Snreerampore a letter shewing the unreasonableness of all the Hindoo Sastras having appeared, I have inserted in the 1st and 2nd numbers of this magazine all the questions in the above letter as well as their answers, and afterwards the replies that may be made by both parties shall in like manner be published.

Humble Suggestions to His Countrymen
Who Believe in the One True God

Reprinted from The English Works of Raja
Rammohun Roy (*Allahabad: Panini Office, 1906*).

Those who firmly believe on the authority of the Vedas, that "God is ONE *only* without an equal," and that "He cannot be known either through the medium of language, thought, or vision: how can he be known except as existing, *the origin and support of the universe?*"—and who endeavour to regulate their conduct by the following precept, "He who is desirous of eternal happiness should regard another as he regards himself, and the happiness and misery of another as his own," ought to manifest the warmest affection towards such of their own countrymen as maintain the same faith and practice, even although they have not all studied the Vedas for themselves, but have professed a belief in God only through an acquaintance with their general design. . . . It is our unquestionable duty invariably to treat them as brethren. No doubt should be entertained of their future salvation, merely because they receive instructions, and practise their sacred music, in the vernacular dialect. . . .

Amongst foreigners, those Europeans who believe God to be in every sense ONE, and worship HIM ALONE in spirit, and who extend their benevolence to man as the highest service to God, should be regarded by us with affection, on the ground of the object of their worship being the same as ours. We should feel no reluctance to co-operate with them in religious matters, merely because they consider Jesus Christ as the Messenger of God and their Spiritual Teacher; for oneness in the object of worship and sameness of religious practice should produce attachment between the worshippers.

Amongst Europeans, those who believe Jesus Christ to be God himself, and conceive him to be possessed of a particular form, and maintain Father, Son, and Holy Ghost to be one God, should not be treated in an unfriendly manner. On the contrary, we should act towards them in the same manner as we act towards those of our countrymen who, without forming any external image, meditate upon Rama and other supposed incarnations, and believe in their unity.

Again, those amongst Europeans who believing Jesus Christ to be the Supreme Being moreover construct various images of him, should not be hated. On the contrary, it becomes us to act towards those Europeans in the same manner as we act towards such as believe Rama, &c., to be incarnations of God, and form external images of them. For the religious principle of the two last-mentioned sects of foreigners are one and the same with those of the two similar sects among Hindoos, although they are clothed in a different garb.

When any belonging to the second and third classes of Europeans endeavour to make converts of us, the believers in the only living and true God, even then we should feel no resentment towards them, but rather compassion, on account of their blindness to the errors into which they themselves have fallen: since it is almost impossible, as every day's experience teaches us, for men, when possessed of wealth and power, to perceive their own defects.

Autobiographical Sketch

Reprinted from The English Works of Raja Rammohun Roy *(Allahabad: Panini Office, 1906).*

MY DEAR FRIEND,

In conformity with the wish, you have frequently expressed, that I should give you an outline of my life, I have now the pleasure to give you the following very brief sketch:—

My ancestors were Brahmins of a high order, and, from time immemorial, were devoted to the religious duties of their race, down to my fifth progenitor, who about one hundred and forty years ago gave up spiritual exercises for worldy pursuits and aggrandisement. His descendants ever since have followed his example and, according to the usual fate of courtiers, with various success, sometimes rising to honour and sometimes falling; sometimes rich and sometimes poor; sometimes excelling in success, sometimes miserable through disappointment. But my maternal ancestors, being of the sacerdotal order by profession as well as by birth, and of a family than which none holds a higher rank in that profession, have up to the present day uniformly adhered to a life of religious observances and devotion, preferring peace and tranquility of mind to the excitements of ambition, and all the allurements of worldly grandeur.

In conformity with the usage of my paternal race, and the wish of my father, I studied the Persian and Arabic languages, these being indispensable to those who attached themselves to the courts of the Mahommedan princes; and agreeably to the usage of my maternal relations, I devoted myself to the study of the Sanskrit and the theological works written in it, which contain the body of Hindoo literature, law and religion.

When about the age of sixteen, I composed a manuscript calling in question the validity of the idolatrous system of the Hindoos. This, together with my known sentiments on that subject, having produced a coolness between me and my immediate kindred, I proceeded on my travels, and passed through different countries, chiefly within, but some beyond, the bounds of Hindoostan, with a feeling of great aversion to the establishment of the British power in India. When I had reached the age of twenty, my father recalled me, and restored me to his favour; after which I first saw and began to associate with Europeans, and soon after made myself tolerably acquainted with their laws and form of government. Finding them generally more intelligent, more steady and moderate in their conduct, I gave up my prejudice against them, and became inclined in their favour, feeling persuaded that their rule, though a foreign yoke, would lead more speedily and surely to the amelioration of the native inhabitants; and I enjoyed the confidence of several of them even in their public capacity. My continued controversies with the Brahmins on the subject of their idolatry and superstition, and my interference with their custom of burning widows, and other pernicious practices, revived and increased their animosity against me; and through their influence with my family, my father was again obliged to withdraw his countenance openly, though his limited pecuniary support was still continued to me.

After my father's death I opposed the advocates of idolatry with still greater boldness. Availing myself of the art of printing, now established in India, I published various works and pamphlets against their errors, in the native and foreign languages. This raised such a feeling against me, that I was at last deserted by every person except two or three Scotch friends, to whom, and the nation to which they belong, I always feel grateful.

The ground which I took in all my controversies was, not that of opposition to *Brahminism,* but to a *perversion* of it; and I endeavoured to show that the idolatry of the Brahmins was contrary to the practice of their ancestors, and the principles of the ancient books and authorities which they profess to revere and obey. Notwithstanding the violence of the opposition and resistance to my opinions, several highly respectable persons, both among my own relations and others, began to adopt the same sentiments.

I now felt a strong wish to visit Europe, and obtain by personal observation, a more thorough insight into its manners, customs, religion, and political institutions. I refrained, however, from carrying this intention into effect until the friends who coincided in my sentiments should be increased in number and strength. My expectations having been at length realised, in November, 1830, I embarked for England, as the discussion of the East India Company's charter was expected to come on, by which the treatment of the natives of India, and its future government, would be determined for many years to come, and an appeal to the King in Council, against the abolition of the practice of burning widows, was to be heard before the Privy Council; and his Majesty the Emperor of Delhi had likewise commissioned me to bring before the authorities in England certain encroachments on his rights by the East India Company. I, accordingly arrived in England in April, 1831.

I hope you will excuse the brevity of this sketch, as I have no leisure at present to enter into particulars, and

I remain, &c.,
RAMMOHUN ROY.

AUROBINDO

Aurobindo (1872–1950), born Aurobindo Ackroyd Ghose and called by his followers Sri Aurobindo, was the son of a wealthy Bengali physician who was an anglophile. He sent his son to an English convent school in Darjeeling at age five and to England at seven. Aurobindo attended St. Paul's School in London and King's College, Cambridge University. Returning to India at twenty-one in the employ of the maharaja of Baroda, he wrote speeches and performed other secretarial work as well as taught at Baroda College, all the while immersing himself in Indian culture. He learned Sanskrit and modern Indian languages. Early in his thirties, Aurobindo became involved in the Indian independence movement, becoming a leader of the extremist wing of the Congress Party. Arrested first for sedition and then for masterminding terrorist acts, he spent a year in jail in Calcutta. There he underwent an important religious experience that led him to retire from politics. Acquitted of these crimes, he settled in the French colony of Pondicherry under the threat of rearrest. (Eloquent and outspoken, he was viewed by the British as a continuing threat, despite the religious and mystical turn of his speeches and writing.)

Aurobindo's ethical doctrines stem from tenets of his metaphysics. First, the philosopher-yogi, while retaining the traditional ideal of a mystical enlightenment or union with God, rejects the notion that the world of everyday experience is somehow illusory. He affirms the reality of this world. The affirmation has ethical consequences, for it implies that we do not need to renounce the world to attain our truest self-interest. The principles of the Pondicherry *ashram,* or community of disciples, that grew up around Aurobindo reflect this; unlike most religious communities in India, that *ashram* stresses education, physical activity, business enterprises, and other "this-worldly" activities as well as contemplation and self-discipline.

Second, Aurobindo argues that the relation between the world and the Divine is not constant, but progresses over time. Each stage of material evolution includes but also transforms earlier stages. To best attune to the ongoing divine creative action, people must practice a new form of yoga, *integral yoga,* which Aurobindo sees as leading not only to a divine illumination but also to an intregation of a diviner consciousness in our everyday lives. The mysticism that follows from this combination, Aurobindo believes, does not seek an alternative to ordinary living; rather, the goal is to make ordinary living more divine. The first selection below is an overview of Aurobindo's world view, the second some of his own statements on ethics, and the third a delineation of the new yoga proposed.

Aurobindo himself does not view his yogic teaching as "ethical." In *The Life Divine,* he sketches what he sees as the limitations of ethical sensibilities—their relative and often unfounded character—in the context of his metaphysics. Against what he sees as conventional ethical standards comprehended by the ordinary mind, he sets his ideal of a "spiritual" transcendence with its own standards of right action and its own goals, which we, until we are ourselves transformed, can understand only imperfectly.

The Teaching of Sri Aurobindo

Reprinted from Robert A. McDermott (ed.), The Essential Aurobindo. *Copyright © 1973 by Schocken Books.*

The Teaching of Sri Aurobindo starts from that of the ancient sages of India: that behind the appearances of the universe there is the reality of a being and consciousness, a self of all things, one and eternal. All beings are united in that one self and spirit but divided by a certain separativity of consciousness, an ignorance of their true self and reality in the mind, life, and body. It is possible by a certain psychological discipline to remove this veil of separative consciousness and become aware of the true Self, the divinity within us and all.

Sri Aurobindo's teaching states that this one being and consciousness is involved here in matter. Evolution is the process by which it liberates itself; consciousness appears in what seems to be inconscient, and once having appeared is self-impelled to grow higher and higher and at the same time to enlarge and develop toward a greater and greater perfection. Life is the first step of this release of consciousness; mind is the second. But the evolution does not finish with mind; it awaits a release into something greater, a consciousness which is spiritual and supramental. The next step of the evolution must be toward the development of Supermind and spirit as the dominant power in the conscious being. For only then will the involved divinity in things release itself entirely and it become possible for life to manifest perfection.

But while the former steps in evolution were taken by nature without a conscious will in the plant and animal life, in man nature becomes able to evolve by a conscious will in the instrument. It is not, however, by the mental will in man that this can be wholly done, for the mind goes only to a certain point and after that can only move in a circle. A conversion has to be made, a turning of the consciousness by which mind has to change into the higher principle. This method is to be found through the ancient psychological discipline and practice of yoga. In the past, it has been attempted by a drawing away from the world and a disappearance into the height of the self or spirit. Sri Aurobindo teaches that a descent of the higher principle is possible which will not merely release the spiritual Self out of the world, but release it in the world, replace the mind's ignorance or its very limited knowledge by a supramental Truth-Consciousness which will be a sufficient instrument of the inner self, and make it possible for the human being to find himself dynamically as well as inwardly and grow out of his still animal humanity into a diviner race. The psychological discipline of yoga can be used to that end by opening all the parts of the being to a conversion or transformation through the descent and working of the higher, still-concealed supramental principle.

This, however, cannot be done at once or in a short time or by any rapid or miraculous transformation. Many steps have to be taken by the seeker before the supramental descent is possible. Man lives mostly in his surface mind, life, and body, but there is an inner being within him with greater possibilities to which he has to awake—for it is only a very restricted influence from it that he receives now and that pushes him to a constant pursuit of a greater beauty, harmony, power, and knowledge. The first process of yoga is therefore to open the ranges of this inner being and to live from there outward, governing his outward life by an inner light and force. In doing so he discovers in himself his true soul, which is not this outer mixture of mental, vital and physical elements, but something of the reality behind them, a spark from the one divine fire. He has to learn to live in his soul and purify and orientate by its drive toward the truth the rest of the nature. There can follow afterwards an opening upward and descent of a higher principle of the being. But even then it is not at once the full supramental light and force. For there are several ranges of consciousness between the ordinary human mind and the supramental Truth-Consciousness. These intervening ranges have to be opened up and their power brought down into the mind, life, and body. Only afterwards can the full power of the Truth-Consciousness work in the nature. The process of this self-discipline or *sādhanā* is therefore long and difficult, but even a little of it is so much gained because it makes the ultimate release and perfection more possible.

There are many things belonging to older systems that are necessary on the way—an opening of the mind to a greater wideness and to the sense of the self and the infinite, an emergence into what has been called the cosmic consciousness, mastery over the desires and passions; an outward asceticism is not essential, but the conquest of desire and attachment and a control over the body and its needs, greeds, and instincts are indispensable. There is a combination of the principles of the old systems, the way of knowledge through the mind's discernment between reality and the appearance; the heart's way of devotion, love, and surrender; and the way of works, turning the will away from motives of self-interest to the truth and the service of a greater reality than the ego. For the whole being has to be trained so that it can respond and be transformed when it is possible for that greater light and force to work in the nature.

In this discipline the inspiration of the master and, in the difficult stages, his control and his presence are indispensable—for it would be impossible otherwise to go through it without much stumbling and error which would prevent all chance of success. The master is one who has risen to a higher consciousness and being and he is often regarded as its manifestation or representative. He not only helps by his teaching and still more by his influence and example, but by a power to communicate his own experience to others.

This is Sri Aurobindo's teaching and method of practice. It is not his object to develop any one religion or to amalgamate the older religions or to found any new religion—for any of these things would lead away from his central purpose. The one aim of his yoga is an inner self-development by which each one who follows it can in time discover the One Self in all and evolve a higher consciousness than the mental, a spiritual and supramental consciousness which will transform and divinize human nature.

from *The Life Divine*

. . . We have to recognise, if we thus view the whole, not limiting ourselves to the human difficulty and the human standpoint, that we do not live in an ethical world. The attempt of human thought to force an ethical meaning into the whole of Nature is one of those acts of wilful and obstinate self-confusion, one of those pathetic attempts of the human being to read himself, his limited habitual human self into all things and judge them from the standpoint he has personally evolved, which most effectively prevent him from arriving at real knowledge and complete sight. Material Nature is not ethical; the law which governs it is a coordination of fixed habits which take no cognisance of good and evil, but only of force that creates, force that arranges and preserves, force that disturbs and destroys impartially, non-ethically, according to the secret Will in it, according to the mute satisfaction of that Will in its own self-formations and self-dissolutions. Animal or vital Nature is also non-ethical, although as it progresses it manifests the crude material out of which the higher animal evolves the ethical impulse. We do not blame the tiger because it slays and devours its prey any more than we blame the storm because it destroys or the fire because it tortures and kills; neither does the conscious-force in the storm, the fire or the tiger blame or condemn itself. Blame and condemnation, or rather self-blame and self-condemnation, are the beginning of true ethics. When we blame others without applying the same law to ourselves, we are not speaking with a true ethical judgment, but only applying the language ethics has evolved for us to an emotional impulse of recoil from or dislike of that which displeases or hurts us.

This recoil or dislike is the primary origin of ethics, but is not itself ethical. The fear of the deer for the tiger, the rage of the strong creature against its assailant is a vital recoil of the individual delight of existence from that which threatens it. In the progress of the mentality it refines itself into repugnance, dislike, disapproval. Disapproval of that which threatens and hurts us, approval of that which flatters and satisfies refine into the conception of good and evil to oneself, to the community, to others than ourselves, to other communities than ours, and finally into the general approval of good, the general disapproval of evil. But, throughout, the fundamental nature of the thing remains the same. Man desires self-expression, self-development, in other words, the progressing play in himself of the conscious-force of existence; that is his fundamental delight. Whatever hurts that self-expression, self-development, satisfaction of his progressing self, is for him evil; whatever helps, confirms, raises, aggrandises, ennobles it is his good. Only, his conception of the self-development changes, becomes higher and wider, begins to exceed his limited personality, to embrace others, to embrace all in its scope.

In other words, ethics is a stage in evolution. That which is common to all stages is the urge . . . towards self-expression. This urge is at first non-ethical, then infra-ethical in the animal, then in the intelligent animal even anti-ethical for it permits us to approve hurt done to others which we disapprove when done to ourselves. In this respect man even now is only half-ethical. And just as all below us is infra-ethical, so there may be that above us whither we shall eventually arrive, which is supra-ethical, has no need of ethics. The ethical impulse and attitude, so all-important to humanity, is a means by which it struggles out of the lower harmony and universality based upon inconscience and broken up by Life into individual discords towards a higher harmony and universality based upon conscient oneness with all existences. Arriving at that goal, this means will no longer be necessary or even possible, since the qualities and oppositions on which it depends will naturally dissolve and disappear in the final reconciliation.

. . . it is the same Nature, the same Force that has burdened man with the sense of good and evil and insists on its importance: evidently, therefore, this sense also has an evolutionary purpose; it too must be necessary, it must be there so that man may leave certain things behind him, move towards others, until out of good and evil he can emerge into some Good that is eternal and infinite.

But how is this evolutionary intention in Nature to fulfil itself, by what power, means, impulsion, what principle and process of selection and harmonisation? The method adopted by the mind of man through the ages has been always a principle of selection and rejection, and this has taken the forms of a religious sanction, a social or moral rule of life or an ethical ideal. But this is an empirical means which does not touch the root of the problem because it has no vision of the cause and origin of the malady it attempts to cure; it deals with the symptoms, but deals with them perfunctorily, not knowing what function they serve in the purpose of Nature and what it is in the mind and life that supports them and keeps them in being. Moreover, human good and evil are relative and the standards erected by ethics are uncertain as well as relative: what is forbidden by one religion or another, what is regarded as good or bad by social opinion, what is thought useful to society or noxious to it, what some temporary law of man allows or disallows, what is or is considered helpful or harmful to self or others, what accords with this or that ideal, what is prompted or discouraged by an instinct which we

call conscience,—an amalgam of all these viewpoints is the determining heterogeneous idea, constitutes the complex substance of morality; in all of them there is the constant mixture of truth and half-truth and error which pursues all the activities of our limiting mental Knowledge-Ignorance. A mental control over our vital and physical desires and instincts, over our personal and social action, over our dealings with others is indispensable to us as human beings, and morality creates a standard by which we can guide ourselves and establish a customary control; but the control is always imperfect and it is an expedient, not a solution: man remains always what he is and has ever been, a mixture of good and evil, sin and virtue, a mental ego with an imperfect command over his mental, vital and physical nature.

The endeavour to select, to retain from our consciousness and action all that seems to us good and reject all that seems to us evil and so to re-form our being, to reconstitute and shape ourselves into the image of an ideal, is a more profound ethical motive, because it comes nearer to the true issue; it rests on the sound idea that our life is a becoming and that there is something which we have to become and be. But the ideals constructed by the human mind are selective and relative; to shape our nature rigidly according to them is to limit ourselves and make a construction where there should be growth into larger being. The true call upon us is the call of the Infinite and the Supreme; the self-affirmation and self-abnegation imposed on us by Nature are both movements towards that, and it is the right way of self-affirmation and self-negation taken together in place of the wrong, because ignorant, way of the ego and in place of the conflict between the yes and the no of Nature that we have to discover. . . .

from *The Synthesis of Yoga*

THE PRINCIPLE OF THE INTEGRAL YOGA

The principle of Yoga is the turning of one or of all powers of our human existence into a means of reaching the divine Being. In an ordinary Yoga one main power of being or one group of its powers is made the means, vehicle, path. In a synthetic Yoga all powers will be combined and included in the transmuting instrumentation.

In Hathayoga the instrument is the body and life. All the power of the body is stilled, collected, purified, heightened, concentrated to its utmost limits or beyond any limits by Asana and other physical processes; the power of the life too is similarly purified, heightened, concentrated by Asana and Pranayama. This concentration of powers is then directed towards that physical centre in which the divine consciousness sits concealed in the human body. The power of Life, Nature-power, coiled up with all its secret forces asleep in the lowest nervous plexus of the earth-being,—for only so much escapes into waking action in our normal operations as is sufficient for the limited uses of human life,—rises awakened through centre after centre and awakens, too, in its ascent and passage the forces of each successive nodus of our being, the nervous life, the heart of emotion and ordinary mentality, the speech, sight, will, the higher knowledge, till through and above the brain it meets with and it becomes one with the divine consciousness.

In Rajayoga the chosen instrument is the mind. Our ordinary mentality is first disciplined, purified and directed towards the divine Being, then by a summary process of Asana and Pranayama the physical force of our being is stilled and concentrated, the life-force released into a rhythmic movement capable of cessation and concentrated into a higher power of its upward action, the mind, supported and strengthened by this greater action and concentration of the body and life upon which it rests, is itself purified of all its unrest and emotion and its habitual thought-waves, liberated from distraction and dispersion, given its highest force of concentration, gathered up into a trance of absorption. Two objects, the one temporal, the other eternal, are gained by this discipline. Mind-power develops in another concentrated action abnormal capacities of knowledge, effective will, deep light of reception, powerful light of thought-radiation which are altogether beyond the narrow range of our normal mentality; it arrives at the Yogic or occult powers around which there has been woven so much quite dispensable and yet perhaps salutary mystery. But the one final end and the one all-important gain is that the mind, stilled and cast into a concentrated trance, can lose itself in the divine consciousness and the soul be made free to unite with the divine Being.

The triple way takes for its chosen instruments the three main powers of the mental soul-life of the human being. Knowledge selects the reason and the mental vision and it makes them by purification, concentration and a certain discipline of a God-directed seeking its means for the greatest knowledge and the greatest vision of all, God-knowledge and God-vision. Its aim is to see, know and be the Divine. Works, action selects for its instrument the will of the doer of works; it makes life an offering of sacrifice to the Godhead and by purification, concentration and a certain discipline of subjection to the divine Will a means for contact and increasing unity of the soul of man with the divine Master of the universe. Devotion selects the emotional and aesthetic powers of the soul and by turning them all Godward in a perfect purity, intensity, infinite passion of seeking makes them a means of God-possession in one or many relations of unity with the Divine Being. All aim in their own way at a union or unity of the human soul with the supreme Spirit.

Each Yoga in its process has the character of the instrument it uses; thus the Hathayogic process is psycho-physical, the Rajayogic mental and psychic, the way of knowledge is spiritual and cognitive, the way of devotion spiritual, emotional and aesthetic, the way of works spiritual and dynamic by action. Each is guided in the ways of its own characteristic power. But all power is in the end one, all power is really soul-power. In the ordinary process of life, body and mind this truth is quite obscured by the dispersed, dividing and distributive action of Nature which is the normal condition of all our functionings, although even there it is in the end evident; for all material energy contains hidden the vital, mental, psychic, spiritual energy and in the end it must release these forms of the one Shakti, the vital energy conceals and liberates into action all the other forms, the mental supporting itself on the life and body and their powers and functionings contains undeveloped or only partially developed the psychic and the spiritual power of the being. But when by Yoga any of these powers is taken up from the dispersed and distributive action, raised to its highest degree, concentrated, it becomes manifest soul-power and reveals the essential unity. Therefore the Hathayogic process has too its pure psychic and spiritual result, the Rajayogic arrives by psychic means at a spiritual consummation. The triple way may appear to be altogether mental and spiritual in its way of seeking and its objectives, but it can be attended by results more characteristic of the other paths, which offer themselves in a spontaneous and involuntary flowering, and for the same reason, because soul-power is all-power and where it reaches its height in one direction its other possibilities also begin to show themselves in fact or in incipient potentiality. This unity at once suggests the possibility of a synthetic Yoga.

Tantric discipline is in its nature a synthesis. It has seized on the large universal truth that there are two poles of being whose essential unity is the secret of existence, Brahman and Shakti, Spirit and Nature, and that Nature is power of the spirit or rather is spirit as power. To raise nature in man into manifest power of spirit is its method and it is the whole

nature that it gathers up for the spiritual conversion. It includes in its system of instrumentation the forceful Hathayogic process and especially the opening up of the nervous centres and the passage through them of the awakened Shakti on her way to her union with the Brahman, the subtler stress of the Rajayogic purification, meditation and concentration, the leverage of will-force, the motive power of devotion, the key of knowledge. But it does not stop short with an effective assembling of the different powers of these specific Yogas. In two directions it enlarges by its synthetic turn the province of the Yogic method. First, it lays its hand firmly on many of the main springs of human quality, desire, action and it subjects them to an intensive discipline with the soul's mastery of its motives as a first aim and their elevation to a diviner spiritual level as its final utility. Again, it includes in its objects of Yoga not only liberation, which is the one all-mastering preoccupation of the specific systems, but a cosmic enjoyment of the power of the Spirit, which the others may take incidentally on the way, in part, casually, but avoid making a motive or object. It is a bolder and larger system.

In the method of synthesis which we have been following, another clue of principle has been pursued which is derived from another view of the possibilities of Yoga. This starts from the method of Vedanta to arrive at the aim of the Tantra. In the tantric method Shakti is all-important, becomes the key to the finding of spirit; in this synthesis spirit, soul is all-important, becomes the secret of the taking up of Shakti. The tantric method starts from the bottom and grades the ladder of ascent upwards to the summit; therefore its initial stress is upon the action of the awakened Shaki in the nervous system of the body and its centres; the opening of the six lotuses is the opening up of the ranges of the power of Spirit. Our synthesis takes man as a spirit in mind much more than a spirit in body and assumes in him the capacity to begin on that level, to spiritualise his being by the power of the soul in mind opening itself directly to a higher spiritual force and being and to perfect by that higher force so possessed and brought into action the whole of his nature. For that reason our initial stress has fallen upon the utilisation of the powers of soul in mind and the turning of the triple key of knowledge, works and love in the locks of the spirit; the Hatha-yogic methods can be dispensed with,—though there is no objection to their partial use,—the Raja-yogic will only enter in as an informal element. To arrive by the shortest way at the largest development of spiritual power and being and divinise by it a liberated nature in the whole range of human living is our inspiring motive.

The principle in view is a self-surrender, a giving up of the human being into the being, conscious-ness, power, delight of the Divine, a union or com-munion at all the points of meeting in the soul of man, the mental being, by which the Divine himself, directly and without veil master and possessor of the instrument, shall by the light of his presence and guidance perfect the human being in all the forces of the Nature for a divine living. Here we arrive at a farther enlargement of the objects of the Yoga. The common initial purpose of all Yoga is the liberation of the soul of man from its present natural ignorance and limitation, its release into spiritual being, its union with the highest self and Divinity. But ordinarily this is made not only the initial but the whole and final object: enjoyment of spiritual being there is, but either in a dissolution of the human and individual into the silence of self-being or on a higher plane in another existence. The Tantric sys-tem makes liberation the final, but not the only aim; it takes on its way a full perfection and enjoyment of the spiritual power, light and joy in the human exis-tence, and even it has a glimpse of a supreme experi-ence in which liberation and cosmic action and enjoyment are unified in a final overcoming of all oppositions and dissonances. It is this wider view of our spiritual potentialities from which we begin, but we add another stress which brings in a completer significance. We regard the spirit in man not as solely an individual being travelling to a transcen-dent unity with the Divine, but as a universal being capable of oneness with the Divine in all souls and all Nature and we give this extended view its entire practical consequence. The human soul's individual liberation and enjoyment of union with the Divine in spiritual being, consciousness and delight must always be the first object of the Yoga; its free enjoy-ment of the cosmic unity of the Divine becomes a second object; but out of that a third appears, the effectuation of the meaning of the divine unity with all beings by a sympathy and participation in the spiritual purpose of the Divine in humanity. The individual Yoga then turns from its separateness and becomes a part of the collective Yoga of the divine Nature in the human race. The liberated individual being, united with the Divine in self and spirit, becomes in his natural being a self-perfecting in-strument for the perfect outflowering of the Divine in humanity.

This outflowering has its two terms; first, comes the growth out of the separative human ego into the unity of the spirit, then the possession of the divine nature in its proper and its higher forms and no longer in the inferior forms of the mental being which are a mutilated translation and not the au-thentic text of the original script of divine Nature in the cosmic individual. In other words, a perfection has to be aimed at which amounts to the elevation of the mental into the full spiritual and supramental nature. Therefore this integral Yoga of knowledge, love and works has to be extended into a Yoga of spiritual and gnostic self-perfection. As gnostic knowledge, will and Ananda are a direct instrumen-tation of spirit and can only be won by growing into the spirit, into divine being, this growth has to be the first aim of our Yoga. The mental being has to enlarge itself into the oneness of the Divine before the Divine will perfect in the soul of the individual its gnostic outflowering. That is the reason why the triple way of knowledge, works and love becomes the keynote of the whole Yoga, for that is the direct means for the soul in mind to rise to its highest intensities where it passes upward into the divine oneness. That too is the reason why the Yoga must be integral. For if immergence in the Infinite or some close union with the Divine were all our aim, an integral Yoga would be superfluous, except for such greater satisfaction of the being of man as we may get by a self-lifting of the whole of it towards its Source. But it would not be needed for the essential aim, since by any single power of the soul-nature we can meet with the Divine; each at its height rises up into the infinite and absolute, each therefore offers a sufficient way of arrival, for all the hundred sepa-rate paths meet in the Eternal. But the gnostic being is a complete enjoyment and possession of the whole divine and spiritual nature; and it is a complete lifting of the whole nature of man into its power of a divine and spiritual existence. Integrality becomes then an essential condition of this Yoga.

At the same time we have seen that each of the three ways at its height, if it is pursued with a certain largeness, can take into itself the powers of the others and lead to their fulfilment. It is therefore sufficient to start by one of them and find the point at which it meets the other at first parallel lines of advance and melts into them by its own widenings. At the same time a more difficult, complex, wholly powerful process would be to start, as it were, on three lines together, on a triple wheel of soul-power. But the consideration of this possibility must be postponed till we have seen what are the conditions and means of the Yoga of self-perfection. For we shall see that this also need not be postponed entirely, but a certain preparation of it is part of and a certain initiation into it proceeds by the growth of the divine works, love and knowledge.

MAHATMA GANDHI

Mohandas Karamchand Gandhi (1869–1948), known universally by the honorific title "Mahatma," was born in Porbandar, India. His father, Karamchand, was Porbandar's chief minister. The family was religious, worshipping the Hindu god Vishnu and also accepting many of the ideas of Jainism—in particular, its advocacy of *ahimsa,* noninjury to all living things. Gandhi was a mediocre student: "good at English, fair in arithmetic, and weak in geography; conduct very good, bad handwriting," according to one of his elementary school teachers. He was married at thirteen. At eighteen, Gandhi enrolled in the University of Bombay. Until then, his classes had been in his native language, Gujarati; the University courses were in English, and Gandhi had some trouble adapting. Nevertheless, he soon went to London to study law.

When he was twenty-two, Gandhi traveled to South Africa. There he suffered various forms of racial discrimination and became a committed social activist. For the rest of his life, he was essentially a professional politician. In South Africa and then in India, Gandhi worked to promote equality and break down racial, caste, and other barriers that kept people from enjoying full legal rights. He worked in relative obscurity until 1919, when, at age fifty, he announced a *satyagraha* (a "holding fast to the truth"), a general campaign of passive resistance against British rule. Although Gandhi abhorred violence and urged nonviolent forms of civil disobedience, the struggle quickly became violent. Hundreds were killed; Gandhi was arrested, tried for sedition, and sentenced to a six-year prison term. The authorities released him after only two years to receive an appendectomy.

Gandhi announced other *satyagrahas* against British rule in 1928 and 1940. Once again, he advocated nonviolent forms of protest; once again, the struggles turned violent. Throughout this period, Gandhi was the chief voice of the Indian independence movement. In 1942, at the end of the third campaign of passive resistance, the British agreed to grant India self-determination after the end of World War II. They kept their promise; India became independent on July 18, 1947, when Gandhi was seventy-eight and his political influence was in decline. Against his wishes, imperial India was partitioned along religious lines into the modern nations of India and Pakistan. Partition led to near anarchy in some areas; hundreds of thousands died. Gandhi himself proved to be a victim; having spent several years advocating harmony between Muslims and Hindus, he was shot by a Hindu fanatic just six months after India gained independence.

In his political speeches and writings, Gandhi argues vigorously in favor of equality. He favors an equality of respect; everyone deserves equal respect as a human being, without regard to caste, race, or other characteristics. Moreover, Gandhi favors economic equality. He does not insist that everyone have equal wealth, for he sees this as impractical. But he does contend that no people should have more than they can use. The rich, who have more, should place their funds in trust for public use. The poor should develop cottage industries to achieve a measure of individual and group self-reliance in an economic context of scarce resources.

Gandhi's main ethical thesis, however, is *ahimsa,* that violence is unjustified. The ends do not justify the means. Indeed, Gandhi questions whether ends can be separated from means. He claims that violence harms not only its victims but also its perpetrators. The moral harm it causes the "inner" person far outlasts any good that it promotes. Also, he believes, it leads eventually to bad consequences in the world. Even for overwhelmingly good ends, therefore, or even in the face of severe opposition, violence is morally unacceptable.

But Gandhi's moral outlook is more demanding than this suggests. We have an obligation to serve others—not merely now and then but as our primary task. This does not mean that we must all leave our occupations and do social work. It does mean, however, that we must transform our way of working in whatever we do to place the good of others at the forefront of our concern. This requires renunciation and self-control to subjugate our desires and happiness to the desires and happiness of others.

from *Gita—My Mother*

Reprinted with permission of Mr. Anand T. Hinorani, Editor-Publisher: "Ghandi Series," C-18/D, Munirka, New Delhi-110 067.

CHAPTER XV / THE GITA AND THE DOCTRINE OF EQUALITY

I believe in the doctrine of equality as taught by Lord Krishna in the *Gita*. The *Gita* teaches us that members of all the four castes should be treated on an equal basis. It does not prescribe the same *dharma* for the *Brahmin* as for the *Bhangi*. But it insists that the latter shall be entitled to the same measure of consideration and esteem as the former with all his superior learning. It is, therefore, our duty to see that the 'untouchables' do not feel that they are despised or looked down upon. Let them not be offered leavings from our plates for their subsistence. How can I accord differential treatment to any person, be he a *Brahmin* or a *Bhangi,* who worships the same God and keeps his body and soul pure and clean? I for one would regard myself as having sinned if I gave to a *Bhangi* unclean food from the leavings from the kitchen, or failed to render him personal assistance when he was in need.

We have to develop in ourselves the quality of looking upon all as equals as laid down in the *Gita*. . . .

I am not after extinguishing all differences. Who can destroy natural differences? Is there no difference between a *Brahmin*, a dog and a dog-eater? And yet the *Gita* says:

> "The men who have realized the Truth look with an equal eye on a learned and cultured Brahmin, a cow, an elephant, a dog and a dog-eater."

There is a difference between them, but the man who knows the Science of Life will say that there is no difference between them in status, as there is none between an elephant and an ant, a savage and a savant. Of course, the savage may be awe-struck before a savant; but the latter should not have any sense of superiority. No, we are all equal in the eye of the law and God. That is the ideal we have to live up to.

The great message of the *Bhagavad Gita* is: Treat the *Brahmin* and the *Bhangi* alike, if you would but know God. But how are they alike? A *Brahmin* is any day superior to the *Bhangi* in learning, and how am I to treat both alike? The *Bhagavad Gita* says that you should treat them even as you would wish to be treated by them, or even as you would treat yourself. . . . That is the the teaching of *Bhagavad Gita.*

CHAPTER XVIII / THE LAW OF SERVICE

The *Bhagavad Gita* provides you with a Code of Conduct. Whenever you are in trouble, doubt, depression or despair, you will turn to the Code and the Compendium. And what can be a better inspiration for you than Chapter Third? It lays down that God created man, and at the same time imposed on him the duty of *Yajna* or sacrifice. Both these words are derived from roots meaning that which purifies, and the Lord also said that "by sacrifice shall you propagate your kind." Sacrifice thus means service, and the Gita says that he who works only for himself is a thief. "Sacrifice ye for the gods, and pleased they will give you the reward of your sacrifice," says the *Gita*. To proceed a little further, sacrifice means laying down one's life so that others may live. Let us suffer so that others may be happy, and the highest service and the highest love is wherein man lays down his life for his fellow-men. That highest love is thus *Ahimsa* which is the highest service. There is an eternal struggle between life and death, but the sum total of life and death does not mean extinction but life. For, life persists in spite of death. We have an ocular demonstration, positive proof of the unquestioned sovereignty of *Ahimsa,* and this triumph of *Ahimsa* is possible through sacrifice. There is thus no higher law than the Law of *Yajna,* the Law of Service. . . .

To serve without desire is to favour not others, but ourselves, even as in discharging a debt we serve only ourselves, lighten our burden and fulfil our duty. Again, not only the good but all of us are bound to place our resources at the disposal of humanity. And if such is the law, as evidently it is, indulgence ceases to hold a place in life and gives way to renunciation. The duty of renunciation differentiates mankind from the beast.

Some object, that life thus understood becomes dull and devoid of art, and leaves no room for the household. But renunciation here does not mean abandoning the world and retiring into the forest. The spirit of renunciation should rule all the activities of life. A householder does not cease to be one, if he regards life as a duty rather than as an indulgence. A merchant, who operates in the sacrificial spirit, will have crores passing through his hands, but he will, if he follows the law, use his abilities for service. He will, therefore, not cheat or speculate, will lead a simple life, will not injure a living soul and will lose millions rather than harm anybody. . . .

Self-indulgence leads to destruction, and renunciation to immortality. Joy has no independent existence. It depends upon our attitude to life. One man will enjoy theatrical scenery, another the ever new scenes which unfold themselves in the sky. Joy, therefore, is a matter of individual and national education. We shall delight in things which we have been taught to delight in as children. And illustrations can be easily cited of different national tastes.

One who would serve will not waste a thought upon his own comforts, which he leaves to be attended to or neglected by his Master on high. He will not, therefore, encumber himself with everything that comes his way; he will take only what he strictly needs and leave the rest. He will be calm, free from anger and unruffled in mind even if he finds himself inconvenienced. His service, like virtue, is its own reward, and he will rest content with it. . . .

One who works according to one's full capacity does all that can be expected of one. But in our work we should develop the *Gita* attitude which we desire to possess. That attitude is that whatever we do, we do selflessly in a spirit of service. Spirit of service means in a spirit of dedication to God. One who does so, loses all idea of self. He has no hatred for anybody. On the contrary, he is generous to others. Even in regard to the smallest piece of service you render, ask yourselves from time to time whether you exhibit all these qualities.

Learn to be generous towards each other. To be generous means having no hatred for those whom we consider to be at fault, and loving and serving them. It is not generosity or love, if we have goodwill for others only as long as they and we are united in thought and action. That should be called merely friendship or mutual affection. The application of the term 'love' is wrong in such cases. 'Love' means feeling friendship for the enemy.

from *All Men Are Brothers*

CHAPTER III / MEANS AND ENDS

Means and end are convertible terms in my philosophy of life. *1*

They say "means are after all means," I would say "means are after all everything." As the means so the end. There is no wall of separation between means and end. Indeed the Creator has given us control (and that too very limited) over means, none over the end. Realization of the goal is in exact proportion to that of the means. This is a proposition that admits of no exception. *2*

Ahimsa and Truth are so intertwined that it is practically impossible to disentangle and separate them. They are like the two sides of a coin, or rather a smooth unstamped metallic disc. Who can say, which is the obverse, and which the reverse? Nevertheless, *ahimsa* is the means; Truth is the end. Means to be means always be within our reach, and so *ahimsa* is our supreme duty. If we take care of the means, we are bound to reach the end sooner or later. When once we have grasped this point final victory is beyond question. Whatever difficulties we encounter, whatever apparent reverses we sustain, we may not give up the quest for Truth which alone is, being God Himself. *3*

I am more concerned in preventing the brutalization of human nature than in the prevention of the sufferings of my own people. I know that people who voluntarily undergo a course of suffering raise themselves and the whole of humanity; but I also know that people who become brutalized in their desperate efforts to get victory over their opponents or to exploit weaker nations or weaker men, not only drag down themselves but mankind also. And

it cannot be a matter of pleasure to me or anyone else to see human nature dragged to the mire. If we are all sons of the same God and partake of the same divine essence, we must partake of the sin of every person whether he belongs to us or to another race. You can understand how repugnant it must be to invoke the beast in any human being, how much more so in Englishmen, among whom I count numerous friends. *8*

The method of passive resistance is the clearest and safest, because, if the cause is not true, it is the resisters, and they alone, who suffer. *9*

CHAPTER IV / AHIMSA OR THE WAY OF NON-VIOLENCE

Non-violence is the greatest force at the disposal of mankind. It is mightier than the mightiest weapon of destruction devised by the ingenuity of man. Destruction is not the law of the humans. Man lives freely by his readiness to die, if need be, at the hands of his brother, never by killing him. Every murder or other injury, no matter for what cause, committed or inflicted on another is a crime against humanity. *1*

The first condition of non-violence is juctice all round in every department of life. Perhaps, it is too much to expect of human nature. I do not, however, think so. No one should dogmatize about the capacity of human nature for degradation or exhaltation. *2*

In the application of *Satyagraha*, I discovered in the earliest stages that pursuit of truth did not admit of violence being inflicted on one's opponent but that he must be weaned from error by patience and sympathy. For, what appears to be truth to the one may appear to be error to another. And patience means self-suffering. So the doctrine came to mean vindication of truth, not by infliction of suffering on the opponent, but on one's self. *9*

Man and his deed are two distinct things. It is quite proper to resist and attack a system, but to resist and attack its author is tantamount to resisting and attacking oneself. For we are all tarred with the same brush, and are children of one and the same Creator, and as such the divine powers within us are infinite. To slight a single human being is to slight those divine powers, and thus to harm not only that being but with him the whole world. *11*

Non-violence is a universal principle and its operation is not limited by a hostile environment. Indeed, its efficacy can be tested only when it acts in the midst of and in spite of opposition. Our non-violence would be a hollow thing and nothing worth, if it depended for its success on the goodwill of the authorities. *12*

The only condition of a successful use of this force is a recognition of the existence of the soul as apart from the body and its permanent nature. And this recognition must amount to a living faith and not mere intellectual grasp. *13*

No man could be actively non-violent and not rise against social injustice no matter where it occurred. *15*

Passive resistance is a method of securing rights by personal suffering; it is the reverse of resistance by arms. When I refuse to do a thing that is repugnant to my conscience, I use soul-force. For instance, the government of the day has passed a law which is applicable to me. I do not like it. If by using violence I force the government to repeal the law, I am employing what may be termed body-force. If I do not obey the law and accept the penalty for its breach, I use soul-force. It involves sacrifice of self.

Everybody admits that sacrifice of self is infinitely superior to sacrifice of others. Moreover, if this kind of force is used in a cause that is unjust, only the person using it suffers. He does not make others suffer for his mistakes. Men have before now done many things which were subsequently found to have been wrong. No man can claim that he is absolutely in the right or that a particular thing is wrong because he thinks so, but it is wrong for him so long as that is his deliberate judgement. It is therefore meet that he should not do that which he knows to be wrong, and suffer the consequence whatever it may be. This is the key to the use of soul-force. *16*

A votary of *ahimsa* cannot subscribe to the utilitarian formula (of the greatest good of the greatest number). He will strive for the greatest good of all and die in the attempt to realize the ideal. He will therefore be willing to die, so that the others may live. He will serve himself with the rest, by himself dying. The greatest good of all inevitably includes the good of the greatest number, and, therefore, he and the utilitarian will converge in many points in their career but there does come a time when they must part company, and even work in opposite directions. The utilitarian to be logical will never sacrifice himself. The absolutist will even sacrifice himself. *17*

If we are to be non-violent, we must then not wish for anything on this earth which the meanest or the lowest of human beings cannot have. *22*

The principle of non-violence necessitates complete abstention from exploitation in any form. *23*

My resistance to war does not carry me to the point of thwarting those who wish to take part in it. I reason with them. I put before them the better way and leave them to make the choice. *24*

Taking life may be a duty. We do destroy as much life as we think necessary for sustaining our body. Thus for food we take life, vegetable and other, and for health we destroy mosquitoes and the like by the use of disinfectants, etc., and we do not think that we are guilty of irreligion in doing so . . . for the benefit of the species, we kill carnivorous beasts. . . . Even man-slaughter may be necessary in certain cases. Suppose a man runs amuck and goes furiously about, sword in hand, and killing anyone that comes in his way, and no one dares to capture him alive. Anyone who despatches this lunatic will earn the gratitude of the community and be regarded as a benevolent man. *27*

I see that there is an instinctive horror of killing living beings under any circumstances whatever. For instance, an alternative has been suggested in the shape of confining even rabid dogs in a certain place and allowing them to die a slow death. Now my idea of compassion makes this thing impossible for me. I cannot for a moment bear to see a dog, or for that matter any other living being, helplessly suffering the torture of a slow death. I do not kill a human being thus circumstanced because I have more hopeful remedies. I should kill a dog similarly situated because in its case I am without a remedy. Should my child be attacked with rabies and there was no helpful remedy to relieve his agony, I should consider it my duty to take his life. Fatalism has its limits. We leave things to fate after exhausting all the remedies. One of the remedies and the final one to relieve the agony of a tortured child is to take his life. *28*

Ahimsa is a comprehensive principle. We are helpless mortals caught in the conflagration of *himsa*. The saying that life lives on life has a deep meaning in it. Man cannot for a moment live without consciously or unconsciously committing outward *himsa*. The very fact of his living—eating, drinking and moving about—necessarily involves some *himsa*, destruction of life, be it ever so minute. A votary of *ahimsa* therefore remains true to his faith if the spring of all his actions is compassion, if he shuns to the best of his ability the destruction of the tiniest creature, tries to save it, and thus incessantly strives to be free from the deadly coil of *himsa*. He will be constantly growing in self-restraint and compassion, but he can never become entirely free from outward *himsa*.

Then again, because underlying *ahimsa* is the unity of all life, the error of one cannot but affect all, and hence man cannot be wholly free from *himsa*. So long as he continues to be a social being, he cannot but participate in the *himsa* that the very existence involves. When two nations are fighting, the duty of a votary of *ahimsa* is to stop the war. He who is not equal to that duty, he who has no power of resisting war, he who is not qualified to resist war, may take part in war, and yet whole-heartedly try to free himself, his nation and the world from war. *34*

I make no distinction, from the point of view of *ahimsa* between combatants and non-combatants. He who volunteers to serve a band of dacoits, by working as their carrier, or their watchman while they are about their business, or their nurse when they are wounded, is as much guilty of dacoity as the dacoits themselves. In the same way those who confine themselves to attending to the wounded in battle cannot be absolved from the guilt of war. *35*

I object to violence because when it appears to do good, the good is only temporary; the evil it does is permanent. I do not believe that the killing of even every Englishman can do the slightest good to India.

The millions will be just as badly off as they are today, if someone made it possible to kill off every Englishman tomorrow. The responsibility is more ours than that of the English for the present state of things. The English will be powerless to do evil if we will but be good. Hence my incessant emphasis on reform from within. *39*

In life, it is impossible to eschew violence completely. Now the question arises, where is one to draw the line? The line cannot be the same for every one. For, although, essentially the principle is the same, yet everyone applies it in his or her own way. What is one man's food can be another's poison. Meat-eating is a sin for me. Yet, for another person, who has always lived on meat and never seen anything wrong in it, to give it up, simply in order to copy me, will be a sin.

If I wish to be an agriculturist and stay in a jungle, I will have to use the minimum unavoidable violence, in order to protect my fields. I will have to kill monkeys, birds and insects, which eat up my crops. If I do not wish to do so myself, I will have to engage someone to do it for me. There is not much difference between the two. To allow crops to be eaten up by animals, in the name of *ahimsa,* while there is a famine in the land, is certainly a sin. Evil and good are relative terms. What is good under certain conditions can become an evil or a sin, under a different set of conditions.

Man is not to drown himself in the well of the *shastras,* but he is to dive in their broad ocean and bring out pearls. At every step he has to use his discrimination as to what is *ahimsa* and what is *himsa*. In this, there is no room for shame or cowardice. The poet had said that the road leading up to God is for the brave, never for the cowardly.... *64*

CHAPTER V / SELF-DISCIPLINE

Civilization, in the real sense of the term, consists not in the multiplication but in the deliberate and voluntary restriction of wants. This alone promotes real happiness and contentment, and increases the capacity for service. *1*

A certain degree of physical harmony and comfort is necessary, but above that level, it becomes a hindrance instead of a help. Therefore the ideal of creating an unlimited number of wants and satisfying them seems to be a delusion and a snare. The satisfaction of one's physical needs, even the intellectual needs of one's narrow self, must meet at a point a dead stop before it degenerates into physical and intellectual voluptuousness. A man must arrange his physical and cultural circumstances so that they may not hinder him in his service of humanity, on which all his energies should be concentrated. 2

The relation between the body and the mind is so intimate that, if either of them got out of order, the whole system would suffer. Hence it follows that a pure character is the foundation of health in the real sense of the term; and we may say that all evil thoughts and evil passions are but different forms of disease. 3

You will wish to know what the marks of a man are who wants to realize Truth which is God. He must be completely free from anger and lust, greed and attachment, pride and fear. He must reduce himself to zero and have perfect control over all his senses—beginning with the palate or tongue. Tongue is the organ of speech as well as of taste. It is with the tongue that we indulge in exaggeration, untruth and speech that hurts. The craving for taste makes us slaves to the palate so that like animals we live to eat. But with proper discipline, we can make ourselves into beings only a "little below the angels." He who has mastered his senses is first and foremost among men. All virtues reside in him. God manifests Himself through him. Such is the power of self-discipline. . . . 11

CHAPTER VIII / POVERTY IN THE MIDST OF PLENTY

That economics is untrue which ignores or disregards moral values. The extension of the law of non-violence in the domain of economics means nothing less than the introduction of moral values as a factor to be considered in regulating international commerce. 1

According to me the economic constitution of India and for that matter of the world, should be such that no one under it should suffer from want of food and clothing. In other words everybody should

be able to get sufficient work to enable him to make the two ends meet. And this ideal can be universally realized only if the means of production of the elementary necessaries of life remain in the control of the masses. These should be freely available to all as God's air and water are or ought to be; they should not be made a vehicle of traffic for the exploitation of others. Their monopolization by any country, nation or group of persons would be unjust. The neglect of this simple principle is the cause of the destitution that we witness today not only in this unhappy land but in other parts of the world too. 2

My ideal is equal distribution, but so far as I can see, it is not to be realized. I therefore work for equitable distribution. 3

I suggest that we are thieves in a way. If I take anything that I do not need for my own immediate use, and keep it, I thieve it from somebody else. I venture to suggest that it is the fundamental law of Nature, without exception, that Nature produces enough for our wants from day to day, and if only everybody took enough for himself and nothing more, there would be no pauperism in this world, there would be no man dying of starvation in this world. But so long as we have got this inequality, so long we are thieving. I am no socialist and I do not want to dispossess those who have got possessions; but I do say that, personally, those of us who want to see light out of darkness have to follow this rule. I do not want to dispossess anybody. I should then be departing from the rule of *ahimsa*. If somebody else possesses more than I do, let him. But so far as my own life has to be regulated, I do say that I dare not possess anything which I do not want. In India we have got three millions of people having to be satisfied with one meal a day, and that meal consisting of a *chapāti* containing no fat in it, and a pinch of salt. You and I have no right to anything that we really have until these three millions are clothed and fed better. You and I, who ought to know better, must adjust our wants, and even undergo voluntary starvation in order that they may be nursed, fed and clothed. 5

Non-possession is allied to non-stealing. A thing not originally stolen must nevertheless be classified stolen property, if one possesses it without needing it. Possession implies provision for the future. A seeker after Truth, a follower of the Law of Love cannot hold anything against tomorrow. God never stores for the morrow; He never creates more than what is strictly needed for the moment. If, therefore, we repose faith in His providence, we should rest assured, that He will give us everything that we require. Saints and devotees, who have lived in such faith, have always derived a justification for it from their experience. Our ignorance or negligence of the Divine Law, which gives to man from day to day his daily bread and no more, has given rise to inequalities with all the miseries attendant upon them. The rich have a superfluous store of things which they do not need, and which are therefore neglected and wasted, while millions are starved to death for want of sustenance. If each retained possession only of what he needed, no one would be in want, and all would live in contentment. As it is, the rich are discontented no less than the poor. The poor man would fain become a millionaire, and the millionaire a multimillionaire. The rich should take the initiative in dispossession with a view to a universal diffusion of the spirit of contentment. If only they keep their own property within moderate limits, the starving will be easily fed, and will learn the lesson of contentment along with the rich. 6

Economic equality is the master key to non-violent independence. Working for economic equality means abolishing the eternal conflict between capital and labour. It means the levelling down of the few rich in whose hands is concentrated the bulk of the nation's wealth on the one hand, and a levelling up of the semi-starved naked millions on the other. A non-violent system of government is clearly an impossibility so long as the wide gulf between the rich and the hungry millions persists. The contrast between the palaces of New Delhi and the miserable hovels of the poor, labouring class cannot last one day in a free India in which the poor will enjoy the same power as the richest in the land. A violent and bloody revolution is a certainty one day unless there is a voluntary abdication of riches and the power that riches give and sharing them for the common good. I adhere to my doctrine of trusteeship in spite of the ridicule that has been poured upon it. It is true that it is difficult to reach. So is non-violence difficult to attain. 7

The real implication of equal distribution is that each man shall have the wherewithal to supply all his natural wants and more. For example, if one man has a weak digestion and requires only a quarter of a pound of flour for his bread and another needs a pound, both should be in a position to satisfy their wants. To bring this ideal into being the entire social order has got to be reconstructed. A society based on non-violence cannot nurture any other ideal. We may not perhaps be able to realize the goal but we must bear it in mind and work unceasingly to near it. To the same extent as we progress towards our goal we shall find contentment and happiness, and to that extent too, shall we have contributed towards the bringing into being of a non-violent society.

Now let us consider how equal distribution can be brought about through non-violence. The first step towards it is for him who has made this ideal part of his being to bring about the necessary changes in his personal life. He would reduce his wants to a minimum, bearing in mind the poverty of India. His earnings would be free of dishonesty. The desire for speculation would be renounced. His habitation would be in keeping with his new mode of life. There would be self-restraint exercised in every sphere of life. When he has done all that is possible in his own life, then only will he be in a position to preach this ideal among his associates and neighbours.

Indeed at the root of this doctrine of equal distribution must lie that of the trusteeship of the wealthy for superfluous wealth possessed by them. For according to the doctrine they may not possess a rupee more than their neighbours. How is this to be brought about? Non-violently? Or should the wealthy be dispossessed of their possessions? To do this we would naturally have to resort to violence. This violent action cannot benefit the society. Society will be the poorer, for it will lose the gifts of a man who knows how to accumulate wealth. Therefore the non-violent way is evidently superior. The rich man will be left in possession of his wealth, of which he will use what he reasonably requires for his personal needs and will act as a trustee for the remainder to be used for the society. In this argument honesty on the party of the trustee is assumed.

If however, in spite of the utmost effort, the rich do not become guardians of the poor in the true sense of the term and the latter are more and more crushed and die of hunger, what is to be done? In trying to find out the solution of this riddle I have lighted on non-violent non-co-operation and civil disobedience as the right and infallible means. The rich cannot accumulate wealth without the co-operation of the poor in society. If this knowledge were to penetrate to and spread amongst the poor, they would become strong and would learn how to free themselves by means of nonviolence from the crushing inequalities which have brought them to the verge of starvation. *8*

We should be ashamed of resting or having a square meal so long as there is one able-bodied man or woman without work or food. *12*

I hate privilege and monopoly. Whatever cannot be shared with the masses is taboo to me. *13*

No one has ever suggested that grinding pauperism can lead to anything else than moral degradation. Every human being has a right to live and therefore to find the wherewithal to feed himself and where necessary to clothe and house himself. But for this very simple performance we need no assistance from economists or their laws.

"Take no thought for the morrow" is an injunction which finds an echo in almost all the religious scriptures of the world. In a well-ordered society the securing of one's livelihood should be and is found to be the easiest thing in the world. Indeed the test of orderliness in a country is not the number of millionaires it owns, but the absence of starvation among its masses. *15*

My *ahimsa* would not tolerate the idea of giving a free meal to a healthy person who has not worked for it in some honest way and if I had the power, I would stop every *sadavrata* where free meals are given. It has degraded the nation and it has encouraged laziness, idleness, hypocrisy and even crime. *16*

Every man has an equal right to the necessaries of life even as birds and beasts have. And since every right carries with it a corresponding duty and the corresponding remedy for resisting any attack upon it, it is merely a matter of finding out the corresponding duties and remedies to vindicate the elementary fundamental equality. The corresponding duty is to labour with my limbs and the corresponding remedy is to non-co-operate with him who deprives me of the fruit of my labour. And if I would recognize the fundamental equality, as I must, of the capitalist and the labourer, I must not aim at his destruction. I must strive for his conversion. My non-co-operation with him will open his eyes to the wrong he may be doing. *22*

Complete renunciation of one's possessions is a thing which very few even among ordinary folk are capable of. All that can legitimately be expected of the wealthy class is that they should hold their riches and talents in trust and use them for the service of the society. To insist on more would be to kill the goose that laid the golden eggs. *28*

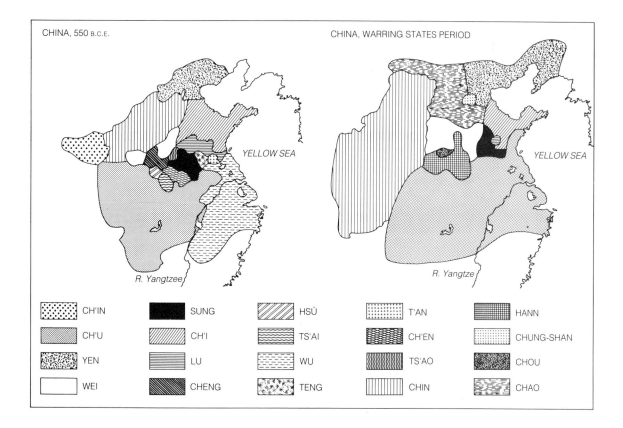

CHINA, 550 B.C.E.

CHINA, WARRING STATES PERIOD

YELLOW SEA

YELLOW SEA

R. Yangtzee

R. Yangtze

CH'IN	SUNG	HSÜ	T'AN	HANN
CH'U	CH'I	TS'AI	CH'EN	CHUNG-SHAN
YEN	LU	WU	TS'AO	CHOU
WEI	CHENG	TENG	CHIN	CHAO

CONFUCIUS

K'ung-Fu-Tzu (Grand Master K'ung), or Confucius, his Latinized name (551–479 B.C.E.), has been called the most influential and revered person in the history of China. Born in the small state of Lu (in modern Shantung) to a noble but poor family, he was completely self-educated. (His father had died when Confucius was three.) He became a granary keeper and a supervisor of flocks during his twenties. Confucius then began teaching. His interest in politics led him to travel to the neighboring state, Ch'i (in the Pinyin transliteration, Qi), where he served as a government consultant for several years during his thirties. These were times of great political and intellectual upheaval; eventually, his life in danger, Confucius left Ch'i.

Returning to Lu, he refused entreaties to support various politicians. He became the first professional teacher in Chinese history, traveling at one point to see Lao Tzu in Chou (Zhou). In his fifties, he became a magistrate and then minister of justice in Chou, where he met great success. He recovered land from Ch'i through negotiations and conquered three important and rival cities. At age fifty-six, however, he fell out of favor and spent the next thirteen years traveling and teaching. Finding the rulers of other states uninterested in his ideas, he returned to Lu at sixty-eight and taught there until his death eight years later. He is reputed to have had over three thousand students.

The Analects is a collection of the sayings of Confucius, probably compiled by his students; *The Great Learning* and *The Doctrine of the Mean,* many scholars think, are works by his pupils—traditionally, by his grandson Tzu Ssu—although some place their composition two or three centuries later. These three works, along with *The Book of Mencius,* were grouped together by a later thinker, Chu Hsi (Zhu Xi), as the Four Books, which formed the basis of Chinese civil service examinations for about six centuries.

Confucian doctrine is sometimes summarized as ethical humanism. Confucius is certainly a humanist—"It is man that can make the Way great and not the Way that can make man great," he says (*Analects* 15:28)—and his works primarily deal with ethics. The Way, or *Tao,* is the path of proper moral conduct. Fundamental to Confucian thought, it is a chief topic of the *Doctrine of the Mean,* though it is barely mentioned in *The Analects.* The concept of *Tao* plays important and very different roles in other East Asian philosophies. In Confucius, however, it is thoroughly ethical. Like Aristotle, who would develop ethical theory roughly 150 years later, Confucius centers his ethics on the concept of virtue. He transforms the traditional notion of a superior man, literally, "son of a ruler," into the notion of a morally upright man, a man of superior character. The idea that human excellence is a function of character rather than birth, upbringing, social position, or even achievement was, and remains, revolutionary. Confucius uses the term *jen,* or *ren* (humanity), as a term for virtue in general. The virtuous person, according to Confucius, is benevolent, kind, generous, and above all balanced, observing the Mean in all things. Again like Aristotle, Confucius thinks of virtue as a mean between extremes; the properly generous person, for example, gives appropriately, neither too much nor too little, to the right people in the right circumstances.

Confucius's view of virtue crucially involves propriety, the observance of proper rites, ceremonies, and principles. The word later Confucians use is *li*, which originally referred to religious sacrifice. It has come to mean ceremony, rite, ritual, decorum, rules of propriety, principle, and proper form or custom. Almost all translators, therefore, render the word differently in different contexts. Most often, *li* refers to traditional social rules. Philosophically, all three aspects of *li* are important. They are traditional: they are mandated by custom and connect us with the past. They are social: they concern relations between people in society and constitute a significant part of the social order. Finally, they are rules: they are codes of conduct governing how people with certain characteristics should behave in certain situations. The Confucian emphasis on virtue ethics, then, should not tempt us to think that rules are unimportant or somehow wrongheaded. They play a vital role in Confucius's thought. Many rules, according to Confucius, arise from particular social relations—the relation of parent and child, for example. Some, however, seem universal. For example, Confucius articulates a version of the Golden Rule, which he calls a rule of reciprocity: "What you do not want done to yourself, do not do to others."

from *The Analects*

Reprinted from The Four Books, *edited and translated by James Legge. Originally published in* The Chinese Classics, *Volume I (Oxford: Clarendon, 1893).*

1:1. The Master said, "Is it not pleasant to learn with a constant perseverance and application?

"Is it not delightful to have friends coming from distant quarters?

"Is he not a man of complete virtue, who feels no discomposure though men may take no note of him?"

1:2. The philosopher Yu said, "They are few who, being filial and fraternal, are fond of offending against their superiors. There have been none who, not liking to offend against their superiors, have been fond of stirring up confusion.

"The superior man bends his attention to what is radical. That being established, all practical courses naturally grow up. Filial piety and fraternal submission!—are they not the root of all benevolent actions?"

1:4. The philosopher Tsang said, "I daily examine myself on three points:—whether, in transacting business for others, I may have been not faithful;—whether, in intercourse with friends, I may have been not sincere;—whether I may have not mastered and practiced the instructions of my teacher."

1:6. The master said, "A youth, when at home, should be filial, and, abroad, respectful to his elders. He should be earnest and truthful. He should overflow in love to all, and cultivate the friendship of the good. When he has time and opportunity, after the performance of these things, he should employ them in polite studies."

1:7. Tsze-hsia said, "If a man withdraws his mind from the love of beauty, and applies it as sincerely to the love of the virtuous; if, in serving his parents, he can exert his utmost strength; if, in serving his prince, he can devote his life; if, in his intercourse with his friends, his words are sincere:—although men say that he has not learned, I will certainly say that he has."

1:8. The Master said, "If the scholar be not grave, he will not call forth any veneration and his learning will not be solid.

"Hold faithfulness and sincerity as first principles.

"Have no friends not equal to yourself.

"When you have faults, do not fear to abandon them."

1:11. The Master said, "While a man's father is alive, look at the bent of his will; when his father is dead, look at his conduct. If for three years he does not alter from the way of his father, he may be called filial."

1:12. The philosopher Yu said, "In practicing the rules of propriety, a natural ease is to be prized. In the ways prescribed by the ancient kings, this is the excellent quality, and in things small and great we follow them.

"Yet it is not to be observed in all cases. If one, knowing how such ease should be prized, manifests it, without regulating it by the rules of propriety, this likewise is not to be done."

1:14. The Master said, "He who aims to be a man of complete virtue in his food does not seek to gratify his appetite, nor in his dwelling place does he seek the appliances of ease; he is earnest in what he is doing, and careful in his speech he frequents the company of men of principle that he may be rectified:—such a person may be said indeed to love to learn."

1:15. Tsze-kung said, "What do you pronounce concerning the poor man who yet does not flatter, and the rich man who is not proud?" The Master replied, "They will do; but they are not equal to him, who, though poor, is yet cheerful, and to him, who, though rich, loves the rules of propriety."

Tsze-kung replied, "It is said in the Book of Poetry,* 'As you cut and then file, as you carve and then polish,'—The meaning is the same, I apprehend, as that which you have just expressed."

The Master said, "With one like Tsze, I can begin to talk about the odes. I told him one point, and he knew its proper sequence."

1:16. The Master said, "I will not be afflicted at men's not knowing me; I will be afflicted that I do not know men."

2:1. The Master said, "He who exercises government by means of his virtue may be compared to the north polar star, which keeps its place and all the stars turn towards it."

2:2. The Master said, "In the Book of Poetry are three hundred pieces, but the design of them all may be embraced in one sentence—'Having no depraved thoughts.'"

2:3. The Master said, "If the people be led by laws, and uniformity sought to be given them by punishments, they will try to avoid the punishment, but have no sense of shame.

"If they be led by virtue, and uniformity sought to be given them by the rules of propriety, they will have the sense of shame, and moreover will become good."

2:4. The Master said, "At fifteen, I had my mind bent on learning.

"At thirty, I stood firm.

"At forty, I had no doubts.

"At fifty, I knew the decrees of Heaven.

"At sixty, my ear was an obedient organ *for the reception of truth.*

"At seventy, I could follow what my heart desired, without transgressing what was right."

2:5. Mang I asked what filial piety was. The Master said, "It is not being disobedient."

Soon after, as Fan Ch'ih was driving him, the Master told him, saying, "Măng-sun asked me what filial piety was, and I answered him, 'not being disobedient.'"

Fan Ch'ih said, "What did you mean?" The Master replied, "That parents, when alive, should be served according to propriety; that, when dead, they should be buried according to propriety; and that they should be sacrificed to according to propriety."

2:6. Mang Wu asked what filial piety was. The Master said, "Parents are anxious lest their children should be sick."

2:10. The Master said, "See what a man does.

"Mark his motives.

"Examine in what things he rests.

"How can a man conceal his character? How can a man conceal his character?"

2:13. Tsze-kung asked what constituted the superior man. The Master said, "He acts before he speaks, and afterwards speaks according to his actions."

---

* The *Book of Poetry,* also called the *Book of Odes,* a Confucian classic, contains 305 poems and songs—some religious, some popular—from the early Chou dynasty (1111–249 B.C.E.). It and the *Book of History* are the earliest existing texts of Chinese literature. According to tradition, Confucius edited these works, finding inspiration in them for his own ethical ideas. —ED.

2:14. The Master said, "The superior man is catholic and not partisan. The mean man is a partisan and not catholic."

2:15. The Master said, "Learning without thought is labor lost; thought without learning is perilous."

2:16. The Master said, "The study of strange doctrines is injurious indeed!"

2:17. The Master said, "Yu, shall I teach you what knowledge is? When you know a thing, to hold that you know it; and when you do not know a thing, to allow that you do not know it;—this is knowledge."

2:19. The duke Ai asked, saying, "What should be done in order to secure the submission of the people?" Confucius replied, "Advance the upright and set aside the crooked, then the people will submit. Advance the crooked and set aside the upright, then the people will not submit."

2:20. Chi K'ang asked how to cause the people to reverence their ruler, to be faithful to him, and to go on to nerve themselves to virtue. The Master said, "Let him preside over them with gravity;—then they will reverence him. Let him be filial and kind to all;—then they will be faithful to him. Let him advance the good and teach the incompetent;—then they will eagerly seek to be virtuous."

2:24. The Master said, "For a man to sacrifice to a spirit which does not belong to him is flattery.

"To see what is right and not to do it is want of courage."

4:2. The Master said, "Those who are without virtue cannot abide long either in a condition of poverty and hardship, or in a condition of enjoyment. The virtuous rest in virtue; the wise desire virtue."

4:3. The Master said, "It is only the (truly) virtuous man, who can love, or who can hate, others."

4:4. The Master said, "If the will be set on virtue, there will be no practice of wickedness."

4:5. The Master said, "Riches and honors are what men desire. If they cannot be obtained in the proper way, they should not be held. Poverty and meanness are what men dislike. If they cannot be obtained in the proper way, they should not be avoided.

"If a superior man abandons virtue, how can he fulfill the requirements of that name?

"The superior man does not, even for the space of a single meal, act contrary to virtue. In moments of haste, he cleaves to it. In seasons of danger, he cleaves to it."

4:6. The Master said, "I have not seen a person who loved virtue, or one who hated what was not virtuous. He who loved virtue, would esteem nothing above it. He who hated what is not virtuous would practice virtue in such a way that he would not allow anything that is not virtuous to approach his person.

"Is any one able for one day to apply his strength to virtue? I have not seen the case in which his strength would be insufficient.

"Should there possibly be any such case, I have not seen it."

4:7. The Master said, "The faults of men are characteristic of the class to which they belong. By observing a man's faults, it may be known that he is virtuous."

4:10. The Master said, "The superior man in the world does not set his mind either for anything or against anything; what is right he will follow."

4:11. The Master said, "The superior man thinks of virtue; the small man thinks of comfort. The superior man thinks of the sanctions of law; the small man thinks of favors which he may receive."

4:12. The Master said, "He who acts with a

constant view to his own advantage will be much murmured against."

4:14. The Master said, "A man should say, I am not concerned that I have no place, I am concerned how I may fit myself for one. I am not concerned that I am not known, I seek to be worthy to be known."

4:15. The Master said, "Shan, my doctrine is that of an all-pervading unity." The disciple Tsang replied, "Yes."

The Master went out, and the other disciples asked, saying, "What do his words mean?" Tsang said, "The doctrine of our master is to be true to the principles of our nature and the benevolent exercise of them to others,—this and nothing more."

4:16. The Master said, "The mind of the superior man is conversant with righteousness; the mind of the mean man is conversant with gain."

4:17. The Master said, "When we see men of worth, we should think of equaling them; when we see men of a contrary character, we should turn inwards and examine ourselves."

4:18. The Master said, "In serving his parents, a son may remonstrate with them, but gently; when he sees that they do not incline to follow his advice, he shows an increased degree of reverence, but does not abandon his purpose; and should they punish him, he does not allow himself to murmur."

4:19. The Master said, "While his parents are alive, the son may not go abroad to a distance. If he does go abroad, he must have a fixed place to which he goes."

4:20. The Master said, "If the son for three years does not alter from the way of his father, he may be called filial."

4:21. The Master said, "The years of parents may by no means not be kept in the memory as an occasion at once for joy and for fear."

4:22. The Master said, "The reason why the ancients did not readily give utterance to their words, was that they feared lest their actions should not come up to them."

4:23. The Master said, "The cautious seldom err."

4:24. The Master said, "The superior man wishes to be slow in his speech and earnest in his conduct."

4:25. The Master said, "Virtue is not left to stand alone. He who practices it will have neighbors."

5:10. The Master said, "I have not seen a firm and unbending man." Someone replied, "There is Shan Ch'ang." "Ch'ang," said the Master, "is under the influence of his passions; how can he be pronounced firm and unbending?"

5:11. Tsze-kung said, "What I do not wish men to do to me, I also wish not to do to men." The Master said, "Tsze, you have not attained that."

5:12. Tsze-kung said, "The Master's personal displays of his principles and ordinary descriptions of them may be heard. His discourses about man's nature, and the way of Heaven, cannot be heard."

6:18. The Master said, "They who know the truth are not equal to those who love it, and they who love it are not equal to those who delight in it."

6:20. Fan Ch'ih asked what constituted wisdom. The Master said, "To give one's self earnestly to the duties due to men, and, while respecting spiritual beings, to keep aloof from them, may be called wisdom." He asked about perfect virtue. The Master said, "The man of virtue makes the difficulty to be overcome his first business, and success only a subsequent consideration;—this may be called perfect virtue."

6:23. The Master said, "A cornered vessel without corners.—A strange cornered vessel! A strange cornered vessel!"

6:24. Tsai Wo asked, saying, "A benevolent man, though it be told him,—'There is a man in the well,' will go in after him I suppose." Confucius said, "Why should he do so? A superior man may be made to go to the well, but he cannot be made to go down into it. He may be imposed upon, but he cannot be fooled."

6:25. The Master said, "The superior man, extensively studying all learning, and keeping himself under the restraint of the rules of propriety may thus likewise not overstep what is right."

6:27. The Master said, "Perfect is the virtue which is according to the Constant Mean! Rare for a long time has been its practice among the people."

6:28. Tsze-kung said, "Suppose the case of a man extensively conferring benefits on the people, and able to assist all, what would you say of him? Might he be called perfectly virtuous?" The Master said, "Why speak only of virtue in connection with him? Must he not have the qualities of a sage? Even Yao and Shun were still solicitous about this.*

"Now the man of perfect virtue, wishing to be established himself, seeks also to establish others; wishing to be enlarged himself, he seeks also to enlarge others.

"To be able to judge of others by what is nigh in ourselves;—this may be called the art of virtue."

7:27. The Master said, "There may be those who act without knowing why. I do not do so. Hearing much and selecting what is good

and following it; seeing much and keeping it in memory—this is the second style of knowledge."

7:36. The Master said, "The superior man is satisfied and composed; the mean man is always full of distress."

7:37. The Master was mild, and yet dignified; majestic, and yet not fierce; respectful, and yet easy.

8:2. The Master said, "Respectfulness, without the rules of propriety, becomes laborious bustle; carefulness, without the rules of propriety, becomes timidity; boldness, without the rules of propriety, becomes insubordination; straightforwardness, without the rules of propriety, becomes rudeness.

"When those who are in high stations perform well all their duties to their relations, the people are aroused to virtue. When old friends are not neglected by them, the people are preserved from meanness."

8:8. The Master said, "It is by Odes that the mind is aroused.

"It is by the Rules of Propriety that the character is established.

"It is from Music that the finish is received."

8:13. The Master said, "With sincere faith he unites the love of learning; holding firm to death, he is perfecting the excellence of his course.

"Such a one will not enter a tottering state, nor dwell in a disorganized one. When right principles of government prevail in the kingdom, he will show himself; when they are prostrated, he will keep concealed.

"When a country is well governed, poverty and a mean condition are things to be ashamed of. When a country is ill

---

* Confucius, Mencius, and other Chinese philosophers refer to Yao, Shun, and Duke Chou as ideal rulers and sages. Yao and Shun were legendary, successive rulers of the third millennium B.C.E. Duke Chou helped to establish the Chou dynasty in 1111 B.C.E. —Ed.

governed, riches and honor are things to be ashamed of."

9:4. There were four things from which the Master was entirely free. He had no foregone conclusions, no arbitrary predetermination, no obstinacy and no egoism.

9:24. The Master said, "Hold faithfulness and sincerity as first principles. Have no friends not equal to yourself. When you have faults, do not fear to abandon them."

11:11. Chi Lu asked about serving the spirits of the dead. The Master said, "While you are not able to serve men, how can you serve their spirits?" Chi Lu added, "I venture to ask about death?" He was answered, "While you do not know life, how can you know about death?"

12:1. Yen Yüan asked about perfect virtue. The Master said, "To subdue one's self and return to propriety, is perfect virtue. If a man can for one day subdue himself and return to propriety, all under heaven will ascribe perfect virtue to him. Is the practice of perfect virtue from a man himself, or is it from others?"

Yen Yüan said, "I beg to ask the steps of that process." The Master replied, "Look not at what is contrary to propriety; listen not to what is contrary to propriety; speak not what is contrary to propriety; make no movement which is contrary to propriety." Yen Yüan then said, "Though I am deficient in intelligence and vigor, I will make it my business to practice this lesson."

12:2. Chung-kung asked about perfect virtue. The Master said, "It is, when you go abroad, to behave to every one as if you were receiving a great guest; to employ the people as if you were assisting at a great sacrifice; not to do to others as you would not wish done to yourself; to have no

murmuring against you in the country, and none in the family." Chung-kung said, "Though I am deficient in intelligence and vigor, I will make it my business to practice this lesson."

12:9. The duke Ai inquired of Yu Zo, saying, "The year is one of scarcity, and the returns for expenditure are not sufficient;—what is to be done?"

Yu Zo replied to him, "Why not simply tithe the people?"

"With two tenths," said the duke, "I find them not enough;—how could I do with that system of one tenth?"

Yu Zo answered, "If the people have plenty, their prince will not be left to want alone. If the people are in want, their prince cannot enjoy plenty alone."

12:15. The Master said, "By extensively studying all learning, and keeping himself under the restraint of the rules of propriety, *one* may thus likewise not err from what is right."

12:17. Chi K'ang asked Confucius about government. Confucius replied, "To govern means to rectify. If you lead on the people with correctness, who will dare not to be correct?"

12:22. Fan Ch'ih asked about benevolence. The Master said, "It is to love all men." He asked about knowledge. The Master said, "It is to know all men."

Fan Ch'ih did not immediately understand these answers.

The Master said, "Employ the upright and put aside all the crooked; in this way the crooked can be made to be upright."

Fan Ch'ih retired, and, seeing Tsze-hsia, he said to him, "A little while ago, I had an interview with our Master, and asked him about knowledge. He said, 'Employ the upright, and put aside all the crooked;—in this way, the crooked will be made to be upright.' What did he mean?"

Tsze-hsia said, "Truly rich is his saying!

"Shun, being in possession of the kingdom, selected from among all the people, and employed Kao-yao, on which all who were devoid of virtue disappeared. T'ang, being in possession of the kingdom, selected from among all the people, and employed I Yin, and all who were devoid of virtue disappeared."

13:3. Tsze-lu said, "The ruler of Wei has been waiting for you, in order with you to administer the government. What will you consider the first thing to be done?"

The Master replied, "What is necessary to rectify names."

"So, indeed!" said Tsze-lu. "You are wide of the mark! Why must there be such rectification?"

The Master said, "How uncultivated you are, Yu! A superior man, in regard to what he does not know, shows a cautious reserve."

13:6. The Master said, "When a prince's personal conduct is correct, his government is effective without the issuing of orders. If his personal conduct is not correct, he may issue orders, but they will not be followed."

13:9. When the Master went to Wei, Zan Yu acted as driver of his carriage.

The Master observed, "How numerous are the people!"

Yu said, "Since they are thus numerous, what more shall be done for them?" "Enrich them," was the reply.

"And when they have been enriched, what more shall be done?" The Master said, "Teach them."

13:11. The Master said, "'If good men were to govern a country in succession for a hundred years, they would be able to trans-

form the violently bad, and dispense with capital punishments.' True indeed is this saying!"

13:13. The Master said, "If a minister make his own conduct correct, what difficulty will he have in assisting in government? If he cannot rectify himself, what has he to do with rectifying others?"

13:16. The duke of Sheh asked about government.

The Master said, "Good government obtains when those who are near are made happy, and those who are far off are attracted."

13:17. Tsze-hsia, being governor of Chü-fu, asked about government. The Master said, "Do not be desirous to have things done quickly; do not look at small advantages. Desire to have things done quickly prevents their being done thoroughly. Looking at small advantages prevents great affairs from being accomplished."

13:18. The duke of Sheh informed Confucius, saying, "Among us here are those who may be styled upright in their conduct. If their fathers have stolen a sheep, they will bear witness to the fact."

Confucius said, "Among us, in our part of the country, those who are upright are different from this. The father conceals the misconduct of the son, and the son conceals the misconduct of the father. Unrightness is to be found in this."

13:19. Fan Ch'ih asked about perfect virtue. The Master said, "It is, in retirement, to be sedately grave; in the management of business, to be reverently attentive; in intercourse with others, to be strictly sincere. Though a man go among rude, uncultivated tribes, these qualities may not be neglected."

14:24. The Master said, "The progress of the superior man is upwards; the progress of the mean man is downwards."

14:25. The Master said, "In ancient times, men learned with a view to their own improvement. Nowadays, men learn with a view to the approbation of others."

14:30. The Master said, "The way of the superior man is threefold, but I am not equal to it. Virtuous, he is free from anxieties; wise, he is free from perplexities; bold, he is free from fear."

Tsze-kung said, "Master, that is what you yourself say."

14:36. Someone said, "What do you say concerning the principle that injury should be recompensed with kindness?"

The Master said, "With what then will you recompense kindness?"

"Recompense injury with justice, and recompense kindness with kindness."

15:2. The Master said, "Tsze, you think, I suppose, that I am one who learns many things and keeps them in memory?"

Tsze-kung replied, "Yes,—but perhaps it is not so?"

"No," was the answer, "I seek a unity all-pervading."

15:17. The Master said, "The superior man in everything considers righteousness to be essential. He performs it according to the rules of propriety. He brings it forth in humility. He completes it with sincerity. This is indeed a superior man."

15:18. The Master said, "The superior man is distressed by his want of ability. He is not distressed by men's not knowing him."

15:19. The Master said, "The superior man dislikes the thought of his name not being mentioned after his death."

15:20. The Master said, "What the superior man seeks, is in himself. What the mean man seeks, is in others."

15:21. The Master said, "The superior man is dignified, but does not wrangle. He is sociable, but not a partisan."

15:22. The Master said, "The superior man does not promote a man simply on account of his words, nor does he put aside good words because of the man."

15:23. Tsze-kung asked, saying, "Is there one word which may serve as a rule of practice for all one's life?" The Master said, "Is not RECIPROCITY such a word? What you do not want done to yourself, do not do to others."

15:38. The Master said, "In teaching there should be no distinction of classes."

15:39. The Master said, "Those whose courses are different cannot lay plans for one another."

15:40. The Master said, "In language it is simply required that it convey the meaning."

16:10. Confucius said, "The superior man has nine things which are subjects with him of thoughtful consideration. In regard to the use of his eyes, he is anxious to see clearly. In regard to his countenance, he is anxious to hear distinctly. In regard to his countenance, he is anxious that it should be benign. In regard to his demeanor, he is anxious that it should be respectful. In regard to his speech, he is anxious that it should be sincere. In regard to his doing of business, he is anxious that it should be reverently careful. In regard to what he doubts about, he is anxious to question others. When he is angry, he thinks of the difficulties (his anger may involve him in). When he sees gain to be got, he thinks of righteousness."

17:2. The Master said, "By nature, men are nearly alike; by practice, they get to be wide apart."

17:6. Tsze-chang asked Confucius about perfect virtue. Confucius said, "To be able to practice five things everywhere under heaven constitutes perfect virtue." He begged to ask what they were, and was told, "Gravity, generosity of soul, sincerity, earnestness, and kindness. If you are grave, you will not be treated with disrespect. If you are generous, you will win all. If you are sincere, people will repose trust in you. If you are earnest, you will accomplish much. If you are kind, this will enable you to employ the services of others."

17:8. The Master said, "Yu, have you heard the six words to which are attached six becloudings?"

Yu replied, "I have not."

"Sit down, and I will tell you.

"There is the love of being benevolent without the love of learning;—the beclouding here leads to a foolish simplicity. There is the love of knowing without the love of learning;—the beclouding here leads to dissipation of mind. There is the love of being sincere without the love of learning;—the beclouding here leads to an injurious disregard of consequences. There is the love of straightforwardness without the love of learning;—the beclouding here leads to rudeness. There is the love of boldness without the love of learning;—the beclouding here leads to insubordination. There is the love of firmness without the love of learning;—the beclouding here leads to extravagant conduct."

20:3. The Master said, "Without recognizing the ordinances of Heaven, it is impossible to be a superior man.

"Without an acquaintance with the rules of Propriety, it is impossible for the character to be established.

"Without knowing the force of words, it is impossible to know men."

The Great Learning

Reprinted from The Four Books, *edited and translated by James Legge. Originally published in* The Chinese Classics, *Volume I (Oxford: Clarendon, 1893).*

1. What the Great Learning teaches, is—to illustrate illustrious virtue; to renovate the people; and to rest in the highest excellence.

2. The point where to rest being known, the object of pursuit is then determined; and, that being determined, a calm unperturbedness may be attained to. To that calmness there will succeed a tranquil repose. In that repose there may be careful deliberation, and that deliberation will be followed by the attainment of the desired end.

3. Things have their root and their branches. Affairs have their end and their beginning. To know what is first and what is last will lead near to what is taught in the Great Learning.

4. The ancients who wished to illustrate illustrious virtue throughout the kingdom, first ordered well their own states. Wishing to order well their states, they first regulated their families. Wishing to regulate their families, they first cultivated their persons. Wishing to cultivate their persons, they first rectified their hearts. Wishing to rectify their hearts, they first sought to be sincere in their thoughts. Wishing to be sincere in their thoughts, they first extended to the utmost their knowledge. Such extension of knowledge lay in the investigation of things.

5. Things being investigated, knowledge became complete. Their knowledge being complete, their thoughts were sincere. Their thoughts being sincere, their hearts were then rectified. Their hearts being rectified, their persons were cultivated. Their persons being cultivated, their families were regulated. Their families being regulated, their states were rightly governed. Their states being rightly governed, the whole kingdom was made tranquil and happy.

6. From the Son of Heaven down to the mass of the people, all must consider the cultivation of the person the root of everything besides.

7. It cannot be, when the root is neglected, that what should spring from it will be well ordered. It never has been the case that what was of great importance has been slightly cared for, and, at the same time, that what was of slight importance has been greatly cared for.

From *The Doctrine of the Mean*

Reprinted from The Four Books, *edited and translated by James Legge. Originally published in* The Chinese Classics, *Volume I (Oxford: Clarendon, 1893).*

I. 1. What Heaven has conferred is called THE NATURE; an accordance with this nature is called THE PATH of duty; the regulation of this past is called INSTRUCTION.

2. The path may not be left for an instant. If it could be left, it would not be the path. On this account, the superior man does not wait till he sees things, to be cautious, nor till he hears things, to be apprehensive.

3. There is nothing more visible than what is secret, and nothing more manifest than what is minute. Therefore the superior man is watchful over himself, when he is alone.

4. While there are no stirrings of pleasure, anger, sorrow, or joy, the mind may be said to be in the state of EQUILIBRIUM. When those feelings have been stirred, and they act in their due degree, there ensues what may be called the state of HARMONY. This EQUILIBRIUM is the great root from which grow all the human actings in the world, and this HARMONY is the universal path which they all should pursue.

5. Let the states of equilibrium and harmony exist in perfection, and happy order will prevail throughout heaven and earth, and all things will be nourished and flourish.

II. 1. Chung-ni said, "The superior man embodies the course of the Mean; the mean man acts contrary to the course of the Mean.

2. "The superior man's embodying the course of the Mean is because he is a superior man, and so always maintains the Mean. The mean man's

acting contrary to the course of the Mean is because he is a mean man, and has no caution."

III. The Master said, "Perfect is the virtue which is according to the Mean! Rare have they long been among the people, who could practice it!"

IV. 1. The Master said, "I know how it is that the path of the Mean is not walked in:—The knowing go beyond it, and the stupid do not come up to it. I know how it is that the path of the Mean is not understood:—The men of talents and virtue go beyond it, and the worthless do not come up to it.

2. "There is no body but eats and drinks. But they are few who can distinguish flavors."

VIII. The Master said, "This was the manner of Hui:—he made choice of the Mean, and whenever he got hold of what was good, he clasped it firmly, as if wearing it on his breast, and did not lose it."

IX. The Master said, "The kingdom, its states, and the families, may be perfectly ruled; dignities and emoluments may be declined; naked weapons may be trampled under the feet;—but the course of the Mean cannot be attained to."

X. 1. Tsze-lu asked about energy.

2. The Master said, "Do you mean the energy of the South, the energy of the North, or the energy which you should cultivate yourself?

3. "To show forbearance and gentleness in teaching others; and not to revenge unreasonable conduct;—this is the energy of southern regions, and the good man makes it his study.

4. "To lie under arms; and meet death without regret:—this is the energy of northern regions, and the forceful make it their study.

5. "Therefore, the superior man cultivates friendly harmony, without being weak.—How firm is he in his energy! He stands erect in the middle, without inclining to either side.—How firm is he in his energy! When good principles prevail in the government of his country, he does not change from what he was in retirement.—How firm is he in his energy! When bad principles prevail in the country, he maintains his course to death without changing.—How firm is he in his energy!"

XI. 1. The Master said, "To live in obscurity, and yet practice wonders, in order to be mentioned with honor in future ages:—this is what I do not do.

2. "The good man tries to proceed according to the right path, but when he has gone halfway, he abandons it:—I am not able *so* to stop.

3. "The superior man accords with the course of the Mean. Though he may be all unknown, unregarded by the world, he feels no regret.—It is only the sage who is able for this."

XII. 1. The way which the superior man pursues, reaches wide and far, and yet is secret.

2. Common men and women, however ignorant, may intermeddle with the knowledge of it; yet in its utmost reaches, there is that which even the sage does not know. Common men and women, however much below the ordinary standard of character, can carry it into practice; yet in its utmost reaches, there is that which even the sage is not able to carry into practice. Great as heaven and earth are, men still find some things in them with which to be dissatisfied. Thus it is that, were the superior man to speak of his way in all its greatness, nothing in the world would be found able to embrace it, and were he to speak of it in its minuteness, nothing in the world would be found able to split it.

3. It is said in the Book of Poetry, "The hawk flies up to heaven; the fishes leap in the deep." This expresses how this *way* is seen above and below.

4. The way of the superior man may be found, in its simple elements, in the intercourse of common men and women; but in its utmost reaches, it shines brightly through heaven and earth.

XIII. 1. The Master said, "The path is not far from man. When men try to pursue a course, which is far from the common indications of consciousness, this course cannot be considered THE PATH.

2. "In the Book of Poetry, it is said, 'In hewing an ax handle, in hewing an ax handle, the pattern is not far off.' We grasp one ax handle to hew the other; and yet, if we look askance from the one to the other, we may consider them as apart. Therefore, the superior man governs men, according to their nature, with what is proper to them, and as soon as they change what is wrong, he stops.

3. "When one cultivates to the utmost the principles of his nature, and exercises them on the principle of reciprocity, he is not far from the path. What you do not like when done to yourself, do not do to others.

4. "In the way of the superior man there are four things, to not one of which have I as yet attained.—To serve my father, as I would require my son to serve me: to this I have not attained; to serve my prince, as I would require my minister to serve me: to this I have not attained; to serve my elder brother, as I would require my younger brother to serve me: to this I have not attained; to set the example in behaving to a friend, as I would require him to behave to me: to this I have not attained. Earnest in practicing the ordinary virtues, and careful in speaking about them, if, in his practice, he has anything defective, the superior man dares not but exert himself; and if, in his words, he has any excess, he dares not allow himself such license. Thus his words have respect to his actions, and his actions have respect to his words; is it not just an entire sincerity which marks the superior man?"

XIV. 1. The superior man does what is proper to the station in which he is; he does not desire to go beyond this.

2. In a position of wealth and honor, he does what is proper to a position of wealth and honor. In a poor and low position, he does what is proper to a poor and low position. Situated

among barbarous tribes, he does what is proper to a situation among barbarous tribes. In a position of sorrow and difficulty, he does what is proper to a position of sorrow and difficulty. The superior man can find himself in no situation in which he is not himself.

3. In a high situation, he does not treat with contempt his inferiors. In a low situation, he does not court the favor of his superiors. He rectifies himself and seeks for nothing from others, so that he has no dissatisfactions. He does not murmur against Heaven, nor grumble against men.

4. Thus it is that the superior man is quiet and calm, waiting for the appointments of Heaven, while the mean man walks in dangerous paths, looking for lucky occurrences.

5. The Master said, "In archery we have something like the way of the superior man. When the archer misses the center of the target, he turns round and seeks for the cause of his failure in himself."

XX. 1. The duke Ai asked about government.

2. The Master said, "The government of Wan and Wu is displayed in the records,—the tablets of wood and bamboo. Let there be the men and the government will flourish; but without the men, their government decays and ceases.

3. "With the right men the growth of government is rapid, just as vegetation is rapid in the earth; and moreover, their government might be called an easily growing rush.

4. "Therefore the administration of government lies in getting proper men. Such men are to be got by means of the ruler's own character. That character is to be cultivated by his treading in the ways of duty. And the treading those ways of duty is to be cultivated by the cherishing of benevolence.

5. "Benevolence is the characteristic element of humanity, and the great exercise of it is in loving relatives. Righteousness is the accordance of actions with what is right, and the great exercise of it is in honoring the worthy. The decreasing measures of the love due to relatives, and the steps in the honor due to the worthy, are produced by the principle of propriety.

6. "When those in inferior situations do not possess the confidence of their superiors, they cannot retain the government of the people.

7. "Hence the sovereign may not neglect the cultivation of his own character. Wishing to cultivate his character, he may not neglect to serve his parents. In order to serve his parents, he may not neglect to acquire a knowledge of men. In order to know men, he may not dispense with a knowledge of Heaven.

8. "The duties of universal obligation are five, and the virtues wherewith they are practiced are three. The duties are those between sovereign and minister, between father and son, between husband and wife, between elder brother and younger, and those belonging to the intercourse of friends. Those five are the duties of universal obligation. Knowledge, magnanimity, and energy, these three, are the virtues universally binding. And the means by which they carry the duties into practice is singleness.

9. "Some are born with the knowledge of those duties; some know them by study; and some acquire the knowledge after a painful feeling of their ignorance. But the knowledge being possessed, it comes to the same thing. Some practice them with a natural ease; some from a desire for their advantages; and some by strenuous effort. But the achievement being made, it comes to the same thing."

10. The Master said, "To be fond of learn- ing is to be near to knowledge. To practice with vigor is to be near to magnanimity. To possess the feeling of shame is to be near to energy.

11. "He who knows these three things knows how to cultivate his own character. Knowing how to cultivate his own character, he knows how to govern other men. Knowing how to govern other men, he knows how to govern the kingdom with all its states and families.

12. "All who have the government of the kingdom with its states and families have nine standard rules to follow;—viz., the cultivation of their own characters; the honoring of men of virtue and talents; affection towards their relatives; respect towards the great ministers; kind and

considerate treatment of the whole body of offi-cers; dealing with the mass of the people as children; encouraging the resort of all classes of artisans; indulgent treatment of men from a distance; and the kindly cherishing of the princes of the state.

13. "By the ruler's cultivation of his own character, the duties of universal obligation are set forth. By honoring men of virtue and talents, he is preserved from errors of judgment. By showing affection to his relatives, there is no grumbling nor resentment among his uncles and brethren. By respecting the great ministers, he is kept from errors in the practice of government. By kind and considerate treatment of the whole body of officers, they are led to make the most grateful return for his courtesies. By dealing with the mass of the people as his children, they are led to exhort one another to what is good. By encourag-ing the resort of all classes of artisans, his re-sources for expenditures are rendered ample. By indulgent treatment of men from a distance, they are brought to resort to him from all quar-ters. And by kindly cherishing the princes of the states, the whole kingdom is brought to revere him.

14. "Self-adjustment and purification, with careful regulation of his dress, and the not mak-ing a movement contrary to the rules of propri-ety:—this is the way for a ruler to cultivate his person. Discarding slanderers, and keeping him-self from the seductions of beauty; making light of riches, and giving honor to virtue:—this is the way for him to encourage men of worth and tal-ents. Giving them places of honor and large emolument, and sharing with them in their likes and dislikes:—this is the way for him to encourage his relatives to love him. Giving them numerous officers to discharge their orders and commissions:—this is the way for him to encourage the great ministers. According to them a generous confidence, and making their emolu-ments large:—this is the way to encourage the body of officers. Employing them only at the proper times, and making the imposts light:—this is the way to encourage the people. By daily examinations and monthly trials, and by making

their rations in accordance with their labors:—this is the way to encourage the classes of artisans. To escort them on their departure and meet them on their coming; to commend the good among them, and show compassion to the incompetent:—this is the way to treat indulgently men from a dis-tance. To restore families whose line of succession has been broken, and to revive states that have been extinguished; to reduce to order states that are in confusion, and support those which are in peril; to have fixed times for their own reception at court, and the reception of their envoys; to send them away after liberal treatment, and wel-come their coming with small contributions:—this is the way to cherish the princes of the states.

15. "All who have government of the king-dom with its states and families have the above nine standard rules. And the means by which they are carried into practice is singleness.

16. "In all things success depends on previous preparation, and without such previous prepara-tion there is sure to be failure. If what is to be spoken be previously determined, there will be no stumbling. If affairs be previously determined, there will be no difficulty with them. If one's actions have been previously determined, there will be no sorrow in connection with them. If principles of conduct have been previously deter-mined, the practice of them will be inexhaustible.

17. "When those in inferior situations do not obtain the confidence of the sovereign, they can-not succeed in governing the people. There is a way to obtain the confidence of the sovereign; —if one is not trusted by his friends, he will not get the confidence of his sovereign. There is a way to being trusted by one's friends;—if one is not obedient to his parents, he will not be true to his friends. There is a way to being obedient to one's parents;—if one, on turning his thoughts in upon himself, finds a want of sincerity, he will not be obedient to his parents. There is a way to the attainment of sincerity in one's self;—if a man does not understand what is good, he will not attain sincerity in himself.

18. "Sincerity is the way of Heaven. The attain-ment of sincerity is the way of men. He who pos-sesses sincerity is he who, without an effort, hits

what is right, and apprehends, without the exercise of thought;—he is the sage who naturally and easily embodies the right way. He who attains to sincerity is he who chooses what is good, and firmly holds fast.

19. "To this attainment there are requisite the extensive study of what is good, accurate inquiry about it, careful reflection on it, the clear discrimination of it, and the earnest practice of it.

20. "The superior man, while there is anything he has not studied, or while in what he has studied there is anything he cannot understand, will not intermit his labor. While there is anything he has not inquired about, or anything in what he has inquired about which he does not know, he will not intermit his labor. While there is anything which he has not reflected on, or anything in what he has reflected on which he does not apprehend, he will not intermit his labor. While there is anything which he has not discriminated, or his discrimination is not clear, he will not intermit his labor. If there be anything which he has not practiced or his practice fails in earnestness, he will not intermit his labor. If another man succeeds by one effort, he will use a hundred efforts. If another man succeeds by ten efforts, he will use a thousand.

21. "Let a man proceed in this way, and, though dull, he will surely become intelligent; though weak, he will surely become strong."

XXI. When we have intelligence resulting from sincerity, this condition is to be ascribed to nature; when we have sincerity resulting from intelligence, this condition is to be ascribed to instruction. But given the sincerity, and there shall be the intelligence; given the intelligence, and there shall be the sincerity.

XXII. It is only he who is possessed of the most complete sincerity that can exist under heaven, who can give its full development to his nature. Able to give its full development to his own nature, he can do the same to the nature of other men. Able to give its full development to the nature of other men, he can give their full development to the natures of animals and things. Able to give their full development to the natures

of creatures and things, he can assist the transforming and nourishing powers of Heaven and Earth. Able to assist the transforming and nourishing powers of Heaven and Earth, he may with Heaven and Earth form a ternion.

XXIII. Next to the above is he who cultivates to the utmost the shoots of goodness in him. From those he can attain to the possession of sincerity. This sincerity becomes apparent. From being apparent, it becomes manifest. From being manifest, it becomes brilliant. Brilliant, it affects others. Affecting others, they are changed by it. Changed by it, they are transformed. It is only he who is possessed of the most complete sincerity that can exist under heaven, who can transform.

XXV. 1. Sincerity is that whereby self- completion is effected, and its way is that by which man must direct himself.

2. Sincerity is the end and beginning of things; without sincerity there would be nothing. On this account, the superior man regards the attainment of sincerity as the most excellent thing.

3. The possessor of sincerity does not merely accomplish the self-completion himself. With this quality he completes other men and things also. The completing himself shows his perfect virtue. The completing other men and things shows his knowledge. Both these are virtues belonging to the nature, and this is the way by which a union is effected of the external and internal. Therefore, whenever he—the entirely sincere man—employs them,—that is, these virtues,—their action will be right.

XXVI. 7. The Way of Heaven and Earth may be completely declared in one sentence.—They are without any doubleness, and so they produce things in a manner that is unfathomable.

XXXIII. 1. It is said in the Book of Poetry, "Over her embroidered robe she puts a plain single garment," intimating a dislike to the display of the elegance of the former. Just so, it is the way of the superior man to prefer the concealment of his virtue, while it daily becomes more illustrious, and it is the way of the mean man to seek notoriety, while he daily goes more and more to ruin. It is characteristic of the superior man, appearing insipid, yet never to produce satiety; while showing a simple negligence, yet to have his accomplishments recognized; while seemingly plain, yet to be discriminating. He knows how what is distant lies in what is near. He knows where the wind proceeds from. He knows how what is minute becomes manifested. Such a one, we may be sure, will enter into virtue.

2. It is said in the Book of Poetry, "Although the fish sink and lie at the bottom, it is still quite clearly seen." Therefore the superior man examines his heart, that there may be nothing wrong there, and that he may have no cause for dissatisfaction with himself. That wherein the superior man cannot be equaled is simply this,—his work which other men cannot see.

3. It is said in the Book of Poetry, "Looked at in your apartment, be there free from shame as being exposed to the light of heaven." Therefore, the superior man, even when he is not moving, has a feeling of reverence, and while he speaks not, he has the feeling of truthfulness.

4. It is said in the Book of Poetry, "In silence is the offering presented, and the spirit approached to; there is not the slightest contention." Therefore the superior man does not use rewards, and the people are stimulated to virtue. He does not show anger, and the people are awed more than by hatchets and battleaxes.

5. It is said in the Book of Poetry, "What needs no display is virtue. All the princes imitate it." Therefore, the superior man being sincere and reverential, the whole world is conducted to a state of happy tranquillity.

6. It is said in the Book of Poetry, "I regard with pleasure your brilliant virtue, making no great display of itself in sounds and appearances." The Master said, "Among the appliances to transform the people, sounds and appearances are but trivial influences. It is said in another ode, 'His virtue is light as a hair. Still, a hair will admit of comparison as to its size. The doings of the supreme Heaven have neither sound nor smell.'— That is perfect virtue."

MO TZU

Mo Tzu (470?–391? B.C.E.), a rival of Confucius, founded a school of philosophy known as Moism. Very little is known about his life. Born in either Sung or Lu, he became the chief officer of Sung. For a time he traveled, serving as consultant to various feudal lords and public officials. He found government officials no more willing to listen, however, than Confucius or Mencius did, and founded a school to train people for public service. Mo Tzu had around three hundred followers. Until about 200 B.C.E., Moism and Confucianism were the two most important philosophical theories in China. After that time, however, Moism died out and affected the development of East Asian thought only slightly.

Nevertheless, Moism is an extremely interesting ethical theory. It opposes Confucianism in almost every respect. Confucius stresses the importance of rituals, ceremonies, and public respect; Mo Tzu finds these wasteful. Confucius emphasizes tradition and continuity with the past; Mo Tzu formulates a principle for evaluating actions that is thoroughly oriented toward the future. Confucius bases his theory of virtue on the concept of humanity (*jen*); Mo Tzu founds his on righteousness or justice (*yi*), which he links directly to the will of Heaven. In this sense, Mo Tzu opposes Confucian humanism.

More fundamentally, Mo Tzu and Confucius have very different approaches to the moral life in general. Confucius argues that the good life is valuable in itself. In effect, he argues that virtue is its own reward. Mo Tzu, however, advocates the good life because of its good consequences. Moism is strikingly similar to modern utilitarianism, the doctrine that actions, or kinds of actions, are good to the extent that they maximize the good. Mo Tzu believes that virtue brings many benefits to the person who has it and to the society at large. He evaluates actions by examining their effects.

Mo Tzu's utilitarianism leads to another important difference. Confucius holds that moral obligation arises from specific and contingent human relations—of parent and child, for example, or sibling and sibling—whereas for Mo Tzu, our obligation to maximize good arises directly from the will of Heaven. Thus, Confucianism implies that our obligations to others depend on who we are, who they are, and how they relate to us. Mo Tzu's doctrine, in contrast, implies that our obligations are universal. In keeping with Confucius's principle of reciprocity and strongly foreshadowing Immanuel Kant's categorical imperative, Mo Tzu contends that the universal is good and the particular is bad. Immoral action involves making an exception for ourselves or our friends. Morality demands that we treat everyone with equal respect—indeed, in Mo Tzu's view, with equal love—regardless of our relation to them. According to Moism, we should love everyone as we love ourselves. Only this attitude can lead to universal peace and harmony.

In politics, Mo Tzu argues for a policy of "honoring the worthy," that is, granting rewards to those who deserve them. There are two aspects of this policy. First, Mo Tzu advocates rewarding morally good behavior. If people win rewards by acting morally, they will tend to act morally. A government can therefore promote ethically correct action by explicitly rewarding it. Second, he speaks of merit or ability more generally; in choosing people for government positions, Mo Tzu contends, we should pick those best able to fulfill the duties associated with that position. This might suggest that Mo Tzu uses the term 'worthy' ambiguously. But for him, morally correct action maximizes the good in the community. This is precisely what the most capable officials can do. Moreover, the ruler (or, in a democracy, the people) can maximize good and hence act morally by appointing those officials. The policy of honoring the worthy thus stems from Mo Tzu's general, utilitarian ethical theory.

from *Universal Love*

Reprinted from The Works of Mencius, *edited and translated by James Legge. From* The Chinese Classics, *Volume II (Oxford: Clarendon, 1895).*

CHAPTER I

It is the business of the sages to effect the good government of the world. They must know, therefore, whence disorder and confusion arise, for without this knowledge their object cannot be effected. We may compare them to a physician who undertakes to cure men's diseases:—he must ascertain whence a disease has arisen, and then he can assail it with effect, while, without such knowledge, his endeavors will be in vain. Why should we except the case of those who have to regulate disorder from this rule? They must know whence it has arisen, and then they can regulate it.

It is the business of the sages to effect the good government of the world. They must examine therefore into the cause of disorder; and when they do so they will find that it arises from the want of mutual love. When a minister and a son are not filial to their sovereign and their father, this is what is called disorder. A son loves himself, and does not love his father;—he therefore wrongs his father, and seeks his own advantage: a younger brother loves himself and does not love his elder brother;—he therefore wrongs his elder brother, and seeks his own advantage: a minister loves himself, and does not love his sovereign;—he therefore wrongs his sovereign, and seeks his own advantage:—all these are cases of what is called disorder. Though it be the father who is not kind to his son, or the elder brother who is not kind to his younger brother, or the sovereign who is not gracious to his minister:—the case comes equally under the general name of disorder. The father loves himself, and does not love his son:—he

therefore wrongs his son, and seeks his own advantage: the elder brother loves himself, and does not love his younger brother;—he therefore wrongs his younger brother, and seeks his own advantage: the sovereign loves himself, and does not love his minister;—he therefore wrongs his minister, and seeks his own advantage. How do these things come to pass? They all arise from the want of mutual love. Take the case of any thief or robber:—it is just the same with him. The thief loves his own house, and does not love his neighbor's house:—he therefore steals from his neighbour's house to benefit his own: the robber loves his own person, and does not love his neighbour;—he therefore does violence to his neighbour to benefit himself. How is this? It all arises from the want of mutual love. Come to the case of great officers throwing each other's Families into confusion, and of princes attacking one another's States:—it is just the same with them. The great officer loves his own Family, and does not love his neighbour's;—he therefore throws the neighbour's Family into disorder to benefit his own: the prince loves his own State, and does not love his neighbour's:—he therefore attacks his neighbour's State to benefit his own. All disorder in the kingdom has the same explanation. When we examine into the cause of it, it is found to be the want of mutual love.

Suppose that universal, mutual love prevailed throughout the kingdom;—if men loved others as they love themselves, disliking to exhibit what was unfilial. . . . And moreover would there be those who were unkind? Looking on their sons, younger brothers, and ministers as themselves, and disliking to exhibit what was unkind . . . the want of filial duty would disappear. And would there be thieves and robbers? When every man regarded his neighbour's house as his own, who would be found to steal? When every one regarded his neighbour's person as his own, who would be found to rob? Thieves and robbers would disappear. And would there be great officers throwing one another's Families into confusion, and princes attacking one another's States? When officers regarded the Families of others as their own, what one would make confusion? When princes regarded other States as their own, what one would begin an attack? Great officers throwing one another's Families into confusion, and princes attacking one another's States, would disappear.

If, indeed, universal, mutual love prevailed throughout the kingdom; one State not attacking another, and one Family not throwing another into confusion; thieves and robbers nowhere existing; rulers and ministers, fathers and sons, all being filial and kind:—in such a condition the nation would be well governed. On this account, how many sages, whose business it is to effect the good government of the kingdom, do but prohibit hatred and advise to love? On this account it is affirmed that universal mutual love throughout the country will lead to its happy order, and that mutual hatred leads to confusion. This was what our master, the philosopher Mo, meant, when he said, "We must above all inculcate the love of others."

CHAPTER II

Our Master, the philosopher Mo, said, "That which benevolent men consider to be incumbent on them as their business, is to stimulate and promote all that will be advantageous to the nation, and to take away all that is injurious to it. This is what they consider to be their business."

And what are the things advantageous to the nation, and the things injurious to it? Our master said, "The mutual attacks of State on State; the mutual usurpations of Family on Family; the mutual robberies of man on man; the want of kindness on the part of the ruler and of loyalty on the part of the minister; the want of tenderness and filial duty between father and son and of harmony between brothers:—these, and such as these, are the things injurious to the kingdom."

And from what do we find, on examination, that these injurious things are produced? Is it not from the want of mutual love?

Our Master said, "Yes, they are produced by the want of mutual love. Here is a prince who only knows to love his own State, and does not love his neighbour's;—he therefore does not shrink from raising all the power of his State to attack his neighbour. Here is the chief of a Family who only knows to love it, and does not love his neighbour's;—he therefore does not shrink from raising all his powers to seize on that other Family. Here is a man who only knows to love his own person, and does not love his neighbour's;—he therefore does not shrink from using all his resources to rob his neighbour. Thus it happens, that the princes, not loving one another, have their battle-fields; and the chiefs of Families, not loving one another, have their mutual usurpations; and men, not loving one another, have their mutual robberies; and rulers and ministers, not loving one another, become unkind and disloyal; and fathers and sons, not loving one another, lose their affection and filial duty; and brothers, not loving one another, contract irreconcilable enmities. Yea, men in general not loving one another, the strong make prey of the weak; the rich do despite to the poor; the noble are insolent to the mean; and the deceitful impose upon the stupid. All the miseries, usurpations, enmities, and hatreds in the world, when traced to their origin, will be found to arise from the want of mutual love. On this account, the benevolent condemn it."

They may condemn it; but how shall they change it?

Our Master said, "They may change it by the law of universal mutual love and by the interchange of mutual benefits."

How will this law of universal mutual love and the interchange of mutual benefits accomplish this?

Our Master said, "It would lead to the regarding another's kingdom as one's own: another's family as one's own: another's person as one's own. That being the case, the princes, loving one another, would have no battle-fields; the chiefs of families, loving one another, would attempt no usurpations; men, loving one another, would commit no robberies; rulers and ministers, loving one another, would be gracious and loyal; fathers and sons, loving one another, would be kind and filial; brothers, loving one another, would be harmonious and easily reconciled. Yea, men in general loving one another, the strong would not make prey of the weak; the many would not plunder the few; the rich would not insult the poor; the noble would not be insolent to the mean; and the deceitful would not impose upon the simple. The way in which all the miseries, usurpations, enmities, and hatreds in the world, may be made not to arise, is universal mutual love. On this account, the benevolent value and praise it."

Yes; but the scholars of the kingdom and superior men say, "True; if there were this universal love, it would be good. It is, however, the most difficult thing in the world."

Our Master said, "This is because the scholars and superior men simply do not understand the advantageousness of the law, and to conduct their reasonings upon that. Take the case of assaulting a city, or of a battle-field, or of the sacrificing one's life for the sake of fame:—this is felt by the people everywhere to be a difficult thing. Yet, if the ruler be pleased with it, both officers and people are able to do it:—how much more might they attain to universal mutual love, and the interchange of mutual benefits, which is different from this! When a man loves others, they respond to and love him; when a man benefits others, they respond to and benefit him; when a man injures others, they respond to and injure him; when a man hates others, they respond to and hate him:—what difficulty is there in the matter? It is only that rulers will not carry on the government on this principle, and so officers do not carry it out in their practice. . . . "

Yes; but now the officers and superior men say, "Granted; the universal practice of mutual love would be good; but it is an impracticable thing. It is like taking up the T'ai mountain, and leaping with it over the Ho or the Chi."

Our Master said, "That is not the proper comparison for it. To take up the T'ai mountain and leap with it over the Ho or the Chi, may be called an exercise of most extraordinary strength; it is, in fact, what no one, from antiquity to the present time, has ever been able to do. But how widely different from this is the practice of universal mutual love, and the interchange of mutual benefits!

"Anciently, the sage kings practised this. . . . "

If, now, the rulers of the kingdom truly and sincerely wish all in it to be rich, and dislike any being poor; if they desire its good government, and dislike disorder; they ought to practise universal mutual love, and the interchange of mutual benefits. This was the law of the sage kings; it is the way to effect the good government of the nation; it may not but be striven after.

CHAPTER III

Our Master, the philosopher Mo, said, "The business of benevolent men requires that they should strive to stimulate and promote what is advantageous to the kingdom, and to take away what is injurious to it."

Speaking, now, of the present time, what are to be accounted the most injurious things to the kingdom? They are such as the attacking of small States by great ones; the inroads on small Families by great ones; the plunder of the weak by the strong; the oppression of the few by the many; the scheming of the crafty against the simple; the insolence of the noble to the mean. To the same class belong the ungraciousness of rulers, and the disloyalty of ministers; the unkindness of fathers, and the want of filial duty on the part of sons. Yea, there is to be added to these the conduct of the mean men, who employ their edged weapons and poisoned stuff, water and fire, to rob and injure one another.

Pushing on the inquiry now, let us ask whence all these injurious things arise. Is it from loving others and advantaging others? It must be answered "No"; and it must likewise be said, "They arise clearly from hating others and doing violence to others." If it be further asked whether those who hate and do violence to others hold the principle of loving all, or that of making distinctions, it must be replied, "They make distinctions." So then, it is this principle of making distinctions between man and man, which gives rise to all that is most injurious in the kingdom. On this account we conclude that that principle is wrong.

Our Master said, "He who condemns others must have whereby to change them." To condemn men, and have no means of changing them, is like saving them from fire by plunging them in water. A man's language in such a case must be improper. On this account our Master said, "There is the principle of loving all, to take the place of that which makes distinctions." If, now, we ask, "And how is it that universal love can change the consequences of that other principle which makes distinctions?" the answer is, "If princes were as much for the States of others as for their own, what one among them would raise the forces of his State to attack that of another?—he is for that other as much as for himself. If they were for the capitals of others as much as for their own, what one would raise the forces of his capital to attack that of another?—he is for that as much as for his own. If chiefs regarded the families of others as their own, what one would lead the power of his Family to throw that of another into confusion?—he is for that other as much as for himself. If, now, States did not attack, nor holders of capitals smite, one another, and if Families were guilty of no mutual aggressions, would this be injurious to the kingdom, or its benefit?" It must be replied, "This would be advantageous to the kingdom." Pushing on the inquiry, now, let us ask whence all these benefits arise. Is it from hating others and doing violence to others? It must be answered, "No"; and it must likewise be said, "They arise clearly from loving others and doing good to others." If it be further asked whether those who love others and do good to others hold the principle of making distinctions between man and man, or that of loving all, it must be replied, "They love all." So then it is this principle of universal mutual love which really gives rise to all that is most beneficial to the nation. On this account we conclude that that principle is right.

Our Master said, a little while ago, "The business of benevolent men requires that they should strive to stimulate and promote what is advantageous to the kingdom, and to take away what is injurious to it." We have now traced the subject up, and found that it is the principle of universal love which produces all that is most beneficial to the kingdom, and the principle of making distinctions which produces all that is injurious to it. On this account what our Master said, "The principle of making distinctions between man and man is wrong, and the principle of universal love is right," turns out to be correct as the sides of a square.

If, now, we just desire to promote the benefit of the kingdom, and select for that purpose the principle of universal love, then the acute ears and piercing eyes of people will hear and see for one another; and the strong limbs of people will move and be ruled for one another; and men of principle will instruct one another. It will come about that the old, who have neither wife nor children, will get supporters who will enable them to complete their years; and the young and weak, who have no parents, will yet find helpers that shall bring them up. On the contrary, if this principle of universal love is held not to be correct, what benefits will arise from such a view? What can be the reason that the scholars of the kingdom, whenever they hear of this principle of universal love, go on to condemn it? Plain as the case is, their words in condemnation of this principle do not stop;—they say, "It may be good, but how can it be carried into practice?"

Our Master said, "Supposing that it could not be practiced, it seems hard to go on likewise to condemn it. But how can it be good, and yet incapable of being put into practice?"

Let us bring forward two instances to test the matter:—Let any one suppose the case of two individuals, the one of whom shall hold the principle of making distinctions, and the other shall hold the principle of universal love. The former of these will say, "How can I be for the person of my friend as much as for my own person? how can I be for the parents of my friend as much as for my own parents?" Reasoning in this way, he may see his friend hungry, but he will not feed him; cold, but he will not clothe him; sick, but he will not nurse him; dead, but he will not bury him. Such will be the language of the individual holding the principle of distinction, and such will be his conduct. He will say, "I have heard that he who wishes to play a lofty part among men, will be for the person of his friend as much as for his own person, and for the parents of his friend as much as for his own parents. It is only thus that he can attain his distinction?" Reasoning in this way, when he sees his friend hungry, he will feed him; cold, he will clothe him; sick, he will nurse him; dead, he will bury him. Such will be the language of him who holds the principle of universal love, and such will be his conduct.

The words of the one of these individuals are a condemnation of those of the other, and their conduct is directly contrary. Suppose now that their words are perfectly sincere, and that their conduct will be carried out,—that their words and actions will correspond like the parts of a token, every word being carried into effect; and let us proceed to put the following questions on the case:—Here is a plain in the open country, and an officer, with coat of mail, gorget, and helmet, is about to take part in a battle to be fought in it, where the issue, whether for life or death, cannot be foreknown; or here is an officer about to be dispatched on a distant commission from Pa to Yüeh, or from Ch'i to Ching, where the issue of the journey, going and coming, is quite uncertain:—on either of these suppositions, to whom will the officer entrust the charge of his house, the support of his parents, and the care of his wife and children?—to one who holds the principle of universal love? or to one who holds that which makes distinctions? I apprehend there is no one under heaven, man or woman, however stupid, though he may condemn the principle of universal love, but would at such a time make one who holds it the subject of his trust. This is in words to condemn the principle, and when there is occasion to choose between it and the opposite, to approve it;—words and conduct are here in contradiction. I do not know how it is that throughout the kingdom scholars condemn the principle of universal love, whenever they hear it.

Plain as the case is, their words in condemnation of it do not cease, but they say, "This principle may suffice perhaps to guide in the choice of an officer, but it will not guide in the choice of a sovereign."

Let us test this by taking two illustrations:—Let any one suppose the case of two sovereigns, the one of whom shall hold the principle of mutual love, and the other shall hold the principle which makes distinctions. In this case, the latter of them will say, "How can I be as much for the persons of all my people as for my own? This is much opposed to human feelings. The life of man upon the earth is but a very brief space; it may be compared to the rapid movement of a team of horses whirling past a small chink." Reasoning in this way, he may see his people hungry, but he will not feed them; cold, but he will not clothe them; sick, but he will not nurse them; dead, but he will not bury them. Such will be the language of the sovereign who holds the principle of distinctions, and such will be his conduct. Different will be the language and conduct of the other who holds the principle of universal love. He will say, "I have heard that he who would show himself a virtu-

ous and intelligent sovereign, ought to make his people the first consideration, and think of himself only after them." Reasoning in this way, when he sees any of the people hungry, he will feed them; cold, he will clothe them; sick, he will nurse them; dead, he will bury them. Such will be the language of the sovereign who holds the principle of universal love, and such his conduct. If we compare the two sovereigns, the words of the one are condemnatory of those of the other, and theirs actions are opposite. Let us suppose that their words are equally sincere, and that their actions will make them good,—that their words and actions will correspond like the parts of a token, every word being carried into effect; and let us proceed to put the following questions on the case:—Here is a year when a pestilence walks abroad among the people; many of them suffer from cold and famine; multitudes die in the ditches and water-channels. If at such a time they might make an election between the two sovereigns whom we have supposed, which would they prefer? I apprehend there is no one under heaven, however stupid, though he may condemn the principle of universal love, but would at such a time prefer to be under the sovereign who holds it. This is in words to condemn the principle, and, when there is occasion to choose between it and the opposite, to approve it;—words and conduct are here in contradiction. I do not know how it is that throughout the kingdom scholars condemn the principle of universal love, whenever they hear it. . . .

. . . How is that the scholars throughout the kingdom condemn this universal love, whenever they hear of it? Plain as the case is, the words of those who condemn the principle of universal love do not cease. They say, "It is not advantageous to the entire devotion to parents which is required:—it is injurious to filial piety." Our Master said, "Let us bring this objection to the test:—A filial son, having the happiness of his parents at heart, considers how it is to be secured. Now, does he, so considering, wish men to love and benefit his parents? or does he wish them to hate and injure his parents?" On this view of the question, it must be evident that he wishes men to love and benefit his parents. And what must he himself first do in order to gain this object? If I first address myself to love and benefit men's parents, will they for that return love and benefit to my parents? or if I first address myself to hate men's parents, will they for that return love and benefit to my parents? It is clear that I must first address myself to love and benefit men's parents, and they will return to me love and benefit to my parents. The conclusion is that a filial son has no alternative.—He must address himself in the first place to love and do good to the parents of others. If it be supposed that this is an accidental course, to be followed on emergency by a filial son, and not sufficient to be regarded as a general rule, let us bring it to the test of what we find in the Books of the ancient kings.—It is said in the Ta Ya,

"Every word finds its answer;
Every action its recompense

He threw me a peach;
I returned him a plum."

These words show that he who loves others will be loved, and that he who hates others will be hated. How is it that the scholars throughout the kingdom condemn the principle of universal love, when they hear it? . . .

. . . And now, as to universal mutual love, it is an advantageous thing and easily practiced,—beyond all calculation. The only reason why it is not practised is, in my opinion, because superiors do not take pleasure in it. If superiors were to take pleasure in it, stimulating men to it by rewards and praise, and awing them from opposition to it by punishments and fines, they would, in my opinion, move to it,—the practice of universal mutual love, and the interchange of mutual benefits,—as fire rises upwards, and as water flows downwards:—nothing would be able to check them. This universal love was the way of the sage kings; it is the principle to secure peace for kings, dukes, and great men; it is the means to secure plenty of food and clothes for the myriads of the people. The best course for the superior man is to well understand the principle of universal love, and to exert himself to practise it. It requires the sovereign to be gracious, and the minister to be loyal; the father to be kind, and the son to be filial; the elder brother to be friendly, and the younger to be obedient. Therefore the superior man,—with whom the chief desire is to see gracious sovereigns and loyal ministers; kind fathers and filial sons; friendly elder brothers and obedient younger ones,—ought to insist on the indispensableness of the practice of universal love. It was the way of the sage kings; it would be the most advantageous thing for the myriads of the people.

from *Honoring the Worthy*

Reprinted from The Ethical and Political Works of Motse, *translated from the original Chinese text by Yi-Pao Mei (London: Arthur Probsthain, 1929).*

Master Mo Tzu said: These days the rulers and high officials who govern the nation all desire their states to be rich, their population numerous, and their administration well ordered. And yet what they achieve is not wealth but poverty, not a numerous population but a meager one, not order but chaos. In actual fact, they fail to get what they seek and instead achieve what they abhor. Why is this?

Mo Tzu said: It is because the rulers and high officials who govern the nation fail to honor the worthy and employ the capable in their administration. If a government is rich in worthy men, then the administration will be characterized by weight and substance; but if it is poor in such men, then the administration will be a paltry affair. Therefore the task confronting the high officials is simply to increase the number of worthy men. But what means are to be used to increase the number of worthy men?

Mo Tzu said: Let us suppose that one wishes to increase the number of skilled archers and chariot drivers in the state. One must set about enriching and honoring such men, respecting and praising them. Once this has been done, one will have no difficulty in obtaining a multitude of them. How much more appropriate, therefore, that one should do this for worthy men, who are ardent in the practice of virtue, skilled in discourse, and broad in learning! Men such as these are the treasures of the nation and the keepers of its altars of the soil and grain. They too should be enriched and honored, respected and praised, and when this has been done, they may be obtained in plenty.

Therefore, when the sage kings of ancient times administered their states, they announced: "The unrighteous shall not be enriched, the unrighteous shall not be exalted, the unrighteous shall be no kin to us, the unrighteous shall not be our intimates!" When the rich and exalted men of the kingdom heard this, they all began to deliberate among themselves, saying, "We have trusted in our wealth and exalted position, but now the lord promotes the righteous without caring whether they are poor or humble. We too, then, must become righteous." Likewise the kin of the ruler began to deliberate, saying, "We have trusted in the bond of kinship, but now the lord promotes the righteous without caring how distant the relationship. We too, then, must become righteous." Those who were intimate with the ruler deliberated, saying, "We have trusted in the intimacy we enjoyed, but now the lord promotes the righteous without caring how far removed they may have been from him until now. We too, then, must become righteous." And when those who were far removed from the ruler heard it, they also deliberated, saying, "We used to believe that, since we were so far removed from the ruler, we had nothing to trust in. But now the lord promotes the righteous without caring how far removed they may be. We too, then, must become righteous." So the vassals of distant and outlying areas, as well as the noblemen's sons serving in the palace, the multitudes of the capital, and the peasants of the four borders, in time came to hear of this, and all strove to become righteous. . . .

Mo Tzu said: In caring for the people, presiding over the altars of the soil and grain, and ordering the state, the rulers and high officials these days strive for stability and seek to avoid any error. But why do they fail to perceive that honoring the worthy is the foundation of government?

How do we know that honoring the worthy is the foundation of government? Because when the eminent and wise rule over the stupid and humble, then there will be order; but when the stupid and humble rule over the eminent and wise, there will be chaos. Therefore we know that honoring the worthy is the foundation of government.

Therefore the sage kings of ancient times took great pains to honor the worthy and employ the capable, showing no special consideration for their own kin, no partiality for the eminent and rich, no favoritism for the good-looking and attractive. They promoted the worthy to high places, enriched and honored them, and made them heads of government; the unworthy they demoted and rejected, reduced to poverty and humble station, and condemned to penal servitude. Thus the people, encouraged by the hope of reward and awed by the fear of punishment, led each other on to become worthy, so that worthy men increased in number and unworthy men became few. This is what is called advancing the worthy. And when this had been done, the sage kings listened to the words of the worthy, watched their actions, observed their abilities, and on this basis carefully assigned them to office. This is called employing the capable. Those who were capable of ordering the state were employed to order the state; those who were capable of heading a government bureau were employed as heads of bureaus; and those who were capable of governing an outlying district were employed to govern the outlying districts. Thus the administration of the state, of the government bureaus, and of the outlying districts was in every case in the hands of the most worthy men of the nation.

When a worthy man is given the task of ordering the state, he appears at court early and retires late, listens to lawsuits and attends to the affairs of government. As a result the state is well ordered and laws and punishments are justly administered. When a worthy man heads a government bureau, he goes to bed late and gets up early, collecting taxes on the barriers and markets and on the resources of the hills, forests, lakes, and fish weirs, so that the treasury will be full. As a result the treasury is full and no source of revenue is neglected. When a worthy man governs an outlying district, he leaves his house early and returns late, plowing and sowing seed, planting trees, and gathering vegetables and grain. As a result there will be plenty of vegetables and grain and the people will have enough to eat. When the state is well ordered, the laws and punishments will be justly administered, and when the treasury is full, the people will be well off. The rulers will thus be supplied with wine and millet to use in their sacrifices to Heaven and spirits, with hides and currency to use in their intercourse with the feudal lords of neighboring states, and with the means to feed the hungry and give rest to the weary within their realm, to nourish their subjects and attract virtuous men from all over the world. Then Heaven and the spirits will send down riches, the other feudal lords will become their allies, the people of their own realm will feel affection for them, and worthy men will come forward to serve them. Thus all that they plan for they will achieve, and all that they undertake will be brought to a successful conclusion. If they stay within their realm, their position will be secure, and if they venture forth to punish an enemy, they will be victorious. It was by this method alone that the sage kings of the Three Dynasties, Yao, Shun, Yü, T'ang, Wen, and Wu, were able to rule the world and become the leaders of the other lords.

But if one knows only the policy to be adopted, but does not know what means to use in carrying it out, then he cannot be sure of success in government. Therefore three principles should be established. What are these three principles? They are that if the titles and positions of worthy men are not exalted enough, then the people will not respect such men; if their stipends are not generous, then the people will not have confidence in them; and if their orders are not enforced, then the people will not stand in awe of them. Therefore the sage kings of antiquity honored the worthy with titles, treated them to generous stipends, entrusted them with important affairs, and empowered them to see that their orders were carried out. These benefits were bestowed not because the ruler wished to reward his ministers, but because he hoped thereby to bring about success in the affairs of government.

MENCIUS

Meng Tzu (372?–289? B.C.E.), or Mencius (his Latinized name), was perhaps the greatest ancient disciple of Confucius. Born in what is now Shantung province, he lived during the turbulent Warring States period. He studied under a student of a student of Tzu Ssu, Confucius's grandson. He became a professional teacher. For about forty years he traveled throughout China offering advice to various nobles and officials. In his fifties he served as an official in Ch'i (Qi).

Mencius abides by the chief doctrines of Confucius, but he develops Confucianism in a number of original and important ways. First, Mencius argues that human nature is originally and essentially good. He observes that anyone seeing a baby fall into a well would rush to help without thinking. This shows that human nature is itself altruistic. Specifically, Mencius holds that four kinds of virtue are inherent in human nature: humanity (*jen*), righteousness or justice (*yi*), decency, and knowledge. We innately feel compassion, which is the beginning of humanity; shame and dislike, the beginnings of righteousness or justice; modesty, the beginning of decency; and approval and disapproval, the beginnings of knowledge. The relation of these virtues to innate feeling leads Mencius to place great emphasis on conscience and moral intuition.

Second, Mencius treats humanity as a virtue that good people can attain rather than as an unattainable idea. According to Confucius, only the sages of antiquity have true humanity. Mencius, in contrast, maintains that we are all born with a disposition to humanity. We must preserve and cultivate this intuition, to be sure, but our innate moral intuition gives us the ability to achieve humanity in the fullest sense.

Third, Mencius stresses the concept of righteousness or justice (*yi*). This concept plays some role in Confucius's thought but is the foundation of Mo Tzu's utilitarianism. Mencius tries to synthesize these approaches by treating humanity and justice as independent, fundamental notions. Confucius talks about the obligations of rulers, the characteristics of good rulers, and other political topics, but he has no conception of rights. Mencius, however, treats justice as the primary political virtue and understands it, not in terms of good consequences, as Mo Tzu does, but in terms of respect for the rights of others. Mencius does not develop a theory of rights; in his view, rights arise from tradition and custom, not from an abstract set of rules or a code of laws. Confucius sometimes seems to agree with Thomas Jefferson that "that government is best that governs least," but only because a good government will produce a well-ordered society that needs little governing. Mencius prefers limited government for a very different and more Jeffersonian reason: anything else is likely to violate the rights of the people. Humanity and justice are linked: in W. A. C. H. Dobson's words, "A man is *jen* when he is what he should be, and *yi* when he does what he should do."*

Mencius also attacks Mo Tzu's utilitarianism and his attendant doctrine of universal love. For Confucius, moral obligations stem from specific human relations, such as that of parent to child. Mencius argues the Moism places too little value on these relations. Suppose, for instance, that two people are drowning, that you can save only one, and that one of the two is your own child. What should you do? Moism implies that it makes no ethical difference which you save. Any simple utilitarian theory like Mo Tzu's directs us to maximize the amount of good in the community. From the perspective of such a theory, it makes no difference who has what amount of good. So, it makes no difference whether your own child lives or dies, provided that another is saved in its place.

In Mencius's view, this result is absurd. Of course you should save your own child. Your relation as parent and child gives you special obligations to each other that go beyond obligations we all have to one another as human beings. Mencius's objection thus goes beyond the specifics of Moism to the impartiality inherent in many forms of utilitarianism. Even if not all obligations stem from particular social relations, Mencius argues, some surely do. If so, then purely universal and impartial ethical theories can at most tell part of the story.

---

* W. A. C. H. **Dobson**, *Mencius* (London: Oxford University Press, 1963), 132.

from *The Book of Mencius*

Reprinted from The Works of Mencius, *edited and translated by James Legge. From* The Chinese Classics, *Volume II (Oxford: Clarendon, 1895).*

2A6. Mencius said, "All men have a mind which cannot bear to see the sufferings of others.

"The ancient kings had this commiserating mind, and they, as a matter of course, had likewise a commiserating government. When with a commiserating mind was practised a commiserating government, to rule the kingdom was as easy a matter as to make anything go round in the palm.

"When I say that all men have a mind which cannot bear to see the sufferings of others, my meaning may be illustrated thus:—even now-a-days, if men suddenly see a child about to fall into a well, they will without exception experience a feeling of alarm and distress. They will feel so, not as a ground on which they may gain the favour of the child's parents, nor as a ground on which they may seek the praise of their neighbours and friends, nor from a dislike to the reputation of having been unmoved by such a thing.

"From this case we may perceive that the feeling of commiseration is essential to man, that the feeling of shame and dislike is essential to man, that the feeling of modesty and complaisance is essential to man, and that the feeling of approving and disapproving is essential to man.

"The feeling of commiseration is the principle of benevolence. The feeling of shame and dislike is the principle of righteousness. The feeling of modesty and complaisance is the principle of propriety. The feeling of approving and disapproving is the principle of knowledge.

"Men have these four principles just as they have their four limbs. When men, having these four principles, yet say of themselves that they cannot develop them, they play the thief with themselves, and he who says of his prince that he cannot develop them plays the thief with his prince.

"Since all men have these four principles in themselves, let them know to give them all their development and completion, and the issue will be like that of fire which has begun to burn, or that of a spring which has begun to find vent. Let them have their complete development, and they will suffice to love and protect all within the four seas. Let them be denied that development, and they will not suffice for a man to serve his parents with."

2A7. Mencius said, "Is the arrow-maker less benevolent than the maker of armour of defence? And yet the arrow-maker's only fear is lest men should not be hurt, and the armour-maker's only fear is lest men should be hurt. So it is with the priest and the coffin-maker. The choice of profession, therefore, is a thing in which great caution is required.

"Confucius said, 'It is virtuous manners which constitute the excellence of a neighbourhood. If a man, in selecting a residence, does not fix on one where such prevail, how can he be wise?' Now benevolence is the most honourable dignity conferred by Heaven, and the quiet home in which man should dwell. Since no one can hinder us from being so, if yet we are not benevolent;—this is being not wise.

"From the want of benevolence and the want of wisdom will ensue the entire absence of propriety and righteousness;—he who is in such a case must be the servant of other men. To be the servant of men and yet ashamed of such servitude, is like a bow-maker's being ashamed to make bows, or an arrow-maker's being ashamed to make arrows.

"If he be ashamed of his case, his best course is to practise benevolence.

"The man who would be benevolent is like the archer. The archer adjusts himself and then shoots. If he misses, he does not murmur against those who surpass himself. He simply turns round and seeks the cause of his failure in himself."

3A5. The Mohist, Î Chih, sought, though Hsü Pi, to see Mencius. Mencius said, "I indeed wish to see him, but at present I am still unwell. When I am better, I will myself go and see him. He need not come here again."

Next day, Î Chih again sought to see Mencius. Mencius said, "To-day I am able to see him. But if I do not correct his errors, the true principles will not be fully evident. Let me first correct him. I have heard that this Î is a Mohist. Now Mo considers that in the regulation of funeral matters a spare simplicity should be the rule. Î thinks with Mo's doctrines to change the customs of the kingdom;—how does he regard them as if they were wrong, and not honour them? Notwithstanding his views, Î buried his parents in a sumptuous manner, and so he served them in the way which his doctrines discountenance."

The disciple Hsü informed Î of these remarks. Î said, "Even according to the principles of the learned, we find that the ancients acted towards the people 'as if they were watching over an infant.' What does this expression mean? To me it sounds that we are to love all without differences of degree; but the manifestation of love must begin with our parents." Hsü reported this reply to Mencius, who said, "Now, does Î really think that a man's affection for the child of his brother is merely like his affection for the infant of a neighbour? What is to be approved in that expression is simply this:—that if an infant crawling about is likely to fall into a well, it is no crime in the infant. Moreover, Heaven gives birth to creatures in such a way that they have one root, and Î makes them to have two roots. This is the cause of his error.

And, in the most ancient times, there were some who did not inter their parents. When their parents died, they took them up and threw them into some water-channel. Afterwards, when passing by them, they saw foxes and wild-cats devouring them, and flies and gnats biting at them. The perspiration started out upon their foreheads, and they looked away, unable to bear the sight. It was not on account of other people that this perspiration flowed. The emotions of their hearts affected their faces and eyes, and instantly they went home, and came back with baskets and spades and covered the bodies. If the covering them thus was indeed right, you may see that the filial son and virtuous man, in interring in a handsome manner their parents, act according to a proper rule."

The disciple Hsü informed Î of what Mencius had said. Î was thoughtful for a short time, and then said, "He has instructed me."

3B2. Ching Ch'un said to Mencius, "Are not Kung-sun Yen and Chang Î really great men? Let them once be angry, and all the princes are afraid. Let them live quietly and the flames of trouble are extinguished throughout the kingdom."

Mencius said, "How can such men be great men? Have you not read the Ritual Usages?—'At the capping of a young man, his father admonishes him. At the marrying away of a young woman, her mother admonishes her, accompanying her to the door on her leaving, and cautioning her with these words, "You are going to your home. You must be respectful; you must be careful. Do not disobey your husband."' Thus, to look upon compliance as their correct course is the rule for women.

"To dwell in the wide house of the world, to stand in the correct seat of the world, and to walk in the great path of the world; when he obtains his desire for office, to practise his principles for the good of the people; and when that desire is disappointed, to practise them alone; to be above the power of riches and honours to make dissipated, of poverty and mean condition to make swerve from principle, and of power and force to make bend:—these characteristics constitute the great man."

4A4. Mencius said, "If a man loves others, and no responsive attachment is shown to him, let him turn inwards and examine his own benevolence. If he is trying to rule others, and his government is unsuccessful, let him turn inwards and examine his wisdom. If he treats others politely, and they do not return his politeness, let him turn inwards and examine his own feeling of respect.

"When we do not, by what we do, realise what we desire, we must turn inwards, and examine ourselves in every point. When a man's person is correct, the whole kingdom will turn to him with recognition and submission.

"It is said in the Book of Poetry, 'Be always studious to be in harmony with the ordinances of God, And you will obtain much happiness.'"

4A5. Mencius said, "People have this common saying,—'The kingdom, the State, the family.' The root of the kingdom is in the State. The root of the State is in the family. The root of the family is in the person of its Head."

4A11. Mencius said, "The path of duty lies in what is near, and men seek for it in what is remote. The work of duty lies in what is easy, and men seek for it in what is difficult. If each man would love his parents and show the due respect to his elders, the whole land would enjoy tranquillity."

4A12. Mencius said, "When those occupying inferior situations do not obtain the confidence of the sovereign, they cannot succeed in governing the people. There is a way to obtain the confidence of the sovereign:—if one is not trusted by his friends, he will not obtain the confidence of his sovereign. There is a way of being trusted by one's friends:—if one does not serve his parents so as to make them pleased, he will not be trusted by his friends. There is a way to make one's parents pleased:—if one, on turning his thoughts inwards finds a want of sincerity, he will not give pleasure to his parents. There is a way to the attainment of sincerity in one's self:—if a man does not understand what is good, he will not attain sincerity in himself.

"Therefore, sincerity is the way of Heaven. To think *how* to be sincere is the way of man.

"Never has there been one possessed of complete sincerity, who did not move others. Never has there been one who had not sincerity who was able to move others."

4A18. Kung-sun Ch'au said, "Why is it that the superior man does not himself teach his son?"

Mencius replied, "The circumstances of the case forbid its being done. The teacher must inculcate what is correct. When he inculcates what is correct, and his lessons are not practised, he follows them up with being angry. When he follows them up with being angry, then, contrary to what should be, he is offended with his son. At the same time, the pupil says, 'My master inculcates on me what is correct, and he himself does not proceed in a correct path.' The result of this is, that father and son are offended with each other. When father and son come to be offended with each other, the case is evil.

"The ancients exchanged sons, and one taught the son of another.

"Between father and son, there should be no reproving admonitions to what is good. Such reproofs lead to alienation, and than alienation there is nothing more inauspicious."

4A19. Mencius said, "Of services, which is the greatest? The service of parents is the greatest. Of charges, which is the greatest? The charge of one's self is the greatest. That those who do not fail to keep themselves are able to serve their parents is what I have heard. But I have never heard of any, who, having failed to keep themselves, were able notwithstanding to serve their parents.

"There are many services, but the service of parents is the root of all others. There are many charges, but the charge of one's self is the root of all others. . . . "

4A20. Mencius said, "It is not enough to remonstrate with a sovereign on account of the mal-employment of ministers, nor to blame errors of government. It is only the great man who can rectify what is wrong in the sovereign's mind. Let the prince be benevolent, and all his acts will be benevolent. Let the prince be righteous, and all his acts will be righteous. Let the prince be correct, and everything will be correct. Once rectify the ruler, and the kingdom will be firmly settled."

4A26. Mencius said, "There are three things which are unfilial, and to have no posterity is the greatest of them.

"Shun married without informing his parents because of this,—lest he should have no posterity. Superior men consider that his doing so was the same as if he had informed them."

4A27. Mencius said, "The richest fruit of benevolence is this,—the service of one's parents. The richest fruit of righteousness is this,—the obeying one's elder brothers.

"The richest fruit of wisdom is this,—the knowing those two things, and not departing from them. The richest fruit of propriety is this,—the ordering and adorning those two things. The richest fruit of music is this,—the rejoicing in those two things. When they are rejoiced in, they grow. Growing, how can they be repressed? When they come to this state that they cannot be repressed, then unconsciously the feet begin to dance and the hands to move."

4B5. Mencius said, "If the sovereign be benevolent, all will be benevolent. If the sovereign be righteous, all will be righteous."

4B6. Mencius said, "Acts of propriety which are not really proper, and acts of righteousness which are not really righteous, the great man does not do."

4B8. Mencius said, "Men must be decided on what they will NOT do, and then they are able to act with vigour in what they ought to do."

4B9. Mencius said, "What future misery have they and ought they to endure who talk of what is not good in others!"

4B11. Mencius said, "The great man does not think beforehand of his words that they may be sincere, nor of his actions that they may be resolute:—he simply speaks and does what is right."

4B12. Mencius said, "The great man is he who does not lose his child's-heart."

4B19. Mencius said, "That whereby man differs from the lower animals is but small. The mass of people cast it away, while superior men preserve it.

"Shun clearly understood the multitude of things, and closely observed the relations of humanity. He walked along the path of benevolence and righteousness; he did not need to pursue benevolence and righteousness."

4B28. Mencius said, "That whereby the superior man is distinguished from other men is that he preserves in his heart;—namely, benevolence and propriety.

"The benevolent man loves others. The man of propriety shows respect to others.

"He who loves others is constantly loved by them. He who respects others is constantly respected by them.

"Here is a man, who treats me in a perverse and unreasonable manner. The superior man in such a case will turn round upon himself—'I must have been wanting in benevolence; I must have been wanting in propriety;—how should this have happened to me?'

"He examines himself, and is specially benevolent. He turns round upon himself, and is specially observant of propriety. The perversity and unreasonableness of the other, however, are still the same. The superior man will again turn around on himself—'I must have been failing to do my utmost.'

"He turns round upon himself, and proceeds to do his utmost, but still the perversity and unreasonableness of the other are repeated. On this the superior man says, 'This is a man utterly lost indeed! Since he conducts himself so, what is there to choose between him and a brute? Why should I go to contend with a brute?'

"Thus it is that the superior man has a life-long anxiety and not one morning's calamity. As to what is a matter of anxiety to him, that indeed he has.—He says, 'Shun was a man, and I also am a man. But Shun became an example to all the kingdom, and his conduct was worthy to be handed down to after ages, while I am nothing better than a villager.' This indeed is the proper matter of anxiety to him. And in what way is he anxious about it? Just that he may be like Shun:—then only will he stop. As to what the superior man would feel to be a calamity, there is no such thing. He does nothing which is not according to propriety. If there should befall him one morning's calamity, the superior man does not account it a calamity."

4B32. The officer Ch'u said to Mencius, "Master, the king sent persons to spy out whether you were really different from other men." Mencius said, "How should I be different from other men? Yao and Shun were just the same as other men."

4B33. A man of Ch'i had a wife and a concubine, and lived together with them in his house. When their husband went out, he would get himself well filled with wine and flesh, and then return, and on his wife's asking him with whom he ate and drank, they were sure to be all wealthy and honourable people. The wife informed the concubine, saying, 'When our good man goes out, he is sure to come back having partaken plenti-fully of wine and flesh. I asked with whom he ate and drank, and they are all, it seems, wealthy and honourable people. And yet no people of distinc-tion ever come here. I will spy out where our good man goes." Accordingly, she got up early in the morning, and privately followed wherever her husband went. Throughout the whole city, there was no one who stood or talked with him. At last, he came to those who were sacrificing among the tombs beyond the outer wall on the east, and begged what they had over. Not being satisfied, he looked about, and went to another party;—and

this was the way in which he got himself satiated. His wife returned, and informed the concubine, saying, "It was to our husband that we looked up in hopeful contemplation, with whom our lot is cast for life;—and now these are his ways!" On this, along with the concubine she reviled their husband, and they wept together in the middle hall. In the meantime the husband knowing noth-ing of all this, came in with a jaunty air, carrying himself proudly to his wife and concubine.

In the view of a superior man, as to the ways by which men seek for riches, honours, gain, and advancement, there are few of their wives and concubines who would not be ashamed and weep together on account of them.

6A1. The philosopher Kao said, "Man's nature is like the *ch'i*-willow, and righteousness is like a cup or a bowl. The fashioning benevolence and righteousness out of man's nature is like the making cups and bowls from the *ch'i*-willow."

Mencius replied, "Can you, leaving untouched the nature of the willow, make with it cups and bowls? You must do violence and injury to the willow, before you can make cups and bowls with it. If you must do violence and injury to the wil-low in order to make cups and bowls with it, on your principles you must in the same way do vio-lence and injury to humanity in order to fashion from it benevolence and righteousness! Your words, alas! would certainly lead all men on to reckon benevolence and righteousness to be calamities."

6A2. The philosopher Kao said, "Man's nature is like water whirling round in a corner. Open a passage for it to the east, and it will flow to the east; open a passage for it to the west, and it will flow to the west. Man's nature is indifferent to good and evil, just as the water is indifferent to the east and west."

Mencius replied, "Water indeed will flow indi-ferently to the east or west, but will it flow in-differently up or down? The tendency of man's nature to good is like the tendency of water to flow downwards. There are none but have this ten-dency to good, just as all water flows downwards.

"Now by striking water and causing it to leap up, you may make it go over your forehead, and by damming and leading it, you may force it up a hill;—but are such movements according to the nature of water? It is the force applied which causes them. When men are made to do what is not good, their nature is dealt with in this way."

6A3. The philosopher Kao said, "Life is what we call nature."

Mencius asked him, "Do you say that by nature you mean life, just as you say that white is white?" "Yes, I do," was the reply. Mencius added, "Is the whiteness of a white feather like that of white snow, and the whiteness of white snow like that of white jade?" Kao again said, "Yes."

"Very well," pursued Mencius. "Is the nature of a dog like the nature of an ox, and the nature of an ox like the nature of a man?"

6A4. The philosopher Kao said, "To enjoy food and delight in colours is nature. Benevolence is internal and not external; righteousness is external and not internal."

Mencius asked him "What is the ground of your saying that benevolence is internal and righteousness external?" He replied, "There is a man older than I, and I give honour to his age. It is not that there is first in me a principle of such reverence to age. It is just as when there is a white man, and I consider him white:—according as he is so externally to me. On this account, I pronounce of righteousness that it is external."

Mencius said, "There is no difference between our pronouncing a white horse to be white and our pronouncing a white man to be white. But is there no difference between the regard with which we acknowledge the age of an old horse and that with which we acknowledge the age of an old man? And what is it which is called righteousness?—the fact of a man's being old? or the fact of our giving honour to his age?"

Kao said, "There is my younger brother;—I love him. But the younger brother of a man of Ch'in I do not love: that is, the feeling is determined by myself, and therefore I say that benevolence is internal. On the other hand, I give honour to an old man of Ch'u, and I also give honour to an old man of my own people: that is, the feeling is determined by the age, and therefore I say that righteousness is external."

Mencius answered him, "Our enjoyment of meat roasted by a man of Ch'in does not differ from our enjoyment of meat roasted by ourselves. Thus, what you insist on takes place also in the case of such things, and will you say likewise that our enjoyment of a roast is external?"

6A5. The disciple Mang Chi asked Kung-tu, saying, "On what ground is it said that righteousness is internal?"

Kung-tu replied, "We therein act out our feeling of respect, and therefore it is said to be internal."

The other objected, "Suppose the case of a villager older than your elder brother by one year, to which of them would you show the greater respect?" "To my brother," was the reply. "But for which of them would you first pour out wine at a feast?" "For the villager." Mang Chi argued, "Now your feeling of reverence rests on the one, and now the honour due to age is rendered to the other;—this is certainly determined by what is without, and does not proceed from within."

Kung-tu was unable to reply, and told the conversation to Mencius. Mencius said, "You should ask him, 'Which do you respect most,—your uncle or your younger brother?' He will answer, 'My uncle.' Ask him again, 'If your younger brother be personating a dead ancestor, to which do you show the greater respect,—to him or to your uncle?' He will say, 'To my younger brother.' You can go on. 'But where is the respect due, as you said, to your uncle?' He will reply to this, 'I show the respect to my younger brother because of the position which he occupies,' and you can likewise say, 'So my respect to the villager is because of the position which he occupies. Ordinarily, my respect is rendered to my elder brother; for a brief season, on occasion, it is rendered to the villager.'"

Mang Chi heard this and observed, "When respect is due to my uncle, I respect him, and when respect is due to my younger brother,

I respect him;—the thing is certainly determined by what is without, and does not proceed from within." Kung-tu replied, "In winter we drink things hot, in summer we drink things cold; and so, on your principle, eating and drinking also depend on what is external."

6A6. The disciple Kung-tu said, "The philosopher Kao says, 'Man's nature is neither good nor bad.'"

"Some say, 'Man's nature may be made to practise good, and it may be made to practise evil, and accordingly, under Wan and Wu, the people loved what was good, while under Yu and Li, they loved what was cruel.'

"Some say, 'The nature of some is good, and the nature of others is bad. Hence it was that under such a sovereign as Yao there yet appeared Hsiang; that with such a father as Ku-sau there yet appeared Shun; and that with Chau for their sovereign and the son of their elder brother besides, there were found Ch'i, the viscount of Wei, and the prince Pi-kan.'

"And now you say, 'the nature is good.' Then are all those wrong?"

Mencius said, "From the feelings proper to it, it is constituted for the practice of what is good. This is what I mean in saying that the nature is good.

"If men do what is not good, the blame cannot be imputed to their natural powers.

"The feeling of commiseration belongs to all men; so does that of shame and dislike; and that of reverence and respect; and that of approving and disapproving. The feeling of commiseration implies the principle of benevolence; that of shame and dislike, the principle of righteousness; that of reverence and respect, the principle of propriety; and that of approving and disapproving, the principle of knowledge. Benevolence, righteousness, propriety, and knowledge are not infused into us from without. We are certainly furnished with them. And a different view is simply owing to want of reflection. Hence it is said, 'Seek and you will find them. Neglect and you will lose them.' Men differ from one another in regard to them;—some as much again as others, some five times as much, and some to an incal-

culable amount:—it is because they cannot carry out fully their natural powers.

"It is said in the Book of Poetry,

'Heaven in producing mankind,
Gave them their various faculties and relations with
    their specific laws.
These are the invariable rules of nature for all to hold,
And all love this admirable virtue.'

Confucius said, 'The maker of this ode knew indeed the principle of our nature!' We may thus see that every faculty and relation must have its law, and since there are invariable rules for all to hold, they consequently love this admirable virtue."

6A7. Mencius said, "In good years the children of the people are most of them good, while in bad years the most of them abandon themselves to evil. It is not owing to any difference of their natural powers conferred by Heaven that they are thus different. The abandonment is owing to the circumstances through which they allow their minds to be ensnared and drowned in evil.

"There now is barley,—Let it be sown and covered up; the ground being the same, and the time of sowing likewise the same, it grows rapidly up, and, when the full time is come, it is all found to be ripe. Although there may be inequalities of produce, that is owing to the difference of the soil, as rich or poor, to the unequal nourishment afforded by the rains and dews, and to the different ways in which man has performed his business in reference to it.

"Thus all things which are the same in kind are like to one another;—why should we doubt in regard to man, as if he were a solitary exception to this? The sage and we are the same in kind.

"In accordance with this the scholar Lung said, 'If a man make hempen sandals without knowing the size of people's feet, yet I know that he will not make them like baskets.' Sandals are all like one another, because all men's feet are like one another.

"So with the mouth and flavours;—all mouths have the same relishes. Yi-ya only apprehended before me what my mouth relishes. Suppose that his mouth in its relish for flavours differed from that of other men, as is the case with dogs or horses which are not the same in kind with us, why should all men be found following Yi-ya in their relishes? In the matter of tastes all the people model themselves after Yi-ya; that is, the mouths of all men are like one another.

"And so also it is with the ear. In the matter of sounds, the whole people model themselves after the music-master K'wang; that is, the ears of all men are like one another.

"And so also it is with the eye. In the case of Tsze-tu, there is no man but would recognise that he was beautiful. Any one who would not recognise the beauty of Tsze-tu must have no eyes.

"Therefore I say,—Men's mouths agree in having the same relishes; their ears agree in enjoying the same sounds; their eyes agree in recognising the same beauty:—shall their minds alone be without that which they similarly approve? What is it then of which they similarly approve? It is, I say, the principles of our nature, and the determinations of righteousness. The sages only apprehended before me that of which my mind approves along with other men. Therefore the principles of our nature and the determinations of righteousness are agreeable to my mind, just as the flesh of grass and grain-fed animals is agreeable to my mouth."

6A8. Mencius said, "The trees of the Niu mountain were once beautiful. Being situated, however, in the borders of a large State, they were hewn down with axes and bills;—and could they retain their beauty? Still through the activity of the vegetative life day and night, and the nourishing influence of the rain and dew, they were not without buds and sprouts springing forth, but then came the cattle and goats and browsed upon them. To these things is owing the bare and stripped appearance of the mountain, and when people now see it, they think it was never finely wooded. But is this the nature of the mountain?

"And so also of what properly belongs to man;—shall it be said that the mind of any man was without benevolence and righteousness? The way in which a man loses his proper goodness of mind is like the way in which the trees are

denuded by axes and bills. Hewn down day after day, can it—the mind—retain its beauty? But there is a development of its life day and night, and in the calm air of the morning, just between night and day, the mind feels in a degree those desires and aversions which are proper to humanity, but the feeling is not strong, and it is fettered and destroyed by what takes place during the day. This fettering taking place again and again, the restorative influence of the night is not sufficient to preserve the proper goodness of the mind; and when this proves insufficient for that purpose, the nature becomes not much different from that of the irrational animals, and when people now see it, they think that it never had those powers which I assert. But does this condition represent the feelings proper to humanity?

"Therefore, if it receive its proper nourishment, there is nothing which will not grow. If it lose its proper nourishment, there is nothing which will not decay away.

"Confucius said, 'Hold it fast, and it remains with you. Let it go, and you lose it. Its outgoing and incoming cannot be defined as to time or place.' It is the mind of which this is said."

6A9. Mencius said, "It is not to be wondered at that the king is not wise!

"Suppose the case of the most easily growing thing in the world;—if you let it have one day's genial heat, and then expose it for ten days to cold, it will not be able to grow. It is but seldom that I have an audience of the king, and when I retire, there come all those who act upon him like the cold. Though I succeed in bringing out some buds of goodness, of what avail is it?

"Now chess-playing is but a small art, but without his whole mind being given, and his will bent, to it, a man cannot succeed at it. Chess Ch'iu is the best chess-player in all the kingdom. Suppose that he is teaching two men to play.— The one gives to the subject his whole mind and bends to it all his will, doing nothing but listening to Chess Ch'iu. The other, although he seems to be listening to him, has his whole mind running on a swan which he thinks is approaching, and wishes to bend his bow, adjust the string to the arrow, and shoot it. Although he is learning along with the other, he does not come up to him. Why?—because his intelligence is not equal? Not so."

6A11. Mencius said, "Benevolence is man's mind, and righteousness is man's path.

"How lamentable is it to neglect the path and not pursue it, to lose this mind and not know to seek it again!

"When men's fowls and dogs are lost, they know to seek for them again, but they lose their mind, and do not know to seek for it.

"The great end of learning is nothing else but to seek for the lost mind."

6A15. The disciple Kung-tu said, "All are equally men, but some are great men, and some are little men;—how is this?" Mencius replied, "Those who follow that part of themselves which is great are great men; those who follow that part which is little are little men."

Kung-tu pursued, "All are equally men, but some follow that part of themselves which is great, and some follow that part which is little;—how is this?" Mencius answered, "The senses of hearing and seeing do not think, and are obscured by external things. When one thing comes into contact with another, as a matter of course it leads it away. To the mind belongs the office of thinking. By thinking, it gets the right view of things; by neglecting to think, it fails to do this. These—the senses and the mind—are what Heaven has given to us. Let a man first stand fast in the supremacy of the nobler part of his constitution, and the inferior part will not be able to take it from him. It is simply this which makes the great man."

6A16. Mencius said, "There is a nobility of Heaven, and there is a nobility of man. Benevolence, righteousness, self-consecration, and fidelity, with unwearied joy in these virtues;— these constitute the nobility of Heaven. To be a kung, a ch'ing, or a ta-fu;—this constitutes the nobility of man.

"The men of antiquity cultivated their nobility of Heaven, and the nobility of man came to them in its train.

"The men of the present day cultivate their nobility of Heaven in order to seek for the nobility of man, and when they have obtained that, they throw away the other:—their delusion is extreme. The issue is simply this, that they must lose that nobility of man as well."

6B1. A man of Zan asked the disciple Wu-lu, saying, "Is an observance of the rules of propriety in regard to eating, or eating merely, the more important?" The answer was, "The observance of the rules of propriety is the more important."

"Is the gratifying the appetite of sex, or the doing so only according to the rules of propriety, the more important?" The answer again was, "The observance of the rules of propriety in the matter is the more important."

The man pursued, "If the result of eating only according to the rules of propriety will be death by starvation, while by disregarding those rules we may get food, must they still be observed in such a case? If according to the rule that he shall go in person to meet his wife a man cannot get married, while by disregarding that rule he may get married, must he still observe the rule in such a case?"

Wu-lu was unable to reply to these questions, and the next day he went to Tsau, and told them to Mencius. Mencius said, "What difficulty is there in answering these inquiries?

"If you do not adjust them at their lower extremities, but only put their tops on a level, a piece of wood an inch square may be made to be higher than the pointed peak of a high building.

"Gold is heavier than feathers;—but does that saying have reference, on the one hand, to a single clasp of gold, and, on the other, to a waggon-load of feathers?

"If you take a case where the eating is of the utmost importance and the observing the rules of propriety is of little importance, and compare the things together, why stop with saying merely that the eating is more important? So, taking the case where the gratifying the appetite of sex is of the utmost importance and the observing the rules of propriety is of little importance, why stop with merely saying that the gratifying the appetite is the more important?

"Go and answer him thus, 'If, by twisting your elder brother's arm, and snatching from him what he is eating, you can get food for yourself, while, if you do not do so, you will not get anything to eat, will you so twist his arm? If by getting over your neighbour's wall, and dragging away his virgin daughter, you can get a wife, while if you do not do so, you will not be able to get a wife, will you so drag her away?'"

6B2. Chiao of Tsao asked Mencius saying, "It is said, 'All men may be Yaos and Shuns;'—is it so?" Mencius replied, "It is."

Chiao went on, "I have heard that king Wan was ten cubits high, and T'ang nine. Now I am nine cubits four inches in height. But I can do nothing but eat my millet. What am I to do to realize that saying?"

Mencius answered him, "What has this—the question of size—to do with the matter? It all lies simply in acting as such. Here is a man, whose strength was not equal to lift a duckling:—he was then a man of no strength. But to-day he says, 'I can lift 3,000 catties' weight,' and he is a man of strength. And so, he who can lift the weight which Wu Hwo lifted is just another Wu Hwo. Why should a man make a want of ability the subject of his grief? It is only that he will not do the thing.

"To walk slowly, keeping behind his elders, is to perform the part of a younger. To walk quickly and precede his elders, is to violate the duty of a younger brother. Now, is it what a man cannot do—to walk slowly? It is what he does not do. The course of Yao and Shun was simply that of filial piety and fraternal duty.

"Wear the clothes of Yao, repeat the words of Yao, and do the actions of Yao, and you will just be a Yao. And, if you wear the clothes of Chieh, repeat the words of Chieh, and do the actions of Chieh, you will just be a Chieh."*

Chiao said, "I shall be having an interview with the prince of Tsau, and can ask him to let me have a house to lodge in. I wish to remain here, and receive instruction at your gate."

Mencius replied, "The way of truth is like a great rod. It is not difficult to know it. The evil is only that men will not seek it. Do you go home and search for it, and you will have abundance of teachers."

6B4. Sung K'ang being about to go to Ch'u, Mencius met him in Shih-ch'iu.

'Master, where are you going?" asked Mencius.

K'ang replied, "I have heard that Ch'in and Ch'u are fighting together, and I am going to see the king of Ch'u and persuade him to cease hostilities. If he shall not be pleased with my advice, I shall go to see the king of Ch'in, and persuade him in the same way. Of the two kings I shall surely find that I can succeed with one of them."

Mencius said, "I will not venture to ask about the particulars, but I should like to hear the scope of your plan. What course will you take to try to persuade them?" K'ang answered, "I will tell them how unprofitable their course is to them." "Master," said Mencius, "your aim is great, but your argument is not good.

"If you, starting from the point of profit, offer your persuasive counsels to the kings of Ch'in and Ch'u, and if those kings are pleased with the consideration of profit so as to stop the movements of their armies, then all belonging to those armies will rejoice in the cessation of war, and find their pleasure in the pursuit of profit. Ministers will serve their sovereign for the profit of which they cherish the thought; sons will serve their fathers, and younger brothers will serve their elder brothers, from the same consideration:—and the issue will be, that, abandoning benevolence and righteousness, sovereign and minister, father and son, younger brother and elder, will carry on all their intercourse with this thought of profit cherished in their breasts. But never has there been such a state of society, without ruin being the result of it.

"If you, starting from the ground of benevolence and righteousness, offer your counsels to the kings of Ch'in and Ch'u, and if those kings are pleased with the consideration of benevolence and righteousness so as to stop the operations of their armies, then all belonging to those armies will rejoice in the stopping from war, and find their pleasure in benevolence and righteousness. Ministers will serve their sovereign, cherishing the

---

* Chieh (1802–1752 B.C.E.), legendary for evildoing, was the last ruler of the Hsia Dynasty (2183–1752 B.C.E.) —ED.

principles of benevolence and righteousness; sons will serve their fathers, and younger brothers will serve their elder brothers, in the same way:—and so, sovereign and minister, father and son, elder brother and younger, abandoning the thought of profit, will cherish the principles of benevolence and righteousness, and carry on all their intercourse upon them. But never has there been such a state of society, without the State where it prevailed rising to the royal sway. Why must you use that word 'profit.'"

Mencius said, "All things are already complete in us.

"There is no greater delight than to be conscious of sincerity on self-examination.

"If one acts with a vigorous effort at the law of reciprocity when he seeks for the realization of perfect virtue, nothing can be closer than his approximation to it."

7A5. Mencius said, "To act without understanding, and to do so habitually without examination, pursuing the proper path all the life without knowing its nature;—this is the way of multitudes."

7A6. Mencius said, "A man may not be without shame. When one is ashamed of having been without shame, he will afterwards not have occasion to be ashamed."

7A7. Mencius said, "The sense of shame is to a man of great importance.

"Those who form contrivances and versatile schemes distinguished for their artfulness, do not allow their sense of shame to come into action.

"When one differs from other men in not having this sense of shame, what will he have in common with them?"

7A15. Mencius said, "The ability possessed by men without having been acquired by learning is intuitive ability, and the knowledge possessed by them without the exercise of thought is their intuitive knowledge.

"Children carried in the arms all know to love their parents, and when they are grown a little, they all know to love their elder brothers.

"Filial affection, for parents, is the working of benevolence. Respect for elders is the working of righteousness. There is no other reason for those feelings;—they belong to all under heaven."

7A17. Mencius said, "Let a man not do what his own sense of righteousness tells him not to do, and let him not desire what his sense of righteousness tells him not to desire;—to act thus is all he has to do."

7A20. Mencius said, "The superior man has three things in which he delights, and to be ruler over the kingdom is not one of them.

"That his father and mother are both alive, and that the condition of his brothers affords no cause of anxiety;—this is one delight.

"That, when looking up, he has no occasion for shame before Heaven, and, below, he has no occasion to blush before men;—this is a second delight.

'That he can get from the whole kingdom the most talented individuals, and teach and nourish them;—this is the third delight.

"The superior man has three things in which he delights, and to be ruler over the kingdom is not one of them."

7A26. Mencius said, "The principle of the philosopher Yang was—'Each one for himself.' Though he might have benefitted the whole kingdom by plucking out a single hair, he would not have done it.

"The philosopher Mo loves all equally. If by rubbing smooth his whole body from the crown to the heel, he could have benefited the kingdom, he would have done it.

"Tsze-mo holds a medium between these. By holding that medium, he is nearer the right. But by holding it without leaving room for the exigency of circumstances, it becomes like their holding their one point.

"The reason why I hate that holding to one point is the injury it does to the way of right principle. It takes up one point and disregards a hundred others."

7A45. Mencius said, "In regard to inferior creatures, the superior man is kind to them, but not loving. In regard to people generally, he is loving to them, but not affectionate. He is affectionate to his parents, and lovingly disposed to people generally. He is lovingly disposed to people generally, and kind to creatures."

7B25. Hao-shang Pu-hai asked, saying, "What sort of man is Yo-chang?" Mencius replied, "He is a good man, a real man."

"What do you mean by 'A good man,' 'A real man?'"

The reply was, "A man who commands our liking is what is called a good man.

"He whose goodness is part of himself is what is called a real man.

"He whose goodness has been filled up is what is called a beautiful man.

"He whose completed goodness is brightly displayed is what is called a great man.

"When this great man exercises a transforming influence, he is what is called a sage.

"When the sage is beyond our knowledge, he is what is called a spirit-man.

"Yo-chang is between the two first characters, and below the four last."

7B31. Mencius said, "All men have some things which they cannot bear;—extend that feeling to what they can bear, and benevolence will be the result. All men have some things which they will not do;—extend that feeling to the things which they do, and righteousness will be the result.

"If a man can give full development to the feeling which makes him shrink from injuring others, his benevolence will be more than can be called into practice. If he can give full development to the feeling which refuses to break through, or jump over, a wall, his righteousness will be more than can be called into practice.

"If he can give full development to the real feeling of dislike with which he receives the salutation, 'Thou,' 'Thou,' he will act righteously in all places and circumstances.

"When a scholar speaks what he ought not to speak, by guile of speech seeking to gain some end; and when he does not speak what he ought to speak, by guile of silence seeking to gain some end;—both these cases are of a piece with breaking through a neighbour's wall."

7B32. Mencius said, "Words which are simple, while their meaning is far-reaching, are good words. Principles which, as held, are compendious, while their application is extensive, are good principles. The words of the superior man do not go below the girdle, but great principles are contained in them.

"The principle which the superior man holds is that of personal cultivation, but the kingdom is thereby tranquilized.

"The disease of men is this:—that they neglect their own fields, and go to weed the fields of others, and that what they require from others is great, while what they lay upon themselves is light."

7B34. Mencius said, "Those who give counsel to the great should despise them, and not look at their pomp and display.

"Halls several times eight cubits high, with beams projecting several cubits;—these, if my wishes were to be realized, I would not have. Food spread before me over ten cubits square, and attendants and concubines to the amount of hundreds;—these, though my wishes were realized, I would not have. Pleasure and wine, and the dash of hunting, with thousands of chariots following after me;—these though my wishes were realized, I would not have. What they esteem are what I would have nothing to do with; what I esteem are the rules of the ancients,—Why should I stand in awe of them?"

7B35. Mencius said, "To nourish the mind there is nothing better than to make the desires few. Here is a man whose desires are few;—in some things he may not be able to keep his heart, but they will be few."

LAO TZU

Lao Tzu (sixth century B.C.E.) founded Taoism. We know little about his life. A native of Ch'u, he apparently served as curator of the archive in the capital of Chou (Zhou). Legend has it that he was conceived by a shooting star and born sixty-two years later. Confucius visited him to ask about ceremonies, according to tradition, and Lao Tzu composed the *Tao-te Ching,* the *Classic of the Way and Its Virtue,* upon his retirement. Many scholars believe, however, that the book was compiled over perhaps two centuries by a variety of people. The book's title, literally "Way-virtue-classic," has been translated variously as *The Way of Life, The Book of Tao, The Book of the Way,* and *The Way and Its Power.*

Taoism opposes Confucianism in many respects. Confucius emphasizes traditional social rules, activity, and government; Lao Tzu stresses nonconformity, tranquillity, and individual transcendence. Confucius uses the term *Tao* (the Way) to refer to moral truth or proper moral conduct; Lao Tzu uses it to refer to the One, which underlies everything but admits no description. Lao Tzu speaks of the One as natural and eternal, but also as changing and spontaneous. Throughout the *Tao-te Ching,* however, he makes clear that language is inadequate to describe it. At most, language can suggest or evoke it.

The One also has moral force. It is the foundation for ethics applied to affairs of government as well as to individual action. The One, as embodied in a particular thing, is that thing's *te*—its power, force, character, or virtue. It is not only an active principle guiding the thing, but also a principle for what the thing ought to do and to be. The excellence of a thing thus stems from its *Tao.*

This twofold character of *te*—power and virtue or, in different terminology, guiding and regulating principle—leads to the distinctive ethical principles of Taoism. Lao Tzu advocates inaction. He recommends weakness, simplicity, and tranquility. It often seems as if he recommends passivity and laziness. But the inaction Lao Tzu advocates is one of letting nature take its course, of letting the guiding principles of things guide them without interference. The coincidence of guiding and regulating principles in *te* means that things naturally tend to their own state of excellence. Interference with this natural process prevents them from attaining excellence and is therefore bad. The individual should adopt a policy of noninterference.

Similarly, because we cannot describe the One, we should not seek enlightenment through language. Language, reason, reflection, and other forms of intellectual activity lead us away from the ultimate truth, from the recognition of the world's unity. Taoism is therefore an anti-intellectual doctrine. Ordinarily, we think in order to understand; we reflect to try to uncover answers to questions that arise in experience or that reason poses to us. In Lao Tzu's view, however, thinking leads us away from understanding. We understand most clearly when we set reason, language, and thinking aside. This aspect of Taoism had significant influence on some forms of Buddhism, in particular on Zen.

The policy of noninterference Lao Tzu recommends to individuals also applies to governments. Left alone, things tend toward their own excellences. Government action and regulation counter the natural tendency of things toward the moral good. For that reason, Lao Tzu advocates minimal government. "The less a leader does and says," he writes, "the happier his people."

from *Tao-te Ching*

1

Existence is beyond the power of words
To define:
Terms may be used
But are none of them absolute.
In the beginning of heaven and earth there were
    no words,
Words came out of the womb of matter;
And whether a man dispassionately
Sees to the core of life
Or passionately
Sees the surface,
The core and the surface
Are essentially the same,
Words making them seem different
Only to express appearance.
If name be needed, wonder names them both:
From wonder into wonder
Existence opens.

2

People through finding something beautiful
Think something else unbeautiful,
Through finding one man fit
Judge another unfit.
Life and death, though stemming from each other,
    seem to conflict as stages of change,
Difficult and easy as phases of achievement,
Long and short as measures of contrast,
High and low as degrees of relation;
But, since the varying of tones gives music to a
    voice
And what is is the was of what shall be,
The sanest man
Sets up no deed,
Lays down no law,
Takes everything that happens as it comes,

As something to animate, not to appropriate,
To earn, not to own,
To accept naturally without self-importance:
If you never assume importance
You never lose it.

3

It is better not to make merit a matter of reward
Lest people conspire and contend,
Not to pile up rich belongings
Lest they rob,
Not to excite by display
Lest they covet.
A sound leader's aim
Is to open people's hearts,
Fill their stomachs,
Calm their wills,
Brace their bones
And so to clarify their thoughts and cleanse their
    needs
That no cunning meddler could touch them:
Without being forced, without strain or constraint,
Good government comes of itself.

10

Can you hold the door of your tent
Wide to the firmament?
Can you, with the simple stature
Of a child, breathing nature,
Become, notwithstanding,
A man?
Can you continue befriending
With no prejudice, no ban?
Can you, mating with heaven,
Serve as the female part?
Can your learned head take leaven
From the wisdom of your heart?
If you can bear issue and nourish its growing,
If you can guide without claim or strife,
If you can stay in the lead of men without their
    knowing,
You are at the core of life.

16

Be utterly humble
And you shall hold to the foundation of peace.
Be at one with all these living things which,
    having arisen and flourished,
Return to the quiet whence they came,
Like a healthy growth of vegetation
Falling back upon the root.
Acceptance of this return to the root has been
    called 'quietism,'
Acceptance of quietism has been condemned as
    'fatalism.'
But fatalism is acceptance of destiny
And to accept destiny is to face life with open
    eyes,
Whereas not to accept destiny is to face death
    blindfold.
He who is open-eyed is open-minded,
He who is open-minded is open-hearted,
He who is open-hearted is kingly,
He who is kingly is godly,
He who is godly is useful,
He who is useful is infinite,
He who is infinite is immune,
He who is immune is immortal.

17

A leader is best
When people barely know that he exists,
Not so good when people obey and acclaim him,
Worst when they despise him.
'Fail to honor people,
They fail to honor you;'
But of a good leader, who talks little,
When his work is done, his aim fulfilled,
They will all say, 'We did this ourselves.'

18

When people lost sight of the way to live
Came codes of love and honesty,
Learning came, charity came,
Hypocrisy took charge;
When differences weakened family ties
Came benevolent fathers and dutiful sons;
And when lands were disrupted and misgoverned
Came ministers commended as loyal.

19

Rid of formalized wisdom and learning
People would be a hundredfold happier,
Rid of conventionalized duty and honor
People would find their families dear,
Rid of legalized profiteering
People would have no thieves to fear.
These methods of life have failed, all three,
Here is the way, it seems to me:
Set people free,
As deep in their hearts they would like to be,
From private greeds
And wanton needs.

20

Leave off fine learning! End the nuisance
Of saying yes to this and perhaps to that,
Distinctions with how little difference!
Categorical this, categorical that,
What slightest use are they!
If one man leads, another must follow,
How silly that is and how false!
Yet conventional men lead an easy life
With all their days feast-days,
A constant spring visit to the Tall Tower,
While I am a simpleton, a do-nothing,
Not big enough yet to raise a hand,
Not grown enough to smile,
A homeless, worthless waif.
Men of the world have a surplus of goods,
While I am left out, owning nothing.
What a booby I must be
Not to know my way round,
What a fool!
The average man is so crisp and so confident
That I ought to be miserable
Going on and on like the sea,
Drifting nowhere.
All these people are making their mark in the
    world,
While I, pig-headed, awkward,
Different from the rest,
Am only a glorious infant still nursing at the
    breast.

21

The surest test if a man be sane
Is if he accepts life whole, as it is,
Without needing by measure or touch to
    understand
The measureless untouchable source
Of its images,

The measureless untouchable source
Of its substances,
The source which, while it appears dark
    emptiness,
Brims with a quick force
Farthest away
And yet nearest at hand
From oldest time unto this day,
Charging its images with origin:
What more need I know of the origin
Than this?

29

Those who would take over the earth
And shape it to their will
Never, I notice, succeed.
The earth is like a vessel so sacred
That at the mere approach of the profane
It is marred
And when they reach out their finger it is gone.
For a time in the world some force themselves
    ahead
And some are left behind,
For a time in the world some make a great noise
And some are held silent,
For a time in the world some are puffed fat
And some are kept hungry,
For a time in the world some push abroad
And some are tipped out:
At no time in the world will a man who is sane
Over-reach himself,
Over-spend himself,
Over-rate himself.

36

He who feels punctured
Must once have been a bubble,
He who feels unarmed
Must have carried arms,
He who feels belittled
Must have been consequential,
He who feels deprived
Must have had privilege,
Whereas a man with insight
Knows that to keep under is to endure.
What happens to a fish pulled out of a pond?
Or to an implement of state pulled out of a
    scabbard?
Unseen, they survive.

37

The way to use life is to do nothing through
    acting,
The way to use life is to do everything through
    being.
When a leader knows this,
His land naturally goes straight.
And the world's passion to stray from
    straightness
Is checked at the core
By the simple unnamable cleanness
Through which men cease from coveting,
And to a land where men cease from coveting
Peace comes of course.

38

A man of sure fitness, without making a point of
    his fitness,
Stays fit;
A man of unsure fitness, assuming an appearance
    of fitness,
Becomes unfit.
The man of sure fitness never makes an act of it
Nor considers what it may profit him;
The man of unsure fitness makes an act of it
And considers what it may profit him.
However a man with a kind heart proceed,
He forgets what it may profit him;
However a man with a just mind proceed,
He remembers what it may profit him;
However a man of conventional conduct proceed,
    if he be not complied with
Out goes his fist to enforce compliance.
Here is what happens:
Losing the way of life, men rely first on their
    fitness;
Losing fitness, they turn to kindness;
Losing kindness, they turn to justness;
Losing justness, they turn to convention.
Conventions are fealty and honesty gone to waste,
They are the entrance of disorder.
False teachers of life use flowery words
And start nonsense.
The man of stamina stays with the root
Below the tapering,
Stays with the fruit
Beyond the flowering:
He has his no and he has his yes.

47

There is no need to run outside
For better seeing,
Nor to peer from a window. Rather abide
At the center of your being;
For the more you leave it, the less you learn.
Search your heart and see
If he is wise who takes each turn:
The way to do is to be.

49

A sound man's heart is not shut within itself
But is open to other people's hearts:
I find good people good,
And I find bad people good
If I am good enough;
I trust men of their word,
And I trust liars
If I am true enough;
I feel the heart-beats of others
Above my own
If I am enough of a father,
Enough of a son.

51

Existence having born them
And fitness bred them,
While matter varied their forms
And breath empowered them,
All created things render, to the existence and
    fitness they depend on,
An obedience
Not commanded but of course.
And since this is the way existence bears issue
And fitness raises, attends,
Shelters, feeds and protects,
Do you likewise:
Be parent, not possessor,
Attendant, not master,
Be concerned not with obedience but with
    benefit,
And you are at the core of living.

57

A realm is governed by ordinary acts,
A battle is governed by extraordinary acts;
The world is governed by no acts at all.
And how do I know?
This is how I know.

Act after act prohibits
Everything but poverty,
Weapon after weapon conquers
Everything but chaos,
Business after business provides
A craze of waste,
 Law after law breeds
A multitude of thieves.
Therefore a sensible man says:
If I keep from meddling with people, they take
    care of themselves,
If I keep from commanding people, they behave
    themselves,
If I keep from preaching at people, they improve
    themselves,
If I keep from imposing on people, they become
    themselves.

58

The less a leader does and says
The happier his people,
The more a leader struts and brags
The sorrier his people.
Often what appears to be unhappiness is
    happiness
And what appears to be happiness is
    unhappiness.
Who can see what leads to what
When happiness appears and yet is not,
When what should be is nothing but a mask
Disguising what should not be? Who can but ask
An end to such a stupid plot!
Therefore a sound man shall so square the circle
And circle the square as not to injure, not to
    impede:
The glow of his life shall not daze,
It shall lead.

63

Men knowing the way of life
Do without acting,
Effect without enforcing,
Taste without consuming;
'Through the many they find the few,
Through the humble the great;'
They 'respect their foes,'
They 'face the simple fact before it becomes
    involved.
Solve the small problem before it becomes big.'

The most involved fact in the world
Could have been faced when it was simple,
The biggest problem in the world
Could have been solved when it was small.
The simple fact that he finds no problem big
Is a sane man's prime achievement.

If you say yes too quickly
You may have to say no,
If you think things are done too easily
You may find them hard to do:
If you face trouble sanely
It cannot trouble you.

HSÜN TZU

Hsün Tzu (also known as Sun Tzu or Xunzi; 310?–212? B.C.E.) was born in Chao (Zhao), one of the states that gave the Warring States period its name. His was a time of intense regional conflict. Hsün Tzu was an extremely talented student, leaving home at fifteen to study at Chi Hsia (Jixia) academy, the intellectual center of ancient China. There he had the opportunity to present his ideas to Tian Wen, prime minister of Ch'i (Qi) and one of the most powerful officials in the country. Like Confucius, Mo Tzu, and Mencius, however, Hsün Tzu found that the government paid little heed to philosophers.

The combined armies of several states invaded Ch'i in 284 B.C.E., routing the army and scattering the scholars at Chi Hsia. Hsün Tzu fled to Ch'u, which in turn suffered a series of devastating military defeats; he returned to Ch'i around 275. While in Ch'u, however, Hsün Tzu became acquainted with the works of Mo Tzu and his followers. It is unclear what Hsün Tzu himself wrote, but on his return to Ch'i, he was recognized as the "most eminent elder scholar," even though he was only in his mid thirties. He returned to the Chi Hsia Academy and attracted students, including Han Fei and Li Ssi, who would become famous in their own right.

In his late forties, Hsün Tzu spent several years at the court of Ch'in (Qin), the most powerful of the warring states. Though he was able to have audiences with various Ch'in leaders, including the king, Hsün Tzu found his advice unheeded. He received no offer of a government post for putting his ideas into practice. But his experiences there did more than produce frustration; they led him to reconsider his entire philosophy. Hsün Tzu recognized that Ch'in, a wealthy but intellectually unsophisticated state that manifested none of the traditional Confucian virtues, nevertheless seemed both successful and well-ordered. It had attracted a series of exceptionally brilliant ministers by operating as a meritocracy, granting advancement without regard to social class to those who demonstrated skill and achieved success.

Ch'in, during Hsün Tzu's stay, carried on a war of expansion, winning victory after victory. Finally, in 260 B.C.E., it attacked his native Chao. Hsün Tzu decided to return to help resist the assault. Initially, matters appeared very grave for Chao: Its entire army surrendered, and all but a few were buried alive; the Ch'in forces laid siege to the Chao capital; the Chao king proved ineffectual. Hsün Tzu advised other Chao leaders on defense, writing several works on warfare in the process. By ignoring and sometimes disobeying the king, with the city near starvation, they managed a remarkable turnaround, defeating Ch'in in 257. Hsün Tzu's *The Art of War* is still read as a superb treatise of military strategy.

Hsün Tzu, a contemporary of Aristotle, adopts a naturalistic approach to philosophy. His ethical theory directly opposes that of Mencius. Confucius declares that all people are by nature alike but differ by training. Mencius amplifies this doctrine, claiming that everyone is by nature good. Hsün Tzu argues, in contrast, that people are originally evil. Human nature, he insists, is entirely bad; everything good is acquired by education, training, or socialization. By nature, we are selfish, combative, envious, lecherous, and hostile.

It is important to distinguish our natural dispositions from our natural capacities, Hsün Tzu believes. Prior to training or education, we are disposed to evil. We nevertheless have the capacity for good. We can nurture and develop that capacity, becoming good in spite of our natures. But this requires effort. Hsün Tzu thus opposes not only Mencius but Taoism. For Lao Tzu, things, including people, naturally tend toward the good. This implies an ethics of noninterference; we should let things follow their natural courses. For Hsün Tzu, in contrast, people naturally tend toward evil. This implies an ethics of active interference; people must be restrained from doing evil and taught to overcome their natural tendencies and become good.

This need for restraint, according to Hsün Tzu, justifies the existence of government. People have the capacity for good but naturally tend toward evil. They can become good only with the help of rules of proper conduct and government to make them obey the rules. Eventually, the good person obeys the rules willingly, not from fear of being punished. But people can reach that state only by the training the rules provide. Like Confucius, then, Hsün Tzu stresses the importance of *li*, propriety, the observance of social rules. Confucius, however, thinks of propriety as an individual virtue, an attitude or state of mind of respect for rules and traditions. Hsün Tzu thinks of propriety much more as an external virtue akin to obedience.

from *That the Nature Is Evil*

Reprinted from The Works of Mencius, *edited and translated by James Legge. From* The Chinese Classics, *Volume II (Oxford: Clarendon, 1895).*

The nature of man is evil; the good which it shows is factitious. There belongs to it, even at his birth, the love of gain, and as actions are in accordance with this, contentions and robberies grow up, and self-denial and yielding to others are not to be found; there belong to it envy and dislike, and as actions are in accordance with these, violence and injuries spring up, and self-devotedness and faith are not to be found; there belong to it the desires of the ears and the eyes, leading to the love of sounds and beauty, and as the actions are in accordance with these, lewdness and disorder spring up, and righteousness and propriety, with their various orderly displays, are not to be found. It thus appears, that to follow man's nature and yield obedience to its feelings will assuredly conduct to contentions and robberies, to the violation of the duties belonging to every one's lot, and the confounding of all distinctions, till the issue will be in a state of savagism; and that there must be the influence of teachers and laws, and the guidance of propriety and righteousness, from which will spring self-denial, yielding to others, and an observance of the well-ordered regulations of conduct, till the issue will be a state of good government.—From all this it is plain that the nature of man is evil; the good which it shows is factitious.

To illustrate.—A crooked stick must be submitted to the pressing-frame to soften and bend it, and then it becomes straight; a blunt knife must be submitted to the grindstone and whetstone, and then it becomes sharp; so, the nature of man, being evil, must be submitted to teachers and laws, and then it becomes correct; it must be submitted to propriety and righteousness, and then it comes under government. If men were without teachers and laws, their condition would be one of deflection and insecurity, entirely incorrect; if they were without propriety and righteousness, their condition would be one of rebellious disorder, rejecting all government. The sage kings of antiquity, understanding that the nature of man was thus evil, in a state of hazardous deflection, and incorrect, rebellious and disorderly, and refusing to be governed, set up the principles of righteousness and propriety, and framed laws and regulations to straighten and ornament the feelings of that nature and correct them, to tame and change those same feelings and guide them, so that they might all go forth in the way of moral government and in agreement with reason. Now, the man who is transformed by teachers and laws, gathers on himself the ornament of learning, and proceeds in the path of propriety and righteousness is a superior man; and he who gives the reins to his nature and its feelings, indulges its resentments, and walks contrary to propriety and righteousness is a mean man. Looking at the subject in this way, we see clearly that the nature of man is evil; the good which it shows is factitious.

Mencius said, "Man has only to learn, and his nature appears to be good;" but I reply,—It is not so. To say so shows that he had not attained to the knowledge of man's nature, nor examined into the difference between what is natural in man and what is factitious. The natural is what the constitution spontaneously moves to:—it needs not to be learned, it needs not to be followed hard after; propriety and righteousness are what the sages have given birth to:—it is by learning that men become capable of them, it is by hard practice that they achieve them. That which is in man, not needing to be learned and striven after, is what I call natural; that in man which is attained to by learning, and achieved by hard striving, is what I call factitious. This is the distinction between those two. By the nature of man, the eyes are capable of seeing, and the ears are capable of hearing. But the power of seeing is inseparable from the eyes, and the power of hearing is inseparable from the ears;—it is plain that the faculties of seeing and hearing do not need to be learned. Mencius says, "The nature of man is good, but all lose and ruin their nature, and therefore it becomes bad;" but I say that this representation is erroneous. Man being born with his nature, when he thereafter departs from its simple constituent elements, he must lose it. From this consideration we may see clearly that man's nature is evil. What might be called the nature's being good, would be if there were no departing from its simplicity to beautify it, no departing from its elementary dispositions to sharpen it. Suppose that those simple elements no more needed beautifying, and the mind's thoughts no more needed to be turned to good, than the power of vision which is inseparable from the eyes, and the power of hearing which is inseparable from the ears, need to be learned, then we might say that the nature is good, just as we say that the eyes see and the ears hear. It is the nature of man, when hungry, to desire to be filled; when cold, to desire to be warmed; when tired, to desire rest:—these are the feelings and nature of man. But now, a man is hungry, and in the presence of an elder he does not dare to eat before him:—he is yielding to that elder; he is tired with labour, and he does not dare to ask for rest:—he is working for some one. A son's yielding to his father and a younger brother to his elder, a son's labouring for his father and a younger brother for his elder:—these two instances of conduct are contrary to the nature and against the feelings; but they are according to the course laid down for a filial son, and to the refined distinction of propriety and righteousness. It appears that if there were an accordance with the feelings and the nature, there would be no self-denial and yielding to others. Self-denial and yielding to others are contrary to the feelings and the nature. In this way we come to see how clear it is that the nature of man is evil; the good which it shows is factitious.

An inquirer will ask, "If man's nature be evil, whence do propriety and righteousness arise?" I reply:—All propriety and righteousness are the artificial production of the sages, and are not to be considered as growing out of the nature of man. It is just as when a potter makes a vessel from the clay;—the

vessel is the product of the workman's art, and is not to be considered as growing out of his nature. Or it is as when another workman cuts and hews a vessel out of wood;—it is the product of his art, and is not to be considered as growing out of his nature. The sages pondered long in thought and gave themselves to practice, and so they succeeded in producing propriety and righteousness, and setting up laws and regulations. Thus it is that propriety and righteousness, laws and regulations, are the artificial product of the sages, and are not to be considered as growing properly from the nature of man.

If we speak of the fondness of the eyes for beauty, or of the mouth for pleasant flavours, or of the mind for gain, or of the bones and skin for the enjoyment of ease;—all these grow out of the natural feelings of man. The object is presented and the desire is felt; there needs no effort to produce it. But when the object is presented, and the affection does not move till after hard effort, I say that this effect is factitious. Those cases prove the difference between what is produced by nature and what is produced by art.

Thus the sages transformed their nature, and commenced their artificial work. Having commenced this work with their nature, they produced propriety and righteousness. When propriety and righteousness were produced, they proceeded to frame laws and regulations. It appears, therefore, that propriety and righteousness, laws and regulations, are given birth to by the sages. Wherein they agree with all other men and do not differ from them, is their nature; wherein they differ from and exceed other men, is this artificial work.

Now to love gain and desire to get;—this is the natural feeling of men. Suppose the case that there is an amount of property or money to be divided among brothers, and let this natural feeling to love gain and to desire to get come into play;—why, then the brothers will be opposing, and snatching from, one another. But where the changing influence of propriety and righteousness, with their refined distinctions, has taken effect, a man will give up to any other man. Thus it is that if they act in accordance with their natural feelings, brothers will quarrel together; and if they have come under the transforming influence of propriety and righteousness, men will give up to the other men, to say nothing of brothers. Again, the fact that men wish to do what is good, is because their nature is bad. The thin wishes to be thick; the ugly wish to be beautiful; the narrow wishes to be wide; the poor wish to be rich; the mean wish to be noble:—when anything is not possessed in one's self, he seeks for it outside himself. But the rich do not wish for wealth; the noble do not wish for position:—when anything is possessed by one's self, he does not need to go beyond himself for it. When we look at things in this way, we perceive that the fact of men's wishing to do what is good is because their nature is evil. It is the case indeed, that man's nature is without propriety and benevolence:—he therefore studies them with vigorous effort and seeks to have them. It is the case that by nature he does not know propriety and righteousness:—he therefore thinks and reflects and seeks to know them. Speaking of man, therefore, as he is by birth simply, he is without propriety and righteousness, without the knowledge of propriety and righteousness. Without propriety and righteousness, man must be all confusion and disorder; without the knowledge of propriety and rightousness, there must ensue all the manifestations of disorder. Man, as he is born, therefore, has in him nothing but the elements of disorder, passive and active. It is plain from this view of the subject that the nature of man is evil; the good which it shows is factitious.

When Mencius says that "Man's nature is good," I affirm that it is not so. In ancient times and now, throughout the kingdom, what is meant by good is a condition of correctness, regulation, and happy government; and what is meant by evil, is a condition of deflection, insecurity, and refusing to be under government:—in this lies the distinction between being good and being evil. And now, if man's nature be really so correct, regulated, and happily governed in itself, where would be the use for sage kings? Where would be the use for propriety and righteousness? Although there were the sage kings, propriety, and righteousness, what could they add to the nature so correct, regulated, and happily ruled in itself? But it is not so; the nature of man is bad. It was on this account, that anciently the sage kings, understanding that man's nature was bad, in a state of deflection and insecurity, instead of being correct; in a state of rebellious disorder, instead of one of happy rule, set up therefore the majesty of princes and governors to awe it; and set forth propri-

ety and righteousness to change it; and framed laws and statutes of correctness to rule it; and devised severe punishments to restrain it: so that its outgoings might be under the dominion of rule, and in accordance with what is good. This is the true account of the governance of the sage kings, and the transforming power of propriety and righteousness. Let us suppose a state of things in which there shall be no majesty of rulers and governors, no influence of propriety and righteousness, no rule of laws and statutes, no restraints of punishment:—what would be the relations of men with one another, all under heaven? The strong would be injuring the weak, and spoiling them; the many would be tyrannizing over the few, and hooting them; a universal disorder and mutual destruction would speedily ensue. When we look at the subject in this way, we see clearly that the nature of man is evil; the good which it shows is factitious. . . .

An inquirer may say again, "Propriety and righteousness, though seen in an accumulation of factitious deeds, do yet belong to the nature of man; and thus it was that the sages were able to produce them." I reply:—It is not so. A potter takes a piece of clay, and produces an earthen dish from it; but are that dish and clay the nature of the potter? A carpenter plies his tools upon a piece of wood, and produces a vessel; but are that vessel and wood the nature of the carpenter? So it is with the sages and propriety and righteousness; they produced them, just as the potter works with the clay. It is plain that there is no reason for saying that propriety and righteousness, and the accumulation of their factitious actions, belong to the proper nature of man. Speaking of the nature of man, it is the same in all,—the same in Yao and Shun and in Chieh and the robber Chih, the same in the superior man and in the mean man. If you say that propriety and righteousness, with the factitious actions accumulated from them, are the nature of man, on what ground do you proceed to ennoble Yao and Yü,* to ennoble generally the superior man? The ground on which we ennoble Yao, Yü, and the superior man, is their ability to

---

* Yü, founder of the Hsia dynasty, ruled from 2183–2175 B.C.E Like Yao, Shun, and Duke Chou, Yü was legendary as an ideal ruler and sage. He was known for his great practical achievements in flood control as well as for his great moral character. —ED.

change the nature, and to produce factitious conduct. That factitious conduct being produced, out of it there are brought propriety and righteousness. The sages stand indeed in the same relation to propriety and righteousness, and the factitious conduct resulting from them, as the potter does to his clay:—we have a product in either case. This representation makes it clear that propriety and righteousness, with their factitious results, do not properly belong to the nature of man. On the other hand, that which we consider mean in Chieh, the robber Chih, and the mean man generally, is that they follow their nature, act in accordance with its feelings, and indulge its resentments, till all its outgoings are a greed of gain, contentions, and rapine.—It is plain that the nature of man is bad, the good which it shows is factitious.

Heaven did not make favourites of Tsang Shan, Min Tsze-ch'ien, and Hsiao-chi, and deal unkindly with the rest of men. How then was it that they alone were distinguished by the greatness of their filial deeds, that all which the name of filial piety implies was complete in them? The reason was that they were entirely subject to the restraints of propriety and righteousness.

Heaven did not make favourites of the people of Ch'i and Lu, and deal unkindly with the people of Ch'in. How then was it that the latter were not equal to the former in the rich manifestation of the filial piety belonging to the righteousness of the relation between father and son, and the respectful observance of the proprieties belonging to the separate functions of husband and wife? The reason was that the people of Ch'in followed the feelings of their nature, indulged its resentments, and contemned propriety and righteousness. We are not to suppose that they were different in their nature.

What is the meaning of the saying, that "Any traveller on the road may become like Yü?" I answer:—All that made Yü what he was, was his practice of benevolence, righteousness, and his observance of laws and rectitude. But benevolence, righteousness, laws, and rectitude are all capable of being known and being practised. Moreover, any traveller on the road has the capacity of knowing these, and the ability to practise them:—it is plain that he may become like Yü. If you say that benevolence, righteousness, laws, and rectitude are not capable of being known

and practised, then Yü himself could not have known, could not have practised them. If you will have it that any traveller on the road is really without the capacity of knowing these things, and the ability to practise them, then, in his home, it will not be competent for him to know the righteousness that should rule between father and son, and, abroad, it will not be competent for him to know the rectitude that should rule between sovereign and minister. But it is not so. There is no one who travels along the road, but may know both that righteousness and that rectitude:—it is plain that the capacity to know and the ability to practise belong to every traveller on the way. Let him, therefore, with his capacity of knowing and ability to practise, take his ground on the knowableness and practicableness of benevolence and righteousness;—and it is clear that he may become like Yü. Yea, let any traveller on the way addict himself to the art of learning with all his heart and the entire bent of his will, thinking, searching, and closely examining;—let him do this day after day, through a long space of time, accumulating what is good, and he will penetrate as far as a spiritual Intelligence, he will become a ternion with Heaven and Earth. It follows that the characters of the sages were what any man may reach by accumulation.

It may be said:—"To be sage may thus be reached by accumulation;—why is it that all men cannot accumulate to this extent?" I reply:—They may do so, but they cannot be made to do so. The mean man might become a superior man, but he is not willing to be a superior man. The superior man might become a mean man, but he is not willing to be a mean man. It is not that the mean man and the superior man may not become the one the other; their not becoming the one the other is because it is a thing which may be, but cannot be made to be. Any traveller on the road may become like Yü:—the case is so; that any traveller on the road can really become like Yü:—this is not a necessary conclusion. Though any one, however, cannot really become like Yü, that is not contrary at all to the truth that he may become so. One's feet might travel all over the world, but there never was one who was really able to travel all over the world. There is nothing to prevent the mechanic, the farmer, and the merchant from practising each the business of the others, but there has never been a case when it has really been done. Looking at the subject in this way, we see that what may be need not really be; and although it shall not really be, that is not contrary to the truth that it might be. It thus appears that the difference is wide between what is really done or not really done, and what may be or may not be. It is plain that these two cases may not become the one the other.

Yao asked Shun what was the character of the feelings proper to man. Shun replied, "The feelings proper to man are very unlovely; why need you ask about them? When a man has got a wife and children, his filial piety withers away; under the influence of lust and gratified desires, his good faith to his friends withers away; when he is full of dignities and emoluments, his loyalty to his sovereign withers away. The natural feelings of man! The natural feelings of man! They are very unlovely. Why need you ask about them? It is only in the case of men of the highest worth that it is not so."

There is a knowledge characteristic of the sage; a knowledge characteristic of the scholar and superior man; a knowledge characteristic of the mean man; and a knowledge characteristic of the mere servant. In much speech to show his cultivation and maintain consistency, and though he may discuss for a whole day the reasons of a subject, to have a unity pervading the ten thousand changes of discourse:— this is the knowledge of the sage. To speak seldom, and in a brief and sparing manner, and to be orderly in his reasoning, as if its parts were connected with a string:—this is the knowledge of the scholar and superior man. Flattering words and disorderly conduct, with undertakings often followed by regrets:— these mark the knowledge of the mean man. Hasty, officious, smart, and swift, but without consistency; versatile, able, of extensive capabilities, but without use; decisive in discourse, rapid, exact, but the subject unimportant; regardless of right and wrong, taking no account of crooked and straight, to get the victory over others the guiding object:—this is the knowledge of the mere servant.

There is bravery of the highest order; bravery of the middle order; bravery of the lowest order. Boldly to take up his position in the place of the universally acknowledged Mean; boldly to carry into practice his views of the doctrines of the ancient kings; in a high situation, not to defer to a bad sovereign, and in a low situation not to follow the current of a bad people; to consider that there is no poverty where there is virtue, and no wealth or honour where virtue is not; when appreciated by the world, to desire to share in all men's joys and sorrows; when unknown by the world, to stand up grandly alone between heaven and earth, and have no fears:—this is the bravery of the highest order. To be reverently observant of propriety, and sober-minded; to attach importance to adherence to fidelity, and set little store by material wealth; to have the boldness to push forward men of worth and exalt them, to hold back undeserving men, and get them deposed:—this is the bravery of the middle order. To be devoid of self-respect and set a great value on wealth; to feel complacent in calamity, and always have plenty to say for himself; saving himself in any way, without regard to right and wrong; whatever be the real state of a case, making it his object to get the victory over others:—this is the bravery of the lowest order.

The *fan-zao* and the *chü-shu* were the best bows of antiquity; but without their regulators, they could not adjust themselves. The *tsung* of duke Hwan, the *chueh* of T'âi-kung, the *lu* of king Wǎn, the *hu* of prince Chwang, the *kan-tsiang, mo-ye, chü-chüeh* and *p'i-lü* of Ho-lü—these were the best swords of antiquity; but without the grindstone and whetstone they would not have been sharp; without the strength of the arms that wielded them they would not have cut anything.

The *hwa-liu*, the *li-ch'i*, the *hsien-li*, and the *lü-r*— these were the best horses of antiquity; but there were still necessary for them the restraints in front of bit and bridle, the stimulants behind of whip and cane, and the skillful driving of a Tsao-fu, and then they could accomplish a thousand lî* in one day.

So it is with man:—granted to him an excellent capacity of nature and the faculty of intellect, he must still seek for good teachers under whom to place himself, and make choice of friends with whom he may be intimate. Having got good masters and placed himself under them, what he will hear will be the doctrines of Yao, Shun, Yü, and T'ang; having got good friends and become intimate with them, what he will see will be deeds of self-conse-

* A measure of distance; not to be confused with li (propriety). —Ed.

cration, fidelity, reverence, and complaisance:—he will go on from day to day to benevolence and righteousness, without being conscious of it: a natural following of them will make him do so. On the other hand, if he lives with bad men, what he will hear will be the language of deceit, calumny, imposture, and hypocrisy; what he will see will be conduct of filthiness, insolence, lewdness, corruptness, and greed:—he will be going on from day to day to punishment and disgrace, without being conscious of it; a natural following of them will make him do so.

The Record says, "If you do not know your son, look at his friends; if you do not know your prince, look at his confidants." All is the influence of association! All is the influence of association!

from *On the Rules of Proper Conduct*

Reprinted from The Works of Hsüntze, *translated from the Chinese by Homer H. Dubs (London: Arthur Probsthain, 1928).*

Whence do the rules of proper conduct (*Li*) arise? Man by birth has desire. When desire is not satisfied, then he cannot be without a seeking for satisfaction. When this seeking for satisfaction is without measure or of limits, then there cannot but be contention. When there is contention, there will be disorder; when there is disorder, then there will be poverty. The former Kings hated this confusion hence they established the rules of proper conduct (*Li*) and justice (*Yi*) in order to set limits to this confusion, to educate, and nourish men's desires, to give opportunity for this seeking for satisfaction, in order that desire should never be extinguished by things, nor should things be used up by desire; that these two should support each other and should continue to exist. This is whence the rules of proper conduct (*Li*) arise.

Thus the rules of proper conduct (*Li*) are to educate and nourish. . . . When the superior man has gotten its education and nourishment, he also esteems its distinctions.

What are meant by its distinctions? There are the classes of the noble and the base; there are the inequalities of the senior and the younger; there is what is appropriate to those who are poor and those who are rich, to those who are unimportant and those who are important. Hence the imperial chariot has a fine rush mat wherewith to take care of the emperor's body; by his side is carried a fragrant flower wherewith to take care of his sense of smell; in front it has ornamented yokes to care for his sense of sight; the harmonious sound of little bells, when going slow the Wu and Hsiang, when going fast the Shao and Hu are to care for his sense of hearing; the dragon flag with nine scallops on the lower border

to refresh his spirits; a sleeping rhinoceros, a male tiger, alligator adorned harness, a silken canopy, dragon yoke-ends, to care for his majesty. Hence the horses of the imperial chariot must be very trustworthy and well trained, and then only driven—thus caring for his safety. He has very capable braves, willing to die, who have agreed to be temperate, in order to care for his life. Very prudent men expend his money and use it in order to care for his wealth. He has very sagacious men who are respectful and courteous in order to preserve his calmness. He has very discreet men who observe the rules of proper conduct (*Li*), justice (*Yi*), and all principles of refinement, in order to care for his emotions. Hence if it appears that a man is only seeking for a livelihood, he shall certainly die. If it appears that he is only seeking gain, he shall certainly meet with injury. If he is a lazy careless scholar, seeking only a quiet life, he shall certainly be in danger. If he thinks that emotional pleasure is joy, he shall certainly be destroyed. For if a man concentrates on the rules of proper conduct (*Li*) and justice (*Yi*), then he will gain both; if he concentrates on satisfying the emotional nature, then he will lose both. Hence the Confucian doctrine causes men to gain both; the Mician doctrine* causes men to lose both—this is the difference between Confucian and Mician doctrines.

The rules of proper conduct (*Li*) are the greatest thing in government and in making social distinctions; they are the foundation of strength and security: they are the way (*Tao*) of being majestic: they are the focus of honour. Kings and dukes gained the empire by following them. By not following them, they lost their territory. Hence strong armour and trained armies were insufficient to gain virtue; high city walls and deep moats were insufficient to make those rules feared. If they followed this principle

*Doctrine of Mo Tzu —Ed.

(Tao) they were successful; if they did not follow this principle (Tao), then they failed. . . .

All rites and rules of proper conduct (*Li*) begin in accumulating rules; they are perfected in becoming beautiful and in producing joy. Hence when they have reached perfection, men's emotions and sense of beauty are both fully expressed. The rite is of the second degree when either the emotion or the sense of beauty overcomes the other. It is of the lowest degree when it reverts to the state of emotion and returns to its primitive state.

Li is that whereby Heaven and Earth unite, whereby the sun and moon are bright, whereby the four seasons are ordered, whereby the stars move in the courses, whereby rivers flow, whereby all things prosper, whereby love and hatred are tempered, whereby joy and anger keep their proper place. It causes the lower orders to obey, and the upper orders to be illustrious; through a myriad changes it prevents going astray. But if one departs from it, he will be destroyed. Is not *Li* the greatest of all principles? When it is established grandly, it becomes the centre of all, and the whole world will not be able to subtract from or add to it. Its source and aim accord with one another. Its end and beginning reach each other. It is most beautiful, but preserves the distinctions. It can be most closely scrutinized, and will be found to be explicable. When the country follows it, there is good government and prosperity; when it is not followed there is anarchy and calamity. He who follows it is safe; he who does not follow it is in danger. He who follows it will be preserved; he who does not follow it will be destroyed. The small-minded man cannot fathom this.

The principle of *Li* is truly deep; if the discussions of "hardness and whiteness" or "likeness and unlikeness" enter, they are submerged. Its principle is truly great; if unauthorizedly made laws or depraved doctrines enter, they are destroyed. Its principle is truly high; if tyrannous, remiss, insolent people who despise the common people and think they are exalted, enter, they fall. For when the plumb-line is truly laid out, one cannot be deceived as to whether a thing is crooked or straight; when the balances are truly suspended, one cannot be cheated in weight; when the compass and square are truly applied, a person cannot be cheated as to squareness or roundness; when the superior man has investigated into *Li,* he cannot be cheated as to what is false. For the plumb-line is the extreme of straightness; the balances the extreme of equableness; the compass and square are the extreme of squareness and roundness: the rules of proper conduct (*Li*) are the utmost of human morality (*Tao*). Moreover those who do not follow the rules of proper conduct (*Li*) neither are satisfied with it, are people without a direction in life; they who follow the rules of proper conduct (*Li*) and are satisfied with it are gentlemen who have a direction to their life. To be able to meditate deeply in the rules of proper conduct (*Li*) is to be able to reflect; to be able to keep from deviating from the rules of proper conduct (*Li*) is to have the power to be firm. He who is able to think deeply and to be firm and adds to that a love of *Li*, is a Sage. For as heaven is the utmost in height, the earth is the utmost in depth, the boundless is the utmost in breadth, so the Sage is the utmost in morality (*Tao*). Hence the student who resolutely studies *Li* becomes a Sage; without especially studying it, he is a person without direction.

HAN FEI TZU

Han Fei Tzu (280?–233 B.C.E.) was an aristocrat in Han, in northwest China, during the last days of the Warring States period. He studied under Hsün Tzu and developed a doctrine known as *legalism*. The ruler of Ch'in, where Hsün Tzu long resided, admired Han Fei Tzu's work; he put legalist ideas into practice and invited Han Fei Tzu to the Ch'in court. The doctrines proved very successful; the ruler was able, with their help, to unify China, bringing the Warring States period to an end. Han Fei Tzu, however, was not so fortunate. Li Ssu, another official of Ch'in and student of Hsün Tzu, became jealous of Han Fei Tzu's success and forced him to commit suicide.

Han Fei Tzu is to Chinese thought as Machiavelli is to Western philosophy. He accepts only one teaching of Hsün Tzu: that human nature is evil. Everyone, according to Han Fei Tzu, is essentially selfish. People act morally only under the threat of punishment or the hope of rewards. The task of government, therefore, is to fashion a system of rewards and punishments that induce people to act properly. This might seem to imply that Han Fei Tzu has an independent account of what it is to act properly. But he does not. The only good that is rational for the ruler to seek is his or her own. Therefore, the ruler should establish laws—very strict laws, in Han Fei Tzu's opinion—that will lead people to act in the best interests of the ruler.

Legalism thus opposes Confucianism and Moism at every turn. Confucius advocates a theory of virtue; Mo Tzu advocates a variety of utilitarianism. For both, the questions of what is and what ought to be are entirely independent. Legalists, however, stress power and control. Confucians and Moists define the good government as one conducive to good moral character and action; legalists define good behavior and character as those which promote the interests of the government.

Han Fei Tzu's theory has several important consequences. First, there is no limit, in principle, to the power of government or to its use of force. Legalism, the very opposite of Taoism in this respect, seems to justify repression, militarism, and even ruthlessness. Second, there may nevertheless be factual limits on what government ought to do. Government interference in economic affairs, Han Fei Tzu thinks, is counterproductive; people produce more and thus enhance the power of the state if left alone. The market incorporates rewards and punishments that encourage production and other socially useful behaviors. Finally, there must be equality before the law. The ruler serves his or her own interests best, not by the exercise of arbitrary power, but by applying laws strictly and uniformly. If anyone is above the law, people's respect for the law will suffer. And this works against the interests of the ruler. Han Fei Tzu thus adopts elements of Hsün Tzu's justification for government and rules. Hsün Tzu's concern, however, is promotion of the good, while Han Fei Tzu's concern is simply promotion of power.

from *On Having Standards*

Reprinted from Basic Writings of Mo Tzu, Hsün Tzu, and Han Fei Tzu, *translated by Burton Watson. Copyright © 1967 by Columbia University Press.*

In our present age he who can put an end to private scheming and make men uphold the public law will see his people secure and his state well ordered; he who can block selfish pursuits and enforce the public law will see his armies growing stronger and his enemies weakening. Find men who have a clear understanding of what is beneficial to the nation and a feeling for the system of laws and regulations, and place them in charge of the lesser officials; then the ruler can never be deceived by lies and falsehoods. Find men who have a clear understanding of what is beneficial to the nation and the judgment to weigh issues properly, and put them in charge of foreign affairs; then the ruler can never be deceived in his relations with the other powers of the world.

Now if able men are selected for promotion on the basis of reputation alone, then the officials will disregard the ruler and seek only the good will of their associates and subordinates. If appointments to office are controlled by cliques, then men will work only to establish profitable connections and will not try to achieve office by regular routes. In such cases, official posts will never be filled by able men, and the state will fall into disorder. If rewards are handed out on the basis of good report alone, and punishments on the basis of slander, then men who covet rewards and fear punishment will abandon the public interest and pursue only private schemes, banding together to further each other's interests. If men forget who their sovereign is and enter into association with foreign powers in order to further the interests of their own group, then subordinates will be of little aid to their superiors. If the groups are large and their allies numerous, so that a single clique embraces men both inside and outside the state, then, though its members commit a glaring fault, they will find plentiful means to conceal it. As a result, truly loyal ministers will face peril and death even though they are guilty of no fault; while evil ministers will enjoy safety and profit which they have done nothing to deserve. If loyal ministers, though guiltless, still face peril and death, then good officials will go into hiding; and if evil ministers, though without merit, enjoy safety and profit, then corrupt officials will come to the fore. This is the beginning of downfall.

In such cases, the officials will turn their backs on law, seeking only to establish weighty personal connections and making light of public duty. Numbers of them will flock to the gates of powerful men, but none will appear in the ruler's court. They will lay a hundred plans for the advancement of private family interests, but give not one thought to how the ruler should order his state. Thus, although there are plenty of men attached to the administration, they will not be the kind who will honor their ruler; though all the official posts are filled, none who fill them will be the kind who can be entrusted with affairs of state. So, although the sovereign holds the title of ruler of men, he will in fact be a pawn of the ministerial families.

Therefore I say: There are no men in the court of a doomed state. When I say there are no men, I do not mean that the actual number of men at court is any less than usual. But the powerful families seek only to benefit each other and not to enrich the state; the high ministers seek only to honor each other and not to honor their sovereign; and the petty officials cling to their stipends and work to make influential friends instead of attending to their duties. And the reason such a state of affairs has come about is that the ruler does not make important decisions on the basis of law, but puts faith in whatever his subordinates do.

A truly enlightened ruler uses the law to select men for him; he does not choose them himself. He uses the law to weigh their merits; he does not attempt to judge them for himself. Hence men of true worth will not be able to hide their talents, nor spoilers to gloss over their faults. Men cannot advance on the basis of praise alone, nor be driven from court by calumny. Then there will be a clear understanding of values between the ruler and his ministers, and the state can be easily governed. But only if the ruler makes use of law can he hope to achieve this.

When a man of true worth becomes a minister, he faces north before the sovereign, presents tokens of his allegiance, and banishes from his mind the thought of all other loyalties. If he serves at court, he does not venture to excuse himself because of the lowliness of the post assigned him; if he serves in the army, he does not dare to shirk danger. He follows the lead of his superiors and obeys the laws of his sovereign; with empty mind he awaits orders and does not question whether they are right or wrong. Thus, though he has a mouth, he never uses it to speak for private advantage; though he has eyes, he never employs them to spy private gain; in all things he is under the control of his superior. A minister may be compared to a hand, which reaches up to serve the head or reaches down to tend the foot; its duty is to relieve the body from heat or cold and, when swords threaten, it dare not fail to strike out at them. For his part, the ruler must never make selfish use of his wise ministers or able men. So the people are never tempted to go beyond their communities to form friendships, nor need they worry about what happens a hundred *li** away. Honorable and humble do not get in each other's way, and stupid and wise find their proper place. This is the perfection of good government.

Men who are contemptuous of ranks and stipends, quick to discard their posts and abandon the state in search of another sovereign, I would not call upright. Those who propound false doctrines and controvert the law, who defy their sovereign or oppose him with strong censure, I would not call loyal. Those who practice charity and dole out benefits in order to win over their subordinates and make a name for themselves, I would not call benevolent. Those who withdraw from the world,

live in retirement, and employ their wits to spread false slander against their superiors, I would not call righteous. Those who devote all their time to establishing favorable relations with the princes of other states, impoverishing their own state in the process, and who, when they see the moment of crisis approaching, attempt to intimidate their sovereign by saying, "Only through me can friendly relations be established with So-and-so; only through me can So-and-so's anger be appeased!", until the ruler comes to believe in them and entrusts all state affairs to their decision; who lower the name of the ruler in order to enhance their own eminence, who raid the resources of the state in order to benefit their own families—such men I would not call wise.

Deeds such as these prevail in a dangerous age, but were precluded by the laws of the former kings. The law of the former kings says, "Ministers shall not wield the instruments of authority nor dispense benefits, but follow the commands of the king; none shall do evil, but uphold the king's path." In antiquity the people of a well-ordered age upheld the public law and renounced private schemes, concentrated their attention upon one goal and their actions upon one object, and together awaited the charge that was laid upon them.

If the ruler of men tries to keep a personal check on all the various offices of his government, he will find the day too short and his energies insufficient. Moreover if the ruler uses his eyes, his subordinates will try to prettify what he sees; if he uses his ears, they will try to embellish what he hears; and if he uses his mind, they will be at him with endless speeches. The former kings, knowing that these three faculties would not suffice, accordingly set aside their own abilities; instead they relied upon law and policy, and took care to see that rewards and punishments were correctly apportioned. Since they held fast to the essential point, their legal codes were simple and yet inviolable, and alone they exercised control over all within the four seas. Even the cleverest men could find no opening for their falsehoods, the glibbest talkers no audience for their sophistries, and evil and deceit were left without a foothold. Though a thousand miles from the ruler's side, men did not dare say anything different from what they had said in his presence; though courtiers in the palace, they did not dare to conceal good or

---

* Here, a measure of distance. —ED.

gloss over evil. Courtiers and officials flocked to the service of their sovereign, each diligently attending to his own duties, and none dared overstep his position. Affairs of government were not pressing and time was left to spare. The way in which the ruler relied upon his position made it so.

The process by which ministers invade the rights of their sovereign is as gradual as the shifting of the contours of the landscape. Little by little they cause him to lose his sense of direction, until he is facing east where before he faced west, and yet he is unaware of the change. Hence the former kings set up south-pointing markers to determine the direction of sunrise and sunset. In the same way, an enlightened ruler will make certain that the ambitions of his ministers do not roam beyond the bounds of the law, and that they do not go about dispensing favors even though such acts may be within the law. They are permitted to make no move that is not in accord with law. Laws are the means of prohibiting error and ruling out selfish motives; strict penalties are the means of enforcing orders and disciplining inferiors. Authority should never reside in two places; the power of decree should never be open to joint use. If authority and power are shared with others, then all manner of abuse will become rife. If law does not command respect, then all the ruler's actions will be endangered. If penalties are not enforced, then evil will never be surmounted.

Though a skilled carpenter is capable of judging a straight line with his eye alone, he will always take his measurements with a rule; though a man of superior wisdom is capable of handling affairs by native wit alone, he will always look to the laws of the former kings for guidance. Stretch the plumb line, and crooked wood can be planed straight; apply the level, and bumps and hollows can be shaved away; balance the scales, and heavy and light can be adjusted; get out the measuring jars, and discrepancies of quantity can be corrected. In the same way one should use laws to govern the state, disposing of all matters on their basis alone.

The law no more makes exceptions of men of high station than the plumb line bends to accommodate a crooked place in the wood. What the law has decreed the wise man cannot dispute nor the brave man venture to contest. When faults are to be punished, the highest minister cannot escape; when good is to be rewarded, the lowest peasant must not be passed over. Hence, for correcting the faults of superiors, chastising the misdeeds of subordinates, restoring order, exposing error, checking excess, remedying evil, and unifying the standards of the people, nothing can compare to law. For putting fear into the officials, awing the people, wiping out wantonness and sloth, and preventing lies and deception, nothing can compare to penalties. If penalties are heavy, men dare not use high position to abuse the humble; if laws are clearly defined, superiors will be honored and their rights will not be invaded. If they are honored and their rights are inviolable, then the ruler will be strong and will hold fast to what is essential. Hence the former kings held laws in high esteem and handed them down to posterity. Were the ruler of men to discard law and follow his private whim, then all distinction between high and low would cease to exist.

CHU HSI

Chu Hsi (Zhu Xi: 1130–1200) was the most influential neo-Confucian and probably the most influential Chinese philosopher of any school during the past two millennia. Born in Fukien (Fujian) he studied under his father, who was head of several departments in the government. Invaders from the north imposed humiliating peace terms on Fukien, the acceptance of which Chu Hsi strongly opposed. He left the capital, becoming a keeper of records. He spent most of his life as a temple guardian, spending his ample free time studying and writing.

Chu Hsi declined many official posts but at age forty-nine did accept appointment as a prefect. Three years later, he was demoted for criticizing his fellow officials as incompetent. At age fifty-eight, he again accepted a post, this time as vice minister of the department of the army, but was demoted shortly thereafter. During the next few years, Chu Hsi held several positions, all very briefly, and evidently made many enemies; at sixty-six he was accused of ten crimes and removed from all his posts. Some of his enemies even demanded his execution. Despite his almost constant conflicts with others, his writings had gained him considerable fame. When he died four years later, nearly a thousand people attended his funeral.

Chu Hsi's relation to Confucius is in many ways like that of Thomas Aquinas to Aristotle. Chu Hsi synthesized various elements of Confucianism, bringing the theory to a very high state of development. He standardized *The Analects, The Great Learning, The Doctrine of the Mean,* and *The Book of Mencius* as the Four Books, the classics at the heart of Confucianism which served as the basis of civil service examinations in China for almost six hundred years.

The most important aspects of Chu Hsi's thought are metaphysical and epistemological, not ethical. But Chu Hsi does develop interesting views on ethics and political philosophy that go substantially beyond earlier Confucian doctrines. Chu Hsi's chief concept is that of the Great Ultimate, which in some ways is similar to the One in Taoism. It is one, eternal, and in everything. Taoism treats the One, in a particular thing, as both its power and its virtue—as both guiding and regulating principle. Chu Hsi separates these two. Embodied in a thing, the Great Ultimate involves both principle (*li*) and material force (*ch'i*). Principle is incorporeal, eternal, and unchanging; it constitutes the essence of things. It is purely good. Material force is corporeal, transitory, and changeable. It constitutes the substance of things, acts as an agent of change, and may be either good or evil.

Each of us, according to Chu Hsi, has a moral mind that is pure principle and drives us toward the good. But we also have desires, physical dispositions, and capacities that mix principle with material force. Desires and physical dispositions are not necessarily bad; they may be either good or evil. Their presence in human nature, however, makes evil possible. And indulging them is the greatest moral danger. Ethical training aims to strengthen the moral mind, helping it to win out over desire and physical disposition. Chu Hsi thus contrasts passion and strength: "A man with passions has no strength, whereas a man of strength will not yield to passions."

Chu Hsi asserts, moreover, that our minds are unified with the mind of the universe. That is, the principle in each of us is exactly the principle in the universe as a whole. This makes knowledge, including moral knowledge, possible. And it guarantees that the directives our moral mind gives us are correct; its directives are the directives of the universe.

Chu Hsi's ethics, then, is thoroughly rationalistic. To act morally is to accord with the directives of the moral mind, which stem in turn from universal principle. It is also to accord with the principles of other people and things. Though Chu Hsi is clearly in the Confucian tradition, he stresses universal, impartial obligations over duties arising from specific social relations. Like Confucius, however, he emphasizes the importance of sincerity, both for the investigation of things and for moral action.

from *Reflections on Things at Hand*

Reprinted from *Chu Hsi*, Reflections on Things at Hand: the Neo-Confucian Anthology, *translated with notes by Wing-Tsit Chan. Copyright © 1967 by Columbia University Press.*

CHAPTER VIII / GOVERNING THE STATE

11. As there are things, there are their specific principles. As a father, one should abide in deep love. As a son, one should abide in filial piety. And as a minister, one should abide in reverence. All things and affairs have their own abiding points. When people succeed in abiding in their proper abiding points, they will be contented and happy. If they fail to do so, they will be rebellious. The reason why a sage-ruler can smoothly govern the world is not that he can invent the principles for them. He only enables them to abide in their proper abiding points.

15. What is concerned in everything from managing the self and regulating the family to bringing peace to the world is moral principles of government. What is concerned in everything from instituting fundamental laws of government, differentiating and rectifying the various offices of government, and starting various activities according to the seasons, to creating institutions and establishing systems, thus covering all the affairs of the world, is methods of government. The way in which the sage governs the world consists of these two items alone.

16. Master Ming-tao [Ch'eng Hao] said: Ancient kings governed the world with moral principles, whereas later generations have merely controlled the world with laws and orders.

CHAPTER X / METHODS OF HANDLING AFFAIRS

9. People usually follow their loved ones. According to the feelings of ordinary people, when they love someone they will see his good points, and when they dislike someone they will see his mistakes. People mostly take the words of their wives and sons even though the words are wrong, whereas the words of those whom they dislike are considered wrong even if the words are right. But to follow a person simply because one loves him means that the association is based on personal feelings. How can this be in accord with correct principle? Therefore the text of the lowest, undivided line of the *sui* [to follow] hexagram* says, "One will achieve merit if one goes beyond his own gate to find associates."

14. The commentary on hexagram *k'uei* [to part] says: "The superior man, while in general agreement, can also differ."

    Master Ch'eng I's commentary says, "In dealing with the world, the sage and the worthy are always agreed where the constant principle of Heaven is concerned, but on matters where common folks are in agreement, they sometimes differ. One who cannot be in general agreement with others disturbs

---

* A hexagram is a diagram consisting of two trigrams, each of which consists of three divided or undivided lines, signifying the weak or strong (*yin* or *yang*, respectively). The *Book of Changes*, or *I Ching*, is a Confucian classic consisting of the sixty-four possible hexagrams together with explanations and commentaries that was probably produced between the sixth and third centuries B.C.E. While not itself philosophical, the *I Ching* exerts great influence on neo-Confucian philosophers such as Chu Hsi. —Ed.

constancy and violates principle. One who cannot be different alone is a follower of popular society and a habitual wrongdoer. The important thing is to be able to differ while in general agreement."

19. If a change is not very beneficial, it is to be regretted. How much more so if a change is harmful! That is why the ancients were serious about making a change.

25. Sometimes one may go beyond the Mean in order to be in harmony with the proper situation. But one should not go too far. For example, one may be overrespectful to some extent in behavior, oversorrowful at funerals, and overthrifty in expenditure. It will be wrong to go too far. The reason for going beyond the Mean to a small extent is to be in harmony with the proper situation. If one is in harmony with the proper situation, he will enjoy good fortune.

26. The way to guard against the inferior man is first of all to be correct oneself.

27. The Duke of Chou was perfectly impartial and unselfish. He advanced and withdrew according to the Way and was not beclouded by the desire for profit. In conducting himself he seriously and humbly harbored in his mind the sense of respect and awe. In preserving his sincerity he was open and easy and without any worry. This is why even in a situation of danger and perplexity he never lost his sageness. The *Book of Odes* says,

> The Duke is humble and very handsome.
> His red shoes move comfortably and leisurely.

33. The Teacher [Ch'eng I] saw a student hurrying. He asked him the reason. The student answered, "I want to finish many items of business."

   The Teacher said, "I am not averse to handling human affairs, but, sir, when have I been in such a hurry as you?"

34. [Ch'eng Hao] An-ting's pupils usually knew how to study antiquity and love the people. Consequently, what difficulty would they have in governing?

38. It is most difficult to "be careful about small things."

39. If one wants to assume great responsibility, one must be sincere.

40. In speaking to anyone, if one's principle is overwhelming, one will make the matter clear to him. If one is irascible, one will arouse anger.

43. Master I-Ch'uan [Ch'eng I] said: People dislike having many things to do. Some even regret this. Although there are many things in the world, they are all human affairs. If we do not handle them, whom shall we ask to handle them?

48. As soon as one has the intention of becoming impartial, that is selfishness. In the past there was someone who was in charge of examinations to select officials. He would not handle the qualification of his sons and juniors. This is selfishness.

   Many say that, while in ancient times it was possible to practice honesty and refrain from avoiding suspicion, it is impossible to do so in later generations. The fact is that what is lacking is the right man, not the right time. (Thereupon he told the stories of Ch'eng Shao-shih's having charge of selection and of Ch'eng Hao's recommendation of talents.)

52. A student should understand human affairs. Affairs in the world are similar to those in a family. Either I or someone else will have to handle them. Either this or that person has to handle them.

53. "If a man does not think far ahead he will find trouble near at hand." One's thoughts should go beyond the matter at hand.

54. The Sage was always slow in reproaching people. This shows that he merely wanted things to be correct and had no intention of exposing people's mistakes or evil deeds.

59. Liu An-li asked how to govern the people. Master Ming-tao said, "Enable them to express their feelings fully."

Liu asked about managing officials. [Ming-tao] said, "Make yourself correct so as to influence people."

61. The text of the *k'an* [pit] hexagram says that, as the mind is penetrating, one's action will be of high value. Danger may build up outside, but if one faces it with a penetrating mind and without perplexity, one will succeed even under great difficulty and achieve merit as one proceeds. Now, water drops from a mountain ten thousand feet high. If it has to fall, it simply falls, ignoring all impediment in the front. One should act according to moral principles only. For this reason, one's mind is penetrating.

62. People cannot do what they themselves [consider to be right] because they are lazy if the thing is difficult to do and shy if the thing is unconventional though easy. Only if one's mind is broad will he not mind people's criticism or ridicule. His objective will be moral principles only. As he looks around the world, nothing will be able to alter his course. As he does [what is right], however, people will not necessarily blame him. Precisely if moral principles in oneself are not dominant, [there will be] the defects of laziness and shyness. If [these defects] decline, [moral principles] will increase. If they do not decline, they will always remain. Then one's thoughts will be restrained and narrow, and nothing can be done.

Past scholars of moral courage risked death to do things. What they did may not be in perfect accord with righteousness. But they could not have done what they did without resolute determination. If one understands moral principles, why should he not do [what he himself considers to be right]?

CHAPTER XI / THE WAY TO TEACH

1. Master Lien-hsi [Chou Tun-I] said: Righteousness, uprightness, decisiveness, strictness, and firmness of action are examples of strength that is good, and fierceness, narrow-mindedness, and violence are examples of strength that is evil. Kindness, mildness, and humility are examples of weakness that is good, and softness, indecision, and perverseness are examples of weakness that is evil. Only the Mean brings harmony. The Mean is the principle of regularity, the universally recognized law of morality, and is that to which the sage is devoted. Therefore the sage institutes education so as to enable people to transform their evil by themselves, to arrive at the Mean and to rest there.

5. Master Ming-tao [Ch'eng Hao] said: People worrying about their young who are flippant but talented should teach them only to study the Classics and recite books, and not to write essays.

Most things young people enjoy will destroy their purpose. As to calligraphy and composition, they are the most ordinary things for the scholar. But if one is totally given to their enjoyment, one will naturally lose his purpose. People like Wang Hsi-chih, Yü Shih-nan, Yen Chen-ch'ing, and Liu Kung-ch'üan were really good men, that is true. But have you seen a good calligrapher who understands the Way? If throughout life one's energy is devoted to this one thing, it will not only waste his time but will prevent understanding the Way. From this we know that he will lose his purpose.

7. In setting up a doctrine, one wants it to contain much hidden meaning so that those who understand virtue will not get tired of it and those without virtue will not be misled.

10. [Ch'eng I] If any principle which he does not yet understand is discussed with a student, not only will he fail to penetrate deeply what he has heard, but he will despise the principle.

11. [Ch'eng Hao] In the dance and in archery, one's sincerity can be seen. The ancients taught people for no other reason than to enable them to perfect themselves. In sprinkling, sweeping, and answering questions, one can reach the level of the activities of the sage.

18. Master Heng-Ch'ü [Chang Tsai] said: "To be respectful, reverent, inclined to restraint, and yielding in order to illustrate the rules of propriety," is humanity to the highest degree and the ultimate of the principle of love. If one does not make an effort to illustrate the rules of propriety, he will not be able to lead others or make the Way great, and his teaching will fail.

CHAPTER XII / CORRECTING MISTAKES AND THE DEFECTS OF THE HUMAN MIND

1. Master Lien-hsi [Chou tun-I] said: Chung Yu was happy to hear about his mistakes and his good reputation was unlimited. Nowadays when people have faults, they do not like others to correct them. It is as though a man should hide his illness and avoid a physician. He would rather destroy his life than awake. How lamentable!

2. Master I-Ch'uan [Ch'eng I] said: As one daily accumulates his virtue and goodness, his blessing and emolument will daily reach a higher degree. When one's virtue surpasses one's emolument, although he is prominent, the prominence is not excessive. From ancient times on, there has never been one who is [undeservedly] prominent who does not err in the Way and be ruined.

4. There are many ways in which a ruler can bring ruin to his state, but the pleasure of comfort is the most common.

5. In cautioning himself, the sage always does it at the height of things. If one does not know how to be cautious at the height of things, he will therefore be accustomed to security and wealth, and pride and extravagance will appear. He will enjoy laxity and indulgence, and regulations and standards will collapse. He will forget calamity and chaos, and their roots will sprout. Therefore he will be absorbed and will not be aware that disorder has come.

11. Generally speaking, if one acts because of pleasure, how can he avoid being incorrect?

16. A man with passions has no strength, whereas a man of strength will not yield to passions.

17. "The mistakes of men follow the group to which they belong." A superior man is often mistaken in being liberal, while an inferior man is often mistaken in being stingy. The superior man is excessive in love, while the inferior man suffers from ruthlessness.

18. Master Ming-tao [Ch'eng Hao] said: To have a proud bearing toward others because of one's wealth and honorable position is, of course, not good. To have a proud bearing toward others because of one's learning will do no small harm either.

20. People want every external thing that serves them to be good but they do not want their own bodies and minds to be good. While they wait for these external things to become good, their own bodies and minds, without their realizing it, have already become no good.

21. People are blind to the Principle of Nature simply because they are confused by desires. Chuang Tzu said, "Those who indulge in many desires have very little of the secret of Nature." His words are quite true.

26. Although one may be public-spirited in all things, if he does a thing according to his personal wishes, that is selfishness.

27. Being an official destroys one's purpose.

29. People ignorant of the Way are like drunkards. While they are drunk, they will do anything. When they become sober, they will feel ashamed. Before people know what learning is, they regard themselves as perfect. After they know, they will recall what they previously did and will be ashamed and even afraid.

31. Master Heng-Ch'ü [Chang Tsai] said: If a student neglects propriety and righteousness, he will stuff himself with food all day and do nothing. He will be like a low-class person and his concerns will not go beyond clothing, food, and the pleasures of feasting and travel.

33. Mencius talked about returning to the unchanging standard purposely after he had [criticized] the goody-goody people of the village because the goody-goody people of the village do not first of all establish the fundamentals. They originally intend to do nothing particular, but only watch and follow others, whom they do not wish to offend. They do this all their lives.

WANG YANG-MING

Wan Yang-Ming (1472–1529) developed a philosophy called *dynamic idealism*, which dominated Chinese thought for a century and a half. His views influenced Japanese thought extensively and remain influential in East Asian philosophy.

The China of the late Ming dynasty into which Wang was born was turbulent and decadent. Seminomadic tribes raided the country from the north. Rulers were generally incompetent and oppressive. Taxes were high; political favoritism and corruption were common; large numbers of people survived only through crime or other underground economic activity. Freedoms of thought and speech were under increasing attack.

The young Wang was notably studious and philosophical; he spent his wedding night engrossed in conversation with a Taoist priest. At twenty, he began studying Chu Hsi's philosophy, which for almost two hundred years had been Confucian orthodoxy, serving as the basis for civil service examinations. Wang was so inspired by Chu Hsi's stress on the investigation of things that he and a friend once sat in front of bamboo for seven days to investigate its principles. Wang turned to the study of military affairs and Taoism but finding these alternatives unsatisfying, returned to Confucianism. He began teaching at twenty-eight, attracting some disciples and attacking the then-popular, highly artificial practices of recitation and flowery composition. This got him into serious trouble; when he was thirty-four he was hauled before the emperor, beaten forty times, and banished to what is now Kweichow (Guizhou). Living in isolation and great hardship, he developed many of his most original doctrines. Later he said they were "achieved from a hundred deaths and a thousand sufferings." By the age of forty-two, he was an official at Nanking (Nanjing) and a famous and influential scholar. Despite notable successes, his critique of Chu Hsi earned him more and more enemies, and he was forced into retirement at forty-nine. He continued writing until his death eight years later.

Wang's ethical theory is a version of intuitionism. Reacting strongly against the rationalism of Chu Hsi, he argues that we have innate intuitive knowledge of the good. Nevertheless, Wang accepts many of Chu Hsi's premises. He agrees that we have a moral mind, which contains innately the moral truth, and that the human mind in general tends to stray from the path because it also contains passions. But, Chu Hsi maintains, we must depend on strength and rational inquiry to combat the passions. Wang, in contrast, contends that "the learning of the sages is extremely simple; it is readily understood and easily followed." We must simply "revert to the original nature of the mind"; that is, recover what our minds innately share.

What ethical conceptions do our minds innately share? The highest good, Wang answers. Ethical living consists in fostering and extending our inborn knowledge of the good. Since mind is principle, Wang's project so far sounds rationalistic. But he believes that a person of humanity is in some sense united with everything; that person, recognizing the unity, loves everything. Here Wang's thought shows the influence of Taoism and Buddhism; only the small, in his view, make distinctions. A mind united with everything is humane and is the "clear character" mentioned in *The Great Learning*.

Desires can becloud this naturally clear character. The point of moral education is clarifying the mind in the sense of removing the obscurity desire introduces. Thus, for Wang, the key to a good life is in the mind already. He agrees with Mencius that the mind is originally good: "Intuitive knowledge of good is characteristic of all men." We must seek to extend our knowledge, not because we do not know right from wrong—we have at birth a conscience that immediately recognizes them—but because we must rectify our minds, removing the clouds and smudges stemming from desire.

Immoral action, then, arises from two factors: ignorance and a lack of sincerity. People who act unethically have moral minds that recognize their actions as unethical. Why, then, do people perform such actions? First, they are confused; they have allowed desire to becloud the originally clear character of the mind. To remedy this, they need knowledge. Second, they are not sincere enough. If they truly loved the good, they would accord the moral mind its proper status and seek the mind's clear character. Cases of immoral action thus involve *both* ignorance and insincerity.

from *Instructions for Practical Life*

Reprinted from The Philosophy of Wang Yang Ming, *translated by Frederick Goodrich Henke (Carbondale, Ill.: Open Court Publishing Company, 1916).*

The Highest Virtues are Innate

I made inquiry regarding the saying from the *Great Learning,* "Knowing where to rest, the object of pursuit is determined." "The philosopher Chu," I said, "held that all affairs and all things have definite principles. This appears to be out of harmony with your sayings."

The Teacher said: "To seek the highest virtue in affairs and things is only the objective side of the principles of righteousness. The highest virtues are innate to the mind. They are realized when the manifesting of lofty virtue has reached perfection. Nevertheless, one does not leave the physical realm out of consideration. The original notes say that the individual must exhaust heaven-given principles to the utmost and that no one with any of the prejudices of human passions will attain to the highest virtue."

I made inquiry saying, "Though the highest virtue be sought within the mind only, that may not enable the individual to investigate thoroughly the laws of the physical realm."

The Mind is the Embodiment of Natural Law

The Teacher said: "The mind itself is the embodiment of natural law. Is there anything in the universe that exists independent of the mind? Is there any law apart from the mind?"

I replied: "In filial obedience in serving one's parents, or faithfulness in serving one's prince, or sincerity in intercourse with friends, or benevolence in governing the people, there are many principles which I fear must be examined."

The Teacher, sighing, said: "This is an old evasion. Can it be fully explained in one word? Following your order of questions I will make reply. For instance, in the matter of serving one's father, one cannot seek for the principle of filial obedience in one's parent, or in serving one's prince one cannot seek for the principle of faithfulness in the prince, or in making friends or governing the people one cannot seek for the principle of sincerity and benevolence in the friend or the people. They are all in the mind, for the mind is itself the embodiment of principles. When the mind is free from the obscuration of selfish aims, it is the embodiment of the principles of Heaven. It is not necessary to add one whit from without. When service of parents emerges from the mind characterized by pure heaven-given principles, we have filial obedience; when service of prince emerges, faithfulness; when the making of friends or the governing of the people emerge, sincerity and benevolence. It is only necessary to expel human passions and devote one's energies to the eternal principles.

I said, "Hearing you speak thus, I realize that I understand you in a measure, but the old sayings trouble me, for they have not been completely disposed of. In the matter of serving one's parents, the filial son is to care for their comfort both in winter and summer, and inquire after their health every evening and every morning. These things involve many details. I do not know whether these details are to be investigated in the mind or not."

The Teacher said: "Why not investigate them? Yet in this investigation there is a point of departure; namely, to pay attention to the mind in getting rid of selfish aims and to foster the eternal principles. To understand the providing of warmth for one's parents in winter, is merely a matter of exhausting the filial piety of one's mind and of fearing lest a trifle of selfishness remain to intervene. To talk about providing refreshing conditions for one's parents during the summer, is again a matter of exhausting the filial piety of the mind and of fearing lest perhaps selfish aims be intermingled with one's efforts. But this implies that one must seek to acquire this attitude of mind for one's self. If the mind has no selfish aims, is perfectly under the control of heaven-given principles (natural law), and is sincerely devoted to filial piety, it will naturally think of and provide for the comfort of parents in winter and summer. These are all things that emanate from a mind which truly honors the parents; but it is necessary to have a mind that truly honors the parents before these things can emanate from it. Compare it to a tree. The truly filial mind constitutes the roots; the many details are the branches and leaves. The roots must first be there, and then later there may be branches and leaves. One does not first seek for the branches and leaves and afterwards cultivate the roots.

"The *Book of Rites* says: The filial son who sincerely loves surely has a peaceful temper. Having a peaceful temper, he surely has a happy appearance. Having a happy appearance he surely has a pleasant, mild countenance.' It is because he has a profound love as the root that he is naturally like this."

The Highest Excellence

Cheng Chao-shuo asked whether it is not also necessary to seek for the highest virtue in objective affairs and things. The Teacher said: "The highest excellence consists in nothing else than a mind completely dominated by heaven-given principles (natural law). As for the method by which it may be sought in affairs and things, attempt to name a few and see."

Chao-shuo said: "Serving one's parents is an instance. Why should one carry out the warmth and refreshing formality, as well as the duty of honoring and caring for one's parents? One must search for an ought in such matters. The highest virtue thus carries with it the work of study, investigation, thought and discrimination."

The Teacher said: "If there is nothing further involved than the formalities of providing comfort for parents in winter and summer, and the duties of honoring and nourishing them, then one or two days will suffice to investigate them completely. What study, investigation, thought, and discrimination are required for this? At the time of providing warmth and coolness, it is necessary to have the mind completely dominated by heaven-given principles; and at the time of honoring and nourishing the same holds true. Without applying study, investigation, thought, and discrimination to the mind, it will be difficult to avoid a slight error on the subjective side, with a resultant gross mistake on the objective side. Even in the case of a sage, it is highly important to urge the necessity of being discriminating and undivided. If the highest virtue is only a matter of mood, manner or ceremony, the actor of today who disguises himself in much providing of warmth, coolness, honoring, and nourishing according to usage, may be classed as having the highest virtue." That day I again comprehended.

The Unitary Character of Knowledge and Practice

Because I did not understand the admonition of the Teacher regarding the unitary character of knowledge and practice, Tsung-hsien, Wei-hsien and I discussed it back and forth without coming to any conclusion. Therefore I made inquiry of the Teacher regarding it. He said: "Make a suggestion and see." I said: "All men know that filial piety is due parents, and that the elder brother should be treated with respect; and yet they are unable to carry this out in practice. This implies that knowledge and practice really are two separate things."

The Teacher replied: "This separation is due to selfishness and does not represent the original character of knowledge and practice. No one who really has knowledge fails to practice it. Knowledge without practice should be interpreted as lack of knowledge. Sages and virtuous men teach men to know how to act, because they wish them to return to nature. They do not tell them merely to reflect and let this suffice. The *Great Learning* exhibits true knowledge and practice, that men may understand this. For instance, take the case of loving what is beautiful and despising a bad odor. Seeing beauty is a result of knowledge; loving the beautiful is a result of practice. Nevertheless, it is true that when one sees beauty one already loves it. It is not a case of determining to love it after one sees it. Smelling a bad odor involves knowledge; hating the odor involves action. Nevertheless, when one perceives the bad odor one already hates it. One does not determine to hate it after one has smelt it. A man with his nostrils stuffed may see the malodorous object before him, but does not smell it. Under such circumstances it is a case of not perceiving it, rather than of disliking it. No one should be described as understanding filial piety and respectfulness, unless he has actually practiced filial piety toward his parents and respect toward his elder brother. Knowing how to converse about filial piety and respectfulness is not sufficient to warrant anybody's being described as understanding them. Or it may be compared to one's understanding of pain. A person certainly must have experienced pain before he can know what it is. Likewise to understand cold one must first have endured cold; and to understand hunger one must have been hungry. How, then, can knowledge and practice be separated? This is their original nature before selfish aims have separated them. The sage instructs the individual that he must practice before he may be said to have understanding. If he fails to practice, he does not understand. How thoroughly important a task this is! Why do you so insistently say that knowledge and practice are two separate things, while the sage considers them as one? If one does not understand the purport of well-established truths but merely repeats one or two, what advantage accrues?"

I said: "The ancients said that knowledge and practice are two different things. Men should also understand this clearly. One section treats of knowledge, another of practice. Thus may one acquire a starting-point for one's task."

The Teacher said: "But thereby you have lost the meaning of the ancients. I have said that knowledge is the purpose to act, and that practice implies carrying out knowledge. Knowledge is the beginning of practice; doing is the completion of knowing. If when one knows how to attain the desired end, one speaks only of knowing, the doing is already naturally included; or if he speaks of acting, the knowing is already included. . . .

Innate Knowledge

Again he said: "Knowledge is native to the mind; the mind naturally is able to know. When it perceives the parents it naturally knows what filial piety is; when it perceives the elder brother it naturally knows what respectfulness is; when it sees a child fall into a well it naturally knows what commiseration is. This is intuitive knowledge of good, and is not attained through external investigation. If the thing manifested emanates from the intuitive faculty, it is the more free from the obscuration of selfish purpose. This is what is meant by saying that the mind is filled with commiseration, and that love cannot be exhausted. However, the ordinary man is subject to the obscuration of private aims, so that it is necessary to develop the intuitive faculty to the utmost through investigation of things in order to overcome selfishness and reinstate the rule of natural law. Then the intuitive faculty of the mind will not be subject to obscuration, but having been satiated will function normally. Thus we have a condition in which there is an extension of knowledge. Knowledge having been extended to the utmost, the purpose is sincere."

. . . .

T'ang Hsü made inquiry saying: "Is it true that in fixing the determination one should constantly cherish good thoughts, do good, and expel evil?"

The Teacher said: "The cherishing of good thoughts is in accordance with natural law. Such thoughts are themselves virtue. What other virtue shall one deliberate upon? They are not evil. What evil shall one expel? Thoughts are like the roots and rootlets of a tree. He who is fixing his determination need only fix his thoughts for a long time. When one is able to follow the desire of the heart without overstepping propriety, one's determination has become habitual.

"It is of first importance that mental and animal energy, virtue, words, and acts would for the most part be controlled (gathered together). That they will lack unity at times is inevitable. Heaven and earth, man and things, are all alike in this". . . .

Selfishness is a Root of Evil

The Teacher said: "Pleasure, anger, sorrow, and joy are in their natural condition in the state of equilibrium and harmony. As soon as the individual adds a little of his own ideas, he oversteps and fails to maintain the state of equilibrium and harmony. This implies selfishness.

"In subduing one's self, one must clear out selfish desire completely, so that not a bit is left. If a little is left, all sorts of evil will be induced to make their entrance."

Lack of Effort Involves Selfishness and Hinders Progress

The Teacher said: "Sirs, how is it that recently when you approach me you have so few questions to ask regarding the things about which you are in doubt? When a man fails to put forth effort, he invariably believes that he well knows how to devote himself to study, and that all that is necessary is to follow the order and act (i.e. study). He certainly does not know that selfish desire increases every day like the dust of the earth. If one neglects to sweep for a day, another layer is added. If one really works with determination one realizes that the doctrine is inexhaustible. The more one searches, the profounder it becomes, until its essence and purity are fully comprehended."

Some one made inquiry saying: "After knowledge has been completed one can say that the thoughts are sincere. At present neither moral law nor the passions of men are thoroughly understood. Under such circumstances how is anyone in a position to begin to subdue himself?"

The Teacher said: "If a person unceasingly applies himself truly and earnestly, he will daily better comprehend the subtle essence of the moral principles of the mind, as well as the subtlety of selfish desires. If he does not use his efforts in controlling himself, he will continually talk and yet never comprehend the meaning of moral principles or of selfish desire. The situation may be likened to a man traveling. When (by walking) he has covered a stage, he understands that stage. When he reaches a fork in the road and is in doubt he makes inquiry, and having made inquiry he again proceeds. In this way he gradually reaches his destination. Men of today are unwilling to abide by the moral principles which they already know, and to expel the passions they have already recognized; but are downcast because they are unable to understand completely. They merely indulge in idle discussions. Of what advantage is this? They should wait until in the process of subduing and controlling themselves there are no more selfish motives to subdue, for then it would not be too late to sorrow because of their inability to understand fully". . . .

The Mind Should Rule the Senses

He made inquiry saying, "In what way may the mind devote itself to things?"

The Teacher said: "When the people's prince is upright, reverent, and majestic, and the six boards distinguish their respective official duties, the Empire is well governed. In the same way the mind should govern the five senses. In our day when the eye wishes to see, the mind applies itself to color, and when the ear wishes to hear, the mind devotes itself to sound. It is as though the people's prince were himself to take a seat on the Board of Civil Offices, when he wishes to choose an official, or on the Board of War, when he wishes to move the troops. In this way the original character of the prince would be sacrificed and in addition the six boards also would be unable to perform their official duties". . . .

How the State of Equilibrium Is to Be Acquired

. . . I made inquiry saying: "An ordinary man surely is unable completely to attain the equilibrium and the harmonious development of pleasure, anger, sorrow, and joy. For instance, he who in some small thing should be either pleased or angry ordinarily has no inclination to be either pleased or angry, but when the time comes the feelings may be manifested in due degree. May not this be called a state of equilibrium and harmony?"

The Teacher said: "At the time in that particular affair it certainly may be called a state of equilibrium and harmony, but it cannot be described as the great root or the universal path. The nature of all men is good. The state of equilibrium and harmony is originally possessed by all men. How, then, can they be said not to have it? However, the mind of the usual man has things that becloud, and therefore, though nature is manifested at times, the condition is such that it is sometimes manifested and sometimes extinguished. It does not represent the functioning of the entire being. When a condition has been reached in which there is a continuous state of equilibrium, it is designated as the great root (great fundamental virtue). When a condition of continuous harmony has been acquired, it is designated as the universal way. Only when a condition of the most complete sincerity under heaven is reached, is it possible for the individual to establish himself in this great fundamental virtue of humanity."

I further said: "I do not yet clearly understand the meaning of the equilibrium."

He said: "You must recognize this from the nature of the mind itself, for it cannot be revealed by means of words. The equilibrium is to be identified with heaven-given principles."

I said, "Why is it the same as heaven-given principles?"

The Teacher said, "When passions have been cast out one understands heaven-given principles."

I said, "Why should heaven-given principles be designated as a state of equilibrium?"

He said, "Because they are not prejudiced or selfish."

I said, "What kind of an attitude and bearing does this lack of selfishness give?"

He said, "It may be compared to a bright mirror, all of which is perfectly clear and not spotted with a particle of dust."

I said: "Selfishness then implies being infected. If one is infected with love of lust, love of gain, love of fame, and similar things, the selfishness is apparent. When they have not manifested themselves, when the lust, fame, and gain have not been experienced, how can one know that he is selfish?"

The Teacher said: "Though they may not have been experienced, yet ordinarily the individual has not been free from love of lust, gain, and fame. Since he has not been free from them, he may be said to have them; and since he may be said to have them, he cannot be free from leaning on them. It may be compared to a man who is sick with intermittent fever. Though at times the fever is not manifest, nevertheless as long as the root of the disease has not been extirpated he cannot be said to be free from the disease. It is necessary to sweep out and wash out the every-day love of lust, fame, and similar things—a lot of passions—so that not the least bit will be retained. Then the mind will be completely filled with unmixed heaven-given principles. Thereupon it may be said to be in the state of equilibrium in which there are no stirrings of pleasure, anger, sorrow, and joy; and this is the great fundamental virtue of humanity". . . .

The Nature of Good and Evil

I (K'an) was pulling weeds out from among the flowers, and for that reason said, "How difficult it is to cultivate the good in heaven and on earth, and how hard it is to get rid of the evil!"

The Teacher said: "You should neither cultivate the good nor expel the evil." A little later he said, "This view of good and evil has its source in the body (is personal), and thus is probably mistaken."

I was not able to comprehend. The Teacher said: "The purpose of heaven and earth in bringing forth is even as in the instance of flowers and grass. In what way does it distinguish between good and evil? If you, my disciple, take delight in seeing the flowers, then you will consider flowers good and grass bad. If you desire to use the grass you will, in turn, consider the grass good. This type of good and evil has its source in the likes and dislikes of your mind. Therefore I know that you are mistaken."

I said, "In that case there is neither good nor evil, is there?" The Teacher said: "The tranquility resulting from the dominance of natural law is a state in which no discrimination is made between good and evil; while the stirring of the passion nature is a state in which both good and evil are present. If there are no stirrings of the passion nature, there is neither good nor evil, and this is what is called the highest good."

I said, "Buddhism also fails to discriminate between good and evil. In what way is it different from what you say?"

He said: "Buddhism gives attention to the lack of good and evil and then pays no attention to anything else, and for that reason cannot enter actively into matters of government. The lack of good and evil in the case of the sage implies that he does neither that which he desires nor that which he does not desire. Having no stirring of the passion nature, he naturally carries out the doctrine of the kings (Yao and Shun). Having become most highly skilled in this, it transpires that in his compliance with natural law there is adaptation for the purpose of rendering mutual assistance."

I said, "Since the grass is not bad, it should not be pulled out."

He said, "That accords with the view held by the Buddhists and Taoists. If the grass impedes progress, what hinders you from plucking it out?"

I said, "In that case you again have action in accordance with likes and dislikes."

He said, "It is not action in accordance with likes and dislikes; but this does not mean that there is a complete lack of likes and dislikes, for a man without these would be devoid of consciousness. Saying that one does not act in accordance with likes and dislikes means simply that in both likes and dislikes one follows the lead of natural law and does not act while one is harboring a single selfish purpose. Thus one is as though he had neither likes not dislikes."

I said, "How can weeding be construed as obedience to natural law and as showing a lack of private motives?"

He said, "If the grass hinders progress, natural law demands that it be uprooted. It should be uprooted, and that is all. Should one be unable to pull it out immediately, the mind should not be embarrassed. If one harbors the least selfish purpose, the very structure of the mind will be involved and there will be much stirring of the passion nature."

I said, "In that case good and evil are not at all present in things."

He said, "They are only in your mind. Obedience to natural law is to be identified with good; and the stirring of the passion nature is evil."

I said, "After all, then, things are devoid of both good and evil."

He said, "As the mind is, so also are the things; but the ordinary scholar of today fails to realize this. He neglects the mind, strives for things, and in so doing makes a mistake in his view of the investigation of things. To the end they all eagerly search for the principle of things in external matters. They are able to obtain it by incidental deeds of righteousness only. During their entire lives they act but without really manifesting it, and learn without investigating it."

I said, "How does this apply in the case of loving beauty and despising evil odors?"

He said, "These are all in accordance with natural law. Natural law is in harmony with this, for originally there were no selfish motives manifested in carrying out likes or dislikes."

I said, "How can love of beauty and dislike of evil odors be other than selfish purposes?"

He said, "On the contrary, they are sincere, not selfish, purposes; and sincere purposes are in accordance with natural law. Though they are in accordance with natural law, they must not contain the least trace of selfish purposes. If a person is under the influence of anger or of joy, he will not attain their true use (will not be correct in conduct). He must be open-minded and without favoritism, for then he is manifesting the original nature of the mind. Know this and you know the state of equilibrium."

Po Sheng said, "The teacher has said that if the grass impedes progress, natural law demands that it be uprooted. Why, then, does he say that it is a thought emanating from the body (a purely personal affair)?"

He said, "You must learn, from introspection, what manner of mind you harbor at the time you wish to pull the weeds. Chou Mei-shu did not pull up the grass in front of his own window. What was his state of mind?" . . .

from a *Record of Discourses*

Reprinted from The Philosophy of Wang Yang Ming, *translated by Frederick Goodrich Henke (Carbondale, Ill.: Open Court Publishing Company, 1916).*

Intuitive Knowledge of Good Is Characteristic of All Men

The Teacher said: "The sages, also, have first devoted themselves to study, and thus know the truth. The common people, also, have knowledge of it from birth."

Some one asked, "How can that be?"

He replied: "Intuitive knowledge of good is characteristic of all men. The sage, however, guards and protects it so that nothing obscures it. His contending and anxiety do not cease, and he is indefatigable and energetic in his efforts to guard his intuitive knowledge of the good. This also involves learning. However, his native ability is greater, so that it is said of him that he is born with knowledge of the five duties and practices them with ease. There is nobody who does not in the period from his infancy to his boyhood develop this intuition of good, but it is often obscured. Nevertheless, this original knowledge of good is naturally hard to obliterate. Study and self-control should follow the lead of intuitive knowledge. Only when the capacity for learning is great does the saying apply, 'Some know them from study and practice them from a desire of advantage or gain.'"

from *Inquiry Regarding the Great Learning*

Reprinted from The Philosophy of Wang Yang Ming, *translated by Frederick Goodrich Henke (Carbondale, Ill.: Open Court Publishing Company, 1916).*

The Great Learning Is Adapted to the Adult Mind

Referring to the *Great Learning*, a former scholar held that it is adapted to adults. I ventured to ask why learning adapted to adults should consist in illustrating illustrious virtue.

Wang said: "The adult is an all-pervading unity —one substance—with heaven, earth, and things. He views the earth as one family and his country as one man. The youth makes a cleavage between things, and distinguishes between himself and others, while the adult's ability consists in considering heaven, earth, and all things as one substance. This is not because his own purpose is of that kind, but because the benevolent nature of the mind is of that type. It is one with heaven, earth, and things. But is this true only of adults? The mind of a youth is also of this type, but he views himself as small. When he sees a child fall into a well, he certainly will experience a feeling of alarm and distress, which implies that his kindly nature is of the same sort as that of the child and that the child belongs to the same class as he. When he hears the pitiful cry and sees the frightened appearance of a bird or an animal that is about to be slaughtered, his mind surely cannot endure it; and this implies that his kindly nature is one with that of birds and animals, and that birds and animals may be said to be conscious and have feelings. If he sees plants destroyed, he surely feels sympathetic. This implies that his benevolence includes plants, and that plants may be said to have life. When he sees tiles and stones being broken,

he surely will have regard for them. This implies that this benevolence is one with inanimate things. They are all the benevolence of the same body (substance). Even a youth will have this type of a mind, which means that the source is in the heaven-given nature. But of course his intelligence must not be obscured. For this reason it is called illustrious virtue. Though the young man's mind is divided, hampered, and vile, his benevolence may not be obscured and darkened, for he may have had no stirrings of desire; and his mind may not be obstructed with selfishness. As soon as he has stirrings of desire and his mind is obscured because of selfishness, and these (desires) contend severely among themselves and angrily impede one another, then will he kill and destroy living things and will be equal to anything. This may easily reach the place where brothers desire to kill one another; but thereby benevolence is completely destroyed. For this reason if the youth is free from the obscuration of selfish desire, his benevolence is as that of the adult, even though he is but a youth. When once the individual has been obscured by selfish desires, he is as divided and ignorant as the youth, even though he be an adult. Thus it is evident that learning adapted to adults merely clears away the obscuration of selfish desire from the mind so as to illustrate the mind's illustrious virtue and to cause it to revert to the original all-pervading unity of heaven, earth, and things. It is not possible to add anything to this original substance."

I said: "I venture to ask why learning for adults should consist in loving the people."

He said: "He who manifests illustrious virtue establishes himself in the proper place in the great all of heaven, earth, and things. He who loves the people perceives and understands the use of his nature (common to heaven, earth and things). The manifesting of illustrious virtue consists in loving the people, and loving the people in manifesting illustrious virtue. For this reason, if I love my own father, the fathers of others, and even the fathers of all men, my benevolence will truly be one with that of my father, the fathers of others, and even with that of the fathers of all men. When they are truly one, then first will the illustrious virtue of filial piety be illustrated. When I love my elder brother, the elder brothers of others, and even the elder brothers of all men, my benevolence will be one with them. When it is truly one with them, then the illustrious virtue of a younger brother will first be illustrated. Everything, from prince, minister, husband, wife, friends, up to mountains, rivers, spirits, gods, birds, animals, and plants, should be truly loved in order to promote my natural benevolence; then there will be nothing left unmanifested by my illustrious virtue, and I will be truly one with heaven, earth, and all things. This is what is called illustrating illustrious virtue throughout the kingdom. This is what is meant by, 'Their families being regulated, their states were rightly governed and the whole Empire was made tranquil.' It is called 'exhausting nature.'"

I said: "I venture to ask in what way learning for adults consists in the individual's 'resting in the highest excellence.'"

The Teacher said: "Resting in the highest excellence implies manifesting illustrious virtue and loving the people in the highest degree. When the heaven-given nature reaches a condition of complete excellence, its intelligence will not be darkened. This is a manifestation of highest excellence. It is really the original form of illustrious virtue, and is called intuitive knowledge of good. When the highest excellence manifests itself, right is right and wrong is wrong. Things of less and greater importance come and go as they will without ceasing, but none of this change is other than natural. This, moreover, implies that mankind holds fast to its natural disposition and has its various faculties and relations with their specific laws. However, it is not allowable that there be the least purpose to add to or subtract from them. If there is the least disposition to add to or diminish them, this implies selfishness and shallow wisdom, and cannot be said to be the highest virtue. Naturally, one who does this does not attain to the condition of watch-ing over himself when he is alone. How can he who is discriminating and undivided be like that? Later generations fail to realize that the highest excellence is in their own minds, but use their selfish wisdom to estimate and calculate how they may find it in things external to themselves. They hold that every affair and every thing has its own definite principles. This is due to the darkening of their ability to estimate right and wrong. They branch off from, and are at variance with, their heaven-given nature. Passion is excessive, while moral principles perish. Thus the learning which inculcates illustrious virtue and love of the people becomes greatly confused in the Empire. Among former scholars there were some who desired to manifest their illustrious virtue, but who did not know how to rest in the highest excellence. They used their selfish purposes to excess and lost the mind in vacuous, lifeless, and lonely contemplation. They did not regulate their families, govern their states, nor make the kingdom happy and tranquil. This means that they drifted into Buddhism and Taoism. Certainly some wished to love the people, but they did not know how to rest in the highest excellence. They sank their selfish minds into base and trifling things. This implies that they lost their power, strategy, wisdom, and craft, and that they did not have the sincerity of real benevolence and sympathy. Thus they became followers of the five rulers, devoting themselves to might, merit, and gain, and all failed to realize their mistake in not resting in the highest virtue. Therefore resting in the highest excellence is to the manifesting of illustrious virtue and loving the people as a pair of compasses and square are to the square and the circle, or rule and measure are to length, or the balances are to weight. If the square and the circle do not correspond with the compasses and the square, they will be defective; if the length and shortness fail to coincide with the rule and the measure, they lose their adjustment; if the weight is not true to the balances, it loses its accuracy. If manifestation of illustrious virtue and love of the people do not rest in the highest excellence, they lose their original character. Therefore, resting in the highest excellence requires the previous use of loving the people and illustrating illustrious virtue. This is what is called by saying that learning is adapted to adults."

The Mind Is Possessed of the Highest Excellence

I said, "How is the following saying to be interpreted? 'The point where to rest (in the highest excellence) being known, the object of pursuit is then determined, and that being determined, a calm unperturbedness may be attained to. To that calmness there will succeed a tranquil repose. In that repose there may be careful deliberation and that deliberation will be followed by the attainment (of the highest excellence).'"

The Teacher said: "People fail to understand that the highest excellence is in their mind and seek it in external things. They believe that all affairs and all things have definite principles, and seek the highest excellence in the midst of affairs and things. This shows that their heaven-given nature has branched off and been disrupted. They are mixed up and confused and do not know that there is a definite direction which they ought to take. Since you know that the highest excellence is in the mind and that there is no need of seeking it in external things, your purpose has taken a definite direction and you are not precipitated into a condition in which nature branches off, is disrupted, or is all mixed up and confused. Moreover, if you are in that condition, your mind will not make mistakes, but will be quiet and calm. If the mind does not make mistakes, but is able to rest, then in its daily use, whenever it gets a moment's rest, it will be in tranquil repose. If the mind is in tranquil repose, your intuitive faculty—whenever thought manifests itself or an affair influences the mind—will naturally carefully inquire, minutely investigate, and thus be able earnestly to deliberate, whether the thing under consideration is in accordance with the highest excellence. If it is able to deliberate carefully, it will choose only the finest, and do only what is proper. But in this the highest excellence is attained."

As Roots and Branches Are One Thing, thus Manifesting Virtue and Loving the People Are One

I said: "'Things have their roots and their branches.' A former scholar (the philosopher Chu) considered illustrious virtue as the root and 'renovating the people' as the branches. But these two, the one being within and the other without, are really opposed to one another. 'Affairs have their end and their beginning.' A former scholar held that knowing where to rest in the highest excellence was the beginning, and ability to attain (the highest excellence) was the end. Every affair has its beginning and its end, and these are mutually connected. According to the teaching of the Master (Wang) one should change the character *hsin* . . . (meaning "to renovate") to the character *ch'in* (meaning "to love"). Would not this be at variance with the saying regarding the roots and the branches?"

The Teacher said: "What has been said regarding the end and the beginning is, in general, correct. To use the original 'love,' in place of 'renovate,' and then to say that the manifesting of illustrious virtue is the root and loving the people the branches, is also a legitimate method of procedure. But root and branches should not be distinguished as being two different things. The trunk of this tree is called the root (source), and its twigs are called branches, but the whole thing is but one thing. If root and branches are two things, they should have been considered as two things. How, then, are they connected in the saying, 'Things have roots and branches'? If the idea expressed in 'renovating the people' is different from that of loving the people, then the task of illustrating virtue is naturally an entirely different thing from renovating the people. If one understands that illustrious virtue is manifested by loving the people, and on the other hand that one loves the people in manifesting illustrious virtue, what occasion is there for separating them? The former scholar's exposition is due to his ignorance of the fact the manifesting virtue and loving the people are *ab initio* one thing, whereas he considered them as two. This means that though he knew that root and branches ought to be considered as one thing, he could but distinguish them as two."

Wang Offers Comments on the Great Learning, Introduction, ¶4

I said: "'The ancients who wished to illustrate illustrious virtue throughout the kingdom first ordered well their own states. Wishing to order well their states, they first regulated their families. Wishing to regulate their families, they first cultivated their persons.' In using the Master's idea of understanding the expressions, 'manifesting virtue' and 'loving the people,' I have been able to understand this. May I venture to ask regarding the arrangement of the task, and the way in which one should proceed, as implied in the following passage from the Great Learning? 'Wishing to cultivate their persons, they first rectified their hearts. Wishing to rectify their hearts, they first sought to be sincere in their thoughts. Wishing to be sincere in their thoughts, they first extended their knowledge to the utmost. Such extension of the knowledge lay in the investigation of things.'"

The Teacher said: "This saying is merely giving in detail the order of the task from the 'manifesting of illustrious virtue' on to 'resting in the highest excellence.' The person, the mind, thought, knowledge, and things constitute the logical order of the task. Though each has its particular place, they are in reality one thing. Investigating, extending, being sincere, rectifying, and cultivating are the task in its logical sequence. Though each has its name, in reality it is only one affair. What is it that is called the person? The form and body in its various exercises. What is it that is called mind? The intelligence of the person, which is called lord or master. What is meant by cultivating the person? That which is described by saying, 'Do good and expel evil.' That my person is able to do good and abhor evil is due to the fact that its master—the will—desires to do good and abhor evil. After that the body in its various exercises is able to do good and abhor evil. Therefore he who desires to cultivate his person must first rectify his heart. Moreover, the mind in its original form is what is called nature. If nature is virtuous in everything, then the mind in its original form is at all times characterized by rectitude. From whence, then, the use of effort in rectifying it? The mind is originally in a condition of perfect rectitude; it is only after there has been a stirring of its purposes and thoughts that it is wrong. Therefore he who wishes to rectify his mind will correct that which his will and thought bring forth. Whenever he manifests a virtuous thought, he will love it as one loves a beautiful color; when he thinks an evil

thought, he will hate it as one despises an evil odor. Since his purpose is perfectly sincere, he will be able to rectify his heart. The purpose manifests both that which is virtuous and that which is evil, and has no knowledge of the difference between good and evil. It confuses and mixes the right and the wrong. Though the individual desires to make his purpose sincere, he is unable to do so. Therefore he who wishes to make his purpose sincere must extend his knowledge of the good to the utmost by developing his intuitive faculty to the utmost. The utmost here is like the utmost of the saying, 'When mourning has been carried to the utmost degree of grief, it should cease.'

"The *Book of Changes* says, 'Knowing the utmost one should reach it. He who knows the utmost really knows. He who reaches it, reaches the utmost.' This signifies extending knowledge to the utmost. It is not what later scholars call filling and extending knowledge, but extending to the utmost the mind's intuitive knowledge of good,—the knowledge of good which Mencius calls the good-evil mind and which all people have. The good-evil mind does not need to deliberate in order to know, nor does it need to learn in order to be able to act. It is for this reason that it is called intuitive knowledge of good. It is the heaven-given nature—the original character of the mind. It is naturally intelligent and clearly conscious. Whenever any purposes or thoughts are manifested, they are all known and recognized by the intuitive faculty. If they be good, the intuitive faculty naturally knows. Are they evil? This, too, the intuitive faculty naturally knows. This shows that it is no concern of others. Therefore, though there is no evil to which the mean man will not proceed, yet when he sees a superior man, he will certainly disguise himself, conceal his evil, and display his virtue. In this it is manifest that his intuitive faculty does not leave him unenlightened. If he desires to distinguish between good and evil in order to rectify his purpose, there is but the one way, that of extending the knowledge of his intuitive faculty to the utmost. How is it that when a purpose manifests itself, the intuitive faculty already knows whether it is good or not? Nevertheless, if the individual is not able to love the good sincerely, but rather turns his back on it and expels it, he uses the good to do evil and obscures his intuitive faculty, which knows the good. How is it when the intuitive faculty knows that what the purpose has manifested is evil, nevertheless, if the individual does not sincerely hate the evil, he violates the good and does the evil, and thus uses the evil to do evil and thereby obscures his intuitive faculty, which knows the evil? If this is true, then, though it is said that he knows, he is as though he did not know. How can his purpose be made sincere under such circumstances? If, in that which the intuitive faculty understands to be good and evil, there is nothing that is not sincerely loved and sincerely hated, then the individual does not deceive his own intuitive faculty and his purpose can be made sincere.

"Again, if the individual wishes to extend his intuitive knowledge to the utmost, shall it be said that he, like a shadow and an echo, is vain and lacks genuineness? If in reality there is such an extension of intuitive knowledge, it must consist in investigating things. Things are affairs (experience). Whenever a purpose is manifested it certainly is relative to some affair and the affair toward which it is directed is called a thing. Investigating means rectifying— rectifying that which is not correct, that it may belong to the things that are correct, rectifying that which is not true, and expelling evil. It implies that turning to the true and the right is what is meant by doing good. This is called investigating.

"The *Book of History* says, 'He (Yao) investigated heaven above and the earth beneath. He (Shun) investigated (in the temple of) the accomplished ancestors.' The individual investigates the evil of his heart. The 'investigating' of 'investigating things' truly combines all of the above ideas. If one sincerely wishes to love the good which the intuitive faculty knows, but in reality fails to act with regard to the thing on which his purpose is fixed, this implies that the thing has not been investigated, and that the determination to love good is not sincere. If one sincerely wishes to despise the evil which the intuitive faculty recognizes, but fails really to expel the thing upon which the purpose is fixed, this implies that the thing has not been investigated and that the purpose of despising the evil is not sincere. If the individual wishes the good which his intuitive faculty knows and he really does that upon which his purpose is fixed, is there anything which he may not accomplish? If in the matter of the evil which his

intuitive faculty knows he really expels that upon which his purpose is fixed, is there anything which he may not complete? After that there is nothing that he does not thoroughly investigate. In that which the intuitive faculty knows, there will be no deficiency nor anything that is obscure, and it will have been extended to the utmost. After that the mind will be joyous, without remorse or regret, but modest and humble; and all the manifestations of the purpose will be free from self-deceit, so that the individual may be said to be sincere in thought. Therefore it is said, 'Things being investigated, knowledge became complete. Their knowledge being complete, their thoughts were sincere; and their hearts being rectified, their persons were cultivated.' These are the principles of the task. Though there may be said to be an order of first and last in this, it is in reality one connected whole and there is no distinction between first and last. Though the task for which these principles stand is not to be divided in an order of first and last, its use nevertheless implies great discrimination. Assuredly, there cannot be the least bit lacking. This is the correct exposition of investigating things, extending knowledge, making the thoughts sincere, and rectifying the mind. Therefore making known the true precepts of Yao and Shun is made the Confucian heart-seal."

The Investigation of Things Is the Real Starting-point of the Task Outlined in the Great Learning

If from the *Great Learning* the idea contained in "investigating things" is expunged, there will be no real starting-point. There must be genuine investigation, before this can be appreciated. From the opening (creation) of heaven and earth, in heaven above and the earth beneath everywhere there are things. Even the person who seeks for the path is a thing. Taken together they have coherent principles, namely in what is called the source of the doctrine. Since the high and the low, altitude and depth, together constitute the great round, unmoved stillness, from what other point can knowledge of the doctrine be gained? If the individual wishes to investigate conditions previous to heaven and earth, he will find it in the Taoist abstract learning of Lao-tzu and Chuang-tzu. This thing can be seen from the manifestations of the doctrine. This is in conformity with the saying of the *Book of Changes*: "When the form is directed upward it is called the doctrine; when it points downward it is called a finished vessel." If you cast aside the vessel, there is the more nothing that can be called the doctrine. The thing referred to is my nature, my heaven-decreed nature. It is in accordance with the saying of Mencius that "all things are already complete in us."

Man alone knows what is meant by being enticed by the influence of things, but is unable to carry on self-investigation with full sincerity or to carry out vigorously the law of reciprocity. He stops with recognizing his body as the person and external objects as things, and forthwith separates things and himself into two distinct realms, so that in last analysis his person represents but one thing among ten thousand. How, then, can he extend his knowledge to the utmost, be sincere in purpose, rectify his mind, cultivate his person, regulate his family, govern the kingdom, and tranquilize the empire, in order to complete and exhaust the doctrine of the *Great Learning*? Therefore it is said that the task is exhausted in extending knowledge to the utmost through the investigation of things.

What is called investigating, does not consist in seeking within the realm of so-called external things. This excellency should be sought in extensive study of what is good, accurate inquiry about it, careful reflection upon it, clear discrimination of it, and earnest practice of it. This excellency is sincerity. In this way, these things may be considered as things. The manifesting of this excellency consists in knowing how to rest in the highest virtue. If one knows how to rest in the highest virtue, he will be able to attain the desired end. If thus understood, all nature will be comprehended in this. It is for this reason that the *Doctrine of the Mean* says: "Sincerity is the end and the beginning of things. The superior man regards the attainment of sincerity as the most excellent thing." Naturally he completes himself and things also. Once mentioned he employs them and does nothing that is not proper. The task of investigating things having been completed, all other things will be adjusted. Therefore, when the philosopher Chu in giving instruction regarding the investigation of things, said "to the utmost," he did that which was exceedingly proper.

Whatever falls into the class of speculation or mere abstract thinking, as in considering extreme height, cannot be said to be to the utmost. What is here called the utmost means that the personality has developed to the utmost degree. Knowledge and practice also should be called activity and tranquility. This is what the Teacher refers to in the saying of the *Book of Changes*: "If you know the highest (utmost), attain to it." To attain to the utmost is the essence of staunch virtue. Beyond this there is no task which has reference to the essence, or is wonderful and godlike. But the people find too shallow a meaning in the "utmost" of the philosopher Chu and thus say: "When you take up anything investigate it." This is the practice whereby the latest scholars branch off, though the philosopher Chu from the first gave no such explanation. Having received the plain exposition of the Teacher, I use it to explain the incomplete idea of the philosopher Chu.

from the *Reply to Ku Tung-ch'iao*

Reprinted from The Philosophy of Wang Yang Ming, *translated by Frederick Goodrich Henke (Carbondale, Ill.: Open Court Publishing Company, 1916).*

The Mind of the Sage Described

The mind of the sage considers heaven, earth, and all things as one substance. He makes no distinction between the people of the Empire. Whosoever has blood and life is his brother and child. There is no one whom he does not wish to see perfectly at peace, and whom he does not wish to nourish. This is in accordance with his idea that all things are one substance. The mind of everybody is at first not different from that of the sage. If there is any selfishness in it, which divides it through the obscuration of passion and covetousness, then that which is great is considered small and that which is clear and open as unintelligible and closed. Whoever has this mind gets to the place where he views his father or son or elder brother and younger brothers as enemies. The sage, distressed because of this, uses the occasion to extend his virtuous attitude, which considers heaven, earth, and all things as one substance, by instructing the people and causing them to subdue their selfishness, remove the obscuration, and revert to the original nature of their minds.

The People and Officials of the State under Yao, Shun, and Yü Were Simple and Virtuous

The main divisions of this instruction, Yao, Shun, and Yü have mutually received and transmitted in the saying, "The mind which cherishes the path of duty is small. Devote yourself to the best, be un-divided, sincerely hold fast the due Mean." The details of the task were given to Hsieh by Shun. He said, "Between father and son there should be affection; between sovereign and minister, righteousness; between husband and wife, attention to their separate functions; between young and old, a proper order; between friends, fidelity." At the time of Yao, Shun, and the Three Dynasties, only this was considered instruction by the teachers and by the students. All that time men did not differ in their opinions, nor homes in their practices. He who adjusted himself to this was called a sage; he who was diligent in carrying it out was called virtuous; he who disregarded it was considered degenerate, even though it was the intelligent Tan Chu. The man at the village well or in the rural district, the farmer, the artisan, the merchant, everybody had this learning (of the human relationships) and looked only to the perfecting of character as important. How is this to be accounted for? They were not subject to the confusion inherent in much hearing and seeing, nor to the annoyance of remembering and reciting, nor to the extravagance of speech and composition, nor to the striving and gaining of honor and advantage. The result was that they were filial toward their parents, respectful to their elders, and faithful toward their friends. They considered this as reverting to the original nature of the mind. This means that they certainly had these things by nature and did not need to acquire them from without. Thus, who was there that could not do them?

The government schools were devoted to perfecting virtue. In accordance with differences of capacity the students were to complete their virtue—whether they excelled in the rites of propriety and music, in capacity for ruling, or in ability to carry on agriculture. And this was done in order the more to refine their ability in the school, that when their virtue came into evidence and they were given employment, it would cause them from first to last to remain in their calling without change.

Those who employed others devoted themselves mutually to virtue alone, that they might give peace to the people of the Empire. Judging whether the individual's ability was suitable, they did not consider those of higher position and those of lower social standing as more or less worthy of consideration, nor labor and leisure as honorable or dishonorable.

Those who were employed also knew only this one thing, mutually to devote themselves to virtue for the purpose of giving peace to the people of the Empire. If they were able to carry this out in practice, then, though they were continually in the midst of increasing perplexities, they did not consider them laborious, and though they were placed in the midst of trifling, vulgar things, they did not consider them low and ignoble. At that time the people of the Empire, with clear, resplendent virtue, all viewed one another as relatives of one home. Those whose ability was lowly, engaged in agriculture, labor, or commerce. All were diligent in their various occupations for the purpose of nourishing one another. Moreover, they did not strive for exalted position and desire external things.

As for the varying degrees of natural ability, there were Kao, K'uei, Chi, and Hsieh. When they took up official position they did their best. They represented the occupations of a single home, attending to and managing the matters of clothes and food, having dealings with those that have and those that lack, and providing the utensils of the home. They brought together their plans and united their efforts, in order that in accordance therewith they might devise means whereby above they might serve their parents and below they might support their wives and children. They were solicitous only lest perhaps in carrying this responsibility some might be indolent or selfish. For this reason Chi was a diligent farmer and not ashamed that he did not understand official admonitions. He viewed the excellent official admonition of Hsieh as his own. K'uei was in charge of the music and was not ashamed because he did not understand the rites of propriety. He considered I's clear understanding of ceremonies as though it were his own. The learning of their minds was pure and clear.

They had the virtue of perfecting their original nature, and therefore their mental energy and their purpose were penetrating and unifying. They did not distinguish between themselves and others, nor between things and themselves. They can be compared with the body of a single person. Eyes, ears, hands, and feet all assist in the functions of the body. The eyes are not ashamed because they are not intelligent. If anything of importance occurs to the ears, they certainly attend to it. The feet are not ashamed because they cannot grasp things. If there is anything that the hands feel for, the feet certainly move forward. The original vital fluids pervade, and the bloods vessels branch out and penetrate the entire body. It is self-evident that itches and pains, expiration and inspiration cause excitement and exhilaration, and the spirit responds. The learning of the sages is extremely simple; it is readily understood and easily followed. Their learning was easily acquired and their ability readily gained, because the main divisions of their learning consisted in reverting to the original nature of the mind. They did not discuss understanding and talent.

Later Decay of State Was Due to Heterodoxy and Sham

The decay of the Three Dynasties was due to the extinction of rule by right, and increase of rule by might. After Confucius and Mencius had died, the learning of the sages became obscure and strange, and heterodox teachings unreasonable. The teachers did not consider the learning of the sages as instruction, nor did the students consider it as learning. The followers of those that ruled by might secretly appropriated things that seemed to be like those of the first king. Externally they made use of his doctrines, but it was done in order to assist their own selfish desires. There was no one in the Empire who did not respect and cherish this point of view. The doctrine of the sages was obstructed with a luxuriant growth of weeds. The people imitated one another and daily sought knowledge through which they might become wealthy and powerful—plans directed toward deception, and schemes for rebellion, things that impose upon heaven and injure mankind. Temporary success was utilized in the earnest pursuit of honor and gain. Of men such as Kuan, Shang, Su, Chang, and their class, there were an indefinite number.

The Learning of the Sages Was Entirely Neglected

After a long time of quarreling, plundering, sorrow, and affliction without ceasing, these men sank into the condition of animals and savages, and even their violent schemes could not all be carried out. All scholars were extremely distressed in their noble-mindedness. They sought to find the sage emperor's laws and regulations, and arrange and renovate what was distressing them. Their purpose was to restore the path of the former kings. As the learning of the sages was left in the distance, the transmitted precepts of the violent practices became more numerous, intense, and pervasive. Even those who had the knowledge of the virtuous man could not avoid being tainted by the practices then prevalent. That they explained and renovated their doctrines in order to spread enlightenment over the world, only extended the boundary of force. The gate and wall of the learning of the sage could not be seen. Under such circumstances expository learning prevailed and was transmitted for the sake of making reputation. Learning that consisted in remembering and reciting was considered extensive; and formal learning was viewed as elegant. Men of this type confusedly and noisily came up in great numbers and disputed among themselves in order to establish their point of view in the Empire. I do not know how many groups there were. They came from ten thousand by-paths and a thousand different ways, but I do not know what they attained.

Wang Describes the Worldly Students

The students of the world may be compared to a theatre where a hundred different acts are presented. The players cheer, jest, hop, and skip. They emulate one another in cleverness and ingenuity; they laugh in the play and strive for the palm of beauty. On all sides the people emulate one another in striving to see. They look toward the front and gaze toward the rear, but cannot see it all. Their ears and their eyes are confused; their mental and physical energy is disturbed and confounded. Day and night they spend in amusement until they are steeped in it and rest in it, as though they were insane. They do not know what has become of their family property. Under the influence of the sayings of such scholars, princes and kings are confused and devote their lives to vain, useless literary style. They do not themselves know what they say. Some among them realize the empty distance between their doctrines and those of the sages, and their errors and perversity. They realize that they have branched off and have impeded the doctrine of the sages, and even rouse themselves to extraordinary effort, because they desire to see the truth and reality underlying all action. But the highest standpoint these views may in time reach, pertains merely to getting wealth, honor, or gain—the occupation of the five tyrants (of the sixth century B.C.). The learning of the sages is left farther and farther in the distance and is more and more obscured, while practices are directed toward acquiring honor and gain. The farther they go, the more they fall into error. Though some among them have been deceived by Buddhism and Taoism, yet even the sayings of Buddha and Lao-tzu, in last analysis, are unable to overcome the mind that is devoted to honor and gain. Though they have weighed the opinions of the mass of scholars, the discussions of these also are unable to break into their point of view—that of devoting themselves to honor and gain. When we consider present conditions, we find that the poison of honor and gain has penetrated the innermost recesses of the mind, and the practice thereof has become second nature.

For several thousand years people have mutually boasted of their knowledge; they have crushed one another because of power, and wrangled with one another for gain. They have mutually sought for superiority in cleverness, and each has sought for reputation. When they come into prominence and are appointed to official position, those who should be in control of the taxes also desire to serve as military officials, and those who are in charge of the laws, ceremonies, and music, also wish positions on the Board of Civil Office. He who holds the position of a prefect or a magistrate thinks of being the treasurer of a province or a provincial judge; he who is censor hopes to become a prime minister. As a matter of fact, he who is unable to carry out the particular task of his position cannot hold other official positions at the same time, and he who does not understand these sayings (of the sage) cannot expect the praise that attaches to them. Where memory and ability to recite are extensive, they tend to increase pride; and extensive knowledge tends toward doing evil. Much hearing and seeing tends toward disorderly behavior in discussion, and wealth in literary style tends to patch up and brighten one's hypocrisy. It was because of this that Kao, K'uei, Chi, and Hsieh were unable to unite two things in one office. But present-day young students who are just beginning to learn, all desire to understand their sayings and investigate their methods and mysteries. Under false pretenses, they have said that they wish to reform the affairs of the Empire, but this is not the real idea of their minds. They are looking for something to help their selfishness and fulfill their desires.

Alas! because of these abuses, and because of this purpose and these devices of study, they naturally should hear the instruction of the sages. But they view it as an excrescence, a tumor, a handle-hole, and thus they consider their intuitive faculty as insufficient. They are certain to reach the point where they say that the learning of the sages is of no value. Alas! how can the scholars living on earth still seek the learning of the sages, or how can they still discuss it? Who is there among the scholars of this generation who, desiring to devote himself to study, is not in toilsome labor and great difficulty, is not also bigoted, does not stick to literary style, and is not in great danger? Alas, one can but feel sympathy for them! It is fortunate that heaven-given principles are in the mind of man; that in last analysis there is something which cannot be destroyed; and that the clearness of the intuitive faculty is the same as in the most ancient times. Thus, when they hear my exhaustive discussion they must surely commiserate their own condition and be in distress because of it. They must be sorry to a degree that is painful. They must rise up with renewed effort, as water flows into a river in spite of every hindrance. Only the superior scholar can promote this. To whom shall I look for it?

KITARO NISHIDA

Kitaro Nishida (1870–1945), born in a small village near Kanazawa, Japan, established the Kyoto School of philosophy. He attended Tokyo University and became a high school teacher. Later he became a professor at Kanazawa Junior College. At age forty-one, he published *An Inquiry into the Good,* which tries to reconcile Zen Buddhism with Western philosophical practice. This earned him an appointment at Kyoto University, where he taught for eighteen years. At fifty-nine, he retired, but he continued writing until his death at age seventy-five.

Nishida's works are difficult, partly because he blends Eastern and Western themes and terminologies. For that very reason, however, they are also exciting. Nishida was impressed by Western logic and precision but wanted to preserve something he found at the basis of Asian culture, which he called "seeing the form of the formless and hearing the sound of the soundless."* Influenced by Zen Buddhism, he sought to explicate the nature of reality and of the good that Zen enlightenment provides—but in precise, rational terms.

Zen is a form of Mahayana Buddhism. The Japanese word *Zen* derives from the Chinese *ch'an,* which in turn derives from the Sanskrit word *dhyana;* literally, *zen* means "meditation." In China, however, the Indian idea of meditation yielded to a Taoist notion of concentration and enlightenment. The northern Chinese Zen school stressed gradual enlightenment based on a process of eliminating error and establishing mental quietude. The southern school, which developed later but eventually won out over its northern competitor, stressed sudden enlightenment. On this conception, the mind is a unity that is simple in the sense that it is absolutely indivisible. The Buddha is everywhere; anything can bring about its realization. The Zen practitioner seeks a state of mind in which reality becomes transparent and crystalline.

As Nishida describes his method in *An Inquiry into the Good,* "I wanted to explain all things on the basis of pure experience as the sole reality."† Nishida begins with experience and tries to construct from it the individual self, the will, and, ultimately, the good. Pure experience is the source of all knowledge, ethical and otherwise. It is prior to the distinction between the knower and the known; it is active, creative, dynamic, and unified. To attain knowledge of pure experience, Nishida recommends that we "discard all artificial assumptions, doubt whatever can be doubted, and proceed directly on the basis of direct and indubitable knowledge."‡ This knowledge alone is knowledge of pure experience.

* *From the Actor to the Seer* (1927), in *Nishida Kitaro Zenshu,* Volume 4 (Tokyo: Iwanami, 1978), 6.

† Preface to *An Inquiry into the Good,* trans. Masao Abe and Christopher Ives (New Haven, Conn., Yale Univ. Press, 1990).

‡ *An Inquiry into the Good,* 38.

The good, according to Nishida, must be understood as the way of reality. This is true for the world as a whole and for the individual. Consequently, the good for an individual is the actualization or fulfillment of that person's reality, or personality. For Nishida, personality is what underlies individual action; we grasp it not by examining the contents of our subjective self but by forgetting them. This has two important ethical consequences. First, ethics must find the good, not outside the individual, in intuited moral properties, consequences of actions, or an abstract moral law, but within the individual, in the innate demands of the will. Nishida thus advocates *energetism*, the view that moral value rests solely on such innate demands. Second, good should be identified with self-realization, which is in turn identified with the transcendence of the distinction between subject and object characteristic of the Zen ideal.

from *An Inquiry into the Good*

CHAPTER 23 / THE GOOD (ENERGETISM)

. . . Let us now consider the good that must be the goal of our will, that is, the standard that must determine the value of our conduct. As I said before, we must seek the basis of value judgments in direct experience found in our consciousness. The good must be articulated from the internal demands of consciousness, not from without. We cannot explain how a thing ought to be simply from how it is or how it occurred. The ultimate standard of truth is found in the internal necessity of consciousness. Foundational thinkers such as Augustine and Descartes started from this point, and we, too, must seek the fundamental standard of good therein.

Heteronomous ethics locates the standard of good and evil as outside us; taking that perspective, such ethics cannot explain why we ought to do the good. In comparison, the approach taken by the rational theory, in which the value of good and evil is determined from reason as one of the internal activities of consciousness, is a step forward—but even so, reason cannot determine the value of the will. As Høffding has indicated in his claim that consciousness begins and ends with the action of the will, the will is a more fundamental fact than the activity of abstract understanding—it is not that the activity of abstract understanding gives rise to the will, but that the will controls this activity. It might be acceptable for hedonic theories to state that feeling and the will are probably manifestations of the same phenomenon with differing strengths, but as seen before, pleasure arises from the satisfaction of the innate demands of consciousness, and such innate demands as impulses and instincts are more fundamental than feelings of pleasure and discomfort.

To explain the good it is clear that we must investigate the character of the will. The will is the fundamental unifying activity of consciousness and a direct manifestation of the fundamental unifying power of reality. The will entails action for oneself, not for the sake of another. The basis for the determination of the value of the will can be sought only in the will itself. As stated in the discussion of the nature of conduct, the action of the will has the following character: at the base of the will are innate demands (the causes of consciousness) that appear in consciousness as goal concepts which unify consciousness; when such unification reaches completion—when ideals are realized—we feel satisfaction. When we go against these ideals, we feel dissatisfaction. Because that which determines the value of conduct lies wholly in these fundamental, innate demands of the will, when we completely realize these demands (our ideals), our conduct is praised as good, and when we act contrary to them, our conduct is censured as bad. Accordingly, the good is the realization of our internal demands, our ideals; it is the development and completion of the will.

The ethical theory that bases itself on such fundamental ideals is called energetism, and its origin is found in Plato and Aristotle. Aristotle wrote that the goal of human life is happiness (*eudaimonia*), and that we reach this happiness through perfect action, not through the pursuit of pleasure.

Many so-called moralists overlook this aspect of action. Focusing on duty and laws, they believe that the fundamental nature of the good is to suppress the desires of the self and to restrict action. Lacking an understanding of the true significance of our actions, we imperfect beings of course often fall into predicaments—so it is only natural that people should talk of suppressing desires and restricting action. But it is only because there is a greater demand to be fostered that we need to suppress smaller demands; therefore to suppress all demands indiscriminately in fact runs contrary to the fundamental nature of the good. The good must include a quality of imperative authority, but natural enjoyment is a more necessary quality. There is no inherent value in moral duty and moral law itself, for they arise on the basis of the great demands discussed earlier.

From this perspective, the good and happiness do not conflict, and like Aristotle we can say that the good is happiness. The satisfaction of the demands of the self or the realization of ideals always constitutes happiness. Although this feeling of happiness necessarily accompanies the good, we cannot maintain—as hedonic theories do—that the feeling of pleasure is the goal of the will and that pleasure is the good. Although they resemble each other, pleasure and happiness are different. We can achieve happiness through satisfaction, and satisfaction arises in the realization of demands for ideals. "Eating coarse food, drinking water, and bending one's elbow to make a pillow—pleasure also resides therein," said Confucius. Depending on the circumstances, we are able to maintain happiness even in the midst of pain. True happiness is actually something acquired through the realization of ideals. People of course often view the realization of the ideals of the self or the satisfaction of demands as identical with egoism and selfishness; but for us the voice of the deepest internal demands of the self has great power, and there is nothing in human nature more awe-inspiring than this.

Assuming that the good is the realization of ideals and the satisfaction of demands, from what do these demands or ideals arise and what sort of character does the good have? Because the will is the deepest unifying activity in consciousness—that is, the action of the self—the fundamental demands or ideals that become the cause of the will arise from the character of the self and are the power of the self. In our consciousness, an internal unity always functions at the base of thinking, imagination, will, perception, feeling, and impulse; and all phenomena of consciousness are the development and completion of this unity. The deepest power unifying this whole is our so-called self, and the will is that which most completely expresses this power. Thus the develop-

ment and completion of the will is none other than the development and completion of the self, and the good is the development and completion—the self-realization—of the self. The highest good, in other words, is for our spirit to develop its various abilities and to achieve a perfect development. In this way, Aristotle's *entelechie* is the good. For a human to display his or her innate nature—just as a bamboo plant or a pine tree fully displays its nature—is our good. Spinoza said that virtue is to function in accordance with the self's own nature.

From this perspective, the concept of good approaches that of beauty. Beauty is felt when things are realized like ideals are realized, which means for things to display their original nature. Just as flowers are most beautiful when they manifest their original nature, humans attain the pinnacle of beauty when they express their original nature. In this regard the good is beauty. No matter how valueless conduct might appear when seen in light of the great demands of human nature, when it is truly natural conduct emerging from the innate talents of the person, it evokes a sense of beauty. In the moral realm this conduct likewise gives rise to a kind of magnanimous feeling. The Greeks regarded the good and beauty as identical, an idea most evident in Plato.

Moreover, from a certain angle, the concept of the good coincides with the concept of reality. As discussed earlier, the development and completion of a thing is the fundamental mode of the establishment of all reality, and spirit, nature, and the universe come to exist by this mode. The good, conceived of as the development and completion of the self, amounts to our obeying the laws of the reality called the self. That is, to unite with the true reality of the self is the highest good. The laws of morality thus come to be included in the laws of reality, and we are able to explain the good in terms of the true nature of the reality called the self. Internal demands, which are the basis of value judgments, and the unifying power of reality are one, not two. The view of existence and value as separate comes from an act of abstraction that distinguishes objects of knowing from objects of feeling and willing; but in concrete reality existence and value are fundamentally one. Thus, to seek the good and to return to it is to know the true reality of the self. The notion of the truth and the good as being identical in the rational theory is partially true, but abstract knowledge and the good do not necessarily coincide. To know the true reality of the self means to have an existential realization.

The above ideas are fundamental to Plato's stance (that the idea of the good is the foundation of reality) in Greece and to the *Upanishads* in India. And in medieval philosophy we encounter the expression, "All reality is good" (*omne ens est bonum*). I think such ideas constitute the most profound notion of the good.

CHAPTER 24 / THE GOOD AS A UNITY OF PERSONALITY

Having set forth a general conception of the good, I will henceforth examine the good in greater detail and clarify its distinctive characteristics.

All of us clearly recognize that consciousness is not a simple activity but rather a synthesis of various activities. The demands that arise in us are not simple either, but are quite naturally varied. This brings us to a question, which concerns the good of the self as a whole: the fulfillment of which demand constitutes the highest good?

None of our phenomena of consciousness stands alone; without exception each comes forth in relation to others. A moment of consciousness is not simple—it contains complex elements that are dependent on each other, for they have a kind of meaning in relation to others. Consciousness at a given time and also over a lifetime is organized into such a system, and the "self" is the name for the unity of this whole.

Our demands likewise never arise alone. They also necessarily arise in relation to others. The good for us differs from the satisfaction of just one kind of demand or a demand of a particular time. Clearly, a particular demand becomes good only when it is related to the whole. For example, the good of the body derives not from the health of one of its parts but from the harmony of the body as a whole. From the perspective of energetism, then, the good is primarily a coordinated harmony—or mean—between various activities. Our conscience is the activity of

consciousness that harmonizes and unifies the activities.

The idea that harmony constitutes the good comes from Plato. He likens the good to harmony in music, and such people as Shaftesbury have adopted this idea. Aristotle theorizes that the mean is the good, and the Asian version of this idea appears in *The Book of the Mean*. Aristotle locates all virtues in the mean, contending for example that courage is the mean between roughness and timidity, and that frugality is the mean between miserliness and squander, a view that closely resembles the thought of Tzu-ssu. On the basis of the theory of evolution Herbert Spencer similarly contends that the good is the average of various faculties, which amounts to the same view as the others just mentioned.

Simply saying that the good is a harmony or the mean, however, does not sufficiently clarify its meaning. What meaning do harmony and the mean have here? Consciousness is not an assemblage of sequential actions but a single unified system. Accordingly, harmony or the mean does not carry a quantitative connotation; it must signify a systematic order. Granting this, what is the order that is distinct in each of the various activities of our spirit? At lower levels, our spirit, like the spirit of animals, is simply an instinctual activity—that is, because it functions impulsively in response to objects before us, it is moved entirely by physical desire. But no matter how simple, phenomena of consciousness necessarily possess ideational demands; however instinctual the activity of consciousness might be, the activity of ideas is hidden behind it. (I think that this is necessarily the case with higher non-human animals as well.) With the possible exception of the severely retarded, no humans can be satisfied by purely physical desires, for ideational desires are always functioning at the bottom of their minds. In short, all people embrace some sort of ideals. Even a miser's craving for profit derives from a kind of ideal. Human beings do not exist on the basis of the flesh—rather, they live on the basis of ideas. In his poem "The Violet," Goethe writes that a violet in the field achieves the fulfillment of love when it is crushed under the foot of a young shepherdess. I take this to be the true feeling of all humans.

The activity of ideas is the fundamental activity of spirit, and by this our consciousness should be controlled. The true good for us is to satisfy the demands arising from that activity. Granting this and proceeding a step farther to inquire into the fundamental law of the activity of ideas, we come to the laws of reason. The laws of reason express the most universal and fundamental relations between ideas; they are supreme laws controlling the activity of ideas. Reason is the basic faculty that should control our spirit, and the satisfaction of reason is our highest good. It can thus be said that human good is to follow reason. Rigorously emphasizing this idea, the Cynics and Stoics rejected all other desires of the human mind as evil and even argued that the sole good is to follow reason alone. In the later thought of Plato and Aristotle, however, the highest good derives from the activity of reason, and to control and govern other activities by it constitutes the good as well. In the *Republic,* Plato sees a parallel between the organization of the republic and that of the human soul and argues that the state of affairs governed by reason is the highest good for both the republic and the individual.

Assuming that our consciousness is constituted by a synthesis of various faculties and constructed such that one faculty controls the others, then in energetism to follow reason and on that basis control other faculties is the good. Originally, however, our consciousness is one activity, and a single, unique power always functions at its base. This power manifests itself in such momentary activities of consciousness as perception and impulse; in conscious activities like thinking, imagining, and willing, it assumes a more profound form. To follow reason means to follow this profound unifying power. Otherwise, as I stated when I critiqued the rational theory of ethics, reason conceived of in the abstract provides merely a formal relationship with no content whatsoever. The unifying power of consciousness never exists apart from the content of consciousness; in fact, the content of consciousness is established by this power. When we investigate the content of consciousness by analyzing it into its individual parts, we of course fail to discover this unifying power. It nevertheless appears as a majestic, indisputable fact in the synthesis of the individual parts. For example, an ideal expressed in a painting or a feeling expressed in music is understood not through analysis, but must be intuited and

realized in oneself. If we regard this unifying power as the personality of each individual, then the good resides in the maintenance and development of personality as this unifying power.

The "power of personality" does not indicate a natural, material force as in the life-force of plants and animals, nor does it indicate such an unconscious faculty as instinct. Instinctual activity is a kind of material force that originates in organic activities. In contrast, personality is the unifying power of consciousness. Although I speak of it in this way, personality is not an assortment of highly subjective hopes that functions as the center of each person's superficial consciousness. Such hopes may express the individual's personality to some extent, but the true personality comes forth when a person eradicates them and forgets his or her self. But this is not the activity of Kant's pure reason, which is common to each individual and totally separate from the content of experience. Rather, personality must be something with a particular meaning unique to the person.

The true unity of consciousness is a pure and simple activity that comes forth of itself, unhindered by oneself; it is the original state of independent, self-sufficient consciousness, with no distinction among knowledge, feeling, and volition, and no separation of subject and object. At this time our true personality expresses itself in its entirety. Personality therefore is not found in mere reason or desire, much less in unconscious impulses; like the inspiration of a genius, it is an infinite unifying power that functions directly and spontaneously from within each individual. (People long ago said that the Way does not pertain to knowing or to not knowing.) And as I discussed in the section on reality, if we assume the phenomena of consciousness are the only reality, then our personalities are the activity of the unifying power of the universe. In other words, our personalities are the particular forms in which the sole reality—which transcends the distinction between mind and matter—manifests itself according to circumstances.

Since the good is the realization of this great power, its demands are exceedingly solemn. Kant stated that there are two things that we always view with praise and reverence: the vast, starry heaven above, and the moral law within.

CHAPTER 25 / THE MOTIVATION OF GOOD CONDUCT (THE FORM OF THE GOOD)

As I stated earlier, the good refers to that which satisfies the internal demands of the self. Because the greatest demands of the self—that is, the demands of personality—are the fundamental unifying power of consciousness, to satisfy these demands and thereby actualize personality is for us the absolute good. The demands of the personality are the unifying power of consciousness and, at the same time, an expression of the infinite unifying power at the base of reality; and so to actualize and fulfill our personality means to become one with this underlying power. If we construe the good in this way, we can determine the nature of good conduct.

From this perspective, all good conduct takes personality as its goal. Personality is the basis of all value, and in the universe only personality possesses absolute value. Within us are, of course, various demands, both physical and mental; therefore various things, such as wealth, power, knowledge, and art, are valuable to us. Yet no matter how powerful or lofty the demand, if it becomes divorced from the demands of personality it loses all value. A demand possesses value only as a part of, or a means of, the demands of personality. Wealth, honor, authority, health, skill, and academic knowledge are not in themselves good. When they run contrary to the demands of personality, they become evil. In short, absolutely good conduct is conduct that takes the actualization of personality as its goal, that is, conduct that functions for the sake of the unity of consciousness.

According to Kant, the value of things is determined from without and is thus relative, but because our will determines its value by itself, personality possesses absolute value. As is widely known, Kant taught that we should respect the personality of ourselves and others and treat others as ends in themselves, never using them merely as a means.

What sort of conduct is the good conduct that truly takes personality as its goal? To answer this question, we must consider the objective content of the action of personality and clarify the goal of conduct—but I will first discuss the subjective element in good conduct: the motivation. Good conduct is conduct that derives from the internal necessity of the self. We can be aware of the demands of the whole personality only in the state of direct experience prior to deliberative discrimination. In this state, personality is the voice of a type of internal demand that emerges from the depths of the mind and that gradually envelops the mind as a whole. Conduct that takes personality itself as its goal is conduct that accords with this demand. If we go against it, we negate our own personality. Another condition necessary for good conduct is sincerity. Christ said that only those who are like an innocent child can enter heaven. Sincerity is the good not because of the results arising from it, but because it is good in itself. It is said that to deceive a person is evil, not necessarily because of what results from deceiving someone but rather because to deceive another is to deceive oneself and to negate one's own personality.

Such expressions as "the internal necessity of the self" and "genuine, unaffected demands" are occasionally misunderstood. Some people think that genuine unaffectedness lies in self-indulgently and recklessly overlooking the rules of society and in not restraining one's sensual desires. But the internal necessity of personality—that is, sincerity—is a demand based on the union of knowledge, feeling, and volition. It does not indicate simply following blind impulse in opposition to judgments made by the intellect and the demands of human feeling. It is only when we exhaust the intellect and feeling that the true demand of personality—sincerity—arises in us; it is only when we exhaust all of the power of the self, when the consciousness of the self nearly disappears and one is not conscious of the self, that we see the activity of the true personality. Take, for example, a work of art. When does the true personality or originality of the painter appear? Insofar as the painter intends various things in his or her consciousness, we cannot yet truly see the painter's personality. We first see it only when, after long years of struggle, the painter's skills mature and the brush follows the will. The expression of personality in the moral realm is no different from this. We express personality not by following temporary desires but by following the most solemn internal demands. This is diametrically opposed to self-indulgent decadence and, contrary to what one might expect, it is an endeavor of difficulty and pain.

To follow the sincere internal demands of the self—to actualize the true personality of the self—does not mean to establish subjectivity in opposition to objectivity or to make external objects obey the self. Only when we thoroughly eliminate the subjective fancies of the self and unite with a thing can we satisfy the true demands of the self and see the true self. From a certain angle, the objective world of each individual is a reflection of his or her personality. Or rather, each individual's true self is the system of independent, self-sufficient reality appearing before that person. In this way, the sincerest demands of each and every person necessarily coincide at all times with the ideals of the objective world the person sees. For example, however selfish one might be, if one has any degree of sympathy, the greatest demand is certainly to give satisfaction to others after securing one's own satisfaction. If we assume that the demands of the self are not limited to carnal desires but include idealistic demands, then we must by all means speak in this way. The more selfish we become, the more we feel anguish at blocking the personal desires of others. Contrary to what one might think, I believe that perhaps only someone devoid of personal desire can obliterate the personal desires of others without losing peace of mind. To fulfill the greatest demands of the self and to actualize the self is to actualize the objective ideals of the self—that is, to unite with objectivity. In this regard, good conduct is love. Love is the feeling of congruence between self and other, the feeling of the union of subject and object. Love exists not only when one person faces another, but also when a painter encounters nature. In his renowned *Symposium,* Plato states that love is the feeling that arises when that which is lacking tries to return to its original, perfect state.

If we go a step farther, however, we find that truly good conduct is neither to make objectivity follow subjectivity nor to make subjectivity follow objectivity. We reach the quintessence of good conduct only when subject and object merge, self and things forget each other, and all that exists is the activity of the sole reality of the universe. At that point we can say that things move the self or that the self moves things, that Sesshū painted nature or that nature

painted itself through Sesshū. There is no fundamental distinction between things and the self, for just as the objective world is a reflection of the self, so is the self a reflection of the objective world. The self does not exist apart from the world that it sees. Heaven and earth grow from the same root, and the myriad things are one system. Sages in ancient India said, "*Tat twam asi*" (That thou art); Paul said, "It is no longer I who live, but Christ who lives in me" (Galatians 2:20); and Confucius said, "I follow what my heart desires, without overstepping the bounds of morality."

CHAPTER 26 / THE GOAL OF GOOD CONDUCT (THE CONTENT OF THE GOOD)

In explaining good conduct that takes human personality as its goal, I indicated the kind of motives from which good conduct must emerge; I will now discuss the goal of good conduct. Good conduct is not a mere event inside consciousness but rather an action that takes as its goal the creation of an objective result in this world of facts, and we must now clarify the concrete content of this goal. I discussed earlier the so-called form of the good, and now I will discuss the content of the good.

Personality, which is both the unifying power of consciousness and the unifying power of reality, is first actualized in individuals. At the base of one's consciousness exists unanalyzable individuality. All activities of consciousness are an expression of this individuality: each person's knowledge, feeling, and volition possess qualities unique to the person. This individuality does not manifest itself only in phenomena of consciousness; it also emerges in each person's appearance, speech, and behavior. Without doubt, it is this individuality that portraits are meant to express. It starts to act at the moment a person is born into this world, and it develops in accordance with various experiences and circumstances until the time of death. Scientists reduce this individuality to the constitution of the brain, but I consider it an expression of the infinite unifying power of reality.

From the outset, we must make the actualization of this individuality our goal. This is the most immediate good. Health and knowledge are to be valued, of course, but they themselves are not the good, and we are not satisfied by them alone. That which gives an individual ultimate satisfaction is the actualization of the individuality of the self— that is, the displaying of one's own distinctive characteristics in practice. Anyone can give full play to individuality regardless of natural talents and life circumstances. Just as everyone has a different face, everyone possesses unique characteristics that cannot be imitated by others. The realization of this individuality gives supreme satisfaction to each person and makes each an indispensable part of the evolution of the universe. Until now, people have not emphasized individual good to any great extent, but I hold the good of the individual is most important and that it serves as the basis of all other goods. Truly great people are so not because of the greatness of their achievements, but because they have displayed great individuality. If one climbs to a high place and yells, one's voice will probably carry a long way because the place is high, not because the voice is loud. I believe that people who thoroughly express their own unique characteristics are greater than those who forget their duty to themselves and heedlessly run around for the sake of others.

This individual good differs from self-interest and selfish desires. Individualism and egoism must be strictly distinguished. Egoism is selfishness that takes one's own pleasure as its goal. This is the polar opposite of individualism, for to give full rein to the material desires of the self is, in fact, to eradicate individuality. No matter how many pigs we might gather together, none will have individuality.

Individualism and communalism are spoken of as if diametrically opposed to each other, but I think that they coincide. It is only when individuals in society fully engage in action and express their natural talents that society progresses. A society that ignores the individual is anything but a healthy one.

A strong will is the virtue most necessary for individual good. Such a person as Ibsen's character Brand embodies the ideal of individual morality. In contrast, weakness of will and vanity are the most despicable evils (and both of them arise from the loss of self-esteem). The greatest crime against individuality occurs when people commit suicide in despair.

As said earlier, true individualism is never reproachable nor does it necessarily conflict with society. But are people's individualities independent, unrelated realities? Or are individuals all expressions of a social self that functions at our base? If the former is the case, then individual good must be our greatest good. If the latter is the case, then there is greater social good in us. I think that Aristotle gets at an indisputable truth when he states at the beginning of his study of politics that people are social animals. Seen from the perspective of contemporary physiology, our physical bodies are not entirely individual, for they originate in the cells of our ancestors. We and our descendants are born through the splitting of these cells. We can thus view all members of each species as constituting one living entity. Biologists now state along these lines that in a sense a living thing does not die, and this is also the case with the life of consciousness. When humans live in communities, a social consciousness necessarily functions to unify the consciousness of the members.

Language, manners, customs, social systems, laws, religion, and literature are all phenomena of this social consciousness. Our individual consciousnesses emerge from and are nurtured by it, and they are single cells that constitute this great consciousness. Knowledge, morality, and aesthetic taste all have social significance, and even the most universal learning does not escape social convention. (It is for this reason that at present each nation has its own academic tradition.) The distinctive characteristics of an individual are simply variations that derive from the social consciousness at their base. Even the most original genius cannot step beyond the scope of this social consciousness; in fact, such a person is one who most displays the deepest significance of the social consciousness. (Christ's relationship to Judaism is one example of this.) In short, anyone who stands absolutely unrelated to the social consciousness has the consciousness of the insane.

No one can deny these facts, but we encounter conflicting opinions about whether communal consciousness exists in the same sense as individual consciousness and can therefore be seen as a single personality. Høffding and others deny the existence of a unified consciousness. Høffding states that a forest is a collection of trees and that if the forest were divided there would no longer be a forest; likewise, a society is a collection of individuals, and there is no independent existence called a society that stands apart from individuals. We cannot say, however, that there is no unity simply because unity no longer exists after the dissection of the whole. If we analyze individual consciousness, we do not find a separate, unifying self. But because there is a unity upon which a unique character arises and various phenomena are established, we consider this unity a living reality. For the same reason, we can view social consciousness as a living reality. Like individual consciousness, social consciousness constitutes a system with a center and interconnections. Individual consciousness of course has a foundation called the body, and in this respect it diverges from social consciousness. But the brain is not a simple material object—it is a collection of cells. This is no different from the fact that society is made up of the cells called individuals.

Because our individual consciousnesses are parts of such a social consciousness, most of our demands are social. If we were to remove all altruistic elements from our desires almost nothing would remain. This is clear when we see our desire for life as caused primarily by altruism. We find greater overall satisfaction in the satisfaction experienced by what the self loves and by the society to which one belongs than in personal satisfaction. Fundamentally, the center of the self is not limited to the interior of the individual: the self of a mother is found in her child, and the self of a loyal subject is found in the monarch. As one's personality becomes greater, the demands of the self become increasingly social.

Such social consciousness consists of various levels. The smallest and most immediate is the family, which is the first level at which one's personality develops in society. The purpose of a man and a woman joining together and forming a family is not only to leave descendants, for it involves a more profound spiritual (and moral) goal. In the *Symposium*, Plato relates a story to the effect that although man and woman were originally of one body, Zeus splits them apart, leaving them in a state of yearning for each other. This is an intriguing idea. If we consider what an exemplar of humankind might be, we see that an individual man or woman falls short,

whereas that which combines masculinity and femininity does not. Otto Weininger states that humans, in both mind and body, are constituted by the union of masculine and feminine elements, and that the sexes love each other so that these elements can join together and constitute a complete human being. Just as a man's character falls short of the exemplar of humankind, so does a woman's. The sexes complement each other and can thereby bring about the development of a complete personality.

The development of social consciousness is not limited to the small group of the family. Our mental and physical life can develop in all of the various social groups. At the next level beyond the family, the nation unifies the entirety of our conscious activity and expresses a single personality. Many theories have been set forth concerning the goal of the nation. Some people consider the essence of the nation to be the power of sovereignty and think that the purpose of the nation is to ward off enemies on the outside and protect life and property of the people on the inside. (Schopenhauer, Taine, and Hobbes hold this opinion.) Others consider the essence of the nation to be the individual, and see the harmonious development of individual personalities as constituting its purpose. (This is the type of theory advanced by such people as Rousseau.) But the true goal of the nation is not something material and passive as outlined by the former group, and the personality of an individual is not the foundation of the nation as maintained by the latter. We individuals are entities that have developed as cells of one society. The essence of the nation is the expression of the communal consciousness that constitutes the foundation of our minds. In the context of the nation, we can accomplish a great development of personality; the nation is a unified personality, and the systems and laws of the nation are expressions of the will of this communal consciousness. (This theory was set forth in antiquity by Plato and Aristotle and in modern times by Hegel.) To exert ourselves for the sake of a nation is to exert ourselves for the sake of the development and perfection of a great personality. Moreover, when a nation punishes an individual, it does so neither for revenge nor for the safety of society, but because personality possesses an inviolable dignity.

At present, the nation is the greatest expression of unified communal consciousness. But the expression of our personality cannot stop there—it demands something greater: a social union that includes all humankind. This idea has already appeared in Paul's Christianity and in the thought of the Stoics, but it is not easily actualized. The present age is still one of armed peace.

If we retrace the development of humankind from the beginning of history, we see that the nation is not the final goal of humankind. A meaningful purpose runs consistently throughout the development of humankind, and the nation appears to be something that rises and falls in order to fulfill part of humankind's mission. (The history of nations is the development of Hegel's so-called "world-spirit.") Genuine universalism, however, does not require that each nation ceases to be. Rather, it means that each nation becomes increasingly stable, displays its distinctive characteristics, and contributes to the history of the world.

CHAPTER 27 / PERFECT GOOD CONDUCT

The good is the actualization of personality. Viewed internally, this actualization is the satisfaction of a solemn demand—that is, the unification of consciousness—and its ultimate form is achieved in the mutual forgetting of self and other and the merging of subject and object. Viewed externally as an emergent fact, this actualization advances from the small-scale development of individuality to a culmination in the large-scale unified development of all humankind. In considering these internal and external views of the actualization of personality, we must resolve a key problem: can we deem that which gives us great satisfaction internally to be a great good in the realm of external facts as well? This is the problem of whether these two facets of the good are always congruent.

Based on my discussion of reality, I hold that these two facets in no way conflict with or contradict each other. Phenomena fundamentally involve no distinction between internal and external. Subjective consciousness and the objective world are the same thing viewed from different angles, so concretely there is only one fact. As stated

before, the world is established by the self's unity of consciousness, and the self is one small system of reality. As emphasized in basic Buddhist thought, the self and the universe share the same foundation; or rather, they are the same thing. For this reason we can feel in our minds the infinite significance of reality as infinite truth in knowledge, as infinite beauty in feeling, and as infinite good in volition. To know reality is not to know something external to the self but to know the self itself. The truth, beauty, and good of reality are the truth, beauty, and good of the self. Doubts may arise as to why if this is so we encounter falsehood, ugliness, and evil in the world. When we consider this problem deeply, however, we see that in the world there is neither absolute truth, beauty, and good, nor absolute falsehood, ugliness, and evil. Falsehood, ugliness and evil always arise in our viewing abstractly just one aspect of things while we are unaware of the whole, and in being partial to just one facet of reality and thereby going against the unity of the whole. (As I said . . . falsehood, ugliness, and evil are in one respect necessary for the establishment of reality; they are generated by a principle of opposition.)

According to Augustine, fundamentally no evil exists in the world and all of nature as created by God is good. Evil is merely the privation of essential qualities. God adorned the world with opposites as in a beautiful poem; and just as shadow increases a picture's beauty, the world is—when seen with insight—beautiful even while including sin.

In considering how the fact of the good and the demands of the good might conflict, we discover two cases. One is when a certain conduct is good in actuality but its motive is not good, and the other is when the motive is good but the conduct is not. In the first case, if an internal motive is selfish while the external conduct in actuality accords with a good goal, then the conduct falls short of good conduct that takes the actualization of personality as its goal. We might praise such conduct, but at such a time we are viewing it not in terms of morality but simply in terms of benefit. From the perspective of morality, this conduct is inferior to that of someone who, no matter how foolish he or she might be, has demonstrated the utmost sincerity. It might be said that conduct that tries to benefit many people—even if it does not spring from a purely good motive—is superior to the conduct of someone who tries to purify himself or herself. To benefit people can mean various things. If we are speaking of merely material benefit, the benefit will be good if it is used toward good ends but evil if it is used toward evil ends. Considered in light of the truly moral benefit that promotes so-called public morality, if conduct is not true good conduct internally, then it is merely a means to promote good conduct rather than good conduct itself. It does not measure up to instances of good conduct, no matter how minor they might be.

Regarding the second case—when the motive is good but the actual conduct is not necessarily good—people often say that individual sincerity and the supreme good of all humankind sometimes conflict. I believe, however, that those who say this lack a correct understanding of sincerity—what such people say is not true if we use "sincerity" in the sense of the truly deepest demands of spirit as a whole. Our true demands are not artificially created by us; they are facts of nature. Like truth or beauty at the base of the human mind, the good contains a universal element. Just as Faust discovered when he returned late at night to his lonely study after a walk in the fields during a time of great anguish over life, in the quiet of night when our minds are at peace the feeling of the universality of the good begins to operate in us spontaneously. Assuming that no person possesses an entirely different basis of consciousness, I think that insofar as we are humans with shared reason we necessarily think in the same way and seek things in the same way. To be sure, there may be times when the greatest demands of humankind get stuck in mere possibility and do not actualize themselves and function. But even then it is not that there are no demands; the demands are hidden, and the self does not know the true self.

For this reason, I think that our deepest demands and greatest goals unite automatically. While internally we discipline the self and attain to the true nature of the self, externally we give rise to love for our fellow humans and come to accord with the supremely good goal—good conduct that is perfect and true. From one angle, such perfect good conduct appears exceedingly difficult, but from a differ-
ʾt angle, it is something anyone must be able to

do. Morality is not a matter of seeking something apart from the self—it is simply the discovery of something within the self. People frequently confuse the essence of the good with its external shell, so they think that unless one is engaged in a worldwide enterprise involving all humankind, one stands unrelated to the greatest good. But because a person's abilities and circumstances determine what sort of enterprise will be undertaken, it is impossible for all people to pursue the same enterprise. Yet no matter how much our enterprises differ, we can function with the same spirit. No matter how small the enterprise, a person who constantly works out of love for his or her fellow humans realizes the great personality of all humankind. Although Raphael's lofty aesthetic personality perhaps found the Madonna the most appropriate medium for its realization, his personality manifests itself not only in the Madonna but in all of his paintings. And though the subjects chosen by Raphael and Michelangelo are quite similar, the two artists express their respective characters in their own distinctive ways. In short, the essence of art and morality lies in spirit, not in things of the external world.

In closing this chapter, I want to say one more thing. When we approach the good academically, we can offer various explanations, but in actuality there is only one true good: to know the true self. Our true self is the ultimate reality of the universe, and if we know the true self we not only unite with the good of humankind in general but also fuse with the essence of the universe and unite with the will of God—and in this religion and morality are culminated. The method through which we can know the true self and fuse with God is our self-attainment of the power of the union of subject and object. To acquire this power is to kill our false self and, after dying once to worldly desire, to gain new life. (As Muhammad said, heaven lies in the shadow of the sword.) Only in this way can we truly reach the realm of the union of subject and object, which is the ultimate meaning of religion, morality, and art. Christianity calls this event rebirth, and Buddhism calls it *kenshō*. According to one story, when Pope Benedict XI asked Giotto to show him a work that demonstrated his ability as a painter, Giotto simply drew a circle. In morality, we must attain to Giotto's circle.

SEUNG SAHN

The southern Chinese Zen school is in some ways anti-intellectual. All distinctions, it maintains, are illusions. Thus, studying the scriptures of Buddhism and other philosophical texts is in itself pointless. Thinking can only take us away from the truth. There is no difference between the real and the unreal, between the holy and the secular, or between the logical and the illogical.

This assertion leads to paradoxes. The Zen doctrine seems to imply that all doctrines are unfounded and need to be transcended. In effect, Zen implies that one must work very hard to achieve effortlessness. This might suggest that Zen Buddhism refutes itself. These paradoxes are not, however, contradictions or refutations of Zen. Zen theses are means for reaching an end—*satori*, enlightenment—rather than literal descriptions of reality. Their point is not to give us descriptive or even normative knowledge but to lead us to undergo certain kinds of experiences.

Of course, there are many ways of undergoing the right kinds of experiences. They need not involve language; if they do, the language need not "make sense" in traditional terms. Zen training methods include meditation, which often includes *koans*—"riddles" meant to develop insight—and various arts. Sometimes, Zen masters use more extreme methods, including beatings, to clarify the mind. According to traditional Zen teachings, the personal element is essential: a Master must pass enlightenment to a student. There is no way to teach yourself. Various writers have nevertheless tried to convey the messages of Zen to a large and predominantly Western audience. One of these writers is Seung Sahn.

Seung Sahn (b. 1927) was born in Seun Choen, North Korea, to Protestant parents. When he was seventeen, he joined the Korean resistance, fighting against the occupying Japanese army. He was captured and barely escaped execution. After his release from prison, he and two friends fled to Manchuria to join the Free Korean Army. Seung Sahn returned to Korea after World War II and studied philosophy at Dong Guk University. He then shaved his head and lived as a hermit in the mountains, studying Confucianism and Buddhism. He was ordained a Buddhist monk at the age of twenty-one. Seung Sahn had his first experience of enlightenment while spending one hundred days on Won Gak Mountain, eating nothing but pine needles. At twenty-two, Seung Sahn became a Zen master; three masters certified his enlightenment. (One of them, Ko Bong, a particularly famous Zen master, never transmitted enlightenment to anyone else.) After serving in the army during the Korean War, Seung Sahn chaired a committee to reform the Chogye order of Korean Buddhism and became abbot of five temples in Seoul. For nine years, he taught in Japan; he founded temples in Hong Kong and Tokyo. At forty-five he came to the United States. He now directs Zen communities in New York, New England, and California.

Seung Sahn's 1976 book, *Dropping Ashes on the Buddha,* poses a puzzle. Smoking a cigarette, someone enters a Zen center, blows smoke in the face of the Buddha statue, and drops ashes on its lap. If you see this, what should you do? One possible answer: All distinctions are illusory. Nothing is holy; nothing is secular. Everything, ultimately, is one, and that is the Buddha. So, there is no difference between dropping ashes on the Buddha and dropping ashes in the ashtray. Another possible answer: Everything is what it is. What is holy is holy; what is secular is secular. Ashes should be dropped on the ashtray, not on the Buddha. Zen teaches that both perspectives are in some sense right. The person dropping ashes on the Buddha, therefore, understands only partially. If you try to explain this, however, the person will simply hit you, since he or she believes that all words—and all distinctions they mark—are meaningless. So, what should you do? Seung Sahn's puzzle brings out forcefully a central paradox of Zen Buddhism. If all distinctions are illusions, then, once we recognize this, how is discourse possible? How could the enlightened, or even partially enlightened, communicate?

This puzzle is partly one of ethics. The immediate problem, after all, is not how communication is possible, but rather what you should do. It is a practical puzzle, concerning obligations to others. The central point of Buddhism is the recognition and alleviation of suffering. The smoker dropping ashes on the Buddha suffers from an incomplete conception; you have an obligation to help. The puzzle has other serious ethical ramifications. If all distinctions are illusions, so is the distinction between good and evil. There is no difference between right and wrong. If so, how can any who understand this decide? How can they criticize, direct, or teach others—or be criticized, directed, or taught by them? We can say that Zen theses are means for achieving certain kinds of experiences—ladders to be kicked away once enlightenment is obtained. Once we see that they are mere ladders, however, how can we make further progress? Seung Sahn sees this as a primary problem for one who seeks enlightenment. He believes its solution is both possible and necessary for achieving enlightenment.

from *Dropping Ashes on the Buddha*

INTRODUCTION

Deep in the mountains, the great temple bell is struck. You hear it reverberating in the morning air, and all thoughts disappear from your mind. There is nothing that is you; there is nothing that is not you. There is only the sound of the bell, filling the whole universe.

Springtime comes. You see the flowers blossoming, the butterflies flitting about; you hear the birds singing, you breathe in the warm weather. And your mind is only springtime. It is nothing at all.

You visit Niagara and take a boat to the bottom of the Falls. The downpouring of the water is in front of you and around you and inside you, and suddenly you are shouting: YAAAAAA!

In all these experiences, outside and inside have become one. This is Zen mind.

Original nature has no opposites. Speech and words are not necessary. Without thinking, all things are exactly as they are. The truth is just like this.

Then why do we use words? Why have we made this book?

According to Oriental medicine, when you have a hot sickness you should take hot medicine. Most people are very attached to words and speech. So we cure this sickness with word-and-speech medicine.

Most people have a deluded view of the world. They don't see it as it is; they don't understand the truth. What is good, what is bad? Who makes good, who makes bad? They cling to their opinions with all their might. But everybody's opinion is different. How can you say that your opinion is correct and somebody else's is wrong? This is delusion.

If you want to understand the truth, you must let go of your situation, your condition, and all your opinions. Then your mind will be before thinking. "Before thinking" is clear mind. Clear mind has no inside and no outside. It is just like this. "Just like this" is the truth.

An eminent teacher said,

If you want to pass through this gate,
do not give rise to thinking.

This means that if you are thinking, you can't understand Zen. If you keep the mind that is before thinking, this is Zen mind.

So another Zen Master said,

Everything the Buddha taught
was only to correct your thinking.
If already you have cut off thinking,
what good are the Buddha's words?

The Heart Sutra says, "Form is emptiness, emptiness is form." This means, "no form, no emptiness." But the true meaning of "no form, no emptiness" is, "form is form, emptiness is emptiness."

If you are thinking, you won't understand these words. If you are not thinking, "just like this" is Buddha-nature.

What is Buddha-nature?

Deep in the mountains, the great temple bell is struck.

The truth is just like this.

CHAPTER 1 / ZEN IS UNDERSTANDING YOURSELF

One day a student from Chicago came to the Providence Zen Center and asked Seung Sahn Soen-sa, "What is Zen?"

Soen-sa held his Zen stick above his head and said, "Do you understand?"

The student said, "I don't know."

Soen-sa said, "This don't-know mind is you. Zen is understanding yourself."

"What do you understand about me? Teach me."

Soen-sa said, "In a cookie factory, different cookies are baked in the shape of animals, cars, people, and airplanes. They all have different names and forms, but they are all made from the same dough, and they all taste the same.

"In the same way, all things in the universe—the sun, the moon, the stars, mountains, rivers, people, and so forth—have different names and forms, but they are all made from the same substance. The universe is organized into pairs of opposites: light and darkness, man and woman, sound and silence, good and bad. But all these opposites are mutual, because they are made from the same substance. Their names and their forms are different, but their substance is the same. Names and forms are made by your thinking. If you are not thinking and have no attachment to name and form, then all substance is one. Your don't-know mind cuts off all thinking. This is your substance. The substance of this Zen stick and your own substance are the same. You are this stick; this stick is you."

The student said, "Some philosophers say this substance is energy, or mind, or God, or matter. Which is the truth?"

Soen-sa said, "Four blind men went to the zoo and visited the elephant. One blind man touched its side and said, 'The elephant is like a wall.' The next blind man touched its trunk and said, 'The elephant is like a snake.' The next blind man touched its leg and said, 'The elephant is like a column.' The last blind man touches its tail and said, 'The elephant is like a broom.' Then the four blind men started to fight, each one believing that his opinion was the right one. Each only understood the part he had touched; none of them understood the whole.

"Substance has no name and no form. Energy, mind, God, and matter are all name and form. Substance is the Absolute. Having name and form is having opposites. So the whole world is like the blind men fighting among themselves. Not understanding yourself is not understanding the truth. That is why there is fighting among ourselves. If all the people in the world understood themselves, they would attain the Absolute. Then the world would be at peace. World peace is Zen."

The student said, "How can practicing Zen make world peace?"

Soen-sa said, "People desire money, fame, sex, food, and rest. All this desire is thinking. Thinking is suffering. Suffering means no world peace. Not thinking is not suffering. Not suffering means world peace. World peace is the Absolute. The Absolute is I."

The student said, "How can I understand the Absolute?"

Soen-sa said, "You must understand yourself."

"How can I understand myself?"

Soen-sa held up the Zen stick and said, "Do you see this?"

He then quickly hit the table with the stick and said, "Do you hear this? This stick, this sound, and your mind—are they the same or different?"

The student said, "The same."

Soen-sa said, "If you say they are the same, I will hit you thirty times. If you say they are different, I will still hit you thirty times. Why?"

The student was silent.

Soen-sa shouted "KATZ!!!"* Then he said, "Spring comes, the grass grows by itself."

CHAPTER 2 / THE ZEN CIRCLE

One evening, at the Providence Zen Center, Seung Sahn Soen-sa gave the following Dharma Speech:

"What is Zen? Zen is understanding myself. What am I?

"I explain Zen by means of a circle. There are five points marked on the circle: zero degrees, ninety degrees, one-hundred-eighty degrees, two-hundred-seventy degrees, and three-hundred-sixty degrees. 360° is exactly the same point as 0°.

"We begin from 0° to 90°. This is the area of thinking and attachment. Thinking is desire, desire is suffering. All things are separated into opposites: good and bad, beautiful and ugly, mine and yours. I like this; I don't like that. I try to get happiness and avoid suffering. So life here is suffering, and suffering is life.

"Past 90° is the area of the Consciousness or Karma I. Below 90° there is attachment to name and

---

* This is the famous Zen belly-shout. Its transcription (KATZ in Korean and Japanese, HO in Chinese) hardly does it justice.

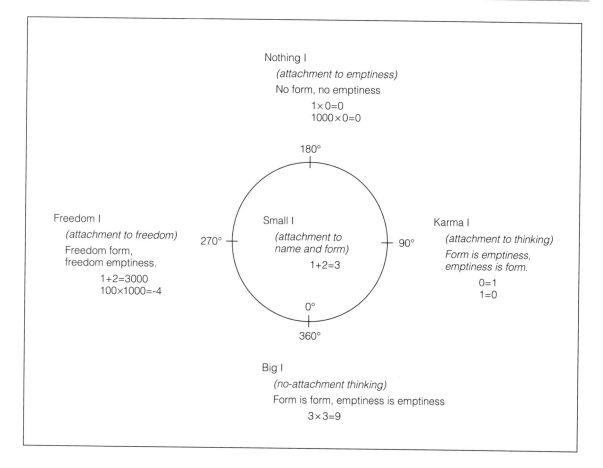

Nothing I
(attachment to emptiness)
No form, no emptiness
$1 \times 0 = 0$
$1000 \times 0 = 0$

180°

Freedom I
(attachment to freedom)
Freedom form,
freedom emptiness.
$1 + 2 = 3000$
$100 \times 1000 = -4$

270°

Small I
(attachment to name and form)
$1 + 2 = 3$

90°

Karma I
(attachment to thinking)
Form is emptiness,
emptiness is form.
$0 = 1$
$1 = 0$

0°

360°

Big I
(no-attachment thinking)
Form is form, emptiness is emptiness
$3 \times 3 = 9$

form. Here there is attachment to thinking. Before you were born, you were zero; now you are one; in the future, you will die and again become zero. So zero equals one, one equals zero. All things here are the same, because they are of the same substance. All things have name and form, but their names and forms come from emptiness and will return to emptiness. This is still thinking.

"At 180° there is no thinking at all. This is the experience of true emptiness. Before thinking, there are no words and no speech. So there are no mountains, no rivers, no God, no Buddha, nothing at all. There is only . . . " At this point Soen-sa hit the table.

"Next is the area up to 270°, the area of magic and miracles. Here, there is complete freedom, with no hindrance in space or time. This is called live thinking. I can change my body into a snake's. I can ride a cloud to the Western Heaven. I can walk on

water. If I want life, I have life; if I want death, I have death. In this area, a statue can cry; the ground is not dark or light; the tree has no roots; the valley has no echo.

"If you stay at 180°, you become attached to emptiness. If you stay at 270°, you become attached to freedom.

"At 360°, all things are just as they are; the truth is just like this. 'Like this' means that there is no attachment to anything. This point is exactly the same as the zero point: we arrive where we began, where we have always been. The difference is that 0° is attachment thinking, while 360° is no-attachment thinking.

"For example, if you drive a car with attachment thinking, your mind will be somewhere else and you will go through the red light. No-attachment thinking means that your mind is clear all the time. When you drive, you aren't thinking; you are just driving. So the truth is just like this. Red light means Stop; green light means Go. It is intuitive action. Intuitive action means acting without any desire or attachment. My mind is like a clear mirror, reflecting everything just as it is. Red comes, and the mirror becomes red; yellow comes, and the mirror becomes yellow. This is how a Bodhisattva lives. I have no desires for myself. My actions are for all people.

"0° is Small I. 90° is Karma I. 180° is Nothing I. 270° is Freedom I. 360° is Big I. Big I is infinite time, infinite space. So there is no life and no death. I only wish to save all people. If people are happy, I am happy; if people are sad, I am sad.

"Zen is reaching 360°. When you reach 360°, all degrees on the circle disappear. The circle is just a Zen teaching-device. It doesn't really exist. We use it to simplify thinking and to test a student's understanding."

Soen-sa then held up a book and a pencil and said, "This book and this pencil—are they the same or different? At 0°, they are different. At 90°, since all things are one, the book is the pencil, the pencil is the book. At 180°, all thinking is cut off, so there are no words and no speech. The answer is only . . . " Here Soen-sa hit the table. "At 270°, there is perfect freedom, so a good answer is: the book is angry, the pencil laughs. Finally, at 360°, the truth is just like this. Spring comes, the grass grows by itself. Inside it is light, outside it is dark. Three times three equals nine. Everything is as it is. So the answer here is: the book is the book, the pencil is the pencil.

"So at each point the answer is different. Which one is the correct answer? Do you understand?

"Now here is an answer for you: all five answers are wrong.

"Why?"

After waiting a few moments, Soen-sa shouted "KATZ!!!" and then said, "The book is blue, the pencil is yellow. If you understand this, you will understand yourself.

"But if you understand yourself, I will hit you thirty times. And if you don't understand yourself, I will still hit you thirty times.

"Why?"

After again waiting a few moments, Soen-sa said, "It is very cold today."

CHAPTER 32 / FIVE KINDS OF ZEN

One Sunday night, after a Dharma talk at the Providence Zen Center, a student asked Seung Sahn Soen-sa, "How many kinds of Zen are there?"

Soen-sa said, "Five."

"What are they?"

"They are: Outer Path Zen, Common People's Zen, Hinayana Zen, Mahayana Zen, and Utmost Vehicle Zen."

"Could you explain each of these?"

Soen-sa said, "Zen is meditation. Outer Path Zen includes many different types of meditation. For example, Christian meditation, Divine Light, Transcendental Meditation, etc.

"Common People's Zen is concentration meditation, Dharma Play meditation, sports, the tea ceremony, ritual ceremonies, etc.

"Hinayana meditation is insight into impermanence, impurity, and non-self.

"Mahayana meditation is: 1) insight into the existence and nonexistence of the nature of the dharmas; 2) insight into the fact that there are no external, tangible characteristics, and that all is emptiness; 3) insight into existence, emptiness, and the Middle Way; 4) insight into the true aspect of all phenomena; 5) insight into the mutual interpenetration of all phenomena; 6) insight that sees that phenomena themselves are the Absolute.

"These six are equal to the following statement from the Avatamsaka Sutra: 'If you wish to thoroughly understand all the Buddhas of the past, present, and future, then you should view the nature of the whole universe as being created by the mind alone.'

"Finally, there is Utmost Vehicle Zen, which is divided into three types: Theoretical Zen, Tathagata Zen, and Patriarchal Zen."

The student then asked, "Which of the five kinds of Zen is the best?"

Soen-sa said, "Do you understand your mind?"

"No."

"When you don't understand your mind, all Zen is no good. When you understand your mind, all Zen is best."

"I want to understand my mind. What kind of Zen is the best training?"

Soen-sa said, "Understanding one's mind is the aim of Utmost Vehicle Zen."

"You mentioned before that this Zen is further divided into three kinds. Which of the three is the best training?"

Soen-sa said, "The three kinds are only one, not three. Intellectual understanding of Zen is Theoretical Zen. The attainment of emptiness, the unity of mind and the universe is Tathagata Zen. 'Like this' is Patriarchal Zen. This means a relaxed mind, the attainment of Big I. Big I is infinite time and infinite space."

The student said, "That's all very difficult. I don't understand."

Soen-sa said, "I will explain to you. The Heart Sutra says, 'Form is emptiness, emptiness is form.' So your substance and the substance of all things is the same. Your original mind is Buddha, Buddha is your original mind."

Then, holding a pencil in his hand, he said, "This is a pencil. Are you and the pencil the same or different?"

"The same."

Soen-sa said, "That's right. This is Theoretical Zen."

"What is Tathagata Zen?"

"The Mahaparinirvana Sutra says, 'All formations are impermanent; this is the law of appearing and disappearing. When appearing and disappearing disappear, then this stillness is bliss.' This means that when there is no appearance or disappearance in your mind, that mind is bliss. This is a mind devoid of all thinking. So I ask you again: Are this pencil and you the same or different?"

The student said, "The same."

Soen-sa said, "If you say 'the same,' I will hit you thirty times. If you say 'different,' I will still hit you thirty times. What can you do?"

The student couldn't answer and became very confused.

Soen-sa hit the floor and said, "If you keep your mind as it is just now, this is Tathagata Zen. Do you understand?"

"I don't know."

"This don't-know mind has no Buddha, no Dharma, no good, no bad, no light, no dark, no sky, no ground, no same, no different, no emptiness, no

form, no anything in it. This is a truly empty mind. Empty mind is the mind which does not appear or disappear. Keeping this mind at all times is Tathagata Zen. Before, you said that the pencil and you are the same. This 'same' is thinking, so I said I would hit you thirty times. Do you understand?"

The student said, "A little."

"A little understanding is good. But if you ask me, 'Are the pencil and you the same or different,' I will hit the floor. When you understand why I hit the floor, you will understand Tathagata Zen."

"Thank you. Would you now explain Patriarchal Zen?"

Soen-sa said, "A person once asked Zen Master Mang Gong, 'What is Buddhism?' Mang Gong said, 'They sky is high, the ground is wide.' Do you understand what this means?"

"I don't know."

Soen-sa said, "That's right. 'Like this' is enlightenment. Patriarchal Zen is enlightenment Zen. An eminent teacher said:

1. 'Sky is ground, ground is sky: sky and ground are constantly changing.
   'Water is mountain, mountain is water: water and mountain are emptiness.
2. 'Sky is sky, ground is ground: how can they ever change?
   'Mountain is mountain, water is water: the truth is just like this.'

"The first verse above is Tathagata Zen, and the second is Patriarchal Zen.

"A man once asked Zen Master Dong Sahn, 'What is Buddha?' He said, 'Three pounds of flax.' The man didn't understand, so he went to another Zen Master, described his encounter with Dong Sahn, and asked, 'What does "three pounds of flax" mean?' The Zen Master said, 'In the North, pine; in the South, bamboo.' The man still didn't understand, so he went to one of his friends who had been practicing Zen for some time. His friend said, 'You open your mouth, your teeth are yellow. Do you understand?' 'I don't know.' 'First understand your mind, then all of this will be clear.'"

Then Soen-sa asked the student, "Do you understand?"

The student said, "Yes. Thank you."

"What do you understand?"

"'Like this' is Patriarchal Zen."

Soen-sa asked "What is 'like this'?"

The student couldn't answer. Soen-sa pinched his arm hard. The student yelled, "Owwwwwwwwww!"

"This is 'like this.' What is in pain?"

"I don't know."

"You must understand what is in pain. Then you will understand Utmost Vehicle Zen, and see that everything in the universe is the truth."

CHAPTER 70 / SEX MIND = ZEN MIND?

One day a student of Seung Sahn Soen-sa's heard a Zen Master speak at Yale University. When he returned to the International Zen Center of New York, the student said to Soen-sa, "This Zen Master's teaching is a little strange. He says that sex mind is Zen mind, because when a man and woman are having sex, they lose their particular identities and become one. So he says that everyone should get married. Is this correct teaching?"

Soen-sa said, "Your mind when you are having sex and your mind when you are driving a car—are they the same or different?"

The student was silent.

Soen-sa said, "I will hit you thirty times."

"Why?"

"You must understand the true meaning of my hitting you. This Zen Master said that during sex you lose your Small I. This may be true. But outside conditions are taking away the Small I. When the outside conditions change, you again become Small I. When you are driving a car with a clear mind, you don't lose yourself. Outside and inside become one. Red light comes and you stop; green light comes and you go. But if you have sex on your mind, red comes and you don't understand red. You lose everything."

The student said, "So what is the difference between sex mind and Zen mind?"

Soen-sa said, "We can talk about three separate minds. The first is attachment mind. This is called losing your mind. Next is keeping one mind. The third is clear mind."

"What is losing your mind?"

"For example, you are standing in a train station

and suddenly there is a loud whistle blast. You are startled out of yourself: no self, no world, only the whistle. This is losing your mind. Or if you haven't eaten for three days and then someone gives you food, you gobble it down without thinking. There is only the eating. Or when you are having sex, there is only the good feeling, the absorption in the other person. This is losing your mind. But afterwards, when you stop having sex, your small mind is just as strong as ever. All these actions are attachment actions. They come from desire and end in suffering."

"What is keeping one mind?"

"When somebody is reciting a mantra, there is only the mantra. He sees good, and there is only *Om mani padme hum;* he sees bad, and there is only *Om mani padme hum.* Whatever he does, whatever he sees, there is only the mantra."

"Then what is clear mind?"

"Clear mind is like a mirror. Red comes, and the mirror is red; white comes, and the mirror is white. When all people are sad, I am sad; when all people are happy, I am happy. The mind that only tries to help all people is clear mind. So the mind that is lost in desire is small mind. One mind is empty mind. Clear mind is big mind, which is infinite time and infinite space."

"It's still not completely clear to me. Would you please give me another example?"

"Okay. Suppose a man and a woman are having sex. They have lost their minds and they are very very happy. Just then, a robber breaks in with a gun and says, 'Give me money!' All their happiness disappears and they are very afraid. 'Oh help me, help me!' This is small mind. It is constantly changing, as outside conditions change.

"Next, somebody is doing mantra. This is one mind. His mind is not moving at all. There is no inside or outside, only true emptiness. The robber appears. 'Give me money!' But the person is not afraid. Only *Om mani padme hum, Om mani padme hum.* 'Give me money or I'll kill you!' He doesn't care. Already there is no life and no death. So he is not in the least afraid.

"Next is clear mind. This person always keeps Bodhisattva mind. The robber appears. 'Give me money!' This person says, 'How much do you want?'

'Give me everything!' 'Okay'—and he gives the robber all his money. He is not afraid. But his mind is very sad. He is thinking, 'Why are you doing this? Now you are all right, but in the future you will have much suffering.' The robber looks at him and sees that he is not afraid, that there is only motherly compassion on his face. So the robber is a little confused. The person has given him money and is now teaching him the correct way. This is true Zen mind."

The student bowed deeply and said, "Thank you very much."

Soen-sa said, "There are four difficult things in this life. The first is to receive a human body. The second is to encounter the Dharma. The third is to meet a keen-eyed Zen Master. The fourth is to attain enlightenment. Number three is very important. A Zen Master may not be deeply enlightened; he may not be a good teacher. If you meet the wrong Zen Master, you will go the wrong way. It is like one blind man leading another blind man into a ditch. So I hope you will be able to tell the difference between a keen-eyed lion and a blind dog."

The student said, "How can I tell the difference?"

Soen-sa said, "Now it is time for breakfast."

The student bowed.

CHAPTER 71 / KEEN-EYED LIONS AND BLIND DOGS

The next morning, the student said to Soen-sa, "You were talking yesterday morning about different kinds of teachers. How can I recognize a keen-eyed Zen Master?"

Soen-sa said, "It is difficult if you stay only in one place. You should go around and hear many Zen Masters. Then you will soon understand. In the Avatamsaka Sutra, there is a story about a young boy who studied with fifty-three teachers. He would learn what he could from one teacher, and then travel on to another. Finally, he met Manjushri, the Bodhisattva of wisdom. Manjushri asked him, 'What have you learned from these fifty-three teachers?' The boy said this teacher had taught him this, and that teacher had taught him that. Manjushri hit him. Everything he had learned disappeared. As soon as

he realized this, he decided to begin his travels again in search of a teacher. At that moment, Manjushri, who himself had disappeared, reached out across ten thousands worlds and touched the boy on the forehead. 'This beginner's mind,' he said, 'is the true mind of enlightenment.' Upon hearing this, the boy became enlightened.

"Some people study Zen for five or ten years without attaining enlightenment. They become very attached to their teacher, and this teacher cannot help them understand. If you study with only one teacher, even if he is a great teacher, it is difficult to meet Manjushri. So Zen students should travel from teacher to teacher until they find a keen-eyed Zen Master. This is very important."

The student said, "But how will I know?"

Soen-sa said, "At first you may not know. But if you practice Zen for a while and listen to many Zen Masters, you will soon understand what is correct teaching and what is not. If you don't taste sugar, you can't understand sweet; if you don't taste salt, you can't understand salty. No one can taste for you. You have to do it yourself."

"But aren't all Zen Masters enlightened?"

"There are different levels of enlightenment. There is first enlightenment, original enlightenment, final enlightenment. First enlightenment is attaining true emptiness. Original enlightenment is attaining 'like this.' Final enlightenment is 'just like this.'"

"Would you please explain some more?"

"Okay. Here is an apple. If you say it is an apple, you are attached to name and form. But if you say it is not an apple, you are attached to emptiness. So is this an apple or not? If you hit the floor or shout KATZ, this is a first-enlightenment answer. If you say, 'The sky is blue, the grass is green,' or 'The apple is red, the wall is white,' you are giving a 'like this' answer. But if you take a bite of the apple, your answer is 'just like this.' In the same way, you would ring the bell or open the book and read it. So first enlightenment, original enlightenment, and final enlightenment all have different answers. Some Zen Masters do not make these distinctions. Some only understand KATZ or silence. Some distinguish between KATZ and 'like this,' but don't understand 'just like this.' A keen-eyed Zen Master distinguishes among the three kinds of enlightenment. But he uses all three kinds with perfect freedom."

"The Zen Master I heard in New Haven said that there is no such thing as complete enlightenment. He said that you can never finish. Is that correct?"

"Buddha said, 'All beings are already enlightened.' An eminent teacher said, 'Without thinking, just like this is Buddha.' Without thinking is clear mind. So if you keep a clear mind, then any action is just like this. To say that you attain more enlightenment, more, more, more, is thinking.

Thinking is desire. Desire is suffering. So Zen Master Nam Chan said, 'Everyday mind is The Way.'"

The student said, "I have one more question. You said that a keen-eyed Zen Master distinguishes three separate kinds of enlightenment. But isn't Zen mind precisely the mind that doesn't create distinctions? Didn't the Third Patriarch say, 'The Great Way is not difficult for those who do not discriminate'?".

Soen-sa said, "First enlightenment, original enlightenment, final enlightenment—are these the same or different?"

The student thought for a moment, then smiled and said, "The wall is white, the rug is blue."

Soen-sa said, "You are attached to color."

"*You* are attached to color!"

"The dog runs after the bone."

"Then are they the same or different?"

Soen-sa said, "The wall is white, the rug is blue."

The student smiled.

Glossary

absolutism In ethics and epistemology, the view that there are absolute truths—truths that do not vary with the person or society considering them; opposed to *relativism*. In political philosophy, government by an absolute ruler.

active intellect In Islamic philosophy, the aspect of the mind that grasps universal truths.

ahimsa Nonviolence; the thesis that violence is unjustifiable; one of the fundamental concepts of Jainism and Gandhi's philosophy.

Arhat The saint (in southern Buddhism); one who has achieved enlightenment.

artha Goal, end, value; material gain.

asana Yogic postures.

asceticism The practice of strict self-denial and renunciation of worldly pleasure.

Atman In the Upanishads, the nature of the soul or self, which can be experienced directly and which illuminates itself.

bliss Complete happiness; in the Upanishads, the unqualified delight of consciousness that constitutes the self.

Bodhisattva In Mahayana Buddhism, one who delays his or her own attainment of nirvana in order to alleviate the suffering of others.

Brahman Ultimate reality underlying all phenomena; according to some Upanishads, responsible for the general features of the world and ourselves.

Brahmin (Brahmana, Brahmun, Brahman) The first and highest caste of the four traditional Hindu castes; a priest.

Buddhism A philosophy and religion founded by Gautama Siddhartha, the Buddha; widespread in South and East Asia; urges the elimination of desire as a means of conquering the suffering inherent in life. Theravada Buddhism is atheistic, stressing the centrality of suffering in existence. Mahayana Bud-

dhism treats the Buddha as divine and stresses the Bodhisattva. Vajrayana Buddhism is overtly mystical.

Carvaka A materialist and hedonist school of classical Indian philosophy also known as Lokayata, "those who follow the way of the world."

categorical imperative The sole fundamental principle of Immanuel Kant's ethics, which he formulates in five different ways: (1) act so that the maxim of your action might be willed as universal law; (2) act so that the maxim of your action might be willed as a law of nature; (3) treat everyone as an end, not merely as a means; (4) act as a legislator in the kingdom of ends; (5) act in accordance with the principle of autonomy.

ch'i Material force; denotes matter and energy as opposed to principle (*li*).

communitarianism The view that moral value rests ultimately on the good of the community as a whole, and only secondarily on the good of individuals; opposed to *individualism*.

Confucianism A philosophy and religion stemming from the teachings of Confucius; common in China, Korea, and Japan; promotes the moral perfection of the individual, centers on the concept of *jen*, and stresses the ethical importance of contingent human relations.

consequentialism The view that moral value rests ultimately on nothing but the consequences of actions; the opposite of *deontologism*.

decolonization The process in which colonies cast off the formal control and influence of the nations that colonized them.

deontologism The view that moral value does not rest ultimately on the consequences of actions alone, but in addition, or instead, on intentions, motives, character traits, and so on; the opposite of *consequentialism*.

detachment Indifference to worldly concerns; an important goal of Sufi mystics.

dharma (1) The right way of action; right living; duty; justice; the Divine way; (2) a teaching about right action, etc.; (3) qualities, characteristics.

dharmakaya The body of splendor, the Buddha body; the physical universe transformed.

dhyana Meditation.

dialectical materialism The view developed by Karl Marx and his followers that reality consists solely of matter, which changes in an intelligible pattern of stages of thesis, antithesis, and synthesis, driven by class struggle.

dialectical theologians Islamic religious thinkers of the eighth, ninth, and tenth centuries C.E. who used Greek philosophical ideas to debate Islamic theology and interpret the Koran.

duties of the heart In Indian, Islamic, and Jewish thought, the purely internal duties pertaining to the state of the soul rather than the actions of the body; duties to have certain states of mind.

dynamic idealism The philosophy developed by Wang Yang-Ming, which identifies mind and principle (*li*) and also knowledge and action.

Eightfold Path Buddhism's recommended way of life, consisting of right views, right intent, right speech, right conduct, right means of livelihood, right endeavor, right mindfulness, and right meditation.

emancipation The attainment of freedom—in Buddhism, freedom from suffering; in the Upanishads, freedom from limitation, achieved through experiences of self-illumination; in political philosophy, freedom from oppression.

energetism The view that ethical value is completely determined by fundamental, innate demands of the will; a basic thesis of Nishida.

enlightenment The state of illumination sought by Mahayana Buddhists, yogins, etc., in which desire and suffering have ended.

epistemology The theory of knowledge, its sources, nature, and limitations.

ethics The pursuit of good judgment concerning action and character.

extraordinary evil In Akan thought, an evil that harms not only individuals but also the entire community.

filial piety Respect and consideration for family; behaving as a son or daughter; a central virtue in Confucian thought.

Four Ends In the *Mahabharata* and other Indian writings, the four things desired as ends in themselves: virtue (*dharma*), pleasure (*kama*), wealth (*artha*), and freedom (*moksha*).

Four Noble Truths The foundation of Buddhism: (1) there is suffering; (2) craving causes it; (3) extinguishing desire extinguishes suffering; and (4) the Middle Way defined by the Eightfold Path extinguishes craving.

gnosis Knowledge of spiritual truth; especially, knowledge attained immediately rather than through ordinary experience; the most important goal of Sufis and other mystics.

Great Ultimate A fundamental concept of neo-Confucianism, originally found in the *Book of Changes* and developed philosophically by Chou Tun-i (1017–1073 C.E.); identified by Chu Hsi with principle in its totality that is complete both in all things considered together and in each thing considered individually.

hedonism In popular usage, the pursuit of pleasure; in ethics, the view that pleasure and pain are the sole ultimate sources of value.

idealism The view that reality is mind-dependent; opposed to *realism*.

imam An Islamic leader, a successor of Muhammad who exercises spiritual and political authority; identified by al-Farabi with the prophet and the ideally ethical person.

individualism The view that moral value rests ultimately on the good of individuals; opposed to *communitarianism*.

integral yoga Sri Aurobindo's method of integrating the personality and releasing the spiritual self into, rather than out of, the world through discipline.

intuitionism The view that people can apprehend ethical truth immediately and directly.

Isvara (Ishvara) God; the ever-liberated purusa according to the *Yogasutra*.

Jainism A religion founded in the sixth century B.C.E. by Mahavira that stresses noninjury (*ahimsa*) along with various practices aimed at a mystical *summum bonum*.

jen Humanity; one of the central virtues of Confucianism; both a particular virtue (benevolence or altruism), and the basis of virtue in general, involving a proper balance of all the virtues. Etymologically, *jen* means "man in society."

kama Sexual desire and enjoyment; enjoyment.

karma (1) Action; (2) a psychological impetus to action created by action; habit.

karmayoga The yoga of action and sacrifice taught in the *Gita*.

koan A paradox used by Zen Buddhists to force the mind away from reliance on reason toward sudden, intuitive enlightenment.

the Koran The fundamental religious text of Islam, which Muslims accept as revelations from the one God, Allah, to the prophet Muhammad through the angel Gabriel.

Legalism A school of ancient Chinese philosophy, founded by Han Fei Tzu, that rejects ethics and religion and maintains that only power is important.

li Rule, principle, ceremony, rite, ritual, or form; originally, a religious sacrifice.

maya Cosmic illusion.

metaethics The study of the project of ethics, concentrating on the meanings of ethical terms and the form of ethical statements and arguments.

metaphysics The study of the fundamental nature of reality.

Middle Way In Buddhism, the way of living defined by the Eightfold Path that extinguishes craving or desire and thereby overcomes suffering.

Moism The philosophy of Mo Tzu, a form of utilitarianism based on the concept of *yi* (righteousness or justice); advocates the good life because of its good consequences and recommends universal love.

moksha Emancipation; liberation from the cycle of birth, death, and rebirth; the mystical *summum bonum* according to several Indian schools.

mysticism The view that it is possible to attain direct and immediate knowledge of God or, more generally, ultimate reality.

naturalism In ethics, the view that ethical value depends on natural, nonmoral features of things; or,

the view that ethical value is determined completely by human nature.

neo-Confucianism The revival of Confucian thought, beginning in the tenth century C.E. and reaching a high point in the thought of Chu Hsi, which continues to be important in interpreting Confucian doctrine; a view characterized by six major concepts—the Great Ultimate, principle (*li*), material force (*ch'i*), nature, the investigation of things, and humanity (*jen*).

nirvana In Buddhism, the final permanent and transcendent state beyond suffering, in which desire and individual consciousness are extinguished; terminates a series of reincarnations once a person reaches moral perfection; literally, in Sanskrit, "extinguishing."

the One Tao; in Lao Tzu, that which underlies all things but admits no description.

oppression The unjust exercise of authority or power.

paramita A personal perfection according to Mahayana Buddhism.

particular An individual object existing in space and time, which has no instances but is instead an instance of various universals.

the perplexed In al-Farabi and Maimonides, those who find it difficult to reconcile religion and reason.

pluralism The view that ultimate values differ in kind.

pranayama Breath control.

Pratyeka-buddha One who seeks enlightenment for himself alone; an *Arhat* as opposed to a *Bodhisattva*.

prophet A person who receives revelation from God; identified by al-Farabi with the imam and the ideally ethical person.

propriety The quality of being proper, appropriate, polite; in Confucian thought, the observance of traditional social rules and correct principles, and, in Hsün Tzu, obedience.

proverb A brief popular epigram, maxim, or adage; often, a tool of instruction.

prudence The ability to promote one's own interests, especially through the use of reason and judicious choice.

purusa Individual conscious being.

realism The view that reality is mind-independent; opposed to *idealism*.

reciprocity Mutual dependence, action, influence, or respect; in Confucius, the principle of the Golden Rule: "What you do not want done to yourself, do not do to others."

relativism The view that what beliefs are true depends on the person holding them or the society that person inhabits; opposed to *absolutism*.

renunciation Self-denial, giving up worldly goods and pleasures; recommended by Sufi mystics.

rights Just entitlements indicating what one may properly claim as due; treated by Mencius as defining justice—respect for the rights of others—and as arising from tradition and custom.

sadhana Mystic disciplines, the practice of yoga.

samadhi Mystic trance.

samana An ascetic or yogin.

sakti (shakti) Divine energy; a concept from Tantra.

satori Enlightenment; the state of sudden, intuitive insight that practitioners of Zen seek.

sincerity A quality of pure, genuine honesty, an important virtue in Confucianism.

skepticism An attitude of doubt, in general or directed at specific kinds of knowledge claims; or, the view that knowledge of certain kinds is uncertain, unreliable, unjustifiable, or unattainable.

sudra (shudra) The fourth caste of the four traditional Hindu castes; a laborer.

Sufism An Islamic philosophy of mystical asceticism, whose devotees, Sufis, seek immediate knowledge, communion, and even union with God.

superior man In Confucius, the ideal person; originally denoted the son of a ruler, but in Confucius and later thinkers, denotes someone of superior character.

sutra Literally, "thread"; an aphorism.

Tantra An Indian philosophic and practical soteriological system (or family of related systems) that uses feminine imagery in its ceremonies and myths, and one that values nature as an expression of *sakti* or the Mother Goddess.

tao In Confucius, the Way, the path of proper ethical conduct; in Lao Tzu, the indescribable, natural, spontaneous One underlying everything.

Taoism The philosophy founded by Lao Tzu that teaches simplicity, tranquillity, nonconformity, and "going with the flow" of the tao; or, the religion that has developed from that philosophy.

Tathagata An epithet for a Buddha; literally, "one who has thus become."

te Virtue, character, power, force, capacity for excellence; active principle guiding a thing and defining what it should do and be; *tao* particularized in an individual object.

universal A property or relation, such as redness or friendship, that may have multiple instances; opposed to *particular.*

universal love Having equal regard for all people, regardless of one's relation to them; treating everyone with the respect we give ourselves; a basic principle of Moism.

utilitarianism The consequentialist view that the fundamental principle of ethics is to maximize the good.

Veda The oldest texts of South Asian traditions which came to be viewed by many Hindus as sacred and revealed.

Vedanta "The end or fulfillment of the Veda," an epithet for the Upanishads; later, the name of a family of schools that based their views on the Upanishads.

the Way In Confucius, the path of proper ethical conduct; *tao.*

wisdom literature Literature consisting of proverbs (each of which often comprises a single line of text) on various subjects in seemingly random order.

yi Righteousness or justice; the quality of acting as one ought to act; the fundamental concept of Moism and one of the foundations of Mencius's thought.

yoga Self-discipline; practices aimed at mystical attainment.

Zen A form of Mahayana Buddhism stressing meditation and the pursuit of sudden enlightenment (*satori*).

Index